HISTORY OF THE FI[RST]

'Immensely readable and infor[mative]... [the] possession of anyone interested i[n]... [what the greatest] military thinker of this century has to say . . .' THE SOLDIER

'Liddell Hart makes the complicated scene intelligible to the reader with the minimum of effort, and yet incorporates an apt and telling comment at every turn' THE TIMES LITERARY SUPPLEMENT

'Remarkable for its clarity and objectivity, and for analysis undistorted by professional prejudice or by bitterness over the unrecallable past. It remains outstanding: for those familiar with its subject, illuminating and thought-provoking; for those new to it and wishing to know what happened in World War I, the best place to begin' WESTERN MAIL

One of the world's outstanding teacher-historians, Sir Basil Liddell Hart was born in Paris in 1895 and educated at St Paul's and Corpus Christi College, Cambridge. He joined the Army (King's Own Yorkshire Light Infantry) and served in the First World War; in 1924 he was invalided and three years later retired with the rank of Captain. He evolved several military tactical developments including the Battle Drill system and was an early advocate of airpower and armoured forces. In 1937 he became personal adviser to the War Minister, but reorganization of the Army was so slow that he resigned a year later to press the need publicly.

Liddell Hart was military correspondent to the *Daily Telegraph* from 1925–35 and to *The Times* until the outbreak of the Second World War. He lectured on strategy and tactics at staff colleges in numerous countries and wrote more than thirty books. He died in 1970.

B. H. Liddell Hart

HISTORY OF THE
FIRST WORLD WAR

Pan Books London and Sydney

First published 1930 as *The Real War, 1914–1918*
by Faber and Faber Ltd. Enlarged edition published 1934
as *A History of the World War 1914–1918*
Published 1970 as *History of the First World War*
by Cassell and Co Ltd
This edition published 1972 by Pan Books Ltd,
Cavaye Place, London SW10 9PG
5th printing 1979
© 1930, 1934, © 1970 Lady Liddell Hart
Maps © Cassell and Co Ltd 1970
ISBN 0 330 23354 8
Printed in Great Britain by
Richard Clay (The Chaucer Press) Ltd, Bungay, Suffolk

TO JOHN BROWN AND THE LEGION

ACKNOWLEDGEMENTS

I wish to acknowledge the kindness of those who read various parts of this book in proof, and their helpfulness in contributing criticisms and suggestions. They include Lieut-Colonel H. G. de Waterville, Mr E. G. Hawke, and one unnamed whose knowledge of sources was as boundless as the trouble he took to aid me.

Original Preface to
A History of The World War

It is more than four years since *The Real War* was published. That title was chosen for reasons explained above. It fulfilled a purpose, but with the passage of time the need for it has passed. As a summary of the significant facts of the war it has met no serious challenge, and even its interpretation of them has been endorsed by the innermost observers of events, in the various countries, to an extent which has come as a pleasant surprise to the author. Now, twenty years have passed since the war came, and a generation has grown up that has no personal memory of it. The war is history. Hence the time has come, as well as the justification, for adopting a title that has no longer a contemporary note. An enlargement of the contents is a further reason. However much it still falls short of completeness, and my own ideal, it may at least be termed 'a history' of the World War. Also it may contribute to the growth of *the* history of the World War.

It is itself a growth from *The Real War*, just as the original volume evolved from a series of monographs on particular aspects and episodes. Personal experience makes me doubt whether it would be possible to compile a satisfactory history of 1914–18 by a less gradual method. Confronted suddenly by a whole mass of evidence now at hand, it would be difficult to maintain a clear view, and so easy for the pattern to be distorted by the very weight of the records. For my own part, I have found the practical value of a method which has allowed me, over a period of years, to fit each fresh bit of evidence into an expanding frame.

In evolving the present volume from *The Real War* there has been some revision, but more enlargement. 'The Opposing Forces and Plans' are now described in separate chapters, each augmented by new material. Two new 'scenes' have been added to make the story of 1914 more complete: one deals with the opening clash of the Austrian and Russian armies; and the other with the autumn struggle at Ypres and on the Yser which determined the possession of the Channel ports. An outline of the war in the air is given under the title 'Panorama'. But the greater part of the enlargement is due to the expansion of the existing chapters and 'scenes' through the incorporation of fresh evidence that has come to attention on the thoughts and feelings of some of the pawns of war. The war was, it is true, waged and decided in the minds of individuals more than in the physical clash of forces. But these decisive impressions were received and made in the cabinets and in the military headquarters, not in the ranks of the infantry or in the solitude of stricken homes.

The other – and more intentional – meaning of the title is that the time has come when a 'real' history of the war is possible. Governments have opened their archives, statesmen and generals their hearts with an unparalleled philanthropy. It is safe to say that most of the possible documentary evidence on the war has now been published or is available for the student. But it has not yet been collated for the information of the public.

The flood of documents, diaries and memoirs has one outstanding advantage. They have come when they can still be tested by the personal witness of those who took part in the crises and critical discussions of the war. A few years hence would be too late. Yet in the application of this test lies the only chance that history may approximate to truth. The more that any writer of history has himself been at hand when history is being made, or in contact with the makers, the more does he come to see that a history based solely on formal documents is essentially superficial. Too often, also, it is the unwitting handmaiden of 'mythology'.

Original Preface to
The Real War

On finishing this book I am conscious of its imperfections – some consolation comes from the reflection that every book worth reading is imperfect. This book may at least claim one merit, and one contrast to most war 'histories'. I have as little desire to hide its imperfections as to hide the imperfections of any who are portrayed in its pages. Hence in writing it my pursuit of the truth has not been interrupted by recourse to the pot of hypocritical varnish that is miscalled 'good taste'. In my judgement of values it is more important to provide material for a true verdict than to gloss over disturbing facts so that individual reputations may be preserved at the price of another holocaust of lives. Taking a long view of history, I cannot regard the repute of a few embodied handfuls of dust as worth more than the fate of a nation and a generation.

On the other hand, I have equally little desire to exaggerate the imperfections of individuals for the sake of a popular effect, or to shift on to them the weight of folly and error which should be borne by the people as a whole.

The historian's rightful task is to distil experience as a medicinal warning for future generations, not to distil a drug. Having fulfilled this task to the best of his ability, and honesty, he has fulfilled his purpose. He would be a rash optimist if he believed that the next generation would trouble to absorb the warning. History at least teaches the historian a lesson.

The title of this book, which has a duality of meaning, requires a brief explanation. Some may say that the war depicted here is not 'the real war' – that this is to be discovered in the torn bodies and minds of individuals. It is far from my purpose to ignore or deny this aspect of the truth. But for anyone who seeks, as I seek here, to view the war as an episode in human history, it is a secondary aspect. Because the war affected individual lives so greatly, because these individuals were numbered by millions, because the roots of their fate lay so deep in the past, it is all the more necessary to see the war in perspective, and to disentangle its main threads from the accidents of human misery. Perhaps this attempt is all the more desirable by reason of the trend of recent war literature, which is not merely individualistic but focuses light in the past four years. Thus, in the chapter outlines, there is some-what fuller treatment of the German advance into France in 1914; the Austro-German offensive against Russia and the Balkan situation in 1915; the Palestine situation in 1916; the spring campaign of 1917 on the Western Front; and the Allied discussions which preceded the German offensives of 1918. The main expansion, however, and most of the new material, will be found in the 'scenes', especially those which deal with Verdun, the Somme, Passchendaele, the 'First Breakthrough' and the 'Breakthrough in Flanders'. To a lesser extent, there is an infusion of fresh facts about the Brusilov, the Arras, the Messines and the Cambrai offensives, and the Second Battle of the Marne.

The revision needed has been comparatively slight. But new evidence that has come out in the past four years has led me to modify my view of such questions as the German strategy at Verdun, the projected move against Austria, the cause of Nivelle's failure in 1917, the Versailles committee and the preparations to meet the German offensive in 1918. On a number of points, fuller knowledge has amplified the earlier view, and while it has tended to illuminate the mistakes that were com-mitted, it has also helped to elucidate their cause. I have also modified or omitted my original comments on certain episodes, and in their place have quoted from the evidence of those who were responsible, leaving the facts to form the conclusion.

CONTENTS

CONTENTS

Chapter Six
THE 'DOG-FALL'
(1916)
204

Chapter Seven
THE STRAIN
(1917)
295

Chapter Eight
THE BREAK
(1918)
362

CONTENTS

MAPS

drawn by Peter McClure

CHAPTER ONE

The Origins of the War

Fifty years were spent in the process of making Europe explosive. Five days were enough to detonate it. To study the manufacture of the explosive materials – which form the fundamental causes of the conflict – is within neither the scope nor the space of a short history of the World War. On the one side we should have to trace the influence of Prussia on the creation of the Reich, the political conceptions of Bismarck, the philosophical tendencies in Germany, and the economic situation – a medley of factors which transmuted Germany's natural desire for commercial outlets, unhappily difficult to obtain, into a vision of world power. We should have to analyse that heterogeneous relic of the Middle Ages known as Austria-Hungary, appreciate her complex racial problems, the artificiality of her governing institutions, the superficial ambitions which overlay a haunting fear of internal disruption and frantically sought to postpone the inevitable end.

On the other side we should have to examine the strange mixture of ambition and idealism which swayed Russia's policy, and the fear it generated beyond her frontiers, especially among her German neighbours – perhaps the deadliest of all the ingredients in the final detonation. We should have to understand the constant alarms of fresh aggression which France had suffered since 1870, study the regrowth of confidence which fortified her to resist further threats, and bear in mind the wounds left in her side by Germany's surgical excision of Alsace-Lorraine. Finally, we should have to trace Britain's gradual movement from a policy of isolation into membership of the European system and her slow awakening to the reality of German feeling towards her.

In such a study of European history during half a century, a generalization can for once be closer to exactness than the most detailed history. The fundamental causes of the conflict can be epitomized in three words – fear, hunger, pride. Beside them, the international 'incidents' that occurred between 1871 and 1914 are but symptoms.

All that is possible, and sensible, here is to trace the most significant turning points in the trail of causation which led to combustion. This trail runs through the structure of alliances which Bismarck built after 1871. Ironically, Bismarck intended it as a shelter for the peaceful growth of his creation, the German Empire, and not as a magazine for explosives. For although his philosophy was epitomized in his 1868 phrase – 'The weak were made to be devoured by the strong' – his own hunger was satiated, after three meals, by the war of 1870–71. It cannot be charged against him that his eyes were larger than his stomach; feeling that Germany now was, as he said, a 'saturated' state, his governing idea henceforth was not expansion but consolidation. And to secure time and peace for this consolidation of the new Germany he aimed to keep France in a state of permanent powerlessness to wage a war of revenge. But the result was to prove that two wrongs do not make a Reich.

Apart from frequent direct menaces to France, he sought to counter-act her annoyingly rapid recovery by the indirect method of depriving her of friends or supporters. To this end his first effort was to bring Austria and Russia together by forging a common link with Germany, while he strove to ensure peace in the Balkans as a means to avoid any dangerous strain on the link. For some years his policy was that of acting as the 'honest broker' in the diplomatic exchange of Europe without committing himself to any party. But friction with the Russian chancellor, Gortchakov, and the complications caused by the Russo-Turkish war of 1877, led him to make a defensive alliance with Austria in 1879, despite the objections of the old Emperor William I, who regarded it as 'treachery' to Russia and even threatened to abdicate. This definite commitment was to have infinite consequences. Neverthe-less, Bismarck temporarily regained his central position by his diplo-matic masterstroke of 1881, the famous 'three emperors' alliance', whereby Russia, Austria and Germany undertook to act together in all Balkan affairs. And although it lapsed in 1887, Germany's connexion with Russia was strengthened in compensation by the secret 'Reinsur-ance Treaty', by which the two powers agreed to maintain benevolent neutrality towards each other in case of war with a third. It was not, however, to apply if Germany attacked France or Russia attacked Aus-tria. By this second masterstroke, executed with great duplicity, Bis-marck averted the risk, then imminent, of an alliance between Russia and France.

Meantime, the alliance between Germany and Austria had been en-larged by the inclusion of Italy in 1882. The object was to safeguard Austria against a stab in the back if at war with Russia, and in return

Italy's new allies would come to her assistance if attacked by France. But as a safeguard to her old friendship with Britain and to her own coasts, Italy had a special protocol appended to the treaty stating that it was in no case to be directed against Britain. In 1883, Rumania, through her King's personal and secret act, was attached to the new Triple Alliance. Even Serbia was temporarily linked on by a separate treaty with Austria, and Spain by an agreement with Italy.

In regard to Britain, Bismarck's aim seems to have been to keep her in friendly isolation from Germany and unfriendly isolation from France. His feelings towards Britain oscillated between friendship and contempt, and the political party system formed the pivot. For the 'old Jew', Disraeli, he had genuine respect, but he could not understand the point of view of the Gladstonian Liberals, and their wavering actions he despised. While Disraeli was in power Bismarck toyed with the idea of linking Britain to his chain of alliances, but although Queen Victoria was plaintively 'sure that Germany would be the safest ally in every way', she was less sure of Bismarck's safety as a repository of trust, and Disraeli shared her doubts. Hence Bismarck continued, with equal satisfaction, his policy of playing off Britain against Russia and France in turn. And with shrewd calculation he favoured Britain's occupation of Egypt because it embroiled her with France, and resisted the growing clamour in Germany for colonial expansion – 'our colonial jingos' greed is greater than we need or can satisfy' – because it threatened future trouble with Britain, yet made his support to Britain in Egypt a means of extracting oversea concessions as morsels with which he could assuage the colonial hunger of a body of German interests too powerful even for him to ignore. The Conservatives' return to power in Britain, and the intensified friction with France, led to a fresh tightening of the links with Germany, and Bismarck's offer of a formal alliance was eagerly welcomed by Lord Salisbury's Cabinet who seem only to have held back from fear of Parliamentary objection to foreign entanglements. Bismarck, however, profited from the informal entente to secure the cession of Heligoland – so vital to German naval operations a generation later – at a paltry price.

Thus at the end of the eighties Bismarck's great structure seemed complete. Germany was buttressed by the Triple Alliance while the attached yet semi-detached position of Russia and Britain gave her advantages without encumbrances. From this secure base she was ready to develop her commercial expansion. And Bismarck had placed France in the combined solitude and circumscription of a political isolation ward.

But with the beginning of the nineties the first crack appeared in the structure, close upon the dismissal of the builder. The accession in 1888 of the young Emperor William II was disagreeable to the Tsar, Alexander III, who disliked his 'aggressive amiability' and distrusted his intentions. Yet the breach came not from Alexander, but from William. Bismarck's control irked him just as it irked the General Staff, and in the soldiers, among whom he had been brought up, he so naturally found allies that in linking himself with them he did not realize that he was forging fresh fetters for himself.

The first effect, after the dismissal of the 'pro-Russian' Chancellor, was his successor's refusal to renew the 'Reinsurance Treaty' with Russia. The second effect, a natural sequel to the first, was that the Tsar swallowed his aversion to republicanism and, in 1891, made an agreement with France which, a year later, was developed into a military convention for mutual assistance in case of attack. In this convention a significant point was that if any member of the Triple Alliance mobilized its forces, both France and Russia were instantly to mobilize. The Tsar at least could not complain that he did not understand the meaning, for the French negotiator, General Boisdeffre, took pains to explain that 'mobilization means declaration of war'.

In the Tsar's case, the draught was swallowed under the fear that Britain was about to ally herself with Germany; it lay heavy on his stomach, so that it was long in producing any diplomatic value for France.

Nevertheless, France had left 'quarantine'. Henceforth there was not one political group, but two, in Europe. Although one was loose, the other compact, the two groups formed a balance of power, if their power was not yet balanced evenly.

A doubly significant sidelight upon Germany's renunciation of the Russian secret treaty is that the council in Berlin which reviewed the matter decided against the treaty on the ground that it was disloyal not only to Austria but to Britain. Whatever the Kaiser's failings, he was more sincere than Bismarck, and the insincerity apparent in his contradictory utterances seems to have been due to his combination of excessive frankness with a quick-changing mind. An essential difference between the two men was that the one sought security through consistent dishonesty, and the other gained insecurity through spasmodic honesty. The consideration shown for Britain was in accord with the Kaiser's views. For, although he had reversed Bismarck's attitude towards Russia, he maintained Bismarck's policy of friendship towards Britain, perhaps owing to more sincere, and less political motives. The

one personal source of cleavage lay in the mutual antipathy of the
Kaiser and his uncle, the Prince of Wales – later King Edward VII.
And, curiously, it was the Bismarck family who worked to widen this
personal breach.

But this could not have developed into a national cleavage without
greater causes being at work. More truly, it was one cause with sundry
accretions. Its origin and its foundation lay in Germany's change of
policy from internal to external expansion. The growth of her commerce and influence to a world-wide scale inevitably brought her
interests and those of Britain into contact at many points. Under tactful
or even Bismarckian guileful handling this contact might not have
caused such friction as to strike sparks, for British statesmanship
was peculiarly insensitive. The party most conscious of Britain's
imperial estate happened to be the party most sympathetic to imperial
Germany. But Bismarck had gone and tact did not fill his place. As so
commonly happens with great men, his disciples forgot his principles
and remembered only his method – the mailed fist. Yet the Kaiser
himself could also exert charm, and through it succeeded not only in
maintaining his popularity in England despite repeated irritation, but in
gaining a strong hold on the new and weakly amiable Tsar Nicholas II.
For a time he thereby acquired influence without obligation.

The first friction with Britain came over Turkey – a shadow cast on
the future. A Liberal government was in power again in 1892, when, as
Grey relates, 'suddenly there came a sort of ultimatum from Berlin,
requiring us to cease competition' with Germans 'for railway concessions in Turkey'. And in the years that followed the Kaiser lost no
opportunity to emphasize that the spreading web of German commerce
had a sharp-fanged spider at its centre. In 1895 his intervention made it
possible for Russia to deprive Japan of her spoils in the war with China.
In 1896 came the next, and more serious, friction with Britain. Ironically, its source was an Englishman's too ardent admiration for Bismarckian imperialism. The Kaiser, unsoothed by Rhodes' equal admiration for himself, became more and more irritated by Rhodes'
schemes of British expansion in South Africa, frustrating his own. After
several sour complaints, and sweet encouragement of the Transvaal
Boers, he found a tempting pretext in the Jameson raid into the Transvaal. At a council on January 3rd, 1896, he suggested that Germany
should proclaim a protectorate over the Transvaal and send troops
thither. When the Chancellor, Hohenlohe, objected 'that would be war
with England', the Kaiser ingenuously replied, 'Yes, but only on land.'
As a less drastic alternative the Kaiser was encouraged to send a con-

gratulatory telegram to President Kruger, so worded as not only to be highly offensive to Britain, but to deny her suzerainty over the Transvaal.

Popular feeling boiled over in both countries, due in the one case to ill-suppressed jealousy and in the other to pained surprise at discovering a fresh rival in a traditional friend. Germans felt a natural chagrin that Britain, with already so many colonies, should be gaining more in the one part of the world where a late-comer might hope to stake a claim. Englishmen had made such a habit of colonization that they blandly assumed it could only fit John Bull's figure, and could not understand that anyone, save the traditional rivals, France and Russia, might be anxious. However unconsciously provoking in ordinary intercourse, this calm assurance was a sedative in a crisis, and it largely saved this one. Warlike measures were actually ordered by Germany, and she suggested to France and Russia a combination against Britain. But lack of response from these countries, the calmness of Lord Salisbury's government, and a sense of her own naval weakness, restrained Germany and averted the immediate danger to peace.

But a danger put off by lack of power is not a danger removed. From this moment dates the real growth of German naval ambition, expressed in the Kaiser's words of 1897 – 'the trident must be in our fist' – and in the Kaiser's action of summoning Admiral Tirpitz to manufacture the trident. The next year saw the first large naval programme. It also heard the Kaiser proclaim himself, during his visit to Damascus, the protector of all Mohammedans throughout the world – a direct provocation to Britain and France. And not only to them. For the Kaiser's undisguised assumption of the role of patron saint of Turkey was fatal to his accord with Russia. His shadow now obscured Russia's view of Constantinople, the goal of her dreams. Like the opponents whom Napoleon derided, the Kaiser failed in policy because he 'saw too many things at once', and forced the other powers, whom Bismarck had played off against each other, to see only one thing – the fist of Germany – wherever they looked. Nevertheless, the affront to Britain in South Africa was followed, in 1898, by the offer from Chamberlain of that very alliance which Bismarck had sought in vain. But it was now the turn of Germany to be suspicious of the offer. On the British side the offer was impelled by a new and uncomfortable consciousness of isolation and weakness, while based on the old consciousness of natural affinity with Germany. But it looked, as it was in part, a confession of weakness, and weakness was not a quality to appeal to the new Germany. And one of Bismarck's few legacies to his successors was the habit of underrating Britain's strength and overrating Russia's.

In Germany's repeated rejections of Chamberlain's proposals between 1898 and 1901, the dominant factor was a personal factor – the concealed figure of Holstein. This crabbed, suspicious and miserly official of the Foreign Office, who loved obscurity because its dimness enhanced his real power in the pursuit of 'real policy', who would not buy himself a new suit although he did not shrink from using his official knowledge for private speculation, who had intrigued for his master's dismissal while posing as his pupil, was now viewed with awe as the spiritual heir of Bismarck when he had only inherited his immoral methods. Above all, he lacked Bismarck's confidence.

In consequence, although he would have liked to accept the British offers he shrank back from fear that Germany would become Britain's catspaw, and be converted into her shock-absorber against Russia. On the other hand he felt that Britain's weakness might now be exploited for Germany's benefit by holding Britain at arm's length and wringing concessions from her, while still keeping her hopeful of closer ties. In this view at least he was supported by the Chancellor, Bülow, and the Kaiser, whose outlook was well summed up in his words to Bülow – 'I have now got the British, despite their twisting and wriggling, where I want them.' And the German navy, expanded afresh in 1900, was the means of putting the screw on harder.

During the next few years, and especially during the South African crisis and war, the British Government had to pay heavily, not for German support, but merely for the privilege that German threats and insults should not be pressed to action. Over the Portuguese colonies, over Samoa, over China, Lord Salisbury's Government showed such contemptible weakness as almost to justify the Kaiser's description of them as 'unmitigated noodles'; the revelations from the diplomatic archives of these years are sorry reading. To them, indeed, can be traced an indirect responsibility for the eventual conflict, for it was natural that the Kaiser and his advisers should be confirmed in their good opinion of the mailed-fist method. He can be acquitted of a desire to press his method as far as actual war, not only because of the evidence of his distaste for it, but because of his tendency to superficial judgement. The limited menace was so obviously yielding the profits of war without the hazards, that the too obvious deduction was just the one to appeal to his mentality.

His responsibility for the war lies in these years. And it is a large responsibility, indeed, the largest. By the distrust and alarm which his bellicose utterances and attitude created everywhere he filled Europe with gunpowder. It is as irrational to fix the chief blame on those who eventually struck the sparks as it is to concentrate investigation of the war's origins on the brief month when the sparks were struck.

In reaction from the unhistorical propaganda which pictured the Kaiser as seeking, or even planning the war, the pendulum has swung too far the other way. To recognize his erratic good intentions should not lead us to underestimate his bad effects. And they came essentially from the fact that he was too well pleased with the reflection of his acts and himself. He saw himself arrayed in 'shining armour' when actually he was wearing the garb of Puck. He proved that making mischief makes war.

In delaying any acceptance of British overtures the Kaiser and Bülow felt secure. They underrated the effect of a common uneasiness in making easy bedfellows. With undue assurance they argued that there could be no real union 'between the whale and the bear', and by their acts they compelled this union. In retrospect, the most extraordinary feature is the number of kicks required to drive Britain away from Germany and into the awkward embrace of the Dual Alliance. Germany had at least full warning, for Chamberlain warned her in 1898 and again in 1901 that 'the period of England's splendid isolation is past ... we should prefer adherence to Germany and the Triple Alliance. But if this proves impossible then we, too, contemplate a *rapprochement* with France and Russia.'

The German belief in its impossibility proved a fallacy. That belief was summed up in Holstein's words – 'the threatened understanding with Russia and France is purely an English swindle ... A reasonable agreement with England can, in my opinion, only be attained when the feeling of compulsion over there has become more general.' He was too clever. By his 'reasonable agreement' he meant not an alliance between equals but the relation of master and servant. Weakly as the British government had behaved, and weaker still as it appeared to one imbued with the 'blood and iron' philosophy, this weakness is not sufficient to explain Holstein's amazing presumption. This is, indeed, an illustration that the real trouble in Germany, and the cause of her troubles, was not any true Machiavellian design, but merely the complaint summed up in the schoolboy phrase 'swelled head'.

Britain's first attempt to strengthen her position in other directions was her alliance with Japan in 1902. Its European significance is that it did not carry Britain away from Germany, but tended to raise a fresh barrier between Britain and the Dual Alliance. It sprang from Chamberlain's original proposal of a treaty between Britain, Germany, and

Japan, in close touch with the United States. Germany held back and so almost did Japan. For the Japanese statesman, Marquis Ito, preferred to seek an alliance with Russia, and was only turned from his purpose because his arrival in St Petersburg was outstripped by the progress of the negotiations in London between Baron Hayashi, the Japanese ambassador, and Lord Lansdowne, the Foreign Secretary. Even then, the Japanese Council of Elder statesmen wavered, under Ito's pressure, before accepting the British alliance – whose indirect result was thus to precipitate the Russo-Japanese war, a result neither desired by nor palatable to Britain.

For by 1904 a dramatic change had occurred in the European situation. Only five years before, France had been so bitter against Britain over Fashoda that she had almost forgotten Alsace-Lorraine. But fear of Germany, more deep-seated, made her statesmen open to approach when, in 1901, Chamberlain fulfilled his warning to Germany. The first step in the eventual negotiations between Lansdowne and Paul Cambon, the French Ambassador, was to remove causes of friction at the most sensitive point – overseas. The greatest obstacle was Egypt, still a cherished object of French ambition, and it was no mean diplomatic feat that recognition of Britain's actual occupation was exchanged for recognition of French right to occupy Morocco if she could. The agreement was signed in April, 1904. Although the popular idea of King Edward VII's responsibility for the agreement is purely legendary – still more so the popular German idea of him as spinning a Machiavellian web around Germany – his visit to Paris created the atmosphere in which agreement was possible. At first his reception was frigid, but his tact and understanding of the French combined with their truly republican love of royalty to hasten a thaw, and succeeding visits uncovered common ground. Thus if it is not true that he made the new *entente*, he undoubtedly made it *cordiale*.

But the Kaiser also helped. Deeply chagrined that the lover whose advances Germany had spurned had dared to woo another, his mischief-making was now redoubled. His efforts were directed to break up the Franco-British entente. And the coincident Russo-Japanese war provided the opportunity. His first move was a failure, for the peace-loving Tsar rejected his advice to send the Black Sea Fleet through the Dardanelles in defiance of Britain. But when the Baltic Fleet, Russia's last naval trump, sailed for the Far East it received false information – the Russians later alleged that it came from German sources – that Japanese torpedo craft were lying in wait in the North Sea. Through a panic mistake they fired on British trawlers, and made no effort to redeem their error, which brought Russia and Britain momentarily to the brink of war. For some days the British Channel Fleet shadowed the Russians, until the tension was eased by a message of regret from the Tsar, against the wishes of the war party in Russia. The Tsar, bitter at his humiliation, now, to the Kaiser's delight, proposed a combination of Russia, Germany, and France 'to abolish English and Japanese arrogance and insolence'. The Kaiser promptly dispatched a draft treaty between Russia and Germany, but urged the Tsar not to divulge it to the French, arguing that the 'Treaty once a *fact*, our combined powers will exert a strong attraction on France', and adding that 'an excellent expedient to cool British insolence and overbearing would be to make some military demonstration on the Perso-Afghan frontier...' But it was the Tsar who cooled, on reflection.

The next German move was singularly inapt, and for it the Kaiser was not responsible. Now, too late, he wanted to woo France instead of trying to separate her from Britain by threat. But he was sent off by Bülow and Holstein to Tangiers, there to 'throw down the glove to France' by a speech which challenged French claims in Morocco. Bülow followed it up by calling for a conference to review the future of Morocco. The challenge came at an awkward moment. The French army was suffering one of its periodical crises, Russia was entangled with Japan, and the French Prime Minister, Rouvier, doubted both the assurance and value of British support. Thus the foreign minister, Delcassé, was sacrificed and France accepted the demand. The mailed fist had scored afresh, but the alarm had driven Britain and France closer together.

The third move was the Kaiser's own. In July, 1905, when on board the Tsar's yacht at Bjorko, he suddenly produced the draft treaty, and in his hybrid 'Willy-Nicky' English, asked – 'Should you like to sign it? It would be a very nice souvenir of our *entrevue*.' The Kaiser relates that, when Nicholas answered 'Yes, I will', 'tears of joy filled my eyes – a thrill ran down my spine', and he felt that all his ancestors including 'Grandpapa' and the 'old Prussian God' were giving him their benediction. This phase of royal diplomacy, however serious its implication, was not without its humorous relief. There is a delightful commercial touch in one of his letters to 'Dearest Nicky' – 'Now that the programme for the renewal of your fleet has been published, I hope you won't forget to remind your authorities to remember our great firms at Stettin, Kiel, etc. They will, I am sure, furnish fine specimens of line of battleships.' Melodrama marks his aggrieved letter to Bülow who, as the treaty ran counter to his own anti-French aims in Morocco, threatened resignation – 'The morning after your resignation reaches him, the Kaiser will no longer be in this world! Think of my poor wife and children.'

But when the Tsar's ministers saw the treaty, they objected that it could not be reconciled with the French alliance, and sufficient hint of it leaked out to cause strong protests from France. Thus the 'masterpiece' was quietly dropped into the diplomatic waste-paper basket.

In justice to the Kaiser it must be mentioned that at the time he had some cause for personal grievance against Britain, even though it was largely the reaction to his long-standing habit of seeking his end by threats. His forceful impulsiveness had a counterpart in Sir John Fisher, just become First Sea Lord, who constantly talked of a preventive war and freely aired suggestions that if Germany would not limit her naval expansion her fleet should be 'Copenhagened' – on the Nelson model. Such wild suggestions naturally made more impression in Berlin than in London. King Edward VII's share as a cause of irritation was social and personal rather than political. A little more tolerance towards his nephew's *gaucherie* might have helped to make relations smoother. Lord Lansdowne records that 'the King talks and writes about his royal brother in terms which make one's flesh creep'. These personal antipathies and pinpricks, of little account on the British side, where the King was a constitutional ruler and also had a sense of humour, had a deeper reaction on the German side of the North Sea, where the ruler could influence policy decisively and had no sense of humour. And by inciting the Kaiser to further mischief-making intrigues and menaces they had an ultimate reaction in Britain, where even the new Liberal government of Campbell-Bannerman could not ignore them, and was unwillingly forced closer into the arms of France.

While the government refused to commit Britain to a formal alliance with France, it held out the hope that British public opinion might favour intervention if France was attacked. And when the French logically argued that emergency aid would be no use unless its method of application had been thought out, Campbell-Bannerman authorized discussions between the two general staffs. While these had no effect upon the eventual decision for war, they were to have a great influence on the conduct of the war. It is significant also that in 1905 the new German war plan made allowance for a British expeditionary force of 100,000 men – the very figure the French asked for – being present on the French side.

Balked of his idea of drawing France, with Russia, into a combination against Britain, the Kaiser now reverted to the idea of action against France over Morocco. He decided, however, that 'from a technico-military standpoint' conditions were not suitable, and that an alliance with Turkey, 'which would place the forces of Mahommedanism to the furthest extent – under Prussian leadership – at my disposal', and a secure internal position were necessary preliminaries. This illuminating example of his unbalanced mind is contained in a letter of December 31st, 1905, to Bülow, which concludes – 'First shoot the Socialists down, behead them, render them impotent – if necessary per Blood bath – and then war abroad! But not before, and not *a tempo.*'

Yet the next change in the European situation was not to strengthen his foundations, but to weaken them, by weakening his influence over Russia in the person of the Tsar. With supreme irony the change came in the most unlikely way – by the drawing together of the new British government and its antipathy, despotic Russia. Impelled partly by its general pacifism and partly by its natural reaction to German menaces, the Liberal government continued the effort begun by Lansdowne to remove the traditional sources of friction with Russia. And in 1907 the points of difference at the points of contact were settled by an arrangement. While there was no definite agreement, the natural effect was to smoothe the way to cooperation in Europe. Although Britain was not tied either to France or Russia by any formal agreement she was tied to their side by the bonds of loyalty, and so could no longer impose a check upon them without suspicion of disloyalty. Thus her old independent influence in a crisis had slipped away.

The dilemma was realized and well summed up by the Foreign Secretary, Sir Edward Grey, in a memorandum of February 20th, 1906:

'There would, I think, be a general feeling in every country that we had behaved meanly and left France in the lurch. The United States would despise us, Russia would not think it worthwhile to make a friendly arrangement with us about Asia, Japan would prepare to reinsure herself elsewhere, we should be left without a friend and without the power of making a friend and Germany would take some pleasure in exploiting the whole situation to our disadvantage ... On the other hand the prospect of a European war and of our being involved in it is horrible.'

Henceforth the great powers were in fact, if not in name, divided into two rival groups. During the next few years Germany, whose aggressive and impolitic policy had created the counter group, so curiously assorted, was also to help and be helped by Austria in hardening it, as a snowball is hardened when squeezed. But she was also to suffer from her own creation. Britain's adhesion to the new group weakened the old, by making Italy a doubtful partner. Hence Germany was compelled to cling more closely to her other partner, Austria, whom formerly she had led. If Germany wished for war, this bondage was an advantage, but if she wished for peace she would be hampered even as Britain was hampered.

The new grouping of Europe was not the old balance of power but merely a barrier between powers. That barrier, moreover, was charged with explosives – the armaments which the several countries, now driven more by fear than by ambition, hurriedly augmented. Another ill consequence was that fear of a sudden detonation led the autocratic powers at least to give the military custodians of these armaments a dangerously free hand in disposing them. Fear had taken charge of reason long before July 1914.

The first spark came from the Balkans in 1908. The revolution in Turkey was seized upon by Bulgaria to throw off Turkish suzerainty and by Austria to annex the provinces of Bosnia and Herzegovina, which she had administered since 1879. This annexation had been discussed between the Austrian and Russian foreign ministers, Ahrenthal and Isvolsky, and Isvolsky had been willing to assent to it in return for Austrian support in securing the opening of the Dardanelles. But before Isvolsky could sound France and Britain, the annexation was declared. In Italy it was justly felt to be an affront, and in Serbia to be a menace. But in Russia the effect was made worse by the German ambassador's peremptory demand that Russia should recognize it under pain of a combined Austrian and German attack.

Russia, caught when she had been acting single-handed, and threatened by a two-handed combination, gave way from fear, and was left with resentment, aggravated by the sense of having forfeited her standing in the Balkans. Isvolsky felt that he had been not only browbeaten but duped, and resigning soon after, went to the Paris embassy as an embittered foe of the Germanic powers. Another personal factor. And Austria, flattered by this first success in imitating Germany's mailed-fist method of diplomacy, was encouraged to continue it.

This Bosnian deceit of Ahrenthal's stands out predominantly among the immediate origins of the war. Its intervention was the more unfortunate because the years 1906–14 saw an improvement in Germany's official relations, at least, with France and Britain. It would have been more marked but for the continued ominous increase in the German navy. It is easy to appreciate now that the Kaiser's encouragement to Tirpitz's anti-British naval ambitions was due largely to vanity, but then it looked more naturally a consistently designed challenge. And even when he tried to repair the damage the Kaiser was unhappy in his method. His way of conciliating British feeling was to declare, in the famous *Daily Telegraph* interview of 1908, that the British were 'mad as March hares' not to recognize his friendship, and that he was in a minority in a land 'not friendly to England'. Without soothing British fears, it caused an outcry in Germany, a public repudiation by Bülow. And it thus weakened the Kaiser's own power to check the war party in Germany.

But it at least led to the Kaiser's replacement of Bülow as Chancellor by the well-meaning Bethmann-Hollweg, who was more desirous of peace if less capable of preserving it. He promptly opened negotiations for an Anglo-German agreement, and met with an eager response from the Liberal government, now renewed in power by the elections of 1910. But practical results were barred, first, by Tirpitz's opposition to any naval adjustment and, second, by the German demand that any agreement must be so worded as to bar Britain from coming to the aid of France.

This was too obviously a strategic move. Sir Edward Grey made the only possible reply – 'One does not make new friendships worth having by deserting old ones.'

Nevertheless the tension was eased. The German public, press and Kaiser – as shown by his documentary comments – still suffered from Anglophobia, owing largely to the feeling of thwarted aims and the much-propagated idea that King Edward VII had planned a vast hostile encirclement of Germany. Perhaps the most illuminating reaction was the belief that the King's 1908 visit to the Emperor Francis Joseph was a move to detach Austria from Germany, whereas we now know from the Austrian archives that the King actually asked Francis Joseph's assistance towards reducing the friction between Britain and Germany, and valued the alliance as a common link. But the discussions helped the relations between the British and German foreign ministries and led them to cooperate in settling several points of dispute. Relations were also helped by the settlement between France and Germany over Morocco.

Characteristically, this settlement followed a new crisis. The crisis, curiously enough, was provoked by the otherwise pacific Foreign Minister, Kiderlen-Wächter, and opposed by the Kaiser, another instance of that incalculable double-headedness which was so dangerous a feature of German policy. As a means of encouraging France to grant concessions in Africa, in June, 1911, Kiderlen-Wächter dispatched a gunboat to Agadir. In reply, Lloyd George, the former opponent of the Boer War and the leading pacifist in the British Cabinet, warned Germany in a public speech against such threats to peace. The effect, in conjunction with firm indications of a readiness to support France, was to damp the spark. But resentment made public opinion in Germany more combustible than ever, and it enthusiastically approved yet another increase in the German Navy. Nevertheless, the subsequent settlement over Morocco removed a serious source of friction between France and Germany, and thus indirectly contributed to the better official atmosphere in which Haldane's 1912 mission to Germany took place. Yet even Haldane had to confess that his 'spiritual home' had become a 'powder magazine', although he communicated his fears only to his colleagues in the Cabinet. The growth of the war party in Germany, however, was accompanied by a consolidation of the peace elements, most marked among the Socialists, and the presence of a pacifically minded Chancellor kept open a possible avenue for further negotiations.

But at this very time a fresh powder trail was laid – in the Balkans. The weakness of Turkey, and the example of Italy in occupying Tripoli, encouraged Bulgaria, Serbia, and Greece to claim autonomy for Macedonia as a step to ejecting the Turks from Europe. The Turks were quickly defeated. Serbia's share of the spoils was to be Northern Albania. But Austria, already fearful of Serb ambitions, had no intention of allowing a Slav state to gain access to the Adriatic. She mobilized her troops and her threat to Serbia was naturally answered by Russia's similar preparations. Fortunately, Germany joined with Britain and France to forestall the danger. Less fortunately, their settlement was the cause of a fresh crisis. For, by setting up Albania as an independent state, they upset the division of the spoil. Serbia now claimed part of Macedonia; Bulgaria refused not only by word but by blow, only to be overcome by the combined weight of Serbia and Greece, while Rumania joined in, and Turkey slipped back to recover her lost property under cover of the dust raised by the 'dog-fight'.

As a result Serbia was the chief gainer and Bulgaria the chief loser. This was much to Austria's distaste and in the summer of the 1913 she proposed an immediate attack on Serbia. Germany restrained her, counselling moderation, but herself gave Russia a fresh cause of offence by extending German control of the Turkish Army. Russia saw her dream of the Dardanelles fading, and her ministers came to the conclusion that it could only be revived if a general European war occurred – a dangerful attitude of mind. Their immediate aim was now to recover their shaken influence in the Balkans, and they sought to win over Rumania as a first step towards building a new Balkan alliance. The prospect created fresh alarm in Austria, already distracted by the internal strain of her diverse racial parts.

Force was her method to suppress the dissatisfaction of her Serb and Croat subjects in the annexed provinces and of her Rumanian subjects in Transylvania. And her desire was to apply the same remedy in time to the external state – Serbia – which formed a natural rallying point for all the dissatisfied elements within. Her leaders felt that war beyond her frontiers would be the best way to silence discord within. In this feeling they were not alone. The popular unrest in Russia, only half stifled by the use of knout and exile, and the clamour for universal suffrage in Germany, made the war parties in both countries look to war as a safety-valve.

During the last year incitements multiplied on all sides – bellicose speeches, articles, rumours, frontier incidents. President Wilson's confidant, Colonel House, left Berlin with the conviction that the military party was determined on war, at the earliest opportunity, and would force the Kaiser to abdicate if he opposed their desire. Their excitement was certainly aggravated by the Three Years' Service Act which France had passed as a remedy for her inferior man power in face of recent developments in the German Army. But the German ambassador reported to Bethmann-Hollweg that: 'In spite of the chauvinistic attitude of many circles and the general dream of a recovery of the lost provinces, the French nation as a whole could be described as desirous of peace.' The most that could be said, even of Poincaré, the President, was what Poincaré himself expressed, 'that France did not want war, but did not fear it'. Elsewhere, however, the surface of the continent was now strewn with powder. And everywhere the air was heavy with fatalism.

The fatal spark was struck at Serajevo, the Bosnian capital, on June 28th, 1914. Its first victim marked the irony of destiny. The fiery Slav nationalists who sought to advance their cause by murdering the Archduke Franz Ferdinand, the heir to Francis Joseph, singled out the one man of influence in Austria who was their friend. For Franz Ferdinand also had dreams – of a reconstructed empire in which the several nationalities were held together not in bondage but in federation. But to most of the Bosnian Slavs he was merely the symbol of the oppressor, and to the extreme nationalists who plotted his death he was the more to be hated because his dream of reconciliation within the empire might thwart theirs of breaking away from the empire, to join with Serbia in creating a wider Yugo-Slav state.

The handful of youthful conspirators sought and received help from the Serbian secret society known as the 'Black Hand'. This was largely composed of army officers, who formed a group hostile to the existing civil government in Serbia. Rumours of the conspiracy seem to have reached the ears of ministers, and orders were sent to the frontier to intercept the conspirators, but as the frontier guards were members of the 'Black Hand' the precautions naturally failed. It seems also, but is not certain, that a vague warning was sent to Vienna. What is certain is the amazing carelessness of the Austrian authorities in guarding the Archduke, and their cynical indifference to the fate that befell this highly unpopular heir to the throne. Potiorek, the military governor of Bosnia and future commander of the offensive against Serbia, could not have done more to facilitate the task of the assassins if he had connived at it. Hence there must always be a suspicion that he did.

After a first attempt, on the Archduke's passage to the city hall, had failed, Potiorek so clumsily directed the return journey that the Archduke's car had to pull up, and two shots rang out, mortally wounding the Archduke and his court-despised morganatic consort. He died at 11 AM – a prophetic hour.

The news of the crime caused horror and indignation in all countries save two – Austria and Serbia. The Serbian press made little effort to conceal its pleasure, and the Serbian public still less, while the government which, exhausted by the Balkan wars, had every incentive for peace in order to consolidate its gains, was foolishly remiss in making or offering an investigation into the complicity of its subjects.

Austrian police investigation was also leisurely, and after a fortnight Wiesner, who was deputed to conduct it, reported that while Serbian societies and officials were implicated there were 'no proofs of the complicity of the Serbian government ... On the contrary there are grounds for believing it quite out of the question.'

But Austrian decision was prompt, although any outward appearance of action was long delayed. Count Berchtold, the Foreign Minister – who had added an air of elegance to the tradition of deceit bequeathed by Ahrenthal – gracefully and gratefully seized the opportunity to retrieve Austria's and his own lost prestige. The day after the crime he declared to the Chief of the General Staff that the time had come to settle with Serbia once for all – words that seemed to Conrad von Hötzendorf the echo of his own repeated promptings to war. But Berchtold met an unexpected obstacle in Count Tisza, who objected strongly, on the score of expediency, not of morality – 'There can be no difficulty in finding a suitable *casus belli* whenever it is needed.' Conrad also considered expediency and remarked to Berchtold – 'We must above all ask Germany whether she is willing to safeguard us against Russia.' Berchtold, too, had no wish to meet a rebuff from Germany such as so damaged his prestige two years before. Hence the aged Emperor was induced to sign a memorandum for the Kaiser, accompanied by a personal letter.

But the Kaiser needed no appeal. For when the German ambassador, Tschirschky, had sent off a report of his conversation with Berchtold on June 30th, saying that he had given a warning against hasty steps, the Kaiser scribbled in the margin – 'Who authorized him to do this? It is idiotic. It is none of his business . . . Tschirschky must be good enough to stop this lunacy. We must clear the Serbians out of the way, and that too forthwith.' Poor Tschirschky, he was not equal to his master's somersaults. Formerly energetic in incitement, he presumably remembered his master's voice, urging restraint two years before, and now thought that he was fulfilling the Kaiser's wish by changing his own tune – only to find that the Kaiser had also changed. How shall we explain it? Most probably by the Kaiser's fear of being again reproached with weakness and by his characteristic indignation that royal blood had been shed, if also by the more creditable motive of his friendship with the murdered man.

Thus to Count Hoyos, the Austrian letter-bearer, he gave the assurance, on July 5th, that Austria 'could depend on the complete support of Germany'. 'In the Kaiser's opinion there must be no delay . . . if it was to come to a war between Austria-Hungary and Russia she could be assured that Germany would stand at her side', although he added that Russia 'was in no way ready for war'. Germany was – so he was assured. In a series of hasty consultations with his military and naval advisers, various precautionary measures were ordered. Meantime, the Kaiser left, as arranged, to visit Norway. A few days later, on the 17th, Waldersee, the Assistant Chief of the General Staff, reported to the Foreign Minister – 'I shall remain here ready to jump. We are all prepared.'

This blank cheque, endorsed by the Chancellor and given with full recognition of the consequences, stands out predominant among the immediate causes of the war. Austria hurried to cash it, and Tschirschky was only too eager to repair his blunder in urging caution. Unlike later decisions this was taken in a calm if not a cool atmosphere, a fact which gives it special significance in assessing the will to war. Significant also is the care taken by Germany and Austria to lull suspicion of any impending move – in Conrad's words, 'peaceful intentions should be simulated'. While giving no advice to Austria to keep her demands within moderation, the German government showed its anxiety that the support of Italy, Bulgaria, Rumania and Turkey should be ensured for a war. Italy was to be given no hint of the action intended, but Austria was urged to be ready with a price for her support when war came.

Now assured of Germany's backing, Berchtold's next problem is so to draft the ultimatum to Serbia that it will be unacceptable. This takes some thought and on July 10th Berchtold confesses to Tschirschky that he is still considering 'what demands could be put that it would be wholly impossible for Serbia to accept'. The only dissenting voice is that of Tisza, but he is told – 'A diplomatic success would be valueless.' He threatens to withhold his support, but suddenly veers round – after Berchtold has warned him of 'the military difficulties which would be caused by a delay', and has impressed the fact that 'Germany would not understand any neglect on our part to use this opportunity for striking a blow'. Austria might forfeit her partnership with Germany if she showed weakness.

The ultimatum is drawn up, and after reading it the old Emperor says – 'Russia cannot accept this ... this means a general war.' But its delivery is delayed until various war preparations are complete – and Poincaré has sailed from St Petersburg, where he has been visiting the Tsar. The Russian ambassador in Vienna is also induced by peaceful assurances to go on leave. But the German steamship lines are warned of the date on which the Austrian note would be delivered, and that they must be ready for swift 'developments'.

At 6 PM on July 23rd the ultimatum is presented to the Serbian government – when the Prime Minister is away. Its terms not only demand the repression of all propaganda against Austria, but Austria's right to order the dismissal of any Serbian officials that she cares to name and to post her own officials in Serbia. This directly violates Serbia's status as an independent country. Only forty-eight hours are allowed for acceptance. Next day the German government delivers notes in St Petersburg, Paris and London, which state that the Austrian demands are 'moderate and proper' – the German government had not even seen the ultimatum when it light-heartedly wrote this – and add the threat that 'any interference ... would be followed by incalculable consequences'. In London the note caused stupefaction, in Russia fierce indignation.

But, two minutes before the ultimatum expired the Serbian reply was handed to the Austrian ambassador. Without waiting to read it, he broke off relations and caught the train from Belgrade, in accordance with his instructions. Formal orders were issued three hours later for Austria's partial mobilization – on the Serbian front. Simultaneously preparatory measures for mobilization took place in Germany and Russia.

Yet the Serbian note had accepted all the Austrian demands except the two which definitely violated her independence. When the Kaiser read it, on July 28th, after his return, he wrote the comment – 'A brilliant performance for a time limit of only forty-eight hours ... A great moral victory for Vienna; but with it every reason for war drops away.' And in reference to Austria's partial mobilization he adds – 'On the strength of this I should never have ordered mobilization.' Once more the mailed fist has triumphed and the Kaiser, having shown the doubters that he is a strong man, is eager to rest on his laurels. Royal honour is satisfied. But he unwisely suggests that Austria might well occupy part of Serbia until her demands are fulfilled – an act that Russia could never be expected to permit. Bethmann-Hollweg agreed with the Kaiser's view, and on the morning of the 28th the advice was sent to Vienna, adding that, 'If Austria continues her refusal to all proposals for mediation or arbitration, the odium of being responsible for a world war will in the eyes of the German people fall on the German Government.'

But the changed tone was fatally belated. Germany had herself blocked these proposals during the most auspicious period. When the German note was delivered, on July 24th, Russia was at once assured of France's support, and Grey was pressed by his allies to declare Britain's solidarity with them. But his parliamentary responsibility and the divided views of the Cabinet, as well as the uncertainty of public support, hindered any such declaration. He feared, too, that any such action might strengthen the war parties in Russia and Germany. Instead, he tried to open a path to mediation. His first move, on the 24th, was to urge through Berlin an extension of the Austrian time limit. It received no support in Berlin and was tardily passed on to Vienna where it arrived two hours before the expiration, when it was at once rejected. On the 25th and 26th he made further proposals for joint mediation by Germany, Britain, France and Italy, while Austria, Russia, and Serbia were to abstain from military operations. Prompt acceptance came at once from Paris and Rome. Sazonov in St Petersburg, who had originally mooted the idea, now agreed in principle but preferred first to try direct discussions with Vienna. Berlin refused. The Kaiser scribbled his usual incendiary comments on the reports that came to him – 'That is a tremendous piece of British insolence. I am not called upon to prescribe *à la* Grey to HM the Emperor [of Austria] how to preserve his honour.' There is much evidence that German opinion was encouraged by Britain's attitude to count on her neutrality in case of war. But in the newspapers of July 27th the British government published the news that the fleet, assembled for manoeuvres, had been ordered not to disperse. This hint in combination with the nature of Serbia's reply caused a change of official tone in Berlin – where, the day before, the General Staff had sent to the Foreign Office the ultimatum they had drafted in readiness for delivery to Belgium.

Thus, later on July 27th, the German government decided to pass Grey's proposals on to Vienna. They sent Grey word that this action implied that they 'associate themselves to a certain extent with your hope'. But after seeing the German Foreign Minister, the Austrian Ambassador telegraphed to Vienna – 'The German government offers the most unqualified assurances that it in no way identifies itself with them, but on the contrary is decidedly opposed to their consideration, and only communicates them in order to satisfy the English ... The German government is so acting because its point of view is that it is of the utmost importance that England, at the present moment, should not make common cause with Russia and France.' On the 28th, after the Kaiser had seen Serbia's reply, there was a further cooling of tone as we have seen. But Bethmann-Hollweg's cautionary message, his first, to Vienna that day was too late and too tepid.

For at 11 AM – again! – on July 28th, Austria's telegraphed declaration of war was delivered to Serbia. And the same day Berchtold refused Sazonov's proposal for direct conversations, giving as his reason the fact that war was now declared! A grim humour underlies both the cause and method of Austria's precipitate decision. Militarily there was every reason for delay in the actual declaration, as the army could not be ready to move until August 12th. But messages from Germany had been inciting Austria to haste; Berchtold and Conrad feared to lose her support and the chance of war if they dallied. Berchtold cynically summed up the position to the Emperor on July 27th – 'I think that a further attempt by the Entente Powers to bring about a peaceful solution remains possible only so long as a new situation has not been created by the declaration of war.' And in obtaining the Emperor's signature to the declaration of war, he quenched any doubts by incorporating the justification that Serbian had attacked Austrian troops.

Having achieved his end, he then deleted the sentence referring to this imaginary attack!

The rush to the abyss now gathered unbrakable speed – driven by the motor of 'military necessity'. In constructing their huge and cumbrous machines the general staffs of Europe had forgotten the first principle of war – elasticity. Alike in mobilization and in use the conscript armies of the Continent were almost unmanageable. Events were soon to show that they could be set in motion, but could not be effectively guided; their steering lock was inadequate. In this deficiency, now a danger to peace, they afforded a contrast both to the fleets of the time and to the small professional armies of the past.

The one thought of the Generals during these critical days was to start their machines. Desire for war, and fear, of being caught at a disadvantage, reacted on each other. Thus in Germany and Russia, as already in Austria, any desire among the statesmen for peace suffered the counter pull of the Generals' entreaties to action, and predictions of dire consequences if their technical advice was disregarded. Already in Austria, the Generals shared with Berchtold the sombre distinction of having initiated the war.

Their next success was in Russia – also a land of military mediocrity. There, the news of the Austrian declaration of war wrought a decisive change. Hitherto Sazonov had kept the Generals in hand. Now he begins to succumb to inevitability, and suggests that partial mobilization shall be carried out – of the troops on the Austrian front only. The General Staff argue that for 'technical reasons' this is impracticable, and urge that only a general mobilization can avoid upsetting the machine. Unwilling to yield to their arguments, yet unwilling to override them, Sazonov makes a compromise. Two *ukases* are prepared for the Tsar's signature, one for partial and one for general mobilization, and a decision between them is put off.

But the General Staff are working on the second. Next morning, the chief of the mobilization branch receives the order for general mobilization signed provisionally by the Tsar, and goes round to obtain the necessary signature of the ministers. One of them cannot be found until the evening. Meantime the German ambassador calls on Sazonov, about 6 PM, and gives him a message from Bethmann-Hollweg, that – 'If Russia continues her mobilization measures Germany will mobilize, and mobilization means war.' The message is delivered with the assurance that it is 'not a threat, but a friendly opinion'; to Sazonov it sounds more like a threat, and it seems to prohibit even partial mobilization on the Austrian frontier. His opposition to his own clamorous

General Staff weakens, and after a conference with its chief, Yanushke-vich, he apparently consents to general mobilization and obtains the Tsar's approval.

Let us shift our gaze for a moment to Berlin. There the same nervous tension exists and the same tug of wills is in progress. But the Kaiser and his political advisers are now seriously alarmed that Austria's action will make them appear the guilty party, and so cost them the support of Italy while ensuring the entry of Britain against them. Thus a demand of the General Staff for immediate mobilization is refused, and late in the evening Bethmann-Hollweg sees the British ambassador. He tries to bargain for Britain's neutrality and suggests that in return Germany would not annex any part of France – but he 'cannot give him such an assurance' as regards the French colonies. The ambassador tells him that acceptance of the offer is highly improbable, wherein he proves a true prophet. Lichnowsky's warnings from London, that British opinion is hardening, send the Kaiser into a paroxysm of frightened rage. He scrawls abusive epithets about 'English pharisaism', calling Grey 'a mean deceiver', and, rather oddly in view of Bethmann-Hollweg's offer, terms the British a 'pack of base hucksters'. But Lichnowsky's report of Grey's renewed proposals for mediation at least induces Bethmann-Hollweg to send a string of telegrams to Vienna ex-horting the Austrians not to continue their open refusal, lest they drag Germany into war at a disadvantage. The Kaiser, also, telegraphs to the Tsar saying that he is trying to persuade Vienna to agree to 'frank negotiations'. It crosses a similar conciliatory telegram from the Tsar, and is answered by a second, suggesting that – 'It would be right to give over the Austro-Serbian problem to the Hague Conference. I trust in your wisdom and friendship.' The fact that the Kaiser's marginal com-ment is 'Rubbish' casts a doubt upon his sincerity. But the Kaiser has also sent a second telegram of appeal to check military measures which 'would precipitate a calamity ...' This produces an actual effect.

The Tsar, about 10 PM, rings up the Chief of Staff, and despite Yanushkevich's horrified protests that the orders have now gone out, directs him to cancel them and substitute a partial mobilization.

But the General Staff, though discomfited, are not defeated. Next morning, in order to retrieve the position, they bring fresh arguments and all their weight to bear. First they try to approach the Tsar, but he takes refuge from their pressure by refusing to see the Minister of War. Yanushkevich then seeks out Sazonov, and insists that any further delay in general mobilization will 'dislocate' the army organization and en-danger Russia's safety. He further contends that partial mobilization will give the French the impression that, when war came, Russia will be unable to help her in resisting Germany's onslaught. Sazonov, now resigned to the certainty of war, agrees to visit the Tsar that afternoon. The Tsar, pale and worried, gives way and gives the order – after Sazonov has soothingly assured him that whatever happens his conscience will be clear. Sazonov telephones the order to Yanushkevich, and advises him to 'disappear for the rest of the day', as a safeguard against the Tsar's vacillation. Sazonov first thinks of trying to keep the general mobilization as secret as possible, without issuing any proclamation, but finds it technically impossible, and the *ukase* is posted up next morning, July 31st. That same day, but a few hours later, the Austrian order for general mobilization is given. Henceforth the 'statesmen' may continue to send telegrams, but they are merely waste paper. The military machine has completely taken charge.

Indeed, it had done so on the 30th – not only in Russia. At 2 PM Moltke, the Chief of the German General Staff, had sent a message to the Austrian General Staff through their attaché that Russia's military measure 'will develop into a *casus foederis* for Germany ... Decline the renewed advances of Great Britain in the interest of peace. A European war is the last chance of saving Austria-Hungary. Germany is ready to back Austria unreservedly.' Subsequently he sent a telegram direct to Conrad – 'Mobilize at once against Russia. Germany will mobilize. Persuade Italy, by offering compensation, to do her duty as an ally.' Thus Moltke counteracted the irresolute telegrams of Bethmann-Hollweg. The Austrian military and civil leaders needed no urging, merely the assurance of Germany's support, and had no intention of acceding to any proposals for mediation unless Germany threatened to withdraw that support. And 'Germany' now meant the General Staff.

As soon as news reached Berlin of the Russian order, a 'state of danger of war' was proclaimed, which comprised the first step of mobilization – a neat military device to gain a lead without giving away a trick. At the same time ultimatums were dispatched both to St Petersburg and Paris. The ultimatum to Russia demanded that she 'must suspend every war measure against Austria and ourselves within twelve hours', and 'definitely notify us of this'. Sazonov, in reply, said that it was technically impossible to stop the mobilization but that, so long as negotiations continued, Russia would not attack. The Tsar reinforced this statement with another telegram to the Kaiser – 'Understand that you are obliged to mobilize, but wish to have the same guarantee from you as I gave you that these measures do not mean war, and that we shall continue negotiating ...' But, without waiting to hear the reply to their ultimatum, the German government dispatched a formally worded declaration of war to their ambassador in St Petersburg, who duly delivered it, after the expiry of the time limit, in the early evening of August 1st. Almost coincidently German mobilization began.

Yet General von Chelius had shrewdly reported from St Petersburg – 'People have mobilized here through fear of coming events with no aggressive purpose, and are already terrified at the result.' And the Kaiser had made the note – 'Right; that is the truth.' But the Kaiser, now equally frightened, and willing, could not stop his own military machine. For Moltke was insistent that 'the unusually favourable situation should be used to strike', pointing out that 'France's military situation is nothing less than embarrassed, that Russia is anything but confident; moreover, the time of year is favourable'. The rashness of the Russian General Staff might at least be excused by 'nerves', but hardly Moltke's. If three men can be singled out as the main personal causes of the war, at this time, they are Berchtold, Conrad and Moltke. But Moltke was really a limited company – the Great General Staff.

Yet, if their action was deliberate, fear was the background of their thought, not merely militaristic ambition. Fear, among the Austrian General Staff, of the doubling of the Serbian Army in consequence of Serbia's gain of territory in the Balkan war. Fear, among the German General Staff, of the Russian Army's unexpectedly rapid recovery, from its 1905 sickness under the ministrations of Sukhomlinov. Like a hard-pressed hero of the towpath, Moltke now pushed Austria into war so that he could jump in to her rescue, and then be sure of her help in return.

The German ultimatum to France demanded to know whether France would remain neutral 'in a Russo-German war', gave her eighteen hours for a reply, and added the menace, 'Mobilization will inevitably mean war'. In case she offered to remain neutral, the German ambassador was instructed to make the impossible demand that France must hand over the fortresses of Verdun and Toul as a pledge. For Moltke's plans were made for a two-front war, and his aim would be upset if only one target appeared! Could military folly go further?

The German ambassador called for his answer on August 1st, and was simply told that France 'would act as her interests required'. That afternoon the French mobilization was ordered, but in republican France the civil government was still superior to the General Staff, and since July 30th the frontier forces had been withdrawn to a line ten kilometres inside the frontier as a pacific gesture and a safeguard against the danger that a frontier skirmish might provide an excuse for war. If a military handicap, the political wisdom of this withdrawal was seen in the fact that German patrols crossed the actual frontier on the 30th and again, by German official admission, on the 31st. Thus when, on August 3rd Germany declared war on France, she could only allege the one concrete excuse that a French aviator had 'thrown bombs on the railway near Karlsruhe and Nuremberg' – a rumour already contradicted in Germany before the declaration was delivered.

Why was the actual declaration delayed two days in delivery? First, because of the fresh suggestion from Grey that so long as there was any chance of agreement between Russia and Austria, Germany and France should refrain from any attack. The suggestion was vaguely worded and Lichnowsky, in his eager desire for peace, enlarged it in telegraphing to Berlin that 'this would appear to mean that in case we did not attack France, England would remain neutral and would guarantee France's neutrality'. The Kaiser and his Chancellor clutched at the straw. The former said to Moltke – 'We march, then, with all our forces, only towards the east.' Moltke, as his memoirs relate, replied, 'that this was impossible. The advance of armies formed of millions of men ... was the result of years of painstaking work. Once planned, it could not possibly be changed.' The Kaiser bitterly retorted – 'Your uncle would have given me a different reply.' Moltke gained his way as regards the continued concentration against France, but a twenty-four hour brake was ordered to be put on the actual crossing of the frontier of France and Luxembourg. Moltke pathetically records – 'It was a great shock to me, as though something had struck at my heart.' However his heart attack was soon relieved, for late that evening further telegrams from London showed that Britain was not promising neutrality. The brake was released. And if it had caused some check on Moltke's arrangements, some of his advanced troops had actually entered Luxembourg that day in advance of timetable!

Nevertheless the British Cabinet was still wavering. A majority of its members were so anxious for peace and uncertain of the public attitude that they had failed to give a clear warning which might have strengthened Bethmann-Hollweg in his feeble efforts to withstand his own war party. Now it was too late and the military machine was in control. Nothing could have averted war after July 31st. Thus the British Cabinet's continued uncertainty, however natural and creditable, merely increased the anxiety of France, fearful of desertion.

Germany came to the rescue. Her long-prepared ultimatum to Belgium, demanding a free passage for her troops as required by her still longer-prepared war plan, was delivered on the evening of August 2nd. The Belgian government sturdily refused to allow its neutrality to be violated. On the morning of August 4th, the German troops began their invasion. The threat, even before the act was known, was decisive in hardening British opinion to the point of intervention, even though that intervention was already inevitable, as the German Staff had correctly calculated. An ultimatum was delivered that Germany should respect Belgian neutrality, and was received by Bethmann-Hollweg with the pitiful complaint that Britain was going to war 'just for a scrap of paper'. At 11 PM – by German time – the ultimatum expired. Britain also was in the war – and Italy was out of it, having already decided for neutrality on July 31st.

Thus in the final act, as in the earlier acts, 'technical military arguments' were decisive. The German army *must* go through Belgium, even though with the certainty that Britain would thereby be drawn in against Germany. Military technique – how competent in peace to gain war; how impotent in war to gain victory, so it was soon to prove!

CHAPTER TWO

The Opposing Forces

The nations entered upon the conflict with the conventional outlook and system of the eighteenth century merely modified by the events of the nineteenth century. Politically, they conceived it to be a struggle between rival coalitions based on the traditional system of diplomatic alliances, and militarily a contest between professional armies – swollen, it is true, by the continental system of conscription, yet essentially fought out by soldiers while the mass of the people watched, from seats in the amphitheatre, the efforts of their champions. The Germans had a glimpse of the truth, but – one or two prophetic minds apart – the 'Nation in Arms' theory, evolved by them during the nineteenth century, visualized the nation as a reservoir to pour its reinforcements into the army, rather than as a mighty river in which are merged many tributary forces of which the army is but one. Their conception was the 'Nation in Arms', hardly the 'Nation at War'. Even today this fundamental truth has yet to be grasped in its entirety and its full implications understood. Progressively throughout the years 1914–18 the warring nations enlisted the research of the scientist, the inventive power and technical skill of the engineer, the manual labour of industry, and the pen of the propagandist. For long this fusion of many forces tended to a chaotic maelstrom of forces; the old order had broken down, the new had not yet evolved. Only gradually did a working cooperation emerge, and it is a moot point whether even in the last phase cooperation of forces had attained to the higher level of coordination – direction by unity of diversity.

The German army of 1914 was born in the Napoleonic Wars, nursed in infancy by Gneisenau and Scharnhorst, and guided in adolescence by the elder Moltke and Roon. It reached maturity in the war of 1870, when it emerged triumphantly from a trial against the ill-equipped and badly led long-service army of France. Every physically able citizen was liable to service; the State took the number it desired, trained them to arms for a short period of full-time service, and then returned them to civil life. The feature, as also the object, of the system, was the production of a huge reserve by which to expand the active army in war. A man served two or three years full-time, according to his branch of the service, followed by five or four years in the regular reserves. He then served in the Landwehr for twelve years, and finally passed into the Landsturm from the age of thirty-nine till forty-five. Further, an Ersatz reserve was formed of those who were not called on for service with the colours.

In this organization and in the thoroughness of the training lay the secret of the first great surprise of the war, one which almost proved decisive. For instead of regarding their reservists as troops of doubtful quality, fit only for an auxiliary role or garrison duty, the Germans during mobilization were able to duplicate almost every first-line army corps with a reserve corps – and had the courage, justified by events, to use them in the opening clash. This surprise upset the French calculations and thereby dislocated their entire plan of campaign.

The Germans have been reproached for many miscalculations; less than justice has been done to the correctness of many of their intuitions. They alone realized what is today an axiom – that, given a highly trained cadre of leaders, a military machine can be rapidly manufactured from short-time levies, like molten liquid poured into a mould. The German mould was a long-service body of officers and NCOs who in their standard of technical knowledge and skill had no equal on the Continent. But if the machine was manufactured by training it gained solidity from another process. The psychological element plays an even greater part in a 'national' than in a professional army. *Esprit de corps* is not enough; the stimulus of a great moral impulse to action is necessary, a deep-rooted belief in the policy for which citizens are called on to fight. The leaders of Germany had worked for generations to inspire their people with a patriotic conviction of the grandeur of their country's destiny. And if their opponents went forth to battle in 1914 with as intense a belief in their country's cause, this flaming patriotism had not the time to consolidate such a disciplined combination as years of steady heat had produced in Germany. The German people had an intimacy with and a pride in their army, notwithstanding the severity of its discipline, that was unknown elsewhere.

This unique instrument was handled by a general staff which, by rigour of selection and training, was unmatched for professional knowledge and skill, if subject to the mental 'grooves' which characterize all professions. Executive skill is the fruit of practice; and constant practice, or repetition, tends inevitably to deaden originality and elasticity of mind. In a professional body, also, promotion by seniority is a rule difficult to avoid. The Germans, it is true, tended towards a system of staff control, which in practice usually left the real power in the hands of youthful general staff officers. As war memoirs and documents reveal, the chiefs of staff of the various armies and corps often took momentous decisions with hardly a pretence of consulting their commanders. But such a system had grave objections, and from it came the grit in the wheels which not infrequently marred the otherwise well-oiled working of the German war machine.

Tactically the Germans began with two important material advantages. They alone had gauged the potentialities of the heavy howitzer, and had provided adequate numbers of this weapon. And if no army had fully realized that machine guns were 'concentrated essence of infantry', nor fully developed this preponderant source of fire power, the Germans had studied it more than other armies, and were able to exploit its inherent power of dominating a battlefield sooner than other armies. In this anticipation of the value of heavy artillery and machine guns the German General Staff seems to have been largely influenced by the acute diagnosis of Captain Hoffmann, its youthful attaché with the Japanese Army in Manchuria. Strategically, also, the Germans had brought the study and development of railway communications to a higher pitch than any of their rivals.

The Austro-Hungarian army, if patterned on the German model, was a vastly inferior instrument. Not only had it a tradition of defeat rather than of victory, but its racial mixture prevented the moral homogeneity that distinguished its ally. This being so, the replacement of the old professional army by one based on universal service lowered rather than raised its standard of effectiveness. The troops within the borders of the empire were often racially akin to those beyond, and this compelled Austria to a politically instead of a militarily based distribution of forces, so that kinsmen should not fight each other. And her human handicap was increased by a geographical one, namely, the vast extent of frontier to be defended.

Nor were her leaders, with rare exceptions, the professional equals of the Germans. Moreover, if common action was better understood than among the Entente Powers, Austria did not accept German direction gladly.

Yet despite all its evident weaknesses the loosely knit conglomeration of races withstood the shock and strain of war for four years, in a way that surprised and dismayed her opponents. The explanation is that the complex racial fabric was woven on a stout Germanic and Magyar framework.

From the Central we turn to the Entente Powers. France possessed but sixty per cent of the potential man power of Germany (5,940,000 against 9,750,000), and this debit balance had forced her to call on the services of practically every able-bodied male. A man was called up at twenty, did three years' full-time service, then eleven in the reserve and finally two periods of seven years each in the Territorial Army and Territorial Reserve. This system gave France an initial war strength of nearly four million trained men, compared with Germany's five; but she placed little reliance on the fighting value of reservists. The French command counted only on the semi-professional troops of the first line, about 1,000,000 men, for the short and decisive campaign which they expected and prepared for. Moreover, they assumed a similar attitude on the part of their enemy – with dire result. But this initial surprise apart, a more profound handicap was the lesser capacity of France for expansion, in case of a long war, due to her smaller population – under 40,000,000 compared with Germany's 65,000,000. Colonel Mangin, later to become famous, had advocated tapping the resources in Africa, the raising of a huge native army, but the Government had considered the dangers to outweigh the advantages of such a policy, and war experience was to show that it had military as well as political risks.

The French General Staff, if less technically perfect than the German, had produced some of the most renowned military thinkers in Europe, and its level of intelligence could well bear comparison. But the French military mind tended to lose in originality and elasticity what it gained in logic. In the years preceding the war, too, a sharp division of thought had arisen which did not make for combined action. Worse still, the new French philosophy of war, by its preoccupation with the moral element, had become more and more separated from the inseparable material factors. Abundance of will cannot compensate a definite inferiority of weapons, and the second factor, once realized, inevitably reacts on the first. In material, the French had one great asset in their quick-firing 75mm field gun, the best in the world, but its very value had led them to undue confidence in a war of movement and a consequent neglect of equipment and training for the type of warfare which came to pass.

Russia's assets were in the physical sphere, her defects in the mental and moral. If her initial strength was no greater than that of Germany, her man-power resources were immense. Moreover the courage and endurance of her troops were famous. But corruption and incompetence permeated her leadership, her rank and file lacked the intelligence and initiative for scientific warfare – they formed an instrument of great solidity but little flexibility – while her manufacturing resources for equipment and munitions were far below those of the great industrial powers. This handicap was made worse by her geographical situation, for she was cut off from her allies by ice- or enemy-bound seas, and she had to cover immense land frontiers. Another radical defect was the poverty of her rail communications, which were the more essential as she relied for success on bringing into play the weight of her numbers. In the moral sphere Russia's condition was less clear. Her internal troubles were notorious and must be a brake on her efforts unless the cause was such as to make a crusade-like appeal to her primitive and incoherent masses.

Between the military systems of Germany, Austria, France and Russia there was a close relation; the differences were of detail rather than fundamental; and this similarity threw into greater contrast the system of the other great European power – Britain. Throughout modern times she had been essentially a sea power, intervening on land through a traditional policy of diplomatic and financial support to Allies, whose military efforts she reinforced with a leaven from her own professional army. This regular army was primarily maintained for the protection and control of the overseas dependencies – India in particular – and had always been kept down to the minimum strength for this purpose. The reason for the curious contrast between Britain's determination to maintain a supreme navy and her consistent neglect, indeed starvation, of the army lay partly in her insular position, which caused her to regard the sea as her essential life-line and main defence, and partly in a constitutional distrust of the army, an illogical prejudice, which had its almost forgotten source in the military government of Cromwell. Small as to size, it enjoyed a practical and varied experience of war without parallel among the continental armies. Compared with them, its obvious professional handicap was that the leaders, however apt in handling small columns in colonial expeditions, had never been prepared to direct large formations in *la grande guerre*.

But the value of such practice, and the British handicap, are easily overrated by the layman. For experience has tended to show that the larger the force, the smaller the scope for generalship, and the less the call upon it. Compared with the manifold personal initiative of a Marlborough or a Napoleon before and during battle, the decisions of an army commander in 1914–18 were necessarily few and broad – his role was more akin to that of managing director of a vast department store.

And in a war where all the leaders were soon out of their depth, and slow to recover, practical acumen counted for more than the theoretical technique acquired in peacetime exercises. These, especially in the French Army, too often bred the delusion that the issue of an order at a distance was equivalent to its fulfilment on the spot.

In the little British Army which originally took the field, personality had for a time more scope. And much was to depend upon it. Unfortunately, the issue was to suggest that the process of selection had not succeeded in bringing to the fore the officers best fitted for leadership. It is significant that, on the way out to France, Haig spoke to Charteris (his military secretary and future chief intelligence officer) of his qualms concerning the Commander-in-Chief, Sir John French, whose right hand he had been in South Africa: 'D.H. unburdened himself today. He is greatly concerned about the composition of British GHQ. He thinks French quite unfit for high command in time of crisis ... He says French's military ideas are not sound; that he has never studied war; that he is obstinate, and will not keep with him men who point out even obvious errors. He gives him credit for good tactical powers, great courage and determination. He does not think Murray will dare to do anything but agree with everything French suggests. In any case he thinks French would not listen to Murray but rely on Wilson, which is far worse. D.H. thinks Wilson is a politician, and not a soldier, and "politician" with Douglas Haig is synonymous with crooked dealing and wrong sense of values.' This judgement is similar to that of another General, eminent as a military historian: 'There could hardly have been worse selected GHQs than those with which we began the South African War and 1914.'

But apart from errors in selection, there is the question whether officers were miscast for their actual roles. In 1912 French himself had expressed the opinion that certainly Haig and perhaps Grierson would 'always shine more and show to greater advantage as superior staff officers than as commanders'. Because of his unrivalled knowledge of the German Army and cordial relations with the French, as well as his gift for putting juniors at their ease, Grierson would have been a peculiarly good Chief of Staff for French. Yet 'when Grierson – his Chief Staff Officer at manoeuvres – had pointed out to French the impracticability of some of his proposals, he had at once been replaced by Sir Archibald Murray'. Grierson, instead, went to France as commander of an army corps. A man of full figure and sedentary habits, fifty-five years old, the combination of good living and hard work had undermined his constitution; he collapsed and died on his way to the front. If this was a great loss to the Army, it was a less immediate danger than Murray's subsequent collapse on August 26th, the critical day of Le Cateau. Worse still, Murray would recover sufficiently to think that he was functioning when actually he was still unfit. These were but two of the most prominent instances of the trouble caused by a system which brought officers to high position at an age when their energy was declining, and their susceptibility to the strain of war increasing. As a fortunate offset the enemy suffered at least as heavily from this handicap: indeed, the directing head of the German armies, Moltke, who had recently been undergoing treatment, caused alarm among his entourage in the very first days of war by his state of semi-collapse.

The other British corps commander, Haig, had taken too good care of his health to cause any such anxiety. Physically, his fitness at fifty-three was exceptional. In the South African War, his thoroughness and methodicity had made him an ideal staff officer to French; but later, when given command of a mobile column, those qualities had not proved all-sufficing. It is worth recalling that when Colonel Woolls-Sampson, 'the incomparable Intelligence officer and fighting scout', was told of Haig's appointment as column commander, he remarked: 'He's quite all right, but he's too — cautious: he will be so fixed on not giving the Boers a chance, he'll never give himself one.' Thirteen years later Woolls-Sampson's point was borne out. For the revised Official History of 1914, published after a generation has passed, has revealed that at Haig's first serious test as a corps commander he was temporarily thrown off his balance by a trifling encounter in the dark, so that he reported 'situation very critical', and repeatedly called for help – from a neighbour who was really hard pressed. It has also revealed that Haig's excessive caution on reaching the Aisne allowed the day of opportunity to slip away, and the enemy to establish their four years' tenure of the position beyond. Yet if command was not Haig's natural role, he had developed qualities which others lacked, and once the battlefront became static the conditions of warfare tended to change the role of a commander into that of a super-staff officer.

Errors of conception were to cost more than any errors of execution. Lessons of the South African War that went wider than the selection of leaders had been overlooked. Read in the light of 1914–18, the 'Evidence taken before the Royal Commission on the War in South Africa' offers astonishing proof of how professional vision may miss the wood for the trees. There is little hint, among those who were to be the leaders in the next war, that they had recognized the root problem of the future – the dominating power of fire defence and the supreme difficulty of crossing the bullet-swept zone. Sir Ian Hamilton alone gave it due emphasis, and even he was too sanguine as to the possibility of overcoming it. His proposed solution, however, was in the right direction. For he urged not only the value of exploiting surprise and infiltration tactics to nullify the advantages of the defence, but the need of heavy field artillery to support the infantry. Still more prophetically, he suggested that the infantry might be provided with 'steel shields on wheels' to enable them to cross no-man's-land and make a lodgement in the enemy's position.

Mr Amery, author of *The Times* history of the war, probed a weak spot in the prevailing European theory by arguing that superior skill now counted more than superior numbers, and that its proportionate value would increase with material progress. The same note was struck by General Baden-Powell, who urged that the way to develop it was to give officers responsibility when young – he was left to find his channel for proving this in the Boy Scout movement, and not in the Army.

Two generals, Paget and Hunter, had a vision of the value and future use of motor vehicles in war, while Haig said that, rather than mounted infantry, he would prefer infantry 'on motors'. In view of the development of the motor between 1903 and 1914 it is strange how little use of it was made at the outset of the next war – or even at the end!

But the most remarkable feature of this Royal Commission was the way that French and Haig discoursed on the paramount value of the *arme blanche*, implying that so long as the cavalry charge was maintained all would be well with the conduct of war. An equally striking underestimate of fire power was contained in Haig's forecast that 'artillery seems only likely to be really effective against raw troops'. His confident opening declaration was that 'cavalry will have a larger sphere of action in future wars'. And he went on to say: 'Besides being used before, during, and after a battle as hitherto, we must expect to see it employed strategically on much larger scale than formerly.' What a contrast there was to be between this expectation and the event! French, Germans, Russians, and Austrians certainly had unexampled masses of cavalry ready at the outbreak of war. But in the opening phase they caused more trouble to their own sides than to the enemy. From 1915 on, their effect was trivial, except as a strain on their own country's supplies: despite the relatively small number of British cavalry, forage was the largest item of supplies sent overseas, exceeding even ammunition, and thus the most dangerous factor in aggravating the submarine menace; while, by authoritative verdict, the transport trouble caused in feeding the immense number of cavalry horses was an important factor in producing Russia's collapse.

In the British Army, also, one unfortunate result of this delusion was that when the cavalry school came to the top in the years just before the war, there was the usual human tendency to penalize the careers of officers who propounded more realistic ideas, while a still larger circle were thereby induced to maintain silence. This was the greater pity because the cavalry sense of mobility was as vital a necessity as the cavalry means of mobility was decadent; and by undue emphasis on the old means the chance of re-creating the means was hindered.

But in other ways the bitter lessons of the South African War brought profit, exerting an influence which to some extent counteracted that inelasticity of mind and ritualism of method which have increased with the increasing professionalization of armies. For the progress in organization in the years before 1914, the British Army owed much to Lord Haldane,* and to him also was due the creation of a second line of partially trained citizens – the Territorial Force. Lord Roberts had pleaded for compulsory military training, but the voluntary principle was too deeply embedded in the national mind for this course to be adopted, and Haldane wisely sought to develop Britain's military effectiveness within the bounds set by traditional policy. As a result, 1914 found England with an expeditionary force of some 160,000 men, the most highly trained striking force of any country – a rapier among scythes. To maintain this at strength the old militia had been turned into a special reserve for drafting. Behind this first line stood the Territorial Force, which if only enlisted for home defence had a permanent fighting organization, unlike the amorphous volunteer force which it superseded. The British Army had no outstanding asset in war armament, but it had developed a standard of rifle-shooting unique among the world's armies.

The reforms by which the army had been brought into line with continental models had one defect, accentuated by the close relations established between the British and French General Staffs since the Entente. It induced a 'continental' habit of thought among the General Staff, and predisposed them to the role, for which their slender strength was unsuited, of fighting alongside an Allied army. This obscured the British Army's traditional employment in amphibious operations through which the mobility given by command of the sea could be exploited. A small but highly trained force striking 'out of the blue' at a

---

* He found an ardent assistant in Haig, whose appointment to the War Office had been strongly urged by King Edward.

vital spot can produce a strategic effect out of all proportion to its slight numbers.

The last argument brings us to a comparison of the naval situation, which turned on the balance between the fleets of Britain and Germany. Britain's sea supremacy, for long unquestioned, had in recent years been challenged by a Germany which had deduced that a powerful fleet was the key to that colonial empire which she desired as an outlet for her commerce and increasing population. This ambition was fostered, as its instrument was created, by the dangerous genius of Admiral von Tirpitz. To the spur of naval competition the British people eventually responded, determined at any cost to maintain their 'two-power' standard. If this reaction was instinctive rather than reasoned, its subconscious wisdom had a better foundation than the catchwords with which it was justified, or even than the need of defence against invasion. The industrial development of the British Isles had left them dependent on overseas supplies for food, and on the secure flow of seaborne imports and exports for industrial existence. For the navy itself this competition was a refining agency, leading to a concentration on essentials. Gunnery was developed and less value attached to polished brasswork. Warship design and armament were transformed; the 'Dreadnought' ushered in the new era of the big-gun battleship. By 1914 Britain had twenty-nine such capital ships and thirteen building, to the eighteen built and nine building, of Germany. Further, Britain's naval strength had been soundly distributed, the main concentration being in the North Sea.

More open to criticism in view of the forecasts of several naval authorities, was her comparative neglect of the potential menace of the submarine. Here German opinion was shown rather by the number building than those already in commission. It is to Germany's credit that though lacking a sea tradition, her fleet an artificial rather than a natural product, the technical skill of the German Navy made it a formidable rival to the British ship for ship, and perhaps its superior in scientific gunnery.

But in the first stage of the struggle the balance of the naval forces was to affect the issue far less than the balance on land. For a fleet suffers one inherent limitation – it is tied to the sea, and hence cannot strike direct at the hostile nation. The fundamental purpose of a navy is therefore to protect a nation's sea communications and sever those of the enemy; although victory in battle may be a necessary prelude, blockade is its ultimate purpose. And as blockade is a weapon slow to take effect, its influence could only be decisive if the armies failed to secure the speedy decision on land, upon which all counted.

In this idea of a short war lay also the reason for the comparative disregard of economic forces. Few believed that a modern nation could endure for many months the strain of a large-scale conflict. The supply of food and of funds, the supply and manufacture of munitions, these were problems that had been only studied on brief estimates. Of the belligerents, all could feed themselves save Britain and Germany, and Germany's deficit of home-grown supplies could only be serious in the event of a struggle of years. But Britain would starve in three months if her outside supplies were cut off.

In munitions and other war material Britain's industrial power was greatest of all, though conversion to war production was a necessary preliminary, and all, again, depended on the security of her sea communications. France was weak, and Russia weaker still, but the former unlike the latter could count on outside supplies so long as Britain held the seas. As Britain was the industrial pivot of the one alliance, so was Germany of the other. A great manufacturing nation, she had also a wealth of raw material, especially since the annexation of the Lorraine ironfields after the 1870 war. But the stoppage of outside supplies must be a handicap in a long war, increasing with its duration, and serious from the outset in such tropical products as rubber. Moreover, Germany's main coal and ironfields lay dangerously close to her frontier, in Silesia on the east and in Westphalia and Lorraine on the west. Thus for the Central Alliance a quick decision and an offensive war were more essential than for the Entente.

Similarly, financial resources had been calculated on a short war basis, and all the Continental Powers relied mainly on large gold reserves accumulated specially for war purposes. Britain alone had no such war chest, but she was to prove that the strength of her banking system and the wealth distributed among a great commercial people furnished the 'sinews of war' in a way that few pre-war economists had realized.

If the economic forces were neglected in the war calculations of the Powers, the psychological forces were an unexplored region, except in their purely military aspect. And even here little study had been devoted to the moral element compared with the physical element. Ardant du Picq, a soldier-philosopher who fell in the 1870 war, had stripped battle of its aura of heroic fictions, portraying the reaction of normal men in the presence of danger. Several German critics had described from experience the reality of battle morale as shown in 1870, and had deduced how tactics should be based on the ever-present and balancing elements of fear and courage. At the close of the century a French military thinker, Colonel Foch, had demonstrated how great was the influence of the moral element in the higher sphere of command, although his teaching was concerned rather with fortifying the will of the commander than with unhinging the will of the opponent. But only the surface of the subject had been penetrated. Its civil aspects were untouched, and in the opening weeks of the conflict the general misunderstanding of national psychology was to be shown in the muzzling of the press – in Britain due mainly to Kitchener, followed by the equally stupid practice of issuing *communiqués* which so veiled the truth that public opinion became distrustful of all official news and rumour was loosed on its infinitely more damaging course. The true value of wisely calculated publicity and the application of the propaganda weapon were only to be learnt after many blunders.

CHAPTER THREE

The Rival War Plans

In an historical survey the German plan must justly take priority, for not only was it the mainspring which set in motion the hands of the war clock in 1914, but it may even be said to have governed the course of the war thereafter. It is true that, from the autumn of 1914 onwards, this course outwardly seemed to be of the nature of a stupendous 'siege' of the Central Powers, an idea incompatible with the terms we have used. But the conception of the Germanic Alliance as a besieged party, although true of the economic sphere, suggests a loss of initiative which their strategy contradicts. Although the initial German plan miscarried, even in its failure it dictated the general trend of operations thereafter. Tactically, most of the fighting resembled siege operations, but the actual strategy on land long erred rather by its disregard of these tactical conditions than by its conformity with them.

The Germans were faced with the problem that the combined forces of themselves and Austria were decidedly inferior to those of France and Russia. To offset this adverse balance, however, they had a central position and the anticipation that Russia's mobilization would be too slow to allow her to exert serious pressure in the opening weeks. While this assumption might suggest a decisive blow at Russia before she was ready, it was equally probable that she would concentrate her main forces too far back for such a German blow to reach – and the experience of Napoleon was not an example to encourage an advance deep into the interior of Russia, with its vast distances and poor communications. The plan long since adopted by Germany was, therefore, to deliver a rapid offensive against France while holding the Russian advanced forces at bay; and later, when France was crushed, to deal with the Russian army. But this plan, in turn, was complicated by the great natural and artificial barriers which the French frontier offered to an invader. It was narrow, only some 150 miles across, and so afforded little room to manoeuvre or even to deploy the masses that Germany planned to launch against her foe. At the south-eastern end it abutted on Switzerland, and after a short stretch of flat country known as the Gap of Belfort the frontier ran for seventy miles along the Vosges mountains. Behind and prolonging this natural rampart ran an almost continuous fortress system, based on Epinal, Toul, Verdun, and twenty miles beyond the last-named lay not only the frontiers of Luxembourg and Belgium but the difficult Ardennes country. Apart from the strongly defended avenues of advance by Belfort and Verdun, the only feasible gap in this barrier was the Trouée de Charmes between Epinal and Toul, left open originally as a strategic trap in which the Germans could be first caught and then crushed by a French counterstroke.

Faced with such a mental and physical blank wall, the logical *military* course was to go round it – by a wide manoeuvre through Belgium. Graf Schlieffen, Chief of the German General Staff from 1890 to 1905, conceived and developed the plan, by which the French armies were to be enveloped and a rapid decision gained; and as finally formulated it came into force in 1905. To attain its object Schlieffen's plan concentrated the mass of the German forces on the right wing for a gigantic wheel and designedly took risks by reducing the left wing, facing the French frontier, to the slenderest possible size. The swinging mass, pivoting on the fortified area Metz-Thionville, was to consist of fifty-three divisions, backed up as rapidly as possible by Landwehr and Ersatz formations, while the secondary army on the left wing comprised only eight divisions. Its very weakness promised to aid the main blow in a further way, for if a French offensive pressed the left wing back towards the Rhine, the attack through Belgium on the French flank would be all the more difficult to parry. It would be like a revolving door – if a man pressed heavily on one side the other side would swing round and strike him in the back. Here lay the real subtlety of the plan, not in the mere geographical detour.

The German enveloping mass was to sweep round through Belgium and northern France and, continuing to traverse a vast arc, would wheel gradually east. With its extreme right passing south of Paris and crossing the Seine near Rouen it would then press the French back towards the Moselle, where they would be hammered in rear on the anvil formed by the Lorraine fortresses and the Swiss frontier.

Schlieffen's plan allowed ten divisions to hold the Russians in check while the French were being crushed. It is proof of his clear sight, if not of his long sight, that he counted on the intervention of Britain, and allowed for an expeditionary force of 100,000 'operating in conjunction with the French'. To him also was due the scheme for using the Landwehr and Ersatz troops in active operations and fusing the resources of the nation into the army. His dying words are reported to have been: 'It must come to a fight. Only make the right wing strong.'

Unhappily for Germany, his successor, Moltke 'the younger', lacked his moral courage while sharing his disregard of international morality. Moltke retained Schlieffen's plan, but he whittled away the essential idea. Of the nine new divisions which became available between 1905 and 1914 Moltke allotted eight to the left wing and only one to the right. True, he added another from the Russian front, but this trivial increase was purchased at a heavy price, for the Russian Army of 1914 was a more formidable menace than when Schlieffen's plan came into force. In the outcome two army corps were taken from the French theatre at the crisis of the August campaign, in order to reinforce the Eastern Front. Schlieffen's deathbed entreaty was lost on his successor.

Moltke also made a change of great political significance in the plan. Schlieffen had intended that the right wing should deploy along not only the Belgian but also the Dutch frontier, as far north as Crefeld. By crossing the strip of Dutch territory known as the 'Maastricht Appendix' it would be able to turn the flank of the Liége forts, which barred the way through the narrow Belgian gateway north of the Ardennes. He hoped that German diplomacy might secure permission for this passage through Holland, and he did not wish to violate the territory of either Belgium or Holland if he could avoid the moral reproach. For it was his calculation that the undisguised deployment there of part of his force would so alarm the French as to induce them to cross the southern frontier of Belgium and occupy the natural defensive position in the Meuse valley, south of Namur. Thereby they would provide a pretext for his own advance into neutral territory. Even should this subtle trap fail, Schlieffen calculated that he would be able to capture Liége in time to avoid any check on his main advance. And he was willing to cut his margin of time so close as to afford German statecraft the fullest chance to escape the charge of rape.

Such imaginative craft was beyond Moltke's capacity, and he decided that Liége must be taken by a *coup de main* immediately after the outbreak of war. Thus for a fancied addition to military security he deliberately invited the condemnation of neutrals, provoked Belgium to resistance, and drew the weight of Britain into the scales against his own forces. Moltke's method of 'drawing' the enemy was certainly the antithesis of Schlieffen's. And it is a glaring example of the dangers, even the military dangers, which may ensue if strategy is allowed to dominate policy.

If the fault of the final German plan was a lack of courage, that of the French plan was due to an excess. In their case, also, a miasma of confused thought seemed to creep over the leadership in the years just before the war. Since the disasters of 1870 the French Command had planned an initial defensive, based on the frontier fortresses, followed by a decisive counterstroke. To this end the great fortress system had been created and gaps like the Trouée de Charmes left to 'canalize' the invasion ready for the counter. But in the decade before 1914 a new school of thought had risen, who argued that the offensive was more in tune with French character and tradition, that the possession of the '75' – a field gun unique in mobility and rapidity of fire – made it tactically possible, and that the alliance with Russia and Britain made it strategically possible. Forgetful of the lessons of 1870 they imagined that *élan* was proof against bullets. Napoleon's much-quoted saying that 'the moral is to the physical as three to one' has much to answer for; it has led soldiers to think that a division exists between the two, whereas each is dependent on the other. Weapons without courage are ineffective, but so also are the bravest troops without sufficient weapons to protect them and their morale. Courage soon oozes when soldiers lose confidence in their weapons.

The outcome was disastrous. The new school, who found their prophet in Colonel de Grandmaison, found in General Joffre, appointed Chief of the General Staff in 1912, a lever for their designs. Under the cloak of his authority, the advocates of the *offensive à outrance* gained control of the French military machine, and, throwing aside the old doctrine, formulated the now famous, or notorious, Plan XVII. It was based on a negation of historical experience, indeed, of common-sense, and on a double miscalculation – of force and place, the latter more serious than the former. Accepting the possibility that the Germans might employ their reserve formations at the outset, the strength of the German army in the west was estimated at a possible maximum of sixty-eight infantry divisions. The Germans actually deployed the equivalent of eighty-three, counting Landwehr and Ersatz troops. But French opinion was, and continued to be, doubtful of this contingency, so much so that during the crucial days when the rival armies were concentrating and moving forward the French Intelligence counted only the forty-five active divisions in its estimates of the enemy strength – a miscalculation by half. If the plan had been framed on a miscalculation less extreme, this recognition does not condone but rather increases its fundamental falsity: for history affords no vestige of justification for a plan by which a frontal offensive was to be launched with bare equality of force against an enemy who would have the support of his fortified frontier zone, while the attackers forswore any advantage from their own.

The second miscalculation – of place – was that although the possibility of a German move through Belgium was recognized, the wideness of its sweep was utterly misjudged. The Germans were expected complaisantly to take the difficult route through the Ardennes in order that the French might conveniently smite their communications! Based on the idea of an immediate and general offensive, the plan ordained a thrust by the First and Second Armies towards the Saar into Lorraine. On their left were the Third Army opposite Metz and the Fifth Army facing the Ardennes, which were either to take up the offensive between Metz and Thionville, or, if the Germans came through Luxembourg and Belgium, to strike north-east at their flank. The Fourth Army was held in strategic reserve near the centre and two groups of reserve divisions were disposed in rear of either flank – relegation to such a passive role expressing French opinion on the capacity of reserve formations.

Britain's contingent share in this plan was settled less by calculation than by the 'Europeanization' of her military organization during the previous decade. This continental influence drew her insensibly into a tacit acceptance of the role of acting as an appendix to the French left wing, and away from her historic exploitation of the mobility given by sea power. At a council of war on August 5th, Sir John French, who was to command the expeditionary force, expressed a doubt of 'the prearranged plan', and, as an alternative, suggested its dispatch to Belgium – where it would have stiffened the Belgian resistance and threatened the flank of the wheeling German mass. Haig seems to have had a similar view. But the plan did not provide for variation, and in any case the General Staff, through Henry Wilson, had virtually pledged themselves to act in direct cooperation with the French. When the General Staffs of the two countries' conducted their informal negotiations between 1905 and 1914, they were paving the way for a reversal of England's centuries-old policy for a war effort such as no Englishman had ever conceived.

Lord Kitchener, who had just been made War Minister in the emergency, had a remarkably accurate intuition of the German plan and tried to avert the danger by advocating that the expeditionary force should concentrate near Amiens, where it would be less exposed. But French was now in accord with Wilson, and his vehement support of the French plan induced Kitchener to give way – later he lamented his consent as a mistaken weakness. Kitchener, however, gave French instructions which, designed to reduce the risks, were in the issue to complicate and even to increase them. For while French's assigned purpose was 'to support, and cooperate with, the French Army', it was qualified by the somewhat contradictory statement 'that the gravest consideration will devolve upon you as to participation ... where your force may be unduly exposed...' Further, 'you will in no case come in any sense under the orders of any Allied General'.

The smoothness and secrecy with which the expeditionary force moved to France (the main part between August 12th and 17th) was a testimony to the transport arrangements and counter-espionage measures, if still more to the shortsightedness of the Germans. Not merely did their intelligence service fail to gain news of the British expeditionary force until it was actually encountered, but the supreme Command showed little concern with its whereabouts. When Moltke was asked if he desired the Navy to interfere with the passage of the British troops, he showed no enthusiasm for the idea, saying that 'it would be indeed splendid if the Army in the west could settle with the 160,000 English at the same time as with the other enemies'. In their pedantic adherence to the principle of concentration both the General Staff and the Naval Staff ignored the importance of distraction. And each remained in its own narrow compartment, with little interest in what the other was doing and less desire to communicate its own intentions.

The General Staff's mind was fixed on the aim of a decisive battle, without a thought for the Channel ports; the detachments it made, so fateful in their effect, were for the negative purpose of protecting its own march, and not to embarrass the enemy. The Naval Staff's dominant idea was to keep the fleet concentrated in the North Sea, ready for eventualities but with little concern to influence events. Its positive action was limited to sending out a few submarines in a half-hearted manner. The idea of a landing on the English coast, or even a feint, does not seem to have been considered – although the mere possibility sufficed to detain a considerable part of Britain's military strength. Nor had the General Staff made plans for embarrassing Britain at long range by encouraging native risings. A swift victory over the main armies in the main theatre of war was the German General Staff's solution for all outside difficulties, and absolved them from thinking of war in its wider aspects.

On the Russian front, the plans of campaign were more fluid, less elaborately worked out and formulated, although they were to be as kaleidoscopic in their changes of fortune as in the western theatre. The calculable condition was geographical; the main incalculable, Russia's rate of concentration. Russian Poland was a vast tongue of country projecting from Russia proper, and flanked on three sides by German or Austrian territory. On its northern flank lay East Prussia with the Baltic Sea beyond. On its southern flank lay the Austrian province of Galicia with the Carpathian mountains to the south, guarding the approach to the plain of Hungary. On the west lay Silesia. As the Germanic border provinces were provided with a network of strategic railways whilst Poland, as well as Russia itself, had only a sparse system of communications, the Germanic Alliance enjoyed a great advantage, in power of concentration, for countering a Russian advance. But if its armies took the offensive, the farther they progressed into Poland or Russia proper the more would they lose this advantage. Hence their most profitable strategy was to lure the Russians into a position favourable for a counterstroke rather than to inaugurate an offensive themselves. The one drawback was that such a Punic strategy gave the Russians time to concentrate and set in motion their cumbrous and rusty machine.

From this arose an initial cleavage between German and Austrian opinion. Both agreed that the problem was to hold the Russians in check during the six weeks which must elapse before the Germans should have crushed France, and so could switch their forces eastwards to join the Austrians in a decisive blow against the Russians. The difference of opinion turned on the method. The Germans, intent on a decision against France, wished to leave a minimum force in the east, and only a political dislike of exposing national territory to invasion prevented them from evacuating East Prussia and standing on the Vistula line. But the Austrians, under the influence of Conrad von Hötzendorf, chief of their General Staff, were anxious to throw the Russian machine out of gear by an immediate offensive, and, as this promised to keep the Russians fully occupied while the campaign in France was being decided, Moltke fell in with this strategy.

Conrad's plan was that of an offensive northwards into Poland by two armies, protected by two more on their right, farther east. The two attacking armies would then wheel eastwards, and all four would join hands in driving the Russians back towards the Black Sea. Complementary to this plan, as originally designed, the Germans in East Prussia were to strike south-east, the two forces converging to cut off the Russian advanced forces in the Polish 'tongue'. But Moltke failed to provide sufficient German troops for this offensive thrust.

Conrad's own offensive was to be impaired by the combination of a variable state of mind with an inelastic basis of movement. The Austrian forces had been divided into three parts: 'Echelon A' (28 divisions) for deployment on the Russian front; *Minimum Balkan* (8 divisions) for deployment on the Serbian front; 'Echelon B' (12 divisions) for use according to circumstances. The plan thus had more adaptability, on paper, than those of other armies; unfortunately, the instrument was not equal to the intention. Conrad's desire to settle with Serbia led him to begin moving 'Echelon B' thither, despite the likelihood of Russia's intervention. Then, on July 31st, he changed his mind and decided to stop it. But 'the Chief of the Field Railways informed him that if utter confusion was to be avoided he must allow "B" to go to its original destination on the Danube frontier, and from there it could be transported to Galicia'. As a result, its withdrawal from the Danube impaired the offensive against Serbia without helping that against Russia, for which it arrived too late. Thus a conflict of purpose in the Austrian Command accentuated the ill-effects of a conflict of interests between Austria and her ally.

On the opposing side also, the desires of one ally vitally affected the strategy of the other. The Russian command, both for military and for racial motives, wished to concentrate first against Austria, while the latter was unsupported, and leave Germany alone until later, when the full strength of the Russian Army would be mobilized. But the French, anxious to relieve the German pressure against themselves, urged the Russians to deliver a simultaneous attack against Germany, and persuaded the Russians to consent to an extra offensive for which they were ready neither in numbers nor in organization. On the southwestern front two pairs of two armies each were to converge on the Austrian forces in Galicia; on the north-western front two armies were to converge on the German forces in East Prussia. Russia, whose proverbial slowness and crude organization dictated a cautious strategy, was about to break with tradition and launch out on a gamble that only an army of high mobility and organization could have hoped to bring off.

When put to the test, the plans of all the military commanders would quickly collapse. At a superficial examination, the fault would seem due to divided purposes in the minds of the leaders – to their failure to maintain the principle of 'concentration' with which they had been indoctrinated. It is easy to point out how they failed in this way – many books by military experts have done so. But such a judgement is too academic. The fact that the fault was common to all sides suggests a deeper explanation. Not one of the leaders was anything but a devout upholder of the principle of concentration in theory: the trouble came when they tried to apply it to reality – to the political and tactical conditions in which strategy operates. Their failure to adapt their plans to the actual situation may be traced to the habit of mind formed in peace training; especially in war games and exercises, where battle was the ruling idea, the conventions too exclusively military, and the values too purely numerical. By treating concentration as a matter of assembling superior numbers, its dependence on the enemy's distraction and on freedom from external interference was too commonly obscured.

Peace training tended towards solutions that were idealistic rather than realistic. For war, like politics, is a series of compromises. Hence the need of adaptation should be foreseen, the power of adjustment developed, in the pre-war preparation. This was rare among the staff-trained leaders of 1914. They had been brought up on a diet of theory, supplemented by scraps of history cooked to suit the prevailing taste: not on the experience contained in real history. For this to be attainable a critical mind is the first requirement; but such a faculty was frowned on by the military tradition of the nineteenth century – although marked in many great leaders of the eighteenth century.

CHAPTER FOUR

1914 – The Clinch

The German invasion of France was designed as a methodical sweep, in which unexpected checks should not upset the timetable. The railway system in Germany had been developed under military guidance and supervision – so strict that not even a narrow-gauge line or road rail could be laid without the approval of the Chief of the General Staff. As a result the number of double lines running to the western frontier had been increased from nine to thirteen between 1870 and 1914. On August 6th the great deployment began; 550 trains a day crossed the Rhine bridges, and by the 12th the seven German armies (1,500,000 men) were ready to advance. Over the Hohenzollern bridge at Cologne a train passed about every ten minutes during the first fortnight of war. This vast railway movement was a masterpiece of organization, but when the deployment, completed on August 17th, merged into the forward march, the friction of war soon revealed weaknesses in the German military machine and its control.

To meet the case of Belgian resistance the German plan, as revised by Moltke, provided an instantly available detachment, under General von Emmich, to clear a passage through the Meuse gateway into the Belgian plain north of the Ardennes, ready for the ordered advance of the main armies concentrating behind the German frontier. The ring fortress of Liége commanded this channel of advance, but, after an initial check on August 5th, a German brigade penetrated between the forts and occupied the town. The interest of this feat is that it was due to the initiative of an attached staff officer, Ludendorff, whose name ere long was to be world famous. The forts themselves offered a stubborn resistance and forced the Germans to await the arrival of their heavy howitzers, whose destructive power was to be the first tactical surprise of the World War.

The very success of the Belgians' early resistance cloaked the weight of the main German columns and misled the Allies' Intelligence. The Belgian field army lay behind the Gette covering Brussels and, even

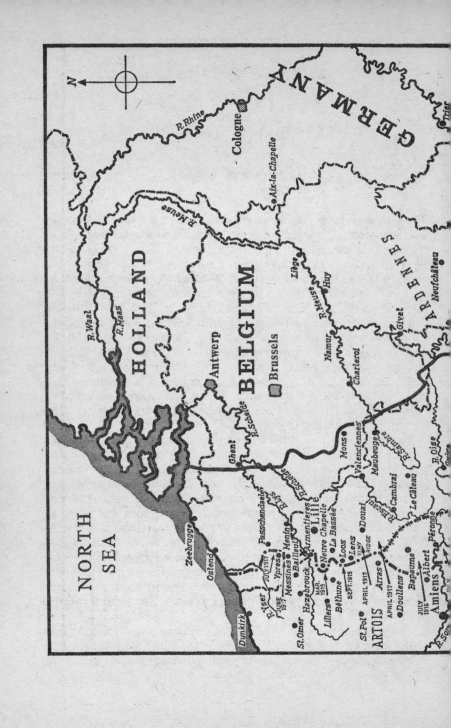

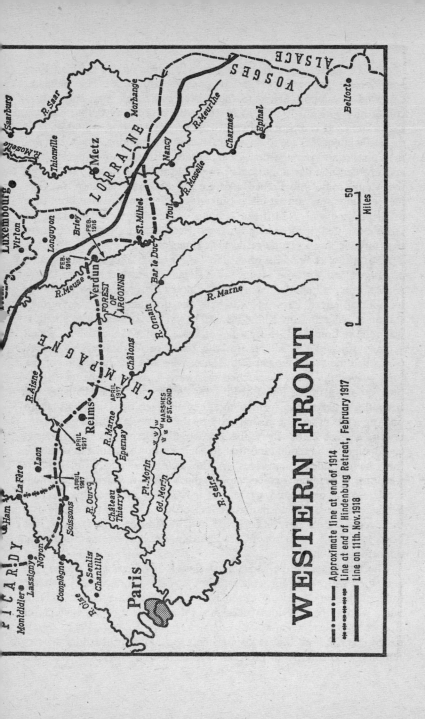

WESTERN FRONT

- ·—·—·— Approximate line at end of 1914
- ◦┼◦┼◦┼◦ Line at end of Hindenburg Retreat, February 1917
- ———— Line on 11th. Nov. 1918

0   50

Miles

ALSACE

VOSGES

Saarburg

R. Saar

R. Moselle

Thionville

Morhange

Metz

LORRAINE

Nancy

R. Meurthe

Charmes

Épinal

Belfort

Luxembourg

Virton

Longuyon

Briey FEB. 1916

FEB. 1916

St. Mihiel

Toul

R. Moselle

Verdun FEB. 1916

FOREST OF ARGONNE

R. Meuse

Bar le Duc

R. Ornain

R. Marne

CHAMPAGNE

Châlons

PICARDY

Ham

Monidider

Lassigny

Noyon

Compiègne

Senlis

Chantilly

R. Oise

Paris

Soissons

R. Aisne

Laon

La Fère

APRIL 1917

APRIL 1917

R. Ourcq

Château Thierry

Reims APRIL 1917

R. Marne

APRIL 1917

Épernay

Pt. Morin

Gd. Morin

MARSHES OF ST. GOND

R. Seine

before the Liége forts fell, the advanced guards of the German First and Second Armies were pressing against this line. The Belgians, deprived of support owing to the mistaken French plan and British conformity with it, decided to preserve their army by falling back on the entrenched camp of Antwerp – where its location would at least make it a latent menace to the German communications. The Germans, their immediate passage now clear, entered Brussels on August 20th, and on the same day appeared before Namur, the last fortress barring the Meuse route into France. Despite the Belgian resistance the German advance was abreast of its timetable; but it might have been four or five days ahead. And if the Belgian withdrawal to a flank momentarily expedited, it ultimately hindered the German progress, far more than any sacrifice in battle could have done.

Meanwhile, away on the other flank, the French offensive had opened on August 7th with the advance of a detached army corps into Upper Alsace, a move intended partly as a military distraction and partly for its political effect. Its actual goal was the destruction of the German station at Basle and the Rhine bridges below. Soon brought to a halt, it was renewed on the 19th by a larger force under General Pau, which actually reached the Rhine. But the pressure of disasters elsewhere compelled the abandonment of the enterprise and the dissolution of the force – its units being dispatched westward as reinforcements. Meantime the main thrust into Lorraine by the French First (Dubail) and Second (de Castelnau) Armies, totalling nineteen divisions, had begun on August 14th and been shattered in the battle of Morhange–Sarrebourg, August 20th, where the French discovered that the material could subdue the moral, and that in their enthusiasm for the offensive they had blinded themselves to the defensive power of modern weapons, a condition which was to throw out of balance the whole mechanism of orthodox warfare. Yet it is fair to add that this abortive French offensive had an indirect effect on the German plan, although this would hardly have occurred if a Schlieffen or a Ludendorff had been in charge at German Headquarters instead of the vacillating opportunist Moltke.

The fact that Moltke had almost doubled the strength of his left, compared with Schlieffen's plan, meant that it was unnecessarily strong for a yielding and 'enticing' defensive such as Schlieffen had conceived, while lacking the superiority necessary for a crushing counter-offensive. But when the French attack in Lorraine developed and Moltke appreciated that the French were leaving their fortified barrier behind he was tempted momentarily to postpone the right-wing sweep, and instead seek a decision in Lorraine. This impulse led him to divert thither the six newly formed Ersatz divisions that should have been used to increase the weight of his right wing. He had hardly conceived this new plan before he abandoned it and, on August 16th, reverted to Schlieffen's 'swing-door' design.

But he also told his left-wing commanders somewhat ambiguously that they must detain as many French troops as possible, and when the Crown Prince Rupprecht of Bavaria argued that he could only do this by attacking, Moltke left the decision to him. We may suspect that Rupprecht was loth to forfeit the opportunity of glory by retiring while the German Crown Prince was advancing. But nothing could have been more foolishly ambiguous than the Supreme Command's attitude. For when Rupprecht refused to refrain unless given a clear order, Moltke's deputy, Stein, said on the telephone to Krafft von Delmensingen, Rupprecht's Chief of Staff – 'No, we won't oblige you by forbidding an attack. You must take the responsibility. Make your own decision as your conscience tells you.' Conscience seems a curious basis for strategy. And when Krafft retorted, 'It is already made. We attack', Stein fatuously exclaimed, 'Not really! Then strike and God be with you.'

Thus, instead of continuing to fall back and draw the French on, Rupprecht halted his Sixth Army on the 17th, ready to accept battle. Finding the French attack slow to develop, he planned to anticipate it by one of his own. He struck on August 20th in conjunction with the Seventh Army (Heeringen) on his left, but although the French were taken by surprise and rolled back from the line Morhange–Sarrebourg, the German counterstroke had not the superiority of strength (the two armies now totalled twenty-five divisions) or of strategic position to make it decisive. Further, the attempt to envelop the French right flank by a movement through the Vosges was begun too late and failed. Thus the strategic result was merely to throw back the French on to a fortified barrier which both restored and augmented their power of resistance. And thereby they were enabled to dispatch troops to reinforce their western flank – a redistribution of strength which was to have far-reaching results in the decisive battle on the Marne.

With similar disregard of superior authority, the German Crown Prince, commanding the pivotal Fifth Army between Metz and Thionville, attacked when he had been ordered to stand on the defensive. The lack of what Colonel Foch had termed 'intellectual discipline' was to be a grave factor in Germany's failure, and for this the ambitions and jealousies of generals were to be largely responsible.

While this 'seesaw' campaign in Lorraine was in progress more decisive events were occurring to the north-west. The attack on Liége awakened Joffre to the reality of a German advance through Belgium, but not to the wideness of its sweep. And the sturdy resistance of Liége confirmed him in the opinion that the German right would pass south of it, between the Meuse and the Ardennes. Plan XVII had visualized such a move, and prepared a counter. Grasping once more at phantoms, the French Command embraced this idea so fervently that they transformed the counter into an imaginary *coup de grâce*. Their Third Army (Ruffey) and the reserve Fourth Army (de Langle de Cary) were to strike north-east through the Ardennes against the rear flank of the Germans advancing through Belgium, and thus dislocate their enveloping manoeuvre. The left wing (Fifth) Army, under Lanrezac, was moved farther to the north-west into the angle formed by the Sambre and Meuse between Givet and Charleroi. With the British Expeditionary Force coming up on its left, it was to deal with the enemy's forces north of the Meuse and to converge on the supposed German main forces in conjunction with the attack through the Ardennes. Here was a pretty picture – of the Allied pincers closing on the unconscious Germans! Curiously, the Germans had the same idea of a pincer-like manoeuvre, with roles reversed, and with better reason.

The fundamental flaw in the French plan was that the Germans had deployed twice as many troops as the French Intelligence estimated, and for a vaster enveloping movement. For information the French relied mainly on their cavalry, of which they had 100,000, but 'this enormous mass of cavalry discovered nothing of the enemy's advance ... and the French armies were everywhere surprised'. The French Third and Fourth Armies (twenty divisions), pushing blindly into the Ardennes against a German centre supposedly denuded of troops, blundered against the German Fourth and Fifth Armies (twenty-one divisions) in a fog on August 22nd, and were heavily thrown back in encounter-battles around Virton–Neufchâteau. The troops attacked blindly with the bayonet and were mown down by machine guns. Fortunately the Germans were also too vague as to the situation to exploit their opportunity.

But to the north-west the French Fifth Army (ten divisions) and the British (four divisions) had, under Joffre's orders, put their head almost into the German noose. The German masses of the First and Second Armies were closing on them from the north, and the Third Army from the east – a total of thirty-four divisions. Lanrezac alone had an inkling of the hidden menace. All along he had suspected the wideness of the

German manoeüvre, and it was through his insistence that his army had been permitted to move so far north-west. It was due to his caution in hesitating to advance across the Sambre, to the arrival of the British on his left unknown to the German Intelligence, and to the premature attack of the German Second Army, that the Allied forces fell back in time and escaped from the trap.

The Retreat to the Marne. The first four British divisions, after concentrating near Maubeuge, had moved up to Mons on August 22nd, ready to advance farther into Belgium as part of the offensive of the Allied left wing. On arrival, however, Sir John French heard that Lanrezac had been attacked on the 21st and deprived of the crossings of the Sambre. Although thus placed in an exposed forward position, he agreed to stand at Mons to cover Lanrezac's left. But next day, the 23rd, Lanrezac had word of the imminent fall of Namur and of the appearance of the German Third Army (Hausen) on his exposed right flank near Dinant, on the Meuse. In consequence, he gave orders for a retreat that night. The British, after resisting the attacks of six German divisions during the day, fell back on the 24th in conformity with their Allies. Not a moment too soon in view of the fact that the rest of the German First Army was marching still farther westward to envelop their open left flank.*

But if the British had begun to retreat later than the Allies, they continued faster and further. This less happy effect was mainly due to Sir John French's sudden revulsion of mind and emotion. He had gone forward almost too eager to fulfil the task given in Kitchener's instructions. He came back with his mind concentrated on the qualifying clause. And the change was due more to the French than to the Germans. The trouble began when Lanrezac, irritated by Joffre's blindness to the close-looming danger, vented on his newly arrived neighbour the

---

* Happily, the task of reducing Namur absorbed six German divisions and 500 guns from August 20th to 25th – when the last forts succumbed. This detachment, added to that already left to stand guard over Antwerp, seriously weakened the German right wing during the critical days when it fell upon and sought to overwhelm the Allied left wing in the battles of Charleroi and Mons. The delay, apparently so slight, imposed by the obsolete and neglected defences of Namur, contributed in turn to the resistance of the equally neglected French fortress of Maubeuge which did not capitulate until September 7th and detained two and a half divisions from the battlefield of the Marne. Less happily, this detachment was set free just in time to reach the Chemin des Dames ridge north of the Aisne – filling part of the gap between Kluck and Bülow (see page 95) – a few hours before the British advanced guards came up on September 12th.

indignation he could not show to his superior. This feeling was illustrated in the greeting which Lanrezac's Chief of Staff gave to Huguet, who came with French to visit Lanrezac – 'At last you're here; it's not a moment to soon. If we are beaten we shall owe it all to you!' And when French, on being excitedly told that the Germans had reached the Meuse at Huy, inquired what they were likely to do, Lanrezac irascibly replied – 'Why have they come there? Oh, to fish in the river.' The sarcasm was modified in translation. But even French's ignorance of the French language could not prevent him understanding the impatience and rudeness which Lanrezac showed in their discussion. Quick to resent this, his resentment changed to alarmed disgust when he found that the French had retired and left him isolated. Henceforward his mind was obsessed with the idea that they had left him in the lurch, and he thought of leaving them. The experience of the next few days hardened his thought of retiring independently to Havre, there to fortify himself in the peninsula with a modern version of the 'Lines of Torres Vedras'. From this disastrous intention he was dissuaded by Wilson's playful cajolery as well as by Kitchener's urgent and less tactful intervention, but still more by the turn of events.

The hurried recoil of the French left wing had at last awakened Joffre to the true situation and to the utter collapse of Plan XVII. From the wreckage he now tried to piece together a new plan. He decided to swing back his centre and left, with Verdun as the pivot, while drawing troops from the right in Alsace and forming a fresh Sixth Army on his left to enable the retiring armies to return to the offensive.

His optimism, soon to wane, might have been again misplaced but for German mistakes. The first was Moltke's folly in detaching seven divisions to invest Maubeuge and Givet and watch Antwerp, instead of using Landwehr and Ersatz troops as Schlieffen had intended. More ominous still was his decision on August 25th to send four divisions to check the Russian advance in East Prussia. These also were taken from the right wing (actually from the force besieging Namur), and the excuse afterwards given was that the German Command thought that the decisive victory had already been won! Further, the German Command lost touch with the advancing armies* and the movements of these became disjointed.

* This vital breakdown was essentially due to the failure of the German higher command to grasp the importance of good communication. The Chief of the Field Telegraphs was not even consulted as to the location of the Supreme Command. And no attempt was made to utilize the many trained operators available in the German civil telegraph and telephone service. The

The British II Corps stand at Le Cateau, made by Smith-Dorrien against his superior's wish, and Lanrezac's riposte at Guise, in which French forbade his I Corps to help, were also factors in checking the German enveloping wing, and each had still greater indirect effects. For Le Cateau apparently convinced the German First Army commander, Kluck, that the British Army could be wiped from the slate, and Guise led Bülow (Second Army) to call on Kluck for support, whereupon Kluck wheeled inwards, thinking to roll up the French left. The idea of a Sedan was an obsession with the Germans, and led them to pluck the fruit before it was ripe. This premature wheel before Paris had been reached was an abandonment of the Schlieffen plan, and exposed the German right to a counter-envelopment.

This rash movement was in progress when Moltke also sacrificed the conception of Schlieffen to the dream of Sedan – in a different sector. His centre and left were ordered to close like pincers round either side of Verdun, while the right wing was to turn outwards and face Paris as a shield to these pincers. This sudden reversal of direction and inversion of role was akin to the folly of a driver who jams on his brakes and slews his front wheels hard round on a greasy road. One further factor must be mentioned, perhaps the most significant of all: the Germans had advanced so rapidly, outrunning their timetable, that their supplies failed to keep pace, so that the fatigue of the troops was increased by hunger.* Indeed, when the chance of battle came, their fighting power was practically numbed by physical exhaustion – a condition much aggravated by the thorough demolitions which the French had carried out as they fell back. Thus, in sum, so much grit had worked into the German machine that a slight jar would suffice to cause its breakdown. This was delivered in the battle of the Marne.

German Official History says that, as the advance proceeded 'Practically nothing was done to extend without delay the inadequate communications between Luxembourg and the right wing of the armies, or to improve them by making use of the various supplementary technical means of communication: wireless, cable, motors, aeroplanes.' Moreover, the cavalry leading the advance had shown no discrimination, and had 'recklessly destroyed both lines and instruments'.

* In one typical regimental history it is mentioned that, in order to march fast, the field kitchens had been left behind, and that there was no issue of bread for four days. The troops had to forage for what could be found in a country exhausted of supplies. And it is not surprising that on reaching the Marne the men were dead-beat, when a man went forty-eight hours on 'one piece of bread – one cup of soup – one cup of coffee – unripe fruit and a raw turnip'.

The Tide Turns. The opportunity was perceived, not by Joffre, who had ordered a continuance of the retreat, but by Galliéni, the Military Governor of Paris, where the newly formed Sixth Army had assembled in shelter. On September 3rd Galliéni realized the meaning of Kluck's wheel inwards, directed the Sixth Army (Maunoury) to be ready to strike at the exposed German right flank, and the next day with difficulty won Joffre's sanction. Once convinced, Joffre acted with decision. The whole left wing was ordered to turn about and return to a general offensive beginning on September 6th. Maunoury was already off the mark on the 5th and, as his pressure developed on the German's sensitive flank, Kluck was constrained to draw off first one part and then the remaining part of his army to support his threatened flank guard. Thereby a thirty-mile gap was created between Kluck's and Bülow's armies, a gap covered only by a screen of cavalry. Kluck was emboldened to take the risk because of the rapid retreat of the British opposite, and still with their backs to, this gaping sector. Even on the 5th, when the French on either flank were turning about, the British continued a further day's march to the south. But in this 'disappearance' lay the unintentional cause of victory. For when the British retraced their steps, it was the report of their columns advancing into the gap which, on September 9th, led Bülow to order the retreat of his army. The superficial advantage which Kluck's First Army, already isolated by its own act, had gained over Maunoury was thereby nullified, and it fell back the same day. By the 11th the retreat had extended, independently or under orders from Moltke, to all the German armies.

The attempt at a partial envelopment, pivoting on Verdun, had already failed, the jaw formed by the Sixth and Seventh Armies merely breaking its teeth on the defences of the French eastern frontier. The attack by Rupprecht's Sixth Army on the Grand Couronné, covering Nancy, was a particularly costly failure. It is difficult to see how the German Command could have reasonably pinned their faith on achieving as an improvised expedient the very task which, in cool calculation before the war, had appeared so hopeless as to lead them to take the momentous decision to advance through Belgium as the only feasible alternative.

Thus, in sum, the battle of the Marne was decided by a jar and a crack. The jar administered by Maunoury's attack on the German right flank causing a crack in a weak joint of the German line, and the penetration of this physical crack in turn producing a moral crack in the German Command.

The result was a strategic but not a tactical defeat and the German right wing was able to reknit and stand firmly on the line of the Aisne. That the Allies were not able to draw greater advantage from their victory was due in part to the comparative weakness of Maunoury's flank attack, and in part to the failure of the British and the French Fifth Army (now under Franchet d'Esperey) to drive rapidly through the gap while it was open. Their direction of advance was across a region intersected by frequent rivers and this handicap was intensified by a want of impulsion on the part of their chiefs – each politely looking to his neighbour and, timorously, to his own flanks. Their feelings can best be described by the apt verse :

> Lord Chatham with his sword undrawn
> Kept waiting for Sir Richard Strachan :
> Sir Richard, longing to be at 'em,
> Kept waiting too – for whom? Lord Chatham.

It seems, too, that greater results might have come if more effort had been made, as Gallièni urged, to strike at the German rear flank instead of the front, and to direct reinforcements to the north-west of Paris for this purpose. This view is strengthened by the sensitiveness shown by the German Command to reports of landings on the Belgian coast, which might threaten their communications. The alarm caused by these reports had even led the German Command to contemplate a withdrawal of their right wing before the battle of the Marne was launched. When the moral effect of these phantom forces is weighed with the material effect – the detention of German forces in Belgium – caused by fears of a Belgian sortie from Antwerp, the balance of judgement would seem to turn heavily in favour of the alternative which French had tentatively suggested. By it the British Expeditionary Force might have had not merely an indirect but a direct influence on the struggle, and might have made the issue not merely negatively but positively decisive.

But, considering the battle of the Marne as it shaped, the fact that twenty-seven Allied divisions were pitted against thirteen German divisions on the decisive flank is evidence, first, of how completely Moltke had lapsed from Schlieffen's intention; second, of how well Joffre had reshuffled his forces under severe pressure; third, of how such a large balance afforded scope for a wider envelopment than was actually attempted.

The frontal pursuit was checked on the Aisne before Joffre, on

September 17th, seeing that Maunoury's attempts to overlap the German flank were ineffectual, decided to form a fresh army under de Castelnau for a manoeuvre *round and behind* the German flank. By then the German armies had recovered cohesion, and the German Command was expecting and ready to meet such a manoeuvre, now the obvious course. The Allied chiefs, however, if cautious in action were incautious in speculation. Critics may complain that they were not sufficiently ingenious, but they were certainly ingenuous. Wilson and Berthelot, the guiding brains of French and Joffre, were discussing on September 12th the probable date when they would cross the German frontier. Wilson modestly estimated it at four weeks hence; Berthelot thought that he was pessimistic and reckoned on reaching the frontier a week earlier.

Flux and Stagnation. Unhappily for their calculations, on the Aisne was re-emphasized the preponderant power of defence over attack, primitive as were the trench lines compared with those of later years. Then followed, as the only alternative, the successive attempts of either side to overlap and envelop the other's western flank, a phase known popularly, but inaccurately, as the 'race to the sea'. This common design brought out what was to be a new and dominating strategical feature – the lateral switching of reserves by railway from one part of the front to another. Before it could reach its logical and lateral conclusion, a new factor intervened. Antwerp, with the Belgian Field Army, was still a thorn in the German side, and Falkenhayn, who had succeeded Moltke on September 14th, determined to reduce it while a German cavalry force swept across to the Belgian coast as an extension of the enveloping wing in France. One of the most amazing features, and blunders, of the war on the German side is that while the Allied armies were in full retreat, Moltke had made no attempt to secure the Channel ports, which lay at his mercy. The British had evacuated Calais, Boulogne and the whole coast as far as Havre; even transferred their base to St Nazaire on the Bay of Biscay, a step which not only revealed the measure of their pessimism but delayed the arrival of the reinforcing 6th Division until the German front had hardened on the Aisne. And, during the Allied retreat, German Uhlans had roamed at will over the north-west of France, settled down in Amiens as if they were permanent lodgers, yet left the essential ports in tranquil isolation. The Supreme Command was so mesmerized by its Clausewitzian dogma – 'We have only one means in war: the battle' – that it could see no purpose in securing the spoils before it had won the 'decisive battle'. A month later the Germans were to sacrifice tens of thousands of their men in the abortive effort to gain what they could have secured initially without cost.

We must pause here to pick up the thread of operations in Belgium from the moment when the Belgian Field Army fell back to Antwerp, divergently from the main line of operations. On August 24th the Belgians began a sortie against the rear of the German right wing to ease the pressure on the British and French left wing, then engaged in the opening battle at Mons and along the Sambre. The sortie was broken off on the 25th when news came of the Franco-British retreat into France, but the pressure of the Belgian Army (six divisions) led the Germans to detach four reserve divisions, besides three Landwehr brigades, to hold it in check. On September 7th the Belgian Command learnt that the Germans were dispatching part of this force to the front in France; in consequence King Albert launched a fresh sortie on September 9th – the crucial day of the battle on the Marne. The action was taken unsolicited by Joffre, who seems to have shown curiously little interest in possibilities outside his immediate battle zone. The sortie led the Germans to cancel the dispatch of one division and to delay that of two others to France, but the Belgians were soon thrown back. Nevertheless the news of it seems to have had a distinct moral effect on the German Command, coinciding as it did with the initiation of the retreat of their First and Second Armies from the Marne. And the unpleasant reminder that Antwerp lay menacingly close to their communications induced the Germans to undertake, preliminary to any fresh attempt at a decisive battle, the reduction of the fortress and the seizure of potential English landing places along the Belgian coast.

The menace to Britain, if the Channel ports fell into German hands, was obvious. It is a strange reflection that, inverting the German mistake, the British command should hitherto have neglected to guard against the danger, although the First Lord of the Admiralty, Winston Churchill, had urged the necessity even before the battle of the Marne. When the German guns began the bombardment of Antwerp on September 28th England awakened, and gave belated recognition to Churchill's strategic insight. He was allowed to send a brigade of marines and two newly formed brigades of naval volunteers to reinforce the defenders, while the Regular 7th Division and 3rd Cavalry Division, under Rawlinson, were landed at Ostend and Zeebrugge for an overland move to raise the siege. Eleven Territorial divisions were available in England, but, in contrast to the German attitude, Kitchener considered them still unfitted for an active role. The meagre reinforcement delayed, but could not prevent, the capitulation of Antwerp, October

10th, and Rawlinson's relieving force was too late to do more than cover the escape of the Belgian Field Army down the Flanders coast.

Yet, viewed in the perspective of history, this first and last effort in the west to make use of Britain's amphibious power applied a brake to the German advance down the coast which just stopped their second attempt to gain a decision in the west. It gained time for the arrival of the main British force, transferred from the Aisne to the new left of the Allied line, and if their heroic defence at Ypres, aided by the French and Belgians along the Yser to the sea, was the human barrier to the Germans, it succeeded by so narrow a margin that the Antwerp expedition must be adjudged the saving factor.

How had the main battleground come to be shifted from France to Flanders? The month following the battle of the Marne had been marked by an extremely obvious series of attempts by each side to turn the opponent's western flank. On the German side this pursuit of an opening was soon replaced by a subtler plan, but the French persevered with a straightforward obstinacy curiously akin to that of their original plan. By September 24th, de Castelnau's outflanking attempt had come to a stop on the Somme. Next, a newly formed Tenth Army, under de Maudhuy, tried a little farther north, beginning on October 2nd, but instead of being able to pass round the German flank soon found itself struggling desperately to hold Arras. The British Expeditionary Force was then in course of transfer northwards from the Aisne, in order to shorten its communications with England, and Joffre determined to use it as part of a third effort to turn the German flank. To coordinate this new manoeuvre he appointed General Foch as his deputy in the north.

Foch continued Joffre's efforts to induce the Belgians to join this wheeling mass, but King Albert with more caution, or more realism, declined to abandon the coastal district for an advance inland that he considered rash. It was. For on October 14th, four days after the fall of Antwerp, Falkenhayn planned a strategic trap for the next Allied outflanking manoeuvre which he foresaw would follow. One army, composed of troops transferred from Lorraine, was to hold the expected Allied offensive in check while another, composed of troops released by the fall of Antwerp and of four newly raised corps, was to sweep down the Belgian coast and crush in the flank of the attacking Allies. He even held back the troops pursuing the Belgians in order not to alarm the Allied Command prematurely.

Meanwhile the new Allied advance was developing piecemeal, as corps detrained from the south and swung eastwards to form a progressively extended 'scythe'. The British Expeditionary Force, now three corps* strong, deployed in turn between La Bassée and Ypres – where it effected a junction with Rawlinson's force. Beyond it the embryo of a new French Eighth Army was taking shape, and the Belgian continued the line along the Yser to the sea. Although the British right and centre corps had already been held up, Sir John French, discounting even the underestimate of the German strength furnished by his Intelligence, ordered his left corps (Haig) to begin the offensive from Ypres towards Bruges. The effort was still-born, for it coincided with the opening of the German offensive, on October 20th, but for a day or two Sir John French persisted in the belief that he was attacking while his troops were barely holding their ground.† When enlightenment came he swung to the other extreme and anxiously urged the construction of a huge entrenched camp near Boulogne 'to take the whole Expeditionary Force'. But his recurrent desire to retreat was overborne by the greater will-power, and perhaps the more consistent self-delusion of Foch, who by flattering deference, as well as forceful personality, had now gained a strong influence over French. And French's regard was increased when Foch let him know privately that Kitchener had proposed – in imagined privacy – to replace him by Sir Ian Hamilton. Too often in this war did the leaders fight each other while the troops fought the foe.

The failure of the higher commanders to grasp the situation left the real handling of the battle to Haig and his divisional commanders. And

* At this time a corps consisted of two divisions, although later of three or even four divisions.

† One cause of French's susceptibility to delusions is suggested in General Gough's record of a conversation with him shortly after the battle – when further experience should have opened his eyes – 'He thought the war would be over in three months, and that Germany could not bear the strain longer ... This seems to show that with French the wish is father to the thought, and that the thought is not the child of the careful consideration of the facts, however unpleasant, as it should be in all great men. It seems to me also to show, to some extent, his failing energy. He does not want to do any more, he does not want to be called on to make further exertions of either intellect or will-power. He hopes it is going to be ended by Russia while we remain passive here. And so his hopes become his thoughts.' Another cause lay in his physical unfitness. French, who was sixty-two, had just suffered from a severe heart attack, and was under doctor's orders to go carefully. Murray, his chief of staff, had collapsed on the critical day of Le Cateau early in the retreat from Mons. Grierson, the original commander of the II Corps, had died suddenly on the way out to France. Such facts suggest the dangers of a system of promotion which brought men to the top at a comparatively advanced age.

they for want of reserves could do little more than cement the crumbling parts of the front, by scraping reserves from other parts and encourage the exhausted but indomitable troops to hold on. Thus Ypres was essentially, like Inkerman, a 'soldiers' battle'. Already, since the 18th, the Belgians on the Yser had suffered growing pressure which threatened a disaster that was ultimately averted, by the end of the month, through the opening of the sluices and the flooding of the coastal area. At Ypres the crisis came later and was repeated, October 31st and November 11th marking the turning points of the struggle. That the Allied line, though battered and terribly strained, was in the end unbroken was due to the dogged resistance of the British and the timely arrival of French reinforcements.

This defence of Ypres is in a dual sense the supreme memorial to the British Regular Army, for here its officers and men showed the inestimable value of the disciplined morale and unique standard of musketry which were the fruit of long training, and here was their tombstone. 'From failing hands they threw the torch' to the 'New Armies' rising in England to the call of country. With the Continental Powers the merging of normal into national armies was the natural product of their system of universal service. But with Britain it was revolution, not evolution. With a supreme flash of vision Kitchener had grasped, in contrast to Governments and General Staffs alike, the probable duration of the struggle. More questionably, he decided that it meant the abandonment of Britain's traditional strategy of semi-detachment, and, donning the continental habit of thought, took the view that Britain could only exercise a decisive influence through the creation of mass armies. The people of Britain responded to his call to arms, and poured into the recruiting stations. By the end of the year nearly 1,000,000 men had enlisted, and the British Empire had altogether 2,000,000 under arms.

Having decided on this vast expansion, Kitchener chose to build a new framework rather than to use the existing Territorial foundation. It is fair to point out that the Territorial Force was enlisted for home defence and that, initially, its members' acceptance of a wider role was voluntary. But the duplication of forces and of organization was undoubtedly a source of delay and waste of effort. Kitchener has also been reproached for his reluctance to replace the voluntary system by conscription, but this criticism overlooks how deeply rooted was the voluntary system in British institutions, and the slowness with which lasting changes can be effected in them. If Kitchener's method was characteristic of the man, it was characteristic of England. If it was unmethodical, it was calculated to impress most vividly on the British people the gulf between their 'gladiatorial' wars of the past and the national war to which they were committed. It took even longer to impress the British military mind, as represented by General Headquarters in France. Henry Wilson wrote that Kitchener's 'ridiculous and preposterous army of twenty-five corps is the laughing stock of every soldier in Europe ... under no circumstances could these mobs take the field for two years. Then what is the use of them?' For by his calculation the British Army was almost due to arrive in Berlin.

While a psychological landmark, the battle of Ypres is also a military landmark. For, with the repulse of the German attempt to break through, the trench barrier was consolidated from the Swiss frontier to the sea. The power of modern defence had triumphed over attack, and stalemate ensued. The military history of the Franco-British Alliance during the next four years is a story of the attempts to upset this deadlock, either by forcing the barrier or by haphazardly finding a way round.

On the Eastern Front, however, the greater distances and the greater differences between the equipment of the armies ensured a fluidity which was lacking in the west. Trench lines might form, but they were no more than a hard crust covering a liquid expanse. To break the crust was not difficult, and, once it was broken, mobile operations of the old style became possible. This freedom of action was denied to the Western Powers, but Germany, because of her central position, had an alternative choice, and from November, 1914, onwards, Falkenhayn adopted, although for his own part unwillingly, a defensive in France while seeking to cripple the power of Russia.

The Russian Front. The opening encounters in the east had been marked by rapid changes of fortune rather than by any decisive advantage. The Austrian Command had detached part of their strength in an abortive attempt to crush Serbia. And their plan for an initial offensive to cut off the Polish 'tongue' was further crippled by the fact that the German part of the pincers did not operate. It was indeed being menaced by a Russian pair of pincers instead, for the Russian Commander-in-Chief, the Grand Duke Nicholas, had urged his First and Second Armies to invade East Prussia without waiting to complete their concentration, in order to ease the pressure on his French Allies. As the Russians had more than a two-to-one superiority, a combined attack had every chance of crushing the Germans between the two armies. On August 17th, Rennenkampf's First Army (six and a half divisions and five cavalry divisions) crossed the East Prussian frontier,

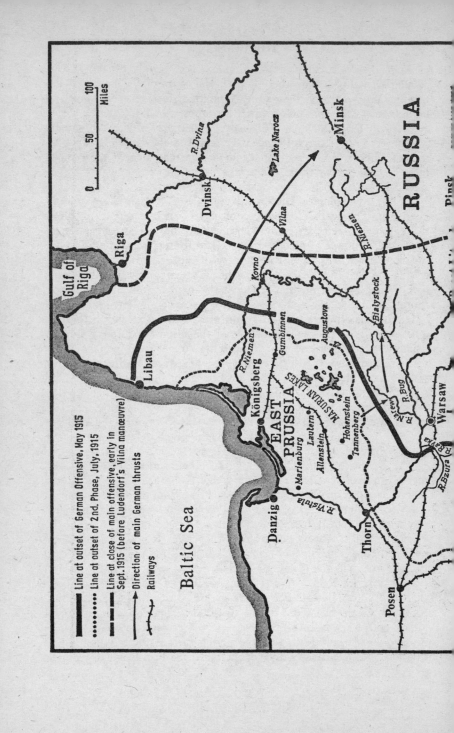

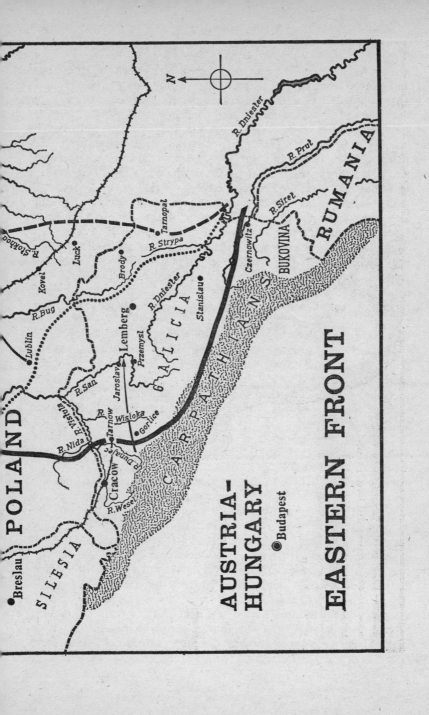

and on August 19th-20th met and threw back the bulk (seven divisions and one cavalry division) of Prittwitz's Eighth Army at Gumbinnen. On August 21st Prittwitz heard that the Russian Second Army (ten divisions and three cavalry divisions) under Samsonov had crossed the southern frontier of East Prussia, in his rear, which was guarded by only three divisions. In panic Prittwitz momentarily spoke on the telephone of falling back behind the Vistula, whereupon Moltke superseded him by a retired general, Hindenburg, to whom was appointed, as Chief of Staff, Ludendorff, the hero of the Liége attack.

Developing a plan which, with the necessary movements, had been already initiated by Colonel Hoffmann of the Eighth Army staff, Ludendorff concentrated some six divisions against Samsonov's left wing. This force, inferior in strength to the Russians, could not have been decisive, but finding that Rennenkampf was still near Gumbinnen, Ludendorff took the calculated risk of withdrawing the rest of the German troops, except the cavalry screen, from that front, and bringing them back against Samsonov's right wing. This daring move was aided by the folly of the Russian commanders in sending out unciphered wireless orders, to which the Germans listened in.

Under the converging pressure Samsonov's flanks collapsed, his centre was surrounded, and his army almost destroyed. If the opportunity was presented rather than created, this brief campaign and its sequel, afterwards christened the battle of Tannenberg, is a significant example of the use of what are technically called 'interior lines' – more simply, a central position.

Then, receiving his two fresh army corps from the French front, the German commander turned on the slow advancing Rennenkampf, and drove him out of East Prussia. As a result of these battles Russia had lost a quarter of a million men and, what she could afford still less, much war material. But the invasion of East Prussia had at least, by causing the dispatch of two corps from the west, helped to make possible the French recovery on the Marne. And, with peculiar irony, these corps had arrived too late to be of service at Tannenberg.

But the effect of Tannenberg was diminished because, away on the southern front, in Galicia, the scales had tilted against the Central Powers. The offensive of the Austrian First and Fourth Armies into Poland had at first made progress, but this was nullified by the onslaught of the Russian Third and Eighth Armies upon the weaker Second and Third Armies which were guarding the Austrian right flank. These armies were heavily defeated (August 26th-30th), and driven back through Lemberg. The advance of the Russian left wing thus threatened the rear of the victorious Austrian left wing. Conrad tried to swing part of his left round, in turn, against the Russian flank, but this blow was parried. And then, caught, with his forces disorganized, by the renewed advance of the Russian right wing, he was forced on September 11th to extricate himself by a general retreat, falling back almost to Cracow by the end of September. Austria's plight compelled the Germans to send aid, and the bulk of the force in East Prussia was formed into a new Ninth Army and switched south to the south-west corner of Poland, whence it advanced on Warsaw in combination with a renewed Austrian offensive. But the Russians were now approaching the full tide of their mobilized strength; regrouping their forces and counter-attacking, they drove back the advance and followed it up by a powerful effort to invade Silesia.

The Grand Duke Nicholas formed a huge phalanx of seven armies – three in the van and two protecting either flank. A further army, the Tenth, had invaded the eastern corner of East Prussia and was engaging the weak German forces there. Allied hopes rose high as the much-heralded Russian 'steamroller', of sixty massed divisions, began its ponderous advance. To counter it the German eastern front was placed under Hindenburg, for whom Ludendorff and Hoffmann devised a masterstroke, based on the system of lateral railways inside the German frontier, and also on a means of knowledge which to a large extent dispersed the fog of war on their side. For the continued interception of the wireless messages sent out by the Russian General Staff gave the German leaders 'a clear picture of how the enemy viewed the situation and what he intended to do'. Superior knowledge proved a compensation for inferior strength, as well as an invaluable insurance on behalf of audacity.

The Ninth Army, retreating before the advancing Russians, slowed them down by a systematic destruction of the scanty communications in Poland. On reaching its own frontier unpressed, it was first switched northwards to the Posen–Thorn area, and then thrust south-east, on November 11th – with its left flank on the Vistula – against the joint between the two armies guarding the Russian right flank.

The wedge, driven in by Ludendorff's mallet, sundered the two armies, forced the First back on Warsaw and almost effected another Tannenberg against the Second, which was nearly surrounded at Lodz, when the Fifth Army from the van turned back to its rescue. As a result, part of the German enveloping force almost suffered the fate planned for the Russians, but managed to cut its way through to the main body. If the Germans were balked of decisive tactical success this manoeuvre had been a classic example of how a relatively small force, by using its mobility to strike at a vital point, can paralyse the advance of an enemy several times its strength. The Russian 'steamroller' was thrown out of gear, and never again did it threaten German soil.

Within a week, four new German army corps arrived from the Western Front, where the Ypres attack had now ended in failure, and although too late to clinch the missed chance of a decisive victory, Ludendorff was able to use them in pressing the Russians back by December 15th to the Bzura–Ravka river line in front of Warsaw. This setback and the drying up of his munition supplies decided the Grand Duke Nicholas to break off the seesaw fighting still in progress near Cracow, and fall back on winter trench lines along the Nida and Dunajec rivers, leaving the end of the Polish 'tongue' in the hands of the enemy. Thus, on the east as on the west, the trench stalemate had settled in, but the crust was less firm, and the Russians had drained their stock of munitions to an extent that their poorly industrialized country could not make good.

The Grip on the Seas. We deal thirdly with the operations at sea, which actually occurred first in chronological order. The reason is that sea power only came to exert a dominant, eventually the dominant, influence on the war after the initial plans on land had miscarried. If the quick decision expected by the military leaders had been reached, it is questionable whether sea power could have affected the issue. How narrowly Germany missed decisive victory, and by what a combination of hardly conceivable blunders, is in the light of history now clear. While it is possible that Britain could, and would, have carried on the war unaided, we need to remember that in August, 1914, the condition was still that of a professional war with popular backing rather than a truly national war; that British intervention was still regarded as a chivalrous effort to succour violated Belgium and challenged France rather than as a life and death struggle for Britain's existence. And when a friend lies prone in a tiger's claws it is mistaken friendship to engage in a tug-of-war for the fragments if there is any chance of enticing the tiger from his prey.

But fortunately, in 1914, the tiger was held at bay and, with this breathing space gained, Britain had the opportunity to exert her traditional weapon – sea power. Its effect on the war was akin not to a lightning flash, striking down an opponent suddenly, but to a steady radiation of heat, invigorating to those it was used in aid of, and drying up the resources of the enemy.

But if its effect was extended and cumulative, its application was instantaneous, comparable almost to turning on an electric switch. This simple act, yet perhaps the most decisive of the war, took place before the actual outbreak – on July 29th when at seven o'clock in the morning that greater Armada, the British Grand Fleet, sailed from Portland for its war station at Scapa Flow. Few eyes saw its passage, fewer minds knew its destination in those northerly Orkney Isles controlling the passage between North Britain and Norway, but from that moment Germany's arteries were subjected to an invisible pressure which never relaxed until on November 21st, 1918, the German fleet arrived in those same northern waters to hand itself into the custody of a force of whom it had seen no more than a few fleeting glimpses during four and a half years of intangible struggle.

The fundamental cause of this unprecedented type of conflict lay in the recent development of new weapons, the mine and the submarine, which reproduced in naval warfare that same predominance of defensive over offensive power which was the key factor on land. The immediate cause, however, was the strategy adopted by Germany's Naval Command, partly through a miscalculation of Britain's probable strategy. Appreciating their own inferiority to the British fleet as well as the impossibility of a surprise blow in face of its preparedness, and believing that their enemy was obsessed with the Nelsonian tradition of seeking battle, the German Command adopted a Fabian strategy. They aimed to refuse conflict until their minelayers and submarines had weakened the strength of the British Navy, until the strain of a close blockade had begun to tell on the superior fleet, and perhaps provided the chance of a surprise stroke, and until the conquest of Britain's Allies on land had made her position more difficult.

The plan had at least a sound geographical basis, for the nature and configuration of the German coast lent itself to this strategy. The short North Sea coastline was heavily indented, the estuaries a maze of difficult channels, and screened by a fringe of islands – of which Heligoland formed a strongly fortified shield to the naval bases at Wilhelmshaven, Bremerhaven and Cuxhaven. Best of all, from the estuary of the Elbe there was a back door into the Baltic Sea, the Kiel Canal. By this the naval forces in the Baltic could be rapidly reinforced, while an enemy advance into that land-locked sea was not only hampered by the neutral possession of its approaches but could be imperilled by submarine and destroyer attack while passing through the narrow channels between the Danish islands. The natural defensive power of Germany's sea frontiers made attack almost impossible, and conversely gave her an excellent base for raiding operations – save for the geographical handicap that the coastline of Great Britain, like a vast breakwater, narrowed the exit for operations on the outer seas.

The one obvious defect of this Fabian strategy was that it involved the immediate abandonment of Germany's foreign trade and reduced the possibility of her interference with the sea-borne supplies of Britain and her Allies. Moreover, the German plan of progressive attrition was vitiated by the strategy adopted by the British Admiralty, which abandoned the direct doctrine of seeking out the enemy for the indirect doctrine of 'the fleet in being'. Realizing how the mine and submarine, combined with Germany's natural advantages, had made a close blockade hazardous, the Admiralty adopted a strategy of distant surveillance, keeping the battlefleet in a position which commanded the North Sea and in instant readiness for action if the enemy appeared, and using the light craft for closer, but not close observation. This strategy was not as passive as it seemed to a critical public, eagerly expecting a new Trafalgar. It appreciated that Britain's general command of the sea was the pivot of the Allied cause, and that to hazard it by exposure to uncompensated losses was the negation of this supreme requirement. Therefore, while desiring battle and being ready for it, the Admiralty quietly set about its primary duties of maintaining the security of the ocean routes, dealing with the sporadic threats to those routes, and, thirdly, ensuring the safe passage to France of the British Expeditionary Force.

The idea of economic pressure exercised by sea power was still in embryo. Not until a later phase did it crystallize into a formal doctrine, and the term 'blockade' assume a new and wider definition. The attack on sea-borne commerce was deep rooted in the traditions of the British Navy, and thus the transition to an indirect attack on the life of the enemy nation – her supplies of food and raw material – was an almost imperceptible progress. When this pressure was exercised against herself in a novel form and by a new weapon – the submarine – it was human, if illogical, that she should decry it as an atrocity. It was not easy for a conservative mind to realize that with the transition from a war of government policies into a war of peoples, intoxicated with Clausewitzian catch-phrases about a 'fight to the finish', the indefinite code of military chivalry must be submerged by the primitive instincts let loose. But in 1914 this 'absolute' war was still only a theory, and had little influence on the opening operations.

The history of the naval struggle must be dated from July 26th, 1914, when the Admiralty, in view of the clouded international situation, sent orders to the fleet assembled for review at Portland not to disperse. If the review was a happy chance the use made of it was one of the decisive acts and wisest judgements of the war, for while free from any of the provocation of an army mobilization, it placed Britain in automatic control of the situation at sea. It was followed, on July 29th, by the unnoticed sailing of the fleet for its war stations in the North Sea, and warning telegrams to all squadrons abroad. To students of war and politics the lesson should not be lost for, whatever its other limitations, a professional force has this power of unprovocative readiness which a national force inevitably lacks. 'Mobilization' is a threat, creating an atmosphere in which peaceful argument withers and dies. Between negotiations and mobilization there is a gulf, between mobilization and war an imperceptible seam, and the act of any irresponsible man can draw a nation across it.

Admiral Jellicoe, the new commander of the Grand Fleet, had one initial weakness to contend with; his base at Scapa was without defences against torpedo attack, and the fortified base being prepared at Rosyth was still incomplete. The historic concentration of British sea power had been on the Channel coast, where lay the best-prepared and defended harbours, and the Government had been slow to provide funds for bases on the North Sea to accompany the change in the concentration areas.

The danger compelled him to take his fleet west of the Orkneys, although it came down as far as the Forth during the transport to France of the Expeditionary Force – which was directly protected by the older battleships of the Channel Fleet, and by a layered system of patrols in the southern waters of the North Sea. The safe passage of the Expeditionary Force was the first direct achievement of the Navy. The next followed on August 29th when Beatty's battle-cruiser squadron and Tyrwhitt's destroyer flotillas made a swoop into the Bight of Heligoland, sank several German light cruisers, and achieved the much greater indirect effect of confirming the Germans in their strictly defensive strategy – not an unmixed blessing, for it led them to concentrate on the development of submarine attack. Apart from this engagement the story of 1914 in the North Sea is a record of unceasing vigilance on the one side; of minor submarine and minelaying successes and losses, on the other.

The war in the Mediterranean opened with a mistake that was to have far-reaching political consequences. Two of Germany's fastest ships were there, the battle cruiser *Goeben* and the light cruiser *Breslau*, and received orders from Berlin to steer for Constantinople. They evaded the British efforts made to cut them off, partly owing to inelasticity in applying the Admiralty instructions.

On the high seas the chase was more prolonged. Germany had not been allowed time to send out commerce-destroyers from home waters, but for some months her few cruisers on foreign service were a thorn in the side of the British Navy. It was not easy to reconcile the needs of the North Sea concentration with the duty of patrolling and protecting the tremendous length of sea routes along which supplies as well as troops were flowing from India and the Dominions to the support of the Mother Country. By the destruction of the *Emden* on November 9th, the Indian Ocean was finally cleared, but this success was offset by disaster in the Pacific, where Admiral Cradock's cruiser squadron was crushed by the heavier metal of Admiral von Spee's armoured cruisers, *Scharnhorst* and *Gneisenau*. This setback was, however, promptly redeemed by the Admiralty, who dispatched Admiral Sturdee with two battle cruisers, *Inflexible* and *Invincible*, on a lightning dash to the south Atlantic, while another battle cruiser, *Australia*, swept down from Fiji on Admiral von Spee's rear. Trapped on December 8th at the Falkland Isles, by this finely conceived surprise, Spee was sunk, and with him the last instrument of German naval power upon the oceans.

From this time onwards, the ocean communications of Britain and her Allies were secured for trade, for supplies and for the conveyance of troops. But as to all ocean routes there must be a land terminus, the development of the submarine made this security gradually less effective than it seemed on the morrow of Sturdee's victory.

The nature of the war at sea began to undergo definite changes early in 1915. During the first phase Britain had been too busy in clearing the seas and maintaining the security of the sea routes to devote much attention to the use of her sea command as an economic weapon against Germany. In any case her naval power was fettered by the artificial restrictions on blockade embodied in the Declaration of London of 1909, which the British Government with singular blindness announced on the outbreak of war that it would accept as the basis of maritime practice. Their release from these self-imposed fetters was aided by Germany's action.

On November 2nd, 1914, a German battle-cruiser squadron made a raid on the Norfolk coast, as a reconnaissance to test the scope of Britain's naval defence. Another followed on December 16th against the Yorkshire coast, Scarborough, Whitby and the Hartlepools being bombarded. Each time the Germans slipped away safely, but when they attempted a third, on January 24th, the English battle-cruiser squadron, under Beatty, trapped them off the Dogger Bank, sank the *Blücher* and badly damaged the *Derrfflinger* and *Seydlitz*. Although the stroke missed full success, it convinced the Germans of the futility of their attrition strategy, and Ingenohl, the commander of their High Seas Fleet, was replaced by Pohl, who proposed to Falkenhayn an offensive submarine campaign, which for success must be unlimited.

As a result, on February 18th, Germany proclaimed the waters round the British Isles a war zone where all ships, enemy or neutral, would be sunk at sight. This gave Britain a lever to loosen the Declaration of London, and she replied by claiming the right to intercept all ships suspected of carrying goods to Germany, and bring them into British ports for search. This tightening of the blockade caused serious difficulties with neutrals, America especially, but Germany eased the friction by torpedoing the great liner *Lusitania*, May 7th, 1915. The drowning of 1,100 people, including some Americans, was a spectacular brutality which shocked the conscience of the world, and appealed more forcibly to American opinion than even the desolation of Belgium. This act, succeeded by others, paved the way for the entry of the United States into the war, though it was to be later than seemed likely on the morrow of the tragedy.

One result of Britain's early established command of the sea was that it gave her the opportunity to sweep up Germany's oversea colonies with little hindrance or expenditure of force. Their seizure was valuable in that it gave the Allies important assets to bargain with in case of an unfavourable or negative issue to the war. At the end of August a New Zealand expedition captured Samoa, and in September an Australian expedition took possession of New Guinea; the Australian Navy also cleared several important German wireless stations in the Pacific Isles. Japan, entering the war on Britain's side, sent a division with a naval squadron, to besiege the German fortress of Tsing-tao on the coast of China. The first landing took place on September 2nd, and a tiny British contingent arrived on the 23rd, but the defences were modern, the land approach narrow, and the actual siege was not begun until October 31st. Seven days' bombardment was followed by an assault, which led to the capitulation of the garrison, after a rather feeble resistance.

In Africa, Togoland was occupied in August; the equatorial forest of the Cameroons was a sterner obstacle, and not until the beginning of 1916 were the German forces conquered by joint British and French forces after a prolonged but economically conducted campaign. General Botha, the South African Premier, once in arms against England, now for her, organized a force which conquered German South West Africa.

Almost concurrently Botha rendered a still greater service to the British cause by putting down the rebellion of a section of disaffected Boers, which, save for the Irish rising of Easter, 1916, was the only revolt within the borders of the Empire during these four trying years.

Only German East Africa, the largest and richest of Germany's colonies, remained, and that, owing to the difficulties of the country and the skill of General von Lettow-Vorbeck, the German commander, was not to be completely subdued until the end of 1917. An Expeditionary Force was sent thither in November to support the local British East African forces, and was repulsed at Tanga. To compensate his lack of troops, the German commander, Lettow-Vorbeck, found allies in the local bees, and his skilful tactics produced panic among the Indian battalions. Not until late in 1915 could the British Government, occupied with greater problems, spare either the time or the force to deal with this hornet's nest.

The year 1915 witnessed the dawn of another new form of war which helped to drive home the new reality that the war of armies had become the war of peoples. From January onwards, Zeppelin raids began on the English coast and reached their peak in the late summer of 1916, to be succeeded by aeroplane raids. The difficulty of distinguishing from the air between military and civil objectives smoothed the path for a development which, beginning with excuses, ended in a frank avowal that in a war for existence the will of the enemy nation, not merely the bodies of their soldiers, is the inevitable target. Although the Zeppelin raids in 1915 and 1916, through misdirection, did little material damage and caused less than two thousand casualties, it has been estimated that, by their disorganizing effect, about 'one sixth of the total normal output of munitions was entirely lost'.

The first psychological symptom of the World War, as it seemed to many, was an immeasurable sigh of relief. Had the peoples of Europe sat on the safety-valve too long? The war-weary mind of today cannot reconstruct the tension and anxiety, the strain and stress of hope and fear of the long years of the peace that was no peace and yet was not war. It may be read as a revolt of the spirit against the monotony and triviality of the everyday round, the completion of a psychological cycle when the memories of past wars have faded, and paved the way for the emergence and revival of the primordial 'hunting' instinct in man.

This first phase of enthusiasm was succeeded by one of passion, the natural ferocity of war accentuated by a form of mob spirit which is developed by a 'nation in arms'. The British Army was relatively immune because of its professional character, whereas in the German

Army, the most essentially 'citizen', it gained scope because of the cold-blooded logic of the general staff theory of war. With the coming of the autumn a third phase became manifest, more particularly among the combatants. This was a momentary growth of a spirit of tolerance, symbolized by the fraternization which took place on Christmas Day, but this in turn was to wane as the strain of the war became felt and the reality of the struggle for existence came home to the warring sides.

CHAPTER FOUR

SCENE 1

The Battle that was not, Yet Turned the Tide – the Marne

No battle has caused more controversy, produced so large a literature in so short a time, or given rise to more popular interest and legend than that of the Marne. But then this crisis of September, 1914, wrought the downfall of the German war plan and thereby changed the course of history. For if it be true, as it certainly is in part, that Germany lost the war when she lost this battle, it is natural that claimants to the distinction of having won it should be many.

The first legend to arise was that Foch had won it by driving the German centre into the marshes of St Gond, and even today, in total disregard of the facts and times of the battle, this is still given currency by reputable historians outside France.

But while, like a pebble dropped in water, the ripples of this story were still spreading, knowledgeable opinion in France was violently arguing whether the credit was due to Joffre, the Commander-in-Chief, or Galliéni, his quondam superior and then subordinate, who had delivered from Paris the blow at the German flank, exposed by Kluck's wheel inwards before Paris. One school contended that Joffre had conceived the idea of the counter-offensive, and at most admitted under pressure of facts that Galliéni's initiative in seeing the opportunity had given an impulse to Joffre's decision to seize it. The other school argued that Joffre, after the failure of his first attempt to stage a counter-offensive on the line of the Somme, had given up all idea of a fresh attempt at an early date, and that but for Galliéni's fiery determination and persuasion the retreat would have continued. A dispassionate judgement is now possible, and if we recognize that on Joffre fell the grave responsibility of taking the decision, the weight of evidence shows that Galliéni's inspiration dictated both the site and promptness of the thrust. Furthermore, it rebuts the alternative case of Joffre's advocates

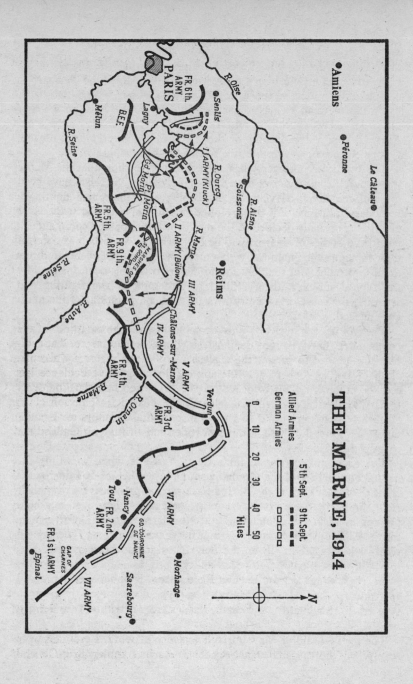

THE MARNE, 1914

Allied Armies 5th. Sept. ⸺ 9th. Sept.
German Armies ⸺ ⸺

0 10 20 30 40 50
Miles

N

Amiens
Péronne
Le Câteau
R. Oise
R. Aisne
Soissons
Reims
PARIS
FR. 6th. ARMY
Senlis
Melun
B.E.F.
Lagny
R. Seine
Gd. Morin
R. Ourcq
I ARMY (Kluck)
II ARMY (Bülow)
R. Marne
Pt. Morin
FR. 5th. ARMY
FR. 9th. ARMY
MARSHES OF ST. GOND
R. Aube
III ARMY
Châlons-sur-Marne
IV ARMY
V ARMY
FR. 4th. ARMY
R. Marne
R. Ornain
FR. 3rd. ARMY
Verdun
VI ARMY
Nancy
Toul
FR. 2nd. ARMY
GD. COURONNE DE NANCY
Morhange
Saarebourg
GAP OF CHARMES
FR. 1st. ARMY
VII ARMY
Epinal

that Galliéni marred the prospect by precipitating the blow, for we know that twenty-four hours' delay would have enabled the Germans to complete the protective redistribution which Galliéni interrupted.

On the German side a similar controversy has raged as to whether the order to retreat was a mistake, and whether Kluck of the First Army, Bülow of the Second, or the envoy of the Supreme Command, Colonel Hentsch, was responsible for the fatal decision.

The multiple controversy has at least served to show that the Marne was a psychological rather than a physical victory. So, also, have been most of the immortal victories of history, with the actual fighting a secondary influence. For the profoundest truth of war is that the issue of battles is usually decided in the minds of the opposing commanders, not in the bodies of their men. The best history would be a register of their thoughts and emotions, with a mere background of events to throw them into relief. But the delusion to the contrary has been fostered by the typical military history, filled with details of the fighting and assessing the cause of a victory by statistical computations of the number engaged.

The Marne was so clearly a psychological issue that the minds of the commanders have received due analysis. But even so, the 'combat complex' has tended to narrow the analysis of minds to the area where the clash of bodies took place. Thereby certain suggestive evidence has escaped comment. This evidence may be expressed in a startling question. Was the victory primarily due to the heated imagination of an English railway porter and to a party of temporary visitors to Ostend? Or, at the least, did these humble worthies constitute with Galliéni the mainspring of victory?

The suggestion is not so fantastic as it seems when we study the mental atmosphere of the German commanders. Before and during the crisis they were constantly looking backward apprehensively over their right shoulders, fearful of an Allied stroke against their ever-lengthening communications in Belgium and Northern France. Unfortunately for the Allies, there was small warrant for this nervousness. The belated plea for landing the BEF on the Belgian coast had been overruled by the Wilsonian pledge and policy of tying it as an appendix to the French left wing. Yet the Belgian Field Army, if under German guard at Antwerp, had at least caused a serious detachment of German strength to this guard – and more, was a chronic irritation to German nerves.

The fertile brain of Mr Churchill was also at work. Resources were scanty, but he dispatched a brigade of marines under Brig-General

Aston to Ostend, with orders to give their presence the fullest publicity. They landed on August 27th, and stayed ashore until the 31st.

Now to turn to the 'other side of the hill'. On September 5th, the day when the French troops were moving forward to strike at Kluck, Colonel Hentsch, the representative of the Supreme Command, came to the threatened army with this ominous and despairing warning – 'The news is bad. The Sixth and Seventh Armies are blocked. The Fourth and Fifth are meeting with strong resistance ... The English are disembarking fresh troops continuously on the Belgian coast. There are reports of a Russian expeditionary force in the same parts. A withdrawal is becoming inevitable.' We know from other sources that the 3,000 marines had grown in the German Command's imagination to 40,000, and that the Russians were said to be 80,000.

Thus the German flank army was left to face its ordeal with the belief that its rear was seriously menaced, and that in any case the Supreme Command was contemplating a withdrawal. At the least such knowledge must have been insidiously enervating during a period of strain. If the Supreme Command came to have doubts of the Belgian news, it also became imbued with the idea of a retirement, and when Hentsch came again on September 9th with full powers to coordinate it, 'should rearward movements have begun', not only had these begun, but they also coincided with fresh disturbing news from Belgium. For if the Belgian sortie from Antwerp that day was shortlived, it had all the incalculable psychological effect of menacing news at a moment of crisis. The German retreat gathered momentum and spread. With it turned the tide of the war.

History should do justice to Mr Churchill's happy inspiration and General Aston's handful of 'marine promenaders'. But equally helpful was that amazing 'Russian' myth which originated and spread so mysteriously. Mr Churchill, we know, had actually proposed to bring a Russian expeditionary force in such a way. Did the proposal perhaps leak out and become exaggerated into realization in the process? General opinion, however, has long ascribed the legend to the heated imagination of a railway porter working on the simple fact of the night passage of troop trains with Gaelic-speaking occupants. If so, a statue in Whitehall 'to the Unknown Porter' is overdue.

Keeping this external factor on the circumference of our thought, let us turn to trace the sequence of events in the actual battle zone. The immediate chain of causation begins with the escape by retreat of the French and British armies from the frontier trap into which Joffre's plan had led them. The first, highly coloured, reports from the army commands in the battles of the frontiers had given the German Supreme Command the impression of a decisive victory. It was under this hallucination that Moltke, on August 25th, cheerfully and need-lessly dispatched four divisions to the Russian front – to the detriment of his right-wing punch, already weakened by seven divisions left for the investment of derelict fortresses – truly a bad investment. Then the comparatively small totals of prisoners raised doubts in Moltke's mind and led him to a more sober estimate of the situation. The Kaiser's easy optimism now irritated him – 'He has already a shout-hurrah mood that I hate like death.' The new pessimism of Moltke combined with the renewed optimism of his army commanders to produce a fresh change of plan, which contained the seeds of disaster.

While Kluck's army, on the German extreme right or outer flank, was pressing on the heels of the British – so close that the 'outside' British corps (Smith-Dorrien) was forced to halt and give battle – Kluck's neighbour on the inside, Bülow, was following up Lanrezac's French Fifth Army. When on August 26th the British left wing fell back southwards badly mauled from Le Cateau, Kluck had turned south-westwards again. If this direction was partly due to misconception of the line of retreat taken by the British – the idea that they were retreating to the Channel ports – it was also in accordance with his original role of a wide circling sweep. And by carrying him into the Amiens–Péronne area, where the first parts of the newly formed French Sixth Army were just detraining after their 'switch' from Alsace, it had the effect of dislocating Joffre's design for an early return to the offen-sive – by compelling the Sixth Army to fall back hurriedly towards the shelter of the Paris defences.

But Kluck had hardly swung out to the south-west before he was induced to swing in again. For in order to ease the pressure on the British, Joffre had ordered Lanrezac to halt and strike back against the pursuing Germans, and Bülow, shaken by the threat, called on Kluck for aid. Lanrezac's attack, on August 29th, was stopped before Bülow needed this help, but he asked Kluck to wheel in nevertheless, in order to cut off Lanrezac's retreat. Before acceding, Kluck referred to Moltke. The request came at a moment when Moltke was becoming perturbed in general over the way the French were slipping away from his embrace and, in particular, over a gap which had opened between his Second (Bülow) and Third (Hausen) Armies through the latter having already turned south, from south-west, to help the Fourth Army, its neighbour on the other flank. Hence Moltke approved Kluck's change of direction – which meant the inevitable abandonment of the original wide sweep round the far side of Paris. Now the flank of the wheeling German line would pass the near side of Paris and across the face of the Paris defences. By this contraction of his frontage for the sake of security Moltke sacrificed the wider prospects inherent in the wide circling sweep of the original plan. And, as it proved, instead of contracting the risk he exposed himself to a fatal counterstroke.

On the night of September 2nd Moltke sent a message to the right-wing commanders which confirmed the change of plan and fore-shadowed a new one. 'The French are to be forced away from Paris in a south-easterly direction. The First Army will follow in echelon behind the Second Army, and will be responsible henceforward for the flank protection of the force.' But the First Army was a full day's march ahead of the Second: if Kluck tried to carry out the second part of the message he would be neglecting the first part. Hence he decided to march on, while detailing an incomplete Reserve Corps and a depleted cavalry division to serve as a flank guard. How lightly he regarded any danger from Paris is also shown in the facts that no aircraft were allotted to the flank guard, and no air reconnaissance ordered to the westward.

Meantime Moltke was growing depressed and his decision to aban-don the original plan was definitely taken on September 4th. In place of it, Moltke substituted a narrower envelopment, of the French centre and right. His own centre (Fourth and Fifth Armies) was to press south-east while his left (Sixth and Seventh Armies), striking south-westwards, sought to break through the fortified barrier between Toul and Epinal, the jaws thus closing inwards on either side of Verdun. Meantime his right (First and Second Armies) was to turn outwards and, facing west, hold off any countermove which the French might attempt from the neighbourhood of Paris. Moltke's order continued to ignore that Kluck was ahead of Bülow in the race southward and had already crossed the Marne. For it not only told Kluck to 'remain facing the east side of Paris' (ie facing west), but to remain north of the Marne while Bülow wheeled into line, facing west, between the Marne and the Seine. Thus to fulfil the order Kluck had not merely to halt, while Bülow caught up and passed him, but to perform a sort of backward somersault. Such gymnastics are somewhat upsetting to the equilibrium of a large army; and in this case the French countermove which Moltke wished to guard against had already begun before his new plan could take effect. More-over Kluck, reluctant to be thus deprived of the chance of being the agent of decisive victory, continued his advance south towards the Seine on the 5th, saying that 'the movement to face west might be made at leisure'. For the moment he still left the weak detachment of three brigades and a few cavalry to guard his flank. Next morning it was struck by the French Sixth Army moving out from Paris.

During these days the Franco-British retreat had continued. On August 30th, Joffre – yielding to the pressure of a Government alarmed at seeing him abandon the capital by his direction of retreat – detached Maunoury's Sixth Army to reinforce the Paris garrison. Parting with it signified his abandonment of the flank counterstroke, for this was the force he had assembled for its execution. Moreover, a memorandum drawn up that same day shows that he had transferred his faith to a counter-offensive against the German centre 'in the hope of accomplishing ... the rupture which we formerly attempted facing north-east and debouching from the Meuse'. On September 1st, Joffre issued orders for the retreat of the Allied armies to be continued to a line south of the Seine, Aube and Ornain rivers. Not only was the effect to take the armies away from and far to the south-east of Paris, but a commander who is contemplating an early counter-offensive does not place the obstacle of a river barrier between himself and the enemy. And a further note to the several army commanders next day added that it was Joffre's intention to 'organize and fortify' this line, whence he planned to deliver not an immediate but an eventual counter-offensive. That same day he replied to a suggestion of a stand on the Marne, made by Sir John French and communicated through the Minister of War:

I do not believe it possible to envisage a general action on the Marne with the whole of our forces. But I consider that the cooperation of the English Army in the defence of Paris is the only course that can give an advantageous result.

To the Minister of War and to Galliéni he repeated the same verdict. When zealous apologists say that the idea of a counter-offensive was at the *back* of Joffre's mind, the historian can agree. This array of evidence is more than sufficient to dispel the legend that Joffre had any intention of giving battle on the Marne or that he planned the counterstroke which tilted the balance so dramatically.

The definite nature of his reply was the more significant because, on September 1st, a staff officer with Lanrezac's army had found the German order for a change of direction in the wallet of a dead officer, and this was sent to Joffre's headquarters early next day. And on the morning of the 3rd, the changed direction, to the south-east, of Kluck's marching columns had been noticed and reported by British aviators. In the afternoon they added that these columns were crossing the Marne and in the evening Maunoury reported that there were no German troops left in the area west of the line Paris–Senlis. All this was reported to Joffre without making any impression on his plans – save that on the night of the 2nd he altered the limit of his retirement to a line still farther south!

But from Galliéni, the new military governor of Paris, even a fragment of information gained on the 3rd had drawn an instant response. He ordered Maunoury to carry out further air and cavalry reconnaissances as soon as it was light on the 4th. Quickly convinced by these early reports that the Germans were moving obliquely past the front of the Paris defences, exposing their own flank, Galliéni was equally quick to act. At 9 AM he ordered Maunoury's army to get ready for a move eastward to strike the Germans in flank. He then informed Joffre by telephone of his preparatory moves, and urged him to sanction a counter-offensive. (This consent was necessary not only to ensure a combined effort but because Joffre had persuaded the new Minister of War to subordinate Galliéni to himself.)

Galliéni's fiery and inspired arguments made an impression, but no more, on the slow-thinking Commander-in-Chief of the field armies. To save time while Joffre was still cogitating Galliéni rushed off by motor to Melun to explain the new situation to the British, and if possible gain their cooperation. Unfortunately, Sir John French was absent from his headquarters, and at first Galliéni could not even find Archibald Murray, his chief of the general staff. It was a curious scene. Galliéni, for his part, found the British staff unsettled and depressed, not hesitating to say that if England had known the condition of the French army she would not have entered the war. They were hardly in the mood to discern the underlying qualities of this most unmilitary-looking military genius, bespectacled and untidy, with shaggy moustache, black buttoned boots and yellow leggings. Little wonder perhaps that one eminent soldier with a pungent gift of humour remarked that 'no British officer would be seen speaking to such a — comedian'.

Galliéni pointed out to Murray that it was vital to seize the opportunity which the Germans had given by offering their right flank, told him that the 'Army of Paris' was already in motion against the German flank, and begged that the British should cease to retreat and join with his forces in an offensive next day. Murray, however, showed *une grande répugnance ... à entrer dans nos vues'*, and declared that he could do nothing in the absence of his commander. After waiting three hours in vain for Sir John French's return, Galliéni had to leave at 5

PM with the mere promise of a telephone message later. This brought
no satisfaction, for its purport was that the British would continue their
retreat next day. Their decision had been confirmed by receiving a
letter, written that morning, from Joffre who said: 'My intention, in
the present situation, is to pursue the execution of the plan that I have
had the honour to communicate to you – that of retiring behind the
Seine – and only to engage on the selected line with all forces united.'
The meagre influence which the news of Kluck's change of direction
had achieved was shown by a subsequent paragraph which said: 'In the
case of the German armies continuing their movement towards the SSE
... perhaps you will agree that your action can be most effectively
applied on the right bank of the river, between the Marne and Seine.'
This casual qualification to the definite opening statement gave the
British little encouragement to fall in with Galliéni's audacious suggestion. There is a dramatic contrast between the sluggish working of
Joffre's mind, gradually but all too slowly veering round, and Galliéni's
swift *coup d'œil* and instantaneous reaction.

After Galliéni's morning message, Joffre had been moved so far as to
send a telegram, timed 12.45 PM, to Franchet d'Esperey (who had
superseded Lanrezac in command of the Fifth Army), saying – 'Please
inform me if you consider that your army is in a state to make it [an
attack] with any chance of success' – an inquiry which hardly suggests
a sense of vital opportunity or an urge to action. This reached Franchet
d'Esperey while Henry Wilson, of French's staff, was with him, and,
after discussion, a reply was drafted, saying 'the battle cannot take
place before the day after tomorrow', and that the Fifth Army would
continue its retreat on the morrow, attacking on the 6th. To this
message he added, in his own hand, a qualifying note even less encouraging: 'In order that the operation may be successful the necessary
conditions are: (1) The close and absolute cooperation of the Sixth
Army debouching on the left bank of the Ourcq on the morning of the
6th. It must reach the Ourcq tomorrow ... or the British won't budge.
(2) My army can fight on the 6th, but its situation is not brilliant. No
reliance can be placed on the reserve divisions.'

What was likely to be the effect on a Joffre of such a discouraging
reply to his tentative inquiry? To harden his hesitation.

That hesitation was the more natural because Berthelot, his chief
adviser, was vehemently in favour of continuing the retreat and maintaining the original plan. Then early in the afternoon came an ominous
report of German progress across the Marne. As Joffre's own memoirs
relate: 'This was all that was needed to cause Berthelot to return to the

charge.' The memoirs, it is true, argue that Joffre merely continued to put off a decision, but they admit that he issued new instructions that were designed to accord with Berthelot's plan. Still more significantly, the decision was taken to move the headquarters over thirty miles farther south. Then, while Joffre was having an early dinner, Franchet d'Esperey's message arrived.

The next link in the chain of causation fits in with a click – the click of a telephone switch putting a call through. For if Galliéni's *coup d'œil* gained the opportunity it was, as he himself said, '*coups de téléphone* which gained the Battle of the Marne'. On returning to his headquarters in Paris he had found a belated message from Joffre which was favourable to his proposal for a counterstroke, but preferred it to be delivered south of the Marne – where it would have lost the greater effect given by a blow against the enemy's flanks and rear.

Galliéni seized the telephone, got through to Joffre, and by the fervour and force of his arguments at last won his sanction for the 'Army of Paris' to strike north of the Marne as part of a general counter-offensive by the left-wing armies. Joffre promised to obtain the co-operation of the British. Galliéni promptly issued orders (8.30 PM) to Maunoury's army, which he reinforced. After several hours' delay Joffre's orders were sent out for the offensive on September 6th – it was too late now for the 5th, and too late to be generally effective even for the 6th. The delay had far-reaching consequences – not all ill.

On the 5th while Maunoury's troops were moving east towards the enemy, both the British and Franchet d'Esperey's were marching south in accord with their original orders – away from the enemy, and even away from each other. But for Galliéni, the gap they thus opened might have proved perilous. When they turned about next day, they had much ground to recover, and were not as quick in retracing their steps as the situation demanded. This 'disappearance' of the British not only enabled but encouraged Kluck – who had been taken completely unawares – to pull back half his main body (II and IV Corps) from the sector where the British had been, to reinforce the hard-pressed flank guard which was trying to hold off Maunoury's menacing advance against the German rear. The arrival of these fresh forces began to check Maunoury's advance on the 7th, and Galliéni pushed forward every possible reserve he could scrape up in order to strengthen Maunoury.

Here occurred the famous if legend-crusted episode of the Paris taxi-cabs. A fresh division had just detrained near Paris, but it was forty miles from the battlefront. If it marched thither it would be too late, and there was only sufficient rail transport to take half the division.

That afternoon, the police held up taxicabs in the streets, bundling the passengers out in some cases, and, after collecting 600 cabs, sent them to the suburb of Gagny where they filled up with soldiers. Galliéni came to see the performance and, with mingled gratification and amusement, exclaimed: 'Well, at least it's not commonplace!' During the night this forerunner of the future motorized column swept, as only Paris taxicabs can sweep, through the outlying villages and past their amazed inhabitants, making two journeys, with 3,000 soldiers at a time. Unfortunately these taxicabs maintained their traditional preference for speed over reliability and, passing and repassing, became so mixed that on the morning of the 8th several hours were spent in sorting out their passengers before the division could attack.

The pressure on the Germans gained extra force from the fact that it was directed against their rear flank. If Galliéni had received the two further army corps for which he had asked days before and which were only just arriving piecemeal, the German forces south of the Marne might have been cut off and the battle been as decisive tactically as it was strategically. Even in the actual situation, the menace was such that at 10 PM on the 6th Kluck called back his two remaining army corps, so creating a thirty-mile-wide gap between himself and the neighbouring army of Bülow. Only two weak cavalry corps, with a few Jäger battalions, were left to fill it and Kluck failed to arrange that this thin screen should be put under a single command. The consequences were fatal. Although he was able to hold and even press back Maunoury's troops, the gap he had left in the southern front uncovered Bülow's flank. Although still untouched by Franchet d'Esperey's slow advance on the 7th, Bülow, sensitive to his raw side, drew back his right to the north bank of the Petit Morin. And when news came that the British were advancing into the centre of the gap, it proved the signal for the German retreat, which began on September 9th. If the continuance of the British withdrawal on September 5th had marred the chance of a crushing victory, it was a pleasant irony of fate that their very withdrawal made possible the 'victory' as actually achieved.

It is necessary, however, to take account of the situation on other parts of the battlefront for, unless the German intentions elsewhere had been frustrated, Joffre's victory would have been impossible and defeat probable. To the frustration of their left wing attack in the east, or Lorraine sector, the Germans themselves were the chief contributors; for by pressing the French back on their own fortress line they had already made their task of breaking through it almost impossible. And yet another of the many 'accidents of the Marne' made their repulse

certain; for when Dubail's and de Castelnau's armies, after their defeat
in the battle of Morhange–Sarrebourg, ended their hasty retreat, their
line sagged inwards; and into this re-entrant, formed quite unintentionally, the main German attack was launched, pushing towards that very
'gap of Charmes' which the French in earlier years had prepared for
their reception.

Thus the French were given an opportunity to strike back effectively
at the Geman flanks, and thereby they temporarily paralysed the original German advance, which came to a halt on August 27th. This not
only gave the French breathing space to strengthen their position, but
enabled Joffre, with safety, to transfer part of the force from the right
wing to the more critical left wing. News of this transfer inspired
Moltke to frame his new plan of September 5th, and lured him into
another vain attack on the French fortified barrier, despite protest from
the Crown Prince Rupprecht of Bavaria, commanding the Sixth Army.
The new attack was launched frontally against the Grand Couronné de
Nancy, the ridge which formed a flank buttress for the gap of Charmes.
And the Kaiser arrived with his white cuirassiers, like an actor waiting
his call, to make a triumphal entry into Nancy. But successive assaults,
inadequately prepared, collapsed under the well-knit and superior fire
of the French artillery, and on September 8th Moltke ordered Rupprecht to stop the offensive and the vain loss of life. Rupprecht had
been urged into it against his own judgement by the excessive confidence of the artillery expert, Major Bauer, that his super-heavy howitzers would have the same effect as on the obsolete Belgian fortresses.
Yet, curiously, he now only gave up the attack under protest – so
Micawberish was the judgement of the military leaders of 1914–18.

The German centre (Fifth and Fourth Armies), west of Verdun, was
no better able to fulfil its role as the right arm of the pincer-like squeeze
ordained in Moltke's modified plan. In the Verdun area Sarrail had
replaced Ruffey as commander of the French Third Army, and the first
instructions he received indicated not only a continued retreat but the
abandonment of Verdun. Sarrail thought differently, however, and
determined to cling on to the Verdun pivot as long as possible, without
losing touch with the Fourth Army to the west. It was a happy piece of
initiative, and the brake thus placed on the south-eastward advance of
the enemy's Fifth Army (under the German Crown Prince) was an
essential factor in upsetting Moltke's plan. The stout resistance of Sarrail's troops, and still more the deadly fire of their artillery, not only
held up but paralysed the Crown Prince's advance. And a belated
attempt on the 9th to break the deadlock by a night attack, ended in a

suicidal fiasco, with the Germans firing on each other. Sarrail, however, asked in vain for reinforcements which might have enabled him to convert his resistance into a dangerous counterstroke from Verdun westwards against the German flank – for by holding on to Verdun he had formed one side of a sack into which the German armies between him and Maunoury, on the other side, had pushed.

The German Third Army (Hausen) formed a link between the German centre and right wing, and was assigned the indefinite role of being ready to support either. This role was perhaps in part the reflection of the fact that, being composed of Saxons, the Prussians tended to discount its value. In the event it was virtually divided. Its left was used to help the Fourth Army in the abortive attack on the French Fourth Army (de Langle de Cary); an attack which, after perhaps the severest fighting of the whole battle, was driven to ground by the French artillery. Its right joined with Bülow's left in an attack on Foch, who had taken over command of a new Ninth Army, in the French centre, formed by simple subtraction from de Langle de Cary's army.

Among all the legends of the Marne that which has grown up round Foch's part is the most comprehensive and has the least substance. The first claim, still widely believed, is that Foch decided the issue of the whole battle by a counterstroke which threw the Prussian Guard 'into the marshes of St Gond'. In fact, however, the Germans took their leave without interference – after the issue had been decided farther west. The second, and more modest claim, is that Foch made the victory possible by preventing a German breakthrough in the French centre. Even this is inaccurate – because the Germans were not trying to break through here. Bülow was merely carrying out his new protective task of wheeling his line to face west. And, in the course of this wheel, his left wing naturally bumped against Foch's front.

A further paradox is that although Foch issued repeated orders for attacks, his troops in reality were on the defensive, a defence needlessly desperate owing to his own disobedience of orders.

At 1.30 AM on September 6th, Foch had received Joffre's famous order for the general 'about turn'. Unlike the other armies, he received it in time to act on his share of it, which was to cover the flank of Franchet d'Esperey's attack by holding the southern exits of the marshes of St Gond. Instead, he concentrated the bulk of his forces for an offensive north of the marshes, leaving the weak XI Corps to hold the wide and vulnerable sector east of the marshes. His troops were tired and much reduced by the hard retreat, and their offensive quickly died away; in their reflux they failed to hold firmly the southern exits of the marshes. Thus Foch continued to keep his main strength on that flank. But the Germans could only cross by the narrow causeways, and in consequence made a side-step – as they might have done earlier. On the 7th, their attack east of the marshes broke down under the fire of the French artillery. As the only way of evading it, a bayonet attack in the half-light before dawn was arranged. This caught Foch's right by surprise and it gave way rapidly. Fortunately the Germans did not follow up as rapidly and so captured few of the tormenting guns. Even so, the situation was serious and Foch called for help; Franchet d'Esperey lent a corps to support his left and Joffre sent another to fill the gap now yawning on his right. On the 9th the continued German attack against Foch's right made fresh progress and met little resistance – until, shortly before 2 PM, it was stopped by receiving Bülow's now notorious order for a general retirement. The Germans drew off undisturbed and even unobserved. To meet the earlier emergency Foch had taken the 42nd Division from his intact left wing and switched it across to his right; but it only arrived in time to fire its guns in the twilight after the vanished foe – contrary to the popular legend of its decisive counterstroke against the flank of the German breakthrough. And one has to add that although Bülow had exposed his flank in making the wheel, Foch thought only of making a frontal counterattack. On the battle as a whole his main, and most serious, effect was that he detracted from the main offensive instead of helping to cover it.

In our survey of the battlefront we have now travelled back to the decisive western flank. Let us focus our eyes on the various headquarters behind the German front and examine the wavering gusts of opinion which culminated in the German retirement. The Supreme Command was back at Luxembourg, whither it had moved from Coblenz, on August 30th, and depended for communication with the armies on wireless, supplemented by occasional visits by staff officers in motor-cars. No regular motor or motorcycle dispatch service had been organized, and wireless communication suffered not only from the time lost in enciphering and deciphering but from interference from the Eiffel Tower in Paris. As the army commanders, faithful to the tradition of 1870, were jealous of control, information was as sparse as it was slow except when they had successes to report – and exaggerate. Throughout the crisis of the battle, from September 7th–9th, no single report of any value came back from the front and, as late as the 12th, Moltke had no knowledge of what had happened to Kluck's army, or where it was. Perhaps this ignorance made little difference, for on the

5th, Falkenhayn, then at Luxembourg in his capacity of Minister of War, noted in his diary: 'Only one thing is certain: our General Staff has completely lost its head. Schlieffen's notes do not help any further, and so Moltke's wits come to an end.'

Moreover, Moltke had already reconciled himself to defeat. For the gloom at Luxembourg is well shown by the fact that when, on September 8th, Lieut-Colonel Hentsch left, as his emissary, to visit in turn the five armies west of Verdun, he was given full powers to coordinate the retreat, 'should rearward movements have been initiated'. He found none had occurred, if he found little confidence, at the headquarters of the Fifth, Fourth, and Third Armies. Passing on he spent the night of the 8th with Bülow, and there found such an intensification of gloom that when he left in the morning he could at least feel confidence on one point – that orders for a retreat would soon be given. And about 9 AM on the 9th air reports told Bülow that six enemy columns (five British and one of French cavalry) were approaching the Marne – and so entering the mouth of the gap. By 11 AM he had issued orders for the retreat of his army to begin at 1 PM, sending word to Kluck of his action.

Hentsch, delayed by blocks and panics on the road, did not reach Kluck's headquarters till almost noon. There, according to his evidence, he found that orders for a retirement had already gone out, and in confirming them merely added the direction of the retreat – north-eastward. But Kluck's Chief of Staff, Kuhl, asserts that these orders were only the mistake of a subordinate and that he had merely ordered a swing-back of his left in view of the fact that the British were almost behind it. He further says that Hentsch, in view of Bülow's situation, gave him orders to retreat. And Hentsch is not alive to contradict him. But the facts that the withdrawal began at 2 PM, that the roads behind had been cleared, and that neither Kuhl nor Kluck troubled to ask for a written order, go far to support Hentsch – by showing their eagerness to be off. Kuhl, indeed, has admitted that the imminent breakthrough of the British and Franchet d'Esperey made the retreat inevitable. And, owing to the British penetration, Kluck's army had to retreat northward, thus leaving the gap still open.

The most curious of all the many accidents of the Marne is its accidental reproduction of the perfect pattern Napoleonic battle – the pattern which Napoleon several times fulfilled and which General Camon and other students believe was normally in his mind. Its characteristics were that while the enemy was gripped in front, a manoeuvre was directed against one of his flanks, a manoeuvre which was intended not to be decisive in itself but to create the opportunity for a decisive stroke. For the threat of envelopment caused a stretching of the enemy's line to ward it off and so created a weak joint on which the decisive stroke then fell. On the Marne Galliéni caused this stretching and the British pierced the joint. The pattern was executed perfectly, yet quite unconsciously.

Hence we see clearly that the continued retreat of the British on the 5th and their slow advance on the 6th and 7th were strategically invaluable, holding back unintentionally as Napoleon would have done purposely. If their 'decisive' thrust had been disclosed earlier, the joint would hardly have been weakened by the removal of Kluck's last two corps – the departure of which, even as it was, Bülow delayed until early on the 8th. And the fact that Maunoury's stroke was definitely checked while these two corps were still on the march towards him is sufficient evidence that his stroke in itself could not have caused a decision.

But the continued slowness of the advance on the 8th, 9th and 10th was the negation of the Napoleonic pattern. And it proved fatal to the chance of converting the German retreat into a disaster. Thereby it paved the way for the four long years of trench warfare. In part it was due to the obstacle provided by successive rivers. But in still greater part it was due to want of impulsion, and misguided direction. Sir John French seems to have had little faith in the prospect, and still less in his Allies' efforts. In consequence he trod on the brake rather than the accelerator, besides keeping most of his cavalry on his right flank, and even in rear of it, as a link with his French neighbour instead of a spearhead of the pursuit.* Indeed, not until the 11th was the cavalry really launched in pursuit. Franchet d'Esperey's advance was even more

* The average advance on the 6th was eleven miles; on the 7th, less than eight miles; on the 8th, ten miles; on the 9th, seven miles. The Official History argues that, under the conditions, 'little more could be expected'. This view does not agree with the evidence of numerous officers who took part. Thus General Charteris has a diary note, referring to the 7th – 'Actually, our own troops, though the men were very keen, moved absurdly slowly ... The cavalry were the worst of all, for they were right behind the infantry.' He also says that Haig went 'from one Divisional HQ to another trying to urge them forward', but the divisional diaries imply the opposite; it is certain that on the 9th Haig imposed a halt of several hours after crossing the Marne until his aircraft reported 'all clear'. He was then stopped again by French. The slowness of the advance is ascribed by General Gough to the fact that 'no attempt was made by GHQ to explain to the corps and divisional commanders the extraordinary opportunity now available for a decisive blow at the enemy'.

cautious: his right was tied back to Foch; his centre slowly followed
up, but did not catch up, Bülow's retiring wing; his left neglected to
push along a completely open path.

A further cause of delay, however, was the tactical method employed
in the advance. The old idea of keeping an even alignment still ruled, as
it did until 1918, so that if one corps or division was checked its neighbours tended to halt. Thus frequent opportunities were missed for pushing on past the flanks of a temporary resistance and maintaining the
momentum of the advance. And because the British and French missed
this opportunity it was to be left for 1918 to see and the Germans to
apply the method of Nature – for thus does any current or stream take
the line of least resistance, finding a way past an obstacle and then
flowing on, while the back eddies wash away the now isolated obstacle.

Perchance also the victory might have been more decisive – to the
shortening of the war – if its creator had not been removed from control
at the beginning of it. Having already limited the power of Galliéni's
blow, Joffre seized the first chance to deprive him of his powers of
directing it. Would that he had been as quick in exploiting the weakness
of the rival army! For on September 11th Joffre informed Galliéni that
he would resume direct control of Maunoury's army, leaving Galliéni
to fret his soul within the confines of Paris while watching the fruits of
victory slipping from the grasp of his slow-thinking superior. Throughout the battle Galliéni's governing idea had been to direct all reserves
to the north – towards the enemy's rear – although several times frustrated by Joffre. With Galliéni's disappearance the advance became
purely frontal, giving the Germans the breathing space to reorganize
and stand firm on the line of the Aisne. Not until then, September
17th, did Joffre's mind awake to the idea of concentrating by rail a
fresh mass of manoeuvre behind the German flank. As a result, in the so-
called 'Race to the Sea', the French were always 'an army corps too few
and twenty-four hours too late', until the trench front stretched to the
sea.

But his was not the sole failure to take advantage of the temporary
state of disorder and indecision behind the German line. It is the sober
verdict of General Edmonds, the British official historian, that – 'Had
some of the fourteen British Territorial Force divisions and fourteen
mounted brigades, with the 6th Division still in England, been landed
at the Channel coast ports to fall on the German communications and
rear, a decisive tactical result might have been obtained and the war
finished.'

Even as it was, on reaching the Aisne an opportunity had remained, only to be missed. Indeed, the Official History states that 'The prospects of a breakthrough never were brighter' than on the morning of the 13th. Thanks to German carelessness and the initiative of various junior commanders, the passage of the river had been achieved on both flanks. And 'from all the information furnished to General Haig the gap had not been closed which had existed between the German First and Second Armies ever since the Battle of the Marne...' But the race was lost owing to 'a failure of the High Command to appreciate the situation'. On the 13th 'the divisions made a rather cautious and leisurely advance', and 'in the GHQ orders there was no hint whatever of the importance of time'.

'By the evening of the 13th September the situation had completely changed. German reinforcements were known to have arrived, and serious resistance was to be expected on the 14th; yet the GHQ orders merely repeated the formula that "the Army will continue the pursuit".' 'There was no plan, no objective, no arrangements for cooperation, and the divisions blundered into battle.' With their failure, the flux crystallized and deadlock ensued.

A still greater opportunity was thrown away by the French to the eastward; for, on reaching the Aisne, Conneau's cavalry corps and a group of reserve divisions were opposite a ten-mile gap in the German front. After crossing the river the cavalry rode on thirteen miles northwards to Sissonne – but then, 'seeing the danger' of being cut off, 'the order was given to retire to the bridges'. This inglorious sense of precaution forfeited an opening such as cavalry would never again enjoy on the Western Front. For, at Sissonne, Conneau's cavalry corps was fifteen miles north of the thrown-back flank of the German Second Army, and forty miles behind the line of the Third Army. 'It had only to move eastwards across the enemy lines of communication to cause at least alarm and confusion.'

The question has often been posed whether the trench stalemate would have come to pass if France had possessed a Napoleon. Although the unappreciated defensive power of modern weapons and the unwieldy masses of 1914 weighted the scales against the mobility and decisiveness of warfare, the Galliéni interlude raises a doubt. For not only did Galliéni afford the one instance of 'Napoleonic *coup d'œil*' witnessed on the Western Front in 1914–18, but his intuition, his boldness of manoeuvre and his swift decision were so vivid a contrast to that of the other leaders, French, British and German, as to suggest that it was possible to snatch a decision by manoeuvre from the jaws of trench warfare – before the artizan swallowed the artist.

The hypothesis is strengthened by the fact that Galliéni's influence was exercised under the most shackling conditions. The command of a fortress was governed by rules and limitations which ordained a strictly defensive role, even gave the governor power to refuse assistance to the field armies, and discouraged him from any wider horizon than that of his immediate responsibility for the defence of the fortress. It was the irony of fortune that the Commander-in-Chief in the field should have led the way to universal siege warfare; that the commander of a fortress should have conceived and launched the most decisive manoeuvre of the war. Yet war is a game where the 'joker' counts, and when Joffre withheld the trump Galliéni played the 'joker'. As he remarked later, half humorously, half bitterly, 'There has not been a battle of the Marne. Joffre's instructions ordained a retreat on the Seine and the evacuation of Verdun and of Nancy. Sarrail did not obey: he saved Verdun; Castelnau held on to the Grand Couronné: he saved Nancy. I have taken the offensive. As for asserting now that it is the Commander-in-Chief – who had gone back far to the rear while I advanced – who conducted, foresaw, and arranged it all ... it is hard to believe!'

The truest phrase of all was his first – 'There has not been a Battle of the Marne.' Nor had there been a 'battle' of Sedan in 1870. The folly of MacMahon in face of the first Moltke was paralleled, and even excelled, by the folly of the second Moltke in face of shadows.

CHAPTER FOUR

SCENE 2

The Field of Legend – Tannenberg

Like that of the Marne, the popular story of the great German victory of Tannenberg is a monument of monumental error. For it consists, actually, of a figure of wood, on a pedestal of clay, varnished with legend.

The first and most popular of these legends provided a romantic picture of an old general who, as the hobby of his years of retirement, spent his time in devising a gigantic trap for a future Russian invasion, exploring paths through and sounding the bottom of the marshes in which the Russian hordes were to be engulfed – and then, when war came, carrying his dream to fulfilment. The next legend, which rose as the shadow of Ludendorff rose behind the figure of Hindenburg, was of a masterly plan for a second Cannae conceived and dictated in the train that was carrying Ludendorff to pick up his nominal master *en route* to East Prussia. History, alas, must dissipate both.

For the Germans, essentially a people of combination, found their Galliéni in a conjunction between the brain of a young staff officer and the drive of an old corps commander. And they, in turn, were much helped because Russian leadership was able to combine the faults of a Moltke and a Joffre. Indeed, the military history of modern Russia is epitomized in the brief record of the invasion of East Prussia.

The man who was, in large measure, responsible for the blundering execution was also responsible for that disastrous invasion being made, and being made before the Russian forces were ready. This was General Jilinsky, who had been Chief of the General Staff until 1913. For he had made the military convention with France whereby Russia was pledged to put 800,000 men in the field on the fifteenth day of mobilization. This arrangement put a strain on the cumbrous Russian war machine which caused numerous cracks and local failures when it began moving. And it also put a strain on the Russian Headquarter staff which

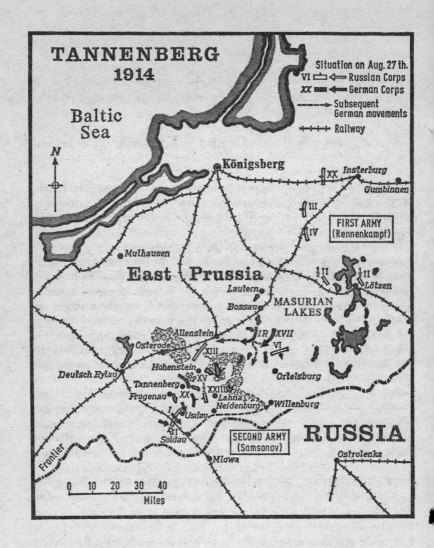

led them to make decisions in a state of nervous flurry. But the arrangement did not end with this promise, for the new plan envisaged an offensive against the Germans simultaneously with the main thrust against the Austrians.

To increase the drawbacks the plan was to be carried out by a man who had not worked it out; who had even been deprived deliberately of any influence upon it by General Sukhomlinov, the Minister of War. Sukhomlinov, indeed, was scheming to get command himself. But he was not the only one who had a belief in his own divine fitness for command. And his rival claimed divine right. For when the war came the Tsar proposed to take command himself – to the alarm of his ministers. Under pressure from them the Tsar regretfully appointed the Grand Duke Nicholas, who was at least a trained soldier, but handicapped him by nominating his two principal assistants. One of these, Yanushkevich, was a courtier general, unpopular with the working army. The second, Danilov, was an able but orthodox soldier, and really directed the Russian strategy.

From the earliest days of August the Grand Duke was incessantly pressed by the French, through the Russian Foreign Office, to do something to relieve the German pressure on the French, and to do it quickly. Thereby, although the Russian invasion of East Prussia did not begin before the promised time it began before it was ready.

East Prussia formed a long tongue of land pointing across the Niemen river, to the heart of Russia, and flanked on the north by the Baltic and on the south by Russian Poland. Along the land frontier two armies had been assembled, the First or Vilna Army under Rennenkampf and the Second or Warsaw Army under Samsonov. The two formed a group under the higher control of Jilinsky. His plan was that Rennenkampf should advance against the eastern tip of East Prussia, drawing upon himself the German defending forces; then, two days later, Samsonov was to cross the southern frontier and bestride the Germans' rear, cutting them off from the Vistula. The fault of this plan lay not in the conception but in the execution. Its potential value was well proved by the alarm – indeed, the dislocation of mind – caused in the German headquarters when the menace was disclosed. But it suffered two natural handicaps, apart from faulty leadership and military unreadiness. The first was that the two armies were separated by the fifty-mile chain of the Masurian Lakes; these also, in conjunction with the fortified Königsberg area on the west, narrowed Rennenkampf's line of advance to a gap only about forty miles wide. Secondly, the Russians' own invasion from the south was now to be handicapped by the fact that they had left the border country a desert, with poor railways and worse roads, as a barrier against a German invasion.

On August 17th, Rennenkampf crossed the eastern frontier with six and a half divisions and five cavalry divisions. The problem of meeting such a double thrust had long been studied, and Schlieffen's solution had been that of utilizing the obstacles of the county, especially the Masurian Lakes, to strike hard and with full strength at whichever Russian army first came within reach, and then to turn against the other. But Prittwitz, the commander in East Prussia, was akin to his superior, Moltke, in his fear of taking calculated risks. Unwilling to rely on Landwehr and garrison troops to supplement natural obstacles in delaying Samsonov, he also left the two divisions of the XX Corps (Scholtz) on the southern front. The remainder of his Eighth Army, seven divisions and one cavalry division, concentrated to oppose Rennenkampf. And, to handicap himself further in gaining quick and decisive results, he launched a frontal attack on the invaders – owing to a mistaken idea of their position.

This attack was delivered near Gumbinnen on August 20th. The German centre corps, the XVII (Mackensen), had to deliver the most straightforward attack and suffered a heavy repulse, which offset – at least psychologically – the success of the corps on either wing. Even so, Rennenkampf was on the point of ordering a retreat to save his own centre from encirclement when, next morning, he found that the Germans were retreating instead.

For on the day of Gumbinnen Samsonov had reached the frontier, so hurried on by Jilinsky, that his troops were tired and hungry, their transport incomplete and the supply services in chaos. He had with him eight divisions and three cavalry divisions, while two more divisions were following on.

His appearance was reported by the XX Corps to Prittwitz, and his force was rather under than over estimated. Prittwitz was unnerved by the news, although the XX Corps was not. That evening two of his staff, General Grünert and Lieut-Colonel Max Hoffmann were talking outside their office in the headquarters at Neidenburg – uncomfortably close to the southern frontier – when Prittwitz appeared and called them into his office. There also was the Chief of Staff, Count Waldersee, another wavering bearer of a famous name. With anxiety writ on his face, Prittwitz said – 'I suppose, gentlemen, you also have received this fresh news from the southern front? The army is breaking off the battle and retiring behind the Vistula.'

Both the junior staff officers protested, urging that the Gumbinnen thrust should first be driven home, that there was adequate time, and that, in any case, a precipitate retreat without fighting would give Samsonov, who was much nearer the Vistula, the chance to cut off the main German forces. Prittwitz, however, curtly told them that the decision rested with him and not with them. He then left the office, leaving them to continue the argument with Waldersee – and, eventually, to persuade him to take bolder measures. It was decided that, to gain time, and room, an attack should be launched against Samsonov's left or western flank. And for this purpose three divisions should be railed back from the Gumbinnen area to reinforce the XX Corps, while the remainder of the force there (I Reserve and XVII Corps) were to retreat westwards by road. Here was the foundation of the Tannenberg manoeuvre.

On returning to the office Prittwitz agreed to their moves, and spoke no more of retiring behind the Vistula. Next day he grew quite cheerful when word came that his forces had been disengaged safely from Rennenkampf's front, and that Samsonov had almost come to a standstill. But on the 22nd, when the headquarters had been moved north to Mühlhausen, a bombshell was exploded by a telegram which announced that a special train was on its way with a new Commander-in-Chief and a new Chief of Staff on board – the first being General von Hindenburg and the second, General Ludendorff. Half an hour after came the delayed telegram which told Prittwitz and Waldersee that they had been superseded.

Not until later did the astonished staff discover the clue to this dramatic upset. It lay in the fact that while Prittwitz was out of the office, during the discussion on the 20th, he had not only telephoned to Mackensen and to the Lines of Communication authorities, to tell them that he was going to retire behind the Vistula, but had telephoned also to the Supreme Command – then at Coblenz on the Rhine. He had even told Moltke that he could only hold the Vistula line if he received reinforcements. To crown his nerve-broken folly, he forgot to tell his staff of this telephone talk when he came back, and so prevented them informing Moltke of his change of plan. And Moltke, whose own loss of nerve and lapse into pessimism were still to come, though imminent, was remarkably quick to penalize it in a subordinate.

He looked round at once for a man of decision and found him in Ludendorff, who had just wrenched victory from defeat at Liége. Then as an afterthought, he chose a nominal superior for Ludendorff, who was summoned to Coblenz. Arriving there on the 22nd, he had the situation in East Prussia explained to him, dispatched his initial orders direct to the unfortunate Prittwitz's corps commanders, caught the train for his new 'command', and picked up his 'commander', Hindenburg, at Hanover.

Let us pause to contemplate this delightful and amusing picture of the German system of command. The staff officer chosen first and alone consulted, while the figurehead waits unclaimed in the 'lost property office' at Hanover; the staff officer telegraphing *his* orders, and then collecting his 'baggage' on the way; but the supreme jest was that the plan had already been framed and the necessary movements made by a still more junior staff officer, Hoffmann, who was to remain under Ludendorff in his post as head of the Operations branch.

The calculated daring of the plan, moreover, owed much to an earlier experience of Hoffmann's. For Schlieffen, with discerning insight, had picked this impishly brilliant young captain, whom many deemed merely a witty *flâneur*, to go as observer with the Japanese forces in the war against Russia. There he learnt much about the Russian army, and not least a story that two Generals, Rennenkampf and Samsonov, had boxed each other's ears on the railway platform at Mukden. Thus, in his judgement, Rennenkampf would be in no hurry to aid Samsonov by pressing on from Gumbinnen. He had also learnt in Manchuria the incredible carelessness of Russian methods and this knowledge led him in August, 1914, to accept the intercepted Russian wireless orders, sent out 'in clear', as authentic, whereas his seniors were distrustfully inclined to regard them as an artful deception.

Paradoxically, the fulfilment of Hoffmann's plan and its development by Ludendorff – the plan on which Ludendorff was to rise to world fame – were hindered by Ludendorff's initial orders. For, in order to amputate Prittwitz's control, Ludendorff had telephoned from Coblenz to the several army corps, telling them to act independently until he arrived. The I Reserve and XVII Corps on Rennenkampf's front utilized this order to take a day's rest in their retreat westwards. Another check on rapidity was that the whole of the Eighth Army headquarters had to move back to Marienburg to meet the new commanders.

On arrival there on the 23rd, Ludendorff was pleasantly surprised to find that the movements already in progress fitted in with his own half-formed plan, and he confirmed Hoffmann's arrangements. Next day it became clear that Rennenkampf was not moving forward in pursuit, and Ludendorff enlarged the plan by accelerating the retirement of the I Reserve Corps (Below), so that it could strike Samsonov's right flank. Then, on the 25th, intercepted wireless messages showed him the slowness of Rennenkampf's movements, and he began to think that he could use the XVII Corps (Mackensen) also, leaving only the cavalry to watch and hoodwink Rennenkampf. Thereby he might strike hard at not one but both of Samsonov's flanks, and bring off a decisive double envelopment. Unfortunately for his now matured plan, even forced marches could not overtake the lost day of rest.

. Samsonov meantime had been staggering forward, driven on by telegraphic lashes from Jilinsky who had jumped to the conclusion that the Germans were doing what Prittwitz had contemplated – retreating to the Vistula. And in driving Samsonov on to cut them off, Jilinsky not only neglected to hasten Rennenkampf, but even diverted his energy by orders to invest Königsberg. Meantime Samsonov's army was spread out over a front of nearly sixty miles, and his right, centre and left were widely separated. If they had been linked by mobility, this width might have been an advantage, but with sluggish troops and bad roads it became a danger. And an attempt to side-step farther west as he advanced led through self-dislocation to self-destruction.

Scholtz's XX Corps had been slowly giving way, and wheeling back westwards, before the advance of the Russian centre (XIII and XV Corps) towards the line Allenstein–Osterode. Fearing both the strain and the effect of a further retirement, Ludendorff ordered François' I Corps to attack on the 26th and break through the Russian left wing (I Corps and two cavalry divisions) near Usdau. François protested that part of his troops, three-quarters of his field guns, all his heavy guns, and his ammunition columns had not yet arrived; he also urged that instead of making a frontal attack he should get round the Russian flank. Ludendorff summarily overrode these objections. His sense of time was perhaps greater than his sense of tactical reality. But François, who had no wish to repeat Mackensen's experience at Gumbinnen, avoided the Russians active resistance by passive resistance to Ludendorff's orders, and contented himself with the capture of an outlying ridge. And any danger to Scholtz's XX Corps was avoided by the inactivity of Samsonov's exhausted troops – one corps, for example, had marched more than 150 miles in twelve days over roads that were merely deep sand.

But the 26th did not pass without hard fighting. For away on the other flank the Russian right wing (VI Corps and cavalry division), separated by two days' march distance from the rest of the army, had encountered near Lautern the two German corps that were marching back from the east front. The Russian right wing was thrown back in confusion, but the attacks of Below and Mackensen were badly coordinated, their troops were tired by the forced marches, and they did not press the pursuit. Thus the Russian right wing, although disorganized, was able to retire safely. Part of one division, however, had been hemmed in with their backs to the Bössau Lake, and in the panic a number were drowned. From this small incident arose the legend that Hindenburg had driven Samsonov's army into the lakes and marshes, drowning thousands.

The real crisis of the battle, as a whole, came on the 27th. For that morning François, now amply supplied with shells, opened a fierce bombardment on the position of the Russian left wing near Usdau. The Russian troops could not stand high explosive on top of an empty stomach, and they broke in flight without waiting for the German infantry. François ordered the pursuit to be made towards Neidenburg, to get across the rear of the Russian centre, but a Russian counter-attack against his outer flank caused him to wheel south towards Soldau. At daybreak on the 28th, however, he discovered that the beaten Russian left wing had retired precipitately from Soldau across the frontier, and he once more turned his forces eastwards to Neidenburg.

The time that he had lost on the 27th was compensated for by the fact that the Russians had engulfed themselves still further – to their doom. For although Samsonov knew the night before that his right had been beaten and his left was menaced, he had ordered his centre to strike northward again. As he can be acquitted of undue optimism, there are two possible explanations – that he was too rigidly loyal to his orders in trying to carry out his mission, or that he was unwilling to retreat when Rennenkampf, his old enemy, was advancing. His attack probably saved the Germans a repulse, for Scholtz had been ordered by Ludendorff to chime in after François' attack. As it was, the Russian centre made several cracks in Scholtz's front, although at the price of further exhaustion to itself. These cracks seem to have momentarily cracked Ludendorff's nerve, for he ordered François both to send back assistance and, with the rest of his corps, to march north-east towards Lahna, against the immediate rear of the Russian centre. This direction, which traversed thick forest country, would have given François less time and chance to bar the Russian line of retreat. Fortunately, he again disregarded his orders, and continued towards Neidenburg. Soon after midday Ludendorff discovered that the Russians were not attempting to deepen the cracks, but, rather, were showing signs of retreat. So he sent François fresh orders not only to move on Neidenburg but, through it, eastward on Willenburg. And by the night of the

29th, François' troops held the road from Neidenburg to Willenburg, with a chain of entrenched posts between, forming a barricade across the line of retreat of the Russians who were now flowing back, and becoming inextricably mixed in the forest maze which François had avoided. With its rear closed and its roads congested, the Russian centre (XIII, XV and half the XXIII Corps) dissolved into a mob of hungry and exhausted men, who beat feebly against the ring of fire and then let themselves be rounded up in thousands.

The crowning scene of the tragedy was enacted by Samsonov himself, who had moved up from Neidenburg on the 27th to control the battle, only to find himself caught up in the swirling eddies of the retreat. Unable to do anything he turned and rode south again on the 28th, only to get lost in the depths of the forest. In the darkness he turned aside, and his absence was unnoticed by his staff until a solitary shot rang out – he had taken his own life rather than survive the disaster.

But when he died the disaster was not so complete as his despair, nor so certain. If the Russian centre had only been able to reorganize itself for an aimed attempt to break out, it might well have succeeded. For François' barricade was thin and was itself menaced from the outside. The source of the menace was Artamanov's I Corps which, after its defeat at Usdau and retreat over the frontier, had been reinforced, and now returned to the rescue. Air reports warned François of the danger on the 29th, but he stoutly refused to give up his 'blockade', although he dispatched such force as he could possibly spare to check the advancing Russians at Neidenburg. Even so, the town was lost on the 30th, but Ludendorff was already sending reinforcements, and Artamanov, having made little attempt to press his advantage, retreated south once more on the 31st.

The cause of François' weakness, however, and the escape of part of Samsonov's army, was due to the failure of Mackensen and Below from the east to join up with François. Thus the barricade was neither as firm nor as complete as it might have been. Owing to faulty cooperation between Mackensen and Below, and lack of clear guidance from above, their corps abandoned the pursuit of the Russian right wing and turned northwards towards Allenstein – marching, in good German style, 'to the sound of the guns' instead of weaving a net round the enemy's rear in Hannibalic style. Ludendorff, divided between fear of Rennenkampf's advance and his desire to annihilate Samsonov, issued a contradictory series of orders which did not help to sort out the tangle into which Mackensen and Below had got their forces. In the outcome, he thereby risked more and gained less. For he took longer to close up his battle accounts and left a gap in the south-east through which part of the Russian XIII Corps actually escaped, and most of it might have escaped – if Mackensen, on his own initiative, had not turned southwards again in an effort to close the gap, and the Russians had not been blinded by panic.

Nevertheless, 92,000 prisoners were taken, two and a half army corps annihilated, and the other half of Samsonov's army severely shaken, especially in morale. The Germans were certainly favoured by the enemy's folly – above all, in dispersing the fog of war at intervals by unciphered wireless messages. Yet if we make due allowance for these flashes of light, we should take due account of the 'blindness' and the difficulties of this wild region. The victory of Tannenberg remains a great achievement, as it was a unique one in the history of the war. But Ludendorff was not the designer of victory, and still less Hindenburg. To Hoffmann is due the chief credit of the design, if Prittwitz and Ludendorff have some share for accepting it in turn, and Ludendorff also for certain additions of detail. Nor was Ludendorff even the agent of victory, for François' share was the most essential. And against Ludendorff's share must be offset the fact that his original telegram from Coblenz was the original and echoing cause of the failure to complete Samsonov's encirclement. For the battle of Tannenberg was not a second Cannae, deliberately planned, as it has so often been acclaimed. The aim was to break the force of the Russian invasion, and not to surround the Russian army, and the idea of the double envelopment only an afterthought, which became possible of fulfilment when Rennenkampf continued to remain passive. As much an afterthought as the very name given to the victory. For Ludendorff's order for the pursuit on the 28th had been headed 'Frögenau', when Hoffmann suggested that he might aptly wipe out a stain on German annals by using instead the name of the town in front of them, Tannenberg, where in 1410 the Teutonic knights had suffered an historic rout.

CHAPTER FOUR

SCENE 3

The Man Who Juggled with Armies,
and Broke Them – at Lemberg

No man in Europe had worked harder for war than Conrad von Hötzendorf, the directing head of the Austro-Hungarian armies. None surpassed him in eagerness. Fate determined that he, of all the military chiefs, should come to grief most utterly in the first clash of the armies. Yet he was, perhaps, the ablest strategist among them. Moltke, Joffre, and the Grand Duke Nicholas were conscientious pedestrian soldiers, with marked differences of temperament but not of *tempo*. They were slow-moving and slow-thinking, whereas Conrad had a sense of mobility and an aptitude for bold manoeuvre. His strategy blended the spirit of an artist with the suppleness of an acrobat. If his ideas were bounded by the walls of the nineteenth-century school of war, they represented its best fruits. Also its worst defect – a failure to appreciate the growing part that material factors play in modern war. Lacking a sense of tactical reality, he would attempt feats of strategic virtuosity for which his instrument was inherently unfitted. When it bent under the strain, he merely pressed on it the harder — until it broke in his hands.

The Austrian Army was the most obsolete in equipment among those of the Great Powers; its field guns were fewer in proportion and shorter in range; some two-thirds of the rifles were of old pattern, a quarter of a century old, and its reserve was so inadequate that, even in September, the troops holding the Carpathian passes had to be issued with single-loaders; its transport was so scanty that it had to be supplemented by a cumbersome collection of assorted farm-carts, which congested the roads. Yet with all these hindrances to vigorous action the training of the Austro-Hungarian army had been devoted purely to the offensive. This infatuation with a tactical impossibility seems to have been due to the influence of Conrad von Hötzendorf, who had himself compiled the manuals on which the army had been trained.

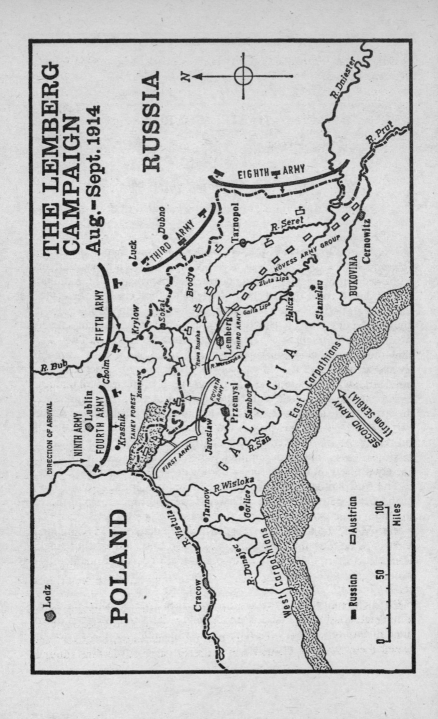

THE LEMBERG CAMPAIGN
Aug.–Sept. 1914

RUSSIA

POLAND

GALICIA

BUKOVINA

EIGHTH ARMY

THIRD ARMY

FIFTH ARMY

NINTH ARMY

FOURTH ARMY

FOURTH ARMY

FIRST ARMY

SECOND ARMY (from SERBIA)

KÖVESS ARMY GROUP

THIRD ARMY

DIRECTION OF ARRIVAL

Lodz

Lublin

Cholm

Krasnik

Krylow

Sokal

Brody

Luck

Dubno

Tarnopol

Sokal

Zluta Lipa

Gnila Lipa

Lemberg

Rawa Ruska

Komarov

Tomaszov

Jaroslaw

Przemysl

L.Sambor

Halicz

Stanislau

Cernowitz

Tarnow

Gorlice

Cracow

TANEV FOREST

East Carpathians

West Carpathians

R. Dniester

R. Prut

R. Seret

R. Bug

R. San

R.Wereszyca

R. Vistula

R. Wisloka

R. Dunajec

N

Miles
0   50   100

Russian
Austrian

If the tactical instrument of his plan was brittle, its strategic foundation was hollow. The Polish salient, deep thrust between the jaws of Austrian and German territory, was on the map a morsel so inviting that any amateur strategist would have jumped at the idea of biting it off. It excited Conrad beyond discretion. He pictured to himself a strategic super-Sedan, with his own armies thrusting up from Galicia and the Germans driving down from East Prussia, to cut off the Russian masses in the wide plains of Poland. But this project was not easy to adjust to the practical problem of a double-fronted war conducted by a double-headed alliance.

Germany had long decided to concentrate her initial efforts against France. At a meeting in 1909, Moltke had told Conrad that he hoped to settle with France within six weeks, and then to switch his forces to the Russian front in support of Austria. In view of the German decision, Conrad might wisely have decided to stand on the defensive until the reinforcement came. If he had done so, geography and Russian lethargy would have worked in his favour, to gain time. The rivers and streams that run north from the Carpathians would have provided a series of delaying obstacles; and the Russian armies' slow rate of concentration would have withheld early danger. But, even to gain time, Conrad could only conceive one form of action – the offensive. And, with this obsession, Russia's lengthy process of mobilization served him as a justification. The sooner he struck the less force he would have to meet. It was calculated that the Russians would have thirty-one divisions on the Austrian front by the twentieth day of mobilization (August 18th) rising to fifty-two by the thirtieth day. Conrad counted on having available a force equal to the Russians by the first date, whereas he would be in an inferiority of three to four by the second. To him this was an incentive to prompt action, although to anybody save a military optimist of the 1914 kind bare equality of strength, and strength of such a dubious quality, might have seemed inadequate odds in launching a would-be decisive offensive.

But Conrad also counted on the strength of a vague promise from Moltke, in 1909, that the German forces in East Prussia would take the offensive. Although no direction was mentioned, and even the intention lapsed, Conrad continued to assume that such an offensive would take place.

If the German General Staff bears the responsibility of having failed to undeceive him – instead, Moltke indulged in schoolboyish exhortations to 'thrust the knout-carriers into the marshes of the Pripet and drown them there' – Conrad was certainly eager to deceive himself, rather than forgo the opportunity of displaying his art. His two strongest armies, the First and the Fourth, were assembled on the left of his line in Galicia for a northward thrust, while the Third covered their eastern flank; it was to be joined by the Second when this eventually arrived from its 'circular tour' on the Serbian front. Conrad had admitted the possibility that the Russians, instead of assembling to be cut off in the Polish salient, might concentrate for an offensive against his eastern flank; in that case he proposed to swing his armies round to face them, on a line through Lemberg; but, as such a possibility did not accord with his desires, he was more than ready to discount it. This did not prove difficult, thanks to the defective means of information on which he relied. He had over a hundred thousand cavalry, but a mere forty-two aircraft, and of these only a few were serviceable.

The Austrian advance 'was preceded by a great mass of cavalry' sent forward on August 15th on a hundred-mile excursion to search a front 250 miles wide. Within a few days 'so many of the horses had sore backs that several entire divisions were put out of action'. Only a small proportion came within reach of the enemy, who did not use a cavalry screen; thus these Austrian cavalry bumped into the Russian infantry, who took heavy toll of them. The Austrian Official History candidly remarks that 'the results of the distant cavalry reconnaissance were not worth the cost of casualties'.

But the slight indications that he gleaned sufficed to satisfy Conrad that the Russians were assembling according to plan – his plan. So, on the 20th, he gave the fateful order for the northward offensive into the depths of Poland. Groping in the dark, the Austrian infantry pushed on towards Lublin, while Conrad, in false confidence, expressed his belief that 'there is no sign of any Russian movement from the east against the right flank'.

His delusion was soon to be rudely dispersed, for two whole Russian armies were marching against this flank. In contrast to the Germans, Conrad seems to have discovered too late the possibility of intercepting the enemy's wireless orders, although he learnt the trick in time to escape the closing of the net into which he had blindly walked.

By comparison, the Russian plan was of shrewd and simple design. It offered two essentially different alternatives, but the initial dispositions were made to suit either. In any event, all the Polish salient west of Warsaw and the Vistula was to be evacuated. The Russian forces were divided into two groups, one assembling on the north-western front facing East Prussia, and the other on the south-western front facing East Galicia. Each group comprised three armies, with a fourth guarding its outer flank. If the Germans concentrated for an offensive against Russia, the alternative that would be adopted was Plan G ('Germania') by which the Russian forces would fall back to a north-and-south line through Brest–Litovsk, retiring farther if and when necessary, until the arrival of the troops from Siberia and Turkestan enabled them to take the counter-offensive in strength. If the Germans made their main effort against France, and remained inactive in the east, Plan A ('Austria') came into operation. In this, the south-western group of armies, reinforced by one from the north-western, would take the offensive against the Austrians: the remainder of the north-western group would invade East Prussia.

In the light of orthodox theory, this plan of delivering a double attack on two widely separated points and in divergent directions, may seem unwise – and be too hastily condemned. Its justification lay in the weakness of the German forces in East Prussia and in the importance of a distraction to their effort against France – as the event proved. Also it would shield the flank of the main offensive, and shorten the front if it succeeded, while paving the way for the ultimate advance of the main armies into Silesia. Here were strong arguments. Moreover, it would have been difficult, because of poor communications, for more troops to be used effectively on the Galician side. The defects of the plan were less in the general design than in the conduct of the northern offensive and the crudeness of the instrument. Unfortunately, these defects were aggravated by the pressure which the French applied to the Russian command to accelerate its action.

The Grand Duke Nicholas resisted their suggestion that he should advance direct against Silesia, ignoring the enemy on his flanks; but in loyalty to his allies he began to assemble two fresh armies on the centre with a view to such a move, as soon as possible. Also, he tried to hasten the execution of his present moves, and thereby put a greater strain on the Russian organization than it could safely bear. If the consequences were most harmful on the East Prussian side, where they led to 'Tannenberg', their effects were felt earlier on the Galician side.

Here the Russians, like the Austrians, had a picture of their enemy's plan that was exactly the reverse of the reality. And no more than the Austrians did they have the means of information to correct it. Ivanov, commanding the south-western group of armies, imagined the enemy moving east: they would be met by his strong Third and Eighth Armies, advancing west: and then his Fourth and Fifth Armies would descend from the north across their rear. A delightful picture; and, although it was incorrectly conceived, it came near to being fulfilled – the other way round.

The opening, however, was unpropitious. Under pressure from the Grand Duke Nicholas, and contrary to Ivanov's wish, the Fourth Army on the extreme west began moving down before its mobilization was complete. In this unready state it collided on the 23rd with the Austrian First Army pushing northward. Both were surprised. But in this battle of Krasnik, superiority of force was on the Austrian side, and it enabled General Dankl to turn the flank of the Russians and drive them back.

The news of this reverse was an unpleasant shock to the Grand Duke and Ivanov; but, with eyes still glued on their original picture, they too easily slipped into the deduction that the Austrian stroke came merely from an offensive flank guard. And to punish the audacious intruder Plehve's Fifth Army was ordered to wheel westward against his flank and rear, so as to cut him off. Another picture.

Unfortunately for the Russians, this wheel presented their own flank to the northward-advancing Austrian Fourth Army (Auffenberg). The clash took place on the 26th. In this battle of Komarov, the Russians suffered the worse because their own commander was continuing to urge the westward wheel while the enemy was forcing them to face round to the south. Under this double pressure the Russian Fifth Army became badly bent, especially on the flanks, and by the evening of the 28th it was in grave danger of being encircled by Auffenberg's. It might have crumpled sooner if the Austrian cavalry had not fallen a prey to a panic, due to their own carelessness, which temporarily unhinged Auffenberg's advance. That hitch in drawing close the net had fateful consequences.

For the grey waves of the main Russian advance were now rolling on towards Lemberg, perilously close to Auffenberg's line of supply and retreat. The caution and cumbrousness of the Russian armies, by acting as a brake on their advance, had helped to keep Conrad in ignorance of the impending menace. And his own temperament had contributed to make this worse. Enthused by the opening success of his northward advance, he had drawn three divisions from the weak Third Army near Lemberg to increase Auffenberg's strength. And at the same time he approved a suggestion that what remained should advance east from Lemberg to strike at the supposedly small Russian forces now reported in that direction. His Second Army from the Danube was only just beginning to arrive on the scene – at Stanislau in the south.

The Third Army's rash advance to the Zlota Lipa on the 26th was followed by still rasher attacks, unprepared and disjointed, on the heads of the Russian columns, which had a five-to-two advantage in numbers. The Austrians recoiled in disorder to the Gnila Lipa. Lemberg itself, twenty-five miles behind the battlefield, was filled with panic-stricken fugitives that night. Next morning Conrad ordered the battered Third Army to fall back on Lemberg, and sent word to Auffenberg to return the three divisions loaned to him. Conrad, indeed, was about to halt his two north-bound armies when news came that the Russians were not pursuing their progress. Thereupon he changed his mind, and also his previous orders.

Ivanov, still believing that he was faced by the mass of the Austrian forces, had decided to pause for forty-eight hours, so that his columns might close up and deploy for battle on the Gnila Lipa. Had he pushed on at once it is likely that he would have crashed through the shaken Austrians as through a paper screen. The Grand Duke, when he heard of the halt, sent orders that the advance on Lemberg was to be resumed immediately.

A remote Commander-in-Chief may propose, but his executive subordinates dispose – the troops under their control. The Russian attack did not develop until the 30th, and even then its decisive impulse came, not from Ruzski's army facing Lemberg, but from Brusilov, who had made a side-step northward with the bulk of his army (the Eighth) by night, and then delivered a smashing blow with his right corps against one sector of the Austrian front. Its collapse produced a general reflux. The roads to the rear were congested with fugitives, intermingled with guns and transport. The Austrian Official History candidly relates that a mere cry of 'the Cossacks are coming' often sufficed to cause another panic surge. They were not coming, however, anything like as fast as in the Austrians' fears. Once more the Russians gave their enemy time to recover. They took nearly three days to advance the eighteen miles which their fugitive opponents had covered in less than one. Then, their belated approach produced fresh panics, which opened such gaps on the enemy front that Conrad was constrained to abandon Lemberg, late on September 2nd. But his enemy had given him time that he could not have gained.

He used it, not to hedge, but to plunge more heavily, staking everything on the completion of his success in the north. Here, by the 30th, Auffenberg's wings were well round Plehve's flanks, while Dankl's right was driving a wedge between the two Russian armies. Confident of an early decision, Auffenberg begged for two days' grace to achieve it. It was far easier for the local commander to ask than for Conrad to concede such an interval; he bore the responsibility for the whole, and had to face the alarming fact that only thirty miles and a panicky mob separated Ruzski and Brusilov from the communications of his own northern armies. Notwithstanding this grim situation, Conrad accepted Auffenberg's plea and allowed him to retain the extra divisions.

Like a left-handed swordsman beset by two adversaries, Conrad would guard his right side with a frail wicker shield while thrusting full out at the man in front of him. His will-power commands admiration: it would command unreserved admiration if one was sure that it was not fostered by self-delusion.

Moreover, in the modern war of masses, the will of the commander-in-chief, however strong, cannot dominate those of the men upon whom he depends; his will will not work unless his mind is attuned to theirs. In the events that now followed, the gulf between Conrad's ideas and the capacity of his instrument became manifest.

On the night of the 30th, the commander of the menaced Russian Fifth Army sought to extricate himself by an order for withdrawal. That order might not have availed to save him if fortune had not on this occasion favoured the discreet. Next morning the jaws of the trap, instead of closing, were drawn back. Two Archdukes controlled the jaws, Joseph on the right and Peter on the left. A solitary Austrian aeroplane, reconnoitring, magnified a handful of Russian cavalry into a division marching against Joseph's rear; he pulled back a large part of his force to guard it. On the other wing, the Austrian cavalry reported a similar threat, equally mythical, whereupon Peter drew back his whole force, to cover his rear. Thus the Russians safely withdrew, leaving an empty battlefield. Too late, Auffenberg the next morning ordered a rapid pursuit. Counter-orders came from Conrad.

These new orders were born of hope rather than of anxiety. It was unfortunate that Plehve's army had not been surrounded, but to Conrad's eyes it was routed. It is fair to point out that he could only see the enemy's condition through the magnifying glass provided by subordinates eager to flatter his hopes and enlarge their own achievements.

Encouraged by this view of a Plehve definitely removed from the board, Conrad conceived the picture of a new and greater encirclement. Auffenberg should turn about and descend from the north upon the slowly advancing armies of Ruzski and Brusilov, while the newly arrived Austrian Second Army should strike from the south against their other flank, and lap round their rear. It was a masterly conception, which in breath-taking boldness was worthy of Napoleon. Unfortunately, Conrad's picture did not coincide with the reality of his opponents' situation, and was affected by a change in their plans. Ivanov had

ordered Ruzski to incline northward, with Brusilov conforming, so that
he might take in flank and rear the forces that were pursuing Plehve.
The effect on Conrad's plan was that this movement brought Ruzski
round to face the south-bound Austrians instead of presenting them his
flank; also, it contracted the space in which Auffenberg could
manoeuvre between his late and his new opponent. Even this might not
have mattered if Conrad's instrument, the Austrian army, had been
fitted for bold and swift manoeuvre. Its palpable unfitness formed Conrad's worst breach with reality.

Moreover, a new danger was arising. There were now two armies
instead of one facing his own extreme left. For the newly formed
Russian Ninth Army had been brought down the Vistula to support
the Fourth. While the latter pinned Dankl's army, the former was to
push past his flank and round the Austrian rear. Then the whole of the
Austrian armies might be cut off from their natural line of retreat. Thus
while Conrad was trying to catch part of Ivanov's forces in a deadly
embrace, Ivanov was side-stepping to get round his left and take him in
the rear.

The clash of these two plans produced a series of acrobatics such as
huge armies have not attempted before or since, and to which these
particular armies were most unsuited.

Auffenberg duly turned about and marched south, leaving the Archduke Joseph's divisions as a rearguard; the supposedly beaten Plehve
also turned about and followed. On September 6th Auffenberg, expecting to strike Ruzski's flank, found Ruzski knocking against his own at
Rava Russka. Fortunately for him, Ruzski was equally surprised, and
this gave Auffenberg a chance to face round. Away to the far south,
Conrad's other pincer had been no more effective; the Austrian Second
Army came fresh, too fresh, to the fighting, but was travel-worn. Its
advance soon petered out in a series of disjointed attacks, unsupported
by artillery, which culminated in a rippling wave of panic during the
night.

When the tangle was straightened out, the Austrian Second, Third
and Fourth Armies stood in a line facing east. The one clear fact that
emerged was that the Russian armies were inclining northward. This
inspired Conrad to the conception of yet another offensive design,
regardless of the state of his troops. On the evening of September 8th,
Auffenberg was given the task of holding the Russians who faced him,
while the other two armies left their prepared defensive positions and
wheeled northwards to roll up the Russian line. But the day of the 9th
brought disillusionment. Brusilov was also intent on taking the offen-

sive, and the two sides met head on. The condition of the Austrian forces discounted their superiority of numbers, and the battle ended in stalemate, leaving each side with an exaggerated impression of the other's power.

With faith unquenched, Conrad that night sent a fresh order to his armies for a 'concentric attack against the enemy on the Lemberg front'. Next morning he went forward himself with the idea that his presence might be an encouragement. Not unnaturally, his presence at – or rather behind – one point of a fifty-mile line made no appreciable difference. He sent an urgent message to the commander of the Second Army to 'attack without halting, vigorously and regardless of loss'. The commander of the Second Army did not think the order worth passing on to the troops. Such orders were to be repeated so many thousand times on all sides during the World War that it would seem as if to those who uttered them they had the virtue of a magic incantation. An economy of the phrase might have endowed it with more potency. It is rare to trace any effect on those to whom it was addressed – still less on the enemy.

By his persistent pursuit of the tactically impossible, Conrad had engulfed his armies in a pit whence escape was hopeless unless fortune threw them a line. Fortune relented and did so – by a telegram that did not travel along a line.

While Conrad's disordered forces were throwing themselves against the Russians near Lemberg, in fulfilment of his plan, and becoming more entangled in the process, dark masses of the enemy were looming across their rear. Away to the north-west, Dankl's isolated army was struggling to hold up the Russian Fourth and Ninth Armies, double its strength, who were pushing down from the north. On the 9th Dankl warned Conrad that he could hold them no longer, but must fall back behind the San. Worse still there was a thirty-mile gap between Dankl's inner flank and Ruzski's. Into this gap Plehve's army and a whole cavalry corps were marching, unseen and unforeseen by Conrad.

But the ingenuous Russian command came to his rescue in the nick of time. Early on the 11th the Austrians intercepted a wireless order which the Russians, according to their habit, had sent out unciphered. The order showed that Plehve's left wing was expected to reach points well behind Rava Russka by that evening. Still clutching at straws Conrad delayed a few hours in the hope of a miracle on his other flank, and meantime sent an order for the remnant of the Archduke Joseph's divisions to drive back the intruding mass. Auffenberg did not think such an order fit to pass on. So, in the afternoon, as no news of a miracle came, Conrad at last gave the order to disengage the armies and fall back behind the San, as fast as possible.

By cne of history's strangest coincidences, it was at almost the same hour that Moltke accepted the inevitable and gave the order that converted the enforced withdrawal of his right wing into a general retreat of the German armies in France.

The Austrian retreat, however, if less final, was far longer and harder. To quote the moving words of the Austrian Official History – 'Day and night behind a huge train of transport vehicles marched the infantry, with bowed heads, yet undiscouraged (sic); the artillery, sinking in up to their axles in the morass that the roads became ... the cavalry regiments, like horsemen of the Apocalypse, in molten confusion, made their way on, their presence palpable from afar by the penetrating smell of the festering galls of hundreds of led horses.'

The deep-churned mud of the roads luckily served as a brake on the inherently sluggish Russians. And frequent flickers of light from their wireless orders helped to guide the Austrians in evading interception. But Auffenberg's troops could only do so by turning so far south that they became intermingled with the retreating tide of the Third Army. Less than two-thirds of the Austrian troops whom Conrad had confidently pushed forward in August reached the shelter of the San. Even there they did not tarry. They were so obviously unfit to fight that on September 16th, when the first Russians approached, Conrad ordered a fresh retreat to the Dunajec, a farther eighty miles west, leaving behind the great fortress of Przemysl and its garrison as an obstacle to the pursuers. Conrad would, almost surely, have saved himself and his country this additional draught of gall if he had abstained from his last futile assaults near Lemberg. But his rosy imagination had prevented him.

This had certainly revived when, after the war, he wrote in his memoirs: 'The Austro-Hungarian armies were not beaten. They had to be withdrawn to escape a situation that might well have led to a defeat if the battle had continued. From this they were saved!' He saved them from annihilation but not from ruin. He had lost some 350,000 men out of 900,000, and the survivors had retreated over 150 miles, abandoning the province of Galicia. But the ultimate effects were worse than the immediate results. Conrad had juggled with armies – and broken them. If he was able to collect the pieces and stick them together with German glue, they never again had a sound ring.

CHAPTER FOUR

SCENE 4

'First Ypres' – The Real and the
Shadow Battle

Within nine months of its beginning, the war produced two Battles of Ypres. And of these 'First Ypres' was itself a twin battle. In its inception and its course it was closely related to the struggle simultaneously in progress along the Yser between Ypres and the sea. But it had also a dual nature. There was the battle fought by the Allied troops who held the shallow trenches in front of Ypres. There was a different battle being fought, in imagination, by the two chief commanders on the Allied side – at their headquarters behind Ypres. The latter were attacking shadows while the former were defending themselves against the sternest realities. Rarely, if ever, have the view at the front and the view behind the front been so widely apart.

The clash at Ypres followed, yet was not truly a continuation of, the outflanking attempts that followed the deadlock on the Aisne. For while Joffre and Foch continued to concentrate their gaze on the immediate western flank of the German line in France, and their thoughts on the next overlapping move, Falkenhayn had shifted his attention to Flanders and was planning a wider manoeuvre – as wide, in fact, as the coastline would allow. A new Sixth Army, composed of troops switched from the eastern flank in Lorraine, was to counter Joffre's next narrow swing. Meantime another fresh army would sweep down the Belgian coast behind the Allies' flank. That army, the Fourth, was made up of the troops set free by the fall of Antwerp together with four newly raised army corps; in these an enthusiastic crowd of young volunteers was blended with a 25 per cent nucleus of trained reservists.

The abandonment of Antwerp, and its possible consequences, did not obtrude into Foch's horizon. On October 10th he sketched out his picture of the future – 'I propose to advance our left (Tenth Army) by Lille to the Scheldt at Tournai or Orchies, the British army . . . forming line from Tournai through Courtrai ... In this way all the French, British and Belgian detachments would be united on the left banks of either the Scheldt or the Lys. After that we can see.'

Had this intention been fulfilled the Allied forces would have been moving eastward while the new German forces were marching southward behind their backs.

On the 13th Foch wrote to Joffre concerning Sir John French's intentions: 'The Marshal wishes at all costs to go to Brussels. I shall not hold him back.' Fortunately for the Allied troops, King Albert held them both back by his sagacious reluctance to let go of the coast and embark on an inland excursion. And the Germans soon supplemented his restraining check, besides confirming his wisdom.

When the British II Corps began moving forward to fulfil its part of the wheeling sweep, it found that the French left was falling back. By the 18th it had been brought to a halt itself, before Lille even was reached. The III Corps, and Allenby's Cavalry Corps, coming up on its left, were likewise held up, and on the 20th found themselves resisting an enemy offensive. The day previously the German onslaught on the Yser line, near the sea, had begun.

Until now the six weak Belgian divisions, stiffened by Admiral Ronarc'h's brigade of French marines, had been occupying the line from the sea almost to Ypres. But, just in time, two French Territorial divisions, covered by Mitry's Cavalry Corps, took over the right half of the line, as far as Dixmude, reinforcing Ronarc'h's brigade and linking up with Rawlinson's force at Ypres.

The attack on the Belgian sector was made by Beseler's three divisions from Antwerp. Screened by these until the last moment, a greater force was converging against the Dixmude–Ypres sector.

At this moment of approaching crisis Foch was still intent on carrying out his eastward offensive, and his chief concern seems to have been with the uncertain spirit of the British Commander-in-Chief. Sir John French had moved his forces to Flanders only after prolonged hesitation, anxious lest by taking position on the left flank of the French he might again be exposed as at Mons in August. Once committed to the move, he had quickly become optimistic, with the help of Foch's tactful handling and assiduous flattery. Then, however, he was disquieted by the resistance his II Corps met in the initial advance towards Lille : he spoke of constructing a huge entrenched camp at Boulogne to shelter the whole Expeditionary Force.

Sensitive as a weathercock, his mind had swung round again by the 19th, under Foch's gusts of optimistic encouragement. Although Raw-

linson's attempt that day to advance eastward on Menin had been abortive, French ordered Haig's corps to advance north-eastward 'with the
object of capturing Bruges', saying that 'the enemy's strength on the
front Menin–Ostend is estimated at about a corps and no more'. Yet his
own intelligence officers estimated, and underestimated, the enemy's
strength as being three and a half corps. As one of the officers later
explained: 'The old man only believed what he wished to believe.'
Foch's power of 'suggestion' for the moment dominated French's mind.
For two more days French persisted in the belief that he was attacking,
while, in reality, his troops were barely holding their ground.

The imagined offensive remained imaginary, because it clashed with
the opening of the German offensive against Ypres and a simultaneous
renewal of the German offensive against the southern part of the British
line. Everywhere the British were thrown on the defensive, and in
several places lost ground. But French that evening renewed his attack
orders to Haig, apparently with the idea that his left wing would still
find the enemy's open flank. So on the 21st Haig's corps duly tried to
advance past Rawlinson's flank, only to be first held up and then
menaced on its left. The troops dug in where they stood, and, as their
left had been swung back, the Ypres salient of now immortal memory
was formed.

That same day, Joffre, visiting Flanders, had come to see French
and, as an encouragement to fresh offensive efforts, had told him that
the French detachment was being increased by the dispatch of the IX
Corps. The weathercock, however, was now veering – back to a former
direction. Until the French reinforcements arrived, the British commander was unwilling to give any more far-reaching order than that
'action against enemy will be continued tomorrow on general line now
held.' It was a euphemistic way of recognizing the defensive!

Foch still persisted in the offensive idea. Although the enemy's
strength was now unmistakable, he ordered his own troops – now forming the embryo of d'Urbal's Eighth Army – to make a general offensive
on the 23rd in the three widely spread directions of Roulers, Thourout,
and Ghistelles. At the same time he asked the Belgians and British to
take part, the latter again to swing east. If they had done so they would
have laid open their flank. Happily the enemy gave them no chance of
trying.

Foch's request did not reach British General Headquarters until a
few hours before the French attack was supposed to start. It was also
complicated by the receipt of a request from d'Urbal that the British
would attack in a different direction, and by d'Urbal's instructions to

his own right wing to advance on a line which would take it through the British front. The official history remarks, with moderation, that such proposals 'could not be taken seriously'. On hearing of them Haig telegraphed to GHQ that 'there must be some misapprehension of the situation, that there was no time for concerted action, and every chance of confusion'. But his anxiety was needless. The leading French troops did not appear until the afternoon, and the enemy's fire at once stopped their attempt to advance. But they were a welcome reinforcement to the line of defence. Their arrival made the two sides approximately equal in strength, numerically, from Ypres to the sea.

Next day, the 24th, the French IX Corps was ordered 'to continue to advance'. Foch telegraphed direct to the corps commander, Dubois, 'all the units of the IX Corps are detrained' – which was anticipation, not fact. 'Make your dispositions that all these units are employed today, and that the action receives a new impulse. There must be decision and activity.' The result at least gave an air of vindication to Foch's theory, for Dubois' men advanced over half a mile before they were finally held up, while the British, fighting defensively, lost some ground. But the German records suggest that in the proportion of loss inflicted the defensive was the more profitable, and that by the night of the 24th the new German corps had blunted their fighting edge.

Realizing that their effort was spent, the German Fourth Army commander pinned his hopes to a continued effort against the Yser sector, 'where a decision seemed imminent'. This, if achieved, would open the path to Dunkirk and Calais. Under cover of darkness the Germans had gained a footing across the Yser near Tervaete on the night of the 22nd. Counter-attacks failed to dislodge them, all the Belgian reserves were used up, and the French 42nd Division, which would have been invaluable for the purpose, had unfortunately been committed to a vain offensive in the coastal corridor near Nieuport. By the 24th the Germans had brought the infantry of two and a half divisions across the Yser to expand this foothold, and the Belgian centre gave way under the strain. Fortunately it managed to rally on the embankment of the Dixmude–Nieuport railway, whither the 42nd Division was switched in time to stiffen the resistance. And Ronarc'h's marines splendidly withstood a succession of assaults on the key point of Dixmude.

But the situation was still critical, and next day King Albert sanctioned the attempt to create a water barrier by opening the locks at Nieuport so as to flood all the country between the Yser and the railway embankment. These arrangements took time. But, happily, the line of the railway embankment was held, without suffering much pressure, until at high tide on the evening of the 28th the Belgian engineers succeeded in opening one of the locks at Nieuport and letting in the sea. If it crept in slowly, each day brought a fresh reinforcement to the flood, until 'it seemed to the Germans as if the whole country had sunk with them and behind them'. With the impetus of desperation they renewed their attack and breached the embankment line of defence at Ramscapelle. But the rising flood came to the rescue, and during the night the Germans began to retire across the Yser to escape being cut off.

The crisis on the Yser was the prelude to a greater crisis at Ypres. This, again, followed on a fresh attempt by the Allies to take the offensive, which weakened them for the subsequent defensive struggle.

No sooner had the first crisis at Ypres passed than Foch resumed the offensive – in his own mind he had never discontinued it. That he had again infused French with his own assurance is clear from the telegram which French had sent to Kitchener: 'The enemy are vigorously playing their last card.' In the night of the 24th French wired again, suggesting that the battle was 'practically won'.

But on the 25th the Allied offensive made practically no progress against newly wired German defences. On the 26th Dubois and Haig continued the attack, but only advanced a few hundred yards. In contrast, the sharp southern corner of the salient, where Rawlinson's men (the 7th Division) stood, was smashed in by a German attack, and for a time converted into an equally sharp re-entrant. Luckily the assailants did not follow up their success. They were preparing and screening a greater stroke.

A new German army under Fabeck was being brought up, to be inserted like a wedge on the south side of the Ypres salient, between the Fourth and Sixth Armies. This wedge was made up of six divisions, heavily buttressed with artillery. Its entry into the battle on the 29th would give the Germans a two-to-one superiority of numbers. With unforeseeing irony, French had just wired to Kitchener that they were 'quite incapable of making any strong and sustained attack'.

For two days more the Allied offensive was continued without effect, although Dubois had been reinforced by a third division. Faced with a strong line, and themselves provided with little ammunition, the fighting commanders were wise enough to water down the orders received from behind. And although on the night of the 28th these orders again prescribed the offensive, the troops in front suspected the coming storm. It broke, over the British front, at half past five next morning. It was now the Germans' turn to leave the shelter of their trenches and offer themselves as targets. An infantry trained to fire 'fifteen rounds rapid' in the minute with the the rifle was thus enabled to prove its hitting power, and to produce a leaden counterstorm that obscured its lack of machine guns so well that its German assailants thought it had 'quantities'; they declared that 'over every bush, hedge and fragment of wall floated a thin film of smoke, betraying a machine gun rattling out bullets'. Thus at the end of the day the British front was intact, save at one point – Gheluvelt crossroads. But Haig, under whom all three divisions had now been placed, had no reserve left intact.

During the day French had been to Cassel for another injection of Fochian serum. Foch told French that he was satisfied with 'the advance' of his own troops between Ypres and the sea, but admitted that he was 'far from well informed as to their doings'. French on his return ordered the British advance to be continued! He also wired to Kitchener that 'if the success can be followed up, it will lead to a decisive result'. Haig, with the greater realism that came from a closer view, told his troops to entrench, and added that he would postpone 'orders as to the resumption of the offensive' until he saw what the situation was in the morning.

The enemy command at the same time was issuing an Order of the Day which said: 'The breakthrough will be of decisive importance. We must and therefore will conquer, settle for ever the centuries-long struggle, end the war, and strike the decisive blow against our most detested enemy. We will finish with the British, Indians, Canadians, Moroccans, and other trash, feeble adversaries who surrender in mass if they are attacked with vigour.'

The attack was aimed at the Zandvoorde and Messines ridges – to break through the southern hinge of the salient with the object of reaching the Kemmel heights. Thus the main weight fell on the 7th Division and on the thin chain of three dismounted cavalry divisions which linked Haig's force with the III Corps. A bad break was made in the cavalry line. But the war-experienced assailants did not show the reckless courage of the volunteers who had been repulsed earlier, and their caution in following up their success enabled Haig and Allenby to 'putty up' the gaps. Haig also made an appeal to Dubois, who generously sent his own small reserve to strengthen the line south of Ypres, where it certainly did more good than in supporting an imaginary offensive on the north side.

Foch, back on the hill of Cassel, had little idea of what had happened. Towards the end of the afternoon a first report of these events was brought to him, but, as he says: 'It was impossible for me to estimate their full significance.' About 10 PM one of his staff came back with word that 'there was certainly a gap in the British cavalry front, which they could not fill for want of men. If this breach was not quickly closed, the road to Ypres would be open.' Foch at once telephoned to the British GHQ at Saint-Omer to ask for fuller news, but was told that 'nothing more definite was known'. So, just before midnight, Foch himself set off for St Omer. To counteract French's depression, and to fill the physical gap, he promised that if French would hold on he would send him eight battalions of the 32nd Division, which was just arriving in the French sector. Foch did not get back to Cassel until about 2 AM. Summarizing his action up to this moment, he said, pointing to the map: 'I've stuck a wafer there and there; then, at Hollebeke, the English broken through, the Boches passing through – a wafer here.'

A few hours later, after daybreak, the worst crisis of the whole struggle arose. The main German attack was once more aimed, with odds of five to one, at the sagging line of Allenby's cavalry. But this line, now reinforced by a few battalions of British infantry and Dubois' timely contribution, stood firm until the attacks died away at nightfall. Half, a bare half, of Foch's promised contribution arrived in time to relieve part of the line in the evening.

The crisis of the battle occurred farther north – at Gheluvelt on the Ypres–Menin road. Lying on a forward spur of the low ridge that covers Ypres, Gheluvelt was the last point retained in British hands from which the eyes of ground observers could overlook the enemy's line. Under increasing pressure the front of the 1st Division caved in, and shortly before noon Gheluvelt was lost. The divisional commander, Lomax, on hearing the news, rode back to the headquarters he shared with Monro of the 2nd Division, and laconically remarked: 'My line is broken.' Half an hour later a shell burst into the room where they were holding a conference with their staffs. Lomax and several others were fatally injured. Only one of those present was unhurt. Control was temporarily disorganized.

Haig meantime had left his headquarters at the White Château and ridden forward up the Menin road 'at a slow trot with part of his staff behind him as at an inspection'. If the sight of him brought reassurance to the stragglers and wounded who were trickling down the road, the sight of them and the nearer fall of the enemy shells told its significant tale to him. On his return he heard definite news of the break in the line. It moved him to issue orders for his troops to fall back to a rearward line just covering Ypres, and to hold it to the last, if they could not hold on where they were. But, unknown to him, the immediate danger had already been averted.

Soon after the Germans captured Gheluvelt, a counter-attack by a remnant of the 1st South Wales Borderers had retrieved the position on the flank. But, clearly, it could only be maintained if an adequate reinforcement arrived. So Brigadier-General FitzClarence, commanding the 1st (Guards) Brigade, sent up the few oddments he still had at hand, and then raced back to find the divisional commander. Lomax's resources were exhausted, but he had arranged with Monro that in case of any break the 2nd Division reserves should aid him by coming down on the enemy's flank from the north. And earlier in the morning, one battalion (the 2nd Worcestershires) had been placed at his disposal. Thus Lomax, barely half an hour before being himself mortally wounded, was able to give FitzClarence the means of saving the situation. Swiftly, FitzClarence studied the map and the ground and gave his orders to Major Hankey, commanding the 2nd Worcestershires; his staff officer, Captain Thorne, went with them as guide. The counter-stroke caught the Germans relaxing after their own success, and, coming unexpectedly, tumbled them out of Gheluvelt before they could rally. If the German artillery was quick to exact a toll, the German infantry had shown a remarkable incapacity to exploit their opportunities. The disciplined cohesion of their superior numbers enabled them to break into the thin Allied defences; once inside, and themselves disordered, they failed to produce the initiative that might have guided them through, and became the victims of their own too machine-like discipline. It was a serious reflection on the system and spirit of their pre-war training.

But the enemy's initial success, naturally, made a strong impression behind the defender's front, where impressions perforce operate sooner than facts, and often more decisively. Sir John French himself came up to the White Château about 2 PM. No better news had yet come to relieve the gloom, and French had scarcely need to be told of the critical situation, for he could feel it in the atmosphere. Haig himself was in a mood that recalled the night of Landrecies during the retreat from Mons. Every reserve had been used, and French had none to offer. White with anxiety, he hurried off on foot to regain his car and go in search of aid from Foch. But he had barely departed when, just as Haig was preparing to ride forward himself, Brigadier-General Rice 'came galloping back, as red as a turkeycock and sweating like a pig, with the news that Gheluvelt had been retaken and the line re-established'. Charteris adds: 'It was just as if we had all been under sentence of death and most suddenly received a free pardon.' Haig alone showed no sign of the reaction; pulling at his moustache, he remarked: 'I hope that it's not another false report.' Despite Rice's assurances, he seemed still doubtful, although he sent an aide-de-camp to tell French.

The aide-de-camp caught up French just as he had reached his car. How far the news was convincingly communicated, and how far French understood its significance, is uncertain. He drove off at breakneck pace on the way to Cassel. But as his car slowed down in passing through Vlamertinghe a French staff officer recognized him and told him that Foch was there, conferring with d'Urbal and Dubois in the town hall. French went thither to catch Foch. In making his appeal for aid he painted a black picture of the situation and the state of Haig's corps. The reality was certainly dark, but perhaps the picture seemed blacker because Foch and French had so long persisted in seeing it brightly coloured. French naturally told Foch of Haig's orders for a withdrawal, and it was equally natural for Foch to regard any limited withdrawal as tantamount to disaster. He protested vehemently against any withdrawal, crying: 'If you retreat voluntarily you will be swept up like straws in the gale' - he could not picture the palsy that afflicted the Germans in following up their attacks.

According to Foch, French replied that if his exhausted troops were asked to continue the battle, 'there is nothing left for me to do save to go up and be killed with the I Corps'. It is possible that the dramatic note was heightened in interpretation. Whether or not Foch replied: 'You must not talk of dying, but of winning', he certainly proposed to apply his usual remedy. 'I'll attack to right and left.' He promised that at daybreak six battalions of the 32nd division - actually two less than he had promised at midnight - should counter-attack on the right flank of the I Corps, while part of Dubois' corps counter-attacked on its left.

He then sat down and drafted a note: 'It is absolutely essential that *no retirement is made*, and to that end to dig in wherever you happen to be. This does not prevent you from organizing a rear position which should join up, at Zonnebeke, with our IX Corps. But any movement made to the rear by a considerable body of troops will lead to an enemy push and to certain disorder among the retiring troops. This must absolutely be prevented ...' He handed this epistle to French with the words: 'There, if I were in your shoes, those are the orders I'd send to Haig.'

Of Foch's influence on French there is little question. It is reflected in the note which French now dispatched to Haig along with Foch's memorandum. 'It is of the *utmost importance* to hold the ground you are on now. It is useless for me to say this, because I know you will do it if it is humanly possible. I will see if it is possible to send you any more support myself when I reach headquarters. I will then finally arrange with Foch *what* our future role is to be.'

But of Foch's practical influence on the battle situation at the time there is no evidence. The Worcestershires' counter-attack had saved it before Foch and French had their talk. And before their notes reached Haig he had settled his new line of resistance. For tactical security he had decided to straighten the front of the 1st Division by withdrawing to a line just behind Gheluvelt, while the 2nd Division was to stand on its existing line. And as the enemy pressure had ceased, what Foch said merely confirmed what had already happened. We may admire the spirit that inspired it, but we cannot regard this celebrated note as materially and historically decisive.

For the next ten days Haig's line remained without change and unshaken, save for a minor withdrawal of his right on the 5th to conform to a recoil of the French troops on his right.

On November 1st the main German effort was again made on the flank of the salient, against its southern hinge. This time they tried an assault under cover of darkness, as early as 1 AM, and the experiment was repaid by the capture of the Messines ridge. The inward bulge of Allenby's line was deepened by over a mile. But the arrival of the French 32nd Division soon after daybreak relieved the strain, although its counter-attack could not redeem the lost ground. If the other French 'attack' on Haig's left also made no measurable progress, its appearance likewise tended to discourage the enemy from pressing his own attack.

Foch wrote: 'The battle continues. It seems to me calmer. More troops are constantly arriving. In a few days we shall be able to renew the attack in full force.'

On the 2nd the French attack to reduce the Messines bulge was forestalled by a German attack, causing a French recoil, during which Wytschaete was lost and the bulge somewhat deepened. But most of the French 39th Division and half of Conneau's Cavalry Corps arrived from the south to relieve the strain; and the 43rd Division was just detraining. The French now took over the larger part of Allenby's line. Thus they held henceforth two-thirds of the battle line formed by the Ypres salient and the Messines re-entrant, leaving the weary and inter-mixed units under Haig's command to maintain the central sector. Worst hit of all was the 7th Division, whose infantry were reduced from 12,300 men to 2,400 – a bare fifth of their original strength.

During the next few days Foch pursued his attacks – without progress. While those of November 1st and 2nd by their boldness damped the enemy's will to advance, these later attacks had no such moral effect to compensate their lack of visible progress. For the German command was marking time until, by combing their line elsewhere, they could bring up six more divisions for a renewed effort. In this, the points of their attack were to be successively closed inwards like a pair of calipers. Initially, abandoning the attempt to deepen the Messines bulge, they would place the points against the two hinges of the salient.

Meantime, Foch and d'Urbal were playing into the enemy's hands by a reckless persistence in abortive local attacks. The sequel to this self-exhausting impulse is to be traced in the dangerous recoil which came on November 6th at the southern hinge in face of the Germans' new pressure – itself a preliminary to their final stroke. At St Eloi the grey tide came within two miles of Ypres, lapping round the rear of the British, who were holding the nose of the salient. Haig warned his chief that, to avoid being cut off, he would have to fall back to a line through Ypres itself. Foch, however, sent to assure Haig that he would regain the lost ground by an attack next day. At 9.30 AM on the 7th he sent a message that the French line had been re-established. But in fact nothing had been done. His men were too dead-beat to respond to orders. And when eventually they were spurred to an offensive effort, it naturally failed, thus failing to remove the menacing wedge that lay embedded in the flank of the salient.

On the 8th Haig went with French to see Foch at Cassel, and found him as exuberantly confident as ever. But it was his indefiniteness rather than his assurance that kept them from fulfilling their intention to fall back to a straighter and safer line. So, unable to obtain any satisfaction, and unwilling to leave his allies in the lurch, Haig was fain to hold on as best he could, scraping the human putty off one crack to cement another. Happily, if deceptively, the next two days were comparatively quiet along the British sector. Not so for the French.

For on November 10th the enemy struck heavily against the northern hinge of the salient, and as far as Dixmude. The blow was parried, the French profiting by the natural line of the Yser canal, across which their left retired. Its more significant result was to convince the French command that their own line north of Ypres was the spot selected for the enemy's final effort. And thither were diverted such few reserves as they could spare, at the expense of the already weakened southern hinge.

But this blow against the northern hinge had been intended by the Germans as simultaneous with one against Gheluvelt and the southern hinge (as far south as the Comines canal): a blow for which a new corps under Plettenberg had been brought up – it comprised a division of the Prussian Guard and another picked division. As Plettenberg was not ready, the left-hand blow had been postponed.

On the 11th the attack was launched, in a grey November mist, and prepared by the heaviest bombardment yet experienced. But at all save two points it was repulsed. One was at the actual hinge, where the wedge was driven in as far as the later famous Hill 60. The French detachment there appealed for help to the French and British corps on either side, but neither could spare any reserves. The 'ever-willing' Dubois, however, once more sent his only reserve, and with its help the line was restored. The other and deeper penetration was made in the British line just north of the Menin road. Here the German 1st Guard Brigade broke through the weak front of the British 1st (Guards) Brigade – a strange coincidence of history, even though only the remnants of one Guards' battalion were left in the latter brigade. But the Prussian Guardsmen, bewildered by the woods, failed to exploit their success and were driven back by a flank counter-attack. In this the 52nd Light Infantry played the leading part, as they had done in repelling the final assault of the Imperial Guard at Waterloo.

Although the blow had been heavier than on October 31st, the situation had never been so critical, perhaps largely because it had made less impression on the minds of the commanders in rear. And with the failure of this blow on November 11th – date of prophetic symbolism – the crisis at Ypres finally passed. It is true that the German Higher Command would, in its own mind, still deliver several powerful attacks before it admitted defeat. But the men who were called on to execute its orders were no longer capable of vigorous effort, or inclined to pursue such an unhopeful prospect. Thus the spasmodic attacks that continued during the following week, chiefly against Dubois' front, were but the fading flickers of a storm that is travelling away. The relief of the I Corps, so long demanded by Haig and refused by Foch with the word 'Impossible', was now carried out, and the French took over for a time the whole salient.

'First Ypres' had been essentially a 'soldier's battle' – a greater Inkerman. In a memorable sentence General Edmonds has epitomized the situation: 'The line that stood between the British Empire and ruin was composed of tired, haggard, and unshaven men, unwashed, plastered with mud, many in little more than rags.' Its only divergency from accuracy lies in its one deviation from stark simplicity. The British Empire has shown a capacity for survival, even when its military expeditions have actually been driven back to their ships, and when its enemy has been in possession of the Channel ports. And it is by no means sure that, if the expeditionary force had been defeated at Ypres, the Germans were capable of following so closely on its heels as to bring disaster. In the light of the succeeding years there is, indeed, reason for regret that Haig did not fulfil his idea of withdrawing to the straighter and stronger line along the canal through Ypres. It would have saved cost and simplified defence. And its hindrance to the later attempts at the offensive in Flanders, an impossible country for the offensive, might have been an additional advantage.

The danger at 'First Ypres' was certainly aggravated by the failure of Foch, French, and d'Urbal to realize this impossibility. Herein lay their most material influence on the battle. For the real handling of the battle was left in the hands of Haig and Dubois. Even they, for want of reserves, could do little more than cement the crumbling parts of the defence by judicious thinning of other parts of an ominously thin front. Perhaps to Dubois, for the way he took, not once alone, the calculated risk of parting with his own reserves, is due the highest credit of command earned in the defensive battle.

Foch undoubtedly had a moral influence on the battle, no less by his obstinate refusal to listen to reason than by the unconquerable strength of his will. This never wilted. Detach it from the actual ebb and flow of the battle line, and we can admire it unreservedly. It made an impression on all who came in contact with it. But one is not able to detect any point at which it touched the men in the battle line. And where it touched the fighting commanders the effect seems to have become a source more of exasperation than exaltation. The one sure point where Foch's will fortified another will was at the back of the front - at the allied general headquarters. While some of the claims made for its influence on the Belgian command may be discounted, especially in regard to King Albert, they cannot be disregarded. On Sir John French the influence is more measurable, but here the measure of its effect is inevitably as infinitesimal as Sir John French's influence on the battle.

The German design was foiled, and Ypres saved, in spite of the delusions of the Higher Command - by the troops in the front line. The men who defended Ypres against the German onslaughts were front-line troops in the strictest sense - their defence had length without depth. Its shallowness was the measure of their numerical weakness, but also the supreme tribute to their moral strength. The 'thin red line' of the past was never so thin as the line at Ypres - and never so hardly tried. The 'thin khaki line' withstood a strain that lasted for weeks compared with the hours of the past.

By a patriotic falsification of history, into which military chroniclers easily lapse, too many accounts of 'First Ypres' have represented it as a nearly all-British battle. Ungenerously, and untruly, they have obscured the great part played by our Allies, just as a century earlier they distorted the outline of Waterloo, and the vital share of the Prussians. To correct the proportions does not diminish the credit of the British troops. It is in quality, not in quantity, that military virtue lies. And no battle in Britain's annals has given clearer proof of fighting quality, and of its value, than 'First Ypres'. It was a battle in the natural line of British tradition – a defensive attitude combined with timely ripostes. Thus it suited the nature of the troops who conducted it. If it did not directly fit their pre-war tactical training, predominantly offensive in imitation of the continental fashion, it appealed to their native instincts, which count for more than a fashionable dogma under the test of battle. And because of the extent of their training, compared with the conscript armies of the Continent, they had acquired elements of skill that were of value in any form of action. Above all was this true of their shooting skill – with the rifle. In defence it had greater scope and effect than in attack. Such was the ability of the British infantry to produce 'fifteen rounds rapid' a minute that the Germans credited them with 'quantities of machine guns' whereas, in fact, each battalion had come to France equipped only with two, and in many cases had lost these by the time Ypres was reached. The delusion in the minds of the enemy, which such weapon-skill created, redressed the delusions of the Allied Higher Command, and was a decisive factor in the issue. Indeed, it was the decisive factor when coupled with the morale of the men who handled the weapons.

No praise can be too high for the indomitable spirit which inspired their collective endurance. This was, in a sense, a special product. The enemy had no lack of courage. Their discipline was equally strong – and perhaps too strong for their own tactical effectiveness. But the little British Army had a corporate sense that was unique. To this its very smallness, as well as its conditions of service and traditions, contributed. 'First Ypres', on the British side, was not merely a soldiers' battle but a 'family battle' – against outsiders. The family spirit was its keynote, and the key to the apparent miracle by which, when formations were broken up and regiments reduced to remnants, those remnants still held together. They attained their end – in both senses. Ypres saw the supreme vindication and the final sacrifice of the old Regular Army. After the battle was over, little survived, save the memory of its spirit.

CHAPTER FIVE

1915 – The Deadlock

Before the end of 1914 the state of deadlock on the Western Front was realized, if in varying degree, by the Governments and General Staffs of the warring countries, and each was seeking a solution. The reaction varied in form and in nature, according to the mental power and predisposition of the different authorities. With the Germanic Powers the opinion of Falkenhayn was the decisive factor, and the impression derived not merely from his critics, but from his own account, is that neither the opinion nor the direction was really clear as to its object.

On his appointment after the Marne reverse, he still adhered to the Schlieffen plan of seeking a decision in the west, but he did not follow the Schlieffen method of weakening his left wing in order to mass on the vital right wing. The autumn attack at Ypres was made largely with raw formations, while war-experienced troops lay almost idle between the Aisne and the Vosges. Colonel Gröner, Chief of the Field Railways, even went so far as to submit a detailed plan to Falkenhayn for transferring six army corps to the right wing, but it was rejected. When we remember how close to breaking point the British front came at Ypres, it can only be said that for a second time the German Supreme Command saved the Allies. At this juncture, too, Ludendorff was pleading for reinforcements to make his wedge-blow at the Russian flank near Lodz decisive, but Falkenhayn missed the chance by delaying until the Ypres failure had passed from assurance to fact.

Reluctantly dissuaded from a fresh attempt to break the trench barrier in the west, Falkenhayn seems to have been vague as to any alternative object. His feeling that the war must ultimately be decided in France led him to distrust the value, as he doubted the possibility, of a decision against Russia. Hence while he realized that the Eastern Front was the only practicable theatre for operations in the near future, he withheld the necessary reinforcements until his hands were forced by the threatening situation of the Austro-Hungarian front. And even then he doled out reserves reluctantly and meagrely; enough to secure success, but never in sufficient quantity or in time for decisive victory.

It is to his credit, however, that he realized a long war was now inevitable, and consequently set to work to develop Germany's resources for such a warfare of attrition. The technique of field entrenchment was carried to a higher pitch than with any other army; the military railways were expanded for the lateral movement of reserves; the supply of munitions and of the raw material for their manufacture was tackled so energetically and comprehensively that an ample flow was ensured from the spring of 1915 onwards – a time when the British were only awakening to the problem. Here was laid the foundation of that economic organization and utilization of resources which were to be the secret of Germany's resisting power to the pressure of the British blockade. For the scientific grasp of the economic sphere in war Germany owed much to Dr Walter Rathenau, a great captain of industry. She was also a pioneer in the psychological sphere for, as early as the autumn of 1914, German agents launched a scheme of propaganda in Asia to undermine British prestige and the loyalty of Britain's Mahommedan subjects. The defect of German propaganda, its crudeness, was less apparent when concerned with primitive peoples than when applied to the civilized peoples of Europe and America.

The same period witnessed also the one great success for German diplomacy, the entry of Turkey into the war, although this was fundamentally due to a combination of pre-war causes with military events. Since 1909 the country had been under the control of the Young Turk party, to whom traditions, including that of friendship with Britain, were abhorrent. Germany, filled with her own dream of a Germanic Middle East – of which the Baghdad railway was the symbol – had skilfully exploited the opportunity to gain a dominating influence over the new rulers of Turkey. Their leader, Enver Pasha, had been military attaché in Berlin; German instructors permeated the Turkish army; and a definite understanding existed between Germany and the Young Turk leaders as to common military action – urged by the common bond of necessary safeguard against danger from Russia. The arrival of the *Goeben* and *Breslau* reinforced the moral pressure of Wangenheim, the German Ambassador, and eventually on October 29th the Turks committed definite acts of war – at Odessa against Russia, and in Sinai against Britain.

Falkenhayn has shown 'the decisive importance of Turkey joining in the struggle' – first as a barrier across the channel of munition supply to Russia, and secondly as a distraction to the military strength of Britain and Russia. Under German dictation, Turkey struck as early as mid-

December against the Russians in the Caucasus, but Enver's over-ambitious plan ended in disaster at the battle Sarikamish. Turkey was no more fortunate in her next venture – to cut Britain's Suez Canal artery with the east. The Sinai Desert was a check on an invasion in strength, and the two small detachments which got across were easily repulsed, at Ismailia and Tussum, although allowed to make good their retreat. But if both these offensives were tactical failures, they were of great strategic value to Germany by pinning down large Russian and British forces.

As an offset to Turkey joining the Central Powers, Italy definitely threw over the artificial ties of the Old Triple Alliance and joined the Entente. On May 24th she declared war on Austria – her hereditary enemy – although avoiding an open breach with Germany. If her main object was to seize the chance of redeeming her kinsmen in Trieste and the Trentino from Austrian rule, there was also a spiritual desire to reassert her historic traditions. Militarily, however, her aid could not have an early or far-reaching effect on the situation, for her army was unready to deliver a prompt blow, and the Austrian frontier was a mountainous obstacle of great natural strength.

On the Entente side the reality of the trench deadlock produced different and diverse reactions. If the desire to hold on to territorial gains swayed German strategy, the desire to recover their lost territory dominated the strategy of the French. It is true that their mental and material concentration on the Western Front, where lay the main armed force of the enemy, was justified by military tenets, but without any key to unlock the barrier they were merely knocking themselves to pieces. Winter attacks in Artois, on the Aisne, in Champagne and the Woevre afforded costly proof that against the Germans' skill in trench fighting, Joffre's 'nibbling' was usually attrition on the wrong side of the balance sheet. As for any new key, the French were singularly lacking in fertility of idea.

Britain's trouble was rather an excess of fertility, or rather an absence of decision in choosing and bringing to fruition these mental seeds. Yet in great measure this failing was due to the obscurantism of professional opinion, whose attitude was that of blank opposition rather than expert guidance.

British-inspired solutions to the deadlock crystallized into two main groups, one tactical, the other strategical. The first was to unlock the trench barrier by producing a machine invulnerable to machine guns and capable of crossing trenches, which would restore the tactical balance upset by the new preponderance of defensive over offensive power. The idea of a machine for this definite purpose was conceived by Colonel Swinton in October, 1914, was nourished and tended in infancy by Mr Winston Churchill, then First Lord of the Admiralty, and ultimately, after months of experiment hampered by official opposition, came to maturity in the tank of 1916.

The strategical solution was to go round the trench barrier. Its advocates – who became known as the 'Eastern' in contrast to the 'Western' school – argued that the enemy alliance should be viewed as a whole, and that modern developments had so changed conceptions of distance and powers of mobility, that a blow in some other theatre of war would correspond to the historic attack on an enemy's strategic flank. Further, such an operation would be in accordance with the traditional amphibious strategy of Britain, and would enable it to exploit the advantage of sea power which had hitherto been neglected. In October, 1914, Lord Fisher, recalled to the office of First Sea Lord, had urged a plan for landing on the German coast. In January 1915, Lord Kitchener suggested another, for severing Turkey's main line of eastward communication by a landing in the Gulf of Alexandretta. The post-war comments of Hindenburg and Enver show how this would have paralysed Turkey. It could hardly, however, have exercised a wider influence, and it was anticipated by another project – partly the result of Churchill's strategic insight and partly due to the pressure of circumstances.

This was the Dardanelles expedition, about which controversy has raged so hotly that the term just applied to Churchill may be disputed by some critics. This is answered by the verdict of Falkenhayn himself – 'If the straits between the Mediterranean and the Black Sea were not permanently closed to Entente traffic, all hopes of a successful course of the war would be very considerably diminished. Russia would have been freed from her significant isolation ... which offered a safer guarantee than military successes ... that sooner or later a crippling of the forces of this Titan must take place ... automatically.' The fault was not in the conception, but in the execution. If the British had used at the outset even a fair proportion of the forces they ultimately expended in driblets, it is clear from Turkish accounts that victory would have crowned their undertaking.

The cause of this piecemeal application of force, and dissipation of opportunity, lay in the opposition of Joffre and the French General Staff, supported by Sir John French. Despite the evidence of the sequel to the Marne, of the German failure at Ypres, and of his own ambitious yet utterly ineffectual offensive in December, Joffre remained confident of his power to achieve an early and decisive victory in France. His plan was that of converging blows from Artois and Champagne upon the great salient formed by the entrenched German front, to be followed by an offensive in Lorraine against the rear of the enemy armies. The idea was similar to that of Foch in 1918, but the vital difference lay in the conditions existing and the methods employed. A study of the documents conveys the impression that there has rarely been such a trinity of optimists in whom faith was divorced from reason as Joffre, Foch, his deputy in Flanders, and French – albeit the latter's outlook oscillated violently. In contrast, the British Government considered that the trench front in France was impregnable to frontal attacks, had strong objection to wasting the man power of the new armies in a vain effort, and at the same time felt increasing concern over the danger of a Russian collapse. These views were common alike to Churchill, Lloyd George and Kitchener, who on January 2nd, 1915, wrote to Sir John French – 'The German lines in France may be looked upon as a fortress that cannot be carried by assault and also that cannot be completely invested, with the result that the lines may be held by an investing force while operations proceed elsewhere.'

Lloyd George advocated the transfer of the bulk of the British forces to the Balkans, both to succour Serbia and to develop an attack on the rear of the hostile alliance. In a memorandum on January 1st he suggested Salonika or the Dalmatian coast as bases of operation. That same day, curiously, Galliéni proposed to the French Government a landing at Salonika, as a starting point for a march on Constantinople with an army strong enough to encourage Greece and Bulgaria to combine with the Entente. The capture of Constantinople was to be followed by an advance up the Danube into Austria-Hungary in conjunction with the Rumanians. Franchet d'Esperey expressed similar views. But the commanders on the Western Front, buoyantly confident of an early breakthrough, argued vehemently against any alternative strategy, stressing the difficulties of transport and supply and insisting on the ease with which Germany could switch troops to meet the threat.* If there was force in their contention, it tended to ignore the experience of military history, that 'the longest way round is often the

---

* The Germans, in contrast, pointed out in their staff calculations that it was far easier for the Allies to move troops by sea to the Balkans than for them to move troops by rail! The facts show that troop shipments from France to Salonika averaged a week, and from England about twelve days; whereas the Germans took nine days to move an army corps even from the French to the Russian frontier. To move any considerable force to the Balkans would have taken over a month. If sufficient shipping had been made available, the Allies could have sent a force far quicker by sea.

shortest way there', and that the acceptance of topographical difficulties has constantly proved preferable to that of a direct attack on an opponent firmly posted and prepared to meet it.

The weight of 'Western' opinion prevailed and the Balkan projects were stifled. But misgivings were not silenced, and at this juncture a situation arose which revived the Near Eastern scheme in a new if attenuated form.

The Dardanelles. On January 2nd, 1915, Kitchener received an appeal from the Grand Duke Nicholas for a diversion which would relieve the Turkish pressure on Russia's army in the Caucasus. Kitchener felt unable to provide troops and suggested a naval demonstration against the Dardanelles, which Churchill, appreciating the wider strategic and economic issues, proposed to convert into an attempt to force the passage. His naval advisers, if not enthusiastic, did not oppose the proposal and, in response to a telegram, the Admiral on the spot, Carden, submitted a plan for a methodical reduction of the forts and clearance of the minefields. A naval force, mainly of obsolete vessels, was got together with French aid and, after a preliminary bombardment, entered the straits on March 18th. Drift mines, however, caused the sinking of several ships, and the attempt was abandoned.

It is a moot point whether a prompt renewal of the advance would not have succeeded, for ammunition in the Turkish forts was exhausted, and in such conditions the mine obstacle might have been overcome. But the new naval commander, Admiral de Robeck, decided against it, unless military aid was forthcoming. Already, a month before, the War Council had determined on a joint attack, and began the dispatch of a military force under Sir Ian Hamilton. But as the authorities had drifted into the new scheme, so were they tardy in releasing the necessary troops, and even when sent, in inadequate numbers, several more weeks' delay had to be incurred – at Alexandria – in order to redistribute the force in its transports suitably for tactical action. Worst of all, this fumbling policy had thrown away the chance of surprise, which was vital for a landing on an almost impregnable shore. When the preliminary bombardment took place in February, only two Turkish divisions were at the straits, this was increased by four by the date of the naval attack, to six when Ian Hamilton was at last able to attempt his landing. For this he had only four British divisions and one French division – actually inferior in strength to the enemy in a situation where the inherent preponderance of defensive over offensive power was multiplied by the natural difficulties of the terrain. His weakness of numbers and his mission of aiding the passage of the fleet compelled him to choose a landing on the Gallipoli peninsula in preference to one on the mainland or on the Asiatic shore; and the rocky coastline limited his possible landing places.

On April 25th he made his spring, at the southern tip of the peninsula near Cape Helles, and – with Australian and New Zealand troops – near Gaba Tepe, some fifteen miles up the Aegean coast; the French, as a diversion, made a temporary landing at Kum Kale on the Asiatic shore. Owing to the Turks' uncertainty the British were able to gain a lodgement on several beaches, strewn with barbed wire and swept by machine guns. But the momentary asset of tactical surprise was forfeited, and the difficulties of supply were immense, while the Turks held the commanding heights and were able to bring up their reserves. The invaders managed to hold on to their two precarious footholds, but they could not expand them appreciably, and the stagnation of trench warfare set in. They could not go on, and national prestige forbade them to go back.

Ultimately, in July, the British Government decided to send a further five divisions to reinforce the seven now on the peninsula. By the time they arrived the Turkish strength in the region had also risen, to fifteen divisions. Ian Hamilton decided on a double stroke – a reinforced blow from Gaba Tepe and a new landing at Suvla Bay, a few miles north – to sever the middle of the peninsula and secure the heights commanding the Narrows. He deceived the Turkish Command and achieved surprise on August 6th, but the first blow failed and the second lost a splendid chance by the inexperience of the troops, and still more by the inertia and fumbling of the local commanders. For over thirty-six hours, before reserves arrived, only one and a half Turkish battalions barred the path. Energetic new commanders, for whom Ian Hamilton had previously asked, were sent out when the opportunity had passed. The British were once more condemned to hang on to tenuous footholds, and, with the autumn rains setting in, their trials were increased. The Government had lost faith and were anxious to withdraw, but fear of the moral effect delayed their decision. Ian Hamilton was asked for his opinion, however, and when he pronounced in favour of continuing – in which course he still had confidence – he was replaced by Sir Charles Monro, who immediately declared for evacuation.

It was a remarkable example of prompt decision. While Monro visited Anzac, Suvla, and Helles during a single morning, without going farther than the beach, his Chief of Staff sat on board ship drafting the recommendation for evacuation. Well may Churchill say – 'He came, he saw, he capitulated.' Kitchener at first refused to sanction the withdrawal and himself hurried out to investigate. The Government was most relieved to see him go because they hoped to utilize his absence to relieve him of his post. Most of the Coalition Cabinet were united in dissatisfaction with his secretiveness and his administration, although disunited over the question of evacuating Gallipoli. Mr Bonar Law, the leader of the Conservative Party, took a strong line on both questions. The Prime Minister, however, feared a public outcry over Kitchener's removal only less than he feared Mr Bonar Law's resignation, and so temporized by giving way to Bonar Law's demand for evacuation, and by excluding Churchill from the War Committee of the Cabinet. Evacuation, therefore, was virtually decided upon before Kitchener reached Gallipoli. The fresh wave of opinion at home undoubtedly had an effect on his mind, and after his revived proposal for a fresh landing near Alexandretta had been vetoed by the War Committee, he reluctantly veered round and consented to evacuation.

Curiously, in the last phase it was the navy that tried to avert this. For de Robeck, who had passively resisted since March all promptings to a further naval attack, was now relieved by Admiral Wemyss, who not only opposed evacuation but, basing himself on a plan devised by Commodore Keyes, offered 'to force the straits and control them for an indefinite period'. The proposal came too late. The forces of opposition at home were now too strong, and in obedience to orders a withdrawal of the troops was carried out from Suvla and Anzac on the night of December 18th, and from Helles on that of January 8th. If the bloodless evacuation was an example of masterly organization and cooperation, it was also a proof of the greater ease of such operations in modern warfare. And as a final touch of irony Monro and his Chief of Staff, who had nothing to do with its skilful execution, received high decorations in reward. Thus the curtain rang down on a sound and far-sighted conception, marred by a chain of errors in execution almost unrivalled even in British history.

The German Campaign. While the British were striving to unlock the back door to Russia, the Germanic Powers were hammering the Russians, whose resistance was collapsing in large measure from a lack of munitions which could only be made good by foreign supplies through that locked entrance, the Dardanelles. This fact and its effect was acutely appreciated by Russia's most formidable opponent. In the autumn of 1915, Hoffmann emphatically declared that the success of Germany's efforts against Russia depended on keeping 'the Dardanelles firmly closed'. For if 'the Russians saw that there was no means of exporting their wheat, or importing war material, there would be a gradual collapse in that country.'

On the Eastern Front, the campaign of 1914 had shown that a German force could count on defeating any larger Russian force, but that when Russians and Austrians met on an equality victory rested with the Russians. Falkenhayn was forced, reluctantly, to dispatch German reinforcements as a stiffening to the Austrians, and thus was dragged into an offensive in the east, rather than adopting it as a clearly defined plan. Ludendorff, in contrast, had his eyes firmly fixed on a particular object, and from now on advocated unceasingly a wholehearted effort to break Russia. Ludendorff's was a rigid strategy of decision, Falkenhayn's an opportunistic strategy of attrition. The one took too little account of political factors, the other too much.

In the conflict of wills between these two men, lies the clue to the resultant strategy of Germany - highly effective, yet not decisive. This tug of wills was marked by the 'offensive' use of the telegraph and by the unceasing pull of wires, with the Kaiser as the chief puppet. While Falkenhayn was constantly trying to nullify a potential supplanter by denuding Hindenburg of the power to strike the enemy effectively, Ludendorff countered by screwing Hindenburg up to threats of resignation. Well might Hoffmann watching the intrigues, note in his diary – 'When one gets a close view of influential people – their bad relations with each other, their conflicting ambitions, one must always bear in mind that it is certainly much worse on the other side among the French, English and Russians, or one might well be nervous'. His intuition was correct. 'The race for power and personal position seems to destroy all men's characters. I believe that the only creature who can keep his honour is a man living on his own estate; he has no need to intrigue and struggle – for it is no use intriguing for fine weather.'

The Russian plan for 1915 embodied some of the lessons of experience and was soundly conceived, but the means were lacking and the instrument defective. The Grand Duke Nicholas aimed to secure both his flanks solidly before attempting a fresh blow towards Silesia. From January until April, under bitter winter conditions, the Russian forces on the southern flank of the Polish salient strove to gain possession of the Carpathians and the gateways into the Hungarian plain. The Austrians, with a German infusion, parried their efforts, and the loss was disproportionate to the small gains. But the long-besieged fortress of Przemysl, with 120,000 men, at last fell into Russian hands on March 22nd. In Northern Poland the Russians were preparing to strike upwards at East Prussia, when they were forestalled by a fresh Ludendorff stroke eastwards towards the frontier of Russia proper. The blow was launched on February 7th, over snow-buried roads and frozen swamps, and was distinguished by the envelopment and capture of four Russian divisions in the Augustovo forests – near the Masurian Lakes. Moreover, it extracted the sting from the Russian attack farther west.

These moves were, however, merely a 'curtain-raiser' to the real drama of 1915. But before turning to this it is necessary to glance at events on the Western Front, the importance of which is partly as a signpost to the future and partly because of their reaction on the Eastern Front.

While a way round the trench barrier was being sought in Gallipoli and experiments with a novel key were being carried out in England, the Allied Commands in France were trying more orthodox solutions. In February and March the French lost 50,000 men in nibbling their way 500 yards into the German defences in Champagne; in his report Joffre claimed that the offensive 'was none the less fecund in results'. In April the French sacrificed 64,000 men in an attack against the St Mihiel salient which proved a complete fiasco. Smaller, yet more significant, was the British attack at Neuve Chapelle on March 10th. Save as a pure experiment the attempt stood self-condemned. For it was an isolated attempt on a small front with inadequate resources. The arrival in France of several new regular divisions – made up from foreign garrisons, of the Indian Corps, and of the 1st Canadian Division, had brought the British strength up to thirteen divisions and five cavalry divisions, besides a number of selected Territorial battalions. This increase enabled French to divide his forces into two armies, and gradually to extend his share of the front. But Joffre was insistent that French should relieve the French of the Ypres salient, which they had taken over in November, and he made the intended French attack contingent on this relief. Sir John French considered that he had not sufficient troops for both purposes, and so decided to carry out the attack single-handed. An additional motive was his resentment of the constant French criticisms that the British were not 'pulling their weight'.

In design, however, the attack, entrusted to Haig's First Army, was both original and well thought out. After an intense bombardment of thirty-five minutes' duration on a 2,000 yards' frontage, the artillery lengthened their range and dropped a curtain of fire to prevent reinforcements reaching the enemy's battered trenches, which were rapidly overrun by the British infantry.

Complete surprise was attained, and most of the first positions captured; but when, in the second phase, the frontage was extended, the artillery support proved inadequate. Further, owing to scanty information and to the two corps commanders waiting upon each other, a long pause occurred which gave the Germans five clear hours to organize fresh resistance. Then, too late and mistakenly, Haig ordered the attack to be pressed 'regardless of loss'. And loss proved the only result. An underlying factor was that the narrowness of the attack sector made the breach more easy for the defenders to close, although this defect was unavoidable owing to the general shortage of munitions, especially heavy guns and high-explosive shell for them.

The British had been slower than the Germans to awaken to the scale of munition supply required for this new warfare. Even so, deliveries fell far behind contract, owing largely to the handicap imposed by trade-union rules on the dilution of skilled labour. These could only be modified after long negotiation, and the shortage of shells became so obvious in the spring of 1915 as to lead to a public outcry initiated by Colonel Repington, the military correspondent of *The Times*, after consultation with Sir John French. Lord Northcliffe, with fearless disregard of the odium, threw the full weight of his newspaper into the campaign which culminated in the establishment of a Ministry of Munitions, under Lloyd George, to coordinate and develop both the supply and the manufacture of raw materials. Although this press campaign failed to recognize some of the major causes of the shortage, as well as the fact that the need was for more heavy guns and not merely for more shells, its general effect was of incalculable value. Nothing else could have so roused the people or cleared away obstructions. Apart from shells, the crudeness and inferiority of all the British trench-warfare weapons, compared with the German, made such a radical reorganization overdue, and its urgency was emphasized by the near approach of the time when Britain's new national armies would take the field. If the task was undertaken late, it was carried out with energy and thoroughness, although improvisation was long in overtaking the evil consequences of earlier neglect. Apart from labour difficulties the immediate fault lay largely with military shortsightedness, which manifested itself in a constant tendency to underestimate needs and underrate novelties.

It is significant that as far back as 1908 the Financial Secretary of the War Office, impressed by an official observer's report of the growing use of machine guns in the German Army, wrote to the Master-General of the Ordnance that 'if the military members of the Council would like to have more machine guns for the Army that at any rate the Finance

Department of the War Office would make no objection'. He received the reply that two machine guns per battalion were enough. And to that scale the War Office authorities stubbornly adhered, although in 1909 the School of Musketry urged an increase to six.

Even when the machine gun had obviously gained a dominance of the battlefield, General Headquarters in France resisted its growth from the puny pre-war scale of two in each battalion. One army commander, Haig, declared that it was 'a much overrated weapon' and that this scale was 'more than sufficient'. Even Kitchener laid down that four were a maximum and any in excess a luxury – until the Ministry of Munitions came to the rescue of the machine-gun advocates and boldly multiplied the scale of provision by sixteen. It was due also to Mr Lloyd George that the Stokes gun, a quick-firing light mortar, had the chance to surmount the official barrier and develop into the outstanding and ubiquitous trench weapon of the war. And later, the Ministry of Munitions succoured the tank when it was repeatedly threatened by the suffocating embrace of the War Office.

Nevertheless the ultimate responsibility for the munition failure lay with the British people, and their representatives in Parliament. Although, before the war came, the new Committee of Imperial Defence had done much preparatory spadework, a strict limit was set to its efforts by the passivity as well as parsimony of Parliament and people in face of the growing danger of war. Preparedness crawled forward to meet the onrushing menace. Most fundamental of all faults was the neglect to organize the industrial resources of the country for conversion and expansion in case of war. While an increase in the fighting forces may, by its air of threat, accelerate the danger of war, readiness for industrial mobilization is unprovocative and, if war comes, a more essential foundation for the power to wage it.

The pre-war neglect is a far graver charge against the Government which declared war on August 4th, 1914, than any failure to increase the army estimates or to introduce conscription. Yet in making that declaration the Government, however conscious of the political and moral issues, appears to have been unconscious that it was dooming the manhood of the nation to a terrible drain of life through want of weapons. It is a moral question how far, in such circumstances, any Government is justified in taking the decision for war and in retaining office. The only excuse lies in the sanction of public indifference to such needs. And unhappily, experience has shown the practical difficulties suffered by a democratic Government which tries to outstrip public opinion. Thus the ultimate responsibility falls on the British people.

Even the military conservatism which obstructed improvements and reorganization during the war may be charged to lack of public concern with the training and selection of officers in peace. In the light of 1914–18 the whole people bear the stigma of infanticide.

No belated wartime spurt could overtake the consequences of pre-war neglect until many thousands of lives had been wasted vainly. Even the Somme offensive was to be hampered by a limited supply of ammunition, while of this much was wasted because of the failure of hastily produced fuses. Not until the end of 1916 did the flow of munitions reach a volume, still expanding, which finally removed any material handicap on the strategy of the British leaders.

The tactical sequel of Neuve Chapelle was less fortunate. It was clear that the small-scale experiment had only missed success by a narrow margin, and that there was scope for its development. But the Entente commands missed the true lesson, which was the surprise attainable by a short bombardment that compensated its brevity by its intensity. And only partially did they appreciate the fact that the sector attacked must be sufficiently wide to prevent the defender's artillery commanding, or his reserves closing, the breach. Instead, they drew the superficial deduction that mere volume of shell-fire was the key to success. Not until 1917 did they revert to the Neuve Chapelle method. It was left to the Germans to profit by the experience against the Russians in May.

But before that occurred, the Western Front was destined to increase the tally of military blunders. In the first, it was the Germans' turn to find and misuse a new key to the trench deadlock. This was the introduction of gas, and, unlike the British introduction of tanks later, the chance, once forfeited, did not return, owing to the relative ease of providing an antidote. On October 27th, 1914, in the Neuve Chapelle sector, the Germans fired 3,000 shrapnel shells containing a nose and eye irritant as well as bullets. This was the first battlefield experiment, but the effect was so weak that the fact was not even known until revealed by the Germans after the war. Then, in a local attack in Poland on January 31st, 1915, the Germans tried the use of improved lachrymatory gas shell, but the experiment was a failure owing to the nullifying effect of the intense cold. At the next attempt the gas was lethal and was discharged from cylinders owing to the failure of the authorities to provide the inventor, Haber, with adequate facilities for the manufacture of shells. Further, the initial disappointment led the German Command to place little trust in its value. In consequence, when gas was discharged against the French trenches at Ypres on April

22nd, there were no reserves at hand to pour through the wide breach it created. A strange green vapour, a surging mass of agonized fugitives, a four-mile gap without a living defender – such was the sequence of events. But the resistance of the Canadians on the flank of the breach and the prompt arrival of English and Indian reinforcements saved the situation in the absence of German reserves.

The chlorine gas originally used was undeniably cruel, but no worse than the frequent effect of shell or bayonet, and when it was succeeded by improved forms of gas both experience and statistics proved it the least inhumane of modern weapons. But it was novel and therefore labelled an atrocity by a world which condones abuses but detests innovations. Thus Germany incurred the moral odium which inevitably accompanies the use of a novel weapon without any compensating advantage.

On the Entente side, wisdom would have counselled a period of waiting until their munition supply had grown and the new British armies were ready, but the desire to regain lost territory and the duty of relieving the pressure on Russia, combined with ill-founded optimism to spur Joffre to premature offensives. The German losses were exaggerated, their skill and power in defence underrated, and a series of diffused and unconnected attacks were made. The chief was by the French between Lens and Arras, under Foch's direction, when the earlier experience of failure to make an effective breach in the trench barrier was repeated. The attack was launched on May 9th by d'Urbal's army (of eighteen divisions) on a four-mile frontage. It was quickly checked with murderous losses except on the front of Pétain's corps which, thanks to meticulous preparation, broke through to a depth of two miles. But the penetration was too narrow, reserves were late and inadequate and the gap closed. Foch, however, persevered with vain attacks which gained a few acres of ground at excessive loss. Meantime Haig's First Army had attacked towards Aubers ridge simultaneously with the larger French attempt. The plan was to penetrate at two points north and south of Neuve Chapelle, four miles apart – the total frontage of the two being two and a quarter miles – and then to converge in exploiting the double penetration. But the Germans, profiting also from the experimental value of Neuve Chapelle, had developed their defences. Thus the attack died away quickly from a surfeit of German machine guns and an insufficiency of British shells. Under pressure from Joffre the attack was renewed on May 15th on the Festubert sector south of Neuve Chapelle, and continued by small bites until May 27th. The larger French offensive between Lens and Arras was not abandoned until June

18th, when the French had lost 102,500 men - nearly double the defenders' loss.

The effect of these attacks was, moreover, to convince even the dubious Falkenhayn of the strength of his western line, and of the remoteness of any real menace from the Franco-British forces. His offensive on the Eastern Front had already opened. Tactically unlimited, its strategic object was at first only the limited one of relieving the pressure on the Austrian front, and, concurrently, of reducing Russia's offensive power. Conrad proposed and Falkenhayn accepted a plan to break through the Russian centre as the best means to this end. In this plan the Gorlice -Tarnow sector between the upper Vistula and the Carpathians was selected as offering the fewest obstacles to an advance and best protection to the flanks of a penetration.

The breakthrough was entrusted to Mackensen, whose Chief of Staff and guiding brain was Seeckt, the man who was to rebuild the German army after the war. Mackensen's force comprised the newly formed German Eleventh Army - made up with eight divisions from the west, and the Fourth Austro-Hungarian Army. The Ypres gas attack and a large cavalry raid from East Prussia were initiated to cloak the concentration on the Dunajec of fourteen divisions and 1,000 guns against a front held by only six Russian divisions. This front was composed of several lines of trenches but not highly fortified. Between the opposing sides there was a wide no-man's-land, as much as two miles across, in which 'the inhabitants were still living in their farms, the cattle pasturing undisturbed' - until the Germans removed these people as a precaution against any leakage of news.

Mackensen's army arrived on the scene and took over its allotted sector during the last week in April, being inserted between two Austrian armies. For his 18-mile front of attack Mackensen had one field gun to every 45 yards, and one heavy gun to every 132 yards. If this was not large by later standards it was ample to solve the problem of breaking *into* a position such as the Russians had organized. The greater problem was that of maintaining the momentum of the advance so as to break *through* the rearward positions before the Russian reserves could arrive and man them. To meet this need Seeckt issued instructions that 'all staffs must strive to keep the advance continuously moving'. No definite daily objectives were to be assigned to corps and divisions 'lest by fixing them the possibility of further progress might be stopped'. 'The quick advance of one part of the front will ease the situation at other parts where there is more resistance ... disposition in depth should enable the success at one place to be extended to a neighbouring front'. This conception of a varying progress coupled with a flexible use of reserves foreshadowed the famous 'infiltration' method of 1918, with its keynote of backing up success instead of trying to redeem local failure. To the further benefit of the Germans Ivanov (the Russian Army Group commander) would not believe reports of the impending attack and was thus caught with his reserves badly placed.

During the night of May 1st the storm troops moved forward across no-man's-land and dug in close to the enemy front line. At 10 AM on the 2nd, after a four hours' intense bombardment had flattened the Russian trenches, the attack was launched and the infantry swept forward through the dust and smoke. 'Here and there loam-grey figures jumped up and ran back, weaponless, in grey fur caps and fluttering, unbuttoned greatcoats. Soon there was not one of them remaining. Like a flock of sheep they fled in wild confusion.' The surprise was complete, the exploitation rapid, and despite a gallant stand on the Wisloka river, the whole Russian line along the Carpathians was rolled up, until on May 14th the Austro-German advance reached the San, eighty miles from its starting point. Russian defeat almost turned into disaster when the San was forced at Jaroslav, but the impetus of the advance had momentarily spent itself and reserves were lacking. A new factor was introduced by Italy's declaration of war against Austria, but Falkenhayn persuaded the Austrian Command, with some difficulty, not to move troops from the Russian front, and to maintain a strict defensive on their Italian frontier, which was secured by the mountain barrier. He realized that he had committed himself too far in Galicia to draw back, and that only by bringing more troops from France could he hope to fulfil his object of transferring troops back there. For this could only be possible when Russia's offensive power was crippled and her menace to Austria removed. Strengthened by these reinforcements, Mackensen attacked again in cooperation with the Austrians, retook Przemysl on June 3rd and captured Lemberg on June 22nd, cutting the Russian front into two separated portions.

But neither Falkenhayn nor Conrad had foreseen such results, and in consequence no arrangements had been made to maintain supplies during so long an advance. Hurried improvisation could not atone for lack of preparation, and the consequent delays allowed the enemy to retire without dissolving, though he left copious drippings.

The Russians, from their vast man-power resources, had almost made good the loss of 400,000 prisoners, so that Falkenhayn's anxiety about the stability of his Austrian Allies led him to yield to Seeckt's insistence and to continue the offensive, although still with limited objects and with one eye on the situation in France. Mackensen's direction was changed, however, from eastwards to northwards, up the wide corridor between the Bug and Vistula, where lay the main Russian forces. In conjunction, Hindenburg was ordered to strike south-east from East Prussia, across the Narew and towards the Bug. Ludendorff disliked the plan as being too much of a frontal attack; the Russians might be squeezed by the closing in of the two wings, but their retreat would not be cut off. He urged once more his spring scheme for a wide enveloping manoeuvre through Kovno on Vilna and Minsk. Conrad took the same view. Falkenhayn opposed this plan, fearing that it would mean more troops and a deeper commitment. And on July 2nd the Kaiser decided in favour of his plan. But the result justified Ludendorff's expectation – the Grand Duke extricated his troops from the Warsaw salient before the German shears could close on him. Falkenhayn, on the other hand, considered that Ludendorff had not put his full weight into the attack. The controversy became bitter. Hindenburg wrote not only to Falkenhayn but to the chief of the Kaiser's Military Cabinet, declaring that his title of Commander-in-Chief on the Eastern Front had become a 'cutting irony'. Falkenhayn unkindly took him at his word, by taking away one of his armies, and forming a fresh group of armies, thus reducing his status.

By the middle of August, 750,000 prisoners had been taken, Poland had been occupied, and Falkenhayn decided to break off large-scale operations on the Eastern Front. Bulgaria's entry into the war was now arranged and he wished to support the combined attack of Austria and Bulgaria against Serbia, as well as to transfer troops back to meet the French offensive expected in September. Yet, in hope of redeeming the lost opportunity and placating his personal opponents, he was led to sanction one more effort to break the Russians. Ludendorff was given belated permission to carry out his Vilna scheme, with such resources as he had, while Conrad planned to strike eastward from Luck in an attempt to repeat 'Gorlice' and cut off the Russian forces south of the Pripet marshes.

Ludendorff's move began on September 9th, Below's army of the Niemen and Eichhorn's Tenth Army forming two great horns which gored their way into the Russian front, the one east towards Dvinsk and the other south-east towards Vilna. The Russians were driven back in divergent directions and the German cavalry, advancing between the horns, far overlapped Vilna and drew near the Minsk railway. But the German strength was slender, and the Russians free to concentrate against this isolated menace. In face of stiffening resistance and shrinking supplies Ludendorff was driven to suspend operations. The crux of the situation was that the Russian armies had been allowed to draw back almost out of the net before the long-delayed Vilna manoeuvre was attempted.

The Austrian offensive did not develop until September 26th, and then failed dismally. Conrad unwisely persisted in renewing it, and, by the middle of October, the Austrians had sacrificed 230,000 men without affecting the general issue. Russia had been badly lamed, but not destroyed, and, although never again a direct menace to Germany, she was able to delay the full concentration of German strength in the west for two years, until 1918. Falkenhayn's cautious strategy was to prove the most hazardous in the long run, and indeed to pave the way for Germany's bankruptcy.

By October, the Russian retreat, after a nerve-racking series of escapes from the salients which the Germans systematically created and then sought to cut off, came to a definite halt on a straightened line, stretching from Riga on the Baltic to Czernowitz on the Rumanian frontier. The Russian armies, however, had gained this respite at a ruinous price, and their Western Allies had effected little in repayment of Russia's sacrifice on their behalf in 1914.

For the Franco-British relief offensive of September 25th had been no more fruitful than its predecessors. The main blow was launched by the French in Champagne, in conjunction with a Franco-British attack in Artois, on either side of Lens. One fault was that the sectors were too far apart to have a reaction on each other, but a worse was that the Command tried to reconcile two irreconcilable factors – they aimed at a breakthrough, but preceded it with a prolonged bombardment which gave away any chance of surprise. Joffre's plan was that the breakthrough in these two sectors was to be followed by a general offensive on the whole Franco-British front which would 'compel the Germans to retreat beyond the Meuse and possibly end the war'. The unquenchable optimist! Both in Champagne and Artois the attacks penetrated the German forward positions without difficulty, but subsequent delay in bringing reserves forward allowed the German reserves to close the gaps, a task simplified by the narrowness of the frontage of attack. The slight gains of ground in no way compensated for the heavy price paid for them – the Allied loss was approximately 242,000 against 141,000 Germans. And if the Allied Commands had gained more experience, so had the Germans, in the art of defence. The British share in this offensive is, however, notable as marking the appearance in strength of the New Armies; at Loos they were 'blooded', and if inexperience detracted from their effectiveness, their courage and driving force were an omen of Britain's power to improvise a national effort comparable with the long-created military machines of the Continent.

The direction of this effort inspired less confidence, and Sir John French gave place to Sir Douglas Haig as Commander-in-Chief, just as already in September the Russian Command had been transferred from the Grand Duke Nicholas, nominally to the Tsar, as a moral symbol, but actually to General Alexeiev, the new Chief of Staff.* Simultaneously, French's Chief of Staff, William Robertson, who had been long slighted by him owing to Henry Wilson's stronger influence, went home to become Chief of the Imperial General Staff, in order to give a stronger direction to the general strategy of Britain – if also to give it a Western Front bias. Somewhat curiously, Haig chose as his own Chief of Staff an old friend, Kiggell, who had not hitherto seen any service in France.

Italy's First Campaign. Italy's military contribution to the Allied balance sheet of 1915 was handicapped not only by her unreadiness, but by the awkward strategic position of her frontier, difficult for initiating an offensive and hardly more favourable for a secure defensive. The Italian frontier province of Venezia formed a salient pointing to Austria and flanked on the north by the Austrian Trentino, on the south by the Adriatic. Bordering on the Adriatic was a stretch of relatively low ground on the Isonzo sector, but the frontier then followed the Julian and Carnic Alps in a wide sweep round to the north-west. Any advance eastwards inevitably suffered the potential menace of an Austrian descent from the Trentino upon its rear.

Nevertheless the easterly sector, though difficult enough, seemed to offer more prospect of success – besides threatening a vital part of Austria – than an advance northward into the Alps. When Italy was preparing to enter the war, General Cadorna, who assumed command, drew up his plan on this basis of an offensive eastwards and a defensive attitude in the north. The overhanging menace of the Trentino was mitigated by the expectation of simultaneous pressure upon Austria from Russia and Serbia. But on the eve of Italy's declaration of war this

* General Brusilov, Russia's most successful commander, has described him as 'a fine strategist. His chief fault was indecision and want of moral courage.' 'I consider that had he been the Chief of Staff of a real Commander-in-Chief, he would have been beyond criticism. But with a commander [the Tsar] whose mind he had to make up for him, and whose feeble will he had to strengthen, Alexeiev was not the right man.' Trotsky, more contemptuously, depicts him as a 'grey mediocrity, the oldest military clerk of the Army, worn out through mere perseverance'.

hope faded, the Russian armies falling back under Mackensen's blows, while the Serbs, despite requests from the Allies, failed to make even a demonstration. This lack of pressure enabled the Austrians to dispatch five divisions to the Isonzo from the Serbian front, these being relieved by three newly formed German divisions. Three more divisions were sent from Galicia. Even so there were only some thirteen divisions in all available to oppose the Italians, who had a numerical superiority of more than two to one.

In order to secure good covering positions on the north a limited advance was made into the Trentino, with success, but another into the north-east corner of the frontier salient – towards Tarvis in the Carnic Alps – was forestalled. This local failure was to have unfortunate results later – in 1917, for it left the Austrians with a good strategic sally port into the Tagliamento valley.

Meantime the main Italian advance, by the Second and Third Armies, had begun at the end of May, but out of their total of twenty-four divisions only seven were ready. Bad weather increased the handicap, the Isonzo coming down in flood, and the initial advance soon came to a standstill. The Isonzo front crystallized, like the others, into trench warfare. The Italian mobilization, however, was now complete and Cadorna mounted a deliberate attack, which opened on June 23rd. This first battle of the Isonzo continued until July 7th with little gain to show. A fresh series of efforts after a ten days' pause were hardly more effective, and the front then relapsed into the spasmodic bickering characteristic of trench warfare, while Cadorna made preparations for a new and larger effort in the autumn. When it was launched in October he had a two-to-one superiority in numbers, but was weak in artillery. This defect, coupled with the superior experience of the defender, rendered the new offensive as barren as its predecessors. It was sustained too obstinately and, when finally broken off in December, the Italian loss in the six months' campaign totalled some 280,000 – nearly twice that of the defenders, who had shown on this front a fierce resolution which was often lacking when they faced the Russians.

The Conquest of Serbia. While stalemate, although with marked changes beneath the surface, had once more settled in on both the Russian and French fronts, the later months of 1915 witnessed fluid operations elsewhere which were to have an unforeseen influence on the war.

One of the most remarkable 'blind spots' in the strategy of the Allies was the failure to perceive the importance of Serbia as an irritation, and consequent distraction, to the Austro-German alliance in a most sensitive region. Such a menace to uneasy Austria's rear flank was an invaluable distraction to the forces and plans of the enemy alliance as a whole. It was, indeed, a necessary distraction if Serbia's allies were to concentrate with effective results in the main theatres. Geography made Serbia a potential 'Austrian ulcer', at a politically and militarily tender spot. To maintain the irritation, quality rather than quantity of aid was needed. Not the dispatch of large Allied forces, which could scarcely be supplied until communications were improved; but the provision of technical troops and material. The Serbs themselves were magnificent fighting troops, and naturally suited to the terrain: what they required were the means of fighting effectively. To provide these was a far more urgent, and more economic, step than to equip the newly raised armies of Britain. By neglecting it the Allies allowed their Austro-German opponents to operate on and excise the ulcer: this blindness was the source of wider, and widening, trouble to themselves.

Austria had proved capable of holding the Italians on the Isonzo, and once the Russian danger began to fade under the pressure of the summer offensive, her Command was anxious to deal conclusively with Serbia. Austria's attempted invasions in August and September, and again in November, 1914, had been brusquely repulsed by Serbian counterstrokes, and it was not pleasant for a great power, especially one with so many Slav subjects, to swallow such military rebuffs. Her impatience coincided with Falkenhayn's desire to gain direct railway communication with Turkey, hard pressed at the Dardanelles. Throughout the summer the rival coalitions had been bidding for Bulgaria's support, and in this bargaining the Entente suffered the moral handicap of military failure, and the material handicap caused by Serbia's unwillingness to give up any part of Macedonia – of which she had despoiled Bulgaria in 1913. As Austria had no objection to offering territory that belonged to her enemy, Bulgaria accepted her bid. This accession of strength enhanced the chance of a decision against Serbia, and in August Falkenhayn decided to reinforce the Austrian Third Army with Gallwitz's army from the Russian front. In addition two Bulgarian armies were available. Mackensen and Seeckt were sent to direct the operations. To meet this new threat Serbia, apart from her own relatively small forces, had only a treaty guarantee of Greek aid and promises from the Entente Powers. The first disappeared with the fall of Venizelos, the pro-Ally Greek Premier, and the second, as usual, were too late.

On October 6th, 1915, the Austro-German armies attacked southwards across the Danube, with a flanking movement across the Drina on the right. The sturdy resistance of the Serbs in delaying actions and the natural difficulty of the mountainous country checked the advance, but before Franco-British reinforcements could arrive the Bulgarian armies struck westwards into southern Serbia, across the rear of the main Serbian armies. This drove a deep wedge between the Serbs and their Allies, moving up from Salonika, and automatically loosened the resistance in the north. With their line bent at both ends until it resembled a vast bow, threatened with a double envelopment, and with their retreat to the south cut off, the Serbian armies decided to retire west through the Albanian mountains. Those who survived the hardships of this mid-winter retreat were conveyed to the island of Corfu, and after being re-equipped and reorganized, joined the Entente force at Salonika in the spring of 1916. The conquest of Serbia – though not, as it proved, of Serbian military power – relieved Austria of danger on her southern frontier, and gave Germany free communication and control over a huge central belt from the North Sea to the Tigris. For the Entente this campaign dug a military sump-pit which for three years was to drain their military resources, there to lie idle and ineffective. Yet ultimately that sump-pit was to overflow and wash away one of the props of the Central Alliance.

The Salonika Expedition. When at the beginning of October the Entente Governments had awakened to Serbia's danger, British and French divisions had been dispatched hurriedly from Gallipoli to Salonika, which was the only channel of aid to Serbia – by the railway to Uskub. The advanced guard of this relieving force – which was under the command of General Sarrail – pressed up the Vardar and over the Serbian frontier, only to find that the Bulgarian wedge had cut it off from the Serbians, and it was forced to fall back on Salonika, pursued by the Bulgarians. On military grounds an evacuation of Salonika was vigorously urged by the British General Staff, but political reasons induced the Allies to remain. The Dardanelles failure had already diminished their prestige, and by convincing the Balkan States of German invincibility had induced Bulgaria to enter the war and Greece to break her treaty with Serbia. To evacuate Salonika would be a further loss of prestige, whereas by holding on the Allies could check German influence over Greece, and maintain a base of operations from which to aid Rumania, if, as expected, she entered the war on their side. To this end the Salonika force was augmented with fresh British and French divisions, as well as contingents from Italy and Russia, and there also the rebuilt Serbian army was brought. But apart from the capture of Monastir in November, 1916, and an abortive attack in

April, 1917, the Entente forces made no serious offensive until the
autumn of 1918. Its feeble effect was partly due to the natural difficulties of the country in the form of mountain ridges guarding the
approach to the Balkans, partly to the feeling of the Allied Governments that it was a bad debt, and partly to the personality of Sarrail,
whose conduct and reputation for political intrigues failed to command
the confidence and cooperation essential if such a mixed force was
to 'pull its weight'. On their side the Germans were content to leave
it in passivity, under guard of the Bulgarians, while they steadily withdrew their own forces for use elsewhere. With gentle sarcasm they
termed Salonika their 'largest internment camp', and with half a
million Allied troops locked up their gibe had some justification – until
1918.

Mesopotamia. Nor was Salonika the only 'drain' opened in 1915.
Mesopotamia was the site of a fresh diversion of force from the centre
of military gravity, and one which could only be excused on purely
political grounds. It was not, like the Dardanelles and Salonika, undertaken to relieve a hard-pressed ally, nor had it the justification of the
Dardanelles expedition of being directed at the vital point of one of the
enemy states. The occupation of Mesopotamia might raise British prestige, and it might annoy Turkey, but it could not endanger her power of
resistance. Although its origin was sound its development was another
example of 'drift' due to the inherent faultiness of Britain's machinery
for the conduct of war.

The oilfields near the Persian Gulf were of essential importance to
Britain's oil supply, and thus, when war with Turkey was imminent, a
small Indian force of one division was dispatched to safeguard them.
To fulfil this mission effectively it was necessary to occupy the Basra
vilayet at the head of the Persian Gulf, in order to command the
possible lines of approach.

On November 21st, 1914, Basra was captured, but the rising stream
of Turkish reinforcements compelled the Indian Government to add a
second division. The Turkish attacks in the spring of 1915 were repulsed, and the British commander, General Nixon, judged it wise to
expand his footing, for greater security. Townshend's division was
pushed up the Tigris to Amara, gaining a brilliant little victory, and the
other division up the Euphrates to Nasiriya. Southern Mesopotamia
was a vast alluvial plain, roadless and railless, in which these two great
rivers formed the only channels of communication. Thus a hold on
Amara and Nasiriya covered the oilfields; but Nixon and the Indian
Government, inspired by these successes, decided to push forward to

Kut-el-Amara. This move led the British 180 miles farther into the interior, but had a partial military justification in the fact that at Kut the Shatt-el-Hai, issuing from the Tigris, formed a link with the Euphrates by which Turkish reserves might be transferred from one river line to the other.

Townshend was sent forward in August; he defeated the Turks near Kut, and his cavalry carried the pursuit to Aziziya, halfway to Baghdad. Enthusiasm spread to the Home Government, anxious for a moral counterpoise to their other failures, and Nixon received permission for Townshend to press on to Baghdad. But after an indecisive battle at Ctesiphon, the growing superiority of the Turkish strength compelled Townshend to retreat to Kut. Here, isolated far from help, he was urged to remain, as several fresh divisions were being sent to Mesopotamia. Kut was invested by the Turks on December 8th, 1915, and the relieving forces battered in vain against the Turkish lines covering the approach on either bank of the Tigris. The conditions were bad, the communications worse, the generalship faulty, and at last on April 29th, 1916, Kut was forced to surrender. However unsound the strategy which dispatched Townshend on this adventure, it is just to emphasize the actual achievements of his small force in face of superior numbers. With inadequate equipment and primitive communications, and utterly isolated in the heart of an enemy country, it wrote a glorious page of military history. When these handicaps are compared with the four-to-one superiority in number, and highly organized supply system of the force which ultimately took Baghdad, the comparison explains the awe in which Townshend and his men were held by the Turks.

The Home Front, 1915. Perhaps one of the most significant landmarks in the transition of the struggle from a 'military' to a 'national' war was the formation of a National Ministry in Britain, which occurred in May, 1915. For the prototype of Parliaments to abandon the deep-rooted party system and pool the direction of the war was proof of the psychological upheaval of traditions. The Liberal Prime Minister, Asquith, remained, but the Conservative element acquired a preponderant voice in the Cabinet, although the dynamic personality of Lloyd George began to gain such a hold on public opinion that the real leadership slipped into his hands. Churchill, whose vision had saved the menace to the Channel ports and made possible the future key to the deadlock, was shelved, as already had been Haldane, the creator of the Expeditionary Force.

Political changes were general in all countries, and were symptomatic of a readjustment of popular outlook. The early fervour had disappeared, and been repulsed by a dogged determination which, if natural to the British, was in strange contradiction to popular, if superficial, conceptions of the French temperament.

Economically, the strain had yet to be felt severely by any country. Finance had shown an unexpected power of accommodation, and neither the blockade nor the submarine campaign had seriously affected food supply. If Germany was beginning to suffer some shortage, her people had more tangible omens of success to fortify their resolution than had their enemies. In 1916, however, the strain on them was to be intensified by the failure of the 1915 harvest – the worst for forty years. Fortunately for Germany's powers of endurance the danger was to be relieved, and the British blockade partly nullified, by the inexpensive capture of a wheat-growing country on the Eastern Front. Ironically, the enemy were to throw Germany this lifebuoy, by encouraging Rumania to enter the war, after Falkenhayn had almost drowned the war-will of the German people in a bath of blood and tears by his renewed offensive on the Western Front.

CHAPTER FIVE

SCENE 1

The Birth of a 'Plan' –
the Dardanelles

A giant, three ships, and the fear of a rape were the main factors in bringing Turkey into the war against her traditional ally, Britain. The giant was Baron Marschall von Bieberstein, who for fifteen years, until 1912, was German Ambassador at Constantinople. To a race whose sole criterion of conduct and admiration was might, whose 'chivalry' was only extended to the mighty, Marschall von Bieberstein's huge frame, scarred face and trampling manner formed a living picture of the growing power of Germany. Perhaps one man alone could have counteracted the impression with that of Britain's more mature and quieter strength. This man was Kitchener, who, curiously, seems to have felt an ungratified desire for the post. Instead, the British Ambassador during the critical years was one from whose personality the requisite prestige and strength were absent – and who, during the critical weeks, was even absent on leave.

The ships were the new German battle cruiser *Goeben*, and the British-built battleships *Sultan Osman* and *Reschadieh*. A shrewd step to enhance German prestige and weaken the one remaining foothold of British influence – that of the naval mission – the *Goeben* was sent out early in 1914 to Constantinople and for long lay anchored near the entrance to the Golden Horn. Then, in the war-charged atmosphere of late July, the ever-present Turkish fear of Russian lust for the Dardanelles developed almost to panic point. It was none the less powerful because mingled with Turkish lust for wider dominion. Certain of war between Germany and Russia, uncertain of Britain's entry, and egged on by the Germanophil Enver Pasha, the Turkish Grand Vizier responded to previous German overtures by asking the German ambassador, on July 27th, for a secret alliance against Russia. Next day the proposal was accepted, and on August 2nd the treaty was signed –

unknown to most of the Turkish Cabinet. On the morrow the first
mines were laid in the Dardanelles; and Enver had already mobilized
the Turkish forces on his own initiative. But the news of Britain's entry
into the war was a shock which nearly burst the new treaty like a paper
balloon. Indeed, so much 'hot air' was generated during the next few
days that it even sufficed to blow out another *ballon d'essai* – the
astonishing offer to Russia of a Turkish Alliance. But this offer did not
suit Russia's ambition, even though it promised her the one chance of
having a channel through which she could receive munitions from her
Western allies. She preferred isolation to the sacrifice of her dream of
annexation, and did not even report the offer to her allies.

But Turkey's sudden reversal of attitude, and the predominance of
her fear of British power over the fear of Russian ambition, were shortlived. And the revival of confidence was greatly helped by annoyance.
Turkey, smarting under her wounds of the Balkan war, had been awaiting the delivery of her first two modern battleships with an eagerness
and pride all the more general because the money had been raised by
collections among the people. On August 3rd, however, the British
government informed Turkey that it was taking over the ships – and
the announcement caused an explosion of indignation. Every man who
had contributed his mite felt an injury akin to a personal betrayal. This
popular outcry was at its height when, on August 10th, the *Goeben*,
accompanied by the cruiser *Breslau*, appeared at the entrance to the
Dardanelles, having slipped past the British fleet near Sicily.

An officer of the German Military Mission, Lieut-Colonel von Kress,
brought the news to the War Minister, Enver Pasha, and told him that
the forts were asking instructions as to whether they should allow the
warships to enter. Then a vital interchange took place. Enver – 'I can't
decide that now. I must first consult the Grand Vizier.' Kress – 'But we
must wire immediately.' A moment of inward turmoil. Then – 'They
are to allow them to enter.' A further and guileful question from Kress
– 'If the English warships follow the Germans, are they to be fired on if
they also attempt an entrance?' 'The matter must be left to the decision
of the Cabinet.' 'Excellency, we cannot leave our subordinates in such a
position without issuing immediately clear and definite instructions.
Are the English to be fired on or not?' Another pause. 'Yes.' As
General Kannengiesser, a German witness of this eventful discussion,
says – 'We heard the clanking of the portcullis descending before the
Dardanelles.'

International law was evaded, British objections frustrated, Turkish
pride satisfied, and Enver's dubious colleagues calmed by arranging the

fictitious sale to Turkey of these warships. Turkey was not yet ready for nor agreed upon war, and Britain had every motive to avoid it.

Thus, during the weeks that followed, the Turks were successively enabled and emboldened to advance along the path to war by the passivity of Britain in face of growing provocation. The German crews were kept, the German Admiral appointed to command the Turkish Navy, the British naval Mission removed from control, and then forced to withdraw; British ships were detained, their wireless dismantled; German soldiers and sailors filtered into Constantinople, and the straits were closed. Meantime Turkish ministers, ever ready with glib assurances, congratulated themselves on the gullibility of the British, whose restraint was rather due to an acute sense of vulnerability, as a power with millions of Moslem subjects. Conciliation was pressed to the point of folly, however, when the British Admiralty's intention to appoint Admiral Limpus, ex-chief of the Naval Mission to Turkey, to command the British Dardanelles Squadron was abandoned for fear of giving offence to the Turks! And when the need for conciliation had passed, a misplaced chivalry seems to have taken its place in preventing the use of the one man who knew the Turks and the Dardanelles intimately.

Even the Germans began to be worried when a series of raids on the Egyptian frontier could not goad Britain to war. So the German Admiral, with Enver's connivance, led the Turkish fleet on a raid into the Black Sea against Britain's more sensitive ally, shelling Odessa and other Russian ports. The story of this provocation, as related to and recorded by Lord D'Abernon after the war, is illuminating. The official sanction came to the German Embassy in a sealed envelope addressed to the Admiral. An official took the initiative and precaution to open it and send on merely a copy. The first report that reached Constantinople was that the *Goeben* had been sunk, and so, thinking that the order had sunk with her, the Grand Vizier conciliatingly replied to Russian protests by denying that any such order had been given. Thereupon the German Embassy sent to him, saying – 'The order of which you deny the existence, because you think it was sunk with the *Goeben*, is in a safe place … at the German Embassy … Pray cease to deny that the Turkish government has given the order to attack Russia.' Thus the war-fearing Grand Vizier was compelled to stand aside helplessly while German cunning removed any excuse to the Triple Entente for avoiding war – at the end of October.

The best chance for both Britain and Russia was now in making war, instantly. The defences of the Dardanelles were obsolete and still incomplete. The only two munition factories in Turkey lay on the shore close to Constantinople and open to easy destruction by any warships which penetrated thither. The misuse of the opportunity is a tale of almost incredible haphazardness on the part of Britain, of equal short-sightedness on the part of Russia.

On November 3rd the Allied fleet carried out a short bombardment of the outer forts at the Dardanelles, the only use of which was to help the German authorities in trying to overcome Turkish inertia over the defences. They had sunk back into lethargy again when, six weeks later, a British submarine gave a fresh alarm and gained its commander a VC by diving under the mines and sinking a ship near the Narrows. But the effect of these warnings has been overrated. Turkish lethargy was almost as boundless as British folly. Not until the end of February did the Turks post more than one division on the Gallipoli peninsula, and not until March did the improvements in the defences of the straits approach completion. In part, this state of weakness seems to have been due to a feeling that it was waste of energy to try to prevent a passage, which could not be prevented against any serious attempt. If the few well-informed experts, German or Turk, were dubious of their power to stop a purely naval attack, they were still less confident of resisting a combined attack. And the Turkish staff history frankly says: 'Up to 25th February, it would have been possible to effect a landing success-fully at any point on the peninsula, and the capture of the straits by land troops would have been comparatively easy.'

At one time the Entente might have found such troops, in quantity, without touching their own resources. For in mid-August the Greek Prime Minister, Venizelos, had formally and unreservedly placed all his country's forces at the disposal of the Entente. The offer was not accepted, owing mainly to Sir Edward Grey's desire to avoid antagoniz-ing Turkey, whose hatred for Greece was stronger than for any other of her adversaries of 1912. But the hope, if not the desire, soon began to fade and before the end of the month Russia asked Greece whether she would send an expedition to help in forcing the Dardanelles. King Constantine agreed, but made the proviso that Bulgaria's neutrality must be assured, to avoid the danger of a stab in the back. The Greek plan, a thorough one, was that 60,000 men should land near the outer tip of the peninsula to take in rear the forts guarding the straits, while another 30,000 landed near Bulair to seize and hold the isthmus; but, by the time Turkey entered the war, Constantine had withdrawn his reluctant consent, believing that Bulgaria was already pledged to Ger-many.

In England the only leader who showed a consistent appreciation of the importance of opening the Dardanelles was Churchill. From August onwards he frequently tried to arouse the interest of the War Office – which, for several years, had not even made a perfunctory review of the question. Three weeks after Turkey had entered the war he raised it again at the first meeting of the new War Council, but all eyes were still focused on the French front, and he got no support from Kitchener. The Turks were granted a fresh lease of repose. But during December the blankness of the prospect on the Western Front was realized by many in England, and a few in France. Simultaneously the growth of the new armies evoked a natural question as to their use. The two factors combined to freshen, if not to clear, the atmosphere. Suggestions for a new strategic line of approach came from several quarters.

The most definite and practical was contained in a paper of December 29th, written by the Secretary of the War Council, Lieut-Colonel Maurice Hankey, who emphasized the deadlock in France, and, while urging the development of new mechanical and armoured devices to force a passage through the wire entanglements and trenches, suggested that Germany could be struck most easily through her allies, especially Turkey. He advocated the use of the first three new army corps for an attack on Constantinople, if possible in cooperation with Greece and Bulgaria, as a means not only to overthrow Turkey and bring the weight of the Balkans into the Entente scale, but to open communication with Russia. Further advantages would be to bring down the price of wheat and release 350,000 tons of shipping. The argument revealed a grasp of grand strategy, whereas the horizon of most soldiers, especially the highest, was narrowly bounded by tactics.

Sir John French, of course, objected to any effort outside his own command in France, but at this juncture an appeal came from the Grand Duke Nicholas for a British demonstration to relieve the pressure on his forces in the Caucasus. Ironically, this danger had almost passed before his appeal was received. Still more ironically, the emergency had been due to his own objection to spare troops from the main front.

Kitchener's response was to suggest the Dardanelles as the best place for such a demonstration, and also that 'reports could be spread at the same time that Constantinople was threatened'. Fisher now chimed in, to suggest not a demonstration but a combined attack on a large scale, in conjunction with which old warships should be used to 'force the Dardanelles'. He concluded characteristically and prophetically – 'But as the great Napoleon said, "Celerity – without it Failure".' Churchill knew how little hope there was of obtaining troops for a large-scale attack, but eagerly caught hold of the naval possibility. Later in the day, January 3rd, he telegraphed, with Fisher's agreement, to the Admiral on the spot, Carden – 'Do you consider the forcing of the straits by ships alone a practicable operation?' Back came Carden's answer – 'I do not consider Dardanelles can be rushed. They might be forced by extended operations with large numbers of ships.'

Carden's detailed plan was submitted to the War Council on January 13th. The fatal decision was to be taken in a fateful atmosphere. Strategy instead of being the servant of policy had become the master, a blind and brutal master. From many sides there was an urgent call upon policy. Russia was faltering before she had even got into her stride; Serbia had barely escaped a fall; Greece and Rumania were leaning back the more that Bulgaria seemed to be leaning forward to grasp Germany's outstretched hand; Italy was sitting on the fence. The one front where troops were available was in France: and there ammunition was not – for the scale of ammunition that would suffice in other theatres would not even make a dent in the trench barrier in France. But strategy, as embodied in Sir John French, balked the desires of policy, and as he was loyally rather than logically supported by Kitchener, the rest of the Cabinet was persuaded by a sense of numb, though not dumb, despair, aggravated by their amateur status. Hence they clutched too desperately at a straw of professional opinion which offered the chance of making bricks without men. And the words in which the decision was formulated was an epitome of their confused thought – 'to prepare for a naval expedition in February, to bombard and take the Gallipoli peninsula, with Constantinople as its objective'. The suggestion that ships were to 'take' a part of the land is delightfully naïve.

A few days later Churchill made an attempt to strengthen his plan by suggesting to the Grand Duke Nicholas that the Russians should cooperate by a simultaneous land and sea attack on the Bosphorus. Strategically, his suggestion was the best possible. Paradoxically, it proved void because the political aspect here dominated the mind of the Russian strategists! Strong as was their desire to possess Constantinople, they had no wish to cooperate with their allies in gaining it. The corner-stone of Russian policy was the annexation of both Constantinople and the Dardanelles. Sazonov, the Foreign Minister, had tried to make this claim more palatable to his allies by suggesting the internationalization of Constantinople in return for Russian control of the straits, but the weight of military opinion had overborne this partial concession. Thus it is not surprising that military Russia viewed with jealousy and suspicion any move of her allies towards her own goal, and withheld her assistance. Even Sazonov records – 'I intensely disliked the thought that the straits and Constantinople might be taken by our allies and not by the Russian forces ... when the Gallipoli expedition was finally decided upon by our allies ... I had difficulty in concealing from them how painfully the news had affected me.' Russia would not help even in helping to clear her own windpipe. She preferred to choke rather than disgorge a morsel of her ambition. And in the end she was choked – the verdict should be *felo de se*.

In England, too, fresh complications arose. Churchill's quarrel with the plan was that the scale was too petty; Fisher's, that it might become too large – and so obstruct his Baltic project. And from this divergence a quarrel developed between the two – the political and the professional heads of the Admiralty. At the next War Council meeting Fisher rose to tender his resignation, but Kitchener intervened and, drawing him aside, persuaded him to fall in with the general opinion of the meeting. Thus the compromise plan was a compromise even in its acceptance. Most apt is the verdict of General Aspinall-Oglander in his official history – that operations on the Western Front were a gamble with pounds for a possible gain of pence, whereas in the east 'pence were to be wagered in the none too sanguine hope of winning pounds'.

The naval attack began with the bombardment of the outer forts on February 19th – curiously, the anniversary of Admiral Duckworth's successful attempt to pass through the straits, in 1807. Five days of bad weather then intervened and, when the bombardment was renewed on the 25th, the forts were outranged and the Turks retired from them. Next day the fleet began the second phase, the crushing of the intermediate defences – more difficult because these, being inside the mouth of the straits, were more difficult targets to observe. Although results were disappointing, the chance was taken to land demolition parties, on the tip of the peninsula, which destroyed the guns in the abandoned outer forts. Thereby history, at least, gained a dramatic comparison. For on the same spot where this handful of marines moved about freely on February 26th, thousands of men fell two months later. Further landings were made next day, and again on March 3rd, but on the 4th they met slight opposition, and were re-embarked.

Meantime, the bombardment continued in rather desultory fashion – due in part, but not wholly, to the bad weather – and trawlers made a few rather feeble attempts to sweep the first minefield. Lack of aircraft to observe and correct the shooting was, however, a great handicap, and on the 9th Carden reported that he could do not more until his air service was reinforced, and would meanwhile concentrate on clearing the minefield.

But the weeks were slipping away and the Admiralty could not help feeling that Carden's caution was disproportionate to the importance of his task – and of speed in his task. Hence, on March 11th a telegram was sent to urge him to decisive action, and to free him from any fear of being held responsible if serious loss ensued. Carden responded at once and arranged a general fleet attack, under cover of which the mines were to be cleared. And the principle governing the attack was to be that the battleships should only move in, and fire from, waters clear or already cleared of mines. At this point Carden fell sick and was succeeded by his second-in-command, de Robeck.

The attack was begun on March 18th and was foiled not by resistance but by inadvertence; for, evading the British destroyer patrols, a little Turkish steamer had laid a new line of mines well outside the main minefield, dropping them parallel to the shore in Eren Keui Bay, where the Allied fleet had taken up its position in earlier bombardments. This new line of mines lay undiscovered and unsuspected while the fleet advanced past it to engage the forts. By 1.45 PM the forts had been practically silenced, with little damage to the battleships, and the minesweepers were now sent forward to clear the main minefield, while the French Battle Squadron, in the van, was temporarily withdrawn. As this squadron was retiring through Eren Keui Bay, a tremendous explosion was heard, and a dense cloud of smoke seen, in the *Bouvet*, and in less than two minutes she had heeled over and sunk with nearly all her crew. But the relieving line of battleships continued the attack from closer ranges and the fire from the forts, momentarily renewed, became more and more flickering as guns were buried in rubble and telephone wires cut. Suddenly, however, about 4PM, the *Inflexible* and *Irresistible* were seen almost simultaneously to have a heavy list. Mystery accentuated the moral effect.

No one suspected the presence of the new line of mines, and guesses as to the cause ranged from that of a shoal of floating mines, turned loose to drift down with the current, to that of torpedoes fired from some hidden point on shore. Fear of the unknown prompted Admiral de Robeck's decision to order a general retirement forthwith, and even as this was in progress the *Ocean*, sent to the *Irresistible*'s aid, struck the same line of mines, and both foundered during the night. Although the whole British fleet lost only sixty-one men in casualties, the loss in material was large, for out of the eighteen Allied battleships three had sunk and three more were badly damaged. But a far worse loss was that of nerve and of imagination – to see the enemy's side – among the naval authorities. Actually, the enemy were suffering greater depression, and with more reason. More than half their ammunition had been expended and they had no reserve of mines. Many of the gun crews were demoralized, and the widespread opinion among both Turkish and German officers was that they had little hope of opposing a renewal of the attack.

But that attack, contrary to their expectation, was never renewed. When he came out of action de Robeck had the full intention of renewing it, and so had the Admiralty, which informed him that five more battleships were being sent out to replace his losses, and added that it was 'important not to let the forts be repaired, or to encourage the enemy by an apparent suspension of the operations'. But on the 23rd he sent a telegram which not only revealed his reversal of view but reversed the opinion of the Admiralty – except Churchill, who had to bow to the weight of professional opinion. For de Robeck's new opinion was that the fleet could not get through without the help of the army, and that any further effort must be postponed until this was ready. And, in practice, this opinion meant that the navy was to hand over the whole offensive burden to the army, and to stand by, watching, while the army spent itself in vain assaults unaided by any fresh naval attack. Perhaps the underlying factor was that service tendency of mind which sentimentally values things more than lives, a tendency which may have its foundation in totemism, but is also accentuated by the peacetime shortage of material and the penalties attached to any loss of it. The artilleryman's love of his guns, and readiness to sacrifice his life to avert the disgrace of losing them, is paralleled by the sailor's adoration of his ship, even an old and obsolete ship such as these at the Dardanelles. It hinders him from adopting the common sense view that a ship, like a shell, is merely a weapon to be expended profitably. Perhaps, also, a powerful auxiliary factor in the sailors' decision was now the presence of soldiers and their willingness to assume the burden.

For, coincidently with the preparations for a naval attack, the British government had drifted independently towards a land attack. It had its origin, not in a wider consideration of the Dardanelles problem, but in a separate consideration of where the new armies could be used as an alternative to France. The committee reported in favour of Salonika, as an immediate aid to Serbia and an ultimate stab in the back to the Central Powers – up the Danube. The opinion won favour at the meeting of the War Council on February 9th, being reinforced by the news that Bulgaria had contracted a loan with Germany and by the desire of encouraging Greece to support Serbia. And Kitchener, who had declared that he could find no troops for the Dardanelles plan, now announced that he would send the Regular 29th Division to Salonika, in conjunction with a French division. The promise of two divisions, however, was naturally not enough to allay Greek misgivings; Greece was unwilling to accept the offer unless Rumania was persuaded to join, and Rumania was held back by the sight of Russia's misadventures.

But the fact remained, and could no longer be hidden from the Cabinet by Kitchener's veil of mystery and authority, that the 29th Division was available. Nor did he for the moment seek to withhold it. In consequence the War Council, on February 16th, decided that it should be dispatched to the centrally placed harbour of Mudros in the Aegean 'at the earliest possible moment, together with troops from Egypt', with the idea that 'all the forces [were] to be available in case of necessity to support the naval attack on the Dardanelles'. No one, however, suggested that the naval attack should be postponed to obtain surprise and the greater effect of a combined operation. The troops were merely to mount guard over what the navy gained.

But the 29th Division immediately became the rope in a tug-of-war between the 'Eastern' and 'Western' schools of thought, and on to the western end were pulling not only the British headquarters in France, but Joffre. Joffre's foresight was always, and only, quick when his own preserves were threatened, and he saw in the dispatch east instead of west of the newly assembled 29th Division a disquieting omen of the destination of the new army divisions. Kitchener could easily have hardened his heart against French, but he could not against the French. Just as his loyalty to France was an earlier instinct than his love of the east, so it now proved stronger than his belief in the eastern theatre. At the next meeting of the War Council, only three days later, he turned about face and asserted that the 29th Division could not be spared. In its place he suggested the dispatch of raw Australian and New Zealand troops, two divisions from Egypt. And he even notified the Admiralty behind Churchill's back that the 29th was not to go, thereby interrupting the collection of the transports required to carry it.

That same day the naval attack had opened – and the bombardment echoed throughout the Near East. When the news came, that the outer forts had fallen, the Turkish government made ready to flee into the interior of Asia Minor. The Germans expected not only the appearance of the Allied fleet off Constantinople but that its appearance would be the signal for a revolt against Enver, and the consequent signature of peace by Turkey. For the Turks, in any case, could not have carried on the war once Constantinople, their only munition source, was abandoned. Italy and Greece began to incline more strongly towards war, and Bulgaria away from it. On March 1st Venizelos proposed to land three Greek divisions on the Gallipoli peninsula – but here Russia fatally intervened by notifying Athens that 'in no circumstances can we allow Greek forces to participate in the Allied attack on Constantinople'.

Only the neutral part of these favourable echoes reached the War Council in London, but it was sufficient to encourage the believers and win over the doubters. The original idea that the naval attack was only tentative, to be abandoned if found difficult, now faded and all save one were agreed that the attack must be carried through, if necessary with land forces. The one dissenting voice was that of Lloyd George, who objected to the Army having 'to pull the Navy's chestnuts out of the fire'. Curiously, he alone sounded the warning truth of history that the renewal along the same line of an attack that has failed is rarely justified, and that it is better to switch the effort in a fresh direction. If his just objection was not immediately justified it was because of the Turks' lethargy in profiting by their warning.

In contrast, Kitchener laid down emphatically that 'having entered on the project of forcing the straits there can be no idea of abandoning the scheme'. But not until March 10th did he make up his mind to release the 29th Division and, perhaps worse, not until the 12th did he nominate a commander for the expedition. Yet the French, despite Joffre's refusal to contribute from the field armies, had scraped together a division from the interior and had begun to embark it as early as the 3rd. At the War Office in London not a single preparatory step had been taken. One result was that when Ian Hamilton departed on the 13th none of his administrative staff were available, and he had to leave without them. Further, the sum of his information comprised a 1912 handbook of the Turkish army, a pre-war report on the Dardanelles forts, and an inaccurate map! To compensate for this deficiency some of his staff had scoured the book-sellers for guidebooks to Constantinople.

The one swift action in this halting period was Ian Hamilton's passage out to the Dardanelles. A chain of special trains and fast cruisers whisked him thither faster than he could have travelled in peacetime by the Orient Express, and he reached the fleet on March 17th – the eve of its attack. His first discovery was the unsuitability of Lemnos as a base, owing to lack of water, as well as lack of piers and shelter in Mudros harbour. His second, was that the troops already present were so ill distributed in their transports that they would have to be disembarked and redistributed before they could land on an open and hostile shore. Hence his first step, on the 18th, had to be the unfortunate one of changing his base to Alexandria and directing all transports there. So ill-conceived and chaotic had been the original loading that battalions were separated from their first-line transport, wagons from their horses, guns from their ammunition – and even shells from their fuses. One infantry battalion of the 29th Division had actually been split up among four ships. Even with the ample wharfs and camps of Alexandria, unloading and reloading was a slow business, not accelerated by the delayed arrival of the administrative staff.

On March 22nd, after the naval attack and before sailing for Alexandria, Ian Hamilton with his chief assistants met de Robeck in conference. 'The moment we sat down de Robeck told us he was now clear he could not get through without the help of all my troops.' Soldiers could not argue with a naval verdict, even had they any wish, and so without discussion the Army was committed to the task. And the task was committed to the Army. For although Ian Hamilton politely suggested to the Admiral that he should 'push on systematically' with the attack on the forts, and Churchill made similar representations, the Admirals both at the Admiralty and at the Dardanelles were as rigid as rock in passive resistance, and henceforth the fleet was dedicated to what Churchill has aptly termed the 'No' principle – an 'unsurmountable mental barrier'. Sired by strategic confusion and dammed by naval negation, the landing on Gallipoli was born – and marred in delivery by muddled military midwifery. From this welter only one clear note emerged, in a memorandum drawn up for the Prime Minister by Maurice Hankey on March 16th. In it he emphasized that 'combined operations require more careful preparation than any other class of military enterprise. All through our history such attacks have failed when the preparations have been inadequate, and the successes are in nearly every case due to the most careful preparation beforehand. It would appear to be the business of the War Council to assure themselves, in the present instance, that these preparations have been thoroughly thought out'. He pointed out that surprise had already been forfeited and in consequence the task had become far more formidable. Hence he enumerated a comprehensive list of practical points upon which the War Council should cross-examine the naval and military authorities, saying, in conclusion – 'Unless details such as these ... are fully thought out before the landing takes place ... a serious disaster may occur.' It may occur to the historian that Hankey was the only expert adviser of the British government who had thought out the foundations of strategy. For when the Prime Minister, loth to question Kitchener's omniscience, tentatively asked if any scheme had been worked out, Kitchener replied, that 'that must be left to the commanders on the spot', and thereby shut down all discussion. No heed was given to the wider aspects of the plan – its immediate and potential needs in men, guns, ammunition, and supplies. In consequence, the expedition was to live from hand to mouth, nourishment being always too small and too late, yet in sum far exceeding what would originally have sufficed for success.

CHAPTER FIVE

SCENE 2

The Slip Twixt Lip and Cup – The Landing on Gallipoli, April 25th, 1915

Despite the chain of folly which preceded it, was there still a chance of success when the belated land attack on the Dardanelles was launched? The verdict of history is affirmative. Part, if not all, of the opportunity forfeited by the British was redeemed for them by the Turks.

The panic caused by the opening of the naval attack, and the feeling that the passage of the Dardanelles could not be prevented, led the Turks to order new military dispositions which, in the words of Liman von Sanders, head of the German Military Mission, 'did away with any defence of the exterior coast of the Gallipoli peninsula with its dominating heights; it did away with the defence of the Asiatic coast at the mouth of the Dardanelles. It was the feeblest imaginable defensive measure.' That it was not put into operation may have been due to Liman von Sanders' protests – with which, however, Enver replied that he did not concur – but was more probably due to pure inertia.

The absence of renewed naval attacks after the failure of March 18th was, rightly, taken as a sign that a land attack was being prepared, and this assurance was confirmed by abundant reports from various Mediterranean ports, especially Alexandria and Port Said. This was the less surprising in that public reviews of the troops were held at Alexandria and Cairo, while at least one member of Ian Hamilton's staff received official letters from home through the ordinary post, addressed 'Constantinople Field Force'. Any chance of secrecy had indeed disappeared, with the necessity of disembarking the force in Egypt.

Thus, on March 25th, Enver was led to form a separate army for the defence of the Dardanelles, and to place it under the command of Liman von Sanders. After a hurried survey Liman exclaimed to his subordinate, Hans Kannengiesser – 'If the English will only leave me

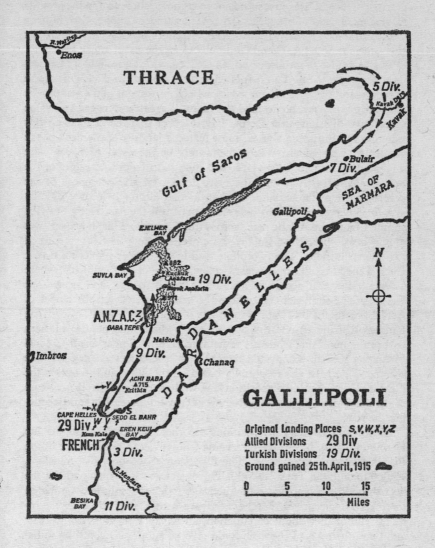

THRACE

5 Div.

Kavak Dere

Kavak

Gulf of Saros

•Bulair
7 Div.

SEA OF
MARMARA

Gallipoli

EJELMER
BAY

▲882
Kuchuk
Anafarta   19 Div.
Buyuk Anafarta

SUVLA BAY

A.N.Z.A.C.
GABA TEPE

9 Div.
Imbros

Maidos

Chanaq

ACHI BABA
▲715
•Krithia

CAPE HELLES
29 Div.   SEDD EL BAHR
Kum Kale   EREN KEUL
FRENCH   BAY

3 Div.

R. Mendere

BESIKA
BAY   11 Div.

GALLIPOLI

Original Landing Places S,V,W,X,Y,Z
Allied Divisions   29 Div
Turkish Divisions   19 Div.
Ground gained 25th.April,1915

0   5   10   15
Miles

N

alone for eight days.' They left him for four weeks. This month of grace, he records, 'was just sufficient to complete the most indispensable arrangements and to bring the 3rd Division under Colonel Nicolai from Constantinople'. Its arrival brought his strength up to six divisions – six times the strength present on Gallipoli before the naval attack began.

But he found them dispersed 'as coastguards', and his first step was to concentrate them. To do this effectively he had to decide where to expect a landing. The Asiatic coast, where movement and an approach to his rear was easy, he deemed the point of greatest danger. And so he placed two divisions near Besika Bay to cover the line of forts on this side. On the European side he most feared a landing at the neck of the peninsula, near Bulair, where the waters of the Gulf of Saros were separated by a mere three-and-a-half-mile strip from the waters of the Sea of Marmara. A landing here would cut off the defenders of the peninsula from Thrace and Constantinople, although if they did not lose their nerve they might be able to maintain themselves by drawing supplies from the Asiatic side, across the Narrows. This, however, was only a possibility. Near Bulair, therefore, Liman von Sanders posted two more divisions. The two other, and lesser danger points were near Gaba Tepe at the six-mile waist – a low waist – of the peninsula, where a wide valley ran across to Maidos at the Narrows; and near Cape Helles, at the southern end, where the gradual ascent up the slopes of Achi Baba might be swept by the fire of the British fleet. Liman von Sanders distributed one division to guard the whole of the southern part of the peninsula while his remaining division, under Lieut-Colonel Mustapha Kemal, was posted near the waist as a general reserve. The scheme of defence was essentially based on mobility, and to obtain the utmost value from his dispositions, as well as to offset the British ease of sea movement, he concentrated his energy on increasing and improving the roads.

Liman von Sanders' dispositions are the best justification for Ian Hamilton's plan. In this the governing factors were the small size of the British force and its mission. The force comprised only five divisions, 75,000 men to the Turks' 84,000. The object was to open a path for the fleet through the Narrows, not to engage independently in a campaign for big strategic prizes. Kitchener's bare instructions 'strongly deprecated', although without explanation, an advance on the Asiatic side; and there the guns of the fleet could give no support beyond the initial landing. The Gulf of Saros was obviously the most vulnerable strategic point but, as Liman von Sanders himself has pointed out, 'it afforded no direct artillery effect against' the defences of the straits. Moreover, the beaches near Bulair were seen to be strongly prepared for defence, while a landing on the west side of the Gulf would be uncomfortably close to the Bulgarian frontier, and with difficult country to traverse. In either case, a small force would be in danger of being itself attacked in flank and rear from the mainland of Thrace, and so being caught between two devils and the deep sea.

Weighing up these conditions, and his handicaps, Ian Hamilton decided on a dual blow in the southern half of the peninsula. The 29th Division was to land on four beaches at the toe and seize Achi Baba, while the French waited in support, meanwhile sending a regiment to land at Kum Kale on the Asiatic side as a feint and distraction. The two divisions of the Australian and New Zealand Army Corps – whose initials were to enrich both dictionary and history with the word 'Anzac' – were to land north of Gaba Tepe, while the Royal Naval Division made a feint near Bulair.

If the idea of security seems to have dictated the landing at the toe, surprise was to be its effect. And surprise was assiduously sought in manifold ways. Commander Unwin was inspired by the proximity of Troy to make the apt suggestion of reproducing the immortal wooden horse – in this case to be a sea-horse. A collier, the *River Clyde*, was to be run ashore at V Beach and to disgorge troops through large openings cut in its sides. Ian Hamilton himself added another stratagem – which had some parallel to Wolfe's at Quebec – whereby a detachment of two battalions was to be landed farther up the coast at a spot apparently inaccessible, and so unlikely to be defended, whence it could menace the rear of the Turks defending the southern beaches. This spot was christened Y Beach. Further, the French transports were to make a pretence of landing troops at Besika Bay. Ian Hamilton also wished to increase the chance of local surprise, and decrease the risk of loss, by landing at night, even though it meant forgoing the support of the guns of the fleet. But Hunter-Weston, commanding the 29th Division, preferred a daylight landing, to avoid the risk of confusion. He gained his way through the support of naval opinion, which was based on the difficulties of the current. For the Anzac landing, the corps commander, Birdwood, wisely preferred any risk to that of the obvious, and if his landing was to suffer in effect through confusion – which was more due to lack of training than to initial loss of direction in the dark – it escaped the heavy losses of the 29th Division.

By April 20th the preparations for the venture were complete and the troops assembled at Mudros on their transports. The weather, almost continuously unfavourable for several weeks, was both the determining and the most uncertain factor. Not until the 23rd did it allow the scheme to be set in motion. For the mechanism, like an alarm clock, required, and was timed to strike, thirty-six hours from the start of the movement.

On the evening of the 24th eleven transports of the Royal Naval Division sailed for the Gulf of Saros, escorted by warships which opened a slow bombardment at daybreak on the Bulair lines. Towards evening boats were ostentatiously swung out, filled with troops, and began pulling for the shore – to return to the ships as soon as darkness cloaked them. During the night an officer, Lieut-Commander B. C. Freyberg, swam ashore from a boat two miles out and lit flares along the beach. His feat, and its effect, was an outstanding proof that in war it is the man, and not men, who count – that one man can be more useful than a thousand.

For the Gaba Tepe landing, 1,500 men of the covering force were carried in three battleships to the rendezvous five miles offshore. They clambered down into the boats at 1.30 AM just as the moon was sinking. Then, towed by the battleships and followed by seven destroyers with the rest of the covering force, they moved silently inshore until the distance was halved. Here the twelve 'tows', each with a steam picket boat at the head, cast loose and continued the approach. But darkness and the strong current caused the tows to arrive off the beach a mile north of the intended point, and so on a more rugged part of the coast, skirted by precipitous cliffs, seamed with steep gullies and covered with scrub. Day was just breaking when at 4.25 AM, under a scattered and erratic fire from a few small and stupefied posts, the forty-eight boats were rowed across the last fifty yards until they touched bottom. Then, in a headlong rush and scramble, the Australians swept inland. Hardly a man had fallen, but units were badly mixed, and soon became worse. The next contingent landed from the destroyers, suffered rather more, at least on the left, but carried the advance over a mile inland. One small party even penetrated far enough to see the glistening straits beyond and beneath.

The Helles landing was less fortunate, although the opponents were little more numerous. Only two Turkish battalions were present in the whole area south of Achi Baba, and only two of the five selected landing places were covered by wire entanglements and machine guns. These were the central beaches W and V on either side of Cape Helles itself. The British covering force comprised the four battalions of Hare's 86th Brigade, which with an extra half battalion were to land at V, W, and X Beaches; one battalion at S Beach; and two battalions at Y Beach for the threat to the enemy's rear. Thus seven and a half battalions were to be thrown ashore initially, followed by five more of the main body, and ultimately by the French division. At 5 AM, under cover of a heavy fleet bombardment, the tows crept towards the shore. The first mischance was the slow progress, against the current, of the tows making for S Beach, on the east flank, which caused those destined for the three main beaches to be held back until nearly 6 AM. Nevertheless, the tows for X Beach, round the western tip of the peninsula, landed without a casualty beneath a low cliff, where their arrival was unexpected by the Turks and opposed only by a picket of twelve men. But at W, the next beach eastwards, the landing parties ran into a well-prepared death trap. Not a shot was fired as the boats rowed in but, as they grounded, they were swept by bullets and the men, jumping overboard, were entangled in submerged wire. Despite heavy loss they struggled forward, drove off the defenders, and gained a lodgement on the cliffs. But Hare, too gallantly exposing himself, was wounded, and the effort subsided.

The landing at V Beach, beside the old fort of Sedd el Bahr, fared still worse. Here the invaders ran, like gladiators, into a gently sloping arena designed by nature and arranged by the Turks – themselves ensconced in surrounding seats – for a butchery. The tows, checked by the current, were caught up by the *River Clyde*, and as it grounded hell yawned. In the incoming boats oars dropped like the wings of scorched moths, while the boats drifted helplessly with their load of dead and wounded. Many men jumped overboard only to be drowned in water stained with their own blood. A few gained the beach and found shelter beneath a low bank – which was to mark the limit of the day's advance. Those who tried to emerge from the *River Clyde*, and reach the shore across a bridge of lighters, were no more fortunate, and fell in heaps. The few survivors on the beach and the thousand left in the *River Clyde* could only wait for nightfall to release them. Two companies of Turks, distributed between V and W Beaches, had checked the main British landing.

But S Beach, at the other side of Morto Bay, was, like X, an unlikely spot and so guarded by only a platoon of Turks. The landing battalion got safely ashore and then, having had preliminary instructions to await the advance from the other beaches, fulfilled them to the letter. Its inertness, however, was approved by Hunter-Weston, owing apparently to an exaggerated estimate of the Turkish strength. Actually the two intact battalions ashore at the two flank beaches, S and X, totalled four times the strength of the Turkish defenders of V and W Beaches, and by an advance inwards could have taken them in rear.

Soon, also, that superiority was increased – but not the pressure. Two battalions of the 87th Brigade (the other two had been used for the original landings at S and Y) were put ashore safely on X Beach by 9 AM, but they had been earmarked as divisional reserve, and the Brigadier did not feel justified in using them, except to dig in, unless and until he received instructions from Hunter-Weston. These never came, so the force at Beach X remained passive.

Meantime, after another vain attempt to land at V Beach – in which the commander of the 88th Brigade was killed – the remaining two and a half battalions of the main body were disembarked at W Beach. 'But,' as the official history gently says, 'in contrast to the gallant exploits of the morning a certain inertia seems to have overtaken the troops on this part of the front, who now amounted to at least 2,000 men ... Faced with a definite task – the capture of the beaches – the 29th Division had put an indelible mark on history. But once that task was done, platoon, company and even battalion commanders, each in their own sphere, were awaiting fresh and definite orders, and on their own initiative did little to exploit the morning's success or to keep in touch with the enemy.' Instead, they allowed themselves to be paralysed by an enemy 'whom they had already driven from his trenches and whom, though unaware of the fact, they outnumbered by at least six to one'.

But a still greater opportunity was missed at Y Beach, three miles up the coast, where '2,000 men were safely disembarked without a hitch and without any opposition. For eleven hours they were left undisturbed by the enemy, and throughout that period they alone were equal in numbers to all the Turkish forces south of Achi Baba. Yet throughout the 25th the initial success remained unexploited. During the ensuing night the troops gallantly repulsed a succession of fierce attacks on their line. But the whole enterprise was suddenly abandoned next morning, and the men re-embarked, at the very moment when the enemy himself was in full retreat'.

The one man who realized the opportunity was Ian Hamilton himself, out at sea; but he had delegated the execution of the landing to the commander of the 29th Division, and had kept no reserve. Somewhat naturally, he was loth to interfere except by suggestion, though he was far quicker than the man on the spot to appreciate the check in the south, and as early as 9.21 AM he signalled to Hunter-Weston – 'Would you like to get some more men ashore at Y Beach? If so, trawlers are available.' But Hunter-Weston's attention was glued to the bloody beaches where the enemy was better prepared, and there he preferred to concentrate his efforts.

At Y Beach itself the landing had been made without a shot being fired or a Turk being discovered. But the commander, Colonel Matthews, was content to await further orders. 'Crowds of troops were ... sitting about the edge of the cliff', and not until late in the afternoon did they even attempt to entrench. Towards dark one Turkish battalion was brought up and launched a series of counter-attacks against the two British battalions. Repeatedly beaten off, the Turks finally fled in disorder soon after 7 AM; but their night assaults caused such loss and confusion among the defenders that panic spread. A string of alarmist messages were signalled to the ships and many stragglers poured down to the beach, swarming into the boats sent for the wounded. This state continued even after the disappearance of the Turks, and Matthews, who saw no response to his urgent appeal for reinforcements, reluctantly decided to follow the example set by his stragglers. By 11.30 AM the whole force had re-embarked. Some hours later a naval party under Lieut-Commander Keyes went ashore and made a prolonged search for wounded without being fired on.

But if anything can justify Matthews' action, and previous inaction, it is his utter neglect by his superior, Hunter-Weston. Throughout the twenty-nine hours on land 'no word of any kind reached him from divisional headquarters'. No officer was sent to visit him, no reply was sent to his urgent appeals. And when, early in the morning of the 26th Ian Hamilton once more intervened with the offer of a French brigade (six battalions), Hunter-Weston had no thought but to land them on W Beach – in the enemy's face. The measured verdict of the official history upon Y Beach is that – 'In deciding to throw a force ashore at that point Sir Ian Hamilton would seem to have hit upon the key of the whole situation ... it is as certain as anything can be in war that a bold advance from Y, on the morning of the April 25th, must have freed the southern beaches that morning, and ensured a decisive victory for the 29th Division.'

At Anzac, too, a great opportunity went begging, although here the initiative of one opponent, the then unknown Mustapha Kemal, contributed to its unfulfilment. The surprise landing had placed 4,000 men before 5 AM, and another 4,000 before 8 AM, on a shore guarded by only one Turkish company. The next company was more than a mile to the south, two battalions and a battery in local reserve were four miles inland, and still farther away lay the general reserve of eight battalions and three batteries, commanded by Mustapha Kemal. He was out watching a regiment at training, when suddenly a number of gendarmes, bareheaded and weaponless, came running frantically towards him, crying – 'They come, they come.' 'Who comes?' 'Inglis, Inglis.' He turned to ask, 'Have we ball cartridges?' 'Yes.' 'All right. Forward.' Leading a company himself, and leaving the rest of the regiment to follow, he raced to the great dividing ridge of Chunuk Bair in time (about 10 AM) to cross the crest and check the leading Australians as they were climbing up the steeper slopes on the west. Until now barely 500 Turks had been available to hold up 8,000 Australians, but henceforth the defenders were to be augmented steadily until by nightfall six battalions (perhaps 5,000 men) had been brought up, and from 4 PM onwards launched in a series of counter-attacks which forced back but failed to break the ragged Australian line. Both sides had suffered about 2,000 casualties, the Turks far more heavily in proportion, but the raw Australians were in unknown country, under fire for the first time, and the moral effect of the shrapnel from the enemy's handful of guns was made worse by the absence of their own. Although 15,000 men were ashore by 6 PM, the front was but a thin and much-intermixed line, and the beach was crowded with leaderless men who had drifted back – many because they had lost themselves rather than lost their nerve. But the sight naturally confirmed the fears of the commanders, themselves in rear, and so gloomy was their report to Birdwood, when he landed at 10 PM, that he sent a message to Ian Hamilton saying – 'Both my divisional commanders and brigadiers have represented to me that they fear their men are thoroughly demoralized by shrapnel fire ... If troops are to be subjected to shell fire again tomorrow morning there is likely to be a fiasco ... if we are to re-embark it must be at once.' All available boats were ordered to be sent to the beach.

Only by a fluke did the message ever reach the Commander-in-Chief, for in the hurry it was not addressed to anyone; but, being thrust into the hands of the beach-master, who was going out to the flagship, he handed it when there to Admiral Thursby. After reading it, Thursby decided to go ashore to discuss the re-embarkation with Birdwood, but at that moment the *Queen Elizabeth*, with Ian Hamilton on board, unexpectedly arrived from Helles, so that Thursby went instead to report to him. Thus by a chain of happy mishaps Birdwood's grave message reached Ian Hamilton in time.

Insight must have guided him in an extraordinarily difficult decision, for no other guidance, or comfort, was available, and no time to obtain it. The reply which he wrote was epitomized in its postscript – 'You have got through the difficult business. Now you have only to dig, dig, dig, until you are safe.'

Like a fresh breeze this definite and confident order dispersed the rumour-laden and gloomy atmosphere on the beach. The rear ceased to talk about evacuation and the front did not know that the rear had been talking about it. When morning broke there was also a respite from the real enemy, for Mustapha Kemal had no further reserves with which to renew his counter-attack, and the shrapnel from his few guns was no longer a terror to troops now safely dug in. Indeed, it was the Turk who suffered demoralization – from the guns of the fleet, and especially the huge 15-inch shells of the *Queen Elizabeth*.

Could the lost opportunity still have been regained? History answers, 'Yes.' And the reason lies in the profound impression made, by Ian Hamilton's original plan, on the mind of the enemy Commander-in-Chief. Liman von Sanders records of the first day, April 25th, that – 'From the many pale faces among the officers reporting in the early morning, it was apparent that, although a hostile landing had been expected with certainty, a landing at so many points surprised and disquieted them.' 'We could not discern at the time where the enemy was actually seeking a decision.' The last sentence is an euphemism, for Liman von Sanders actually thought that the place where the British were merely making a bluff was the place where they were seeking a decision. If he kept his head he lost his sense of direction.

His first act was to order his 7th Division to march from the town of Gallipoli to Bulair. His next, to gallop thither himself. And there he stayed while the critical struggle was in progress at the other end of the peninsula. Not until evening would he even spare five battalions, out of his two divisions around Bulair, to go to the real battle zone, and not until over forty-eight hours after the British landing did he release the remainder.

But the extension of the opportunity was of no avail to the British. Partly for want of fresh troops – when so many, in comparison, were locked up in the Western Front safe-deposit. But partly, also, for want of effort from those who had landed. Ian Hamilton's optimism, although justified, was not shared by his subordinate commanders on the morning of the 26th. It was not merely the Anzac force which remained passive. At Helles, Hunter-Weston, appreciating the tiredness of his troops but not the weakness of the enemy, gave up any idea of advancing until French reinforcements arrived. Expecting a Turkish onslaught, and fearing the result, he issued the order, 'Every man will die at his post rather than retire.' So far from attacking, the Turks went back to a new line in front of Krithia. Well they might, for their total strength here up to the 27th was only five battalions, and casualties had reduced them to a real strength scarcely more than the original two.

Not until the 28th was a new attack attempted, and by then the Franco-British force had almost lost its advantage of numbers and suffered the disadvantages of ignorance of the ground, thirst, increased tiredness, besides complicating its task by combining the attack with a right wheel. The small gains were lost to Turkish counter-attacks, and near the coast the line wavered and broke. The danger here was averted by a single shell from the *Queen Elizabeth*. It burst its 24,000 shrapnel bullets right in the midst of the onrushing mass of Turks, and when the dust cleared not a Turk was to be seen. But by nightfall the whole 29th Division was back at its starting point. Meantime the troops at Anzac were reorganizing and making their front secure. But so also were the Turks, and thus the Anzac force was locked in a tiny cell only one and a half miles long and half a mile deep, while the Turk looked down from the 'roof' upon the arrested trespassers.

The almost blank credit side of the Allied balance sheet was now relieved by a Turkish contribution. Urged on by Enver's peremptory order 'to drive the invaders into the sea', Liman von Sanders launched massed bayonet attacks on the nights of May 1st and 3rd. Several thousand dead were heaped as a sacrifice before the Allied front, which was only, and momentarily, endangered in the French sector.

The Turks' forfeit was soon redeemed – by the British. Two brigades were brought from Anzac and a new brigade, of Territorials, came from Egypt. Even so, the Allied force at Helles could only bring a fighting strength of 25,000 against a Turkish strength now raised to nearly 20,000. And, in the issue, it did not even test their strength. The Allied attack arranged for May 6th suffered every possible disadvantage. It was purely frontal, on a narrow three-mile front, against un-located positions, with an extreme shortage of shells, and a shortage of aircraft to observe the fire, at the shortest notice – Hunter-Weston's orders were not issued to brigades until 4 AM for an attack to begin at 11 AM. Once more the control of the battle and the last remaining reserves were handed over to Hunter-Weston by Ian Hamilton – 'All that was left to him', as the official history says, 'of the high office of Commander-in-Chief was its load of responsibility'.

Fatigue rather than resistance foiled the attack. The troops, worn out by strain and lack of sleep, had not even the energy to press on to the slaughter, and they did not even push back the Turks' advanced posts. As the best remedy for lack of rest Hunter-Weston ordered a fresh effort next morning. This was no more effective, except in draining the ammunition almost to zero. So a third attack was ordered for the third morning. In this the loss at least was confined to a smaller circle, by launching four weak battalions of New Zealanders, in daylight, against a position held by nine Turkish battalions. Then Ian Hamilton, finding that three brigades were still in reserve, himself intervened. The whole Allied line was to 'fix bayonets, slope arms, and move on Krithia precisely at 5.30 PM'. This produced heavy casualties, if nothing else. The attacking force had lost a third of its strength in the three days. Thereafter the front of the two small footholds gained by the Allies inevitably relapsed into stagnation, which soon froze solidly as the Turks converted their hasty defences into an organized trench system.

Now, at last, Ian Hamilton was driven to ask for reinforcements, and to awake the Government to his serious need and situation. Hitherto, although conscious of the inadequacy of his force, he had been too loyal to Kitchener, and perhaps too aware of his old chief's arbitrary methods, to worry him by importunate demands. Before leaving England he had been told that 75,000 men would and must suffice, that even the 29th Division was but a temporary loan, and the fact that Kitchener had warned Maxwell, the commander in Egypt, to help him with additional troops, was not communicated to him by Maxwell despite Kitchener's explicit instructions. Lack of ammunition was another handicap, and when he called attention to it the War Office reply merely told him that it was 'important to push on'. Yet, almost simultaneously with his vain three days' attack, May 6th to 8th, in which he could only use 18,500 shells, Haig was expending 80,000 on Aubers ridge in one day – for less result, a far less object, and twice the loss of life. Up to a point, the astonishing feature of Gallipoli was how near Ian Hamilton came to success with his inferior forces and resources.

His oft-criticized choice of landing place could hardly have been improved on if, by supernatural power, he had been able to know the enemy's mind and dispositions. By avoiding the natural line of expectation, the pitfall of commonplace generalship, and by distracting the enemy's attention to that line, he ensured his own troops an immense superiority of force at the actual landing places – although his total force was less than that of the Turks. The enemy commander let his attention be so fixed on Bulair that for forty-eight hours after the British were ashore their immediate opponents were denied adequate reinforcements. This fact is the best answer to the common criticism that Ian Hamilton should have struck at Bulair, a point so obvious to everyone at home that, curiously, it was also obvious to the enemy. Another popular criticism is that Ian Hamilton dispersed his force at too many points and should have concentrated his effort on one small sector. This is answered not only by the 'pale faces' of which Liman von Sanders tells, but by the next three years' experience of this abortive method on the Western Front – experience which was purchased at an infinitely greater cost.

Perhaps, as an alternative landing place, also in the least-defended area, Suvla Bay might have offered the advantages of Ian Hamilton's choice with less disadvantages. But in April accurate information was lacking and exaggerated faith placed in the effect of the naval guns at Helles.

Another reasonable criticism is that the British power of rapid sea movement might have been utilized more fully – to withdraw troops where checked before they were deeply committed and switch them to reinforce the unopposed landings or to fresh points. Thereby the lack of reserves might have been partly compensated through the power to create fresh ones by 'switching'. This, indeed, had been suggested to Braithwaite, the Chief of Staff, on the day before the landing by Captain Aspinall, an officer of the General Staff. He urged that the plan should be adapted to meet the contingency that either or both the landings at Anzac and Helles might fail. An equal or greater fault in the plan was that it failed to provide for partial success, the most probable case in war, and left no 'floating' reserve in the hands of the Commander-in-Chief ready for prompt application at the most promising point ashore. Unhappily, both the plan and the execution suffered from lack of the elasticity which is an essential axiom in war. And the partial success of both landings in the first phase tended to harden the design – until it became hard and stuck fast.

For years controversy has centred round the incubation period of the Dardanelles project, and the plan which was evolved. More depressing is the later revelation of the opportunities thrown away after the force had landed – lost opportunities hitherto obscured by a halo of romance.

CHAPTER FIVE

SCENE 3

The Gas Cloud at Ypres –
April 22nd, 1915

The sun was sinking behind Ypres. Its spring radiance had breathed life that day into the dead town and the mouldering trench lines which guarded it. A month hence the town would be a shell with all the eerie moonlit grandeur of a greater Colosseum. Three years hence it would be merely a vast ant-heap of tumbled ruins. But on that 22nd day of April, 1915, it had merely the dreariness of incomplete abandonment, momentarily relieved by the fragrance of a spring day's sunshine.

As that fragrance faded with the waning sun, even the guns became silent, and an evening hush spread over the scene as if in awed awaiting of a benediction. The hush was false; purely a prelude to the devil's malediction, with organ pealing, censers swinging. At five o'clock a fearful din of guns broke out and heavy shells struck with reverberating crash on Ypres and many villages rarely or never touched before; and to the nostrils of men nearer the front came the smell of a devilish incense. Those nearer still to the trenches north of Ypres saw two curious wraiths of greenish-yellow fog creep forward, spread until they became one and then, moving forward, change to a blue-white mist. It hung, as it had come, over the front of the two French divisions, one Algerian, one Territorial, which joined up with the British, and held the left of the salient. Soon, officers behind the British front and near the canal bridges, were startled to see a torrent of terrified humanity pouring backward. The Africans, nearest the British, were coughing and pointing to their throats as they fled; mingled with them soon came horse-teams and wagons. The French guns were still firing, but at 7 PM these suddenly and ominously became silent.

The fugitives left behind them a gap in the front over four miles wide, filled only by the dead and by those who lay suffocating in agony from chlorine gas-poisoning. Otherwise the two French divisions had

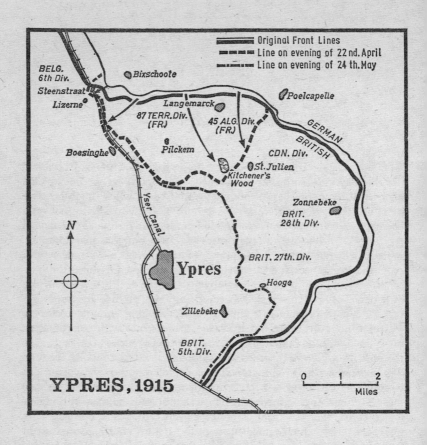

Original Front Lines
Line on evening of 22nd. April
Line on evening of 24th. May

BELG.
6th Div.

Bixschoote

Steenstraat
Lizerne

Langemarck

Poelcapelle

87 TERR.DIV.
(FR)

45 ALG. Div.
(FR)

GERMAN

BRITISH

Boesinghe

Pilckem

CDN. DIV.

St. Julien
Kitchener's
Wood

Yser Canal

N

Zonnebeke

BRIT.
28th Div.

BRIT. 27th. Div.

Ypres

Hooge

Zillebeke

BRIT.
5th. Div.

YPRES, 1915

0   1   2
                Miles

almost completely disappeared. With the aid of gas the Germans had removed the defenders on the north flank of the salient as deftly as if extracting the back teeth from one side of a jaw. The remaining teeth in front and on the south flank of the salient were formed by the Canadian Division (Alderson), nearest the gap, the 28th Division (Bulfin), and the 27th Division (Snow), which together comprised Plumer's 5th Corps. The Germans had only to push south for four miles to reach Ypres, and loosen all these teeth by pressure from the rear. That evening they walked forward two miles and then, curiously, stopped. The space of four and a half miles between the raw edge of the Canadian front and the canal which formed the chord of the salient, was only filled by a few small posts, taken up hastily by packets of French and Canadians hitherto in reserve, and between these posts there were three untenanted gaps of 2,000 yards, 1,000 yards, and 3,000 yards, respectively. Yet on May 1st the Germans had only advanced a few hundred yards farther. And when the fighting at last died down, at the end of May, the only outward change was that the nose of the salient had been flattened – mainly by a voluntary British withdrawal. But, in curious contrast to normal experience, it was the defenders who had lost most heavily. The British loss was 59,000, nearly double that suffered by the Germans who attacked them.

Why did the gas come as so complete a surprise? Why did the Germans fail to exploit such a surprise? Why did the British escape disaster when taken unawares by the French collapse and yet suffer so disproportionately when the Germans had forfeited their advantage? These are the three crucial questions of 'Second Ypres'.

Towards the end of March, prisoners taken on the south of the salient, then held by the French, gave full details of the way that gas cylinders had been stored in the trenches, and of its method of discharge. Perhaps because they were about to be relieved, the French commanders took no action in regard to this warning, although, curiously, the details appear in the Bulletin of the French Tenth Army, away down in Picardy, for March 30th.

An even more complete and localized warning came on April 13th, when a German deserter gave himself up near Langemarck to the French 11th Division, then holding the sector, and related that 'cylinders with asphyxiating gas [had been] placed in batteries of twenty cylinders for every forty metres along the front'. 'At a given signal – three red rockets fired by the artillery – the cylinders will be opened and the escaping gas will be carried by a favourable wind towards the French trenches ... In order to guard against being poisoned by the gas, each German soldier is in possession of a packet of tow soaked in oxygen' – the deserter handed over one of these embryo gas masks in proof of his statement. The French divisional commander, General Ferry, gravely impressed, warned the French division on his left, the British 28th Division on his right, and the Canadian division – which took over part of his front two days later while the Algerian divison took over the rest. More significant still, Ferry warned his corps commander, Balfourier, and the liaison officer from Joffre's headquarters, who came to visit him.

How did these two key men react? Balfourier deemed Ferry a credulous fool and ignored his suggestions that the German trenches should be shelled in order to destroy the cylinders, and that the number of men in the front line, exposed to the gas danger, should be reduced. The liaison officer not only dismissed the story as a myth, but reproved Ferry, first, for warning the British direct, and, second, for taking steps to reduce the garrison of the front line contrary to Joffre's doctrine. And, following the usual happy custom of the French Army, Ferry was thereafter punished by removal for being right.

General Putz, who, with his two divisions, took over the left of the salient from Balfourier, was no more inclined to believe the story than Balfourier, although a fresh warning came from Belgian sources on April 16th. Putz mentioned the story scoffingly to the British liaison officer from Smith-Dorrien's Second Army, but apparently did not think it worth repeating to his own troops. So they waited in ignorance until suffocation overtook them.

The only measures taken were by the British. Aircraft reconnaissances were made, but failed to observe anything unusual, and Plumer passed the warning to his divisional commanders 'for what it was worth'. No precautions against gas were suggested or ordered, and in the next few days even the fact of the warning was forgotten – perhaps all the easier because it sounded such an 'ungentlemanly' novelty. Yet acquaintance with the German practice of getting in the first verbal blow might well have made the British Command suspect the sinister significance of the German wireless *communiqué* of April 17th – 'Yesterday, east of Ypres, the British employed shells and bombs with asphyxiating gas.'

But one factor which undoubtedly lulled suspicion of an attack was the lack of any sign that the Germans were concentrating reserves for it. This lack of signs was due, not to special precautions, but to the lack of such reserves. And thereby the Germans lost the opportunity created by the most complete surprise of the war.

As scientifically hidebound as its opponents, the German Supreme Command had little faith in the new weapon. So little, that for want of facilities the inventor, Haber, had to use cylinders mainly for projection instead of shells. A discharge of gas from cylinders must be dependent on a favourable wind and, as a westerly or south-westerly wind was the most frequent in Flanders, the Germans thus offered a hostage to fortune. Disclosing their new weapon prematurely and for a paltry prize, they gave their opponents the advantage in retaliation until sufficient gas shell was produced to replace gas cylinders.

However weak their faith, it is incredible, but for the result, that the Germans should have neglected to be ready for a possible success. Yet, actually, Falkenhayn allotted no fresh reserves for the attack, and even refused the request for extra ammunition. Falkenhayn's idea was merely to try the gas as an experimental aid to an attack which itself was merely a cloak to his projected blow against the Russians. If the Ypres salient could be erased, so much the better, but he did not take any longer view.

Originally the attack was to be launched by the XV Corps against the southern side of the salient, and the gas cylinders were in position by March 10th. But the attack had to be postponed repeatedly for want of a favourable wind, and towards the end of March an alternative attack was prepared on the north side of the salient. Intended for April 15th, this in turn was delayed a week. It was then launched by the two divisions of the XXVI Reserve Corps, with one division of the XXIII Reserve Corps attacking on their right. As an aid to the main thrust the other division of the XXIII Reserve Corps was to strike at Steenstraat which was both the hinge of the salient and the junction between the French and the Belgians. Unaided by gas this subsidiary attack made little progress. Only one division was available in army reserve, and this was not released until next day, and was then given to the XXIII Reserve Corps, not to the XXVI, which had an open gap before it.

But if lack of reserves was the fundamental cause of the Germans' failure, the immediate cause was the troops' fear of their own gas. They had only been issued with the crudest form of respirator, which many of them did not even wear; no special tactics had been thought out; and, after passing through the gasping and agonized men who littered the French trenches, they were only too willing to comply with the letter of their limited orders, and dig in as soon as they reached the short-distance objective that had been assigned. The failing light, too, prevented them discovering the extent of their success and the weakness of the few stout-hearted knots of Canadians who were strung across their path. And during the succeeding days they were equally content to act as camp-followers to their artillery, merely taking a short step forward to occupy and consolidate such fresh patches of ground as the guns and gas had swept practically clear of defenders. However shortsighted during the first days, when opportunity lay open to their embrace, this pure siege warfare method was good sense later. It foreshadowed the Verdun method of a year later, and, thanks to Foch, the Allies helped to make it most profitable to the Germans.

Foch was then, as Joffre's deputy, in higher control of the French troops in Flanders, and charged with the duty of coordinating the efforts of the French, British and Belgians. On hearing the news of the German breakthrough, he ordered Putz to make sure of holding his ground, now the line of the canal, and to organize a counter-attack to regain the ground he had lost. But the French had lost their artillery and all they could do was to fulfil the first point. Fortunately, the Belgians baffled the German efforts to break the hinge. Putz, however, told the British that he would be counter-attacking, and to aid him two Canadian battalions made a midnight counter-attack. They penetrated the new German line, and captured Kitchener's Wood, but as no French attack developed they had to withdraw from it later. Next day, the British, scraping together a few handfuls of reserves, attempted further petty counter-attacks which naturally failed at heavy cost, as they were delivered in daylight and with negligible support from the French and from artillery. By evening on the 23rd, however, the broad way to Ypres and the British rear was almost filled, although by only twenty-one and a half sorely weakened British battalions (twelve of them Canadian), who faced forty-two German battalions – and a five-to-one superiority in guns.

Sir John French ordered a continuation of these vain efforts on the 24th – but the Germans anticipated him. At 3 AM they attacked the Belgian 'hinge' and were badly discomfited; henceforth they were unable either to widen or deepen their small foothold across the canal. At 4 AM they launched a heavy blow, with gas, against the jagged corner of the Canadians' front. No respirators were yet available and the only protection were handkerchiefs, towels and cotton bandoliers, wetted with the liquid most readily available in the trenches and placed over the mouth. Many men were overcome and, although there was only a small break in the line at the first onset, this gradually spread. For a time good artillery shooting prevented the Germans probing the breach, but in the afternoon they surged forward to and beyond St Julien. The situation looked critical, but a counter-attack by two Yorkshire Territorial battalions, helped by Canadian batteries firing over open sights, rolled the leading Germans back to St Julien. This slight taste of repulse sufficed to quench the Germans' thirst for further advance that day. But their irresolution was hidden from the eyes of the British commanders by the general confusion. In the patchwork line across the Germans' path, Canadians, British Regulars, Territorials, even Zouaves, of various divisions and brigades, were intermingled, clinging on wherever they had been pushed, like dabs of cement into a crumbling wall. The salient had now been compressed by German pressure into a narrow tongue of land, barely three miles across, although nearly six miles deep. Thus, in attempting to hold it, the defenders were now so crowded that they provided an easy harvest for the German guns.

Yet Sir John French, beguiled by the optimism of Foch and Putz, and the assurance that two fresh French divisions were coming up to retake the lost ground, was unwilling to sanction any withdrawal. Early on the 25th, the day of the Gallipoli landing, a fresh Regular brigade was brought up and thrown blindly into an attack near St Julien, there to be 'mown down like corn, by machine guns in enfilade'. With appalling swiftness 2,400 men were scythed – more loss than Ian Hamilton's army paid for the capture of the Gallipoli beaches. And that evening the bulk of the Canadian division was withdrawn into reserve, having lost some 5,000 men in its gallant efforts to battle against gas and heavy guns with their rifles, supplemented meagerly by guns that the official history terms 'the ancient and obsolete weapons of the South African War'. Nor did the burden of this hopeless struggle cease with the relief of the Canadians; it was merely shifted more fully to other shoulders. For another month operations were to continue, methodical German attacks answered by unmethodical British attacks. Lest I be thought to emphasize the futility unduly, let me quote the sober and sombre words of the official history:

The governing idea was that the French should restore the line lost by them, and that the British should assist ... General Foch ordered immediate counter-attacks which General Putz was not in a position to execute; whilst the British wholehearted attempts to carry out their share by means of offensive action, which was as a rule neither a true counter-attack nor a deliberately prepared attack, led to heavy losses without restoring the situation ... It seemed to the British officers at the front that they were being sacrificed to gain time until the French were ready for a big spectacular effort; but this, even if ever intended, did not materialize.

To study the cause of the tragedy we must shift our gaze from the front to the rear. After expending the Indian Lahore Division and the Northumberland Territorial Brigade in another vain attack on the 26th, with a loss of another 4,000 men, Smith-Dorrien realized the futility of such efforts and the improbability of French cooperation. Hence on the 27th he wrote to Robertson, the Chief of the General Staff, asking him to put the real situation before French, and saying – 'I am doubtful if it is worth losing any more men to regain this French ground, unless the French do something really big.' He further suggested that it would be wise to prepare for a withdrawal to a less acutely bent line nearer to Ypres. All that he got in reply was a telephone message from Robertson – 'Chief does not regard situation nearly so unfavourable as your letter represents.' In fact, however, Smith-Dorrien's letter was far more optimistic than the grim conditions justified. Yet this 'comforting' message from the comfortable and peacefully remote General Headquarters was followed by a still worse rebuff – a telegram, sent through unciphered, telling Smith-Dorrien to hand over command of all the troops engaged at Ypres to General Plumer, and also to send the latter his Chief of Staff, General Milne. Relations between French and Smith-Dorrien had become very strained ever since Smith-Dorrien had saved French's situation against his own orders at Le Cateau in August, 1914. Now, French, true to a habit of his namesakes, seized the chance to punish Smith-Dorrien for making a true diagnosis, and administered a public rebuff which left Smith-Dorrien no option but to send a hint that he would resign if desired. French instantly embraced it and ordered him to hand over his shrunken command and go home.

Nevertheless, Plumer's first instructions from French were to prepare the very withdrawal that Smith-Dorrien had tentatively proposed. Then French went off to see Foch at Cassel and came back with a different outlook. Foch argued vehemently against a withdrawal, said that the lost ground could be retaken by the troops already available, urged that a retirement 'should be forbidden', and begged French 'to support the French *offensive to retake the Langemarck region at all costs,* beginning at noon on the 29th'. The days that followed were a comedy behind the front, a tragedy for the troops in front. Day after day, French heard from his fighting subordinates of the sufferings of the men and of the continued absence of the ever-promised French offensive. Thereupon he would incline towards a withdrawal, only to be swung the other way by Foch's buoyant assurances and flattering entreaties.

Once more let us quote the official history:

For ill now, although for weal in the last year of the war, General Foch was the very spirit of the offensive ... Sir John French, though at first he had wholeheartedly complied with General Foch's wishes, appreciated the small result of the French efforts – or, rather, the smallness of the first efforts – and the heavy losses of his own troops crowded together in the small *place d'armes* of the narrowed salient ... Sir John French then became convinced that he must withdraw his troops, and passed from optimism to pessimism. It was naturally most difficult for his subordinates to follow his moods, particularly when his mind was on the border line between one phase of thought and the next, and when, at the entreaty of General Foch, he more than once agreed to wait a little longer before withdrawing his men – and to order one more counter-attack.

However, he clutched at a straw in the wind when, late on May 1st, Foch confessed that Joffre, so far from sending reinforcements, was calling for troops to be sent from Ypres to strengthen his forthcoming offensive near Arras. French forthwith sanctioned the long-planned withdrawal, by nightly stages, although only to a line some three miles short of Ypres, so that the front still formed a salient, if a flatter one. This was more inconvenient for defence and control than the original salient, the head being exposed to pounding from all sides while Ypres itself formed a dangerously narrow throat of supply and communication. The political and sentimental objection to yielding ground, especially Belgian ground, and the military desire to facilitate the task of any belated French effort, led Sir John French to overrule the fighting commanders' wish to withdraw to the natural straight line of defence formed by the ramparts of Ypres and the canal. So they stayed in the reduced salient, 'one huge artillery target', there to be pounded and gassed incessantly, with their scanty ammunition running out, until relief at last came, in the fourth week of May, through the Germans exhausting their own comparative superfluity of shells. For the Germans had at least the good sense to cease attacks when they came to the choice between economizing infantry lives and economizing artillery ammunition. All that the French had done in the interval was to clear the west bank of the canal, on May 15th, while the continued British bayonet attacks east of Ypres did not even succeed in preventing the Germans switching troops from the British sector to check the eventual small French attack – truly a mountain that was long in labour and brought forth a mouse. And having forfeited 60,000 men for the privilege of acting as midwife, the British were then left to hold the most uncomfortably cramped new salient, or target, at continued expense for over two years.

To throw good money after bad is foolish. But to throw away men's lives where there is no reasonable chance of advantage, is criminal. In the heat of battle mistakes in the command are inevitable and amply excusable. But the real indictment of leadership arises when attacks that are inherently vain are ordered merely because if they could succeed they would be useful. For such 'manslaughter', whether it springs from ignorance, a false conception of war or a want of moral courage, commanders should be held accountable to the nation.

CHAPTER FIVE

SCENE 4

The Unwanted Battle – Loos
(September 15th, 1915)

In early September the 'back of the front' in France was seething with rumours of a great Franco-British offensive which was to shatter the German front; and, if the atmosphere among the fighting troops was tense, it had also an exhilarating breath of confidence in the result. For the first time the New Armies and Territorials were to take a prominent part, and few seemed to expect that the joint hammer blows of British and French together could fail, at least, to dissolve the static trench warfare that had persisted for nearly a year. But there was one extreme contrast to this air of confidence – and that was in the headquarters of the British higher commanders.

For the ill-fated Loos offensive was undertaken directly against the opinion of Haig, the man who, as commander of the First Army, had to carry it out. Haig argued that the supply of heavy artillery and of shells was still inadequate, that its adequacy was the governing factor of the situation, and that until this weakness was remedied, it was little use to make plans for offensives. For in June the British Army still had only seventy-one heavy guns to 1,406 field guns, and the factories in England were turning out no more than 22,000 shells a day, compared to 100,000 by the French, and 250,000 by the Germans and Austrians – according to report.

Haig's view was by no means an isolated one. Robertson, Chief of the General Staff of the British Expeditionary Force, fully endorsed it, but his influence with his own Chief had been undermined by Sir Henry Wilson, who was a devout believer in the infallibility of French military judgement, and Robertson had even been excluded from Sir John French's personal mess. Meantime, Wilson, the friend and confidant of French, was proposing to Kitchener that the British Army should be divided into two groups, one to be located away in Lorraine, so as to

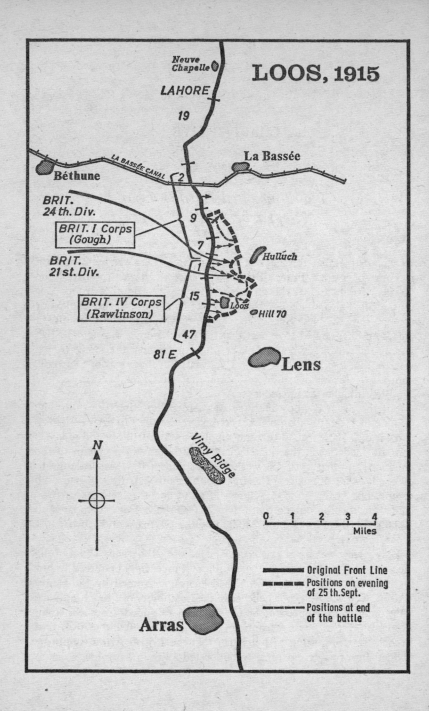

LOOS, 1915

Neuve Chapelle

LAHORE

19

LA BASSÉE CANAL

La Bassée

Béthune

2

BRIT.
24th. Div.

9

BRIT. I Corps
(Gough)

7

Hullúch

1

BRIT.
21st. Div.

15

BRIT. IV Corps
(Rawlinson)

Loos

Hill 70

47

81 E.

Lens

N

Vimy Ridge

0 1 2 3 4
Miles

———— Original Front Line

– – – – Positions on evening
of 25th. Sept.

—·—·— Positions at end
of the battle

Arras

ensure that French should be unable to take an independent attitude towards the French!

Equally emphatic, and pessimistic, was Sir Henry Rawlinson, who, under Haig, would have the main task with his army corps. He noted in his diary – 'My new front is as flat as the palm of my hand. Hardly any cover anywhere ... D.H. tells me that we are to attack "*au fond*", that the French are doing likewise and making a supreme effort. It will cost us dearly, and we shall not get very far.' He, however, was left no choice but to do that his men might die. For, in face of all these warnings, only too truly founded, the better judgement of the British commanders was overborne by Joffre's pressure.

The next revelation is that the instrument of this pressure was Lord Kitchener. It is a curious sidelight on one who had been among the first of British leaders to appreciate the state of deadlock in the west and to exclaim against the stubborn folly of seeking to pass the impassable. Kitchener had seen his January doubts fulfilled, and in June had bitterly remarked, as Poincaré has recorded – 'Joffre and Sir John [French] told me in November they were going to push the Germans back over the frontier; they gave me the same assurances in December, March, and May. What have they done? The attacks are very costly and end in nothing.' Yet he was now the determining factor in adding nought to nought.

How was this strange chain of causation forged? Joffre, spiritual twin of his subordinate Foch, in the sense of being an unquenchable optimist, was undeterred by his hard experiences of the spring from the repetition of them in the autumn. In his plan, two great convergent blows were to be delivered from the widely separated sectors of Artois (Arras–Lens) and Champagne (Reims–the Argonne), the former being originally intended as the main blow. Note this point, for it had a vital influence and suffered a vital alteration.

A successful breakthrough both in Champagne and Artois was to be the signal for a general offensive of all the French and British armies on the Western Front. This, Joffre confidently declared, would 'compel the Germans to retreat beyond the Meuse and possibly end the war'.

Yet, in the event, one and a third German divisions sufficed to break the back of the attack of the six British divisions north of Lens, and south of Lens the French attack by fourteen divisions was hardly even developed in face of five German divisions. What a majestic conception was this plan of Joffre's, and how utterly unrelated to the material conditions of modern warfare! And what painful evidence that professional strategy may be the sheerest 'amateur strategy'.

When Joffre's draft plan was sent on June 4th to Sir John French, the British Commander-in-Chief expressed his general agreement. Then a strong gust of common-sense came from his subordinate, Haig, and the military weathervane swung the other way.

Haig had made a personal reconnaissance of the area south of the La Bassée canal (La Bassée–Lens) and as a result declared definitely that it was 'not a favourable one for an attack'. His verdict was to prove most accurate. In his view the German defences were so strong that, until a great increase of heavy artillery was provided, they could only be taken by siege methods. 'The ground, for the most part bare and open, would be so swept by machine-gun and rifle fire both from the German front trenches and from the numerous fortified villages immediately behind them, that a rapid advance would be impossible.' He suggested that, if an offensive on the left of the French was imperative, subsidiary attacks only should be made south of the canal, and the main one delivered astride and north of it. But he concluded with the cold douche already mentioned.

Joffre, however, would not accept arguments for a postponement of the offensive or a change of site. He even remarked with that magisterial infallibility which is so delightful in retrospect, but in retrospect only, that 'your attack will find particularly favourable ground between Loos and La Bassée!' It was certainly both a simple and a magisterial way of brushing aside the adverse evidence of Haig, who had seen the ground.

Meanwhile the Germans, if not yet expecting an attack, were working with feverish energy to strengthen their defences and to create a second system in rear of the front. This was nearing completion by the end of July and knowledge of it accentuated Sir John French's doubts – under Haig's reiteration of his opinion. Hence a conference was arranged at Frévent on July 27th with Foch who, however, maintained that it was essential that, regardless of the ground and the strength of the enemy's defences, Haig's army should make its main attack just north of Lens in close connexion with the French Tenth Army south of Lens, pinching out this maze-like mining town.

The tug-of-war between Haig and French, and Joffre and Foch continued, with Sir John French seeking a way out through a project of cooperating with artillery fire alone. This was quashed and the tug-of-war decided by the intervention of Kitchener. Visiting Sir John French in August, he told him that 'we must act with all energy and do our utmost to help France in this offensive, even though by so doing we may suffer very heavy losses'.

In this reversal of his own previous attitude, he was apparently influenced by the disasters then occurring on the Russian front, and his feeling of the urgent need to succour our Russian Allies, as well, perhaps, by his reaction from the disappointment at the Dardanelles. But two blacks do not make a white and, as he had long since declared his view that the Western Front was impassable, it is difficult to see how he could feel that a hopeless offensive there could bring fresh hope to the Russians.

He may have felt, however, that it would show the need and pave the way for the appointment of a supreme commander of the Entente forces. The official history has discreetly lifted a corner of the veil of history with the statement – 'It is believed that Lord Kitchener himself had anticipated a call to this post.' In that case a timely concession to the French over Loos was likely to make them more receptive towards the other suggestion later.

But the immediate result, to quote the official history, was that:

Under pressure from Lord Kitchener at home, due to the general position of the Allies, and from Generals Joffre and Foch in France, due to the local situation in France, the British Commander-in-Chief was therefore compelled to undertake operations before he was ready, over ground that was most unfavourable, against the better judgement of himself and of General Haig, and, with no more than a quarter of the troops, nine divisions, instead of thirty-six, that he considered necessary for a successful attack.

French was himself, as we shall see, to extinguish its last hope of success. The last but one had been extinguished by a final alteration of the French plan. This was Joffre's decision to make the Champagne attack, and not the Artois, his main attack, for the reason that the ground in Champagne had fewer obstacles or villages in the way of the attackers. The sudden preference for tactical over strategical considerations is in curious contrast to his view where the British attack was concerned.

This change, again, had a damaging influence on the British attack, for both the British and French official accounts make it clear that the French Artois attack south of Lens by seventeen divisions on a twelve-mile frontage – supported by 420 heavy guns – was not seriously pressed once the strength of the defence was realized. Yet the French had nearly twice as many heavy guns to the mile as the British (117 in all). In Champagne twenty-seven French divisions, with 850 heavy guns, were assembled for the attack – on an eighteen-mile frontage. Thus the proportionate artillery support here was still higher.

When the decision to attack at Loos was definitely taken, Haig's first intention, to curtail his commitment and probable loss, was to attack at first with only two divisions. But a too successful demonstration of the possibilities of chlorine gas projected in a 'wave' from cylinders led him to modify his views, and to believe that if the wind was favourable the gas discharge might even procure 'decisive results' and justify him in attacking on the wider frontage of six divisions – Rawlinson's IV Corps (47th, 15th and 1st Divisions) on the right, or south, and Gough's I Corps (7th, 9th, and 2nd Divisions) on the left.

With sound judgement of the chances, Haig urged that 'under no circumstances should our forthcoming attack be launched without the aid of gas', but he was overruled by French and Foch. He then obtained permission to reserve his decision until the last possible moment and to let the choice – between the large or limited attack – depend on the weather conditions. By the irony of fortune, the wind was most favourable for the use of gas on September 15th, the day originally fixed by Foch for the attack, and this fact encouraged Haig's hopes. But the retention of a dual plan led to a distribution of the artillery on the whole army front instead of a concentration on one-third.

Over 5,000 cylinders of gas, containing nearly 150 tons, were carried up to the front trenches and safely installed in special recesses, without one being hit by enemy fire. Even so, there was barely half the volume of gas necessary to maintain a continuous flow for the forty minutes that, in turn, were considered necessary to outlast the protective power of the oxygen apparatus used by the enemy machine-gunners. Hence the cylinders had to be turned on and off intermittently. Smoke candles were used in the intervals to simulate gas, and, at the end, to form the first smoke screen of the war.

The artillery bombardment began on September 21st, the ammunition being eked out by limiting each heavy gun to ninety rounds, and each field gun to 150 in the twenty-four hours. The results were not encouraging, so far as effect could be discovered, and led the commanders to study the wind all the more attentively.

The last night was a time of tense anxiety. Repeatedly Haig studied fresh charts sent in by a chain of meteorological observers. At 6 PM the forecast was that the wind would be 'on the border line between favourable and unfavourable, with a slight bias towards favourable'. At 9 PM the forecast was better, indicating a probable change to a south-westerly or even westerly wind, which would carry the gas over the German trenches. Thereupon Haig unhesitatingly ordered the full-scale offensive with gas, although as a precaution staff officers of each corps had been ordered to stand by their telephones. At 3 AM, after a further report not quite so encouraging, he fixed sunrise (5.50 AM) as the hour for releasing the gas. During the hours of darkness the wind changed as predicted, but only as far as south-west, and, worse still, was so slight as to be almost a calm.

About 5 AM, as soon as it was light, Haig went out. He could feel only the faintest breath of air, and he asked his senior ADC to light a cigarette. The smoke drifted in puffs to the north-east.

Did it justify the venture? Would the gas merely hang in the British trenches? A slight increase of wind was felt and at 5.15 AM Haig gave the decisive order to 'carry on' and climbed his wooden look-out tower. But the improvement was delusive, and a few minutes later one of his staff telephoned to the I Corps, to ask whether it was possible to stop the discharge and the attack. For this emergency the gas officers had made ample arrangements. But Gough replied that it was too late. If it would certainly have been a close shave, one may suspect, especially in view of Gough's record, that with this ardent fighter the wish was at least the midwife, if not the father, of the thought.

When the gas was actually turned on at 5.50 AM it carried fairly well over the German trenches on the right, if too slow and slight for full effect, but on the left was a failure, in some places drifting back and upsetting the attack. In Horne's 2nd Division, the officer in charge of the gas on the 6th Brigade front declined to assume the responsibility of turning on the cylinders. But when this was reported to divisional headquarters, Horne replied with an order that 'the programme must be carried out whatever the conditions...' As a result of this obstinacy many of the infantry were poisoned by their own gas. Those who were able to advance were soon stopped, and slaughtered by the ungassed German machine-gunners. Nevertheless, Horne ordered a fresh assault, which was only abandoned after his brigade commanders had protested against the 'useless sacrifice of life'.

The general infantry assault had been launched at 6.30 AM, and into it was thrown the entire strength of the First Army, except for local reserves. Neither Haig nor the commanders of his two attacking corps kept any reserve, as they understood that the Commander-in-Chief expected a breakthrough and would use his general reserve to back them up promptly.

On the extreme right the 47th Division nearly carried out its task of throwing forward a defensive flank, but the 'not quite' had an important bearing on the surprisingly successful initial rush of its neighbour, the 15th Division, contributing towards the loss of direction which nullified its near approach to a breakthrough, beyond Hill 70. So swift and deep was the advance of these Scotsmen of 'K's' Army that the German Command made hurried preparations to evacuate the whole area, and as far back as Douai 'there were endless convoys of wagons formed up in double lines ready to march away'.

Another ill-effect was due to the long delay in the 1st Division's advance, only partially retrieved. Its left brigade had suffered similarly to Horne's division and, instead of the divisional reserve being sent through the gap made on the flanks, the morning was wasted in futile attempts to renew the frontal assault. This stoppage in the British centre tended to check the whole momentum of the British advance. Further to the left the 7th and 9th Divisions obtained promising results, although the 9th had suffered, both in opportunity and life, from the misguided insistence of the corps commander, Gough, on renewing the vain frontal assault of the left brigade. In wise contrast Capper, commanding the 7th Division, when confronted with a check on his left, had quickly passed his reserve through the gap made by the successful advance of his right.

The fulfilment of any promise, however, depended on the prompt infusion of reserves. This was the crux of the situation and the sealing cause of failure. Even Joffre had said that if French kept his reserve divisions too far back they would 'run the risk of arriving too late to exploit the success of the leading ones. It is indispensable that these divisions are put, before the attack, at the absolute disposal of General Haig'. Haig repeatedly urged that they should at least be brought up close behind him. French's assurances were so vague as to be simultaneously unsatisfying and misleading. As usual his outlook seems to have been governed by contradictory impulses of undue optimism and pessimism.

French's general reserves comprised the Cavalry Corps – which, under modern conditions, did not count except in the minds of cavalry-trained commanders – and the XI Corps. The last included the Guards Division, newly formed, and the 21st and 24th Divisions, newly arrived in France. With curious judgement French left seasoned divisions lying idle on the quiet Somme front, and chose to use these two raw divisions for the critical phase of the battle. Moreover, he had given Haig to understand that they would be immediately at hand for Haig's use, whereas he placed them sixteen miles in rear. And in his subsequent dispatch he untruthfully stated that they were put at Haig's disposal at

9.30 AM on the 25th. Actually, Haig did not hear until 1.20 PM, and then indirectly. Haig bitterly remarked, soon after – 'If there had been even one division in reserve close up we could have walked right through. General headquarters refuses to recognize the teaching of the war as regards the control of reserves.' His confidence was probably exaggerated, at least as to the effect of such a narrow breach, and he was himself to err somewhat similarly in the following July. But his natural disgust, accentuated by French's untruthful dispatch, led first to an acrimonious interchange of letters and then to an irreconcilable quarrel. He seems, also, to have been galled, and not for the first time, at the way his own sound advice had been overruled by Foch's influence with French. French in retort charged Haig with the folly of trying to push reserves through a far too narrow gap. The sequel was that Haig wrote personally to Kitchener and spoke to Haldane about French's failure and incompetence, and thereby helped to precipitate French's downfall and his own succession.

As for the long and slow march up of those divisions, bad traffic arrangements were more responsible than their own inexperience for accentuating the evil caused by the Commander-in-Chief's dispositions. As General Edmonds caustically says – 'It was like trying to push the Lord Mayor's procession through the streets of London, without clearing the route and holding up the traffic.' Folly was capped by farce when, on the outskirts of Béthune, a military policeman stopped the 72nd Brigade because the brigade commander had no pass to enter the area.

Never, surely, were 'novice' divisions thrown into a vital stroke in a more difficult or absurd manner, and in an atmosphere of greater misconception of the situation in all quarters. This amply explains their subsequent failure when their belated attack was at last launched at 11 AM on the 26th, and redresses the hasty judgements which were spread at the time – a stigma that was slow to fade. That in courage they were not lacking is clear, and equally that its fruits were reduced by their rawness, by that of their staff still more.

The handicap of inexperience in these and the other New Army divisions engaged can be over-emphasized. It does not appear that, as a whole, apart from certain battalions in them, the regular divisions were more effective or even as effective in the battle. 'Battlecraft' is a rare quality, the product of gifted and original leadership, and in its absence mere dash is often more effective than so-called experience.

The ineffectiveness of the larger French attack south of the Lens also affected the British opportunity. For the French did not advance until six and a quarter hours after their Allies, and even then made little progress where they did not make merely a demonstration. The bitter experiences of the spring and summer seem to have led the fighting commanders to discount Foch's faith in a breakthrough, and to annul his vehement order by gentle evasion in places. Joffre also put a brake on him from above, for on the second morning he telephoned him to 'go cautiously', and followed this by the warning – 'Stop the attacks of the Tenth Army, taking care to avoid giving the British the impression that we are leaving them to attack alone.' His reason was apparently that he now pinned his hopes to the attack in Champagne, which on the first day gave a delusive promise of a real breakthrough.

It is worthwhile to note that the partial opening success of the attack in Champagne, and also in Artois, was largely due to the obstinate self-delusion of Falkenhayn, who had disregarded ample warnings from many sources, and requests for reserves. Only two hours before the attack began he assured the Kaiser that the local army commanders 'see things too black', and that the French were not in a condition to attack.

Early reports on the 25th had also led Haig to overestimate his initial success, and as early as 10.30 AM he ordered the 3rd Cavalry Division forward. The commander soon discovered Haig's mistake, but Haig, believing that the cavalry had gone on, hurried the 21st and 24th Divisions forward as soon as he could get hold of them. But before they came up the known situation had changed, and the two leading brigades were taken to strengthen the line gained by the original attack. Haig still hoped to break the intact German second line of defences, and to this end the rest (four brigades) of these divisions continued their march across country, and unknown country, in the dark and rain. Tired, hungry, and as confused as their commanders, they were launched to the attack next morning without effective artillery support, and against defences now stronger and more strongly manned than the original first line. For the Germans had not only been reinforced, but had covered themselves with a thick wire entanglement during the night. The attack broke down at or before this uncut obstacle, and the survivors turned and flowed backwards. Their disappearance left a hole in the ragged British front between Loos and Hulluch, which the Guards Division came up to fill. Meantime German counter-attacks were multiplying dangerously, especially on the flanks. At last, on the 28th, Foch came to the relief not only by taking over the British flank sector near Loos, but with a local success on Vimy ridge, which drew off most of the newly arrived German Guard Corps to check it. And in concert with Sir John French he arranged to make a renewed general offensive on October

2nd. The same course was adopted in Champagne, where the French for three days had vainly hurled themselves at the German second position, suffering fearful loss, which would have been worse if Pétain (Second Army) had not stopped his attack in disregard of higher orders.

But as the pause was to be followed by a renewal at the same point, it merely gave the Germans time to strengthen it and accumulate resources in the rear. Local upsets due to German counter-attacks, and the exhaustion of the troops, caused further delay, and the renewed offensive was repeatedly postponed. Eventually all three attacks were delivered on different dates, the British last on October 13th. And, in the words of the official history, it 'had not improved the general situation in any way and had brought nothing but useless slaughter of infantry'. Curiously, Haig's sense of realism waned in this last phase, or, perhaps more truly, it was subdued by his bulldog tenacity; for although Joffre had abandoned the effort, Haig was working up a new general attack for November 7th, an operation whose inevitable cost does not seem to have had any adequate excuse. Happily, Generals Winter and Weather intervened. But the British casualties already amounted to 50,380 – or 60,392 if the subsidiary attacks by Haig's army be included – whereas the German loss was barely 20,000, despite their costly counter-attacks. The French in Champagne and Artois had lost 191,797 officers and men, and inflicted 120,000 casualties – a proportion which suggests that the actual handling of these attacks was better than that of the British, if helped by more powerful artillery. Both Allies had gained in experience, if not in wisdom, but they had afforded the Germans still better experience in the way to frustrate such attacks. And in 1916 it was the Germans who profited heavily both by the offensive and the defensive lesson.

CHAPTER SIX

1916 – The 'Dog-Fall'

In 1914 the centre of gravity of the World War had been on the Western Front; in 1915 it shifted to the Eastern Front; in 1916 it once more moved back to France. Although the Entente had dissipated some of their strength in Salonika and Mesopotamia, the rising tide of England's new armies and of her munition supplies promised the power for an effort far larger in scale than before to break the trench deadlock. Measures had also been taken to keep these new divisions up to strength. By the end of 1915 the British force in France had risen to thirty-eight divisions through the entry into the field of 'Kitchener's Army', as well as of the Territorial divisions. Although the principle of voluntary enlistment had not yet been abandoned, the method was systematized and based on a national register. This scheme, launched in October, 1915, under the aegis of Lord Derby, aimed to reconcile the demands of the Army with the needs of industry, calling up men by groups as they were wanted, and taking single men first. But the response among the latter was not adequate to preserve this graduated principle, and in January, 1916, by the Military Service Act, the voluntary system – system is hardly the correct term – was replaced by conscription.

At the close of 1915, the first serious effort to obtain unity of action between the Allies was made, and a conference of the leaders of the French, British, Belgian and Italian armies, with representatives present from the Russian and Japanese, was held at Joffre's headquarters on December 5th. As a result they adopted the principle of a simultaneous general offensive in 1916 by France, Britain, Russia and Italy. In view of the rawness of the British troops, it was recognized that time must be allowed for training, and Russia also needed time for re-equipment, so that the offensive could not begin before the summer of 1916, although it was hoped to carry out preliminary attacks to wear down the enemy's strength. But in January both Joffre and Foch gave Haig a clear intimation that it was for him to carry out this preparatory task, and that they did not intend to take the offensive until he had done so.

German action was to dislocate this scheme, and only the British share came fully into operation, and not even that into full effect. By a grim jest, however, it forced the French to carry out the wearing-down process – in an indirect form. For Falkenhayn was about to fulfil his long-cherished plan for a western offensive, but with characteristic limitations. Always a believer in the strategy of attrition, he now carried this ruling idea into tactics, and produced the new form of attack by methodical stages, each with a limited objective. In an appreciation made at Christmas, 1915, he argued that England was the staple of the enemy alliance. 'The history of the English wars against the Netherlands, Spain, France and Napoleon is being repeated. Germany can expect no mercy from this enemy, so long as he still retains the slightest hope of achieving his object.' Save by submarine warfare, however, England and her army were out of reach, for their sector of the front did not lend itself to offensive operations. 'In view of our feelings for our arch-enemy in the war that is certainly distressing, but it can be endured if we realize that for England the campaign on the Continent … is at bottom a side-show. Her real weapons here are the French, Russian and Italian armies.' He regarded Russia as already paralysed, and Italy's military achievements as unlikely to affect the situation. 'Only France remains.' 'France has almost arrived at the end of her military effort. If her people can be made to understand clearly that in a military sense they have nothing more to hope for, breaking point would be reached, and England's best sword knocked out of her hand.' He added that a breakthrough in mass was unnecessary, and that instead the Germans should aim to bleed France to death by choosing a point of attack 'for the retention of which the French command would be compelled to throw in every man they have'. Such an objective was either Belfort, or Verdun, and Verdun was chosen, because it was a menace to the main German communications, because it offered a salient and so cramped the defender, and because of the moral effect if so renowned a place were lost to France. It has also been suggested that the choice was influenced by a peculiarly German moral, or unmoral, consideration. For Verdun was the ancient gate of the west through which the German hordes had passed to attack the Gauls. Similarly the Germans were fond of christening their trench positions after the heroes of the Nibelungen – Siegfried, Brünhilde and so on. The vein of superstition is still more clearly suggested in the Kaiser's choice of a second Moltke to guide his armies, and in the original location of their headquarters in the same hotel and same town, Coblenz, as they had occupied in 1870.

The keynote of the tactical plan at Verdun was a continuous series of limited advances, which by their menace should draw the French reserves into the mincing machine of the German artillery. And each of these advances was itself to be secured from loss by a short but intense artillery bombardment. By this means the objective would be taken and consolidated before the enemy could move up his reserves for counter-attack. Although the Intelligence branch at French General Headquarters gave early warning of the German preparations, the Operations branch were so full of their own offensive schemes that the warning fell on deaf ears. Further, the easy fall of the Belgian and Russian fortresses had led to a commonly held view that fortresses were obsolete, and Joffre, persuading the French government to 'declass' Verdun as a fortress, had denuded it of guns and troops. The forts were only used as shelters and the trench lines which took their place were inadequate and in poor repair.

At 7.15 AM on February 21st, the German bombardment began, on a front of fifteen miles, and at 4.45 PM the infantry advanced, although the first day only on a four and a half miles' front. From then until February 24th the defenders' line east of the Meuse was crumbled away as by the erosion of the tide.

Joffre was now aroused so far as to entrust the defence to Pétain, for whose use reserves were assembled. On March 6th the Germans extended the attack to the west bank of the Meuse; but the defence was now stiffening, the numbers balanced, and the immediate threat to Verdun was checked.

A slight lull followed, and during it the Allies of France made efforts to relieve the pressure on her. The British took over the Arras front from the French Tenth Army, their front becoming now continuous from the Yser to the Somme; the Italians made their fifth attack, though in vain, on the Isonzo front; and the Russians hurled untrained masses on the German front at Lake Narocz, near Vilna, where the slight gains were soon lost through a counterstroke. These efforts did not prevent Falkenhayn pursuing his attrition offensive at Verdun. The advances were slight but they were cumulative in effect, and the balance of loss turned definitely against the defenders. On June 7th Fort Vaux fell, and the German tide crept ever closer to Verdun. And in the Asiago region, Conrad had launched his offensive against Italy's Trentino flank.

Again Russia came to the rescue. In the spring of 1916 she had 130 divisions, but still woefully short of equipment, facing forty-six German and forty Austrian divisions. The preparation and reorganization for her intended share in the year's Allied offensive were cut short by the emergency at Verdun, and in relief of her French Allies she had launched the costly and obstinately prolonged attack at Lake Narocz in March. When at last it was broken off, the preparations for the main offensive were resumed. This was to begin in July, coincidently with the Somme offensive; meantime Brusilov, commanding the south-western front, prepared such attacks as he could stage from his own resources as a distraction of the enemy's attention from the main offensive. But the distraction was released prematurely, on June 4th, in response to Italy's appeal to Russia to prevent the Austrians reinforcing their Trentino attack. Without warning, because without any special concentration of troops, Brusilov's troops advanced against the Austrian Fourth Army near Luck, and the Austrian Seventh Army in the Bukovina, whose resistance collapsed at the first shock.

This last vital effort of the Russian Army in the war had important consequences. It stopped the Austrian attack on Italy, already impaired by an Italian riposte. It compelled Falkenhayn to withdraw troops from the Western Front, and so abandon his plan for a counterstroke against the British offensive preparing on the Somme, as well as the hope of nourishing his Verdun attrition process. It led Rumania to take her fateful decision to enter the war on the Entente side, and caused the supersession of Falkenhayn in the supreme command, and his replacement by Hindenburg – with Ludendorff, officially styled First Quartermaster-General, as the directing brain. Although Rumania's entry was the immediate reason, the underlying one was the fact that Falkenhayn's indefinite strategy in 1915 had made possible the Russian recovery which stultified his strategy of 1916. Falkenhayn was history's latest example of the folly of half-measures; the ablest and most scientific General – 'penny wise, pound foolish' – who ever ruined his country by a refusal to take calculated risks. In 1916 he had turned back westwards to pursue his long-cherished goal, and his strategy had faithfully fulfilled the canons of military orthodoxy by taking for its objective the enemy's strongest army and the strongest point of that army's position. It certainly achieved the object of compelling the French to pour their reserves into the Verdun 'blood-bath', but did not achieve any decisive strategic result.

Falkenhayn had rejected Conrad's proposal for a concentration against Italy such as had previously overthrown Serbia. Conrad's reasons had been that such a blow against the 'hereditary enemy' would act as a tonic to the Austro-Hungarian forces, and that the theatre of war lent itself to decisive results by a thrust southwards from the Trentino against the rear of the Italian armies engaged on the Isonzo. The success attained by the relatively light blow of 1917 – Caporetto – lends historical support to his contention. But Falkenhayn was dubious both of the feasibility and value of the plan, and was unwilling even to lend the nine German divisions which Conrad asked for to relieve Austrian divisions in Galicia. In default of this aid Conrad persisted in attempting his design single-handed, taking some of his best divisions from Galicia, and thereby exposing their front to Brusilov's advance without obtaining adequate force to achieve his Italian plan. Falkenhayn's smouldering resentment at this disregard of his views was fanned into flame by the Galician disaster, and he intervened in Vienna to procure the deposition of Conrad. With retributive irony his own fall followed close on that of Conrad.

Brusilov's offensive continued for three months with fair success, but reserves were not at hand for immediate exploitation, and before they could be moved down from the north the Germans were patching up the holes. His later efforts were never so dangerous, but they absorbed all the available Russian reserves, and the huge losses then incurred went far to complete the ruin of Russia's military power.

Great as was the influence of Brusilov's offensive on German strategy, its effect on the Verdun situation was less immediate. But the long-planned offensive on the Somme came to the rescue, and for want of nourishment the Verdun offensive faded away. Nevertheless, although the Germans at Verdun had fallen short of their object, moral and material, they had so drained the French army that it could play but a slender part in the Allied plan for 1916. The British had now to take up the main burden of the struggle, and the consequence was to limit both the scope and effect of the Entente strategy.

On July 1st, after a week's prolonged bombardment, the British Fourth Army (recently created and placed under Rawlinson) attacked with thirteen divisions on a front of fifteen miles, north of the Somme, and the French with five divisions on a front of eight miles, mainly south of the river, where the German defence system was less highly developed. The unconcealed preparations and the long bombardment had given away any chance of surprise, and in face of the German resistance, weak in numbers but strong in organization, the attack failed along most of the British front. Owing to the dense and rigid 'wave' formations that were adopted the losses were appallingly heavy. Only on the south of the British front, near Fricourt and Montauban, did the attack gain a real footing in the German defences. The French, with slighter opposition, and being less expected, made larger gains.

This setback negatived the original idea of a 'breakthrough' to Bapaume and Cambrai, and Haig for a time fell back on the attrition method – of limited advances aimed to wear down the German strength. Rejecting Joffre's desire that he should again throw his troops frontally on the Thiepval defences, Haig at first resumed the attack with his right wing alone, and on July 14th the penetration of the Germans' second position offered a chance of exploitation, which was not taken. From now onward a methodical but costly advance continued, and although little ground was gained the German resistance was seriously strained when the early onset of winter rains suspended operations in November. The effect, however, can be exaggerated, for it did not prevent the Germans withdrawing troops from the west for the attack on Rumania.

But in one respect the Somme shed a significant light on the future, for on September 15th the first tanks appeared. Their early employment before large numbers were ready was a mistake; losing the chance of a great strategic surprise, and owing also to tactical mishandling, and minor technical defects, they had only a limited success. Although the higher military authorities lost faith in them, and some urged their abandonment, more discerning eyes realized that here was a key which, when properly used, might unlock the trench barrier.

The Somme offensive had a further indirect effect, for its relief to the Verdun pressure enabled the French to prepare counterstrokes, carried out by Mangin's corps on October 24th and December 15th, which regained most of the lost ground with small casualties. These economical successes were due to a partial revival of surprise, to a more elastic use of the limited objective method, and to a high concentration of artillery, with a minimum of infantry to occupy the defences crushed by the guns. But the French success was greatly helped by Hindenburg's misguided insistence, for the sake of prestige, on maintaining the earlier gains instead of withdrawing the tired troops to a more secure line somewhat in rear. He at least profited by the lesson, to the Allies' detriment, in the spring of 1917.

Rumania, sympathetic to the Entente cause, had been waiting a favourable opportunity to enter the war on their side, and Brusilov's success encouraged her to take the plunge. Her command hoped that this, combined with the Allied pressure on the Somme and at Salonika, would fix the German reserves. But Rumania's situation had many inherent defects. The strategical position of her territory was bad, the main section, Wallachia, being sandwiched between Austro-Hungary and Bulgaria. Her army, though externally of a modern pattern, had grave weaknesses beneath the surface. Of her Allies, only Russia could give her direct aid, and they failed her. And, with all these handicaps, she launched an offensive into Transylvania, which bared her flank to Bulgaria.

While the Entente fumbled the Germans acted. The plan was initiated by Falkenhayn and developed by Hindenburg-Ludendorff when they took over the Supreme Command on August 28th. While one force concentrated in Transylvania for a counterstroke, a Bulgarian army with German stiffening – under Mackensen – was to strike through Rumania's 'back door' and invade the Dobruja. This automatically halted the Rumanian offensive in Transylvania, and drew away its reserves; at the end of September the Rumanians were thrown back by the Austro-German counter-offensive, of which Falkenhayn was given executive command. They succeeded in holding the passes of Rumania's mountain border in the west until mid-November, but Falkenhayn just broke through before the snows blocked the passes. Mackensen switched his main forces westwards, and crossed the Danube close to Bucharest, on which both armies now converged. It fell on December 6th, and, despite belated Russian aid, the Rumanian forces were driven north into Moldavia. The brilliantly coordinated German strategy had crippled their new foe, gained possession of the bulk of Rumania, with its oil and wheat, and gave the Russians another 300 miles of front to hold. Sarrail, at Salonika, had not succeeded in fixing the Bulgarian reserves.

The Austrian offensive in the Trentino had interrupted Cadorna's plans for a renewed effort on the Isonzo, but when the former was halted Cadorna switched his reserves back to the Isonzo. In preparation for this offensive the whole sector from Monte Sabotino to the sea was entrusted to the Duke of Aosta's Third Army, under which sixteen divisions were concentrated against six Austrian divisions. Following a preliminary feint near the sea on August 4th, the attack opened well two days later. North of Gorizia Capello's corps swept over the long-impregnable Monte Sabotino, which guarded the approach to the river, and, crossing the river on the night of August 8th, occupied the town. This compelled an Austrian retreat in the Carso sector to the south, but attempts to exploit the success eastward failed against fresh positions of resistance. Three more efforts were made in the autumn, and if they imposed a wearing strain on the Austrians, they caused greater loss to the attackers. During the year Italians had suffered some 483,000 casualties, and inflicted 260,000.

The only territorial success that the Entente could show for their year's campaign – and, even so, it did not reveal itself fully until the New Year – was away in Mesopotamia – the capture of Baghdad. This moral token was seized on with an enthusiasm which, militarily, it hardly warranted. The bitter experience of the past had damped the ardour of the British Government, and Sir William Robertson, the new Chief of the Imperial General Staff, was opposed to any further commitments which drained the strength available for the Western Front. But Maude, the new commander on the spot, by subtle if unconscious steps succeeded in changing this defensive policy into one of a fresh offensive. After thorough reorganization of the Mesopotamian force and its communications, he began on December 12th, 1916, a progressive right wheel and extension of his front on the west bank of the Tigris above and below Kut. These methodical trench-warfare operations had placed him ready for a spring across the Tigris at the Turks' line of retreat, which was thus parallel to his front. But despite his four-to-one superiority of force, the failure of his right to pin down the enemy, and of his cavalry to cut off their retreat, prevented a decisive success. But it led to permission for an advance on Baghdad, and he entered the Mesopotamian capital on March 11th, 1917. A series of skilfully conducted operations then drove the Turks into divergent lines of retreat and secured the British hold on the province.

Ever since the abortive Turkish attempt to invade Egypt early in 1915, the British had kept a fairly large force there, even when the Dardanelles expedition was crying out for troops. When Gallipoli was evacuated, the release of the Turkish forces threatened a fresh move on Egypt. To forestall this danger the authorities in Cairo had gained Kitchener's approval for a landing in Ayas Bay near Alexandretta, but the proposal had been opposed by the General Staff at home and then nullified by the political objections of the French to any British intervention in Syria, which they already counted as part of their share of the spoils of war. Thus throughout 1916 the large British garrison of Egypt (at one time over a quarter of a million strong) remained passive while the Turks, by using a few thousand men in Sinai and by stirring up the Senussi in the Western Desert, created trouble on both flanks which reacted on the unrest within the frontiers of Egypt.

But the British, also, contrived to secure an Arab ally, on the eastern side of the Red Sea. This was the Sherif of Mecca, who had already rendered them valuable service by refusing to proclaim the *Jihad* from the Holy Cities at the Turks' behest, and had thus extinguished the prospect of rallying the Moslem peoples for a Holy War against the

British. Then, in June 1916, the Sherif raised a revolt in the Hejaz against Turkish rule, and thereby created a distraction to the Turks which the British had hitherto failed to provide with their own forces. Its first effect was on the British, who now decided to undertake an advance to El Arish, which would give them command of the Sinai Desert and restore their possession of the frontier. But although another Turkish incursion was punished at Romani in July, Sir Archibald Murray's advance was slow to develop, being governed by the time taken in laying a railway and pipeline (for water) across the desert. It was not until Christmastide that the British occupied El Arish, and pounced on the outlying Turkish posts at Magdhaba and Rafah.

This new 'Exodus inspired' the British Government to carry out an invasion of Palestine, at as cheap a cost in troops as possible. The towns of Gaza, on the coast, and Beersheba, twenty-five miles inland, guarded the approach to Palestine. Murray attacked Gaza on March 26th, 1917, but the attempt fell short when on the brink of success. By nightfall Gaza was practically surrounded, but the victorious position was given up bit by bit, not under enemy pressure, but on the orders of the executive British commanders, through faulty information, misunderstandings, and over-anxiety. Nor did the harm end there, for Murray reported the action to the Government in terms of a victory, and without hint of the subsequent withdrawal, so that he was encouraged to attempt, without adequate reconnaissance or fire support, a further attack on April 17th–19th, which proved a costlier failure against defences now strengthened.

Britain's new Arab allies, however, provided a valuable distraction which counteracted these Turkish successes, with no drain on the British forces beyond a handful of technical advisers. After its opening success the revolt had been in danger of collapse; but the situation was saved and the scales changed by Feisal's sudden flank move up the Red Sea coast to Wejh, whence the Arabs harassed the Hejaz railway. This move was prompted by a young archaeologist turned temporary soldier, Captain T. E. Lawrence. Steeped in the history and theory of warfare, he had the elasticity of mind to adapt his knowledge to irregular conditions and the magnetic personality to combine the Arabs' 'loose shower of sparks into a firm flame' which consumed the Turkish resources. In May 1917, he set off with a party of Arabs on a lone-hand expedition which, after sowing fresh seeds of revolt in Syria, culminated in a descent upon Aqaba. The capture of this sea base on the northern arm of the Red Sea removed all danger to the British communications in Sinai and opened the way for the Arabs to become a lever on the flank of the Turkish forces opposing the British. Already more Turks were occupied in guarding the long line of the Hejaz railway and the territory south of it than were facing the British in Palestine.

The War at Sea, 1915–16. Germany's first submarine campaign – associated by Allied opinion with the name of Admiral von Tirpitz, the exponent of ruthlessness – had been a signal failure, both in its meagre results and the disproportionate ethical damage it did to Germany's cause. A series of notes, exchanged between the American and German Governments, culminated in April, 1916, in a virtual ultimatum from President Wilson, and Germany abandoned her unrestricted campaign. The deprivation of this weapon spurred the German navy to its first, and last, attempt to carry out the initial plan on which it had begun the war. Late on May 30th, 1916, the British Grand Fleet left its bases on one of its periodical sweeps through the North Sea, but with reason to expect a possible encounter. On May 31st, early in the morning, the German High Sea Fleet also put to sea, in the hope of destroying some isolated portion of the British fleet.

For such an encounter the British Admiral, Jellicoe, had formulated an outline plan in the early months of the war. Its basis was the cardinal necessity of maintaining the unimpaired supremacy of the Grand Fleet, which he viewed as an instrument, not merely of battle, but of grand strategy, the pivot of the Allies' action in all spheres, economic, moral and military. Hence, while desirous of bringing the German fleet to battle under his own conditions, he was determined not to be lured into mine and submarine-infested waters.

Early in the afternoon of May 31st, Beatty, with his battle cruisers and a squadron of battleships, after a sweep to the south was turning north to rejoin Jellicoe, when he sighted the German battle cruisers, five in number. In the initial engagement two of Beatty's six battle cruisers were hit in vital parts and sunk; when thus weakened he came upon the main German fleet under Admiral Scheer. He turned north to lure them into reach of Jellicoe, fifty miles distant, who raced to support him. Mist and failing light put an end to an indecisive action, which, however, left the British fleet between the German and its bases. During the night Scheer broke through the destroyer guard, and although sighted was not reported. Thus he slipped safely through a net which Jellicoe dared not draw too close in view of his guiding principle, and of the danger of torpedo attack.

If the battle of Jutland could be counted a tactical advantage to the Germans, it had no effect on their strategic position. The grip of Britain's blockade was unrelaxed. Once more Germany fell back on submarine warfare, and the first development was an extension of range. In July one of her large submarine cruisers appeared off the American coast and sank several neutral ships.

In the narrow seas the Mediterranean was the scene of active operations, but the immediate pressure on Britain was relaxed during the summer. For Scheer, in a fit of pique at the German Government's surrender to President Wilson's threat, refused to let his submarines operate under the code of visit and search. Hence the burden of the restricted campaign fell on the Flanders flotillas, and, fortunately for Britain, the German naval chiefs had been obtusely slow to realize and exploit the advantages of the Belgian coast as a base. The six months lost originally through neglect to organize a base were never fully redeemed, and the scale of the forces here was never in proportion to the possibilities of menacing Britain from this close-range post. On October 6th, Scheer was overruled by an order to reinforce the effort with his flotillas. This veiled renewal of the general submarine campaign was inspired mainly by Admiral von Holtzendorf, the Chief of the Naval Staff, and Captain von Bartenbach, the Chief of the Flanders flotillas. The indirect result was to deprive Scheer automatically of the submarines which he required to safeguard his own sorties and lay traps for the British fleet.

Thus the paralysis of the German fleet henceforth was the result of the Germans' own alternative plan, and not of Jutland. And it did not even leave the British Grand Fleet in possession of the North Sea. For the moral effect of a submarine ambush which marked the German sortie of August 19th was so great, even though it miscarried, that henceforth the Grand Fleet was almost as confined as an old-time debtor in the Fleet Prison, and was definitely debarred from the southern half of the North Sea. Jellicoe and the Admiralty were agreed upon the necessity for this self-imprisonment. The 'command of the sea' became almost a burlesque when the danger of a German invasion of Denmark loomed up that autumn and, after examination by the Admiralty and War Office, the verdict was that – 'For naval reasons it would be almost impossible to support the Danes at all.' The shadow of the submarine was longer than the shadow of Nelson's column. With illuminating candour the British official naval history says – 'The Grand Fleet could only put to sea with an escort of nearly one hundred destroyers, no capital ship could leave its base without an escort of small craft, and the German U-boats had hampered our squadrons to an extent which the most expert and far-sighted naval officer had never foreseen.' Yet, with curious inconsistency, the voices of naval officers have been heard ever since the war proclaiming the sovereignty of the battleship, the ineffectiveness of the submarine.

The Grand Fleet in the autumn of 1916 was all the more heavily fettered because its warders were reduced, owing to the call for light craft to combat the new 'veiled' submarine campaign against commerce. Despite all counter-measures this was so successful that the monthly loss of shipping rose steadily from 109,000 tons during June, to 368,000 tons in January, 1917 – approximately half being British. During the 'veiled' campaign the Mediterranean was both an ill-favoured and, by the Germans, too well-favoured area, for besides simplifying the submarine's task of finding targets it simplified the problem of evading the undertakings given to America – in the Mediterranean there was little risk of injuring American ships or interests by mischance. One U-boat alone in five weeks' cruise sank 65,000 tons of shipping.

Counter-measures proved utterly unable to stem the rising tide of sinking ships, even when more destroyers and other small craft became available. During one week of September, 1916, thirty ships were sunk by two, or at the most, three submarines in an area patrolled by ninety-seven destroyers and sixty-eight auxiliary craft. Among the remedies tried were those of secret routes, of hoisting false colours, and of decoy ships. This last ruse was carried out by what were known as Q-ships, equipped with torpedo-tubes, depth charges, and guns concealed behind collapsible bulwarks, while disguised as merchant ships. The disguise was enhanced by the acting of the crews who coolly simulated panic under conditions where most men would not have needed to do so, and thereby lured the molesting submarine to the surface within close range. Although these Q-ships provided the most romantic phase of the naval war, and sank eleven U-boats, their effect was almost exhausted by the end of 1916, save that it made the enemy more wary – and naturally less inclined to merciful discrimination between armed and apparently unarmed ships. This Q-ship risk to the U-boat was accentuated by the British arming of ordinary merchant ships, which placed the slow, fragile and half-blind U-boat in a perilous dilemma. The more merciful the U-boat the greater danger it ran; the less heed it paid to the nature of its target and the rescue of those on board the more its safety and success were assured. Hence the outcry in Germany for a policy of sinking at sight was naturally strengthened.

Moreover, if Britain was feeling the strain of economic pressure, so also was Germany, and her leaders feared that the race between decisive success on land and economic collapse would end against her. The naval authorities declared that a renewal of the 'unlimited' submarine campaign, which with her increased numbers could now be far more intense, would bring the Entente to their knees. Accepting this opinion, Ludendorff agreed to a step which he had hitherto opposed; the combined weight of·naval and military opinion overbore the protests of the Imperial Chancellor. A proposal of peace discussions, and its foreseen rejection by the Entente powers, was made the moral justification for openly abandoning the restrictions of visit and search, and for withdrawing the promise given to President Wilson. On February 1st, 1917, the 'unrestricted' policy – of sinking all ships, passenger or cargo, without warning – was proclaimed – with the full realization that it involved the weight of America being thrown into the scales against Germany. Doubts of its wisdom in Germany were stifled by the plea of necessity, the promise of certain victory, and the argument of inevitability – that America was bound to come to the help of the Allies in order to ensure their ability to pay their debts to her. But the Germans reckoned on victory before America's weight could count in the scales.

CHAPTER SIX

SCENE 1

The Mincing Machine – Verdun

It is a truism that the war of 1914–18 revolutionized all ideas of time, in a military sense, and especially in the duration of its battles. For several thousand years of warfare a battle, however great the scale, had been a matter of hours. This remained the general case down to the beginning of this century, though a few battles from the Napoleonic Wars onwards increased the span to days – for example, Leipzig, Gettysburg. The real change was inaugurated with the Russo-Japanese campaign, when battles at last had to be reckoned in weeks. With the World War the standard became months – because the battles had usually become sieges, without being recognized or scientifically treated as such. The change, it is to be hoped, is a transitory one, for quantity does not imply quality, and duration does imply immobility and indecisiveness – which are perforce the negation of generalship. So that whether from the standpoint of military science or from that of the drain of human life, long battles are bad battles.

The prolongation, too, has complicated the task of the military historian, for unless he desires to fill massive tomes with profuse detail, it is difficult to pick out salient features where there are either none, or else so many that they tend to merge into a formless mass. And of all the so-called 'battles' of the war, Verdun holds the duration record, extending from February 21st to December 15th, 1916. Even if the suspension of the German offensive be taken as the last date, and the French counter-offensive considered as distinct, the duration is seven months.

This difficulty of singling out any one date is unfortunate, for no battle of the whole war was more heroic or more dramatic in its course, or made so vivid an appeal to the sympathies of the watching nations. It was France's supreme sacrifice and her supreme triumph, and to the splendour of her achievement all the world paid homage.

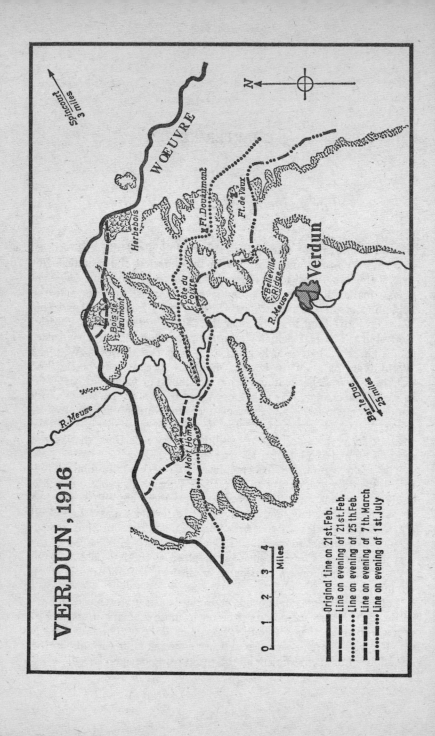

VERDUN, 1916

N

Spincourt
3 miles

WOEUVRE

Herbebois

N Ft. Douaumont

Ft. de Vaux

Côte du Poivre

Belleville Ridge

Bois de Haumont

R. Meuse

R. Meuse

le Mort Homme

Verdun

Bar le Duc
25 miles

——— Original line on 21st. Feb.
– – – Line on evening of 21st. Feb.
••••••• Line on evening of 25th. Feb.
–·–·– Line on evening of 7th. March
······· Line on evening of 1st. July

0   1   2   3   4
Miles

From February 25th onwards, there was a series of crises until June 23rd, and many French authorities select the former date as the chief. Yet who should know better than the Germans the moment when the tide really turned against them? So distinguished a critic as General von Zwehl considered that the real turning point was on March 9th, when the Germans failed to capture the Côte de Poivre. It was on March 4th that the Crown Prince called on his army group for a supreme effort to take Verdun, 'the heart of France'. On March 6th, after a two days' bombardment, the new blow fell, and by the 9th was definitely frustrated.

The determination of such a datum point is affected also by the question as to the object of the German Supreme Command in launching the attack on Verdun. General von Falkenhayn, the Chief of the Great General Staff and the responsible officer, has stated categorically that it was to bleed France white by choosing a point of attack for which, sooner than let go, the French Command would have to fight to the last man. He has also quoted from a paper prepared at Christmas, 1915, to show that he argued that a breakthrough in mass was not necessary for this purpose.

Yet, despite his post-war statements, there is still a just doubt as to the initial object. A prominent German critic, Colonel Foerster, pointed out how difficult it was to reconcile Falkenhayn's statement with the manner in which the attack was carried out, and declared that the initial operation was obviously an accelerated attack for the purpose of breaking through. He based himself on extracts from Falkenhayn's own order of January 27th, 1916, and the latter's vehement marginal criticisms on the explanation of failure rendered by the Crown Prince's headquarters on March 31st. These show Falkenhayn calling for an unchecked and continuous advance.

Others, including Pétain, believe the real idea underlying the plan was that of a revival of the 'Sedan' double envelopment which had been attempted in September 1914. In 1916 such a plan had more favourable chances, for the salient was more acute than at the time of the Marne battle, owing to the St Mihiel wedge that had been driven into its eastern flank. And the fact that the salient lay astride a river, the Meuse, would hamper the defenders in holding back the German pincers. Moreover, this hypothesis provides a logical explanation for what outwardly seems the unaccountable German mistake in launching their first attack only on the east bank of the river. But if a Sedan was the Germans' object, they might expect that their attack on the east bank would draw the French reserves thither so that the later attack on the west bank, when released, would be able to sweep across the rear of the French, using the river as their prison wall. Thereby, not only would part of the French army be cut off, but the rest be cut in two, while the vast breach would ensure the collapse of the whole trench front in France.

Fresh light on this enigmatic battle has, however, come from the German archives and from important witnesses; the evidence collated in a book by Hermann Wendt is particularly illuminating. From this new material it would appear that the explanation of Falkenhayn's purpose lies in his opportunism; and the explanation of the curious course of the German operations, in one more of the internal conflicts that wrecked so many plans.

Falkenhayn, whose course was apparently none too clear in his own mind, seems to have rested on the hope that something might happen – that 'something' might be a moral collapse behind the French front, produced by the combination of natural depression and subsidized propaganda. But if he was wiser than other strategists in realizing the importance of political effects, he does not seem to have had clear ideas as to how to produce them. And, unfortunately for him, his executive subordinates had a purely military outlook. The scheme drawn up by the Crown Prince's Chief of Staff, Schmidt von Knobelsdorf, diverged widely from Falkenhayn's line of thought. It proposed an attempt to pinch off Verdun, by a vigorous attack on both flanks, 'so as to avoid a long-drawn-out battle of material, with its incalculable expenditure of force'.

This big gamble did not suit Falkenhayn's book, so he reduced the plan to an attack on the east bank only, apparently hoping to control the executive commander's impetuosity by keeping a tight hand on the reserves. In this purpose, as in his greater one, he was to fail. It is not easy to determine whether that failure was due more to his own misjudgement in adjusting the means to the end, or to his inability to adjust his subordinate's views to his own. Princely subordinates were difficult to control, and Falkenhayn's position was too unstable for him safely to exert strong pressure. Also, whatever his failings, he at least has the credit of affirming a new principle in tactics.

The German offensive was to be based on fire power rather than on man power, and its main agent was to be an intense artillery bombardment, making up for its relatively short duration by the number of batteries and their rapidity of fire, and so seeking to regain the supreme advantage of surprise which was inevitably lost by an artillery preparation of several days, or even a week – as the Allied method had been at

Loos, in Champagne, and was still to be on the Somme. To increase their chance of surprise the Germans constructed none of the customary 'jumping off' trenches close to the enemy lines, confident that their tremendous artillery bombardment would enable their infantry to cross the wide no-man's-land, in places half a mile across, without meeting effective resistance. With their rear preparations they were less success-ful. But although the Intelligence branch at French General Head-quarters was thus able to deduce the German intentions, the Operations branch disregarded the warning. On February 1st a driblet of two Territorial divisions was sent, but only at the last moment were ade-quate reinforcements – two army corps – ordered there. Even when the first of these arrived there were only three divisions on the right bank of the Meuse, two on the left, and three south of the fortress facing east – with no reserves at hand. It is not difficult to guess what would have happened if the German attack had come on the 13th, as intended, before this first corps arrived. Bad weather saved the defenders in a double sense, for it also hampered the moving forward of the Germans' heavy guns.

There is, however, another important aspect of this preliminary phase which is comparatively little known. A hasty generalization from the easy fall of the Belgian and Russian fortresses may have caused much of the subsequent critical position at Verdun. Originally the French fortresses were not under the control of the field army, but Joffre used the examples of Liége and Namur as an excuse to persuade the French Government to 'declass' Verdun as a fortress, and, having got control in August, 1915, from then on he drained it of its men and armament. This removal of guns continued even until January 30th, 1916, and the casemates were simply used as shelters for troops. Instead of an all-round defence a single trench position was taken up beyond the forts, and in rear only one subsidiary trench line was usable.

For this continuous front, the commander, General Herr, had not enough men or material – to garrison it or keep it in an efficient state of defence. Its wire was incomplete, and it had scarcely any shell-proof cover. Little wonder that when the blow fell the trench position was blotted out. In contrast was the extraordinary imperviousness of the forts. Forts Douaumont and Vaux fell into German hands, and when they were recaptured in October the French found that months of tremendous bombardment had made scarcely an impression. The un-derground cover remained intact, not one field-gun turret was des-troyed, and hardly any of the casemates rendered unoccupiable. It was a grim jest of fate that the French should have thrown away their shield for a target, through a hasty assumption that fortresses were valueless.

The original Governor, General Coutanceau, had not shared this view, but when, before a Parliamentary delegation, he dared to express his opinion, in contradiction to the Army Group commander, General Dubail, he was not only rebuked but dismissed. For some time, rumours had percolated through to Paris about the inadequate state of the Verdun defences, and in December Galliéni, as Minister of War, had written to Joffre asking for information and an assurance that they should be developed. Joffre's reply might well be framed and hung up in all the bureaux of officialdom the world over - to serve as the mummy at the feast. Rebutting the suggestions, he added - 'But since these apprehensions are founded on reports which allege defects in the state of the defences, I request you to ... specify their authors. I cannot be a party to soldiers under my command bringing before the Government, by channels other than the hierarchic channel, complaints or protests concerning the execution of my orders ... It is calculated to disturb profoundly the spirit of discipline in the Army.' The enemy was soon to dispel his doctrine of infallibility, as the mutinies of 1917 were to show that the incapacity of generals and their waste of human life are the most potent factors in disturbing the spirit of discipline. But retribution is slow. Colonel Driant, Deputy for Nancy and a well-known military writer, who had given the warning, was one of the first victims of its neglect, while Joffre for a time gained fresh popular laurels from the heroic sacrifice of Driant and his fellows.

At a quarter past seven on the morning of February 21st, a cold, dry day, the German bombardment began on both banks of the Meuse and on a front of fifteen miles. Steadily the trenches and wire were flattened out or upheaved in a chaos of tumbled earth. 'The craters made by the huge shells gave to all the countryside an appearance like the surface of the moon.' Familiar as it was to be later, in February, 1916, so violent a bombardment was new, and therefore the more appalling. So it went on - until at 4 PM the fury of the shell-storm reached its height. Another three-quarters of an hour and a thin skirmish line of German infantry began to advance almost unnoticed, followed by bombing parties and flame-throwers, to feel the French position before the rest of the infantry was launched. This method economized life, and it also disclosed the unequal effect of the German bombardment, which in parts suffered from the deadly counter-battery fire of the French artillery. Moreover, the initial German attack was made by only six divisions and only along a four-and-a-half-mile front between Bois de Haumont and Herbebois on the east bank. On so narrow a front the few scattered packets of surviving Frenchmen caused more delay than should have been the case on a reasonable frontage, and the early onset of darkness halted the attack after the foremost trenches had been occupied. But next day the attack developed more widely, and from then until the 24th the defenders' line was progressively crumbled away.

The French commanders on the spot asked permission to evacuate the Woevre plain and draw back the line on to the Meuse heights on the right bank. Even this they felt must be only a preliminary to the evacuation of the whole right, or eastern, bank of the Meuse. But behind the front the full gravity of the situation was hardly realized. 'Operations' still asserted that the Verdun offensive was a feint to cover the real blow, in Champagne. Even when the news of the crumbling front came through, Joffre was not moved, much less disturbed. At last, on the evening of the 24th, General de Castelnau – who, since his appointment as Chief of the French General Staff, had been adroitly side-tracked by Joffre's ever-zealous, and jealous, *entourage* – took the initiative and, going direct to Joffre, gained his permission to send Pétain's army to take over the defence of Verdun. Still more alarming reports came in later, and at 11 PM de Castelnau, with unique daring, insisted that the orderly officer should rap on Joffre's locked door and wake him up. Before the great man returned to resume his unvarying ration of sleep, he had given de Castelnau authority to go to Verdun with 'full powers'.

Leaving Chantilly during the night, de Castelnau motored post haste to the headquarters of the Army Group commander, de Langle de Cary. Joffre meanwhile had telegraphed that the front north of Verdun must be held at all costs: 'Every commander who ... gives an order for retreat will be tried by court martial.' He left it to de Langle de Cary to decide whether to swing back his right on to the Meuse heights, and the latter acted on this permission.

De Castelnau's first day at Verdun was not auspicious; for on the 25th occurred the strange incident of Fort Douaumont, and with it the first crisis of the long battle. Like most of the other forts it had no garrison, except for a crew of twenty-three gunners who manned one turret. When, however, the German tide approached the fort, General Chrétien, commanding the right sector, dictated an order that the line of the forts was to be made the principal line of resistance. This was shortly before midnight on the 24th. Unfortunately his staff waited for the preparation of some sketches to attach to the order, and so delayed its issue until 9.45 AM on the 25th. Meantime a patrol of Brandenburgers, finding the drawbridge down and no sign of any defenders –

the gunners had fallen asleep dead-beat – walked in and took possession without firing a shot. A triumphal German *communiqué* announced the capture of Douaumont 'by assault' in the presence of the Kaiser. This piece of official bombast, however, was to be outclassed and out-farced when, owing to a misunderstood telephone message, the *communiqué* of March 9th announced the capture of Fort Vaux – three months too early. But the cream of the jest was that both the divisional commander who made the report and the officer who had *not* taken the fort, received from the Kaiser the highest Prussian order, *Pour le Mérite*! A bad telephone is not without compensations.

On February 25th Pétain took over command at Verdun, and the nucleus of a reserve army was assembling in rear. His first problem was not so much defence as supply. The German heavy guns had closed all avenues except one light railway and the Bar-le-Duc to Verdun road – which later became immortal as 'the Sacred Way'. To push up troops was no use unless they could be fed and supplied with ammunition. The road was already cracking under the strain of the incessant transport, and so gangs of Territorial troops were brought up to keep it in repair and to double it by parallel tracks. Henceforward the flow of traffic rose to as many as 6,000 lorries in the twenty-four hours. Up in front Pétain was organizing the front into sectors, each with its own heavy artillery, and throwing in repeated counter-attacks. If these gained little ground, they disconcerted and checked the attacking Germans. Another assisting factor was that the farther they advanced on the east bank the more did they expose themselves to flanking fire from the French artillery across the river. The advance lost its momentum, slowed down, and already on the German side 'a grievous pessimism had set in', so Zwehl tells us.

Falkenhayn was now led to widen the front of attack, although he doled out only four divisions. On March 6th, after two days' bombardment, the Crown Prince attacked on the west bank of the Meuse, and on the 8th the troops on the east bank joined in this supreme effort. The gains did not repay the losses, and against Mort Homme on the west and the Poivre height on the east the attack beat in vain. Any hope of a breakthrough faded, for the defence was now consolidated and the numbers had been balanced. Whatever we think of his foresight, there can be no question that Joffre's imperturbable temperament was a great asset in calming the anxiety of those days, and in Pétain he made the right choice for the emergency. It is proverbial that fortune favours the brave, and two great pieces of luck befell the French – the fortunate destruction of all the German 17-inch howitzers by the French long-range guns, and the blowing up of the great German artillery park near Spincourt, which held 450,000 heavy shell, unwisely kept fused. One authority, indeed, General Palat, gives it as his opinion that these two factors saved Verdun.

From March 9th onwards, there can be no question that the German policy was primarily attrition, and that so far as Verdun was aimed at it was as a moral objective. Publicity had given it a symbolical value definitely superior to its military value. It must be confessed that the strategy nearly succeeded – but only, after a long interval, through the introduction of a new agent. In the meantime the Germans paid an exorbitant price for little gain. Nevertheless, they put a heavy tax on the French. Pétain did his best to mitigate the strain by a rapid rotation of reliefs, which kept each division under fire for the shortest possible time. But, as a result, a great part of the French Army was drawn through the 'mincing machine', and the drain on the French reserves almost bankrupted their share in the forthcoming Somme offensive.

On the German side, the disappointing results produced an earlier reaction. At the end of March Falkenhayn enquired whether there was 'any chance of progress within a reasonable time'; and he contemplated an alternative attack at Ypres. But the Crown Prince confidently declared that the greater part of the French reserves had been used up, and that he was 'unreservedly of the opinion that the fate of the French Army would be decided at Verdun'. Moreover, the fatally old-fashioned idea of the executive command was betrayed in the remark that 'the destruction of the French reserves ... should be completed by the employment of men, as well as of apparatus and munitions'. Falkenhayn gave way to this plea.

So the Crown Prince, egged on by Schmidt von Knobelsdorf, continued to pour out his men's blood, while Falkenhayn spent the time in study of possible alternatives. But at the end of April the barren result of constant nibbling attacks led to a decision to revert to wider ones.

These proved equally futile, so that even Schmidt von Knobelsdorf was led to admit the hopelessness of further attack. Yet when he visited Falkenhayn in this mood of repentance, he found the latter had also changed his mind – to the opposite view. So Schmidt von Knobelsdorf was reconverted, and the offensive continued. But the wastage of life was now balanced by Joffre's misguided instructions that Fort Douaumont must be recovered; he also removed Pétain's restraining hand by promoting him to command of the Army Group and placing Nivelle in direct charge at Verdun. By launching repeated attacks, Nivelle now played into Falkenhayn's hands, and lost on the rebound.

On June 7th, after a heroic resistance, Fort Vaux really fell – by another German telephone mistake the wrong officer again received the credit – and with it a large stretch of ground was submerged by the German tide, that now seemed to the anxious watchers to resemble the forces of nature rather than of men. On June 11th Pétain was forced to ask Joffre to hasten the relief offensive on the Somme. Then on June 20th, the Germans introduced a new kind of diphosgene gas shell with startling effect. It paralysed the French artillery support, and on the 23rd came a deep advance that brought the Germans almost to the Belleville height, the last outwork of Verdun. Mangin's incessant counter-attacks could do no more than put a brake on the advance, and Pétain made all ready for the evacuation of the east bank, though to his troops he showed no signs of anxiety and ever repeated the now immortal phrase, 'On les aura!' Four divisions were hurriedly dispatched to him by Joffre, thus further weakening the Somme reserve.

But the Germans had used their new lever too late. Strategically, the defenders were now made secure, indirectly, as Falkenhayn stopped the flow of ammunition to Verdun on the 24th – when the British bombardment began on the Somme, preparatory to the long-arranged attack which was delivered on July 1st. From that day on the Germans at Verdun received no fresh divisions, and their advance died out from pure inanition. The way was thus paved for the brilliant French counter-offensives of the autumn, which retook by bites what had been lost by nibbles. It is no disparagement of the sterling defence to recognize, as we must, that the Somme saved Verdun, and, second, that the Germans after throwing away their best chance by too narrow an attack frontage, came desperately close to their goal four months later.

CHAPTER SIX

SCENE 2

The Brusilov Offensive

On June 5th, 1916, began an offensive on the Eastern Front which was to prove the last really effective military effort of Russia. Popularly known as Brusilov's offensive, it had such an astonishing initial success as to revive enthusiastic dreams of the irresistible Russian 'steamroller', that was perhaps the greatest and most dangerous myth of the war. Instead, its ultimate achievement was to sound Russia's death knell. Paradoxical in its consequences, it was still more so in its course – an epitome of the delusive objectives, of the blunders leading to success, and the successes leading to downfall, which marked perhaps the most erratic war in history. In 1915 the Entente had pinned their hopes on Russia, only for the year's campaign to close with the Russian armies, battered and exhausted, barely escaping complete disaster by a seemingly endless retreat. When Falkenhayn turned in 1916 to inaugurate the Verdun attack he left Russia lamed but not crippled, and her surprisingly rapid, if perhaps superficial recovery, enabled her to dislocate the German plans for 1916. As early as March she attacked at Lake Narocz, on the Baltic flank, in a gallant sacrificial attempt to relieve the pressure on France. Her command then prepared, for July, a main offensive, also in the north. But before this was ready the needs of her Allies once more led her into a premature move. While the strain at Verdun was growing ever more serious, the Austrians took the opportunity to launch an attack in the Trentino, against the Italians, who appealed to their Russian ally to prevent the Austrians releasing further forces from the Eastern Front to reinforce the Trentino menace.

Meantime the Tsar had held a council of war of his Army Group commanders on April 14th. It was here arranged that the main Russian offensive should be made by Evert's centre group of armies, while Kuropatkin's northern group wheeled inwards to assist it; and it was proposed that Brusilov's southern group should stay strictly on the defensive as his front was unsuited to the offensive. But Brusilov regarded this as a reason for taking the offensive – because helpful to surprise – and argued that past lack of success was due to the way the Russian armies had allowed the enemy to utilize his central position by not attacking simultaneously. As a result of the discussion Brusilov was given permission to act as he wished, and, with such resources as he had, to stage an offensive that would draw the enemy's attention away from the main blow planned in the north, near Molodeczno. Realizing that his best chance of success lay in surprise, he began preparations at over twenty places, so that even deserters could not give away the real point of attack. And, instead of concentrating his reserves, he divided them.

The appeal of Russia's ally hastened his action. On May 24th Alexeiev telegraphed to ask how soon he could attack. Brusilov replied that he would be ready to do so on June 1st, provided that Evert also attacked. Evert, however, was not ready; it was finally agreed that Brusilov should strike on the 4th, and Evert ten days later. On the night of the 3rd Alexeiev rang up Brusilov and expressed doubts of the wisdom of a plan so unconventional, suggesting that he should concentrate his troops for an attack on a narrow front, instead of distributing them on a wide front. Brusilov demurred and Alexeiev eventually gave way, saying, 'God be with you. Do as you like.'

The troops were moved up during the night for an apparent gamble, in which every factor save the possibility of surprise weighed against success. Brusilov's strength was no more than equal to that of the opposing force – thirty-eight against thirty-seven divisions – and it was widely distributed. But the absence of any concentration gave the Austrians no warning of the impending move, and when, on June 4th, the Russian Eighth Army, under Kaledin, advanced near Luck for what was little more than a reconnaissance in force, they took the Austrians by surprise. The front broke like a crust of pastry at the first touch, and almost unresisted the Russians pushed between the Austrian Fourth and Second Armies. By the following day 40,000 prisoners had been taken, and the number swelled rapidly as Brusilov widened his offensive. Although the Russian Eleventh Army (Sakharov) failed near Tarnopol, the other two armies farther south gained as rapid success as that at Luck. The Seventh Army (Shcherbachev) drove the Austrians back across the Strypa, and the Ninth Army (Lechitski), breaking through in the Bukovina, captured Czernowitz – the southernmost position of the Austrian front. By the 20th, Brusilov had captured 200,000 men.

Never has a mere demonstration had so amazing a success since the walls of Jericho fell at Joshua's trumpet blasts. With both flanks collapsed, the Austro-German armies in the south were in danger of a greater Tannenberg, if only the Russians could exploit their chance. But all the reserves were massed in the north for the intended main offensive, and this was not developed. First, Evert said that on account of bad weather he could not begin until the 18th, and, even so, did not expect to be successful. The Tsar and Alexeiev lacked the resolution either to coerce or to replace Evert, and instead authorized him to prepare an attack at a different place – which meant further delay. But neither Evert nor Kuropatkin showed any inclination to take the offensive; and, as Alexeiev could not move them, he tried instead to move their reserves. Poor lateral communications, however, prevented these reaching Brusilov before the Germans could hurry reinforcements to stem the tide. The German Command showed its usual cleverness, using the first reinforcements for a counterstroke by Linsingen against the northern edge of the Luck breakthrough, and this at least checked the Russian progress at the most critical point. To the south, in the Bukovina, the Russian advance continued until it came to a natural halt against the barrier of the Carpathian Mountains.

Late in July the Russian attack was renewed, first in the centre towards Brody and Lemberg by Sakharov, then farther north towards the Stokhod river and Kovel, by the Russian Guard Army, long prepared for a supreme effort. But the opportunity had passed, and although the attacks still dragged on throughout August, the gains in no way compensated for their heavy cost, and an effort which opened in a blaze of sunshine faded out in autumn gloom.

Its indirect were, however, greater than its direct effects, although not unmixed in benefit. It had compelled Falkenhayn to withdraw seven divisions from the west, and so abandon his plan for a riposte against the British Somme offensive, as well as the hope of nourishing his attrition process at Verdun. It led Rumania to take her fateful decision to enter the war on the Entente side – to her undoing. And it wrought the downfall of Falkenhayn, who had 'spoiled the ship for a ha'porth of tar.'

But these indirect effects were purchased at a heavy price. Brusilov had captured the Bukovina and much of Eastern Galicia; he had captured 350,000 prisoners – but, through prolonging the offensive when opportunity had passed, over 1,000,000 men had been lost. This loss undermined morally, even more than materially, the fighting power of Russia. The imminent sequel was to be revolution and collapse. For the last time Russia had sacrificed herself for her allies, and it is not just that subsequent events should obscure the debt.

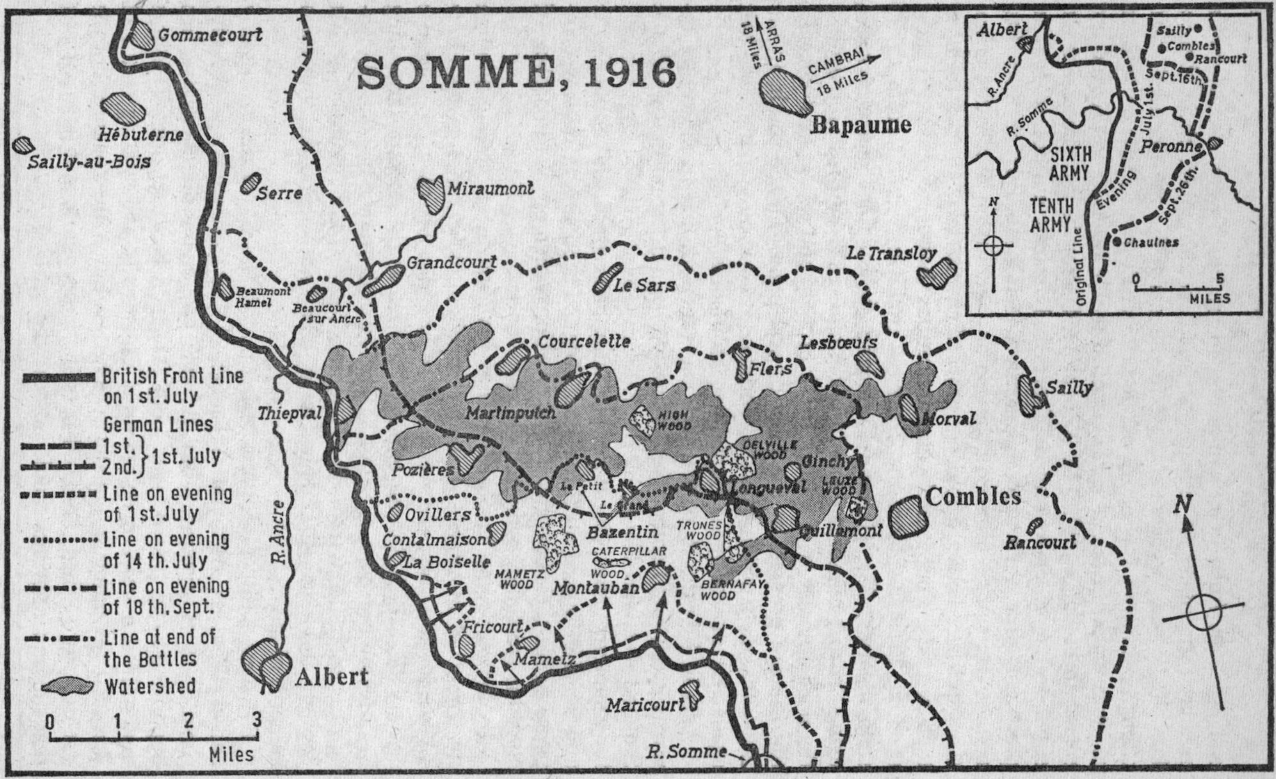
SOMME, 1916
ARRAS 18 Miles
CAMBRAI 18 Miles
Bapaume
Gommecourt
Hébuterne
Sailly-au-Bois
Serre
Miraumont
Grandcourt
Beaumont Hamel
Beaucourt sur Ancre
Le Sars
Le Transloy
Courcelette
Lesboeufs
Flers
Thiepval
Martinpuich
HIGH WOOD
Sailly
Morval
DELVILLE WOOD
Ginchy
Pozières
Le Petit
Le Grand
Longueval
LEUZE WOOD
Combles
Ovillers
Bazentin
TRONES WOOD
Guillemont
Rancourt
Contalmaison
CATERPILLAR WOOD
La Boiselle
MAMETZ WOOD
Montauban
BERNAFAY WOOD
Fricourt
Mametz
Albert
Maricourt
R. Ancre
R. Somme
N
British Front Line on 1st. July
German Lines
1st.
2nd.
1st. July
Line on evening of 1st. July
Line on evening of 14 th. July
Line on evening of 18 th. Sept.
Line at end of the Battles
Watershed
0
1
2
3
Miles
Albert
R. Ancre
R. Somme
SIXTH ARMY
TENTH ARMY
Original Line
Evening
July 1st.
Peronne
Sept. 26th.
Sept. 16th.
Sailly
Combles
Rancourt
Chaulnes
0
5
MILES

CHAPTER SIX

SCENE 3

The Somme Offensive

The 'battle' – or, to be strategically accurate, the series of partial actions – in Picardy which opened on July 1st, constituted the offensive campaign of the Franco-British armies in 1916. Into it was thrown the entire British effort of the year on the Western Front, and such part of the French effort as was available after the exhausting strain of the long defensive 'battle' of Verdun. And it proved both the glory and the graveyard of 'Kitchener's Army' – those citizen volunteers who, instantly answering the call in 1914, had formed the first national army of Britain.

The Somme offensive had its genesis at the Chantilly Conference of the Allied commanders on December 5th, 1915. Joffre, in his appreciation of the situation, claimed that the autumn offensives in Champagne and Artois (including Loos) had brought 'brilliant tactical results', and ascribed the failure to develop these into a strategical success, partly to bad weather and partly to a temporary shortage of ammunition. The essential for the next effort was that 'the Higher Command must have no anxiety as regards ammunition', and for this reason it could not be undertaken in less than three months. By early February he had realized that the date must be later still, if, as was essential, the Russians were to attack simultaneously and the British were to take an adequate share with their newly raised armies. At a meeting with Haig he emphasized the view that a broad frontage of attack was the method of success, and to this end desired a combined offensive by the French and British *'bras dessus bras dessous'*, with the attacking line of one Ally prolonging that of the other Ally. Joffre envisaged the French attacking with forty divisions on a twenty-five miles' front from Lassigny to the Somme, and the British attacking thence to Hébuterne, fourteen miles, with twenty-five divisions, or as near that number as possible.

The British Official History remarks that Joffre's decision to make the offensive in a sector which 'might be considered the strongest' for defence, on the Western Front, 'seems to have been arrived at solely because the British would be bound to take part in it. The reasons advanced by General Joffre will hardly bear examination'. Even Foch, if it was not his habit to weigh tactical difficulties, disliked the choice of sector as being a strategic dead-end. Haig would have preferred to make his attack in Flanders, on the lines of the offensive which he carried out in 1917, assisted by a landing on the Belgian coast.

Joffre also pressed the British to make a preparatory attack north of the Somme in April, and another in May – to draw in the enemy's reserves, so easing the way for the Franco-British main blow. Haig preferred to trust in one great stroke, with all the forces available and when they were fully prepared. Although Haig's attitude was justified by the incompleteness of his resources and by the barrenness of such preparatory attacks the previous autumn, the critic is compelled to recognize that Joffre had the experience of history on his side, and that the experience of the war was to show that decisive offensives were vain until the enemy's reserves had been attracted elsewhere. But Haig was unquestionably right in maintaining that any such preparatory attacks, to fulfil their object, should only precede the general offensive by ten days or a fortnight.

He suggested that the British might deliver one such attack if the French made others. This idea did not appeal to Joffre who, according to Poincaré, had now 'in mind a war of attrition which must be chiefly carried out by our Allies, England, Russia, and even Italy'. So discussions continued. It is amusing to note that the British staff took refuge in the explanation – 'The British Army is ready to do its full share, but we cannot cope with the politicians, who, after the Germans, are our worst enemies.'

Eventually, at a conference on February 14th, an agreement was reached by which Haig accepted Joffre's plan for the Somme offensive – dated for July 1st – while Joffre gave up his demand for preparatory offensives.

The result of the postponement of the Allied offensive, whether inevitable or not, was to yield the initiative to the Germans, and their attack at Verdun, from February 21st onwards, impaired the whole of the Allied plan and campaign in 1916. Yet such a possibility had not even been mentioned at the conference on the 14th.

On February 22nd Joffre asked the British to aid him by relieving part of his troops in the north. Haig accordingly hastened the relief of the French Tenth Army, round Arras, which was sandwiched between his own First and Third Armies. Allenby's Third Army sideslipped northwards, and the newly formed Fourth Army, under Rawlinson, took over its front between Maricourt and Hébuterne. The British now held a continuous eighty-mile front from Ypres almost to the Somme.

As the French were drained of their strength at Verdun, so did their share of the Somme plan evaporate. Ultimately their front of attack shrank from twenty-five miles to eight, and their force from forty divisions to sixteen, of which only five attacked on July 1st. From now onwards the British were to take up the main burden of the Western Front campaign and, because of this fact alone, July 1st, 1916, is a landmark in the history of the war.

Nevertheless, Haig did not adjust his aims to the shrinkage of resources. It is true that he continued preparations for an attack at Messines, and formed an alternative plan, to switch his reserves thither in case of complete failure. But he does not seem to have foreseen the case of mixed success and failure – always the greater probability in war. And for this want of elasticity his plan suffered in execution. Realism was equally lacking. The hopeful intention of the British Command was, in the first stage, to break the German front between Maricourt and Serre; in the second stage to secure the high ground between Bapaume and Ginchy, while the French seized that round Sailly and Rancourt; in the third stage to wheel to the left and roll up the German flank as far as Arras, so enlarging the breach. With this object all available troops, including cavalry, would work northwards, from the line Bapaume–Miraumont, while a cooperating attack was launched against the German front south-west of Arras. Fourthly, was to come a general advance towards Cambrai–Douai. What a contrast between intention and achievement! In outline, the plan was shrewdly designed, and Haig was wise to take such long views. But he does not seem to have looked clearly enough at the ground beneath his feet. The very belief in such far-reaching possibilities suggests a failure to diagnose the actual conditions. There was a fundamental unrealism in a plan which, while discarding the old and ever-new master key of surprise, made no pretence to provide a substitute.

The main attack, on a fourteen-mile front between Maricourt and Serre, was entrusted to Rawlinson's Fourth Army of eighteen divisions, of which eleven were to lead the attack, with five in close reserve. Only two, together with a cavalry division, were in army reserve. But Haig also placed at Rawlinson's disposal, for exploiting success, a force of two cavalry divisions under Gough, with a corps of two divisions to follow. Two divisions of the Third Army were to make a subsidiary attack round Gommecourt. The artillery concentration totalled 1,537 guns, 467 being heavy. This meant one gun to every twenty yards of front, a record at that time, although far eclipsed by later concentrations. It was double that of the Germans for their great Dunajec breakthrough, but the defences on the Russian front a year before could not be compared with the network of wire and trenches on the Somme front. Another significant contrast was that whereas the French had 900 heavy guns, the British had less than half this number for a far wider front – one to every fifty-seven yards.

The British Official History remarks that 'The problem facing the Allies was, in fact, that of storming a fortress, in which, according to history and precedent, there should be a main assault on the largest breach (or weakest spot), several subsidiary ones on minor breaches – which must be strong enough to be converted into main assaults and carried through – and false attacks.' Instead, the distribution of force was as uniform as the methods of attacks were stereotyped. The artillery, in any case deficient, was spread evenly along the whole frontage. 'It must be confessed that the problem was not appreciated at GHQ.' What were the causes of this blindness? They had a pre-war base. 'It must be admitted that the problems of semi-siege warfare and the large concentration of guns necessary for the attack of great field defences had never been studied in practice by the General Staff. Under the influence of General H. H. Wilson (the late Sir Henry Wilson) it had been content to follow French ideas as to the nature of the next war, and ignored and almost resented hearing of the information obtained by its Intelligence branch as to the preparations being made and methods practised at manoeuvres by the Germans.'

To understand both the problem and the course of the battle a brief description of the ground is necessary, for in few battles on the Western Front did topography have so important an influence or make so deep an impression on the minds of the combatants. From Péronne, where the Somme makes a right-angled turn south, a range of hills runs northwest, forming the watershed between the Somme and the basins of the Scarpe and the Scheldt. This ridge, intersected by the narrow valley of the little river Ancre, had been in German possession since the 'Race to the Sea' of October, 1914, and it gave the enemy command and observation over the Allied lines and the land behind them. For the first year this disadvantage mattered little, for when British troops relieved the French here in July, 1915, the front had an air and a condition of peacefulness astonishing to men accustomed to the incessant 'bickering' of Ypres or La Bassée. Report said that in some places the troops of our Ally went back for *déjeuner* to villages hardly touched, close to the line, leaving only sentries in the trenches; that in another hamlet which stood in no-man's-land the sleeping accommodation was nightly shared between the opposing sides by tacit consent. I can vouch for the fact that in the first months after the British had taken over this front it was possible for battalions to drill undisturbed on fields in full view of the German lines – whereas six months later billets several miles farther back were harassed by gunfire. The campaign policy of the French, except when engaged in active operations, was 'live and let live', and in retrospect there seems little doubt that it was wiser than the British policy of continual 'strafing'. For when the Germans held the dominating positions as well as a superiority in ammunition and equipment these worrying tactics wore down the British troops more than the enemy – attrition on the wrong side of the balance sheet. Further, they stirred the Germans to strengthen their trench defences, to develop by art the advantages of nature, so that the offensive came against an almost impregnable fortress instead of against the relatively weak defence system which existed in the autumn of 1915. Masefield, in his book, *The Old Front Line*, expressed the situation aptly – 'Almost in every part of this old front our men had to go up hill to attack ... The enemy had the look-out posts, with the fine views over France, and the sense of domination. Our men were down below, with no view of anything but of stronghold after stronghold, just up above, being made stronger daily.' Today the tumbled desolation that was the Somme battlefield has passed. Though he underestimated the time, Masefield's instinct was correct that 'when the trenches are filled in and the plough has gone over them the ground will not keep the look of war. One summer with its flowers will cover most of the ruin that man can make, and then these places, from which the driving back of the enemy began, will be hard indeed to trace, even with maps'. 'Centre Way, Peel Trench, Munster Alley, and these other paths to glory will be deep under the corn, and gleaners will sing at Dead Mule Corner.' Yet, while even memory finds it difficult to recapture the wartime aspect, a tranquil visit impresses the mind with the steepness of the ascent and the command from the ridge, even more than in days when progress was reckoned in yards and the contour was seen from the eye-level of trenches and shell-holes. From an artillery point of view there were advantages in attacking uphill, because the German trenches were more clearly displayed, but in other ways it was a physical and psychological handicap – not only to the attacking infantry.

Surprise, difficult in face of such commanding positions, was the more difficult because the art of concealing preparations, and of camouflage, had yet to be relearnt. The construction of new hutments on both sides of the Ancre provided the Germans with the first clue, in February, and thenceforward signs continually multiplied. Falkenhayn contemplated an attempt to dislocate the British offensive, but found that he could not spare the necessary troops. If the vast preparations had not given it away, a bombardment of a week's duration would in any case have announced the coming assault. Even earlier, a censorship error in allowing publication of a speech to munition workers by the Minister of Labour, Mr Arthur Henderson, on June 2nd, had given the German Command a hint of its early delivery. The one redeeming factor was that despite accurate predictions and warnings of the attack both from the immediate army command (the Second) and from agents abroad, Falkenhayn continued to believe that it was only a preliminary to the real blow farther north, apparently feeling that British preparations were too blatant to be true. In consequence he withheld reinforcements, and not until July 5th was he convinced that the Somme was Haig's chosen battleground. In the meantime he dismissed the Chief of Staff of the Second Army for having been right and 'asking for more'.

This divergence of views in the German Command left the British a chance which was to be forfeited by a divergence of views in their own command. The extent of this difference, and its effects, has only come to light in recent years. For the offensive was only a few weeks old when the story was spread by officially inspired apologists that Haig was throughout aiming at a campaign of attrition and had not dreamt of a 'breakthrough'. This denial was vehemently maintained for years, long after the war; it forms one of the most elaborate perversions of historical truth that has come to light. The 'smoke screen', composed of particles of truth dishonestly mixed, was finally dissipated by the publication of the Official History in 1932.

This revealed that Joffre was only contemplating an attrition battle, and that Rawlinson inclined to the same view, while Haig, the middle man, both sought and believed in a breakthrough. His judgement dictated the British aim. But Rawlinson's doubts led to the British plan being a compromise of method, which made it largely unsuitable to either aim. In view of his 'comparatively small resources' in artillery, and the depth of the German position, Rawlinson favoured a prolonged bombardment and an advance by limited stages. The first inevitably diminished the chances of surprise – the most potent compensation for small resources – while the second was a check on exploiting any success that was gained, giving the enemy time to recover and to bring up reserves. Haig justly realized the latter defect and also inclined to a short bombardment; but, perhaps, being an untechnically minded cavalryman, he skimmed over the problem of cutting the wire entanglements that covered the approach to the enemy's position. After discussion Rawlinson was allowed his long bombardment, but was ordered to swallow part of the German second position, as well as the first, at one gulp.

The Official History, while showing that a breakthrough could hardly have had decisive results, and even suggesting that it would merely have created a dangerous salient, implies that a breakthrough was possible. But not in the way it was attempted. For his breakthrough aim, Haig actually relied on the one means in which he was, by all advice, too limited. His artillery adviser told him that he was 'stretching' his artillery too much. Rawlinson 'expressed the fear' that he was 'asking too much' of the force available, that its gun power would be spread too thinly for effect, and that an attempt to bite off part of the second position would be 'a gamble'. Nevertheless, it was to that gamble that Haig decided to commit his subordinates and their men.

'Increasing optimism' was shown by Haig as the day of battle drew nearer, though French resources, and consequently their share, were steadily shrinking owing to the drain of Verdun. What is perhaps more remarkable is the way his chief subordinates joined in the chorus of optimism, singing so loudly as apparently to drown the doubts they had felt during cool consideration of the problem. They not merely deferred to his judgement; they made it their own. Loyalty could go no further.

'Privately' Rawlinson 'was convinced that they (Haig's instructions) were based on false premises and on too great optimism'. Yet he 'impressed on all at conferences and other times ... "that nothing could exist at the conclusion of the bombardment in the area covered by it", and the infantry would only have to walk over and take possession'. This current of optimism was passed downwards with the result that even when the bombardment was proving ineffective, battalions 'which reported that the enemy machine guns had not been silenced were told by the divisional staffs that they were scared'. Terrible words for an official history to record as being said to men who were about to pay with their lives for this disregard of their words!

Because of its disastrous effects, the causes of this fantastic optimism demand analysis. With some officers in large degree, and perhaps most officers in some degree, care for their personal interests may have had an influence. Viewed fairly, that is no particular reproach to soldiers;

for in any profession where life-careers are concerned it is human nature to follow the cue given from above.* But a wider cause would seem to have been genuine self-delusion. In some cases this may have been induced by the confused idea of loyalty – 'blind loyalty' – that the nineteenth-century military system had fostered; even here, the Fourth Army instructions, which omitted so many tactical points of vital importance, took pains to lay down with heavy emphasis that 'all criticism by subordinates ... of orders received from superior authority will in the end recoil on the heads of the critics...' But in other cases optimism was so buoyant as to need no inspiration from on high. Thus when Haig, anxious over the inadequate preparedness of one army corps, sent General Charteris thither with power to countermand its attack, 'for it had little chance of complete success', his envoy found the commander 'more than satisfied', and saying exuberantly that he felt 'like Napoleon before the battle of Austerlitz'. So Charteris yielded to his desire, although he 'came back feeling very miserable'.

The Official History suggests that the root of this fatal optimism among the higher command may be traced to an astounding failure to grasp the main lesson of previous experience – a lesson that most regimental soldiers had long since learnt. 'The failures of the past were put down to reasons other than the stout use of the machine gun by the enemy and his scientifically planned defences.' Such expert 'reasoning' is certainly one of the most remarkable recorded cases in all history of missing the wood for the trees.

Rationally it seems inexplicable that the bombardment should have been counted on to leave nobody alive in the opposing trenches. For, beyond Rawlinson's original doubts, there is the fact that he himself spread his limited artillery evenly along the front 'without regard to the strength and importance of any particular part', with the result that 'their fire was necessarily so dispersed that many strong points and machine-gun posts were never touched'. Moreover, a large proportion of the heavy guns available were of obsolete pattern and poor range, while much of the ammunition was defective. Thus the shells could not penetrate the dug-outs in which the German machine-gunners were

---

* Perhaps its ill-effects could only be curtailed if war was conducted by amateurs, or at least by soldiers who had become civilians after being trained: the point is illustrated in General Charteris' remark on one such appointment late in the war. 'He has one very strong asset ... a very big job in civil life to go back to whenever he may wish ... It is difficult for any regular professional soldier not to be influenced by consideration of his own future prospects. — has the independence of a civilian and the training of a soldier.'

sheltering – in waiting. Yet it is only on the assumption of a potentially overwhelming bombardment that we can understand at all the tactics adopted by the British command. One can hardly believe that anyone with a grain of common-sense or any grasp of past experience would have launched troops to the attack by such a method unless intoxicated with confidence in the effect of the bombardment. The method is certainly an object-lesson in supreme negation.

The Official History continues – 'In the early discussions Haig had said that corps were not to attack until their commanders were satisfied that the enemy's defences had been sufficiently destroyed; but this condition seems to have been dropped as time passed.' This carelessness to maintain an essential condition of all warfare, especially siege warfare, is another extraordinary fact. It would have been culpable in the commander of a company.

Let us, in justice, record a redeeming point of precaution – or what might have been one. Haig had suggested tentatively that, before the mass of the infantry were launched, the result of the bombardment and the state of the defences might be tested by sending ahead patrols or small parties, such as the Germans had used at Verdun. But this suggestion was 'rejected by his army commanders'.

Was there anything that might have rescued success, or at least mitigated the sacrifice? Yes – if the British infantry could have reached the enemy trenches before the defenders were able to open fire. There were two ways in which this might have been achieved. By crossing either before the enemy could see to fire or before they were ready to fire. Without fog, natural or artificial, the only chance of the first lay in an assault during the darkness or in the dim light before dawn. We learn that 'a few commanders ... desired that at least the assault should be made at the first streak of light, before the enemy machine-gunners could see their prey'. We are told that 'Rawlinson himself accepted' the suggestion 'and pressed his French neighbours to agree'. But they had double his quantity of heavy guns and wanted good observation for them. So he agreed to the later hour, apparently with little misgiving.

The question that remained was whether the British infantry could cross no-man's-land before the barrage lifted. It was a race with death – the greatest of such races – run by nearly 60,000 men in the first heat. They were hopelessly handicapped. The whole mass, made up of closely packed waves of men, was to be launched together, without discovering whether the bombardment had really paralysed the resistance. Under the Fourth Army's instructions, those waves were to advance at 'a steady pace', symmetrically aligned like rows of ninepins ready to be knocked over. 'The necessity of crossing no-man's-land at a good pace, so as to reach the parapet before the enemy could reach it, was not mentioned.' But to do so would have been physically impossible, for the heaviest handicap of all was that 'the infantryman was so heavily laden that he could not move faster than a walk'. Each man carried about 66 lb, over half his own body weight, 'which made it difficult to get out of a trench, impossible to move much quicker than a slow walk, or to rise and lie down quickly'. Even an army mule, the proverbial and natural beast of burden, is only expected to carry a third of his own weight!

The 'race' was lost before it started, and the battle soon after. The barrage went on, the infantry could not go on, the barrage could not be brought back, and infantry reinforcements were pushed in just where infantry could not go on – a compound tragedy of errors.

The bombardment began on June 24th; the attack was intended for June 29th, but was later postponed until July 1st, owing to a momentary break in the weather. This postponement, made at French request, involved not only the spreading out of the ammunition over a longer period, and a consequent loss of intensity, but a greater strain on part of the assaulting troops, who, after being keyed up for the effort, had to remain another forty-eight hours in cramped trenches under the exhausting noise of their own gunfire and the enemy's retaliation – conditions made worse by torrential rain which flooded the trenches.

July 1st dawned a day of broiling heat, and at 7 AM, the bombardment rose to its height. Half an hour later the infantry advanced from their trenches – and thousands fell, strewing no-man's-land with their bodies, before the German front trench was even reached. For their opponents were the Germans of 1916, most stubborn and skilful fighters; while the shells flattened their trenches, they sheltered in dugouts or shell-holes, and then as the barrage lifted dragged out their machine guns, to pour an unslackening hail of lead into the unduly dense waves of the attackers – for 1916 marked the nadir of infantry attacks, the revival of formations that were akin to the eighteenth century in their formalism and lack of manoeuvring power. Battalions attacked in four or eight waves, not more than a hundred yards apart, the men in each almost shoulder to shoulder, in a symmetrical well-dressed alignment, and taught to advance steadily upright at a slow walk with their rifles held aslant in front of them, bayonets upwards – so as to catch the eye of the observant enemy. An excellent imitation of Frederick's infantry *automata*, with the difference that they were no longer advancing against muskets of an effective range of barely a hundred yards. It is hardly remarkable that by nightfall many bat-talions were barely a hundred strong. Only as the upstanding waves were broken up by the fire did advance become possible. For then human nature and primitive cunning reasserted themselves against authorized tactics; the more enterprising and still uncowed survivors formed little groups, usually under some natural leader, and worked their way by short rushes, and crawling from shell-hole to shell-hole, stalking the opposing machine guns, and often progressing to a con-siderable depth with little further loss. But in many places packets of the enemy and nests of machine guns were left in their wake, to take heavy toll of the supports, in similarly dense formations.

Thus, save in the south, the force of the tide slackened and later ebbed. Fricourt, on the right centre, formed a turning point both in the front and in the fortune of the day. The French, south of the Somme and north of it as far as Maricourt, gained all their objectives with slight loss. This success they owed partly to their more flexible tactics and heavier artillery concentration, partly to the lesser strength of the German defences, and to the fact that the attack here came as a tactical surprise to the Germans who had expected an attack only on the British front. Between Maricourt and Fricourt the British XIII Corps (30th and 18th Divisions) reached its objectives, though with greater loss, capturing Montauban. On its left the XV Corps partially achieved its task of pinching out the bastion of Fricourt village and wood. The 7th Division turned one flank by capturing Mametz, and on the other flank the 21st Division penetrated some half a mile into the German lines, holding on to a narrow tongue of captured land with both its own flanks in the air until Fricourt fell next day.

But the 21st Division marked the boundary of success, and all to the north was failure – with the heaviest British loss of any day's fighting in the war. One significant factor was the greater width of 'no-man's-land'. In the III Corps, fractions of the 34th Division pushed past La Boisselle to Contalmaison, but were forced to fall back. Against Ovil-lers the waves of the 8th Division beat practically in vain. A renewed attack was ordered for the afternoon – 'wiser counsels, however, pre-vailed'. Northward, again, in the X Corps the assault of the 32nd Divi-sion was broken again the defences of Thiepval – 'only bullet-proof soldiers could have taken Thiepval this day'. The 36th Ulster Division, however, celebrated the anniversary of the Boyne by penetrating deep into the German front past Thiepval towards Grandcourt. Unhappily, the corps commander used his reserve to reinforce the division that was hopelessly held up and refused it to the Ulstermen who had made a hopeful opening. Thus their advanced parties were cut off, and at nightfall only small fractions of the German front trenches remained in British hands. The attack of the VIII Corps (29th, 4th and 31st Divisions) on the left flank was shattered more abruptly, though here again a few isolated parties pressed through to Beaumont Hamel and Serre. A muddled argument over a question of one mine explosion led to the heavy artillery 'lifting' ten minutes before the infantry assault – with fatal result. As for the subsidiary attack by the VII Corps at Gommecourt, the failure of the 46th Division nullified the opening success of the 56th, while the value of the heavy sacrifice made by the corps as a whole was nullified by the failure of the main offensive.

The tally of prisoners who passed through the corps cages that day is in some degree an index of the comparative initial success – XIII Corps (Congreve), 934; XV Corps (Horne), 517; III Corps (Pulteney), 32; X Corps (Morland), 478; VIII Corps (Hunter-Weston), 22. In contrast, the French had taken over 4,000 prisoners at little cost. The assault of their XX Corps next to the British was cloaked by a river mist in crossing no-man's-land, and quickly overran the German first position. The French then proposed to push on, but gave up the idea on hearing that their British neighbours were held back by orders from the higher command. The French attack south of the Somme, by two divisions of the Colonial Corps and one of the XXXV, enjoyed a surprise effect through being delivered two hours later than elsewhere. It not only gained all its objectives, but was pushed beyond, and by nightfall was within reach of the German second position.

For the French, in view of these results, July 1st may be counted a victory. But the major attack was that of the British, and here the Germans could justly claim success, for with only six divisions available, and roughly a regiment holding each British division's sector of attack, they had only yielded 1,983 prisoners and a small tract of ground to the assault of thirteen British divisions. The high hopes built up beforehand had fallen to the ground, and the months of preparation and sowing had only garnered a bitter fruit. Yet although a military failure, July 1st was an epic of heroism, and, better still, the proof of the moral quality of the new armies of Britain, who, in making their supreme sacrifice of the war, passed through the most fiery and bloody of ordeals with their courage unshaken and their fortitude established.

All along the attacking line these quondam civilians bore a percentage of losses such as no professional army of past wars had ever been deemed capable of suffering – without being broken as an effective instrument. And they carried on the struggle, equally bitter, for another five months. Experience would improve their tactical action, still more their handling by the Higher Command, but no subsequent feats could surpass the moral standard of July 1st, 'a day of an intense blue summer beauty, full of roaring violence, and confusion of death, agony, and triumph, and from dawn till dark. All through that day little rushes of the men of our race went towards that no-man's-land from the bloody shelter of our trenches. Some hardly left our trenches, many never crossed the green space, many died in the enemy wire, many had to fall back. Others won across, and went farther and drove the enemy back from line to line till the Battle of the Somme ended in the falling back of the enemy.' That falling back, however, was long postponed, and when it came was so timed as to discomfit the attackers far more than it advantaged them.

Why did Haig persevere on the Somme after so disastrous a start, and discard the alternative he had prepared in the north? The Official History has 'little doubt that the Messines attack, carried out so successfully in 1917, would have had in 1916 a far better chance of decisive result, especially if combined with a coastal attack, than had an offensive astride the Somme'. As late as June 5th Haig had warned Rawlinson that if the Fourth Army attack 'met with considerable opposition he might decide to stop it and proceed with the Messines operation'. The experience of July 1st certainly fulfilled his condition. Perhaps his continuance is best explained by the very marked 'bulldog' element in his make-up. He hated to accept a rebuff, to loosen his grip once he had got his teeth into the resistance. If repulsed everywhere he might have found it easier to switch his reserves north to Messines. But, having bitten into a slice of the German front, Haig wanted to go on and bite deeper. Why, then, did he not bite quicker on the one soft part? In part, because of a fog of war that was thickened by human frailty in facing facts.

Behind the front the higher commanders had been rendering reports more rosy than the dim facts warranted, and also apparently than their own belief. 'Capture of prisoners, but not the heavy casualties, were regularly reported.' Ignorance in such conditions was natural, but deception less excusable. Meantime the opportunity of developing the success in the south went begging.

Late on July 2nd, Haig, confronted with a difficult situation, decided to press the attack where success had been gained, instead of making a fresh frontal assault on the intact defences from Ovillers northwards. The tactical experience of the later years – and earlier history – confirms his wisdom, and the only question is why the exploitation of the success in the south was not more prompt. Part of the dense infantry strength which had been used to strew no-man's-land with dead might better have been kept to swell the reserve for such a purpose. Even as it was, the Germans were badly shaken, and if British reserve divisions were few, theirs were less, as their delay in counter-attacking showed. But the Fourth Army made no attempt to push reserves through at the sectors of least resistance and at 10 PM on the 1st merely ordered its corps to 'continue to attack', evenly along the whole front. At Rawlinson's suggestion, Gough was put in charge of the two left corps (X and VIII) which had most obviously failed – 'an unenviable task' for a man who had been intended, and was best fitted for the role of exploitation. The corps commanders pointed out the hopelessness of a fresh attack without adequate preparation. Gough wisely concurred, and the orders were cancelled. As these corps were not in a state to attack unbroken defences again, nothing happened on the 2nd. Meantime the XIII Corps, which had made a real penetration on the extreme right, was held back. This passivity was the more regrettable because, in conjunction with the French, it had already shattered a ragged and fumbling night counter-attack by a German division hurried up from Cambrai – the one enemy reserve immediately available.

Opportunity receded further when, for the 3rd, Rawlinson merely ordered a renewed attack by the left wing in conjunction with his centre. This plan, Haig approved but modified – with not altogether happy results. He was now turning his eyes to the right, and he reduced the morrow's attack to thrusts by small packets against Thiepval and Ovillers. The rearrangement accentuated the defects due to divided control, so that the attacks became not only petty in scale but disjointed in delivery – and proved void of any effect except further casualties. Meantime, troops of the XIII Corps on the right walked into Bernafay Wood almost without opposition, but were restrained from going farther. The French XX Corps next to it was, as a corollary, also constrained to inactivity, but south of the Somme the French captured the German second line and the high ground overlooking Péronne.

Haig was now convinced of the advisability of concentrating his effort on the right. But he met a French stumbling block. Both Joffre and Foch – who was in direct charge of the French share of the offensive – insisted that Haig should capture the ridge from Pozières to Thiepval in the centre as a preliminary to any attack on the right, or Longueval, sector. Haig's contention that he had not enough ammunition to cover effectively a renewed attack on the whole front, and that the Longueval ridge defences were weaker than at Thiepval, made no impression, and Joffre declared that if the British attacked Longueval they would be beaten. Indeed, he went so far as to give Haig a direct order to attack in the centre, whereupon Haig retorted that he was responsible to the British Government, and that, although he was ready to follow Joffre's strategy, in matters of tactics he would take his own line. This settled the question.

A long interval followed, however, before the Fourth Army was ready for the attack on the enemy's second line. The interval was the longer because Haig considered it necessary to clear away all the enemy's outlying footholds before attempting the main stroke, and sought to seize these by a series of nibbling attacks. At the same time the X and VIII Corps on the left were definitely transferred from Rawlinson's Fourth Army to Gough's reserve army, later to become the Fifth, and the available reserves and guns were concentrated on the reduced Fourth Army front.

Thus, during the days immediately following July 1st, when the German defence was seriously shaken in the southern sector – Montauban – La Boisselle – the renewed attacks were slight in strength and spasmodic. The resistance had breathing space to reorganize and harden, to strengthen its hold on the commanding ridge, Ginchy–Pozières, where ran the German second line. The British progress became very slow, and a special obstacle was offered by Mametz Wood. The three days' abortive attacks – by the 38th (Welsh) Division – and consequent delay here were to prejudice the main stroke. But as great a handicap was imposed from above.

If the British Higher Command had been over-ambitious and unduly optimistic before July 1st, it perhaps now tended to the other extreme. Rawlinson, however, had been brought to realize that bold and rapid measures were essential if he was to forestall the German reinforcements and labour which were rebuilding, in rear, the fortified front faster than the British could force a way through it. If the British waited until their front line had been carried near enough to the German second line (Braune Stellung) for a close assault, they might well be confronted with a barrier as firm as the original of July 1st. Rawlinson framed a plan to attack and break the German defences on a four-mile front between Delville Wood on the right, and Bazentin-le-Petit Wood on the left. His right was fully three-quarters of a mile distant from this second line, with the vital tactical feature of Trônes Wood between still in German hands. Thence towards his left no-man's-land gradually narrowed, until in front of Mametz Wood it was only about 300 yards wide; but Trônes Wood enfiladed a large part of the line of advance. If the obvious course was adopted, and an attack delivered only on the left, the prospects were barren; for the experience of 1915 had shown that an attack on a narrow frontage against an enemy with ample guns might gain an initial success, only to be blown out of the captured fragment by the concentration of hostile gunfire thus facilitated.

Instead of the obvious, Rawlinson took a course which for all its risks – calculated risks – was more truly secure and economical of force. The troops were to cross the exposed area by an advance under cover of darkness, followed by a dawn attack, preceded by a hurricane bombardment of only a few minutes' duration. This plan revived the use of surprise, which lay rusting throughout the greater part of the war, until in fact the last year from Cambrai onwards.

In 1916 the ideas of a night advance and of such a brief bombardment were alike so fresh in revival as to be a shock and appear a gamble to orthodox opinion. That he should attempt the manoeuvre with New Army troops, men who had been civilians less than two years before, made his plan seem yet more rash. The Commander-in-Chief was strongly opposed to it, preferring a more limited alternative, but Rawlinson persevered, his own confidence reinforced by the confidence of the actual troop leaders in their ability to carry out the night operation. For once, Horne, who was usually as apt to agree with Haig's views as he was dependable in other ways, agreed instead with his immediate superior, and this fact may have helped to tilt the scales. Rawlinson gained his way, but instead of the already delayed attack being launched on July 13th, as he intended, the reluctance of the Higher Command caused it to be postponed until July 14th – a day's delay that was to have grave consequences. Another drawback was the lack of French cooperation, owing to lack of faith in the prospects of the attack.

The attacking troops were composed of the 9th and 3rd Divisions of the XIII Corps on the right (W. T. Furse and J. A. L. Haldane), and the 7th and 21st Divisions of the XV Corps on the left (H. E. Watts and D. G. M. Campbell), while on the extreme right flank Maxse's 18th Division had the task of clearing Trônes Wood. On the extreme left the III Corps formed a defensive flank between Bazentin-le-Petit Wood and Contalmaison. Cavalry divisions were brought up close and placed under the orders of the two attacking corps.

The German front was held by only six battalions of mixed divisions in General Stein's group, with the 7th Division in reserve south of Bapaume. The trenches of the Braune Stellung ran just in front of

Delville Wood, Longueval, Bazentin-le-Grand and Bazentin-le-Petit Woods, with High Wood, 'like a dark cloud on the skyline' behind, dominating the whole area of approach. From it the Germans could see several miles behind the old British front line of July 1st.

On the right, markers went out some hours after darkness had fallen on July 13th and placed white tapes to guide the troops along their 1,000 yards' approach; then further tapes at right angles to mark the forward line on which the troops were to form up, so that they should start parallel with their objective. The hazardous and difficult task was carried through successfully, and soon after midnight the battalions assembled in the shelter of Caterpillar Valley, moving up in long worm-like lines of companies or platoons in single file. At 3.20 AM the barrage fell on the German trenches, and five minutes later the whole line moved forward to the assault. The vision which had dared to attempt such a surprise stroke, and had supported imagination with good staff work, was justified. The whole of the German second line was rapidly overrun, and the attacking troops passed beyond. From left to right, the 21st Division pressed through Bazentin-le-Petit Wood to the village, the 7th Division cleared Bazentin-le-Grand Wood and pushed up the slopes towards High Wood, the 3rd Division captured Bazentin-le-Grand, and the 9th Division fought their way, albeit with difficulty, through Longueval to the outskirts of Delville Wood.

On this right flank every yard of advance was bitterly opposed, and in the depths of Delville Wood, during the ensuing days, the South Africans made their supreme sacrifice of the war – where today a white stone colonnade of peaceful beauty commemorates, and contrasts with, the bloodiest battle-hell of 1916.

But on the left flank opportunity – and open country – stretched out its arms. Soon after midday the German resistance was clearly disintegrating on the front of the 7th Division, and an effort was made to exploit the chance, although some hours were lost. The 7th Division moved forward soon after 6 PM with two squadrons of cavalry working on their flank – the first mounted cavalry seen on a British battlefield since 1914. Roseate expectations pictured open warfare on the skyline, but once more it proved a mirage in the military desert. The troops of the illustrious 7th Division were a shade battle-weary; their depleted ranks had been filled with many untried drafts. Whatever the cause, the advance tended to lack vigour, and although most of High Wood was cleared that evening, the northern corner of the flanking trenches remained in the Germans' grip. Worst of all, twenty-four hours' postponement had enabled fresh reserves to come up, and as their strength steadily swelled the German hold tightened, the British relaxed. Late on July 15th the wood was evacuated under pressure of counter-attacks, and two months were to pass before possession was regained. The surprise storm of the Somme 'Bastille' on July 14th brought the British to the verge of a strategic decision; thereafter their effort degenerated into a battle of attrition.

After the disappointing end of the July 14th stroke, Haig played for smaller stakes. His overdrawn supplies of ammunition were causing concern, and he had in mind no effective substitute for gun-pounding as an 'opener' for the enemy's sealed front. Early in June he had contemplated the step of transferring his main offensive to the Messines sector in Flanders if the German reserves held him up on the Somme. And the Anzac Corps began to move thither in readiness. But by July 7th he had decided instead to pour his own reserves down to the Somme – now, for the enemy, the line of expectation – and to throw all his weight into the direct offensive there.

He ordered, however, a number of local attacks in the north as a means to fix the enemy's attention and keep his reserves there, and away from the Somme. The method reveals a most curious military delusion, for while simulated preparations for a large-scale offensive would cause the enemy natural apprehension, the actual delivery of a narrow-fronted local attack would merely disclose the bluff. One consequence was the shattering of the 5th Australian Division in an absurdly advertised attack at Fromelles, an attack which was the final link of an almost incredibly muddled chain of causation.

The rest of the Anzac Corps had been moved to the Somme, where Haig's aim was now to enlarge his lodgement on the main ridge. He had favoured the idea of trying to carry out his original third phase – of rolling up the German front northwards – although the original conditions had not been fulfilled. But he had not sufficient elbow-room to deploy an adequate force for it. And it would have diverged from the line of cooperation with the French. Hence he decided to continue his main pressure with his right, eastward towards the French line of convergence, while on his left Gough sought to gain the Pozières–Thiepval end of the ridge, and so widen the British holding upon it.

To this end Gough was given the Anzac Corps (Birdwood), and on July 23rd he launched part of it against Pozières in conjunction with a renewed assault by the three corps of the Fourth Army along the whole of its narrow front, from Guillemont to Bazentin-le-Petit. This failed completely; on the left the 1st Australian Division gained a footing in Pozières. Haig reverted to the method of nibbling, now to be exalted as a definite and masterly strategy of attrition, and to be defended by optimistic miscalculations of the German losses.

Nearly two months of bitter fighting followed, during which the British made little progress at much cost, and the infantry of both sides served as compressed cannon-fodder for artillery consumption. On the left flank the Anzac Corps was the main agent of the new plan of 'methodical progress'. The effect is best described in the measured words of the Australian official history:

Doubtless to the Commander-in-Chief, and possibly to the Cabinet, the use of terms implying leisurely progress brought some comfortable assurance of economy of life as well as of munitions; but to the front line the method merely appeared to be that of applying a battering-ram ten or fifteen times against the same part of the enemy's battlefront with the intention of penetrating for a mile, or possibly two, into the midst of his organized defences...

'Even if the need for maintaining pressure be granted, the student will have difficulty in reconciling his intelligence to the actual tactics. To throw the several parts of an army corps, brigade after brigade ... twenty times in succession against one of the strongest points in the enemy's defence, may certainly be described as 'methodical', but the claim that it was economic is entirely unjustified.

Twenty-three thousand men were expended in these efforts for the ultimate gain, after six weeks, of a tiny tongue of ground just over a mile deep. And what of the moral effect?

Although most Australian soldiers were optimists, and many were opposed on principle to voicing – or even harbouring grievances, it is not surprising if the effect on some intelligent men was a bitter conviction that they were being uselessly sacrificed. 'For Christ's sake, write a book on the life of an infantryman (said one of them...), and by doing so you will quickly prevent these shocking tragedies.' That an officer who had fought so nobly as Lieutenant J. A. Raws, should, in the last letter before his death, speak of the 'murder' of many of his friends 'through the incompetence, callousness, and personal vanity of those high in authority', is evidence not indeed of the literal truth of his words, but of something much amiss in the higher leadership ...' We have just come out of a place so terrible (wrote —, one of the most level-headed officers in the force) that ... a raving lunatic could never imagine the horror of the last thirteen days.'

The history indicates that Birdwood lost much of his Gallipoli popularity through his failure to interpose against Gough's impetuous desire for quick results and his lack of thought. This may have been a factor in leading the Australian troops to reject Birdwood's personal appeal when they voted against the conscription of other men to share the horrors that they had experienced.

But Pozières was matched on the other flank by Guillemont – now a peaceful hamlet amid cornfields, then a shambles of blended horror and mystery. From Trônes Wood it is down one slope, up another, only a few hundred yards of farm road now, yet in July and August, 1916, an infinite distance. Division after division essayed to cross it, felt the petty prize within their fingers, and then slipped back unable to maintain their hold. And when it was at last secured on September 3rd, Ginchy, a few hundred yards farther up the slope, was a similar obstruction until September 9th. Save Thiepval, still defiant, no hamlets have exacted a heavier price for their possession.

Now at last the British line was straightened on a seven-mile front running north-west from Leuze Wood, overlooking Combles, where it joined up with the French. They had just extended farther south the attack south of the Somme, storming three miles of the old German front line near Chaulnes and taking 7,000 prisoners. On August 30th Rawlinson had recorded in his diary – 'The Chief is anxious to have a gamble with all the available troops about September 15th, with the object of breaking down German resistance and getting through to Bapaume.' And he added, somewhat illogically – 'We shall have no reserves in hand, save tired troops, but success at this time ... might bring the Boches to terms.' Despite his professed faith in attrition, Haig was now reduced to gambling on a breakthrough.

The attack was to pivot on the left wing – Gough's army. The primary object of the main blow, by Rawlinson, was to break through what had originally been the Germans' last line between Morval and Le Sars, in cooperation with a French thrust to the south between Combles and the Somme – thus pinching out Combles. If the opening success warranted the attempt the British attack was to be extended northward to seize Courcelette and Martinpuich. Eight divisions were deployed for the original attack, and two detailed for the 'extension'. A special feature was the employment for the first time of tanks, the armoured cross-country machines which had been invented as an antidote to the defensive obstacle of machine guns and barbed wire. In disregard of the opinions of the tank's progenitors, and of their own expressed agreement with these opinions, the British Higher Command had decided to utilize such machines as were available, as a stake to redeem the fading prospects of the Somme offensive. When this decision was taken only sixty of the initial 150 machines had been transported to France. Forty-nine were actually employed, to work in tiny detachments of two or three machines – another breach with the principles laid down by Colonel Swinton. The scant and hasty preparation combined with the mechanical defects of this early model to reduce the total, so that only thirty-two reached the starting point. Of these, nine pushed ahead with the infantry, nine failed to catch the infantry, but helped in clearing the captured ground, nine broke down and five were 'ditched' in the craters of the battlefield. The first nine rendered useful aid, especially in captur-ing Flers, but the greater prize – of a great surprise stroke – was a heavy forfeit to pay for redeeming in a limited degree the failure of the Somme offensive.

After three days' bombardment, the attack was launched at dawn on the 15th in a slight mist. The mist, together with the clouds of smoke, prevented the German gunners in many places from seeing the light-signals fired by their infantry, and the consequent lack of artillery sup-port on the German side eased the path of the British infantry. Thus the XV Corps in the centre made early and good progress; by 10 AM its left division was beyond Flers. Its progress was greatly helped by the tanks, of which the German regimental histories give a vivid impres-sion – 'The arrival of the tanks on the scene had the most shattering effect on the men. They felt quite powerless against these monsters which crawled along the top of the trench enfilading it with continous machine-gun fire, and closely followed by small parties of infantry who threw hand grenades on the survivors.' But on the right the XIV Corps lost heavily and was held up long before it could reach Morval and Lesboeufs. The III Corps, on the left, also fell short of its objectives, although its 47th Division finally cleared the long-sought High Wood. On the extreme left the projected extension of the attack was carried out, and both Martinpuich and Courcelette were taken. As a result of the day the crest of the ridge had been gained, except on the right, and with it the commanding observation which the Germans had so long enjoyed.

The failure on the right was redressed on September 25th, by another big attack which, in conjunction with the French, compelled the Germans to evacuate Combles. Next day Thiepval at last fell to an attack by four divisions of Gough's army. German accounts make it clear that the decisive break in their front was 'caused by the appear-ance of three British tanks ... on the outskirts of Thiepval village'.

Haig still called for pressure 'without intermission' and, as a result of further small gains, by the first week of October the Germans were back in their last completed line of defences, which ran from Sailly-Saillisel, on the right, past Le Transloy and in front of Bapaume; they were busily constructing fresh lines in rear, but these were not yet complete. On the other hand these days had proved the continued strength of the German resistance, and the limited success held but little hope of a real breakthrough or its exploitation. The early onset of the autumn rains made this hope more slender daily. The rains combined with the bombardments to make the ground a morass in which guns and transport were bogged, while even lightly equipped infantry could barely and slowly struggle forward. Attacks under such conditions were terribly handicapped; that most of them failed was inevitable, and if a trench was taken the difficulties of consolidating it liquidated the gain.

By October 12th Haig seems to have been at last convinced that he could not pierce the German defences that year. But Joffre and Foch continued to urge him on, and in partial response Haig continued to call for fresh attacks through the mud towards Le Transloy, until a strong protest was made by Lord Cavan, commanding the XIV Corps, who desired to know whether it was deliberately intended to sacrifice the British right in order to help the French left, and pointedly added – 'No one who has not visited the front can really know the state of exhaustion to which the men are reduced.' But other corps commanders had less moral courage, and Rawlinson, although sympathetic, seems to have yielded against his better judgement to his Chief's determination. Hence the III and Anzac Corps continued a hopeless series of petty attacks until November 16th. Their ineffectiveness was redeemed, as their ineptitude was obscured, by a welcome, last-hour success of Gough's army.

The wedge that had been slowly driven eastward between the Ancre and the Somme had turned the original German defences north of the Ancre into a pronounced salient. For some time Gough's army had been preparing an attack against this and a temporary improvement in the weather allowed it to be launched on November 13th, by seven divisions. Beaumont-Hamel and Beaucourt-sur-Ancre were captured, with 7,000 prisoners, but on the left Serre once more proved impregnable. Haig was pleased – because it would 'strengthen the hands of the British representatives' at the forthcoming Allied Military Conference at Chantilly. So the Somme offensive could at last be suspended with honour satisfied.

The folly of the last phase, from September 25th onwards, was that having at last won the crest of the ridge, and its commanding observation, the advantage was thrown away by fighting a way down into the valley beyond. Thereby the troops were doomed to spend the winter in flooded trenches. 'Somme mud' was soon to be notorious.

Thus the miscalled Battle of the Somme closed in an atmosphere of disappointment, and with such a drain on the British forces that the coincident strain on the enemy was obscured. This strain was largely due to the rigidity of the German higher commanders, especially General von Below of the First Army, who issued an order that any officer who gave up an inch of trench would be court-martialled, and that every yard of lost trench must be retaken by counter-attack. If German mistakes do not condone British mistakes they at least caused a vain loss of life, and still more of morale, which helped to balance the British loss – until on August 23rd Below was compelled to swallow his own orders and modify his method of resistance, in accord with that of the new Hindenburg-Ludendorff régime.

CHAPTER SIX

SCENE 4

The Growing Pains of the Tank

On September 15th, 1916, a new instrument of war received its baptism of fire, and helped to make the British attack on that day one of the landmarks of the Somme offensive. It was one of the few attacks which did not require the use of a large-scale map and a magnifying glass to detect its progress. But, far more significant, it cast its shadow over the whole future of the war. And as it thus becomes a greater landmark in the history of the war than in the history of the Somme, so it is likely to become a still greater landmark in the history of war.

For this new instrument – the tank – changed the face of war by substituting motor-power for a man's legs as a means of movement on the battlefield and by reviving the use of armour as a substitute for his skin or for earth-scrapings as a means of protection. Hitherto he could not fire if he wished to move, and could not move if he wished for cover. But September 15th, 1916, saw the simultaneous combination in one agent of fire power, movement, and protection – an advantage until then enjoyed in modern warfare only by those who fought on the sea.

But although sea warfare on land may be the ultimate consequence of the tank, and was foreshadowed in its first name of 'landship', the original intention was more limited and more immediately practical – to provide an antidote to the machine gun which, in alliance with barbed wire, had reduced warfare to stagnation and generalship to attrition.

The cure was a British production, the most significant achievement of British brains during the World War. Yet it has an essential transatlantic link, symbolical in view of the association on the battlefield that was soon to follow. For the source of both the evil and the antidote was American. The trench deadlock was due above all to the invention of an American, Hiram Maxim. His name is more deeply engraved on the real history of the World War than that of any other man. Emperors, statesmen, and generals had the power to make war, but not to end it. Having created it, they found themselves helpless puppets in the grip of Hiram Maxim, who, by his machine gun, had paralysed the power of attack. All efforts to break the defensive grip of the machine gun were vain; they could only raise tombstones and not triumphal arches. When at last a key to the deadlock was produced, it was forged from the invention of another American, Benjamin Holt. From his agricultural tractor was evolved the tank – an ironic reversal of the proverbial custom of 'beating swords into ploughshares'.

The eventual effect of the tank is best appreciated by studying the evidence of those who had to face it. Was it not Ludendorff himself who spoke of the great tank surprise of August 8th, 1918, as the 'black day of the German army in the history of the war', and added, 'mass attacks by tanks ... remained hereafter our most dangerous enemies'. More emphatic still is the comment of General von Zwehl – 'It was not the genius of Marshal Foch that beat us, but "General Tank".' Nor can it be suggested that these were afterthoughts put forward in mitigation of defeat, for the most striking evidence of all, red-hot from the forge of battle, is to be found in the momentous report submitted, on October 2nd, 1918, by the representatives of the German Military Headquarters to the leaders of the Reichstag – 'The Chief Army Command has been compelled to take a terribly grave decision and declare that according to human possibilities there is no longer any prospect of forcing peace on the enemy. Above all, two facts have been decisive for this issue; first, the tanks...' The confession thus made gains force from comparison with the earlier disparagement of the tanks by the German Command.

For history the first question is how the tank came to be introduced, and the second, why its decisive effect was delayed until 1918. The first question is befogged rather than guided by the popular question, so widely raised during and after the war – 'who invented the tank?' So many claimed the honour, many with some show of reason, and still more without, that the public became confused. And the Government did not help to establish the actual chain of causation, perhaps influenced by the instinct of the Treasury to avoid the recognition of financial obligations. Thus it did not become clear until the evidence in an action brought against the Crown in 1925 was available to supplement that given in 1919 before the Royal Commission on Awards to Inventors. In order to defeat this unjustified claim to reward the Treasury had to provide an opportunity for evaluating the genuine claims to honour.

The historical evolution of the tank has been confused also by the lack of any clear definition of the tank and its purpose, and this vagueness owes something to the fact that prior to the time when the camouflage name 'tank' was invented, the machine was known as a 'landship' or 'land cruiser'. Such a title, due to its being mothered in infancy by the Admiralty, however prophetic of its still distant future, is far from applicable to its past, in the war. Regarded as a landship, or even as an armoured battle-car, the origin of the tank is lost in the mists of antiquity. Among its forbears might be included the ancient warchariot, the Hussite war-carts which formed their famous '*wagenburg*', even, with some show of reason, the battle elephants of Pyrrhus, or the mediaeval knight in armour.

If the search be limited to self-moving, as distinct form men- or animal-moved machines, its origin might be traced to Valturio's windpropelled war-chariot of 1472, or to the proposals made by that manysided genius, Leonardo da Vinci, to his patron Ludovico Sforza. In 1599 Simon Stevin constructed for the Prince of Orange two actual landships, wheel-borne and sail-propelled. As far back as 1634, David Ramsey took out the earliest patent for a self-moving car capable of use in war. So through an endless chain of experiments the origin might be traced. The caterpillar track itself – perhaps, in general opinion the distinctive feature of the tank – goes back to the early nineteenth century, or even to Richard Edgeworth's device of 1770.

If the definition be drawn still closer to mean a petrol-driven tracked machine for military use, the Hornsby tractor, used at Aldershot in 1908, takes precedence of the American Holt tractor in the ancestry of the tank. If the use of 'tank-like' machines as weapons be the test, then Mr H. G. Wells deserves the credit popularly accorded him for priority of conception, although his prophetic story of 1903 in the *Strand Magazine* was itself twenty years behind the writings and drawings of M. Albert Robeida in *La Caricature*; if similarity of design, then one recalls Mr L. E. de Mole's model, superior to the 1916 tank, which was pigeon-holed in the War Office in 1912. To these add also the story of the Nottingham plumber whose hobby it was to make toy machines of this nature, and whose design, submitted to the War Office in 1911, and duly pigeon-holed, was unearthed after the war, the file bearing the terse official comment, 'the man's mad'.

The chief result of this historical survey, however, is to show the futility of trying to determine the credit for the origination of this decisive weapon of the World War without a clear understanding and definition of its particular purpose. Leonardo da Vinci and the Nottingham plumber alike may claim to be among the fathers of mechanical warfare, but for the parentage of the actual tank of the World War we must look closer. The test of its origin it tactical rather than technical. It was a specific antidote for a specific disease which first broke out virulently in the World War. This disease was the complete paralysis of the offensive brought about by the defensive power of serried machine guns, and aggravated by wire entanglements. This disease doomed the manhood of the nation to a slow and lingering end, prolonged only by the capacity to produce fresh victims for the futile sacrifice. Wycherley's phrase, 'necessity, mother of invention', has never had a truer example, and it provides the real test to determine the immediate origin of the World War tank.

The first military physician who diagnosed the disease and conceived the antidote was Colonel Ernest Swinton, whose pen-name of 'Ole-Luk-Oie' had become well known through *The Green Curve* and *Duffer's Drift* – studies of war in fiction form, wherein the pill of knowledge was delightfully coated with jam. A term of hard labour on the British official history of the Russo-Japanese War gave him the opportunity to analyse its tendencies and to deduce the potential domination of the machine gun. Later, he took an interest in the Holt tractor experiments. These two impressions soon fitted together like the two segments of a circle. For when, soon after the outbreak of war, he was sent to France as official 'Eyewitness' at General Headquarters, he was both well placed and well prepared to recognize the first symptoms of stalemate, and to suggest a remedy. On October 20th, visiting London, he saw Colonel Maurice Hankey, the Secretary of the Committee of Imperial Defence, and after describing the situation – domination of defence based on the machine gun – outlined his proposals for an antidote. These were, in brief, to develop such a machine as the Holt tractor into a bullet-proof trench-crossing machine-gun destroyer, armed with one or more small quick-firing guns. In Hankey he found an acute and receptive mind, and a further discussion the next day led to an understanding that Hankey would take up the matter at home and Swinton in France. On October 23rd, Swinton took up the question at General Headquarters, but the suggestion came up against a blank wall.

Meanwhile Hankey put the idea before Lord Kitchener, with equally barren result. But he also submitted to the Prime Minister (Mr Asquith), a memorandum on various ways, strategic and technical, of overcoming the deadlock, which embodied, among others, Swinton's suggestion. This reached Mr Churchill. His mind was already active with the problem of enabling armoured cars to cross broken ground and trenches, because of his concern with the armoured-car detachments of the Royal Naval Air Service operating on the Belgian coast. On January 5th, 1915, Churchill wrote a letter to the Prime Minister supporting and amplifying the suggestion in Hankey's memorandum for the use of armoured caterpillar tractors to overrun trenches. This letter was sent by Asquith to Kitchener. By a coincidence Swinton had called at the War Office on January 4th to press anew his proposals, now extended owing to the continued experience of conditions in France.

The seed thus planted at the War Office by two sowers fell on stony soil, and after some attention finally withered, owing largely to the freezing verdict of Sir Capel Holden, Director of Mechanical Transport. Fortunately, the general idea was kept alive on other soil, for Churchill, in February, formed a committee at the Admiralty, which later became known as the Landships Committee. But this committee, though investigating many lines of thought and experiment, did not make much practical headway, its energies being diverted for a time in the direction of a landship with giant wheels. A worse blow was the removal of Churchill's vision and driving force, though even when he left the Admiralty it was his influence which kept the experiments alive. By this time also, fortunately, the committee – under the guidance of Mr Tennyson d'Eyncourt, the Director of Naval Construction – had got on to the right line, that of the caterpillar. Even so, concrete results seem to have been hindered, and energy leaking, through lack of any exact specification of the military requirements of such a machine, for in the scheme of scientific war the tactical takes precedence of the technical.

This essential, but hitherto missing, link came in a memorandum forwarded from General Headquarters, and once this was available progress became rapid and practical. The memorandum was compiled by Swinton, who had surmounted the barrier of unbelief and convention by an appeal direct to the Commander-in-Chief. It formulated the performance required of the machine, and on this specification the newly framed joint committee of War Office and Admiralty went to work.

On July 19th, Swinton returned to England as acting Secretary to the War Committee of the Cabinet, and got in touch with the Joint Committee later, on the Prime Minister's authorization, calling an Inter-Departmental Conference to coordinate the work on the new machines. On September 19th, an inspection was held at Lincoln of a provisional machine, 'Little Willie', but this was rejected by Swinton as failing to conform to requirements. He was then shown a full-size wooden model, or mock-up, of a larger machine, which had been specially designed by Mr Tritton and Lieutenant Wilson to meet the latest army specification. This was accepted, as it looked capable of complying with the two main conditions – to climb a vertical face of five feet and cross a ditch eight feet wide – and it was decided to concentrate on the production of a sample machine of this type.

Finally, on February 2nd, 1916, at Hatfield was held the official trial of this machine – christened 'Mother' or 'Big Willie', and as a result forty of these machines were ordered, a number subsequently increased to 150. The French, now, had independently begun similar experiments through the initiative of Colonel Estienne, whose project was sanctioned by Joffre on December 12th. Although both idea and machine were later in maturing than the British, it is a significant contrast that the first French order was for 400; and that order was soon doubled.

During the summer of 1916 the crews for the new machines were being trained in a vast secret enclosure, surrounded by armed guards, near Thetford in Norfolk. They formed a unit that was christened the Heavy Section, Machine Gun Corps. For secrecy sake also a new name had been chosen for the machines. The need was to find a name sufficiently mystifying and yet plausible to any outside observer who might see the tarpaulined machines in transit on the railway, and after discussing the merits of 'tank', 'cistern', and 'reservoir', the choice fell on the first.

Through the secrecy so well maintained, surprise was obtained when the 'tanks' made their début on the battlefield. Unhappily the fruits of the surprise were forfeited. Herein lay the tragedy of September 15th, 1916; for the official guardians disregarded the entreaties of the parents and insisted on putting the tank to work before it was mechanically mature and before its numbers were adequate. Thus they not only endangered its future usefulness but threw away the chance of surprising the enemy while he was unprepared with any countermeasures. The consequence was to prolong the hardships and toll of the war.

The reply normally made to this charge is to point out the mechanical defects which the early tanks developed, the numbers that were 'ditched', and to argue that a weapon must be tested under battlefield conditions before mass production is begun. The contention is plausible, but unconvincing in view of the facts. The tank first used in the shell-mangled chaos of the Somme, and against the deep and intricate trench systems of 1916, was built to a specification laid down in the summer of 1915, when trench lines were far less developed and artillery bombardments were not so heavy as to turn the ground into a morass – as in 1916 and 1917.

Moreover, the apologists gloss over the fact that in September, 1916, the tanks were hurried out to France and rushed into battle before their crews were fully trained and before the commanders in France had time to think, or had been given instructions, how to use them. Again, the very likelihood that the proportion of mechanical failures in this early model would be high was surely a logical reason for the production of a large number, so that sufficient might survive to reap the harvest of surprise. As the British nation was paying over several million pounds a day for the pleasure of watching and occasionally tapping on the locked gates of the German front, it would surely have been worth risking an extra day's expenditure in the purchase of a possible means of breaking the lock.

Let us probe a little further the mystery of the premature use of this immature instrument. In December, 1915, Churchill drafted a paper on the use of the tank. Printed for the Committee of Imperial Defence, copies were given to the Commander-in-Chief in France. In February, 1916, as soon as the design and armament of the machine had been settled sufficiently for accurate calculations, Swinton produced a more comprehensive and detailed memorandum. This emphasized that the vital factor was the secret production of tanks until masses could be launched in a great surprise stroke, and that on no account should they be used in driblets as they were manufactured. Haig expressed his full agreement with this memorandum in the spring. Yet in August he suddenly decided to use the mere sixty then available. At that time the offensive on the Somme had practically come to a standstill, and the reports of petty gain at heavy loss grated unpleasantly on the ear of the public.

Haig's decision came as a shock to the Cabinet at home, and Lloyd George, now War Minister, energetically protested, while Montagu, his successor at the Ministry of Munitions, went out to General Headquarters in a vain attempt to avert the premature use of the tanks. Haig was immovable and the powerless parents had to submit to the sacrifice of their offspring's future.

Thus history is left to surmise that the tanks were 'pawned for a song' – of the Somme. Pawned to pay for a resounding local success which might draw an encore from the public – and, incidentally, drown the growing volume of criticism. But the greater prize thus lost beyond recall was a heavy forfeit to pay for redeeming in a limited degree the ill success of the Somme offensive. With Haig this act may have been prompted by a laudable if unwise desire to economize the lives of his infantry without giving up his offensive. He had certainly shown his eagerness to clutch at any new aid. But the attitude of some of his staff cannot be similarly excused.

For the breach of principle does not complete the tally of General Headquarters. Swinton's memorandum laid down a number of conditions which were disregarded in September, 1916, only to be adopted after bitter experience had shown their necessity. The sector for tank attack was to be carefully chosen to comply with the powers and limitations of the tanks – this condition was neither considered nor fulfilled until the Cambrai offensive in November, 1917. Their routes of approach were to be specially prepared, as well as suitable railway trucks or barges to bring them up – despite six months' warning these preparations were not begun until the tanks arrived in August. The need for reserves of tanks was stressed – but the lesson was not even learnt by the time of Cambrai, nor indeed, until August, 1918. The combined tactics of tanks and infantry were expounded – also to be overlooked until Cambrai. In addition to shell, the tank guns were to fire case shot. It was designed but its manufacture was debarred until the commanders in France clamoured for it after the Somme. Some of the tanks were to be equipped with wireless sets; these were designed and operators trained – but General Headquarters would not allow the equipment to be sent out, and it was dispersed. The attitude and mentality prevailing at General Headquarters is illustrated by a story current at the time. A general on Haig's staff gave instructions that the tanks were to be brought to the front by a certain railway route. The technical expert in charge of the movement pointed out that this was impossible because of the loading gauge. The General retorted – 'What the hell is a loading gauge?' The officer explained, and pointed out that by another route they could avoid the two tunnels that made this route impossible. But the General, still refusing to recognize the impossible, curtly said – 'Then, have the tunnels widened.'

The trial of the tank on the Somme did not complete its trials. A thousand of a new model had just been ordered by the Ministry of Munitions in England. But their opponents – by which one means not the Germans but the General Staff in France – made haste to report so adversely that the War Office cancelled the order. Unfortunately for their intention, if fortunately for England, the officer in charge of the construction of tanks was a temporary soldier, Major Albert Stern, whose permanent position in the City enabled him to bear with equanimity the frowns of his temporary superiors. Disregarding the order he went straight to the War Minister, to find that the cancellation had been sent without Lloyd George's knowledge. And having satisfied himself of Lloyd George's opposition to any such foolish measure, Stern called on the Chief of the Imperial General Staff, Sir William Robertson, to intimate that he was not going to carry out the cancellation order.

Nevertheless, let it be said to the credit of those who, on the General Staff, opposed the tank, that if they had not the ingenuity to devise means of beating the Germans they were fertile in devices to beat the sponsors of the tank. Swinton, as merely a soldier, was not a difficult adversary and almost at once was ousted from his position in command of the whole tank unit in England. In July, 1917, d'Eyncourt and Stern were neatly excluded from the meetings of the committee, which now at the War Office controlled tank design and production; a committee whose three military members had not even seen a tank until a few weeks previously. The programme of building 4,000 tanks for the next year's campaign was then cut down by two-thirds. And in October, under pressure from the Generals, Stern was removed from his post at the Ministry of Munitions and replaced by an Admiral who had not seen a tank at all. The General Staff would seem to have profited from contact with their French colleagues, and to have learnt that the most important point when proved wrong is to get rid of the uncomfortable prophet who has proved right. Just as Swinton was sacrificed to balance for the General Staff's folly in launching the first model into the Somme battle, so Stern seems to have been chosen to expiate the folly of throwing the next model into the swamps of Passchendaele. Instead of losing faith in their own judgement the General Staff again lost faith in the tank.

Happily, the younger regular soldiers who had taken charge of the tanks at the front had overcome their first doubts and, realizing the stupidity of Passchendaele, fought for the chance to give the tanks a fair trial. They obtained it at Cambrai in November, a battle which at last fulfilled the pattern designed in February, 1916. Although, for want of the resources wasted at Passchendaele, the victory itself was but a tinsel crown, it yielded the tanks a solid crown which none could any longer dispute. As 1917 was the year of vindication, so 1918 proved the year of triumph. Yet it is a sobering reflection that the price in lives might have been cheaper if tanks had been available in thousands instead of hundreds. The numbers manufactured under the reduced programme of 1917 sufficed to bring victory; but they could not bring back the dead. May the tank's hard childhood be an object lesson for future generations, so that if war engulfs them they may learn by the experience of others and not at their own cost.

CHAPTER SIX

SCENE 5

Rumania Swallowed

Rumania entered the war on August 27th, 1916, and the fall of Bucharest on December 6th, 1916, marked the virtual extinction of her war effort and of the misplaced exhilaration which had greeted her entry on the side of the Allies. Less known and less studied than almost any other campaign of the world struggle, it has a special interest, and deserves far more attention than it has received, because it epitomized the Allies' fundamental weakness and the Germans' strength – the evils inherent in a co-partnership system of conducting war as opposed to the concentration of effort and economy of force which springs from a single control.

Nor is this the sum of its lessons; there are others which have a more practical value, because more easily remedied. It revealed the fallacy of numbers, and the much-abused Napoleonic saying that God is on the side of the big battalions received yet another historical contradiction from the Alexandrine principle of quality rather than quantity. Once again the blend of superior hitting power with superior mobility played havoc with an army which pinned its faith to weight of human bodies. Moreover, the swift three months' conquest of Rumania has a particular value for British study, because it was essentially a war of movement, carried out under the difficult natural conditions, topographical and climatic, for which the small British army is trained and has to be prepared.

During the preceding years of the war, public opinion in Rumania had gradually consolidated in favour of intervention on the Allies' side, and the friendly sentiments of Jonescu and Filipescu found a powerful lever in the people's desire to rescue their kinsmen in Transylvania from a foreign rule far more drastic than Alsace-Lorraine had suffered. At last, in the summer of 1916, the spectacular, but, as we now know, superficial successes of the Russian advance under Brusilov encouraged

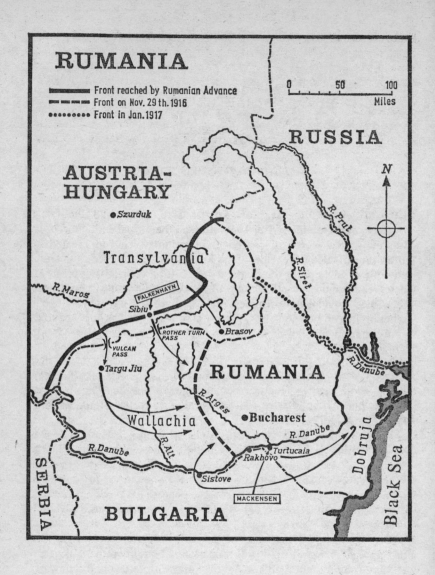

RUMANIA

— Front reached by Rumanian Advance
– – – Front on Nov. 29 th. 1916
••••••• Front in Jan. 1917

0   50   100
Miles

RUSSIA

AUSTRIA-
HUNGARY

•Szurduk

Transylvania

R. Maros

FALKENHAYN
Sibiu

ROTHER TURM
PASS

VULCAN
PASS

•Brasov

•Targu Jiu

RUMANIA

R. Arges

R. Siret

R. Prut

R. Danube

N

•Bucharest

Wallachia

R. Alt

R. Danube

Turtucaia

R. Danube

Rakhovo

Sistove

MACKENSEN

SERBIA

BULGARIA

Dobruja

Black Sea

Rumania to take the decisive step – into the abyss. She might have fared better if she had declared war earlier, when Serbia was still an active force and Russia a real one. The two years of preparation had doubled the numbers of the Rumanian army, but in reality reduced its relative efficiency, for while her foes, under the pressure of hard experience, had developed their means of fire power and equipment, Rumania's isolation and the incapacity of her military leadership had combined to prevent the transformation of her army from a militia of bayonetmen into a modern force.

Her infantry had no automatic rifles, gas equipment, trench mortars, and few machine guns – in the ten active divisions only the usual pre-war proportion of two per battalion, and of the thirteen new divisions eight had none at all. Her artillery was inadequate, and her air force negligible. She had only six weeks' supply of ammunition at the start – an explosion in the Bucharest arsenal had destroyed 9,000,000 rounds of small-arm ammunition – and her Allies failed to maintain the daily supply of 300 tons which they had promised. And the unwieldy size of her divisions, added to the indifferent quality of her corps of officers, was in itself a brake on mobile operations.

Her strategical situation was another source of weakness – her territory forming an 'L' reversed, with the bottom section, Wallachia, sandwiched between Transylvania and Bulgaria. Moreover, the length of her frontier was out of all proportion to the depth of the country, she suffered a shortage of lateral railways, and the capital was within thirty miles of the Bulgarian frontier. Further, she had in the Dobruja – on the other side of the Danube – a 'backyard' strip which offered an easy way of access.

These internal and geographical handicaps were accentuated by the divergent counsels of her Allies as to her action. While the British General Staff favoured a southward advance against Bulgaria which might have crushed the latter between the Rumanians and the Salonika army, the Russians urged a westward advance which would, in theory, be in closer cooperation with their Bukovina advance. The political and moral advantages of a move into Transylvania led the Rumanians to adopt the second course, and bitter as the upshot was, their folly is not so certain as their critics have suggested. The Bulgarian territory offered many obstacles to an effective invasion by such a defective instrument as the Rumanian army proved, and they had ample ground to doubt the energy of Sarrail in pushing forward to meet them.

On the other hand, we now know that a more rapid invasion of Transylvania by the Rumanians would have put the Austro-Germans in a grave position, and that even with the breathing space they were unluckily given they were almost at their wits' end to scrape together forces for this new front. Rumania's fault was less in her choice of objective than in her incapacity to strike for it rapidly and forcefully.

The Rumanian advance began, on the night of August 27th–28th, with three main columns, each of about four divisions, moving in a general north-westerly direction through the Carpathian passes, the conception being to pivot on the left and wheel the right up into line facing west when the Hungarian plain was gained. Three divisions were left to guard the Danube, and three more in the Dobruja 'backyard', whither also the Russians had promised to send one cavalry and two infantry divisions – the Rumanians' stipulation originally had been for a force of 150,000 Russians.

The slow and cautious advance of the Rumanian columns, hampered by the bad mountain roads and the Austrian destruction of bridges, but not by resistance, withheld danger from the five weak Austrian divisions which covered the frontier and enabled the Supreme Command to bring up five German and two Austrian divisions and concentrate them on the line of the River Maros ready for a counter-offensive. In fulfilment of the other half of Falkenhayn's plan, a Bulgarian force of two divisions, and two more to follow, with a German detachment and an Austrian bridging train, was placed under Mackensen to invade the Dobruja. Falkenhayn adds that preparations were made for 'the abundant equipment of Mackensen's army with such weapons, not yet known to the Rumanians, as heavy artillery, mine-throwers, gas'.

Thus, at the outset, Rumania had twenty-three divisions against seven, but within a week she would have sixteen against her, so that her chances of success turned on the rapidity of her action. While her columns were creeping westward into Transylvania, Mackensen stormed the Turtucaia bridgehead on September 5th, destroyed the three Rumanian divisions which covered the Danube front, and then, with his flank secure, pressed eastwards into the Dobruja. It was a shrewd moral blow, for the automatic strategic effect was to draw away the Rumanian reserves intended to support the Transylvanian offensive, and so check its progress for want of nourishment. And the dispersion left them weak everywhere. Thus on September 18th, when Falkenhayn arrived to conduct the Austro-German offensive in Transylvania, he found the Rumanian advance almost at a standstill, and their columns widely separated over a 200-mile front. One must mention that Falkenhayn had now been replaced in the Supreme Command by Hindenburg (and Ludendorff), and given this executive command as a consolation.

Falkenhayn's decision was first to concentrate against the Rumanian southern column, which had crossed the Rother Turm Pass, while using smaller forces to hold off the other columns. Even allowing for his superior information, he took bold risks and suffered anxious moments before success, as so often in war, favoured the brave. The Alpine Corps, by a fifty-mile march in three days over the mountains, turned the Rumanians' southern flank, and combined with the skilful manoeuvre of the reserves in the direct attack to throw back the Rumanians from Sibiu (Hermannstadt), and force them to retreat through the mountains.

His next move was facilitated by the fact that the Rumanian Higher Command, like Napoleon's opponents, 'saw too many things at once'. They kept their Transylvanian armies inactive while diverting their reserves for an abortive attempt to force a crossing of the Danube at Rakhovo and take Mackensen in rear. This enabled Falkenhayn to concentrate against the Rumanian centre column at Brasov (Kronstadt) and by October 9th he had driven this back in turn, but he missed his greater goal of encircling and destroying it, which would have opened a clear passage into Rumania.

The mischance jeopardized the whole German plan and almost saved Rumania, for with all the passes through the mountain barrier still in their hands, her troops sturdily repulsed the Austro-German efforts to press through on their heels, and compelled them to wait for reinforcements. A prompt attempt by Falkenhayn to swing farther south and force a way by the Vulkan and Szurduk passes was also stopped, and the beginning of the winter snows was on the point of blocking operations when a concentrated last-minute effort at the same point, November 11th–17th, broke through to Targu Jiu. A rapid pursuit through the Wallachian plain hustled the Rumanians back to the line of the Alt.

It was the signal for the next move in the ably coordinated plan. Mackensen, leaving only a fraction to hold the northerly part of the Dobruja, withdrew the bulk of his forces westwards to Sistovo, where, on November 23rd, he forced the crossing of the Danube and automatically turned the flank of the Rumanian line on the Alt. A prompt and well-planned Rumanian counterstroke, inspired by General Presan, their new Chief of the General Staff, for a brief time threatened danger to Mackensen's force and almost enveloped its flank. But once the counterstroke was parried the converging pressure of Mackensen and Falkenhayn proved too great for the Rumanians' last desperate resistance on the line of the Argesu, and on December 6th the Austro-Germans entered Bucharest. The pursuit pressed the Rumanians and the Russians, whose action in the Dobruja had been ineffectual, rapidly back to the Sereth–Black Sea line. The greater part of Rumania, with its wheat and oil, lay under the heel of the invader, and the Rumanian Army was crippled, while her Allies had suffered a moral setback greater than any material advantage for which they might have hoped from her intervention.

For military history this brief campaign furnished an object lesson that men do not count more than machines, but instead, that the better machine controlled by a better man – the commander – can discount the value of 'big battalions'. Weapons and training count far more than mere numbers.

CHAPTER SIX

SCENE 6

The Capture of Baghdad

The entry of the British into Baghdad on March 11th, 1917, was an event which impressed the imagination of the whole world, both because of the romantic appeal of the famed city of the Arabian Nights, and because it symbolized the first streaks of dawn coming to illumine the darkness which had lain like a pall over the Allied cause throughout 1916. If the historical data that are now available dim the radiance of popular impressions, revealing that the military achievement was less striking than it appeared at the time, the moral significance and value cannot be minimized. But in justice to those who earlier fought and failed, it is well to realize the fallacy underlying this contemporary public view that the operations which led to the fall of Baghdad were as white as those which culminated in the surrender of Kut were black.

The strategy and organization of the campaign were infinitely more sound and more sure, but on the lower scale of tactical execution the record of the advance is spotted with missed opportunities, despite an overwhelming preponderance of force. While recognizing the difficulties of the country, the historian cannot but feel that a sledge-hammer was used to crush a flea – and the flea escaped being crushed. And if quality rather than quantity be the test of a feat of arms, comparison suggests that the advance and retreat of Townshend's original 6th Division, in face of superior numbers, with inadequate equipment, primitive communications, and utterly isolated in the heart of an enemy country, forged an intrinsically finer link in the chain of British military history.

Credit for the 1917 success is due, above all, to the strategical direction, and to the ability and energy of those who put the organization of supplies and transport on a sound and efficient basis. These assets, moreover, sufficed to attain the military goal, without any further uneconomic drain on the forces in the more vital theatres of war. The

general direction was now transferred to Whitehall. After the surrender of Townshend at Kut – despite the gallant but costly efforts to relieve him – the Chief of the Imperial General Staff, Sir William Robertson, was emphatically in favour of a defensive strategy in Mesopotamia. He inclined to adopt a withdrawal to Amara as the simplest and cheapest way of safeguarding the oilfields, and of commanding the two river arteries – the Tigris and Euphrates. But the new commander, Maude, who had been Robertson's own choice, maintained, after examination, that the advanced position at Kut was both militarily secure and politically wise. He was supported by Duff and Monro, the successive Commanders-in-Chief in India, and Robertson gave way, accepting the judgement of the man on the spot. There is profound psychological interest in studying how the strong personality of Maude and the military results which, step by step, he obtained, combined to change this defensive policy, almost imperceptibly, into a fresh offensive policy. The mirage of Russian cooperation had also an influence, for, beginning as a mere supplementary aid to a Russian offensive, the advance became an all-British achievement.

The whole summer and autumn of 1916 were devoted to thorough reorganization and preparation, initiated by Lake, but greatly expanded and intensified by his successor, Maude. He strove to ameliorate the condition of the troops, to improve both their health and training, to develop the precarious lines of communication, and to amass a large reserve of supplies and ammunition. Thus Maude ably established a secure base for his subsequent and sustained offensive, fulfilling Napoleon's maxim. The design of his plan of operations was equally admirable, blending boldness and circumspection. A study of his orders, both initial and during operations, shows that the lack of decisiveness cannot be charged to his want of energy. Where he tended to err was in excessive centralization and secrecy. If the latter is usually a fault on the right side, it seems here to have been partly responsible for the pause at Aziziyah, on the advance to Baghdad. For his Inspector-General of communications had to complain that even he had not been given warning that such a move was intended, and thus he had made no special preparations in readiness.

This 'imperceptible' offensive began on December 12th, 1916, the first step in a series of well-thought-out trench 'nibbles', methodical and deliberate, on the west bank of the Tigris. When it began, Maude faced the Turkish trenches at a right angle to the Tigris, and gradually brought his left shoulder up, pivoting on the river, and at the same time extending his front farther and farther upstream. At last by February

22nd, 1917, he had cleared the west bank, his extended line facing the main Turkish forces on the other bank, from Sannaiyat to the Shumran bend above Kut. Thus the Turks had not merely to guard against a direct attack from the south upon their fortified position at Sannaiyat, but against a cross-river blow from the west, which might cut their communications. The length of this patient siege-warfare process was not merely due to the intricacy of the defences or the stubborn resistance of the weak Turkish detachments on the west bank. Robertson had no taste for further adventures, and his instructions from home were framed to prevent them. The historian who studies the orders and operations gains the impression that Maude's operations were contrived, consciously or unconsciously, to undermine the stability, not merely of the Turkish position, but of Robertson's instructions.

The outcome of these deliberate and economical operations was that by the third week in February Maude was able, and admirably placed, to play for a bigger stake. His plan was to pin the Turks' left at Sannaiyat while he sprang at their communications, by forcing the river crossing at the Shumran bend – where the right flank ended and their line of retreat prolonged their line of battle. Wisely he realized that a mere feint at Sannaiyat was useless and that a real simultaneous menace to both extremities was essential if the Turkish force was to be held while it was being cut off. Unhappily his purpose was not fulfilled. Splendid as was the gallantry of the troops at the Shumran crossing, the difficulty of the task made progress slow, and the Sannaiyat attack could not pin the defenders long enough.

Even so, the Turks were placed in such peril that, as they confess, 'only the slowness of the enemy' saved them from disaster. The main cause was the tardy and feeble action of the cavalry in pursuit – partly due to Maude's too strict control, partly to the cavalry commander's want of energy and initiative, and partly to the inherent vulnerability of cavalry under modern conditions. On February 24th, when there was a splendid opportunity of turning retreat into rout, the cavalry division broke off to go back to bivouac at 7 PM, after a mere twenty-three casualties. And on subsequent days they were no more effective. The excuses offered are the need to water and the obstacle of modern fire-arms, and their admission rather accentuates than impairs the lesson as to the restricted modern value of cavalry – even in Asia. Only the daring pursuit of the naval flotilla disturbed the Turks' orderly retreat – acting on the river as a few cross-country armoured cars might have done on land.

The strategic victory had at least won Maude sanction for an attempt to gain Baghdad, and on March 5th his advance from Aziziyah began. When a check came at the line of the Diyala, Maude switched the cavalry division and 7th Corps to the west bank, for an outflanking move direct on Baghdad. More mistakes enabled the Turks to hold up this menace, but realizing their hopeless inferiority of strength and the inevitable end, against two powerful converging advances, they gave up Baghdad on the night of March 10th, and retired northward up the river. Next afternoon Maude entered the city, and another name was added to the roll of Baghdad's innumerable conquerors. For the prestige of Britain and the morale of all the Allies the capture was an invaluable stimulant worth the immediate effort, if not the sum of the efforts which had gone to fill the debit side of the victors' balance sheet.

CHAPTER SIX

SCENE 7

The Battle of Blind Man's Buff – Jutland

Only once during over four years of war did the Grand Fleet of Britain and the High Seas Fleet of Germany meet. It would be more exact to say that they 'hailed each other in passing' – with a hail that was awe-inspiring but leaving an impression that was merely pen-inspiring. No battle in all history has spilt so much – ink. On the afternoon of May 31st, 1916, the fleet that had been built to dispute the mastery of the sea stumbled into the fleet that had held it for centuries. In the early evening these two fleets, the greatest the world had seen, groped towards each other, touched, broke away, touched again and broke away again. Then darkness fell between them. And when the 'glorious First of June' dawned a sorely puzzled Grand Fleet paraded on an empty sea.

A fundamental difference between the higher naval and military leadership in the World War was that the Admirals would not give battle unless sure of an initial advantage, and perhaps not then, whereas the Generals were usually ready to take the offensive whatever the disadvantages. In this attitude the Admirals were true to their art, the Generals were not. The sole reason for employing men who have made war their profession is the presumption that by training they have acquired a mastery of their art. Anyone with sufficient authority or inspiration can lead or push men to battle, especially if he is furnished with technically trained assistants who can help him to regulate the marshalling of the forces in movement and fire. For this shepherding of sheep to the slaughter, perhaps artful but essentially inartistic, a practised demagogue would have a definite superiority over the tongue-tied professional warrior. But the custom of employing a professional is based on the idea that through art he will be able to obtain more profit at less cost.

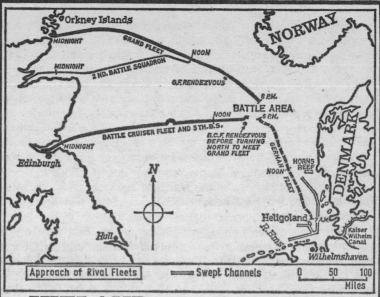

Orkney Islands

MIDNIGHT

GRAND FLEET

NOON

MIDNIGHT

2 ND. BATTLE SQUADRON

G.F. RENDEZVOUS

NORWAY

6 P.M.

BATTLE AREA
6 P.M.

MIDNIGHT

BATTLE CRUISER FLEET AND 5TH B.S.

B.C.F. RENDEZVOUS
BEFORE TURNING
NORTH TO MEET
GRAND FLEET

Edinburgh

N

NOON

HORNS
REEF

DENMARK

Heligoland
R. Ems
7 A.M.

Kaiser
Wilhelm
Canal

Hull

Wilhelmshaven

| Approach of Rival Fleets | ══ Swept Channels | 0   50   100 |
Miles

JUTLAND

Deployment of British Battle Fleet and first retirement of German Fleet

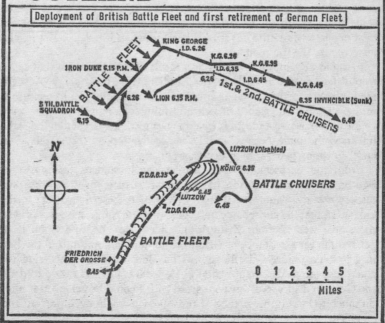

KING GEORGE
I.D. 6.26

K.G.6.26

K.G.6.35

IRON DUKE 6.15 P.M.

I.D. 6.35

I.D. 6.45

K.G. 6.45

6.26

FLEET

BATTLE

1st.& 2nd. BATTLE CRUISERS

6.35 INVINCIBLE (Sunk)

6.26   LION 6.15 P.M.

5 TH. BATTLE
SQUADRON

6.45

6.15

N

LUTZOW (Disabled)

KÖNIG 6.35

F.D.G.6.35

BATTLE CRUISERS

6.45
LUTZOW

6.45

F.D.G.6.45

6.45   BATTLE FLEET

FRIEDRICH
DER GROSSE

6.45

| 0 1 2 3 4 5 |
Miles

Only one consideration should override a commander's fidelity to the fundamental truths which govern his art, and that is national expediency. It is for the government, and not for its employee, to decide whether the needs of policy compel a sacrifice of art and the consequent sacrifice of lives. Curiously, however, in the World War the Generals were so full of the lust of battle that they voluntarily sacrificed art, and repeatedly sought battle at a disadvantage against the wishes of a government reluctantly dragged in their wake. The Admirals, in contrast, were so faithful to their art that they sometimes ignored or evaded the express wish of the government for battle even without an assured advantage. If their sense of reality was refreshing, it tended to throw a heavier burden of expense on the armies, although it is fair to point out that this might not have occurred if the Generals had not been so extravagantly eager to shoulder it.

Perhaps one explanation of the difference was that the Admirals exercised their command in the forefront of the battle and the Generals from headquarters far in rear. This does not imply that the difference was merely a matter of the physical courage required, for some Generals were as ready to risk their own lives as their men's, while others undoubtedly gained moral courage through physical remoteness. But, undoubtedly, imagination and sense of reality are quickened by personal contact with the situation; a commander so placed is better able to appreciate where the advantage lies and when it fades; quicker, also, to recognize the impossible.

It would be natural to expect as a result of this difference that sailors would have a bias towards tactics, soldiers towards strategy. Actually, the reverse occurred. The explanation of the paradox would seem to lie in the different experience of peace training, wherein the soldier serves in small garrisons and exercises in cramped areas, while the sailor traverses the wide oceans and learns navigation as the staple of his craft. For him, geography precedes gunnery.

From the outbreak of war British naval strategy was governed, rightly, by the appreciation of the fact that maintenance of sea supremacy was even more vital than defeat of the German fleet. Instantaneously, that sea supremacy had come into force and upon it was based the whole war effort of Britain, and her Allies, because upon it depended the very existence of Britain. Churchill has epitomized the issue in a graphic phrase – 'Jellicoe was the only man on either side who could lose the war in an afternoon.' Hence the aim and desire to defeat the German fleet was always subsidiary. If it could be achieved it might do much to hasten the victory of the Allies. It might even prevent their defeat. The collapse of Russia as well as the near starvation of Britain by the U-boats may well be traced to the inability of the British navy to crush the German fleet. But if, in trying to defeat the German fleet, the British lost so heavily as to lose its strategic superiority national defeat would be certain.

The aim of German naval strategy since August, 1914, had been to avoid the risk of a decisive action until the British fleet was so weakened that the prospect of success veered from gloomy to fair. Mines and torpedoes were the means on which the Germans relied to achieve this preliminary weakening. And it was the fear of such under-water weapons, the possibility that by trap or chance they might dramatically alter the balance of strength, which infused an extra degree of caution into the British strategy of precaution. In a letter of prophetic foresight on October 14th, 1914, Jellicoe had warned the Admiralty that if a chance of battle came he would regard the turning away of the German battlefleet as a sign that it was trying to lure him into such a trap, where mines and submarines lay in wait; that he would refuse to be drawn into it and, instead, would move quickly to a flank. In other words, he would side-step to avoid the chance of being sur-prised, and so not only disarm the enemy of his best potential weapon, but possibly throw him off his balance. The calculation is an indication of how thoroughly Jellicoe had thought out his theory of war, up to a point.

Both the German and the British strategic keynotes were well attuned to the reality of their respective conditions; the question re-mains whether more energy and subtlety could have been shown in executing them. The situation in May 1916, after nearly two years of war, was that the British fleet was still waiting for a favourable chance of battle and the German fleet was further away from the attainment of its preliminary aim of weakening the British. Despite a few losses due to mines and torpedoes, the British fleet was proportionately much stronger than at the beginning. In the coming clash it was to bring thirty-seven capital ships (battleships and battle cruisers) of the Dread-nought type against the German twenty-three, and in gun power the margin was still greater, 168 guns of 13.5-15 inch calibre and 104 of 12 inch could be brought against 176 German guns of only 12 inch calibre. It is true that the German fleet also included six pre-Dreadnought battleships, but in a fleet action these would be little better than a target for the heavier guns of the British. Moreover, by their presence they reduced the already slower German fleet to a still more marked in-feriority in speed. The British had also a comfortable superiority in cruisers and destroyers – eight armoured and twenty-six light cruisers, against eleven of the last; eighty destroyers against sixty-three.

Another advantage gained since the outbreak of war was in the sphere of knowledge. For the British had not only gained from occasional contacts a clearer idea of the capacity of the enemy's weapons, but had discovered his signal-code. In August, 1914, the German light cruiser *Magdeburg* had been sunk in the Baltic, and clasped in the arms of a drowned under-officer the Russians had found the cipher and signal books of the German navy, as well as their squared maps of the North Sea. These were sent to London and thereafter, by intercepting the enemy's enciphered wireless messages, the British Intelligence was able to obtain advance information of many of the enemy's movements. Although suspicion led the enemy to make variations in their codes and maps, their efforts to seal up the leakage of information were offset by the development of directional wireless as a means of locating the position of ships. And this was the source of the one naval battle of the war – Jutland.

In January, 1916, a new commander was appointed to the German High Seas Fleet. This was Admiral Scheer, the nominee of Admiral von Tirpitz, and an advocate of a more aggressive war policy. The pressure of the British blockade and the relaxation of the German submarine blockade – under pressure from President Wilson – combined to provide an urge to action. And a rumoured division of the British fleet, to protect the coast from raids, came as an encouragement to action. In mid-May Scheer crystallized his plan. A cruiser raid on Sunderland was intended to draw out part of the British fleet to counter it, and lying in wait for this detachment would be the German submarines with the High Seas Fleet behind, ready to pounce. The submarines were duly dispatched, but bad weather prevented reconnaissance by the German airships. Without this safeguard Scheer would not move, and thus the submarines exhausted their sea-going endurance. On May 30th, Scheer decided to abandon his plan, and the use of his submarines, for an alternative. This was to send the Scouting Force, of battle and light cruisers, under Admiral Hipper, to demonstrate off the Norwegian coast, while he followed, out of sight. He calculated that the danger to the British cruiser patrol and shipping might draw part of the British fleet to the spot and give him a chance to destroy it. Hipper steamed north early in the morning of the 31st, with Scheer fifty miles astern.

Already, the previous evening, the impending departure of the Germans, although not their purpose, was known to the British Admiralty, and the Grand Fleet was ordered to sea. Jellicoe with the main section of the fleet sailed eastward by 10.30 PM for a rendezvous some fifty miles off the Norwegian coast, being joined on the way by Jerram's squadron from Invergordon. Beatty with the battle cruisers, reinforced by four of the latest *Queen Elizabeth* type battleships, sailed simultaneously from Rosyth (near Edinburgh) with orders from Jellicoe to reach by 2 PM on the 31st a spot sixty-nine miles south-south-east of the main rendezvous. From this, if no enemy had yet been sighted, Jellicoe would sweep southwards toward Heligoland Bight, while Beatty was ordered to close to within sight of him.

Beatty reached his own rendezvous at the assigned hour and was just turning north towards Jellicoe when the *Galatea*, one of his screen of light cruisers, sighted a stray merchant steamer and, instead of turning with the rest, continued east-south-east to examine her. This was the first of many jests of fate. For simultaneously a German light cruiser, screening Hipper's western flank, also sighted the steamer and decided to investigate. Within a few moments the two unsuspecting rivals had sighted each other – and warned their respective superiors. Thereby the strange steamer not only brought on the battle of Jutland, but probably cost the British a decisive victory. For if this chance meeting had not occurred, the two forces might not have met until they were farther north – when the Germans would have been farther from shelter and nearer the jaws of Jellicoe.

Minutes were now to be momentous. Controversy as to their use has been acrid, but much of the criticism on both sides seems pedantic – more apt for the proverbial armchairs, although here occupied by professional sailors, than for the vague conditions in the North Sea on the afternoon of May 31st, 1916.

At 2.20 PM the *Galatea* signalled 'Enemy in sight. Two cruisers probably hostile bearing south-east, course unknown'. The sound of guns from the distant *Galatea* had just been heard when at 2.32 PM Beatty turned again south-eastwards to cut off the retreat of the enemy cruisers. Unfortunately, his signal to turn, made by flags, was not read owing to smoke and want of wind by Evan-Thomas' squadron of battleships which had been following five miles astern. In consequence Evan-Thomas did not turn until 2.40 PM and thereby found himself ten miles behind Beatty's battle cruisers.

It has been argued that the signal should have been made, more simply and effectively, by searchlight flashes – an argument that seems irrefutable. It has been argued that Evan-Thomas should have turned on his own initiative, as he must have seen Beatty turning – an argument which seems highly disputable in view of his general orders and his ignorance of Beatty's tactical intentions. On the other side, it has been contended, first, that Beatty himself should have acted earlier; second, that he should also have given Evan-Thomas the chance to close up to him – either by continuing on his northward course while Evan-Thomas was turning or, still better, by swinging towards him before turning. But this ideal perhaps unduly discounts the conditions – physical and psychological. Both Jellicoe and Beatty had been steaming leisurely, with hope of an encounter waning as the hours passed, and all the more because the Admiralty had signalled that, by directional wireless, the enemy fleet had been located still at its anchorage. Yet another unlucky mishap.

If fair account be taken of the hazy situation, Beatty would seem to have taken his decision with all reasonable promptness. As for the decision itself he had every reason, from past experience, to fear that the German cruisers would give him the slip, and little reason to suspect that they masked a greater force. At the most he might meet the German battle cruisers, and they were only five in all, while he had six. If his temperament was impetuous rather than calculating, both past experience and the general strategic situation would here seem to justify his action in forfeiting extra strength to gain extra minutes.

Finding that the enemy cruisers were apparently following the *Galatea* north-westwards, Beatty himself gradually changed his course until he was steaming north-east. Thereby he and Hipper were converging towards each other and about 3.30 PM they came in sight of each other. Hipper promptly turned to fall back towards his own battle-fleet and Beatty duly turned on a parallel course. At 3.45 PM both sides opened fire at a range of about nine miles. Owing to bad light the British miscalculated the range, and so not only lost the advantage that their guns outranged the Germans, but made poor shooting. In contrast, the British were silhouetted against the western sky. Just after 4 PM catastrophe burst upon the British. A shell from the *Lutzow*, Hipper's flagship, plunged into the midship turret of the *Lion*, Beatty's flagship. With both legs shattered, Major Harvey of the marines managed before he died to call down the voice tube the order to flood the magazines – and thereby saved the ship from being blown up. But the *Indefatigable*, hit by a salvo of three shells from the *Von der Tann*, dropped out of the line and, hit again, turned over and sank with 1,000 men. Fortunately, at this critical moment, Evan-Thomas, by cutting the corners, had come within range, and his accurate fire disturbed the accuracy of the Germans' – although the poor quality of the British shells, which burst without penetrating their armour, saved the Germans from vital injury. And at 4.26 PM they scored afresh, when the battle cruiser *Queen Mary*, hit by a salvo, blew up and sank with her crew of 1,200 – her grave and their grave marked by a gigantic pall of smoke 800 feet high. Thus Beatty was reduced from six ships to four, against five. About this time also, the *Princess Royal* vanished momentarily in an ominous cloud of smoke and spray, and a signalman on the *Lion* laconically reported, '*Princess Royal* blown up, sir.' Whereupon Beatty as curtly said to his flag captain – 'Chatfield, there seems to be something wrong with our damned ships today. Turn two points to port' – nearer the enemy.

It was a tribute to his cool nerve, although the crisis had really passed with the entry of Evan-Thomas into the fight. That entry marred the trap which Scheer was planning for Beatty. For instead of steering to catch Beatty between the two jaws formed by Hipper and his own main fleet, Scheer was forced to steam direct to Hipper's aid.

At 4.33 PM Goodenough's light-cruiser squadron, two miles ahead of the *Lion*, sighted battleships to the south-east, and signalled the news to Beatty. Goodenough boldly held to his course until he could definitely identify the High Seas Fleet and then sent a wireless message direct to Jellicoe – who had already quickened his pace towards Beatty.

Beatty also held his course until he had sighted Scheer's battleships and then, at 4.40 PM, turned about to run north towards Jellicoe. The turn was well timed to let Beatty's force, now the bait, be seen by Scheer without letting it come within range of Scheer's guns. But the signal to turn, again made by flags, was again missed by Evan-Thomas, who held to his southward course until he had passed Beatty running north. Thereby he came under fire from Scheer's leading battleships, and became both the bait to Scheer and the shield to Beatty during the run north.

Danger during Beatty's turn, which was made in succession round a fixed point, was partly averted by the disconcerting and gallant attacks of the British destroyers. Two had been crippled and, drifting helplessly between the oncoming lines of battleships, with glorious impudence fired their last torpedoes before they were riven by shells. German destroyers chivalrously stopped to pick up the survivors.

Meantime the two great fleets were rushing towards each other, Scheer in ignorance, Jellicoe in knowledge of his enemy's approach – but not of his exact course. But upon such detailed knowledge Jellicoe's own dispositions must depend. Unfortunately the haze over the North Sea was mental as well as physical. Beatty, leading the run north, had lost touch with Scheer's fleet and even with Hipper's, which was steaming roughly parallel to him in the mist. And although Evan-Thomas was still in touch with Scheer he sent no reports. The only messages Jellicoe received came at the very start of the retirement, four from Goodenough and one from Beatty, whose wireless had been shot away – so that he had to transmit the message through a third ship. But the importance of this lack of information of the enemy can be, and has been, exaggerated. For the German fleet did not vary its course and the real trouble came from British error in reckoning their own position – on the part of both Jellicoe's and Beatty's flagships. The result was that when the two came in sight of each other the *Lion* was found to be some seven miles farther west than Jellicoe had anticipated. And, as a corollary, the enemy also were sighted on the starboard bow, ie, on Jellicoe's right front instead of straight ahead. More frequent reports of the position of Beatty's fleet might have provided, through averaging, a more accurate reckoning.

Jellicoe was advancing south in a compact mass of six parallel columns, like a six-pronged comb, four miles wide from flank to flank. This is not a fighting formation, for only a minimum of the total guns would be able to fire, forward, if an enemy was met. To deliver the maximum fire the ships must bring their broadsides to bear, and must form into line of battle. If the enemy were found directly ahead each column had only to wheel to the right or left for the whole fleet to be in line, firing their broadsides at the enemy. The Grand Fleet only required four minutes to make this deployment, but it required that the enemy should be in exactly the right position. An alternative method, if the enemy lay to a flank, was for one of the columns – normally a wing column – to steam on while the remainder wheeled to follow in its wake. In this case the fleet would still be able to form a single chain within four minutes, but would take much longer to straighten their line.

Let us now see what actually happened. Jellicoe had dispatched the 3rd Battle Cruiser Squadron (Hood) to support Beatty, but owing to the error in reckoning already mentioned it moved too far eastward. Thereby it became unintentionally the upper jaw of a trap into which the unconscious Hipper was putting his head. Hipper meantime was still running parallel to, but out of sight of, Beatty. At 5.40 PM Hipper suddenly sighted Beatty afresh – to the westward – and coming under fire, swerved more to the eastward. Then he heard Hood's guns opening fire on his light cruisers. Alarmed, he turned away to the south-east at 6.34 PM, only to see his light cruisers attacked by four of Hood's destroyers, which he imagined to be the forerunners of Jellicoe's main fleet. So he swerved again, to the south-west.

Meantime, Jellicoe and Beatty had not sighted each other until just before 6 PM, although their advanced cruisers had made visual contact at 5.30 PM, when about five miles apart. At 6.1 PM Jellicoe flashed the question – 'Where is the enemy's battlefleet?' No answer came. Beatty was busily intent on his own 'disappearing' opponent, Hipper – following him on a long outer curve which, incidentally, was carrying Beatty across Jellicoe's front. At 6.10 PM Jellicoe repeated his question and four minutes later Beatty, almost simultaneously with Evan-Thomas, reported the enemy's bearing. The two reports enabled Jellicoe to judge Scheer's rough position, although not the course he was steering – which, actually, was north-westward in Hipper's wake.

Within a minute of Beatty's report Jellicoe had made his decision and given the order to deploy – on his left wing. Two minutes later his right wing opened fire, as it was wheeling to the left. It has been argued that he should have deployed earlier; but this would have meant acting on uncertain information, and the risk of putting himself in an unfavourable position. It has been argued that he should have deployed on his right; but this would have meant the risk that the enemy crossed the head of his line before he could cross theirs, and the certainty that until the line was straightened out – twenty-two minutes later – only a part, if a growing part, of his fleet could fire. It has been argued, by Churchill, that he might have deployed on one of the centre divisions and thereby have saved seven minutes, besides gaining the advantage of deploying within closer, yet not too close, reach to the oncoming foe. This, however, was a manoeuvre rather more complex and less practised, and would at least have meant that the fire of the left fork of the tail was temporarily masked.

Jellicoe's actual deployment ensured that he would have time to cross the head of the enemy's line – the historic and deadly manoeuvre of 'crossing the T' – and also that none of his battleships would have their fire masked by others while the chain was straightening. Nor does there seem much actual substance in the criticism that a chance was lost by deploying farther away from the enemy. Rather was it gained. For Scheer had no intention of fighting the Grand Fleet unless at an advantage.

Thus he no sooner saw that Jellicoe's line – obscured for a time by the smoke of the cruiser action in the intervening space – was likely to 'cross the T' than he made, at 6.30 PM, an instant turn about. This was a deft emergency manoeuvre whereby each ship, beginning from the rear, began to turn in almost simultaneous succession; it enabled the whole line to slip out of range in the minimum time. His precipitancy was due to the fact that he mistook Hood's battle cruisers for Jellicoe's leading battleships, and so thought the British manoeuvre was further advanced than in reality. His mistake was to his opponent's disadvantage. For Jellicoe had signalled at 6.29 PM for his line to turn south-south-east by sub-divisions, in order to get closer to the enemy, but had cancelled the order on finding that his tail had not yet straightened out. Nor had it done so when Scheer made his 'somersault' turn, under cover of a torpedo attack and a smoke screen. This hid Scheer's retirement for the few minutes before he was swallowed up in the mist. Although several of his leading battleships had suffered heavy hits, the only complete loss had been one of Hipper's light cruisers, the *Wiesbaden*. And, before disappearing, Hipper had destroyed another British battle cruiser, the *Invincible*, and one armoured cruiser, and had left a second sinking.

But the potentially vital fact in Scheer's retirement was that he had turned westward – away from his own harbours. If he had sighted the British battlefleet on his flank, as would have happened if Jellicoe had deployed in any other way, the natural course for Scheer would have been, not to turn about, but to turn right – and so retire towards his own harbours. Thus the best justification for Jellicoe's choice is that it gave him the opportunity to cut off Scheer's path of retreat. It also placed Scheer against the western sky.

This opportunity Jellicoe promptly exploited. To give direct chase to Scheer, when his own line was already six miles astern of Scheer, and only two hours' daylight remained, was a move that promised little. It would also have exposed the battlefleet to the very risk of running into mines dropped and torpedoes fired by the enemy, which Jellicoe was intent to avoid.

Instead, at 6.44 PM he ordered each division to turn south-east – so that they were once more in six columns echeloned back like a staircase from left to right. In the next quarter of an hour he made two more partial turns. The effect was to bring him round in a gradual curve between the unseen Germans and their line of retreat, while edging closer to them. Only the coming darkness and the increasing mist threatened the advantage gained by his skilful manoeuvre. One criticism, however, appears reasonable – that, either on Beatty's initiative or Jellicoe's orders, the Battle Cruiser Fleet, whose essential role was that of 'feelers' for the battlefleet, might have swung round more sharply and sought to keep touch with the enemy. Actually, the battle cruisers were farther away than the battlefleet from the enemy.

The enemy, however, was about to make touch himself – to his own danger. Having slipped out of one trap he almost slipped into another, created mainly by his own miscalculation. For, after steaming west for about twenty minutes, Scheer suddenly reversed his direction and steamed east again – to appear out of the mist at about the same point as before. He claimed in his subsequent dispatch that his idea was to strike a second blow so as to keep the initiative, and maintain German prestige. The claim is at his own expense, for no good tactician would steam into the middle of the superior British fleet for such a purpose. The logical hypothesis is that he expected to cross the tail of the British fleet, thereby gaining the chance to punish part of it and regaining his path home. For, as already mentioned, he had mistaken Hood's squadron for the van of the battlefleet and so he overestimated the distance that the battlefleet had moved. Hence, when Scheer appeared out of the mist at 7.10 PM he was opposite the centre of the 'stepped' British line.

Its rear squadron, being nearest, opened fire first – at a range of only about five miles. Within the next few minutes the greater part of the British fleet joined in. But with a perhaps excessive fear of partial exposure, Jellicoe ordered his rear squadrons to form astern of him – in non-technical language, to wheel eastward and follow in his wake. Thereby he drew them farther away from the enemy. And at this moment Scheer had also decided to go away. Indeed, he was in such a hurry to get out of Jellicoe's jaws that he not only performed a fresh 'somersault' manoeuvre, less neat than before, under cover of smoke screens and destroyer attacks, but also launched his battle cruisers in a 'death ride'.

The destroyers proved the most effective of these agents of his salvation, for seeing their torpedoes loosed, at long range, Jellicoe swung his ships away by two quick turns of two points each (22.5 degrees in all). This turn away was a long-practised method which the majority opinion in the navy approved as the best expedient, and only a minority opposed on the score that the torpedo danger was overrated, and that its adoption tended to abnegate the offensive value of the battleship. A decision between these opinions is difficult. One can only draw the logical conclusion that if the precaution was essential, it was a confession of the weakness of the battleship, and of the ease with which its offensive movements could be paralysed by an infinitely less expensive instrument of war. At Jutland the justification for the precaution is that only one British battleship was hit by a torpedo, and the justification for the minority opinion is that this battleship was so little affected that it kept its place in the line.

As a means of freeing the German fleet the destroyer attack was not only the most effective but the cheapest, for only one destroyer was sunk – by a counterstroke of the British light cruisers – while the German battle cruisers suffered heavily. The *Lutzow* was disabled before the 'death ride' began, and the other four were hit repeatedly in the few minutes before a signal of recall from Scheer reprieved them.

The tactical effect of the destroyer attack was that while the German fleet was going west the British fleet was going the opposite way. A quarter of an hour later, satisfied that the torpedo attack had spent itself, Jellicoe corrected his turn away, but continued on a course almost due south. Not until 8 PM did he turn west. In this delay there seems to be ground for criticism. For to maintain his tactical advantage of being across the enemy's line of retreat, it was desirable both to shepherd him away from his own coast and to keep in touch with him so that he had less chance of slipping past the British mobile barrier in the dark.

By one school of criticism much emphasis has been given to the fact that after sighting the enemy again at 7.40 Beatty sent a further wireless signal to Jellicoe ten minutes later – 'Submit van of battleships follow battle cruisers. We can then cut off whole of enemy's battlefleet.' But excellent as this sounds, and was its meaning, its historical value is rather diminished by the fact that, before it was decoded and handed to him, Jellicoe had already turned the battlefleet west, while Beatty was merely going south-west according to his last message. Moreover, the German fleet was already cut off from its base. Perhaps Beatty meant 'head off' – his own next order to his light cruisers, to locate the head of the enemy's line, which was now steaming south, suggests this explanation. Moreover, he succeeded in heading off the enemy on his own, for when they came under his fire about 8.23 PM, they promptly sheered off to the westward again. And by checking their course south this encounter helped them in slipping past the British tail later.

The best, indeed the only, chance of closing with the Germans had passed in the half-hour following their 7.20 PM turn away. The great question that remained was whether Jellicoe could continue to bar their way during the night so that he could re-engage at dawn with a whole day's light before him, and thereby profit from his strategic advantage – now added to superior strength.

When the blanket of darkness spread across the sea about 9 PM it not merely accelerated the haziness of the day, but changed it to blindness. The battleships lost their advantage of range, the torpedo craft gained the advantage of coming to close range with minimum risk. And all ships would have difficulty in distinguishing friend from foe.

Jellicoe wisely rejected the hazard of a night battle, for it would have meant staking his double advantage on a pure gamble. Thus his problem was to prevent the enemy finding an open way home during the five and a half hours before daylight. There were three likely routes, each leading to a swept channel through the minefields which covered the approaches to the Heligoland Bight and the German harbours. One, on the east, was past Horn Reefs and down the Frisian coast; a second, more central, eventually led past Heligoland; the third, in the extreme south-west, was entered near the German coast and led eastward past the mouth of the Ems. The distance to this was 180 miles, and being the farthest it was the least obvious choice. Hence Jellicoe might justly fear that an astute enemy might take it – but for one factor. This was the inferior speed of the German fleet compared with his own. If the Germans had enjoyed equal or greater speed the Ems route would have offered them more chance and scope for evading an uncertain guard during the hours of darkness. Lacking it, they were wise to take the greater immediate risk of the shorter route.

Jellicoe, however, was unwilling to uncover one completely in order to cover the others more closely. And he chose a 'beat' which certainly reconciled as far as was possible the difficulties of covering all. Indeed, it left the Germans only one good chance – that of slipping behind Jellicoe and taking the Horn Reefs passage. Hence, one would anticipate that Jellicoe would be specially sensitive to any signs of an attempt to pass astern of him.

At 9.17 PM Jellicoe ordered the fleet to take up night cruising stations – the battleships being closed up in three parallel columns. The course of the fleet was to be due south, and the speed seventeen knots. The destroyers were massed five miles astern, a disposition which prolonged the moving barrier, protected the rear of the battlefleet against torpedo attacks, and, above all, prevented the risks of mistaken identity in the darkness. If the battleships sighted destroyers, or the destroyers battleships, each would know that the dim shapes were those of an enemy. Beatty had already taken station with the battle cruisers ahead of and on the western, or enemy, flank of the battlefleet. The historical significance of his night position is that it made impossible any attempt of the Germans to outstrip or pass south of the British, and so might have provided a further cause for sensitive suspicion of an attempt to pass astern. The formation of the Grand Fleet might be likened metaphorically and symbolically to that of the traditional British lion,

Beatty's battle cruisers and light cruisers being the nose and ears, and the destroyers – the lion's tail. The nose was to smell nothing, the ears to hear something, the tail to be twisted, but the lion as an entity to remain as majestically unmoved as those which surround Nelson's column.

One preliminary remains to be mentioned – Scheer's intention. It was simple, not subtle, and to that extent simplified the problem of parrying it. Desperation, at the morning's dire prospect, seems to have inspired it. For he took the shortest route home – by Horn Reefs – prepared to lose heavily but determined to break through. Unlike Jellicoe, he could at least feel that the luck lurking in a night encounter was more likely to be a friend than otherwise to his bold course. To enhance his prospects and safety he posted his lame battle cruisers and old battleships in rear and covered his van with destroyer and light-cruiser tentacles.

The scene was set. Would the monarchs of the seas, taking the call, clash in blind battle? Thus the anticipation. But only the tinkle of the jester's bell was heard from the darkened stage. And when light came, the stage was empty.

The first tinkle came at 9.32 PM when the *Lion*, Beatty's flagship, inquired by flashing-lamp of the *Princess Royal* – 'Please give me challenge and reply now in force as they have been lost.' The reply seems to have been seen, in part, by an enemy ship. For, about half an hour later, several cruisers were sighted by the *Castor*, which was leading one of the British destroyer flotillas. They took the initiative and challenged her by making part of the British secret challenge for the day. As, however, they next switched on their searchlights and opened fire, the *Castor* replied in a similar unfriendly fashion, but several of her attendant destroyers withheld their torpedoes from a natural doubt as to the true identity of the cruisers. But the effect of this mischance, and missed chance, can be exaggerated. For, from 10.20 PM to 11.30 PM, the British tail was repeatedly in action with the enemy, who were trying to elbow their way through. At 10.20 PM they 'elbowed' Goodenough's light cruisers, but sheered off after the light cruiser *Frauenlob* had been sunk by a torpedo from the badly battered *Southampton*. In the next hour the British destroyers suffered the contusion and caused confusion. The light cruiser *Elbing* was rammed by the battleship *Posen* and left sinking, while the British destroyer *Spitfire* acted up to her name by ramming the battleship *Nassau*. She not only 'got away with' this act of impertinence, but with a long strip of *Nassau*'s plating as proof of her prowess. Once more the German fleet sheered off, but veered in afresh about 11.30 PM and this time broke through, although harassed by the British hornets for more than an hour at the cost of four of their number.

They had contributed much gallantry, but little intelligence. The only report of these encounters that came to Jellicoe was one from Goodenough at 10.15 PM, and, owing to the *Southampton*'s wireless being shot away this did not reach Jellicoe until 11.38 PM. For the light craft, hotly engaged, there was some excuse for failure to send information, although even those which were not engaged sent no word of what they saw. But Evan-Thomas' 5th Battle Squadron was also astern of the main fleet, forming an intermediate link; it was well aware of the constant attacks and its two rear battleships actually saw the leading German battleships in their wake. The *Valiant*, at 11.35 PM, noted 'two German cruisers with at least two funnels and a crane amidships, apparently steering eastward at a high speed'. The crane identified them so unmistakably as battleships of the *Westfalen* class, that the mistake of assuming them to be cruisers would be incredible were it not fact. The *Malaya*, five minutes later, noted 'enemy big ships, three points abaft the starboard beam, steering the same way as ours'. It had evidently sighted the enemy battleships as they were making a momentary swerve in face of the destroyer attack. It noted the 'conspicuous crane' of the leading ship, and drew the correct deduction that it was 'apparently *Westfalen* class'. Neither the *Valiant* nor the *Malaya* reported what they had seen, apparently assuming that the *Barham*, their flagship ahead, had seen it likewise. How the *Barham* failed to see it has never been explained. The one clear fact is that no word from the squadron was sent to the Commander-in-Chief.

Was there, then, no information which might have quickened Jellicoe's suspicion or upon which he might have acted? Two reports reached him from the Admiralty, which had been intercepting German wireless messages. The first, giving the German location at 9 PM, was valueless because, owing to an error, the position indicated was obviously inaccurate. This did not encourage him to accept the second – which was only too accurate. It stated that the German fleet had been ordered home at 9.14 PM and gave the dispositions, course and speed. But, by another fateful slip, it omitted the most significant fact contained in the several enemy messages which it summarized – that Scheer had asked for an airship reconnaissance near Horn Reefs at daylight. Here was the unmistakable scent to his bolt-hole.

This message was received at 11.5 PM and read, after deciphering, about 11.30 PM. One other message reached Jellicoe, being received at

11.30 PM – and so read later than the Admiralty message. It came from the light cruiser *Birmingham*, and reported that 'battle cruisers probably hostile' were in sight, steering south and well to the westward. Unfortunately, the *Birmingham* had sighted them at a moment when they had sheered away from the British torpedo attacks. If Jellicoe already distrusted the Admiralty message, upon which he took no action, it was natural that he should regard the two later reports from the *Southampton* and *Birmingham* as support to his doubts.

Yet, it is curious, and not easy to explain, that he should have been so insensitive to the definite indication of fighting astern. For, apart from these two reports, the recurrent firing was heard and the flashes seen both by his flagship and the other battleships. That this fire was obviously from light guns did not, it is true, reveal the presence of enemy battleships, but it was no proof that they were not there, for at night battleships would naturally be using their secondary armament if engaged with British light craft. More curious still is the fact that Jellicoe made only one attempt, at 10.46 PM to inquire the source of the firing, and the wording of his signal suggests a preconceived idea that it was merely an enemy destroyer attack. Thus, in sum, the conclusion is that while Jellicoe's lack of certain knowledge was due to the neglect of his subordinates, his lack of suspicion is the measure of his own responsibility – and the salvation of Scheer.

One more serious contact occurred before the German fleet was at last safely free. In the dim light before dawn it was sighted by Captain Stirling's 12th Destroyer Flotilla. The exception, when he should have been the rule, Stirling sent a wireless report to Jellicoe at 1.52 AM, before he engaged the enemy and another during the action. His attack torpedoed and sank the German battleship *Pommern*, and thereby achieved more than the whole Grand Fleet had done. But his reports did not reach Jellicoe, presumably owing to a wireless failure. Thus the British battlefleet continued serenely on its course southward, and the German, on its course homeward.

When daylight came Jellicoe turned about, at 2.39 AM, and steamed northward, expecting to see the German fleet and seeing only an empty sea. Then came another Admiralty message to say that the German fleet was close to Horn Reefs, and this time its evidence was accepted. After searching for enemy stragglers, and finding none, the Grand Fleet in turn steamed homeward. Its total loss had been three battle cruisers, three armoured cruisers and eight destroyers to the German one battleship, one battle cruiser, four light cruisers and five destroyers. In officers and men, the British had lost 6,097 killed to the German 2,545, and 177 prisoners to none.

Thus the one naval 'battle' of the World War was but a casual item in the long butcher's bill. Its value as a battle was in every sense negligible. To trace to it the ultimate and bloodless surrender of the German fleet two and a half years later is absurd, confounding mere sequence with causation. If Jutland did little to encourage the Germans to provoke a decisive clash at sea it did little to discourage them. They had won the first game, against the battle cruisers, and superior gunnery had yielded them honours 'above the line'; they had been out-manoeuvred in the second game, with honours easy, and had scored several tricks in the third before the game had been broken off. As they could not hope to gain the rubber because of their opponent's stronger hand, the interruption left them at least a flattering sense of their own skill. As a new and untried creation the German navy inevitably suffered an inferiority complex in face of a navy which enjoyed a matchless roll of victories and the 'Nelson tradition'. Jutland had dissipated this fear of the untried in face of the known unknown.

Within twelve weeks the German fleet was to make a bolder bid to take the British at a disadvantage. Covered by airship patrols it advanced close to the English coast on August 19th with the idea of bombarding Sunderland as a bait to draw the Grand Fleet south on to a waiting ambush of submarines. Battle was again balked by caution and an accident. One of Beatty's advanced cruisers was torpedoed and Jellicoe, suspecting instead a new-laid minefield, turned back and steamed north for two hours. When he again came south the German fleet had gone. For Scheer had received a report of a strong British force – actually the light force from Harwich – coming up from the south, and hastily assumed that this was the Grand Fleet. If so, it had not only evaded his trap but, turning the tables, threatened to cut him off. Hence he turned for home.

For the British Navy, Jutland would better not have been fought at all. However unpalatable the admission, it undoubtedly depreciated British naval prestige in the eyes of Allies and the home public more than the inspiring feats of individual gallantry and the fact of Britain's continued supremacy at sea could redeem. That supremacy was to ensure the ultimate downfall of German power to continue the war. But no victorious battle helped, as such a battle might, to shorten the gloomy and costly process of exhaustive slaughter on land. Jutland merely ensured what was already ensured without a battle, so long as the British navy maintained its passive superiority of strength.

Here was the general aspect. On the technical side, Jutland was more significant if not more productive of enthusiasm. It showed that the German standard of gunnery was far higher than complacent or patronizing opinion in England had recognized, and it tended, less fairly, to reflect unfavourably on British gunnery owing to the lapse of some, and the lack of opportunity of other, elements of the fleet. In material, Jutland showed also that the Admiralty and its technical advisers had failed to foresee or profit by experience as well as the Germans. Against the inferior armour-piercing qualities of the British shells must be set – but not offset – the fact of insufficient protection of the British ships against plunging fire, and especially against the flash from an explosion in a gun turret passing down into the magazine. This was the probable cause of the mysteriously sudden end of the *Queen Mary* and *Indefatigable*. More debatable perhaps were the results of the policy of building huge battle cruisers in which a large degree of protection was sacrificed for a small increase in speed. Speed in itself confers indirectly a high degree of protection, but essentially through diminishing the target, in the sense of making it more difficult for the enemy to hit. For effective protection in this way a diminution of size is required, not merely a diminution of armour for the sake of a few extra knots.

The tactical side of Jutland has aroused still more criticism and controversy than the technical side. Criticism of its foundation is less easy to counter than criticism of the actual direction. The naval neglect of tactical study, the absence of tactical textbooks, and the secrecy which by custom had enshrouded the meagre instructions, have ever been a source of wonder to soldiers, who know from history and experience that good and flexible tactics in an army are essentially the product of ceaseless reflection and discussion by many minds. '*La critique est la vie de la science.*' Students of military history know that the attempt to keep tactics secret defeats its own end – and its own employer. There was no mystery in the tactics by which Alexander's Macedonians, the Romans, the Mongols, Gustavus' Swedes, Frederick's Prussians, Wellington's Peninsular infantry, won their repeated triumphs. Only a matchless harmony of execution through practice and understanding which gave them the advantage no rival and imitator could overtake. Secrecy leads to rigidity of tactics; open discussion and criticism, to flexibility and the well-attuned initiative of subordinates when confronted with the unexpected. The basic criticism of naval tactics during the World War period is that they undermined the basis of tactics – elasticity. Moreover, the fleet fought at Jutland as a single body, as did armies in the days before Napoleon developed the system

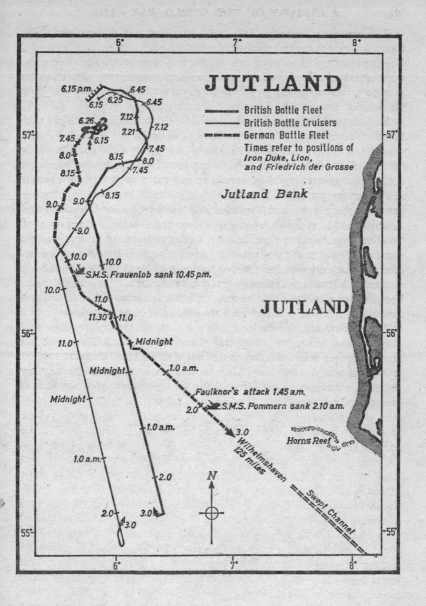

JUTLAND

───── British Battle Fleet
───── British Battle Cruisers
╌╌╌╌╌ German Battle Fleet
Times refer to positions of
Iron Duke, Lion,
and Friedrich der Grosse

Jutland Bank

JUTLAND

6.15 p.m.
6.15   6.25   6.45
        6.45
6.26   7.12
      7.21   7.12
7.45   7.12
8.0   7.45
8.15   8.15   8.0
           7.45
9.0   9.0   8.15

9.0

10.0   10.0
S.M.S. Frauenlob sank 10.45 p.m.
10.0
11.0
11.30   11.0
11.0
Midnight
Midnight
Midnight   1.0 a.m.
Faulknor's attack 1.45 a.m.
2.0   *S.M.S. Pommern sank 2.10 a.m.*
Midnight   1.0 a.m.
3.0
Horns Reef
1.0 a.m.   2.0
Wilhelmshaven
125 miles
2.0   3.0
Swept Channel

N

of independent divisions. Tactically, the fleet was an armless body. Thus however skilfully Jellicoe manoeuvred his fleet he could not justly hope to paralyse his opponent's freedom of movement. And to pin an opponent is the vital prelude to a decisive manoeuvre; this dual act gives a double meaning to the old maxim – 'divide to conquer'. The British fleet was all too truly 'one and indivisible'.

Subject to this dominant proviso, Jellicoe's handling of the fleet during the day of May 31st may fairly be adjudged a very able if cautious performance when we take full account of the obscure conditions. In 1916 this obscurity had reached an extreme, for aircraft reconnaissance had not yet been adequately developed as a corrective to the long ranges developed by progress in guns. As for Jellicoe's oft-criticized deployment on the left wing it was probably the best in the circumstances, although praise of it is apt to overlook the fact that it was not free from trouble. For it meant that Beatty's battle cruisers took longer to get clear of the front of the battlefleet and so masked its fire and caused checks – the very objection which has been brought against Churchill's suggested alternative of deploying from the centre.

The lessons of the night have already been summed up, and the only further question is whether Jellicoe might not have seized the opportunity to forestall the enemy's attempt to break through by using his torpedo craft offensively instead of defensively as his pendent tail. But if, discounting all criticisms, we admit that Jellicoe's handling of the battlefleet was the flawless masterpiece that numerous naval admirers argue, the admission only strengthens the belief that the worst fault of the Jutland battle was that it was ever fought.

CHAPTER SEVEN

1917 – The Strain

Despite incessant provocation for two years, since the *Lusitania* incident, President Wilson held to his neutral policy, and if his excess of patience angered many of his own people it was at least the means of consolidating American opinion and reconciling it as a whole to intervention in the war. Meantime he strove by speech and by the agency of Colonel House – his unofficial ambassador – to find a basis of peace on which the belligerents could agree. This effort was doomed to failure by his misunderstanding of the psychology of the warring peoples and of people at war. He was still thinking in terms of traditional warfare, between governmental policies, while the conflict had long since passed into the wider sphere of the struggle of peoples dominated by primitive instincts and chained by their own catch-phrases to the chariot wheels of Mars-mechanized.

The declaration of the unlimited submarine campaign brought convincing proof of the futility of these peace hopes and of the reality of the German intentions, and when followed by the deliberate sinking of American ships and an attempt to instigate Mexico to action against the United States, President Wilson hesitated no longer and, on April 6th, 1917, America entered the war against Germany.

Her potential force in man power and material was illimitable. But, even more unready than Britain in 1914, it must be long in exerting more than a moral influence, and Germany confidently anticipated that the submarine campaign would take decisive effect within a few months. How near her calculation came to fulfilment the record of 1917 and 1918 bears witness.

The year 1916 had closed in gloom for the Entente. The simultaneous offensive on all fronts, planned a year before, had misfired, the French Army was at a low ebb, the Russian still lower, the Somme had failed to produce visible results in any way proportionate to its cost, and another fresh Ally had been overrun. At sea the negativeness of Jutland was a disappointment, and although Germany's first submarine campaign had been abandoned a stronger one was threatened. To offset these debits, the Entente could only show the capture of distant Baghdad and the limited Italian success at Gorizia in August, whose value, however, was mainly that of a moral fillip to Italy herself.

Among the Allied peoples and their political representatives there was a growing sense of depression. On the one hand it took the form of dissatisfaction with the conduct of the war, and, on the other, of discouragement over the prospects of a victorious conclusion to the war, and a tendency to discuss the possibilities of a peace by negotiation. The first-named tendency was the first to come to a head and was signalized in London, the political mainspring of the Allies, by the replacement of Asquith's Government on December 11th by one with Lloyd George as its chief. The order of precedence in events had a significant effect. For Lloyd George had come into power as the spokesman of a widespread demand for a more vigorous as well as more efficient prosecution of the war.

The second tendency received an impulse from the German peace move of December 12th, after the fall of Bucharest, which proposed an opening of peace discussions. This suggestion was rejected as insincere by the Allied Governments, but it afforded the opportunity for President Wilson, on whose behalf Colonel House had long been sounding the belligerent Governments as to the prospects of mediation, to invite these to define their war aims as a preliminary to practical negotiation. The German reply was evasive, the Allied replies were considered by their opponents unacceptable as a basis of discussion, and the tentative peace moves subsided. But while this wave of depression was surging on the 'home front', the Allied commanders continued optimistic. In November Joffre assembled, at Chantilly, a further conference of the commanders at which it was agreed that the Germans were in great difficulties on the Western Front, and that the situation of the Allies was more favourable than it had ever been.

The fighting strength of the British Army in France had grown to be about 1,200,000 men, and was still growing. The fighting strength of the French Army had been increased by the incorporation of native troops to some 2,600,000, so that, including the Belgians, it was estimated that the Allies disposed of about 3,900,000 men against about 2,500,000 Germans.

Joffre, however, declared that the French Army could maintain its strength for one more great battle, and that thereafter it must progressively decline, as France had no longer a sufficient number of men of military age to replace losses. He therefore warned Haig that during the coming year the burden must fall more and more upon the British Army. It was also agreed that in view of these factors the relative superiority of the Allies on the Western Front would be greater in the spring of 1917 than at any time which could be foreseen with certainty. In consequence it was decided to take the earliest opportunity of pressing the advantage gained on the Somme, and to continue the process of exhausting the enemy's reserves as preparation for an effort which should be decisive. An alternative proposal was made by General Cadorna that the French and British should cooperate in a combined thrust from the Italian front against Austria with the object of knocking this weaker partner out of the war. But it was rejected by the French and British commanders, despite Lloyd George's espousal of it at the Allied conference held in Rome in January. Their objection was that it involved a fresh diversion of strength away from the main front, where alone, they held, success could have decisive results.

An offensive towards Vienna would have had formidable difficulties to overcome, especially from the mountainous country; but in judging the objections to it the historian is compelled to note that the Franco-British strategists showed no signs of recognizing a fundamental truth of strategy – that a concentration at one place is unlikely to succeed unless an adequate distraction to the enemy's counter-concentration is provided elsewhere. In their justifiable conviction that the main effort of France and Britain must be made on the Western Front, they seem to have dismissed too lightly the possibility of helping Italy to create a distraction to their own benefit. Yet, with Russia palpably flagging, the need to develop some fresh channel of pressure had become more urgent. When Robertson dogmatically asserted that the first lesson of history was to concentrate all available force in the main theatre, and that 'any departure from this rule has invariably proved to be disastrous', he exposed his own ignorance of history. Lloyd George might well have reminded him of the effective way in which the Italian theatre had been used by Eugene, with Marlborough's support, as a lever against France in the War of the Spanish Succession; and by Napoleon Bonaparte, as a lever against Austria in the War of the First Coalition. It was a reflection on modern strategists that, with superior facilities, they treated as insuperable the obstacles of nature which their ancestors had repeatedly overcome. To turn the Italian theatre into an effective distraction in favour of the Western Allies, quality rather than quantity of aid from them was needed. The initial task of breaching the Isonzo front would have demanded the concentration there of heavy artillery from the Western Front – but with a promise of much-increased effect in proportion to their number. The subsequent advance would have depended less on weight of numbers than on providing the forces with an adequate spearhead of troops suitable for mountain fighting. In the organization of their respective forces as in the organization of their total resources, a cardinal defect of the Allies in their strategy was that they concentrated by count of numbers instead of concentrating on the most effective utilization of suitable tools.

Poverty of thought, not poverty of resources, produced the bankruptcy of the scheme drawn up at the Chantilly Conference. The military cupboard was abundantly stocked with men and munitions, but its shelves were bare of constructive ideas. The proceedings reveal only too clearly the want of any deep understanding of war and knowledge of its history. The Allied peoples were clamouring for something fresh. This instinct was true if their motives mixed. But all that the combined brains of Chantilly offered them was a skeleton swathed in a few mouldering platitudes.

The Entente plan for 1917 was soon to be complicated by changes in the command. French opinion had tired of the meagre results of Joffre's attrition strategy, and the method of the limited objective had fallen into disfavour because of the unlimited losses on the wrong side, which accompanied it without apparent gain. They contrasted the dull course of Joffre's strategy with the brilliant results gained by Mangin at Verdun, in the autumn, under Nivelle's direction, and as a result Joffre gave place to Nivelle, who promised a real breakthrough. His confidence so inspired Lloyd George, the new British Prime Minister, that Haig was subordinated to him for the forthcoming operations – an arrangement which violated the axiom that a general cannot direct one force while exercising executive command of another. For carrying out a plan essentially audacious, Nivelle had two further handicaps; he failed to convert several of his subordinates to the idea, and he was given less rein by the Government than his predecessor. Again, while Joffre had intimated that the British must take the chief part, Nivelle changed this policy, and in his desire to conserve the glory for France overlooked how severely the French fighting power had been strained.

Joffre's plan had been for a renewal of the Somme offensive on a widened front – the British to attack north of the Somme, including but extending beyond the old battleground, and the French south of it to the Oise. This attack was to open early in February and to be followed a fortnight later by a smaller French attack in Champagne, between Reims and Craonne.

The French had in mind comparatively short-distance objectives;

hence, unless German resistance unexpectedly collapsed, the bulk of the British forces would subsequently be transferred to Flanders for a fresh offensive there. Analysis of the facts does not tend to support the idea that the chance of early victory for the Allies was forfeited through the abandonment of Joffre's plan. The hard frosts that came in late January would have aided its early development; but it would have been too early for any prospect of a simultaneous offensive in the other theatres; and although it might have disturbed the Germans' execution of their plan, they were better prepared to rally in rear than were the Allies to press home the advantage.

Nivelle's plan was more far-reaching than Joffre's. He intended to deliver a convergent attack on both flanks of the great salient Lens–Noyon–Reims, with the French striking the main blow in Champagne immediately after the British and French attacks north and south of the Somme had attracted the enemy's attention and resources. In this 'preparatory' offensive, Nivelle's design was to avoid the old Somme battlefield and, instead, to strike on each side of it. Haig's frontage of attack would thus be reduced, and in return Nivelle wished him to take over the French front south of the Somme, as far as Roye, so as to release additional French forces for the main attack in Champagne, where Nivelle hoped to achieve a decisive breakthrough.

Haig was rather sceptical of such a possibility, and in favour of a later date for the offensive, but he recognized certain advantages in the new plan – especially the fact that it implied a greater effort by the French. On the other hand, he objected strongly to an extension of his front which would reduce the British forces available for his cherished idea of an offensive in Flanders. This objection produced the first crack in the Nivelle plan. To Nivelle's pressing letter of December 21st, Haig made indefinite reply, saying that he could only relieve the French if he himself obtained six additional divisions; and Nivelle, feeling that there was no time to lose, appealed through his own Government to the British. In mid-January, as a result, a conference was held in London: here Haig's appeal that they should wait for the Russian and Italian attacks in May was overruled, and the date fixed for not later than April 1st. It was also settled that Haig should relieve the French south of the Somme, and he was promised two additional divisions for the purpose – after further argument he eventually received eight. Haig was instructed to carry out this agreement 'both in the letter and in the spirit'.

But the difficulties, especially those of personal feeling, had not been smoothed out. Tension between the French and British headquarters increased, the former complaining of obstruction and the latter of attempted domination. This tension was magnified by British dissatisfaction with the French railway service, and on this point Haig now made an appeal to his own Government which led to a fresh conference at Calais on February 26th. But here, to his surprise, the French seized the opportunity to raise the wider issue of a unified control of operations, and produced a scheme by which, for this purpose, the British armies would be placed under Nivelle, whose orders to them would be issued through a British chief of staff at his headquarters. To this proposal, Haig and Robertson naturally took exception, and after heated discussion a compromise was reached by which Haig agreed to act under Nivelle's direction during the forthcoming offensive, subject to the right of appeal. But the chance of a smooth-working arrangement was vitiated by the deep-rooted suspicions of the British Higher Command, and these in turn were accentuated by the way that some of Nivelle's satellites agitated for Haig's removal.

A few days later, Haig, nettled by a rather peremptory letter of instructions from Nivelle, found cause for exercising his right of appeal in the signs of a German withdrawal on the Somme front; laying a perhaps excessive emphasis on the possibility that the Germans might switch troops north and attack him in Flanders, he notified the British Government and Nivelle that he might have to reduce his share in Nivelle's offensive and postpone its execution. Nivelle not unnaturally felt that Haig was evading his obligations, so one more conference was called, in London on March 12th. Here some further safeguards were inserted in the agreement, but the discussion mainly turned on the form rather than on the substance of Nivelle's instructions, and after a personal talk between the two commanders the trouble over these niceties of phrasing was settled. Nivelle was at last free to concentrate his mind on the plan for the forthcoming offensive.

Before it could begin the Germans had dislocated it. Ludendorff's first step had been to set on foot a complete programme for the reorganization of German man power, munitions and supplies. While this was developing, he intended to stand on the defensive, hoping that the new submarine campaign would either decide the issue or pave the way for a decisive blow on land when his reserves of men and material were ready. As a 'coefficient of safety' in face of the Somme offensive, he had previously ordered a new line of defence, of great artificial strength, to be built across the chord of the arc Lens–Noyon–Reims. Early in the new year, anticipating the renewal of the Entente advance on the Somme, Ludendorff hurried on the completion of this rear line and arranged for the utter devastation of the whole area inside the arc. There was a satirical, or satyrical, aptness in the code word for this programme of destruction – 'Alberich', the name of the malicious dwarf in the Nibelung Saga! The Crown Prince Rupprecht thought of resigning rather than carry out these extreme measures, but satisfied his conscience by refusing to sign the order for them. Houses were demolished, trees cut down, and even wells contaminated, while the wreckage was littered with a multitude of explosive booby-traps.

The rearward move was preceded on February 23rd by a local retirement from the awkward salient in front of Bapaume. This timely step relieved the Germans of British pressure and from the risk of interference. Although it gave the Allies a clear hint of what was in prospect they were not able to take advantage of the warning. Nivelle did not believe that the retirement would extend to his front, while Haig, who did, believed also in caution – that only a carefully mounted attack was feasible under modern conditions. The Germans evaded one such attack by another local retirement in the early hours of March 12th. Then on the 16th the main withdrawal began, the German forces marching back unhurried to the new line called by them the 'Siegfried' and by the Allies the 'Hindenburg' line. A consummate manoeuvre, if unnecessarily brutal in application, it showed that Ludendorff had the moral courage to give up territory if circumstances advised it. The British, confronted with a desert, were cautiously slow in pursuit, and their preparations for an attack on this front were thrown out of gear, limiting them to the sector around Arras, where the front was unchanged.

On April 9th Allenby's Third Army opened the spring offensive at this point, taking the long-sought Vimy ridge, but failed to develop its initial success, and continued the attack too long after the resistance had hardened. This costly action was ostensibly prolonged in order to take the pressure off the French. For the French thrust between the Somme and the Oise had also been stultified by the German retirement, and the main attack on April 16th east and west of Reims was a worse fiasco with a dangerous sequel. If it was scarcely Nivelle's fault that the foundations of his strategic plan had been upset, he betrayed *la folie de grandeur* in the way he persisted in it when the conditions had vitally changed. And his tactical plan, over-elaborate and inelastic, had no compensating elements of success against an enemy who was fully forewarned. With a prolonged bombardment giving away any chance of surprise and without first drawing away the German reserves, the idea of a rapid breakthrough was doomed to fail. The high hopes that had been raised caused the greater reaction, and the troops were weary of being thrown against barbed wire and machine guns to no apparent effect.

Accentuated by service grievances, mutinies occurred in the French armies, and no less than sixteen corps were affected. The flame of revolt broke out in a regiment of the 2nd Colonial Division on May 3rd, and although momentarily extinguished soon spread, to the tune of such cries as 'We will defend the trenches, but we won't attack!' 'We are not so stupid as to march against undamaged machine guns!' The fact that the mutinies always occurred when the troops were ordered into the line is clear proof that disgust with their leadership rather than seditious propaganda was the real cause of revolt. A significant sidelight is that cases of desertion in the French Army rose from 509 in 1914 to 21,174 in 1917. So general was the rot that, according to the Minister of War, only two divisions in the Champagne sector could be relied on fully, and in places the trenches were scarcely even guarded.

The saviour of the situation was General Pétain; and his instrument, a change of policy based on psychology. On April 28th the Government had made him Chief of the General Staff as a brake on Nivelle's reckless offensive, and on May 15th they took the wiser and more honest step of appointing him to replace Nivelle. For a month he travelled along the front by car, visiting nearly every division, summoning both officers and men to voice their complaints. Essentially patriarchal and not familiar, he inspired confidence both in his firmness and in his promises. Tours of duty in the trenches were equalized, regularity of leave ensured, rest camps improved. Within a month calm was restored – at the price of only twenty-three executions, although more than a hundred of the ringleaders were deported to the colonies.

But if the French Army was convalescent, Pétain had still to revive its fighting confidence and power. To this end he first reorganized its training and tactics on the basis that fire power should economize man power, and then aimed to try his newly sharpened blade in easy tests that should not risk blunting it again. Thus, for the rest of the year the British bore the brunt of the campaign. Their strength in France was now at its highest – sixty-four divisions, supplied with an abundance of artillery and ammunition. The strain on them, however, was increased by the failure of Russia to make any effective contribution to the pressure on Germany owing to the revolution which broke out in March. Haig decided to keep the Germans occupied by carrying out the original plan for an offensive in Belgium, but even if the principle was right the method and choice of site were opposed to all the experience of history.

The initial move was an attack on the Messines ridge in order to straighten out the Ypres salient and attract the enemy's reserves. Carried out on June 7th by the Second Army under Plumer (with Harington as Chief of Staff) it proved a model example of the 'limited' attack, in which the surprise effect of nineteen huge mines, simultaneously exploded, and supplemented by an overwhelming artillery concentration, was exploited just as far as, and no further than, the point where the German 'numbness' began to wear off.

This coup was tardily followed on July 31st by the main attack at Ypres which, hampered in execution by the heavy rain, was foredoomed by its own destruction of the intricate drainage system of the area. The British Command had persevered for two and half years with the method of a prolonged preparatory bombardment, believing that quantity of shells was the key to success, and that, unlike all the great captains of history, they could forgo the aid of surprise. The offensive at Ypres, which was finally submerged in the swamps of Passchendaele in early November, threw into stronger relief than ever before the fact that such a bombardment blocked the advance for which it was intended to pave the way – because it made the ground impassable. The discomfiture was increased by the new German defensive method of thinning the front defences and using the men so saved for prompt local counterattacks. The defence was built up of a framework of machine guns distributed in concrete 'pillboxes' and disposed in great depth. On the British side the profitless toll of this struggle in the mud was to some extent mitigated by better staff work when the direction of the attack was progressively handed over to Plumer's Second Army.

Three months of dreadful struggle came to an end with the British no appreciably nearer their immediate object of driving the Germans from their submarine bases in the Belgian ports, and if they had worn down the German strength they had worn down their own still more.

The 1917 campaign in the west closed, however, on a note brighter in promise if not in accomplishment. Appreciating from the first days the futility of using tanks in these Flanders swamps, the Tank Corps headquarters looked around for an area where they could try out a new and different method. They drew up a project for a large-scale raid to scour a canal-enclosed 'pocket' near Cambrai, where the rolling downland lent itself to tank movement. The basic idea was the release of a swarm of tanks without any preparatory bombardment to give warning of the attack. When their hopes at Ypres waned, the British Command adopted the scheme, but transformed it into a definite offensive with far-reaching aims, for which they had not the resources because of the drain of Ypres. It was to be carried out by Byng's Third Army with six divisions, and the date was fixed for November 20th. Led by nearly 400 tanks, the attack came as a complete surprise, and despite minor checks achieved a penetration far deeper and at less cost than any past British offensive. But all the available troops and tanks were thrown into the first blow, and no reserves were at hand to exploit the success. The cavalry, as always on the Western Front, proved unable to carry out this role.

Thus the advance died away, and on November 30th the Germans launched a counterstroke against the flanks of the salient created by the British advance. In the north it was parried but in the south broke through, and a disaster was narrowly averted. But if Cambrai closed in disappointment it revealed that surprise and the tank were the combination by which the trench barrier could be unlocked. Meanwhile Pétain, after overhauling his instrument, the French Army, sought to test its readiness for 1918. In August a stroke by Guillaumat's army at Verdun recovered all the remainder of the ground lost in 1916, and in October Maistre's army flattened the south-west corner of the German front, seizing the Chemin des Dames ridge.

The Collapse of Russia. The temporary breakdown of the French fighting power was not the worst of the troubles which together crippled the Entente offensive in 1917. The collapse, first partial and then complete, of Russia was a loss which even the entry of America into the war could not possibly compensate for many months, and before the balance was restored the Western Allies were to be perilously near the brink of defeat. Russia's enormous losses, due to her defective machine but incurred in sacrifice for her Allies, had undermined the moral even more than the material endurance of her forces. Revolution broke out in March, superficially against the corrupt *entourage* of the Tsar, but with more deep-seated moral causes beneath. The Tsar was forced to abdicate and a moderate Provisional Government climbed into the saddle, but without reins. This was only a makeshift, and in May another succeeded it, more Socialist in tendency and outwardly led by Kerensky. While clamouring for a general peace and undermining discipline by a system of committee control suitable to a trade union but not to the field of battle, Kerensky imagined he could send troops against the enemy by platform appeals. Brusilov succeeded Alexeiev in the Supreme Command, and on July 1st the army gained some initial success against the Austrians, especially in the region of Stanislau, only to stop as soon as real resistance was met, and to crumble directly the Germans counter-attacked. By early August the Russians had been driven out of

Galicia and the Bukovina, and only policy halted the Austro-German forces on the frontiers of Russia itself. Since the departure of Hindenburg and Ludendorff in 1916, Hoffmann had been in real control of the Eastern Front; his clever combination of strategy and policy did much to complete the paralysis of Russia, and thus release German troops for use in the west. In September the Germans took the opportunity to practise their new artillery methods, for future use in France; their surprise attack, under Hutier's command, achieved the capture of Riga with scarcely a show of opposition. Next month the Bolsheviks under Lenin overthrew the wordy Kerensky, imposed their self-constituted rule on the Russian people and sought an armistice with Germany, which was concluded in December.

The Breakthrough in Italy. The defection of Russia did not end the Entente tale of woe. Each autumn, with demoralizing regularity, Germany had seized an opportunity to eat up one of the weaker Allies. In 1915 it had been Serbia's fate, in 1916 Rumania's, and now it was to be Italy's turn – or so the Germans intended. Ludendorff's decision, taken in September, was determined by the appeals of the Austrian authorities, who felt that their troops could not endure the strain of another defensive battle on the Italian frontier. In May, Cadorna had attacked once more on the Isonzo front but an Austrian counter-attack in the Carso sector had retaken part of the small gains. Losses, however, were more nearly balanced than formerly. The question of Allied cooperation on the Italian front was raised afresh without result, Haig protesting strongly. Cadorna, nevertheless, initiated in August an 'eleventh battle of the Isonzo'. Capello's Second Army captured a large part of the Bainsizza plateau, north of Gorizia, but a long-sustained effort brought no further success and Cadorna was forced to break off the offensive after four weeks' struggle. But it had so strained the resistance of the debilitated Austrians that, in Ludendorff's words, 'it became necessary to decide for the attack on Italy in order to prevent the collapse of Austria-Hungary'.

Ludendorff had a difficult problem to solve, Russia had not yet capitulated, the front there was already weakly held for its extent, and the British offensive in Flanders made impossible a large withdrawal of troops from France. As he could only scrape together six German divisions, and the Austrians' quality was lower than ever, he came to the conclusion that the only chance of decisive results was to pick out a particularly weak sector which coincidently offered scope for a strategic exploitation of the breakthrough. This was found in the Tolmino–Caporetto sector. On October 24th, after a short bombardment, the blow was launched and pushed deep down the western slopes of the mountains, imperilling the Italian forces to both south and north. On October 28th the advance reached Udine, the former Italian general headquarters, and on October 31st the Tagliamento.

Not the least significant feature of this offensive was the way it was prepared, by a moral bombardment. Propaganda had been exploited for months as a means of sapping the Italian discipline and will to resist. But its effect can be exaggerated – the most formidable propaganda, as with the French in April, was that supplied by the attrition strategy of the Italian Command, which had sickened the troops by its limited results at unlimited cost.

But the result also surprised Ludendorff, who with his slender forces had not calculated on such distant objectives as were now possible of attainment. As the direct pursuit was slowing down he belatedly tried to switch troops from the left wing to Conrad's army which flanked the north of the Venetian salient, but was foiled by the inadequacy of the railways. Even so, Cadorna, with his centre broken through, only saved his wings by a precipitate retreat to the line of the Piave, covering Venice, leaving 250,000 prisoners in the enemy's hands. The same day Cadorna was superseded in supreme command by Diaz. Italy's Allies had begun to rush reinforcements, two army corps, one British and one French, to her aid, and on November 5th their political and military chiefs arrived at Rapallo for a conference, out of which sprang the Allied Council at Versailles, and ultimately a unified command.

The invaders had outrun their transport, and the resistance of the Italians, morally braced by the emergency, succeeded in holding the Piave in face of direct assaults and strenuous efforts by Conrad to turn their left flank from the Trentino. At the beginning of December, the British and French, who had been waiting in reserve in case of a fresh breakthrough, moved forward to take over vulnerable sectors, but the attack was only renewed in the north, and on December 19th it came to an end with the coming of the snows. If Caporetto seriously damaged Italy, it also purged her, and after an interval of recuperation she was to vindicate herself at Vittorio Veneto.

The Capture of Jerusalem. Once more a distant theatre of war provided the sole triumph of the Entente cause during the year – this time in Palestine. The second reverse at Gaza, in April 1917, had led to a change of command, Murray being succeeded by Allenby, who was strong enough and fortunate enough to obtain the adequate force for which Murray had asked in vain. The British Government was anxious for a spectacular success to offset the moral depression of the Nivelle failure and the decline of Russia, and the British General Staff desired to dislocate the Turk's attempt to recapture Baghdad by drawing away their reserves.

Allenby took over in July and devoted the first three months to intensive preparations for an autumn offensive, when the season would be suitable. The command was reorganized, the communications developed, and his own headquarters moved forward from Cairo to the front. By complete secrecy and ruses he deceived the Turks as to the point of attack. The defences of Gaza were bombarded from October 20th onwards, and an attack followed on November 1st to pin the enemy and draw in his reserves. Meanwhile, as a necessary preliminary to the real blow, the inland bastion of Beersheba was seized by a convergent manoeuvre on October 31st, a prelude to the decisive attack on November 6th, which broke through the enemy's weakened centre and into the plain of Philistia. Falkenhayn, now in command at Aleppo, had also been planning an offensive, but the better communications of the British decided the race, and although Falkenhayn tried to stem the tide by a counterstroke against Beersheba, the breaking of his centre compelled a general retreat. The pursuit was hampered by lack of water and of initiative. Even so, by the 14th, the Turkish forces were driven apart in two divergent groups, the port of Jaffa was taken, and Allenby wheeled his main force to the right for an advance inland on Jerusalem. He gained the narrow hill passes before the Turks could block them and, after a necessary pause to improve his communications, brought up reserves for a fresh advance, which secured Jerusalem on December 9th. By the time the winter rains set in the British had expanded and consolidated their hold on the region. As a moral success the feat was valuable, yet viewed strategically it seemed a long way round to the goal. If Turkey be pictured as a bent old man, the British, after missing their blow at his head – Constantinople – and omitting to strike at his heart – Alexandretta – had now resigned themselves to swallowing him from the feet upwards, like a python dragging its endless length across the desert. The difficult process of assimiliation, however, was assisted by the spreading paralysis of the Turkish strength under the needle-pricks of Lawrence and the Arabs.

The Clearing of East Africa. The year 1917 witnessed another overseas success, the clearing of German East Africa, although not the close of the campaign. More than a year elapsed after the rebuff at Tanga before a serious attempt was made to subdue the last German stronghold on the African continent. To spare troops from the main theatres was difficult, and the solution was only made possible by the loyal cooperation of the South African Government. In February 1916, General Smuts was appointed to command the expedition and formed the plan of a drive from north to south through the difficult interior, in order to avoid the fever-rampant plain on the coast. In conjunction with this central wedge, a Belgian force under Tombeur was to advance eastwards from Lake Tanganyika, and a small British force under Northey was to strike in from Nyasaland in the south-west. The Germans under Lettow-Vorbeck were weak in numbers but handled with masterly skill, and with all the advantages of an equatorial climate, a vast and trackless region – mountainous in parts and covered with dense bush and forest – to assist them in impeding the invader. From Dar-es-Salaam on the coast to Ujiji on Lake Tanganyika ran the one real line of rail communication, across the centre of the colony. After driving the Germans back across the frontier and seizing the Kilimanjaro gap, Smuts moved direct on this railway at Morogoro, over 300 miles distant, while he dispatched a force under Van Deventer in a wide sweep to the west to cut the railway farther inland, and then converge on Morogoro. Lettow-Vorbeck delayed this manoeuvre by a concentration against Van Deventer, but Smuts' direct advance compelled him to hurry his force back, and thus enabled Van Deventer to get astride the railway.

However, Lettow-Vorbeck evaded the attempt to cut him off and fell back in September on the Uluguru mountains to the south. The Belgians and Northey had cleared the west and the net had been drawn steadily closer, confining Lettow-Vorbeck to the south-east quarter of the colony. Early in 1917 Smuts returned to England, and Van Deventer conducted the final operations which ended with Lettow-Vorbeck avoiding envelopment to the end, slipping across the frontier into Portuguese Africa. Here he maintained a guerrilla campaign throughout 1918 until the general Armistice. With an original force of only 5,000, five per cent being Europeans, he had caused the employment of 130,000 enemy troops and the expenditure of £72,000,000.

The Mastering of the Submarine. The military side of 1917 is thrown into shadow by the naval, or more strictly the economic, side. The vital issue turned on the balance between Germany's submarine pressure and Britain's resistance. April was the worst month. One ship out of every four which left the British Isles never came home. The Allies lost nearly a million tons of shipping, sixty per cent of it British, and although the German navy's promise of victory by the end of the month was proved a miscalculation, it was clear that, ultimately, the continuance of such a ratio of loss must starve the civilian population and automatically prevent the maintenance of the armies. Britain, indeed, had only food enough to sustain her people for another six weeks.

The Government sought to counter the menace by the indirect means of rationing, increasing home production, and the expansion of ship-building; by the direct means of the system of convoys with naval escorts, and a counter-offensive against the submarine, aided by new devices to detect the presence of submarines and the use of thousands of patrol craft. The most effective countermeasure, that of penning the Germans in their bases by close-in minefields, was hindered by the British failure to obtain a real command of the North Sea, through a decisive victory. The British destroyer flotillas daringly laid thousands of mines in the channels left by the Germans through the Heligoland Bight, but their ceaseless efforts were largely foiled by the German minesweepers, which were able to work freely under the protection of the German fleet. Nevertheless these mines hindered and delayed the passage of the U-boats and increased that demoralizing nerve-strain on the U-boat crews which was, above all, the cause of the decline of the submarine campaign. Too few submarines and trained crews in proportion to the task – and too great a strain upon them – spelt ultimate collapse.

But the British crisis of the spring of 1917 was averted less by an offensive than by a defensive method. For the convoy system was the main agent of salvation. The method of patrolled areas had been continued, despite its proven futility of 1916, during the early months of 1917. As Churchill says – 'In April the great approach route to the south-west of Ireland was becoming a veritable cemetery of British shipping.' And other cemeteries were only small by comparison. Besides 516,000 tons of British shipping, 336,000 tons of Allied and neutral were buried beneath the waves during April, and the direct loss of food and raw materials to the island kingdom was augmented by the growing unwillingness of neutral shipping to take the risk of supplying such a customer. Only the 'guts' of her merchant seamen in going to sea after being several times torpedoed lay between Britain's stomach and starvation. And the blindest blunder of the British Admiralty was in opposing the introduction of the convoy system in face of the futility of their other methods to avert the close-looming disaster. At last the advocacy of younger officers was decisively reinforced by Mr Lloyd George's intervention, and in April voyages under convoy were sanctioned as an experiment on the Gibraltar and North Sea routes. The first left Gibraltar homeward bound on May 10th. Crowned by unmistakable success, the convoys were extended to the transatlantic routes when the arrival of American flotillas under Admiral Sims increased the number of destroyers available for escorts. The loss of shipping in such convoys was reduced to a bare one per cent and when, in August, the convoys were extended to outward-bound shipping the British loss fell next month below the 200,000-ton level. Meantime the offensive campaign – now reinforced by special submarine chasers, aircraft, and the new horned mines – exacted an ever-rising toll of submarines, and by the end of 1917, the menace, if not broken, was at least subdued. If the British people had to tighten their belts, and their food rationing, they were now secure against starvation.

During the early months of 1918 the number of German submarines declined as steadily as their losses rose, until in May fourteen were lost out of 125 on service, while the effect of those that were operating declined disproportionately to their number. In all, the German war loss totalled 199 submarines, of which 175 fell victims to the British navy. And of the various weapons the mine claimed forty-two and the depth charge thirty-one submarines. Hunted from the narrow seas, the U-boats were even shut out from the ocean during the last phase by a vast mine barrage, laid mainly by the American navy, across the 180-mile-wide passage between Norway and the Orkney Islands. It consisted of no less than 70,000 mines, of which the British laid 13,000. This was a direct counter to the main submarine operations against the ocean-brought supplies of Great Britain.

The shorter-range operations of the small submarines from the Belgian coast were crippled by the perfected barrage across the straits of Dover, by the daring attack of Admiral Keyes' force on the night of April 22nd, 1918 – which for a time blocked up the exit from Zeebrugge – and by the progressive demoralization of the U-boat crews. Yet the removal of the menace should not lead to an underestimate of its powers for the future. The 1917 campaign was launched with only 148 submarines and from the most unfavourable strategic position. Great Britain lay like a huge breakwater across the sea approaches to northern Europe, and the submarines had to get outside through narrow and closely watched outlets before they could operate against the arteries of supply. And despite these handicaps they almost stopped the beat of England's heart.

The Economic Reinforcement. In restoring circulation America's first-aid became a potent factor long before her military assistance. It embraced her provision of light craft to reinforce the British anti-submarine fleet, her rapidly developed construction of new mercantile ships and still more her financial aid. By July, 1917, Britain had spent over £5,000,000,000, her daily expenditure had risen to £7,000,000 and the burden of financing her Allies as well as her own efforts was straining even her resources, when America's aid came to ease the pressure. In the first months after her entry into the war the appeals for loans came as a shock to Congress. Unable from remoteness and in-experience to realize the inevitable costs of the war, a large section of the American public felt that its new associates were trying to dip their hands too freely into the capacious pockets of Uncle Sam. Thus Mr McAdoo, the Secretary of the Treasury, could satisfy neither the Allies nor the American public, the former feeling that he was stinting them and the latter crying that he was spending the nation's money like a drunken sailor. Hence further loans were vigorously opposed in Con-gress. Northcliffe graphically, if perhaps hyperbolically, summed up the situation when he cabled – 'If loan stops, war stops.'

Actually, up to mid-July the USA had advanced £229,000,000 to the several Allies, with the restriction that this was to pay for supplies bought in the United States, while Britain in the same period had added £193,000,000 to the £900,000,000 already lent to her Allies – without such restriction. On the top of this fresh strain came the fear of having to sell securities in order to liquidate the earlier 'Morgan loan' – with consequent damage to British credit. Mr Balfour, then Secretary for Foreign Affairs, was so alarmed that he cabled to Colonel House – 'We seem on the verge of a financial disaster which would be worse than defeat in the field. If we cannot keep up exchange neither we nor our Allies can pay our dollar debts. We should be driven off the gold basis, and purchases from the USA would immediately cease and the Allies' credit would be shattered.' The danger was met by the action of the United States Treasury in continuing monthly advances, despite opposition, until a coordinated inter-Allied finance council could be created; by the formation of an official purchasing commission to take over the unofficial functions formerly fulfilled by J. P. Morgan and Company on behalf of the British Government; and by sending Lord Reading to Washington as a combined political and financial representative to oil, by frankness and sympathy, the creaking machinery of demand and supply. The overwhelming success of the Liberty Loan campaign was at least an equal asset. Advances to the Allies were authorized at a maximum average monthly rate of $500,000,000. By the end of the year the problem itself was shifting its basis; for, owing to the vast needs and purchases of the American Government for its own forces, the supply of credit to the Allies began to exceed that of the supply of goods. The difficulty of the Allies was now that of obtaining the material they needed for munitions rather than of obtaining the money to pay for it.

While America's entry into the war thus secured the position of the Allies, it also conferred one great offensive benefit even before America's armies threw their weight into the scale. No longer was the grip of the naval blockade hampered by neutral quibbles, but instead America's cooperation converted it into a stranglehold under which the enemy must soon grow limp, since military power is based on economic endurance. As a party to the war, the United States, indeed, wielded the economic weapon with a determination, regardless of the remaining neutrals, far exceeding Britain's boldest claims in the past years of controversy over neutral rights. Thus the surface blockade of Germany began to tighten coincidently with the flagging of the submarine blockade of Britain.

The Air. Another new form of action reached its crest at the same time as the submarine campaign. As the submarine was primarily an economic weapon, so was the aeroplane primarily a psychological weapon. The explosive bullet had virtually ended the Zeppelin raids in 1916, but from early in 1917 aeroplane raids on London grew in intensity until by May 1918 the air defences were so thoroughly organized that the raiders thereafter abandoned London, as a target, for Paris. If the stoicism of the civil population took much of the sting from a weapon then in its infancy, the indirect effect was serious, interrupting business and checking output in industrial centres, as well as drawing off, for defence, many aircraft from the front. In reply the British belatedly formed a small Independent Air Force, which carried out extensive raids into Germany during the closing months of the war, with marked effect on the declining morale of the 'home front'.

Propaganda. The beginning of 1918 witnessed the development and thorough organization of another psychological weapon, when Lord Northcliffe, who had been the head of the British War Mission in the United States was appointed 'Director of Propaganda in Enemy Countries', and for the first time the full scope of such a weapon was understood and exploited. Northcliffe found his best blade in President Wilson's speeches, which with idealism if not with entire realism unvaryingly distinguished between Germany's policy and the German people, and emphasized that the Allied policy was to liberate all people, including the Germans, from militarism. This blade, sharpened by the armourer, Colonel House, was trenchantly wielded by Northcliffe with the aim of severing the common ties which held together the enemy nations and their rulers. But these ties were stout enough to turn any blade until they had been frayed by military pressure. In July 1917 the effect of President Wilson's speeches, acting upon war-weariness and anti-militarism in Germany, produced a parliamentary revolt and under Erzberger's management the Reichstag passed a peace resolution, which forswore territorial annexations. But the only effect was to break Bethmann-Hollweg, the unhappy rope in the tug-of-war between the military and the political parties. The parliamentary representatives of the German people were as helpless to withstand the iron will of the General Staff as was Imperial Austria, now utterly sick of, and only anxious to abandon, the war which she had provoked. These peace movements received small practical response from the enemy democracies; for President Wilson as their spokesman reiterated the declaration that they would negotiate no peace with military autocracy. His encouragement to the enemy peoples to throw off this control was excellent in precept but vain in fact when addressed to those who were so firmly manacled. They were not Houdinis.

In January 1918 there was, indeed, a significant attempt at popular revolt, when over a million German workers joined in a general strike, but this was soon quenched and even forgotten in the fresh exhilaration of the great offensive. Only when the military machine itself began to crumble could the slaves of the machines free themselves from the grip, or propaganda help them in loosening it. Perhaps only then did an active will to peace reinforce their mere passive weariness of war. The inner strength of militant patriotism lies in the fact that it is not merely a gag but a drug.

CHAPTER SEVEN

SCENE 1

The Halt and Lame Offensive – Arras, April, 1917

On April 9th, 1917, the British armies in France entered upon what they had hoped was to be the final and decisive campaign of the World War. To the ordinary observer the day was a brilliant contrast to all previous offensives, but it proved yet another mirage in the military desert. This was perhaps inevitable before zero hour.

The Arras offensive had its roots deeply embedded in the battles of the Somme, 1916. Its strategic conception sprang from the Somme, for, in conjunction with the other attacks – still-born or prematurely deceased – planned for the spring of 1917, it was an effort to complete the overthrow of German power and man power which it was believed that only the onset of winter had prevented on the Somme. Its strategic failure was the outcome partly of the situation produced by the Somme and partly of the inability of the higher command to forget the barren methods employed on the Somme. And the germ of the Arras plan dated from the time of the Somme.

For as early as June, 1916, a plan known as the Blaireville project had been drawn up for a blow near Arras to take place as a supplement to the Somme offensive. Postponed because of the immense casualties on the Somme, which drew off all available forces to that human sump-pit, it was revived and extended in October as part of the spring plan. The gradual British advance eastwards on the Somme had left a German-held bulge between it and Arras – a bulge of which Gommecourt formed the westernmost point. This bulge seemed to offer the opportunity for a right- and left-hand blow on the respective sides, converging towards Cambrai. If successful this might not only cut off the German forces holding the bulge, but create a gap too wide for the German reserves to block, and so pave the way for an advance towards Valenciennes and against the enemy's line of communications and retreat through the Belgian 'trough'.

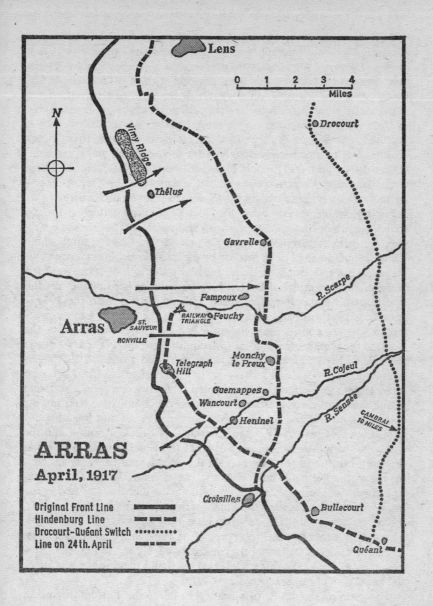

Lens

0 1 2 3 4
Miles

N

Drocourt

Vimy Ridge

Thélus

Gavrelle

Arras

R. Scarpe

Fampoux

RAILWAY TRIANGLE

ST. SAUVEUR

Feuchy

RONVILLE

Telegraph Hill

Monchy le Preux

R. Cojeul

Guemappes

Wancourt

R. Sensée

Heninel

CAMBRAI 10 MILES

ARRAS
April, 1917

Original Front Line
Hindenburg Line
Drocourt-Quéant Switch
Line on 24th. April

Croisilles

Bullecourt

Quéant

On November 18th, 1916, the Allied Commanders-in-Chief met at Chantilly to discuss their plans for 1917, and the outcome was that early in February the British Fourth and Fifth Armies should resume their Somme offensive on the southern side of the Gommecourt bulge, while the Third Army (Allenby) struck on the northern side from Arras. After gaining Monchy-le-Preux Allenby was to push south-east to close the German lines of retreat along the Cojeul Valley, and, if possible, the Sensée Valley also. In conjunction, the First Army (Horne) was to attack immediately north of the Third and form a defensive flank, and the French to attack south of the Somme. Three weeks later the French blow was to be launched in Champagne – an undue delay if the two main blows were to react on each other.

But the whole scheme was dissolved by a combination of French action, British hesitation, and German anticipation. The French action took the form of dismissing their Commander-in-Chief, Joffre, whose bubble reputation had been pricked by the unconcealable evidence of ill-preparedness at Verdun and, less justly, by the lack of success on the Somme. He was replaced by Nivelle, the popular hero of the Verdun *ripostes*, whose appointment caused a change in the plan for 1917 – towards greater aims and also towards giving the French a more spectacular role. In consequence the British had to take over more of the front, to the impairment of their own offensive projects. Tactlessness on one side and sensitiveness on the other produced a time-wasting series of arguments that caused a delay in the Allied offensive. And before it could begin the Germans had disrupted its foundation – by a strategic withdrawal not merely from the Gommecourt bulge, but from the whole of their old and indented front between Arras and Soissons. An absurd attempt was made to picture this as a British triumph and the fruit, even if a little late in garnering, of the Somme offensive. It was the fruit, but not in the sense which the British command suggested – for the method of petty limited attacks pursued throughout the autumn had given the Germans ample opportunity to dig, literally and metaphorically, a pit for their assailants. Straightening their front by retiring to the newly built Hindenburg Line, they left the British to follow laboriously through the intervening desert which, with immense thoroughness of destruction, they had created. By nullifying the Allies' preparations for attack this withdrawal restricted them to the sectors on the two flanks of the evacuated area.

The main role in the British attack thus fell to the Third Army under Allenby. If he could break through the old defences just to the north of where the Hindenburg Line ended, he would automatically take this line in flank and rear. But in anticipation of such a move the Germans had dug a switch line from Quéant, near the northern end of the Hindenburg Line, through Drocourt – covering the rear of the old defences north of Arras. Thus Allenby's whole chance of strategic success depended on whether he could reach and break through this partially completed switch line – some five miles behind the front system – before the German reserves could arrive in strength. Surprise was the only key which could open this gate. Because of this the real drama of the Arras offensive lies in the preliminary discussions and preparations even more than in the battle itself.

Surprise had been discarded in the Somme offensive, except on July 14th – indeed, this master key of all the great captains of history had been rusting since the spring of 1915. The two means by which surprise could be obtained, and the Drocourt–Quéant switch reached in time, were by launching a mass of tanks or by a hurricane bombardment, brief but intense. The first means became impossible owing to the slowness in delivering new tanks after the discouraging reports made upon them in 1916, so that sixty old machines were all that could be scraped together. Allenby and his artillery adviser, Holland, were anxious to have the shortest possible bombardment, and originally proposed that it should last only forty-eight hours. If this, according to later standards, was more than forty hours too long, it was a tentative step in the direction of surprise. But the Higher Command was faithful to the theory of prolonged bombardment, and had a deep-rooted distrust of such an innovation. Nevertheless Allenby stood firm until General Headquarters hit upon the deft device of promoting his artillery adviser to another sphere and replacing him by one who shared their view. Then the plan of a five days' bombardment, preceded by three weeks of 'wire-cutting', was adopted. This, together with the too visible preparations, spelt the doom of surprise. In the bombardment 2,879 guns (989 heavy) took part – a gun to every nine yards.

The most vivid impression of the British disregard for surprise at Arras is perhaps to be found in the German account of the counter-preparations which they were able to make during the three weeks' 'notice' they were so clearly given – 'Field and heavy artillery in long columns awoke the approach roads of the *Hinterland*; flying-corps formations and machine-gun units ... responded to the call. Innumerable crowds of working parties laboured day and night ... at the repair and deepening of the defence system. Night and day in unbroken sequence trains from the Homeland laden with material and munitions reached the main depots ... Mountains of shell were piled up in the ammunition dumps ... The construction of the defences and the organization of the troops was completed ... The enemy could come, the troops had now the word.'

Ludendorff himself visited the sector and was satisfied that although the British might break into the forward positions, if they liked to pay the price, they would then be held up by his new system of defence in depth.

The difficulties, however, were not all of German manufacture. General Charteris, the head of Haig's intelligence service, has provided a significant sidelight in his diary notes at the time: 'Allenby shares one peculiarity with Douglas Haig: he cannot explain verbally, with any lucidity at all, what his plans are. In a conference between the two of them it is rather amusing. D.H. hardly ever finishes a sentence, and Allenby's sentences, although finished, do not really convey exactly what he means.' 'They understand one another perfectly' – other evidence throws a doubt on this point – 'but as each of their particular staffs only understands their immediate superior a good deal of explanation of details has to be gone into afterwards ... At these army conferences no one dares to interfere ...'

In smaller points Allenby still sought for surprise, notably in linking up the underground sewers and quarries of Arras, St Sauveur, and Ronville, in order to shelter two divisions which were to pass underground and leapfrog through the leading divisions. Another feature of the plan was that after the three assaulting corps of the Third Army had broken the enemy's first system of defence, the Cavalry Corps (Kavanagh) and XVIII Corps (Maxse) were to pass through in the centre between the human buttresses, and drive forward towards the switch line. Partly for concealment, the daring risk was taken of moving this pursuit force through the city of Arras, whose houses extended almost up to the front line. This plan, refreshingly ingenious, was vitiated, however, not only by the absence of initial surprise, but by the comparatively narrow front of the opening attack – about twelve miles. Thus the central bottle-neck was, in turn, so narrow that its end could be easily stopped. Ludendorff in his Vilna offensive in the autumn of 1915 had revealed a better method – a dual penetration by two horns goring their way into the enemy's front, while through the wide gap between the horns the pursuit force unexpectedly issued.

A fundamental defect of the Arras plan, moreover, was the width of its base compared with its fighting front – the routes of supply and reinforcement all converging on Arras, with the result that the narrow mouth of this bottle-neck became utterly congested. When the initial

attack failed to make the progress anticipated, this congestion was increased by the arrival of the cavalry in the forward area – although the
experience of 1915 and 1916 had shown that such advance was futile
unless and until a wide path had been swept clear of the enemy.

Yet if the strategic object was practically forfeited before zero
hour on April 9th, the tactical success was at first a vivid and enhearten-
ing contrast to all previous British offensives. The new British gas shell
was most effective in paralysing the defending artillery, for it not only
compelled the gun crews to keep on their gas masks for hours at a time,
but by killing off the horses like flies prevented ammunition being
brought up. The attack was delivered by the VII, VI and XVII Corps
of the Third Army and the Canadian Corps of the First Army. On the
extreme right, or south, lay Snow's VII Corps, with the 21st Division
near Croisilles forming a pivot on which the rest of the corps – the
14th, 30th and 56th (1st London) Divisions – advanced. To their left
lay Haldane's VI Corps, with the 3rd, 12th and 15th Divisions attacking and the 37th Division waiting to leapfrog through and seize the key
position of Monchy-le-Preux. The marshy valley of the Scarpe, the
boundary between the VI Corps and its neighbours, separated the
British right and left wings. North of the Scarpe the attack was entrusted to Fergusson's XVII Corps, composed of the 9th, 34th and 51st
Divisions, with the 4th to leapfrog through the 9th on the Corp' right.
Farthest north of all, Byng's Canadian Corps was to assault the ill-
omened Vimy ridge, which had so long proved an impregnable barrier
to the Allied forces. The capture of a large part of the ridge on April
9th gained all the greater *éclat* from the fame – or, to the Allies, ill-
fame – which this ridge had acquired. The Canadians' feat was as finely
prepared as it was executed. Yet it is but just to recognize that in one
important condition the task was easier than farther south, for the very
fact of attacking uphill gave the attackers here better artillery observation and drier ground than those who had to traverse the sodden or
marshy area near the Scarpe.

At 5.30 AM the assaulting infantry moved forward on the whole
front, covered by a superbly timed creeping barrage, and in less than an
hour almost the whole German first-line system was captured. North of
the Scarpe the success continued, and after the leading divisions had
gained their three successive objectives, the 4th Division passed
through on the corps' right, and by seizing Fampoux breached the last
German line in front of the Drocourt–Quéant switch. But south of the
Scarpe the German resistance, first at the Railway Triangle and Telegraph Hill, then on the Wancourt–Feuchy line – helped by machine

guns from Monchy-le-Preux Hill – was so strong that it badly delayed, although it could not stop, the advance of the 12th and 15th Divisions. Thus the reserve 37th Division could not pass through that day, and behind them the cavalry had moved up not only in vain but to add to the congestion.

The results of the opening day had been greater and quicker, both in prisoners and progress, than in any previous offensive – yet they had extinguished the dim hope of a strategic breakthrough. A contributory factor was the misuse of the tanks. With only sixty machines available it would have been wiser to have concentrated them in aid of the vital effort to gain Monchy-le-Preux instead of spreading them over the front. The error was repeated in the next phase, whereas, if all available tanks had been concentrated on the south side of the salient formed by the first day's attack, they could have taken the German resistance in enfilade, and might have rolled it up.

So on April 10th the Third Army butted direct at a stiffening resistance, with its guns too far back to support the infantry. Not until the morning of April 11th did the arrival of four tanks help a battalion of the 37th Division to seize Monchy-le-Preux – driving in a wedge which was, however, too narrow and too late.

That same morning part of Gough's Fifth Army launched a converging assault from the south against the Hindenburg Line, in an attempt to relieve the pressure of German opposition to the Third Army. It was a desperate remedy for a despairing situation. For this army, after painfully toiling over the evacuated area, had neither been able to make the preparations nor to bring up the artillery necessary for a normal trench attack, far less an assault on the massive defences of the Hindenburg Line. The difficulty led to a novel expedient, which contained the germ of the method which was triumphantly successful later at Cambrai. But instead of 381 tanks as at Cambrai, only eleven could be gathered. As artillery support was deficient, this handful of tanks was to act as a mobile barrage and wire destroyer, leading the 4th Australian Division against the Hindenburg Line near Bullecourt.

The gamble failed – the preparations were too hasty, the resources inadequate, and the front too narrow. For a few hours there was an illusion of success. If the tanks arrived too late for their intended role, they at least helped to distract the enemy's attention, and caused a panic which 'sent part of the German garrison fleeing across the countryside'. The Australians broke into the Hindenburg Line, but then became the target of counter-attack from all sides, while the illusion of a sweeping advance prevented the artillery from protecting them.

With better security the gain might have been held, but the British could hardly have done more, as the obstinate German resistance at Heninel and Wancourt, to the right of the Third Army, prevented any chance of the two armies joining hands. Next morning a gallant assault by the 21st and 56th (1st London) Divisions conquered these two bastions, but the increasing intensity of German counter-attacks brought the first and main phase of the offensive to a close on April 14th. If strategic success had been missed, 13,000 prisoners and 200 guns had been taken.

The next phase had little result to put in relief against the depressing total of British casualties. The French offensive of April 16th on the Aisne, to which Arras had been the prelude, proved a worse downfall, shattering Nivelle's extravagant hopes and predictions, and burying his career in its ruins. The British were not ready to resume their offensive until a week later, and although Haig decided to continue 'the full pressure of the British offensive ... in order to assist our Allies', there was by then no French advance to assist. On April 23rd and 24th Allenby pushed forward his line, at heavy cost and against heavy pressure, to include Guemappe and Gavrelle. At a conference of the army commanders on April 30th, Haig showed that he placed little faith in the possibility of a further French offensive, but decided to continue his own attacks, 'to move steadily forward up to a good defensive line'.

Despite fruitless assaults and sacrifices on May 3rd and 5th, 'bald-headed' assaults which showed more obstinacy than imagination or care, this line was not reached, and the offensive which had been prolonged to so bitter a conclusion was at last broken off. The British offensive centre of gravity was then transferred to the north – to open as brilliantly at Messines on June 7th, and to fade out still more miserably in the swamps of Passchendaele in October.

CHAPTER SEVEN

SCENE 2

The Siege-war Masterpiece – Messines

On June 7th, 1917, took place a battle which on the morrow was hailed as a brilliant military achievement, and which today, unlike so many historically tarnished 'masterpieces' of 1914–18, stands out in even higher relief. For we appreciate now that the capture of the Messines ridge by General Plumer's Second Army was almost the only true siege-warfare attack made throughout a siege war. It was also one of the few attacks until late in 1918 in which the methods employed by the command completely fitted the facts of the situation.

But if today its abiding historic interest lies in its perfect suitability of method, at the time this was overshadowed, and rightly, by its value as a moral tonic. Perhaps this was almost too strong a stimulant to those not in direct charge of the operation, leading them to place too high hopes in the subsequent operations at Ypres, where the conditions were different and the methods also. But such a reflection does not dim the value of Messines, which came as a tonic badly needed after the depressing end of the spring offensive at Arras and on the Aisne.

While Pétain was striving to rally and rejuvenate the French Army, Haig decided to transfer the weight of his attack to Flanders, and, as a preliminary step to his main action at Ypres, to fulfil his long-formed plan of securing the high ground about Messines and Wytschaete as a flank bastion to the Ypres advance. For while in German possession it gave the enemy complete observation of the British trenches and forward battery positions, enabled them to command the communications up to the Ypres salient, and to take in enfilade, or even reverse, the trench positions therein.

Preparations had been begun nearly a year before, although their real development dated from the winter. Thus, when Haig asked Plumer, on May 7th, when he would be ready to deliver the Messines attack, Plumer was able to say, 'A month from today' – and keep his promise exactly. The calm confidence of this businesslike statement betrays no sign of the anxiety suffered, nor does it do justice to the will-power demanded of Plumer in carrying through his purpose.

The key factor in the success was the simultaneous explosion of nineteen great mines, containing 600 tons of explosives and involving the tunnelling of 8,000 yards of gallery since January, in the face of active countermining by the enemy. A couple of months before the attack it was reported to Plumer that the Germans were within eighteen inches of the mine at Hill 60, and that the only thing to do was to blow it. Plumer was firm in his refusal, and equally staunch under the wearing strain of ominous rumours and reports throughout the following weeks. His justification came at 3.10 AM on June 7th, when this mine went up along with eighteen others – only one out of twenty had been blown up by the Germans.

Another example of his will-power was in withstanding strong and insidious pressure from General Headquarters to change his artillery adviser. Before the Arras offensive the same thing had happened with the Third Army, and Allenby's artillery plan had been radically modified – to the loss of all hope of surprise – by the removal of his artillery adviser to another sphere and his replacement by one who gave a different opinion. But before Messines, Plumer resisted all attempts at a change, and finally quelled them by saying flatly that as long as he was responsible he intended to have his own men. If Plumer could be strong in resisting expert advice at need, no commander was more keen to secure it from all sources, and none weighed it more carefully – as a foundation for his own decision. In Harington, he had a Chief of his General Staff of blended intelligence and sympathy. And their happy combination was a symbol of the cooperation which was diffused throughout the Second Army staff, and through them to the fighting troops.

Trust and receptiveness to ideas and criticisms were the keynotes of the Second Army. They were instanced in the schools and courses behind the front, where free questioning and criticism were encouraged, while an answer and a reason to any point raised was always forthcoming. They were also marked in the preparation of an attack. Where other high commanders were apt to lay down a series of objectives which their troops must gain, Plumer's method was to suggest certain provisional lines, and then to discuss them, and each fraction of them, with the corps and divisional commanders concerned, adjusting the several objectives to the local conditions and opinions until a final series was pieced together like a mosaic, on which all were agreed.

Further, the impartial common-sense of his judgement was shown by the fact that, although he could oppose technical advice from General Headquarters when it conflicted with reality, he welcomed it when it coincided. The Western Front in 1914–18 was pre-eminently an engineers' war, yet historians will be perplexed at the small part played by engineers in its direction, and the overweening influence of cavalry and infantry doctrine in the attempt to solve its problems. Messines, however, was in sharp contrast, for here the methods and the training were largely based on a manual, S.S. 155, compiled by the engineers from their special knowledge and experience of siege warfare.

For Messines was to be a strict siege operation, the capture of a fortified salient at the minimum cost of lives by the maximum substitution of mind – in preparation – and material – in execution – for human bodies. Mines, artillery, tanks, and gas all played their part. But a contrary wind curtailed most of the scheme of gas projection, and the effect of the mines and artillery was so overwhelming that the tanks were hardly needed. On a front of just over nine miles a total of 2,338 guns – of which 828 were heavy – were concentrated. There were also 304 large trench mortars. Thus the artillery strength here was approximately one gun to every seven yards of front, or 240 to the mile; five and a half tons of ammunition were thrown on each yard of front.

The fact that the attack would converge against a salient increased its chances, but it complicated the staff, troop and artillery organization of the attack. For the sectors of each attacking corps were of varying depths, and contracted more and more in width up to the final objective which was the chord of the arc forming the salient. As, however, it was a siege operation, without any attempt at exploitation or a breakthrough, it was easier to avoid the congestion which had occurred at Arras. And the problem was further simplified by the plan of so allotting sectors that five of the divisions had sectors of equal breadth from front to rear, while the four which filled the interstices had smaller tasks. Further, when the main ridge was captured, fresh troops were to 'leapfrog' through to gain the final Oosttaverne line across the base of the salient.

Meticulous organization and forethought marked every stage of the preparation, but this was based on personal touch – staff officers continually visiting the units and trenches – not on paper reports and instructions. Another feature was the special intelligence scheme, whereby the information obtained from prisoners, ground and air observation and reconnaissance, photography, wireless interception, and sound ranging, was swiftly conveyed to an army centre, established for a fortnight at Locre Château, and then sifted and disseminated by summaries and maps.

The bombardment and 'wire-cutting' began on May 21st, were developed on May 28th, and culminated in a seven days' intense bombardment, mingled with practice barrages to test the arrangements. The consequent forfeiture of surprise did not matter in the Messines stroke, a purely limited attack, in contrast to that at Arras, where it had been fatal to the hope of a breakthrough. For although there was no surprise there was surprise effect – produced by the mines and the overwhelming fire – and this lasted long enough to gain the short-distanced objectives that had been set. The point, and the distinction between actual surprise and surprise effect, are of significance to the theory of warfare.

It was fortunate, however, for the British that the Germans played into their hands. When the attack preparations were suspected, Rupprecht's chief of staff, Kuhl, had made the suggestion to 'evacuate the salient and withdraw behind the Lys'. But the corps commanders maintained the traditional belief in the value of 'commanding' positions; and their opinion prevailed. Obsessed by the soldierly conviction that ground should never be given voluntarily, they even insisted on holding the forward positions in strength. Thus German stupidity made possible the success of the British plan, preventing the short step to the rear that would have nullified the British mines and wasted the labour devoted to them.

In the British plan nine infantry divisions, with three more close up in reserve, were to advance to the assault. On the right (or south flank) was the II Anzac Corps (Godley) composed of the 3rd Australian, New Zealand, and 25th Divisions, with the 4th Australian Division behind. In the centre came the IX Corps (Hamilton-Gordon), the attack here being led by the 36th, 16th, and 19th Divisions, with the 11th in reserve. On the left was the X Corps (Morland), composed of the 41st, 47th, and 23rd Divisions, backed up by the 24th.

At 3.10 AM on June 7th the nineteen mines were blown, wrecking large portions of the Germans' front trenches. Simultaneously the barrage fell. When the débris and shock of the mines subsided, the infantry advanced and within a few minutes the whole of the enemy's front-line system was overrun, almost without opposition. Resistance stiffened as the penetration was deepened, but the training of the infantry and the efficiency of the barrage, based on the finest shades of calculation, enabled continuous progress to be made, and within three hours the whole crest of the ridge was secured.

The New Zealand Division had cleared the intricate fortifications of Messines itself – here the pace of the barrage was regulated to 100 yards in fifteen minutes instead of the general pace of 100 yards in three minutes. The garrisons of Wytschaete and the White Château held out for some time, but the first village was captured after a fierce struggle by troops of the 36th (Ulster) and 16th (Irish) Divisions in a combined effort – a feat of symbolical significance. Perhaps the most difficult sector was that of the 47th (2nd London) Division, which had not only to overcome the highly fortified position of the White Château, but had the Ypres–Comines canal as an oblique interruption across its line of advance. The Londoners, however, overcame both and by 10 AM the objective of the first phase was reached along the whole attacking line. While it was being consolidated, over forty batteries were moved forward to support the next pounce.

At 3.10 PM the reserve divisions and tanks 'leapfrogged' through, and within an hour almost the whole of the final objective was captured. Some 7,000 prisoners had been taken, apart from dead and wounded, at a cost to the attacker of only 16,000 casualties. The success had been so complete that only feeble counter-attacks were attempted that day. When the expected general counter-attack was launched on the whole front on the morrow, it failed everywhere against defences that had been rapidly and firmly organized, and in the recoil yielded the British still more ground.

The peculiar glory of the Messines attack is that, whereas in 1918 the decline in the German power of resistance brought the conditions to meet the methods almost as much as the methods were developed to meet the conditions, on June 7th, 1917, the methods were perfectly attuned to a resisting power then at its height.

CHAPTER SEVEN

SCENE 3

The 'Road' to Passchendaele

On July 31st, 1917, began what is termed the Third Battle of Ypres. And it is symbolical of its course and its issue that it is commonly spoken of by the title of 'Passchendaele', which in reality was merely the last scene of the gloomiest drama in British military history. Although called the Third Battle, it was not a battle, but rather a campaign, with the fighting more defined than the purpose – of the nature so familiar in the military annals of Flanders, and the Low Countries generally. And, like its German forerunners of 1914 and 1915, it achieved little except loss – in which, again, it repeated the earlier history of this theatre of war. So fruitless in its results, so depressing in its direction was this 1917 offensive, that 'Passchendaele' has come to be, like Walcheren a century before, a synonym for military failure – a name black-bordered in the records of the British Army. Even the inexhaustible powers of endurance and sacrifice shown by the combatants, or the improved executive leadership which did much in the later stages to minimize their sufferings, tend to be not merely overshadowed, but eclipsed in memory by the futility of the purpose and result.

What was the origin and what the object of 'Third Ypres'? An offensive in this sector had formed part of Haig's original contribution to the Allied plan for 1917. Its actual inauguration had been postponed by the unfortunate turn of events elsewhere. When the ill-success of the opening offensive in the spring at Arras and in Champagne was followed by the threatened collapse of the French Army as a fighting force, Haig's 'first-aid' treatment was to allow the British offensive at Arras, by the Third Army, to continue for some weeks longer with the general object of keeping the Germans occupied, and with the local object of reaching a good defensive line. When successive thrusts, against an enemy now fully warned and strengthened, failed to reach this line, Haig decided to

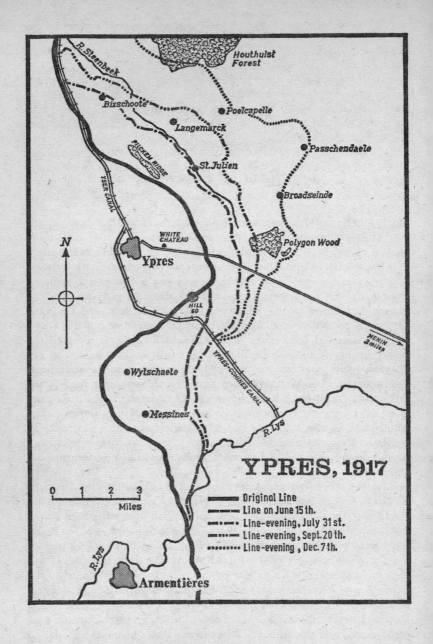

N

Houthulst
Forest

R. Steenbeek

Bixschoote

Poelcapelle

Langemarck

Passchendaele

PILCKEM RIDGE

St. Julien

YSER CANAL

Broadseinde

WHITE
CHATEAU

Polygon Wood

Ypres

HILL
60

MENIN
2 miles

Wytschaete

YPRES-COMINES CANAL

Messines

R. Lys

YPRES, 1917

0   1   2   3
Miles

━━━━ Original Line
──── Line on June 15th.
─·─·─ Line-evening, July 31st.
─··─·· Line-evening, Sept. 20th.
······ Line-evening, Dec. 7th.

R. Lys

Armentières

transfer the main weight of this effort northward to Flanders, as he had originally intended. An intense conviction of the importance of giving the enemy no respite inspired him to press on with an offensive policy, even though French cooperation was lacking. His remarks, at the conference of the army commanders on April 30th, show that in his own mind he had practically written off the French share as a bad debt on the balance sheet of 1917.

It is right to emphasize that, at this moment, Haig's opinion of the strategy to pursue was supported by the Prime Minister, who was in favour of continuing the offensive provided that the French took a vigorous part in it. But it soon became clear that this essential condition would not be fulfilled, and thenceforward he tried in vain to restrain Haig. If the need to distract the enemy's attention from the French, the crisis at sea caused by the submarine campaign, and the need to second the still possible Russian offensive, combined to justify Haig's decision in May, the situation had radically changed before the main offensive was actually launched on July 31st. In war all turns on the time factor. By July the French army, under Pétain's treatment, was recuperating, if still convalescent, the height of the submarine crisis was past, and the revolutionary paralysis of the Russian army was clear. Nevertheless, the plans of the British High Command were unchanged. The historian may consider that insufficient attention was given to the lessons of history, of recent experience, and of material facts in deciding both upon the principle of a major offensive and upon its site. The axis of the attack diverged from, instead of converging on, the German main communications, so that an advance could not vitally endanger the security of the enemy's position in France. Haig curiously was to adopt here the same *eccentric* direction of advance which a year later his advice prevented Foch and Pershing from taking on the other flank of the Western Front. Thus an advance on the Belgian coast offered no wide strategic results, and for the same reason it was hardly the best direction even as a means of pinning and wearing down the enemy's strength on a profitable basis. Moreover, the idea that Britain's salvation from starvation depended on the capture of the submarine bases on this coast has long since been exploded, for the main submarine campaign was conducted from German ports. The story of how this delusion was fostered is a curious one.

In the middle of June, Haig was called home to see a Cabinet which had grown uneasy over his offensive schemes. Its members were agreed in wishing to postpone serious operations until the French had recovered and the Americans had arrived on the scene, and to save up their strength for 1918. Haig marshalled his arguments, and committed himself to 'the definite opinion that if the fighting was kept up at its present intensity for six months Germany would be at the end of her available man power'. Here he went beyond even the estimate of his optimistic intelligence service, which had at least made its forecast dependent on Russia's continued efforts. As the Cabinet were growing sceptical of military arithmetic, Haig's arguments failed to make the impression he had hoped. Suddenly, the Admiralty came to the rescue of his plans – by telling the Cabinet that 'the Navy could not keep going unless the Germans were turned out of the Belgian coast'. Even in high military quarters, as the chief of Haig's intelligence staff has admitted, 'no one really believed this rather amazing view'. But it served as a welcome lever to make the Cabinet give way – as was the result.

The real source of the offensive, more potent than any of the arguments with which he buttressed his case, seems to have been Haig's optimistic belief that he could defeat the German armies single-handed – in Flanders. In large measure it was to be a battle fought for British prestige. If such a single-handed design had little support in the history of war, the geography of Flanders offered still less. A plan that was founded on faith rather than on reason, both plan and faith were to be sunk in the mud of Flanders. Foch, himself the past exponent of 'faith-healing' strategy, forecast the verdict when he deprecated the British offensive as a 'duck's march' and expressively remarked '*Boche* is bad and *boue* is bad; but *Boche* and *boue* together—!'

Haig adopted the plan in face of formidable facts. His meteorological advisers had collated weather statistics, based on the 'records of eighty years', which showed that he could not hope for more than a fortnight, or at the best three weeks, of fine weather.

Worse still, the Ypres offensive was doomed before it began – by its own destruction of the intricate drainage system in this part of Flanders. The legend has been fostered that these ill-famed 'swamps of Passchendaele' were a piece of ill luck due to the heavy rain, a natural and therefore unavoidable hindrance that could not be foreseen. In reality, before the battle began, a memorandum was sent by Tank Corps Headquarters to General Headquarters pointing out that if the Ypres area and its drainage were destroyed by bombardment, the battlefield would become a swamp. This memorandum was the result of information from the Belgian 'Ponts et Chaussées' and local investigation – the facts had, indeed, been brought to light by the engineers in 1915, but apparently forgotten. The area had been reclaimed from marshland by centuries of labour and in consequence the farmers of the district were under penalty to keep their dykes clear. Land used for pasture was such because it was subject to flooding and too wet for cultivation. In the disregard of this warning is epitomized the main and inevitable cause of the barren results of the 'Passchendaele offensive'.

Perhaps the very brilliance of the preliminary stroke at Messines on June 7th had helped to raise unfounded expectations over what was in conception and purpose a totally different operation. Nearly two months passed before the preparations for the main advance were completed, and during that interval the Germans had ample warning to prepare countermeasures. These comprised a new method of defence, as suited to the waterlogged ground as the British offensive methods were unsuited. Instead of the old linear systems of trenches they developed a system of disconnected strong points and concrete pillboxes, distributed in great depth, whereby the ground was held as much as possible by machine guns and as little as possible by men. While the forward positions were lightly occupied, the reserves thus saved were concentrated in rear for prompt counter-attack, to eject the British troops from the positions they had arduously gained. And the farther the British advanced the more highly developed, naturally, did they find the system. Moreover, by the introduction of mustard gas the Germans scored a further trick, interfering seriously with the British artillery and concentration areas.

Thus, when the fully expected blow fell, the Crown Prince Rupprecht was so far freed from his usual pessimism as to record in his diary – 'My mind is quite at rest about the attack, as we have never disposed of such strong reserves, so well trained for their part, as on the front attacked.' This actual front was held by the troops of the German Fourth Army (Sixt von Arnim).

The certainty that the Germans were aware of the coming offensive, and would be moving up reserves, led the chief of Haig's intelligence staff to urge that the attack should be advanced by three days 'in spite of the fact that our preparations were not fully completed; it was a choice of evils'. But 'the army commanders pressed for delay', and Haig reluctantly accepted their view. There was also a difference of view over the extent of the initial aim. Here Gough, like Rawlinson on the Somme, wished to make a series of limited advances, but Plumer urged that after so long a preparation they should go 'all out' – and Haig once again inclined to a breakthrough aim.

The main role in the attack was given to Gough's Fifth Army, with one corps of the Second Army playing a subsidiary part on the right flank, and a French corps on the left. The British artillery strength totalled 3,091 guns, of which 999 were heavy – an average of one gun to every six yards. During the bombardment, four and a quarter million shells were fired (£22,000,000 worth). It meant that four and three-quarter tons were thrown for every yard of the front.

The bombardment proper opened on July 22nd, and continued for ten days until at 3.50 AM on July 31st the infantry of twelve divisions advanced on an eleven-mile front to the accompaniment of torrential rain. On the left substantial progress was made, Bixschoote, St Julien, and the Pilckem ridge being gained, and the line of the Steenbeek reached. The 'green line' (third objective) was attained in most places, an advance of nearly two miles. But on the right, in the more vital sector round the Menin road, the attack was held up, short of the second objective. And the rain continued day after day, postponing the next major attempt, and hastening the conversion of the undrainable ground into a swamp in which first the tanks and ere long even the infantry were bogged.

Even the ardent Gough 'informed the Commander-in-Chief that tactical success was not possible, or would be too costly, under such conditions, and advised that the attack should be abandoned'. But Haig was too determined, and still too optimistic, to be thus dissuaded. And it would seem that none of the army commanders ventured to press contrary views with the strength that the facts demanded. One of the lessons of the war, exemplified at Passchendaele, is certainly the need of allowing more latitude in the military system for intellectual honesty and moral courage. As it was, Haig continued to send home to the War Office confident reports that the enemy were 'fast approaching' the exhaustion of their forces: actually, Ludendorff was making preparations not only to attack the Russians at Riga but to crush the Italians by sending eight or ten divisions to reinforce the Austrians. Haig's reports, indeed, had 'gone much further' than those his intelligence furnished.

The second blow, on August 16th, was a diminished replica of the first in its results. The left wing was again advanced across the shallow depression formed by the little valley of the Steenbeek and past the ruins of what had been Langemarck. But on the right, where alone an advance might have a strategic effect, a heavy price was paid for nought. The tally of prisoners shrank from six to a mere two thousand. Nor did men feel that the enemy's skilful resistance and the mud were the sole explanation of their fruitless sacrifice. Complaints against the direction and staff work in Gough's army were general and bitter, and their justness seemed to receive recognition when Haig extended the Second Army's front northward to include the Menin road sector, and thereby entrusted to Plumer the direction of the main advance towards the ridge east of Ypres. It was a thankless task at the best, for the experience of war attested the futility of pressing on in places where failure had already become established, and it seemed heavy odds that the laurels earned by Messines must become submerged in the swamps beyond Ypres.

Yet, in the outcome, the reputation of Plumer and the Second Army staff, headed by Harington, was enhanced – less because of what was achieved in scale than because more was achieved than could reasonably have been expected in so hopeless a venture. Applying, as at Messines, siege-warfare methods to a task that was more a siege than a battle, their plan was that of a series of shallow advances, not pressed beyond the point where the artillery support was outrun, and leaving both the infantry fresh enough and the artillery close enough to deal with the inevitable counter-attacks.

Bad weather and the need for preparation delayed the resumption of the offensive until September 20th, but that morning the Second Army attack, on a four-mile front, achieved success in the area of previous failure – on either side of the Menin road. Six divisions (two being Australian) were used; but infantry were kept down to the minimum with artillery at the maximum. Plumer had 1,295 guns – a gun to every five yards. Of these 575 were heavy, which meant one to every twelve yards compared with one to eighteen on July 31st. The infantry advanced at 5.40 AM; by 6.15 AM the first objective was gained almost unopposed, and, with the exception of one or two strong points, the third and last objective was gained soon after midday, and the counter-attacks were repulsed by fire. A fresh spring on September 26th, and another on October 4th – the last a larger one on an eight-mile front, by troops of eight divisions (four Anzac) in the Second Army, and of four in the Fifth Army on the left flank – gave the British possession of the main ridge east of Ypres, with Gheluvelt, Polygon Wood, and Broodseinde, despite torrents of rain, which made the battlefield a worse morass than ever. And on each occasion the majority of the counter-attacks had broken down under fire, a result which owed much to the good observation work of the Royal Flying Corps and the quick response of the artillery. Some 10,000 prisoners were swallowed in the three bites, and this widening maw frightened the enemy into modifying his elastic tactics and strengthening his forward troops – to their increased loss under the British artillery fire.

These attacks had at least done something to restore prestige, if they could have little strategic effect on a campaign which was foredoomed, and in which both the time and the scope for extensive penetration had long since vanished. Unhappily, the Higher Command decided to continue the pointless offensive during the few remaining weeks before the winter, and thereby used up reserves which might have saved the belated experiment of Cambrai from bankruptcy. For having wasted the summer and his strength in the mud, where tanks foundered and infantry floundered, Haig turned in November to dry ground – where a decisive success went begging for lack of reserves.

At Ypres the comparative success of the late September attacks produced an unfortunate intoxication. On the evening of October 4th the chief of the intelligence staff expressed the opinion that there were no fresh enemy reserves 'within immediate reach of the battlefront'. (Actually, fresh German divisions began to take over the line next day; before the next attack on October 9th, 'the whole of the battered front was held by fresh troops, and an extra division had been inserted'.) Even the sober Second Army staff seem to have been momentarily carried away, and at a conference with the war correspondents Harington said that the crest of the ridge was 'as dry as a bone'. The Australian Official History records the impression of one who was present: 'I believe the official attitude is that Passchendaele ridge is so important that tomorrow's attack is worth making whether it succeeds or fails ... I suspect that they are making a great, bloody experiment – a huge gamble ... I feel, and most of the correspondents feel, terribly anxious ... I thought the principle was to be "hit, hit, hit, *whenever the weather is suitable*!" If so, it is thrown over at the first temptation.'

The anxiety of the correspondents was to prove more justifiable than the hopes of the military chiefs. There had been rain each day since October 4th, and on the afternoon of the 8th it became torrential; the meteorological experts said that no improvement could be expected. Yet Haig decided to press on, and his army commanders, although dubious, did not care to protest. So next morning the attack was launched, again on an eight-mile front – and proved a tragic fiasco, except in the low ground on the left. The curious nature of military judgement is illustrated in the diary of Haig's chief intelligence officer (October 8th): 'With a great success tomorrow, and good weather for a few more weeks, we may still clear the coast and win the war before Christmas.' (October 10th) 'D.H. sent for me ... He was still trying to find some grounds for hope that we might still win through here this year, but there is none.'

Nevertheless, a fresh attack was ordered for the 12th – with still deeper objectives. Gough doubted its wisdom, but Plumer 'had decided that an attack was practicable', and Haig gave the order on the 10th. At this moment 'little was known of the true experiences and results of the recent fight' (Australian Official History). There was still time to find out, but this duty seems to have been neglected. After renewed rain on the 11th, Gough, to his credit, telephoned to Plumer to suggest a post-ponement. But after consulting Godley, the corps commander mainly concerned, Plumer preferred to continue. Next day the would-be dash for Passchendaele ended with the attacking troops, save those who perished in the mud, back almost on their starting line.

Haig now seems to have realized there was no foundation for antici-pating a great strategic success. But he was determined to reach Passchendaele, and for this purpose brought up the Canadian Corps. Meantime a combined attack by the Fifth Army and the French was tried, with small result, on October 22nd. On the 26th the Second Army made its fresh effort with the Canadians and suffered a fresh disappointment. They tried again on the 30th, while the Fifth Army loyally yet sceptically struggled to advance alongside – '300 yards or so being the limit'.

Progress so trifling, save in its cost, was largely explained by the exhaustion caused in pushing forward over a morass and to the fact that the mud not only got into and jammed rifles and machine guns, but nullified the effect of the shell bursts. The attackers' troubles were augmented by the enemy's increasing use of mustard gas, and by his renewed adoption of his tactics of holding the bulk of his troops well back for a counter-attack. Thus, when on November 4th, a sudden advance by the 1st Division and 2nd Canadian Division gained the empty satisfaction of occupying the site of Passchendaele village, the official curtain was at last rung down on the pitiful tragedy of 'Third Ypres'. It was the long-overdue close of a campaign which had brought the British armies to the verge of exhaustion, one in which had been enacted the most dolorous scenes in British military history, and for which the only justification evoked the reply that, in order to absorb the enemy's attention and forces, Haig chose the spot most difficult for himself and least vital to his enemy. Intending to absorb the enemy's reserves, his own were absorbed.

He was lured on by a lofty optimism that extended even to the cost. After the disappointing attack of July 31st, he advised the Government that the enemy casualties exceeded the British 'not improbably by a hundred per cent'; and in his final dispatch he still declared that it was 'certain that the enemy's loss considerably exceeded ours'. That optimism was nourished by ignorance of the situation, due in part to the failure – a moral failure – of his subordinates to enlighten him.

Perhaps the most damning comment on the plan which plunged the British Army in this bath of mud and blood is contained in an incidental revelation of the remorse of one who was largely responsible for it. This highly placed officer from General Headquarters was on his first visit to the battle front – at the end of the four months' battle. Growing increasingly uneasy as the car approached the swamplike edges of the battle area, he eventually burst into tears, crying, 'Good God, did we really send men to fight in that?' To which his companion replied that the ground was far worse ahead. If the exclamation was a credit to his heart it revealed on what a foundation of delusion and inexcusable ignorance his indomitable 'offensiveness' had been based.

The only relief to this sombre review is that a bare fortnight later was enacted, on a different stage, and with a technique suggested in early August, a 'curtain-raiser' which was to be developed into the glorious drama of autumn, 1918.

CHAPTER SEVEN

SCENE 4

The Tank Surprise at Cambrai

On November 19th, 1917, the German troops in front of Cambrai were contemplating with undisturbed minds the apparent normality and comparative tranquillity of the British lines opposite them; contrasting their own security in the massively fortified and comfortable trenches of the Hindenburg Line with the unsavoury lot of their comrades struggling in the shell-churned mudholes of the Ypres salient; indulging in self-congratulation not only on the impregnability of their famous line, but on the pertinacity of the unteachable English who had so engulfed themselves at Ypres that there could surely be no danger of any other assault elsewhere before winter came.

On November 20th, 381 tanks, followed by a relatively small proportion of infantry rolled forward in the half-light upon the astonished Germans without even the courtesy of a preliminary bombardment to announce their coming. Always good hosts, the Germans might well feel aggrieved at the omission of a warning which had customarily given them four or five days' notice to prepare a suitable reception.

On November 21st the bells of London rang out in joyous acclaim of a triumphant success that seemed a foretaste of victory, perhaps at no distant date. And Ludendorff, back at the German Supreme Command, was hurriedly preparing emergency instructions for a general retreat. Both the bells and Ludendorff were premature – although prophetic – by some nine months.

For on November 30th came a German retort so full of menace that the public thereafter showed a strong distaste for premature celebrations. Applause changed to reproaches; the cause of the disasters was the subject of inquiry; and in public opinion the name of Cambrai came to be associated more with the ultimate reverse than with the initial success. Actually, however, the fuller knowledge now available suggests that the black date in the national calendar should be the 20th,

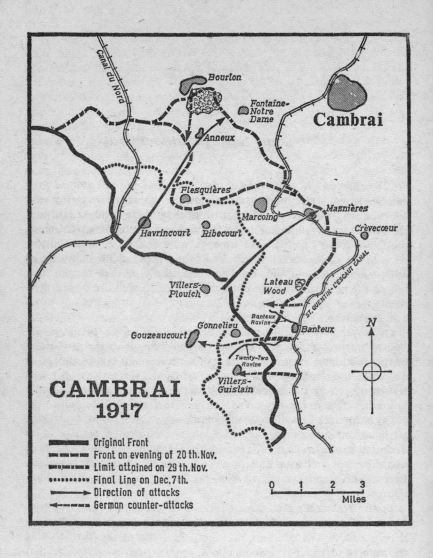

CAMBRAI
1917

Canal du Nord

Bourlon

Fontaine-
Notre
Dame

Cambrai

Anneux

Flesquières

Marcoing

Masnières

Crèvecoeur

Havrincourt   Ribecourt

Villers-
Plouich

Lateau
Wood

ST. QUENTIN - L'ESCAUT CANAL

Banteux
Ravine

Banteux

Gonnelieu

Gouzeaucourt

Twenty-Two
Ravine

Villers-
Guislain

N

▬▬▬▬ Original Front
▬ ▬ ▬ Front on evening of 20th. Nov.
▰▰▰▰ Limit attained on 29th.Nov.
•••••••• Final Line on Dec. 7th.
———▶ Direction of attacks
◀— — — German counter-attacks

0   1   2   3
            Miles

and not the 30th, of November. Yet gloomy as is this page of World War history, it forms one of the most striking examples of the proverb that 'every cloud has a silver lining'. If November 20th, 1917, is in itself a tragedy of errors, its eventual effect on the fortunes of the Allies was beneficent – pointing and paving the way to the victorious method of 1918, and, to take a still longer view, it is seen to be one of the landmarks in the history of warfare, the dawn of a new epoch. Thus we may say that the joy-bells, if immediately wrong, were ultimately right.

In contrast, the Germans failed to profit by the warning and later paid the penalty – as their official historians recognize. While the more far-sighted German officers urged the necessity of replying in kind to the new British method others argued that 'the further mechanization of the battle' would impair the moral qualities of the troops. And their fervent traditionalism fathered the thought that 'the tank terror was more of a phantom than a real danger'. The success of the counter-offensive was a support to men who did not care to face an unconventional reality, and the weight of conservative opinion prevailed – as so often in the history of armies. Thus it was left for the post-war historians of the German Army to record, in bitterness of soul, that 'the outwardly brilliant German offensive battle held within a deep tragedy'.

These eleven days form perhaps the most dramatic of all episodes in the World War. Yet, sensational as was their course in its abrupt change of fortune, the real story of 'Cambrai' lies beneath the surface. First is the question of its origins, of paramount importance because it ushered in a new cycle of warfare. Its initial source is to be found nearly two years, and its immediate source nearly four months, earlier.

The guiding idea of those who sponsored the tank in infancy had been to release it unexpectedly in a large concentration, and this idea had, as we have seen not only been formulated but worked out in detail as early as February, 1916 – seven months before a driblet of tanks were launched on the Somme under conditions which violated all the essentials therein laid down. Fortunately, in 1917, the headquarters of the Tank Corps in France, although unlike General Headquarters they had not seen this memorandum, had come by experience to similar ideas. Further, the eternal yet too often underrated principle of surprise was deeply rooted in their minds, and thus when insight apprised them in the very first days of Third Ypres – the Passchendaele offensive – that the 'mudlark' was futile, an alternative project was quick to blossom.

The chief general staff officer, Colonel Fuller, on August 3rd, 1917, drew up a plan for a great tank raid in a more suitable sector. In the preface to it this significant example of prevision may be read: 'From a tank point of view the Third Battle of Ypres may be considered dead. To go on using tanks in the present conditions will not only lead to good machines and better personnel being thrown away, but also to a loss of morale in the infantry and tank crews, through constant failure. From an infantry point of view, the Third Battle of Ypres may be considered comatose. It can only be continued at colossal loss and little gain.'

Then came the alternative proposal: 'In order to restore British prestige and strike a theatrical blow against Germany before the winter, it is suggested that preparations be at once set on foot to take St Quentin.' It was further pointed out that the operation was strategically a sound one as a preparatory step to an advance towards Le Cateau, and then Valenciennes, the following year. Discussion of this project brought out the objection that it required a combined British and French operation, which might lack the simplicity and smooth working essential for the novel method to succeed. Therefore, on August 4th, a second project was framed, for a tank raid south of Cambrai. The word 'raid' should be stressed, for, as originally conceived, the object was 'to destroy the enemy's personnel and guns, to demoralize and disorganize him, and not to capture ground'. As the preliminary notes stated: 'The duration of the raid must be short – eight to twelve hours – so that little or no concentration of the enemy may be effected for counter-attack.' Had this been followed there would have been no need to lament the 30th November. 'The whole operation may be summed up as "advance, hit, retire". Big raids of this description will not only reduce the enemy's fighting power, but will reduce his initiative with reference to any big battle which at the time may be in progress.' For this raid a force of three tank brigades of two battalions each, and 'one, or better, two, divisions of infantry or cavalry', with extra artillery, was suggested, operating on an 8,000-yard front. The object, as proposed, was 'to raid the re-entrant formed by the L'Escaut–St Quentin Canal between Ribecourt–Crèvecoeur–Banteux'. The raiding force was to be divided into three groups, the main one to scour the country in this canal-enclosed pocket, while smaller groups formed offensive flanks on each side to protect the main operation. 'The essence of the entire operation is surprise and rapidity of movement. Three hours after zero the retirement might well begin, the tanks and aeroplanes operating as a rearguard to the dismounted cavalry retiring with their prisoners.'

The proposed sector lay in the area of the Third Army, under General Sir Julian Byng, and on August 5th the detailed project was taken informally to him by one of the Tank Corps brigadiers. Byng was receptive to the idea, although inclined to expand it from a raid into a breakthrough attack to gain Cambrai. Next day he went to General Headquarters, saw Haig, and suggested a surprise attack with tanks at Cambrai in September. The Commander-in-Chief was favourable, but his Chief of Staff, General Kiggell, offered strong objections on the ground that the army could not win a decisive battle in two places at once, and should rather concentrate every possible man in the Ypres sector – which, incidentally, he never visited until the campaign was over. Thus the enlarged idea helped to postpone the raid, as the refusal to recognize reality at Ypres postponed the attack at Cambrai until too late for decisive results to be possible.

The historian, while respecting Kiggell's emphasis on the principle of concentration, may doubt whether Ypres was a suitable site for the fulfilment of this principle, and may also hold that distraction of the enemy's force has ever been an essential complement to concentration – of one's own effort.

Kiggell's objections sufficed to dissuade Haig, who still valued the tank as only 'a minor factor'. Thus the Cambrai project was postponed indefinitely, while the High Command persevered with their hopeless efforts in the Passchendaele swamps. But neither Byng nor the Tank Corps were willing to let the idea drop, and certain opinions at General Headquarters were in accord, so that as the Ypres offensive became a more palpable failure, a readier ear was lent to an alternative which promised to redeem British prestige. Finally, in mid-October, the Cambrai plan was sanctioned, and fixed for November 20th. But now the situation had changed for the worse, for, if the plan were crowned with success, that success must be barren for want of reserves to reap the harvest. The reapers were engulfed at Passchendaele.

It is just to recognize that if General Headquarters had missed the opportunity, General Headquarters had now perhaps a surer appreciation than the Third Army Command of the limitations imposed by their lack of means. Kiggell urged that Bourlon Hill merely should be the first objective, followed by a lateral exploitation northward, and Haig put a time limit on the operation. But the Third Army orders were more ambitious in scope and objectives, despite the fact that all their available infantry divisions and tanks were being thrown into the initial 'breakthrough' effort.

Byng's plan was (1) to break the German defensive system, the famous Hindenburg Line, in the neck between the Canal de L'Escaut and the Canal du Nord, (2) to seize Cambrai, Bourlon Wood and the passage over the River Sensée; (3) to cut off the Germans in the area south of the Sensée and west of the Canal du Nord; and (4) to exploit the success towards Valenciennes. The force allotted for this ambitious plan comprised the III (Pulteney) and IV (Woollcombe) Corps, each of three infantry divisions, the Cavalry Corps (Kavanagh) of three divisions (plus one under IV Corps), a total of 381 fighting tanks, and roughly 1,000 guns. Thus of the original project only the fundamental idea, the tank method, and the locality remained. Otherwise there were marked alterations, and in these lay the germ of disaster. The raid had been transformed into a large-scale offensive, with far-reaching aims. Instead of securing a 'pocket' and withdrawing, an organized advance was to be made up a narrow 'lane', bounded by two canals. A protection to a raid, these became a danger to such an attack, circumscribing the action of the tanks and preventing the formation of tank-offensive flanks. Otherwise the ground was good, mostly rolling downland, excellent for tank movement; it was marked by two features, the Flesquières–Havrincourt ridge and Bourlon Hill.

The fundamental weakness of the general plan, however, was not topographical, but the complete lack of reserves, unless the four cavalry divisions can be considered such – and the futility of so regarding them was amply shown in their fresh inability, in face of modern weapons, to influence the action. The six divisions employed in the initial attack were all that the Third Army commander had at his disposal – for a plan that visualized a penetration beyond Cambrai to Valenciennes! It is extremely difficult to understand what was in mind as to the future, for without reserves complete success could only mean the creation of an excessively deep and narrow salient, requiring scores of divisions to hold it. It is true that the Guards and one or two other divisions could be made available, and were ultimately brought to the scene, but they were too far away for a prompt intervention. The situation, indeed, had some reminder of Loos. The French also moved a corps to the Senlis–Péronne area just before the attack, but after the first day were told that they were no longer required!

The best comment on this lack of reserves is contained in a story of General Franchet d'Esperey, which one has on the authority of the officer to whom the words were spoken. A long motor ride, in search of information, brought him to a British headquarters at Albert. Entering, he interrogated a senior General Staff officer, flinging at him a string of crisp questions as to the progress of the attack, its frontage, depth. Then came the final, the vital question: 'And where were your reserves?' 'Mon Général, we had none.' The French commander exclaimed, 'Mon Dieu!' turned on his heel and fled.

Turning now to the tank plan, the problems were to gain surprise, to cross the wide and deep obstacle of the Hindenburg Line and to ensure cooperation between the infantry and tanks for their common security. Careful organization and the absence of a preliminary bombardment contributed to the accomplishment of the first object. The difficulty presented by the Hindenburg Line was overcome by devising super-fascines, huge bundles of brushwood, which were carried on the nose of each tank and released on reaching the edge of the Hindenburg trenches; the tanks, working in sections of three, had thus the power to cross three successive obstacles. Thirdly, a strictly drill attack was worked out and practised by which in each section an advanced-guard tank moved about 100 yards ahead of the two main-body tanks, keeping down the enemy's fire and protecting the main body as they led the infantry forward. The infantry, moving in flexible file formations, followed immediately behind the main-body tanks. While the tanks cleared a way for them through the deep belts of enemy wire and sub-dued the hostile machine-gun fire, the infantry acted as 'moppers-up' to the tanks and were also ready to protect them from the enemy's guns at close quarters. The one fault of the tank plan was that, against expert advice, the tanks attacked on the whole frontage instead of against selected tactical points, with the result that no tank reserves were kept for use in the later stages.

The preparations for the battle were made with great skill and secrecy, while to mislead the enemy as to the scale and frontage of the attack, gas and smoke attacks, dummy attacks with dummy tanks, raids and feints, were carried out on a wide front both north and south of the real sector of attack.

Nevertheless, one man nearly undid the secrecy of a multitude. A prisoner from an Irish regiment gave information of the coming attack, and of the concentration of tanks, but fortunately he was not believed and the German army commander, General von der Marwitz, reported on the 16th that there was no likelihood of an attack. But on the 19th a British telephone message, 'Tuesday Flanders', was overheard near Bullecourt, and, as it sounded like a combined date and codeword, quickened German suspicions. That night the troops were ordered to be specially alert, and Marwitz hastily utilized a division, just detraining from Russia, to strengthen his defences. But if the Germans now antici-pated an attack they also expected the usual preliminary bombardment*

* An attack without heavy bombardment was considered out of the ques-tion, as the position was so strong. Thus the orders for Moser's group, shortly

– and its absence assured the British attack the essential surprise effect. That effect was accentuated by an early morning mist, as in almost all the successful thrusts of the war.

At 6.20 AM on November 20th the tanks and infantry moved forward to the attack on roughly a six-mile front, and gained a demoralizing initial success at all points save in the left centre in front of Flesquières. The main cause of this one serious check was that the commander of the 51st Division, Harper, preferred a method of his own instead of conforming to the formations devised by the Tank Corps, and adopted in all the other divisions. His advance tanks were called 'rovers', and went much farther ahead, and the infantry formations were not as well fitted for close cooperation with tanks as those laid down. The separation seems to have been inspired by his expressed feeling that the whole Cambrai plan was 'a fantastic and most unmilitary scheme' – when on the staff of General Headquarters he had resisted the development of machine guns, and now was equally sceptical of tanks. The result was that the infantry were too far behind the tanks, lost the gaps in the wire, and were stopped by machine-gun fire. An officer who examined the battlefield afterwards could only find three small heaps of machine-gun cartridge cases, from which it would appear that a handful of machine guns held up a whole division – a fact which sheds a striking light on the future of infantry action in open country. The loss of touch between the infantry and tanks lay also at the root of the losses which befell the tanks when they came over the ridge and under the close fire of several German batteries, for infantry accompanying them could have picked off the gunners. Here occurred the famous incident of the solitary German artillery officer who was reputed to have 'knocked out' sixteen tanks single-handed. It must go into the catalogue of historic legends, for only five derelict tanks were to be seen at this point after the attack had moved on, and an intelligence officer who examined the ground found marks which showed clearly that three batteries had been in position there to engage the tanks. It is possible that all save one gun, and one gunner, had been silenced, as was claimed, but impressions in the heat of battle are sometimes misleading. The feat has, however, an ironical significance in the fact that it was blazoned to the world by the British General Headquarters. The incentive of a mention in dispatches was not accorded to enemy feats performed at the expense of the infantry or cavalry.

---

before midnight on the 19th, said – 'Tanks may take part. The four or five hours' artillery bombardment will probably begin between 3 and 4 AM.' This is a suggestive example of how habit may contribute to surprise.

The effect of this battlefield incident has also been magnified. On the right the 12th, 20th and 6th Divisions secured their objectives rapidly, though the 12th had severe fighting at Lateau wood. The 20th Division passed through and captured Masnières and Marcoing, securing the passage of the canal at both and even the bridge intact at the latter. On the left of the 51st the 62nd Division made a brilliant advance, advancing by nightfall as far as Anneux, over two miles in the rear of Flesquières. The Flesquières resistance was thus only an islet, cut off and overlapped by the waves which swept round its flanks and on to Marcoing, Anneux and even to the edge of Bourlon Wood. A penetration of five miles had been made – the equivalent of months of heavy fighting and heavier losses on the Somme and at the Third Battle of Ypres. Decisive success was within the grasp of the British forces, the enemy's three main lines of defences had been overrun, only a half-finished line and the open country lay beyond. But the tank crews were exhausted, the infantry showed little capacity to make progress on their own, and apart from one squadron of the Canadian Fort Garry Horse the two cavalry divisions could contribute nothing towards fulfilling their role of exploitation.

The German official monograph emphasizes the fact that a wide gap remained open for 'many hours, completely unoccupied', between Masnières and Crèvecoeur: 'It was great luck, as no reinforcements could be expected to reach there before evening.' The Germans also had luck in that a relief division from Russia had just arrived when the attack came; by midday on the 20th part of it was in position to cover the direct path to Cambrai. With notable promptness the German Command began moving five reserve divisions to the scene from other parts of the front, and six more were warned to follow. It was thus a race with time; and to the joy of the anxious Germans, their assailants seemed astoundingly dilatory. 'The British failed to utilize the afternoon and evening; they might at least have surrounded the German forces still holding out in Flesquières. The defence ... seems to have deprived the 51st Division of all initiative.' As for the British cavalry, it is remarked that they appeared late and were easily stopped by enfilade fire.

On November 21st local reserves made some further progress. Flesquières was evacuated by its surviving defenders in the early hours, and after dawn the 51st and 62nd Divisions pressed on, clearing the German salient formed by this resistance on the first day and carrying the tide of the British advance as far as Fontaine-Notre Dame, one and a half miles beyond the high-water mark of November 20th. Owing to the British penetration into Bourlon Wood and Fontaine there was a three-mile-wide breach between Walter's and Moser's corps. But, by German witness, the British lapsed into inactivity at the moment of supreme opportunity. On the right, little ground was gained during the day, and, by evening, three of the enemy's reinforcing divisions were on the scene. The opportunity had been forfeited.

Haig's time limit of forty-eight hours had now expired, but owing to the menace of the uncaptured Bourlon Hill to the new British position, as well as the hope of an enemy withdrawal and the desire to relieve the enemy pressure on Italy, he decided to continue the offensive and, somewhat belatedly, placed a few fresh divisions at the disposal of the Third Army. But the Tank Corps, the essential cause of the early success that had apparently surprised the British as much as the German Command, was tired out, men and machines – all had been staked on the first throw.

The fresh attacks met with more failure than success against an enemy now braced to meet the danger. On November 22nd the Germans recaptured Fontaine-Notre Dame; on the 23rd, the 40th Division with tanks captured the whole of Bourlon Wood, but the attempts on Bourlon village and Fontaine-Notre Dame failed. Bitter and fluctuating fighting followed; both villages were won, and lost again. And meanwhile the Germans, with prompt initiative and consummate skill, were preparing a deadly counterblast. Unfortunately there seems to have been a disposition in the superior command, with certain exceptions, to discredit the numerous warning signs of the gathering storm, and even to find amusement in the anxiety displayed by those whose clearer vision was soon to be attested. This attitude was apparently due to over-confidence – partly induced by the easy success of November 20th, and partly due to a belief that the Passchendaele offensive had absorbed all the enemy's reserves. The effect of Passchendaele, indeed, was always overrated.

In contrast, General Snow, commanding the VII Corps on the southern flank of the wedge driven into the German front, had forecast both the place and date of the counterstroke nearly a week before. His subordinate commanders, particularly in the 55th Division (Jeudwine), which adjoined the III Corps, had reported a host of corroborative evidence – that the enemy artillery were registering on spots never bombarded before, that German aircraft were flying over the lines in large numbers, and that the British reconnaissance machines were 'shelled off' certain areas where the enemy could concentrate under cover. Late on November 29th the 55th Division was so convinced of the imminent menace that Jeudwine asked that the neighbouring III Corps might put down a counter-preparation with 'heavies' on the Banteux Ravine just before daylight next morning, but his request was refused. The gathering enemy themselves were surprised that 'nothing was done to disturb the German preparations'.

And next morning they repaid the tank surprise by one which was similar in principle if different in method. Unheralded by any long artillery preparation, a short, hurricane bombardment with gas and smoke shell paved the way for the infiltrating advance of the German infantry – the prototype of the German offensive method of spring, 1918, as the British attack had been the prototype of the Allied offensive method of summer and autumn, 1918. Emerging from the sheltered assembly position of Banteux and Twenty-two Ravines at the very moment when the unfulfilled counter-preparation would have opened, the German stream trickled through the weak points in the British line; then, expanding into a broad torrent which submerged the villages of Gonnelieu and Villers Guislain, swept over gun positions and headquarters, and surged forward to Gouzeaucourt. The menace of disaster was immeasurable, but, fortunately, the complementary attacks on the north of the salient, round Bourlon Wood, were brought to a standstill, and the emergency declined with the recapture of Gouzeaucourt by the superb counter-attack of the Guards' Division and a later effort of the 2nd Tank Brigade. For a time, indeed, there was a chance to 'redouble' and score heavily off the Germans, disordered by this success and hampered by their narrow penetration. But rejecting Snow's plea for a flank riposte by the cavalry, the army commander directed his cavalry head-on against the Germans, and they were soon held up. Thus the invaders were able to consolidate their hold and even to resume their erosion of the British position. During the next few days continued German progress, especially towards Villers Plouich, and British lack of reserves rendered the British position in the Masnières–Bourlon salient so precarious that the greater part of the original gains had to be evacuated. A sombre sunset after a brilliant sunrise.

One shadow which still lingers is that undeservedly thrown on the regimental officers and men by superior officers anxious to exculpate themselves. The official court of inquiry pinned the blame on the troops, ascribing the surprise to their negligence and also asserting, contrary to facts, that they had failed to send up 'SOS' flares. Even Byng declared – 'I attribute the reason for the local success on the part of the enemy to one cause and one alone, namely – lack of training on the part of junior officers and NCOs and men.' Haig, however, who had been kept in the dark as to the warnings, was an exception to the 'general' rule. In sending his report home, he generously assumed the whole responsibility – although he also sent home several of the subordinate commanders.

It is thus due for history to record, from the records, that many of the junior leaders were acutely alive to the danger and gave vain warnings to their superiors. And as for their resistance, it was more than anyone had a right to expect of troops who had been kept in action continuously since their attack on November 20th. For military history, indeed, the lesson of Cambrai is that the welcome renaissance of the essential principle of surprise was offset by a fundamental breach of the principle of economy of force – both in adjusting the end to the means and in appreciating the capacity and limits of human endurance.

CHAPTER SEVEN

SCENE 5

Caporetto

In the chill and sodden gloom of an autumn morning amid the mist-wreathed peaks of the Julian Alps came a rumbling. Before its echoes finally subsided, the Allied cause had been shaken to its foundations. The first rumours of disaster, which were far from exaggerating the reality, came like a thunderclap to the Allied peoples, if not to all their leaders, for 1917 hitherto had seen the Allies on the offensive in all theatres.

The year had begun with the expectation of a sure progress towards victory, of a vast combined offensive culminating in the overthrow of the Central Powers, and if the mirage of early victory had been slowly fading before the evidence of stubborn resistance and heavy losses, the public were still unprepared for a definite change of role from attack to defence. More especially was this unexpected in Italy, for while there was obvious ground for qualms over Russia, the Italians had been attacking during August and September, and the cables had given the impression that the tide of battle was flowing strongly in their favour. And for once, in a war when the output of fiction was greater than that of fact, these reports were correct.

If the gain in ground was small the moral and material effect on the already war-rotted Austrians was large, and, as Ludendorff records, 'the responsible military and political authorities of the dual monarchy were convinced that they would not be able to stand a continuation of the battle and a twelfth attack on the Isonzo'. Thus 'in the middle of September it became necessary to decide for the attack on Italy in order to prevent the collapse of Austria-Hungary'. So urgent was the need that Ludendorff was forced to abandon his preparations for the offensive in Moldavia, which he had intended as the *coup de grâce* to Russia's crumbling resistance. Even so, where could he raise sufficient troops for converting the Austrian defensive into an effective offensive? The

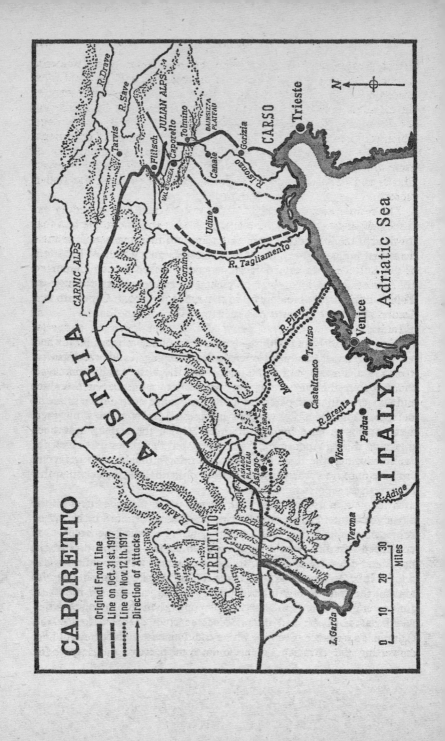

British pressure at Passchendale and the mere length of his immense fronts in France and Russia absorbed his resources until he could force peace on Russia. All he could spare was his slender general reserve of six divisions, which had already been his instrument in countering the Kerensky offensive – Russia's final flicker – and in the coup which captured Riga. His adviser in the strategic design of operations, Major Wetzell, was however of the opinion that the application of even this small force at a 'soft' spot, such as the sector between Flitsch and Canale, would suffice to lame if not to break the Italian menace.

The result proved him right – the trouble was that it unduly exceeded the most sanguine expectations. And it was due to the fact that it was expanded to a more ambitious plan – without increase of means – than was originally intended in the 'germ' scheme, which Waldstätten, of the Austrian General Staff, had brought to the German Command on August 29th. This original scheme was for a breakthrough at Tolmino, followed merely by rolling up the Isonzo front. Caporetto and Cambrai were to have a curious kinship.

Ludendorff sent General Krafft von Delmensingen on a special mission to reconnoitre the ground and report on the scheme. Krafft had led the Alpine Corps in the Rumanian campaign, and was thus an expert in mountain warfare. He found that the Austrians had managed to retain a small bridgehead on the west bank of the Isonzo at Tolmino, and this afforded a jumping-off point for the projected attack. Guns were got up mostly by hand and at night; the infantry came up by seven night marches, taking no vehicles, but carrying their ammunition, equipment, and supplies on the men or on pack animals. Thus the twelve assault divisions and 300 batteries concentrated undiscovered by the Italians, owing partly to able precautions, partly to the country, and partly to the inadequate air reconnaissances of the enemy.

What of the Italians? The Commander-in-Chief, Cadorna, was undoubtedly a man of more than ordinary ability, but, like certain other famous commanders, his intellectual power was offset by his lack of touch with and understanding of the fighting troops. With such men, also, their mental remoteness is often accentuated by the natural isolation in which those in high military position are placed. Considering the comparatively slender weight of the attack, he had enough men and guns to withstand it successfully, but his distribution of them was unsuited to the conditions of the various sectors. Troops already too highly tried were kept too long in the positions of greatest strain. Thus, the combination of faulty distribution with the enemy's unerring eye for the vulnerable spot produced, with other factors, an Austro-German success out of all proportion to the means.

Capello, commanding the Second Army, dissatisfied with the defensive suitability of the positions on which the Italian offensive had stopped, had wished to forestall the attack by a flank thrust northwards from the Bainsizza Plateau, but was overruled by Cadorna, who was not only conscious of his shortage of reserves but had belatedly come to doubt the value of offensive methods. In this he was at least wiser than his subordinate who, alike in offensive spirit, in his manner as a commander, and as the victim of the Germans' new offensive method, was the Gough of the Italian Army. Cadorna had full warning of the enemy's intention from his Intelligence and from deserters – Czech and Transylvanian officers, but he did not feel sufficiently sure of the real direction of the enemy's attack to justify him in committing his reserves beforehand.

Yet it is at least curious that, as information specifically pointed to the Caporetto sector, on its fifteen-mile frontage there were only posted two battalions to the mile compared with eight to the mile farther south. The very fact that this had long been a quiet sector, where both sides sent troops to rest, might have aroused the suspicions of the Italian command. But Capello actually refused the appeal of his left wing here for reinforcements. Perhaps he was the less patient towards arguments because he should have been a patient in hospital. Instead, with misguided pertinacity he stayed in bed at his headquarters, and only yielded the reins of command the day after his front collapsed.

The Italian frontier province of Venezia formed a tongue pointing towards Austria. It was flanked on the south by the Adriatic and on the east and north by the Julian and Carnic Alps – beyond which lay the Austrian Trentino. The six German divisions, with nine Austrian, formed the attacking Fourteenth German Army, under General Otto von Below, with whom was Krafft as Chief of Staff and guiding brain. These troops were to climb the mountain barrier at the tip of the tongue, while two Austrian armies, under Boroevic, were to advance along the stretch of lower ground near the Adriatic shore.

The difficulties of organizing and deploying an attack in the mountains were ably overcome, and after four hours' gas shell and one hour's general bombardment, the attackers moved forward in the drizzle of snow and rain, and in many places rapidly overcame the resistance of infantry who, owing partly to the breakdown of telephone communication, were but fitfully supported by their own artillery. But the misty conditions were the greater factor in the success, as next March in

France; they provided the element of surprise which proved the only and indispensable key to open a way through the enemy's front. Although the right and left wings of the attacking army were delayed by sturdy resistance in the rear positions, the centre group (four divisions) under Stein penetrated completely at Caporetto, and through this breach reserves were pouring by evening. The effect was to make the whole defensive position untenable and to ease the task of the attacking right wing (three and a half Austrian divisions) under Krauss, which now pushed forward almost unchecked down the Val d'Uccea, the shortest line to turn the river barrier of the Tagliamento. This enveloping advance nullified Cadorna's efforts to dam the breach, efforts which also broke down owing to the difficulty of pushing reserves up the narrow mountain roads already congested by troops which had no stomach left for fighting. This convinced Cadorna of the necessity of ordering a general retreat to the Tagliamento, as Capello had earlier urged, and it was successfully achieved after two critical days – October 30th and 31st.

Fortunately the pursuing enemy had suffered from hitches in movements and supply, as well as an increasing friction between the German and Austrian commanders. Their attempt to achieve a surprise capture of the crossings was foiled, and although in a deliberate attack one of Krauss' Austrian divisions got across at Cornino on November 2nd, Cadorna had had breathing space to make preparations for a further retreat to the Piave. Although large bodies of troops were cut off by the enemy's pincer-like advance, the main armies succeeded in reaching the Piave by November 10th, thus reforging their line. Yet its links were very thin. Nearly 600,000 men had been lost, and the Second Army, which had suffered the direct blow, was practically out of action as a force. At this juncture Cadorna gave place to Diaz, whose supreme value was that he understood the mind of the soldiers, and knew how to reinvigorate their morale, playing, in fact, the same role as Pétain in France earlier that year.

Three days later a fresh menace developed, on November 12th when Conrad's troops (Austrian Tenth and Eleventh Armies) sought to move down from the Trentino on the Italian rear. But here Cadorna's preparations for defence had been long initiated and were well matured, so that the threat was frustrated. Ludendorff, too late, tried to switch reinforcements round to Conrad, but was foiled by the inadequate rail communications and deficiency of motor transport – if, fundamentally, by the limited horizon of the original plan.

Meanwhile, French and British divisions had been hurriedly railed to

Italy, their coming preceded by the arrival of Foch and Sir Henry Wilson, but they took some time to concentrate – and were then at first held back in reserve – so that the interval before they relieved divisions of their severely strained Ally was a time of grave stress. The most serious attack came in the sector between the Piave and the Brenta, but here, after five days of struggle, Laderchi's Italian IX Corps brought the attack to halt, and at the beginning of December was relieved by the French, while the British, under Lord Plumer, took over the Montello sector. Contrary to expectation, both were left in peace, and during the remaining months of the campaign the enemy's attack was confined to renewed efforts by Conrad and Krauss farther to the north-west, in the Asiago and Grappa sectors. If these imposed a fresh tax on the weary Italians, it was psychologically worthwhile, for this successful and stalwart resistance by its vindication of their fighting power laid the moral foundations for the Italian 'revanche' of 1918.

Reviewing the drama of Caporetto in the clearer light of history, there is reason to think that excessive emphasis was placed on the effect of enemy and seditious propaganda, and that the major reason of the crumbling resistance early was the same as in France that spring – that the troops were morally tired, and that the result of being hurled endlessly against machine-gun defences had worn down their fighting spirit. The presence of imminent disaster to their country set a new light upon the position, and gave a sacrificial impulse to a duty which on the Piave line, fighting 'with their backs to the wall', they honourably and gallantly fulfilled.

Strategically, however, the most critical stage was past with the passing of Tagliamento, for henceforth what Clausewitz called the 'friction of war' so upset the attackers' communications that their power and speed fell off badly. Some of the causes have been mentioned. But one, which was to operate again next spring in France, deserves emphasis. The well-filled supply depots of the Italian army were too great a temptation to the under-nourished enemy, the desire to eat quenched the desire to pursue, and sudden congestion of the stomach accelerated the congestion of the advance. It is significant that even a German divisional commander, General Lecquis, could exult more at the capture of two or three chickens apiece by his men than of many prisoners, and regarded the possession of a few pigs 'as the height of human felicity'.

CHAPTER SEVEN

PANORAMA

The War in the Air

To relate the action of aircraft in the military sphere is not possible, for it formed a thread running through and vitally influencing the whole course of operations, rather than a separate strategic feature. But a brief outline of the evolution of aircraft action in the field may help to complete the strategic picture. Military appreciation of air values was a slow growth, and the advocates of aircraft had an uphill struggle for recognition. Until the Italians used aircraft extensively against the Turks in Tripoli, 1911–12, general military opinion was aptly represented by General Foch's comment when watching the *Circuit de l'Est* – 'That is good sport but for the Army the aeroplane is worthless.' Even in 1914 the proportion of military aircraft was puny, and their application more limited than with the Italians two years earlier.

In the first month of the war visual reconnaissance was the only role allotted and no provision was made for air combat or bombing. For the inadequacy of its air service and lack of information the German Army paid a heavy price during the invasion of France. But the Royal Flying Corps, although bringing only sixty-three machines across the Channel, twice rendered invaluable service. One reconnaissance unmasked the initial attempt to outflank the British Army at Mons, and another discovered Kluck's historic swerve towards the Marne.

In September the sphere of air cooperation was enlarged to embrace observation of targets for the artillery, communication being at first by coloured lights and eventually by wireless telegraphy. In September also, photography from the air was tried, but its potential value was not recognized by General Headquarters until 1915. By March a special aeroplane camera was supplied, and air photography henceforth developed continuously, although long handicapped by dependence on captured German lenses for the large-scale cameras. A fresh form of cooperation was tried in 1915, although not fully applied until 1916. This was the contact patrol, whereby commanders were informed of the situation of their own infantry during battle, and of threatened counter-attacks by the enemy.

The pursuit of this air cooperation by both sides simultaneously, as well as the desire to baffle the enemy's observation, had naturally led to air fighting, and this, in turn, to a struggle for supremacy in the air. Rifles and pistols were the only weapons available at the outset, so that air combat bore the appearance of an exhilarating and uncertain new form of game-shooting. Soon, however, light machine guns were fitted, although the fighting role was mainly restricted to 'pusher' type aeroplanes, as, on a tractor type, the propeller hindered fire in a forward direction. In May, 1915, the Germans produced a new and fast Fokker fighting machine equipped with an interruptor gear which enabled the gun to fire through the orbit of the revolving propeller without risk of hitting the blades. The Fokkers inflicted heavy losses amongst the British machines, and, for a time, gained air superiority for the Germans.

The Allies replied to this menace not only by new machines but by new methods, settled in joint conference. The 'fighters' were concentrated in special squadrons, instead of being distributed among all, and these squadrons were to seek out their opponents behind the opposing front, thus enabling their own reconnaissance and artillery machines to work undisturbed. This method of offensive patrols was successfully tried by the French at Verdun in February, 1916, and developed by the British on the Somme, where for some weeks the Germans were almost driven out of the air. The offensive was also extended to the enemy's aerodromes – an extension which recalled the historic naval maxim that the enemy's coasts were the frontiers of Britain. Already, in October, 1914, British naval aircraft operating on the Belgian coast had raided the Zeppelin sheds at Dusseldorf and Cologne, destroying one airship; another was destroyed next month in a raid from Belfort on Friedrichshafen.

Although the raids on aerodromes from 1916 onwards did not often succeed in inflicting serious material damage, they had a marked moral effect, for once pilots were safely back in their own aerodrome they were apt to feel that their share of risk was complete. An unforeseen addition was all the worse to bear when the nerve-tension had been relaxed, and when they were taken at a disadvantage on the ground.

The Allied air supremacy of 1916 was not long maintained. The Germans challenged it with improved types of single-seater fighting machines and with the so-called 'circus' system whereby special fighting squadrons were formed – under a picked leader who picked his own pilots – and were successively switched to any part of the front where the higher command desired air superiority to be gained. The most famous of these 'circuses' were those of Boelcke and Baron von Richthofen.

By their superior strategy the Germans regained the upper hand early in 1917, although the total British fighting machines outnumbered theirs by three to one. And the British tragically helped to swell the enemy's 'bag' by sending out swarms of partially trained young pilots from England, under pressure from GHQ. But the Allies soon retorted with fresh machines and gradually, if expensively, won back a superiority in the air which was never lost again – although never so marked as in the summer of 1916. Because of the three-dimensional conditions of air warfare, a command of the air could never be attained in the sense that a command of the sea was possible, and the object became a superiority, which should ensure a local and temporary command of the air over a static front when needed.

The year 1917 was marked also by an increasing development of the method of fighting and flying in formation, which tended to replace the Homeric combats of individual champions – whose mounting score of victims had been followed with the excitement that formerly awaited the return of a Red Indian scalping expedition or the news of a Test Match. Henceforth, knight-errantry yielded to tactics and air fighting gradually assumed the more developed forms of warfare, although carried out on a different plane. By the end of the war an attack was often delivered by formations of fifty or sixty machines which manoeuvred – the actual squadrons compact – with the aim of breaking up the enemy's formation.

Thus they became cavalry of the air, and the resemblance was heightened by another new form of air action, used with great effect in the later stages of the war. This was the attack on ground troops. So long as the rival armies were firmly embedded in trenches, air attack had small scope, although occasionally it came to the relief of hard-pressed packets of infantry. But when the British front broke in March, 1918, all the available fighter squadrons, French as well as British, were concentrated to strike at the advancing enemy. Their overhead counter-attacks during this crisis were an important factor in stemming the German onrush, and one that has been inadequately recognized by military historians. Still greater opportunities came when the enemy tide ebbed in the autumn. After the breaking of the Bulgarian, Turkish, and Austrian fronts alike, air attacks on the retreating columns both hastened and completed the break-up of the enemy armies.

Air attacks on the communications, supply depots, ammunition dumps, and billets of the armies, had been developed much earlier. The battle of Neuve Chapelle in March, 1915, marked the first organized attempt to prevent the arrival of enemy reinforcements, and at Loos in September, a more extended bombing plan was applied against the German railways. Results were small, however, owing to lack of experience, deficiency of equipment, and the want of machines to maintain the intensive bombardment essential for causing an effective stoppage. If a railway was damaged before the battle it could be repaired in time for the passage of reinforcements; and, unless repairs were hindered by continuous bombing, supplies and ammunition would reach the enemy troops before they began to run short. The first lesson was learnt and applied in the later battles of the war, when the bombing of communications played a regular part, but the second lesson was never fully applied owing to lack of bombing aircraft. The very eagerness with which the armies had eventually embraced aircraft as immediately auxiliaries – for reconnaissance, artillery observation, and the protection of these duties – limited the supply of aircraft for roles of indirect cooperation, and curtailed their exploitation of the bombing weapon.

Moreover, their very concentration on these auxiliaries blinded the armies to the greater possibilities of crippling their opponents by hunger. The Germans, especially, neglected opportunities of inflicting decisive injury – as a senior staff officer of the British Second Army revealed a few years ago. This army received the bulk of its supplies from Calais and Boulogne, and in front of these bases was held only three days' reserves of food and ammunition, apart from three days' supplies with the fighting troops. To serve the front there were two double lines and one single; to meet the normal needs of the troops seventy-one trains a day were needed – three-quarters of the total capacity of the three lines. With this narrow margin of safety, the blocking of one line would have sufficed to dislocate the whole system, while the blocking of more than one line would have brought a catastrophe. To cause such a block would have been the easier because outside Calais there was a junction of two of the lines, and near St Omer two converged. Moreover, a block at Arques, near St Omer, would even have cut off the troops from the three days' reserves, which lay in depots farther back along the two lines which converged at this point. It is not difficult to picture the situation which would have arisen if an effective and sustained bombing attack had been launched in April,

1918, to coincide with the German Army's attack, when this area was congested with British and French troops who were trying to dam the breach in the front.

The Allied commanders, also, on the Western Front, were unwilling to spare sufficient aircraft for a real test of the effect of bombing communications. Yet, there was a significant hint of its potency, when on July 16, 1918, the bombing of an ammunition train at Thionville station stopped all traffic along this important section of the German communications for forty-eight hours – the forty-eight hours before the Allied counterstroke on the Marne which turned the tide of the war.

At sea, the Germans, relying on their submarines, fortunately failed to explore the possibilities of air attacks on merchant shipping, or on the ports where that shipping had to unload its freight. And the Allies could not, as their enemy had no shipping in use. There was one fleeting glimpse of such action; as early as August 12th, 1915, a British seaplane, launched from a seaplane carrier near the Dardanelles, gained the distinction of being the first to torpedo a ship. The most valuable service rendered by naval aircraft during the war was in anti-submarine patrolling and escorting convoys – a purely protective role.

Yet seven months before the battle of Jutland, Commodore Sueter of the Naval Air Service had begged the Admiralty to sanction the construction of 200 torpedo-carrying aircraft. His persistence merely led to his removal – to the Adriatic. The year after Jutland, the new Commander-in-Chief of the Grand Fleet asked for that very number to be produced as early as possible. It was too late. The unwanted offspring of Sueter's vision might conceivably have made that one ineffective naval battle decisive. Moreover, a further chance had been forfeited through the oversight by which the *Campania*, a large aircraft carrier, was left behind when the Grand Fleet sailed from Scapa Flow.

It was the Naval Air Service, however, which first proposed, and attempted, to strike at the sources of the enemy's power to make war – his industrial centres. The way was blocked by the narrow view of the Army Command. The idea nevertheless made headway, and in October 1916 was reinforced by the arguments of Colonel Barès, of the French air service, on a visit to London. The Admiralty representative on the Air Board then suggested that the Navy should keep a force of 200 bombers in France for this purpose. But, according to the Official History, the proposal 'drew a strong letter of protest from Sir Douglas Haig ... He stated that the views attributed to Colonel Barès were unsound in theory and should not be accepted in practice'. Haig's opposition killed the scheme – which might have checked the stream of shells that were being hurled at his troops. In 1917, out of fifty air squadrons in France, only two were for bombing, and those were confined to local targets.

Not until late in the war was there any attempt on the Allied side to attack the enemy's 'home' front save for spasmodic raids by a handful of British naval aircraft, as well as by the French. Nor, in the light of human nature, was independent air action likely to be developed so long as this new weapon was handled by and divided between the land and sea forces. The essential fusion between the two parts was delayed until April, 1918, when the Royal Air Force was created. As a sequel, the Independent Air Force was formed in' June, and placed under Trenchard, who had been the dynamic leader of the military air arm in France, if also, ironically, a determined opponent of independent air action. In the few months that remained, the repeated and expanding raids of the new force accelerated the moral disintegration of Germany, and, by their moral effect at least hampered the production of munitions in the Rhineland. Even so, the significance of this force was more in promise than fulfilment, for it was barely a quarter of its intended strength when the Armistice came. Similarly, the effect of the German air raids on England should be assessed in the light of the fact that the largest raid was carried out by less than forty bombers.

What might have been achieved is suggested by the fact that the seven principal munition centres in the Ruhr, as well as those in the Rhineland, were all within air range of the British front. Essen (173 miles), Germany's main arsenal, was only as far as the German machines flew in bombing London from their base near Ghent. Again, one factory at Hagen (175 miles) produced two-thirds of the German submarine accumulators. Two of the largest chemical factories were less than 100 miles from the Allied front. Yet this immense opportunity of crippling the munition supply of the German armies was sacrificed in favour of air fighting over the trench front – sacrificed, in fact, on the 'battle' altar of Clausewitz-in-the-air. Even when the Independent Air Force was at last formed, in face of vehement opposition from GHQ, its strength was curtailed to a mere hundred machines (about 2 per cent of Britain's total Air Force) and more than half its raids were directed against tactical, instead of industrial targets. Apart from what was then achieved, a sidelight on its wider indirect effect is shed by the fact that, in the month of August alone, one shell factory, which was never even bombed, received fifty-three false alarms and suffered an output deficit of 3,000 tons. There is also a paradoxical reflection on the GHQ doctrine of concentration on the battlefront in the fact that the menace of these raids drew off no less than twenty German squadrons from the front – three or four times as many machines as were engaged in them!

CHAPTER EIGHT

1918 – The Break

The middle years of the World War had been, in a military sense, a tussle between a lean Hercules and a bulky Cerberus. The Germanic Alliance was weaker in numbers but directed by a single head, the Entente stronger in numbers but with too many heads. Owing to their own excessive losses, diffusion of effort and the collapse of Russia, the Entente at the end of 1917 were faced with the grim fact that the numerical balance had been reversed, and months must elapse before the prospective stream of America's new divisions should tilt the scales once more in their favour. The emergency paved the way for the creation of a unified command but it still needed disaster to bring it into being.

At the conference at Rapallo in November, the formation of a Supreme War Council was decided upon, to be composed of the principal ministers of the Allies, with military representatives, and to sit permanently at Versailles. If a fundamental defect was that it merely substituted a formal for an informal committee, a further flaw was that the military representatives had no executive status. In the economic sphere, where deliberation rather than instant action was necessary, it led to a real improvement in the combination of shipping, food and munition resources. Militarily, it was futile, for it set up a dual advisership – the Versailles representatives on the one hand and the chiefs of the national General Staffs on the other. Yet it is fair to add that this 'dead end' was due to a British obstruction.

Both the Americans and the French desired to give this committee executive power and an executive head, and Pétain logically supported the proposal, which came from Colonel House and General Bliss. But the fundamental offset to its wisdom was that it eliminated the essential control of strategy by the statesman, while the suggested composition of the council repeated the error of the Nivelle era. For it was to consist of the national Commanders-in-Chief and Chiefs of Staff, and thus whichever member was chosen as President would have his freedom of judgement and execution hampered by his responsibility to and for his own national army. Moreover, in fulfilment, the proposal would mean that the council would have a French chief – as the French realized when they supported, and the British when they opposed, the proposal. In rejecting it Lloyd George was guided not only by a wise objection to a purely military council but by his feeling that British opinion was not ripe for it, and that Haig's resistance to another Nivelle solution would be supported by the public at home. Moreover, the suggested inclusion of the Chiefs of Staff introduced a personal complication, for the last thing that Lloyd George desired was to strengthen the influence of Sir William Robertson upon the conduct of the war. Rather was he hoping to sidetrack Robertson, whom he held responsible for the futile and costly strategy of 1917, in favour of Sir Henry Wilson, his nominee for the Versailles committee. And while he sought to make Versailles independent of the narrow purview of the British General Staff, Clemenceau was equally intent to make it merely a microphone for the French General Staff, to amplify its 'voice'.

In default of agreement the military representatives – now Generals Weygand, Wilson, Bliss, and Cadorna – were merely technical advisers. But as the menace of the German attack grew closer, and with it the need for common action, this advisory body was converted into a military executive committee to handle an inter-Allied general reserve, a fresh compromise which set up a dual control – the Commanders-in-Chief and the Versailles committee. Only an enlargement of mind and goodwill could make it workable.

Time was too short. Since early in November the stream of German troop trains from the Eastern to the Western Front had been steadily swelling. When the 1917 campaign opened, there had been a proportion of nearly three Allies to two Germans – actually in March 178 British, French and Belgian divisions against 129 German divisions. Now the Germans had a slight advantage, with the likelihood of augmenting it. But the Allied statesmen, recalling how often their own offensive had failed with equal or greater superiority of force, were naturally slow to appreciate the gravity of the menace or to respond to the sudden fall in the temperature of military opinion. Nor could they agree to draw reinforcements from the other fronts.

The Italians strove against any withdrawal of the Allied contingents from their front, and the French opposed any reduction of the Salonika force. Lloyd George urged an effort to complete the success in Palestine; this was sanctioned on the understanding that no reinforcements went there from France, though it also meant that none came from there to France. Meantime, the German strength had increased to 177 divisions by the end of January, and fifteen more in March. The Allied strength, by the dispatch of divisions to Italy and the breaking up of others owing to the French shortage of drafts had fallen to the equivalent of 173 – counting as double the four and a half large-size American divisions which had arrived. For the French and British had been constrained to follow the Germans in reducing their divisions from twelve to nine battalions each.

Internal friction among the Allies increased their handicap. In part it was due to the difficulties of a fair settlement as to the length of front which each should hold. In the 1917 campaign the British, bearing the burden of the offensive, had been in charge of barely 100 miles of line, while the French, on the defensive, had held 325 miles. At the close of the campaign Haig had come to an agreement with Pétain that he would extend his line to Barisis, just south of the Oise, which made a total of 125 miles. In view of his change to a defensive attitude, the extension can hardly be considered exacting, although his heavy losses made it a greater strain than it would have been on the 1917 basis of strength. But before this extension was complete, Clemenceau, the new French Premier, intervened with a demand that the British should take over an additional thirty miles, as far as Berry-au-Bac. Clemenceau threatened to resign if this demand were not met, but eventually agreed to submit the case to the Versailles committee, which proposed a compromise whereby the British should take over approximately half the distance in dispute. Thereupon Haig threatened to resign; this threat threw the Supreme War Council and its advisory committee into the melting-pot from which the executive committee emerged. Meantime Haig went direct to Pétain and reached a settlement by which he was merely to complete his extension to Barisis, according to the original agreement. This was a noteworthy concession on Pétain's part, which did honour to his spirit of helpfulness. And the Supreme War Council on February 2nd accepted this private settlement between the two Commanders-in-Chief, wisely swallowing the affront to its own dignity. It is astonishing, in view of this fact, that the legend should still persist that Haig was forced by the 'politicians' to extend his line against his will, and likewise the argument that such extension was the cause of the subsequent breakthrough.

The just proportion between the respective fronts is hardly less difficult to determine now, in retrospect, than it was to agree upon them. With ninety-nine divisions the French had to hold 300 miles, while the British with fifty-eight divisions, of somewhat greater rifle strength, took charge of 125 miles – after the extension to Barisis. Of the French line, however, the half from St Mihiel eastwards was of secondary importance. If, even so, the French had cause for complaint on any mileage basis, the British could fairly claim that they had more vital objectives to cover, less room to fall back, and a higher proportion of the enemy already on their front. But the French, in turn, could point to the fact that the main mass of the German reserves was so placed that it might intervene on either front. To weigh a question compounded of such diverse elements required a strategic mind of the purest scientific detachment, whereas it had to be resolved by men whose determined character and strong sense of nationality made it difficult for them to see the other man's point of view. Lloyd George was an exception, but to his endowment with a wider outlook was linked a tendency to be impatient with the point of view of his own men, especially when this seemed to him parochial or obstructive.

Disagreement between him and Sir William Robertson, his official military adviser, had increased throughout 1917, Robertson being suspicious of political interference with military plans and of Lloyd George's unorthodox ideas, while Lloyd George felt that Robertson's sole idea in strategy was to support Haig blindly and frustrate any alternative schemes. The results of this blank-cheque policy at Passchendaele made the Prime Minister more anxious to provide himself with alternative advice, a desire that had influenced him in setting up the Supreme Council with its military committee, and in appointing to it Sir Henry Wilson, whom he regarded as a soldier of more sympathetic and larger outlook. But when the new organ was converted into an executive committee, Robertson insisted that he, as Chief of the Imperial General Staff, should be the British military member. The Prime Minister objected that the combination of the two posts in one man would vitiate the whole principle, maintaining the sectional instead of the detached view. Robertson's stand brought the long-growing dissension to a climax. The Prime Minister went part of the way to meet him by appointing him the Versailles representative, while Wilson was to become Chief of the Imperial General Staff at home with reduced functions. Sprung on Robertson as a surprise, this proposal provoked his refusal. After several days of discussion and domestic crisis, Robertson was offered his former post on the new terms. His refusal to accept them produced his enforced resignation, and relegation to a home command. Wilson succeeded him, and Rawlinson was appointed to Versailles. Such conflicts of view, if unavoidable in human nature and in an alliance, weakened the common front. And as soon as one difficulty was overcome, other sources of dissension came to the fore.

The prolonged waste of soldiers' lives in the swamps beyond Ypres had led Lloyd George and his Cabinet to withhold reinforcements for fear of encouraging fresh squandering. This undoubtedly weakened Haig's initial power of resistance to the German onslaught, yet it is just to point out that it was weakened more – in quality as well as quantity – by the 400,000 British casualties suffered in the offensive of the later part of 1917. Moreover, we should not forget that the Government had the heavy responsibility of being the trustee for the lives of the nation. The real ground of criticism is that it was not strong enough to make a change in, or place a check upon, a command which it did not trust, while supplying the reinforcements necessary for defence. And for this lack of moral strength the public must share the blame, for they had already shown themselves too easily swayed by clamour against political interference with the generals, and too prone to believe that the politician is invariably wrong on such occasions. The civilian public, indeed, is apt to trust soldiers too little in peace, and sometimes too much in war.

These political handicaps, and the accompanying tendency of politicians to work deviously towards what they dare not demand openly, were also seen in the project for a unified command. The Prime Minister, indeed, had gone so far in November as to disclaim faith in his own long-sought cure. Instead he sought a palliative in the inter-Allied executive committee, under Foch's chairmanship, which should control a common reserve of thirty divisions – one-seventh of the total forces. This scheme was decisively annulled by Haig, who, when called on by Foch for his contribution of nine divisions, replied that he could spare none. He preferred to make an arrangement with Pétain for mutual support.

When the test came, a week later, this broke down, and Haig then took a foremost part in hastening and facilitating the appointment of a generalissimo, which he had formerly opposed. His change of attitude had simply an immediate purpose – 'The whole and sole object is to override Pétain and get the French to send reinforcements to prevent the British and French armies being separated.' (Charteris.)

For the actual breakdown the blame has been commonly thrown upon the French, and there is no question that Haig understood from Pétain on March 24th that if the Germans continued their rapid progress the French reserves would have to be used to cover Paris. But in fairness it is essential to add that, whereas the original compact had only pledged the aid of some six French divisions, Pétain actually sent nine by March 24th, and twenty-one (including four of cavalry) by March 26th. If these reinforcements were perhaps slower coming into action than in dispatch, it does not affect the fact that the original pledge was amply exceeded. Thus the fundamental fault would seem to lie in trusting to an arrangement for such slender support by either Ally.

The German Plan. On the German side the submarine panacea for victory had been replaced by a military panacea, and hopes were perhaps exaggerated by the unexpected collapse of Russia. But although Ludendorff promised victory in the field, he did not disguise the fact that a western offensive would be a far harder task than the conquests in the east. He realized also that it would be a race between the effect of Germany's blow and the arrival of American reinforcements, although he hoped to win the race. To secure the rear of his offensive, a definite peace was wrung from the Bolshevik Government of Russia by a military demonstration, and also forced on Rumania. And to secure, if possible, the economic base of his offensive the Ukraine was occupied for its wheat supplies, with little resistance except from Czechoslovak troops who had formerly been taken prisoners from the Austrian Army.

Ludendorff's next problem was to decide his first point of attack. The sector between Arras and St Quentin was chosen, on the western face of the great salient formed by the German front in France. The choice was governed by tactical reasons – this sector was the enemy's weakest point and the ground offered fewer difficulties than elsewhere – although Ludendorff had in mind the possibility of separating the Allied armies and driving the British back against the Channel coast, where they would be too closely penned in to evade his blows. From the experience of the vain Allied attacks Ludendorff had drawn the deduction that 'tactics had to be considered before purely strategical objects which it is futile to pursue unless tactical success is possible'. Hence he formulated a strategical plan based on the new, or resurrected, principle of taking the tactical line of least resistance. Presumably he hoped by firm control to guide these tactical movements to a strategic destination. If so, he failed.

Where did the fault lie? The general view at the end of the war was that the tactical bias had led Ludendorff to change direction and dissipate his strength. That if the Franco-British Command had previously erred by aiming at the strategically correct target without enough attention to the tactical difficulties the German Command had followed it with an equal if opposite error by concentrating on tactical success at the expense of the strategical goal. But a closer examination of the German documents since available, and of Ludendorff's own orders and instructions, throws a different light on the question. It would seem, indeed, that the real fault was that Ludendorff failed to carry out in practice the new principle he had adopted in theory; that he either did not grasp, or shrank from, the full implication of this new theory of strategy. For in fact he dissipated too large a part of his reserves in trying to redeem tactical failures and hesitated too long over the decision to exploit his tactical successes. Ludendorff's strategy in the east had been so forceful and so far-sighted that his indecision and shortsight in the west is difficult to explain. Perhaps he himself was feeling the strain of directing so many vast operations; perhaps it was that he missed the strategical insight and balanced view of Hoffmann who, after being at his side throughout the 1914–16 campaigns, had stayed in the east when Ludendorff went to the Supreme Command. The modern vice of seniority prevented Germany making the fullest use of the man who perhaps approached nearer to military genius than any other general of the war.

In any case the campaign leaves the impression that Ludendorff had neither his former clearness as to the goal, nor the same grip on the changing situations. But in the organization of the attacks his powers were at their highest level. Surprise was to be the key which should open a gate in the long-locked front. The most thorough arrangements were made for concealing and for exploiting the attacks, and the surprise effect of the short but intense bombardment was increased by lavish use of gas and smoke shell. Further, while Ludendorff had settled to strike first on the Somme sector, to which blow the code name 'Michael' was given, he also began preparations for successive attacks at other points, which besides being in readiness for the future helped to mystify the enemy. Two were on the British front and one on the French – 'St George I' against the Lys sector, 'St George II' against the Ypres sector, and 'Blücher' in Champagne.

The 'Michael' attack was to be made by the German Seventeenth, Second, and Eighteenth Armies (sixty-three divisions in all) on the forty-three-mile front Arras–St Quentin–La Fère, but its main force was intended to be exerted north of the Somme, and, after breaking through, the Seventeenth and Second Armies were to wheel north-west and press the British army against the coast, while the river and the Eighteenth Army guarded their flank.

The assault was launched on March 21st, and the surprise was greatly helped by an early morning mist. But while the thrust broke through completely south of the Somme, where the defence – but also the attacking force – was thinnest, it was held up near Arras, a check which reacted on all the attack north of the river. Ludendorff, violating his new principle, spent the following days in trying to revive his attack against the strong, and strongly held bastion of Arras, maintaining this direction as his principal line of effort. Meantime he kept a tight rein on the Eighteenth Army which was advancing in the south without serious check from its opponents. As late as March 26th he issued orders which restrained it from crossing the Avre and tied it to the pace of its neighbour, the Second, which in turn was held back by the very limited success of the Seventeenth Army near Arras. Thus we see that in reality Ludendorff was bent on breaking the British army by breaking down its strongest sector of resistance in a direct assault. And because of this obsession he failed, until too late, to throw the weight of his reserves along the line of least resistance south of the Somme. The intended wheel to the north-west might have come to pass if it had been made after passing the flank, and thus being directed against the rear, of the Arras bastion. On March 26th the attack north of the Somme (by the left wing of the Seventeenth Army and the right of the Second Army) was visibly weakening as the price of its hard-earned gains. South of the Somme the left of the Second Army reached, and was now to be embarrassed by, the desert of the old Somme battlefields, – a brake on progress and supply. The Eighteenth Army alone was advancing with unslackened impetus.

This situation led Ludendorff to adopt a new plan, but without relinquishing his old. He ordered for March 28th a fresh and direct attack on the high ground near Arras – by the right of the Seventeenth Army, to be followed by a Sixth Army attack just to the north between Vimy and La Bassée. But the promising situation south of the Somme led him to indicate Amiens as an additional main objective. Even so, he restrained the Eighteenth Army from pushing on to turn the flank of the Amiens defences without further orders! On March 28th the fresh Arras attack was launched, unshielded by mist or surprise, and failed completely in face of the well-prepared resistance of Byng's Third Army. Only then did Ludendorff abandon his original idea and direct his main effort, and some of his remaining reserves, towards Amiens. But meantime he ordered the Eighteenth Army to mark time for two days. When the attack was renewed it made little progress in face of a resistance that had been afforded time to harden, and Ludendorff, rather than be drawn into an attrition struggle, suspended the attempt to reach Amiens.

He had, however, missed vital arteries and decisive results by the narrowest of margins. By March 27th the advance had penetrated nearly forty miles and reached Montdidier, cutting one railway to Paris; by March 30th the German flood was almost lapping the outworks of Amiens. Eighty thousand prisoners and 975 guns had been taken. Once the crust was broken, the very elaboration of the methods of communication built up during three years of static warfare caused the greater flux behind the front. The extent of the retreat was primarily the measure of the loss of control by the British commanders.

Disaster had driven the Allies to an overdue step, and on Haig's appeal and Lord Milner's intervention Foch had been appointed on March 26th to 'coordinate' the operations of the Allied armies. In this hour of crisis, Foch's decisive manner and exuberant promises created confidence. Yet, in actual fact, his appointment made little difference to the flow of reinforcements. And although on April 14th he secured the title of Commander-in-Chief of the Allied armies, it gave him no real power of command. By this time a fresh German menace had developed – though not intended as such.

With a large part of his reserves holding the vast bulge south of the Somme, Ludendorff turned, if without much confidence and merely as a diversion, to release, on April 9th, his 'St George I' attack. Its astonishing early success against a weakened front led him to convert it bit by bit into a major effort. The British were desperately close to the sea, but their resistance stopped the German tide, after a ten-mile invasion, just short of the important railway junction of Hazebrouck, and an attempt to widen the front towards Ypres was nullified by Haig swinging his line back just before and by the gradual arrival of French reinforcements. Haig complained strongly that Foch was too slow in sending French reserves northwards, but the event justified Foch's reluctance to commit himself thither and his seeming excess of optimism in declaring that the danger was past. Ludendorff had doled out reserves sparingly, usually too late and too few for real success; so apprehensive that his new bulge would become another sack, that after the capture of Kemmel Hill, when opportunity opened its arms, he stopped the exploitation for fear of a counterstroke.

Thus Ludendorff had fallen short of strategic results; on the other hand he could claim huge tactical successes – the British casualties were over 300,000. The British Army had been badly mauled; and although fresh drafts to the number of 140,000 were hurried out from England and divisions brought back from Italy, Salonika and Palestine, months must elapse before it could recover its offensive power. Ten British divisions had to be broken up temporarily, while the German strength had now mounted to 208, of which eighty were back in reserve. A restoration of the balance, however, was now in sight. A dozen American divisions had arrived in France and, responding to the call, great efforts were being made to swell the stream. At the crisis in March, Pershing, the American Commander-in-Chief, even relaxed his inflexible opposition to partial or premature use of the American troops so far as to declare that they were at Foch's disposal for use wherever required. It was an inspiring gesture – although in practice he continued to keep a tight hold on his troops and, with rare exceptions, only allowed them to take over parts of the front as complete divisions.

For Germany the sands were running out. Realizing this, Ludendorff launched his 'Blücher' attack between Soissons and Reims, on May 27th. Falling by surprise with twenty-two divisions against eleven, it swept over the Aisne and reached the Marne on May 30th, where its impetus died away. This time the German superiority of force had not been so pronounced as before nor so well aided by nature's atmospheric cloak. It would seem that the extent of the opening success was due in part to the strategic surprise – the greater unexpectedness of the time and place of the blow – and in part to the folly of the local army command in insisting on the long-exploded and obsolete method of massing the defenders in the forward positions – there to be compressed cannon-fodder for the Germans' massed artillery.

But once again Ludendorff had obtained a measure of success for which he was neither prepared nor desirous. The surpriser was himself surprised. The attack had been conceived merely as a diversion, to attract the Allied reserves thither preparatory to a final and decisive blow at the British front in Flanders. But its opening success attracted thither too large, yet not large enough, a proportion of the German reserves. Blocked frontally by the river, an attempt was made to push west, but it failed in face of Allied resistance – notable for the appearance of American divisions at Château-Thierry, where they gallantly counter-attacked.

Ludendorff had now created two huge bulges, and another smaller one, in the Allied front. His next attempt was to pinch out the Compiègne 'tongue' which lay between the Amiens and Marne bulges. But this time there was no surprise, and the blow on the west side of the 'tongue', June 9th, was too late to coincide with the pressure on the east. A month's pause followed.

Ludendorff, though anxious to strike his long-cherished decisive blow against the British in Belgium, considered that their reserves here were still too strong, and so again decided to choose the line of least tactical resistance, hoping that a heavy blow in the south would draw off the British reserves. He had failed to pinch out the Compiègne 'tongue' on the west of his Marne salient; he was now about to attempt the same method on the east, by attacking on either side of Reims. But he needed an interval for rest and preparation, and the delay was fatal, giving the British and French time to recuperate, and the Americans to gather strength. The British divisions previously broken up had now been reconstituted, and as a result of an urgent appeal made to President Wilson in the crisis of March, and the provision of extra shipping, American troops had been arriving at the rate of 300,000 a month since the end of April. By mid-July seven American divisions were ready to help in resisting the next, and final, German stroke. Five more were being acclimatized to front-line conditions away on the Alsace-Lorraine sector, and five with the British, while another four were assembled in the American training area.

The tactical success of his own blows had been Ludendorff's undoing. Yielding too late to their influence, he had then pressed each too far and too long, so using up his own reserves and causing an undue interval between each blow. He had driven in three great wedges, but none had penetrated far enough to sever a vital artery, and this strategic failure left the Germans with an indented front which invited flanking counterstrokes.

The Turning of the Tide. On July 15th Ludendorff launched his new attack, but its coming was no secret. East of Reims it was foiled by an elastic defence, and west of Reims the German penetration across the Marne merely enmeshed them more deeply to their downfall – for on July 18th Foch launched a long-prepared stroke against the other flank of the Marne salient. Here Pétain, who directed the operation, turned the key which Ludendorff lacked, using masses of light tanks to lead a surprise attack on the Cambrai method. The Germans managed to hold the gates of the salient open long enough to draw back their forces into safety and straighten their line; but their reserves were depleted, Ludendorff was forced (on the 20th) to postpone, if not yet to abandon, the offensive in Flanders, and the initiative definitely and finally passed to the Allies.

Foch's first concern was to keep it, by giving the enemy no rest while his own reserves were accumulating. To this end he arranged with Haig, Pétain and Pershing for a series of local offensives, aimed to free the lateral railway communications and to improve the position of the front ready for further operations. To Haig he proposed an attack in the Lys sector, but Haig suggested instead the Somme area as more suitable. Rawlinson, commanding the British Fourth Army in front of Amiens, had already submitted to Haig a plan for a large surprise attack there, and Foch agreed to this in place of his own proposal. He also placed under Haig the French First Army (Debeney) to extend the attack to the south. Rawlinson's army was doubled, and by skilful precautions the enemy were kept in the dark until, on August 8th, the attack was delivered – with 456 tanks. The blow had the maximum shock of surprise, and south of the Somme the troops of the Australian and Canadian Corps rapidly overran and overwhelmed the German forward divisions. By August 12th when the advance came to a halt through reaching the tangled wilderness of the old 1916 battlefields, if also through lack of reserves, the Fourth Army had taken 21,000 prisoners at a cost of only 20,000 casualties. Great, if not fully exploited, as a material, it was far greater as a moral success.

Ludendorff has said: 'August 8th was the black day of the German army in the history of the war ... It put the decline of our fighting power beyond all doubt ... The war must be ended.' He informed the Emperor and the political chiefs that peace negotiations ought to be opened before the situation became worse, as it must. The conclusions reached at a Crown Council held at Spa were that 'we can no longer hope to break the war-will of our enemies by military operations', and 'the object of our strategy must be to paralyse the enemy's war-will gradually by a strategic defensive'. In other words the German Command had abandoned hope of victory or even holding their gains, and hoped only to avoid surrender – an insecure moral foundation.

On August 10th Foch issued fresh *directives* for the preparation of an 'advance' by the British Third Army 'in the general direction of Bapaume and Péronne'. Meantime he wished Haig to continue the Fourth Army's frontal pressure, but Haig demurred to it as a vain waste of life and gained his point. Economy of force was henceforth to be added to the advantages of the new strategy now evolved. Thus the momentum of the Fourth Army had hardly waned before the Third Army moved. From then on Foch beat a tattoo on the German front, a series of rapid blows at different points, each broken off as soon as its initial impetus waned, each so aimed as to pave the way for the next, and all close enough in time and space to react on each other. Thus Ludendorff's power of switching reserves to threatened spots was restricted, as his balance of reserves was drained.

On August 10th the French Third Army had struck to the south; then on August 17th the French Tenth Army still farther south; next on August 21st the British Third Army, followed by the British First

Army on August 26th. Ludendorff's order to the troops holding the Lys salient to retire was hastened in execution by the attacks of the re-formed British Fifth Army, and by the first week in September the Germans were back on their original starting line – the strong defences of the Hindenburg Line. And on September 12th Pershing completed the series of preliminary operations by erasing the St Mihiel salient – the first feat of the Americans as an independent army. Pershing had originally intended to make this a stepping stone to an advance towards the Briey coalfields and the eastern end of the Germans' main lateral railway near Metz, but the project was abandoned for reasons that will be referred to later. Thus no exploitation of the success was attempted.

The clear evidence of the Germans' decline and Haig's assurance that he would break the Hindenburg Line where the German reserves were thickest, persuaded Foch to seek victory that autumn instead of postponing the attempt until 1919. All the Allied armies in the west were to combine in a simultaneous offensive.

The Collapse of Bulgaria. Before this attack developed, an event occurred in the Balkans which, in the words of Ludendorff, 'sealed the fate of the Quadruple Alliance'. He had still hoped to hold fast in his strong lines in the west, falling back gradually to fresh lines if neces-sary, and with his strategic flanks in Macedonia and Italy covered, while the German Government was negotiating for a favourable peace. At the same time there was alarm as to the moral effect of the Western Front defeats on the German people, their will-power already under-mined by shortage of food, and perhaps also by propaganda.

But on September 15th the Allied armies in Salonika attacked the Bulgarian front, which crumbled in a few days. Guillaumat, who had succeeded Sarrail in December 1917, had prepared the plan for an offensive; when recalled to France in the crisis of June as Governor of Paris (and potential successor to Pétain) he won over the Allied Governments to consent to the attempt. His successor in Salonika, Franchet d'Esperey, concentrated a Franco-Serb striking force, under Michich, on the Sokol–Dobropolye sector, west of the Vardar, where the Bulgarians trusted to the strength of the mountain ridges and were weak in numbers. On September 15th Michich attacked and by the night of the 17th the Serbs had penetrated twenty miles deep, while the breach had been expanded to a width of twenty-five miles. On the 18th the British attack on the Doiran front was a tactical failure, but it at least helped to pin the enemy's reserves. Meantime the whole of the enemy's front west of the Vardar had collapsed under the converging pressure of the Serbs and French, whose pursuit drove on towards

Uskub. And on the 21st the Bulgarian forces east of the Vardar began to fall back in turn. This gave the British aircraft an opportunity, and by bombing the narrow Kosturino Pass they 'largely contributed, on that side, to turn the Bulgarian retreat into a disorderly flight'. With their army split into two parts the Bulgarians, already tired of the war, sought an armistice, which was signed on September 29th. Franchet d'Esperey's achievement not only severed the first root of the Central Alliance, but opened the way to an advance on Austria's rear.

The First Peace Note. The capitulation of Bulgaria convinced Ludendorff that it was necessary to take a decisive step towards securing peace. While he was scraping together a paltry half-dozen divisions to form a new front in Serbia, and arranging a meeting with the political chiefs, Foch's grand assaults fell on the western defences, September 26th–28th, and the line threatened to crack.

The German Supreme Command lost its nerve – only for a matter of days, but that was sufficient, and recovery too late. On the afternoon of September 29th Ludendorff was studying the problem in his room at the Hotel Britannique at Spa – an ominously named choice of headquarters! Examination only seemed to make it more insoluble, and in a rising outburst of fear and passion he bemoaned his troubles – especially his lack of tanks – and berated all those whom he considered as having thwarted his efforts – the jealous staffs, the defeatist Reichstag, the too humanitarian Kaiser, and the submarine-obsessed navy. Gradually he worked himself into a frenzy, until suddenly, with foam on his lips, he fell to the floor in a fit. And that evening it was a physically as well as mentally shaken man who took the precipitate decision to appeal for an armistice, saying that the collapse of the Bulgarian front had upset all his dispositions – 'troops destined for the Western Front had had to be dispatched there'. This had 'fundamentally changed the situation in view of the attacks then being launched on the Western Front', for though these 'had so far been beaten off their continuance must be reckoned with'.

This remark refers to Foch's general offensive. The American attack in the Meuse–Argonne had begun on September 26th, but had come practically to a standstill by the 28th. A Franco-Belgo-British attack had opened in Flanders on the 28th, but if unpleasant did not look really menacing. On the morning of the 29th, however, Haig's main blow was falling on the Hindenburg Line, and the early news was disquieting.

In this emergency, Prince Max was called to be Chancellor to negotiate a peace move, with his international reputation for moderation and honour as its covering pledge. To bargain effectively and without confession of defeat he needed, and asked, a breathing space 'of ten, eight, even four days, before I have to appeal to the enemy'. But Hindenburg merely reiterated that 'the gravity of the military situation admits of no delay', and insisted that 'a peace offer to our enemies be issued at once', while Ludendorff plaintively chanted the refrain 'I want to save my army'.

Hence on October 3rd, the appeal for an immediate armistice went out to President Wilson. It was an open confession of defeat to the world, and even before this – on October 1st – the Supreme Command had undermined their own home front by communicating the same impression to a meeting of the leaders of all political parties. Men who had so long been kept in the dark were blinded by the sudden light. All the forces of discord and pacifism received an immense impulse.

While the German Government was debating the conditions for an armistice and questioning Ludendorff as to the situation of the army for further resistance if the terms were unacceptable, Foch continued his military pressure.

The Breach of the Hindenburg Line. The plan of the general offensive embraced a series of convergent and practically simultaneous attacks:

1 and 2. By the Americans between the Meuse and the Argonne Forest, and by the French west of the Argonne, both in the direction of Mézières – beginning on September 26th.

3. By the British on the St Quentin–Cambrai front in the general direction of Maubeuge – beginning on September 27th.

4. By the Belgian and Allied forces in the direction of Ghent – beginning on September 28th.

The general aspect was that of a pincer-like pressure against the vast salient jutting south between Ypres and Verdun. The attack towards Mézières would shepherd that part of the German armies towards the rather difficult country of the Ardennes and away from their natural line of retreat through Lorraine; it was also dangerously close to the hinge of the Antwerp–Meuse line which the Germans were preparing in rear. The attack towards Maubeuge would threaten the other main line of communication and retreat through the Liége gap, but it had farther to go. In these attacks, the Americans had the hardest natural obstacle; the British had to face the strongest defences and the heaviest weight of enemy troops.

Pershing's attack opened well, adding surprise to its superiority in numbers – approximately eight to one – but soon lost impetus owing to the difficulties of supply and exploitation in such country. When it was eventually suspended on October 14th, after bitter fighting and severe losses, the American Army was still far distant from the vital railway. A new force, it was suffering the growing pains which the British had passed through in 1915–16. Pershing's difficulties were enhanced by the fact that he had waived his own proposal for an exploitation of the St Mihiel success towards Metz in view of Haig's objection to a move which, however promising in its ultimate aim, would diverge from the general direction of the other Allied attacks. Foch's original plan for the general offensive had accordingly been readjusted, and in consequence Pershing had not only a more difficult sector, but a bare week in which to prepare his blow. The shortness of time led him to use untried divisions instead of switching the more experienced divisions used at St Mihiel. But in the outcome, Haig's insistence was proved unnecessary, for the British attack broke through the Hindenburg Line before the Meuse–Argonne attack had drawn away any German division from his front.

Haig, by pushing forward his left wing first, facilitated the attack on his right on the strongest section of the Hindenburg Line – the Canal du Nord, and by October 5th the British were through the German defence system, with open country beyond. But on this front the attackers had actually fewer divisions than the defenders,* their tanks were used up, and they could not press forward fast enough to endanger the German retreat.

Within a few days the Supreme Command became more cheerful, even optimistic, when it saw that breaking into the Hindenburg Line had not been followed by an actual breakthrough of the fighting front. More encouragement came from reports of a slackening in the force of the Allies' attacks, particularly in the exploitation of opportunities. Ludendorff still wanted an armistice, but only to give his troops a rest as a prelude to further resistance and to ensure a secure withdrawal to a shortened defensive line on the frontier. By October 17th he even felt he could do it without a rest. It was less that the situation had changed than that his impression of it had been revised. It had never been quite

---

* On September 25th, the eve of Foch's general offensive, there were fifty-seven German divisions facing forty British and two American divisions along the Hindenburg Line between, roughly, St Quentin and Lens. In the Meuse–Argonne sector twenty enemy divisions opposed thirty-one French and thirteen large-strength American divisions – a total equivalent to at least sixty normal-size Allied divisions. The German divisions had shrunk to an abnormally small size, but this fact does not affect the historical comparison of odds met by the right and left pincers respectively of the Allied offensive.

so bad as he had pictured it on September 29th. But his first impression, and depression, had now spread throughout the political circles and public of Germany, as the ripples spread when a pebble has been dropped in a pool.

The combined pressure of the Allied armies, and their steady advance, were loosening the will-power of the German Government and people. The conviction of ultimate defeat, slower to appeal to them than to the army chiefs, was the more forcible when it was realized. And the indirect moral effect of military and economic pressure was accentuated by the direct effect of peace propaganda, skilfully directed and intensively waged by Northcliffe. The 'home front' began to crumble later, but it crumbled quicker than the battlefront.

The Collapse of Turkey. The offensive planned for the spring in Palestine had been interrupted by the crisis in France and the consequent withdrawal of most of Allenby's British troops. The depletion was made up by reinforcements from India and Mesopotamia, and by September Allenby was again ready to take the offensive. He secretly concentrated, on the Mediterranean flank, the mass of his infantry, and behind them the cavalry. Meantime Lawrence and his Arabs, appearing out of the desert like unseen mosquitoes, menaced the enemy's communications and distracted their attention. At dawn on September 19th the western mass attacked, rolling the Turks back north-east towards the hilly interior – like a door on its hinges. Through the open doorway the cavalry passed, riding straight up the coastal corridor for thirty miles, before swinging east to bestride the Turkish rear. The only remaining way of retreat was eastwards across the Jordan and this was closed with shattering effect by the British air bombers. Completely trapped, the main Turkish armies were rounded up, while Allenby's cavalry exploited the victory of Megiddo by a swift and sustained pursuit which gained first Damascus and finally Aleppo. Defenceless and threatened with a direct advance of Milne from Macedonia on Constantinople, Turkey capitulated on October 30th.

The Collapse of Austria. The last Austrian attempt at an offensive on the Italian front, in conjunction with the German assaults in France, had been repulsed on the Piave in June. Diaz waited until conditions were ripe for an offensive in return, until Austria's internal decay had spread and she was without hope from Germany. On October 24th Cavan's army moved to seize the crossings of the Piave, and on October 27th the main attack opened, driving towards Vittorio Veneto to divide the Austrians in the Adriatic plain from those in the mountains. By October 30th the Austrian Army was split in two, the retreat became a rout, and the same day Austria asked for an armistice, which was signed on November 4th.

The Curtain Falls on the Western Front. Already on October 23rd President Wilson had replied to the German request by a note which virtually required an unconditional surrender. Ludendorff wished to carry on the struggle in hopes that a successful defence of the German frontier might damp the determination of the Allies. But the situation had passed beyond his control, the nation's will-power was broken, and his advice was in discredit. On October 26th he was forced to resign.

Then, for thirty-six hours, the Chancellor lay in coma from an overdose of sleeping draught after influenza. When he returned to his office on the evening of November 3rd, not only Turkey, but Austria, had capitulated. If the situation on the Western Front was felt to be rather easier, Austrian territory and railways were now available as a base of operations against Germany. Several weeks before, General von Gallwitz had told the German Chancellor that such a contingency, then unrealized, would be 'decisive'. Next day revolution broke out in Germany, and swept rapidly over the country. And in these last days of tremendous and diverse psychological strain the 'reddening' glare behind was accentuated by a looming cloud on the Lorraine front – Where the renewed American pressure, since November 1st, was on a point more sensitive than other parts, a point where 'they must not be allowed to advance if the Antwerp–Meuse line was to be held any longer'. If this continued the Rhine and not the frontier would have to be the next line of resistance.

But hourly the revolution was spreading, fanned, as peace negotiations were delayed, by the Kaiser's reluctance to abdicate. Compromise with the revolutionaries was the only chance, and on November 9th Prince Max handed over to the socialist Ebert. Germany had become a republic in outward response to President Wilson's demand and in inward response to the uprising of the German people against the leaders who had led them into disaster. The German fleet had already mutinied when their commanders sought to send them out on a forlorn hope against the British. And on November 6th the German delegates had left Berlin to treat for an armistice.

In the days previous to their arrival the Allies had been anxiously debating the terms, but here the voice of Foch was clear, and decisive, for President Wilson suggested that the terms should be left to the decision of the military chiefs. Haig, supported by Milner, urged moderation – 'Germany is not broken in the military sense. During the last weeks her armies have withdrawn fighting very bravely and in

excellent order. Therefore ... it is necessary to grant Germany conditions which she can accept ... the evacuation of all invaded territories
and of Alsace-Lorraine is sufficient to seal the victory.' The British also
feared the danger of guerrilla warfare and considered that the German
Army should be kept undemobilized as a safeguard against the spread
of Bolshevism.

Foch agreed that 'the German army could undoubtedly take up a
new position, and that we could not prevent it'. But he disagreed with
Haig's conditions and insisted not only that the Germans must hand
over a third of their artillery and half their machine guns but that the
Allies must occupy the Rhineland, with bridgeheads on the east bank of
the Rhine. Only by holding the Rhine would the Allies have a guarantee
that Germany could not subsequently break off the peace negotiations,
whereas Haig's proposals would facilitate the German withdrawal to
and consolidation of a new position of resistance. Foch also intimated
privately to Clemenceau that the occupation would 'serve as a pledge
for security as well as for reparations'.

Pershing went even further than Foch and protested against granting
any armistice. Foch, however, answered such objections logically –
'War is only a means to results. If the Germans now sign an armistice
under our conditions those results are in our possession. This being
achieved, no man has the right to cause another drop of blood to be
shed.' The real results he sought by his terms went, however, beyond
the armistice. Once the German army was out of the way France might
then be able to frame the peace on her terms and not on those of
President Wilson. Thus the ironical result of the President's action in
allowing the soldiers to settle the armistice conditions was that he
nullified the peace conditions set out in his Fourteen Points – and gave
the Germans a just complaint, if not a realistic objection, that they had
been entrapped to their doom by his promises.

The next point of difference was whether reparations should be mentioned in the armistice. The British objected, but the French insisted.
Clemenceau cleverly and disarmingly argued – 'I wish only to make
mention of the principle', and advocated the vague but comprehensive
formula 'reparations for damages', while the French Finance Minister
strengthened its potential effect by inserting the innocent-looking reservation that 'any future claims or demands on the part of the Allies
remain unaffected'. With greater innocence Colonel House swallowed
this clause and through his support it was added to the terms.

The next question was that of the naval terms, and here the national
positions were reversed. Foch, having made his own terms so severe,

was anxious to lighten the naval terms and to demand merely the surrender of submarines. He asked somewhat scoffingly – 'As for the German surface fleet, what do you fear from it? During the whole war only a few of its units have ventured from its ports. The surrender of these units will be merely a manifestation, which will please the public but nothing more.' But Sir Eric Geddes, the First Lord of the Admiralty, reminded Foch that it was the British fleet which 'held in check' the German fleet, and pointed out that if the latter was left intact the war strain on the former would continue until peace was settled. Lloyd George suggested that as an effective but less humiliating compromise the naval terms should demand the internment and not the surrender of the German surface ships. This solution was agreed upon, although the Admiralty only gave way under protest, and the final demand, apart from the surrender of 150 submarines, was for the internment 'in neutral ports, or failing them, Allied ports' of ten battleships and six battlecruisers, besides light craft. Owing to the difficulty of finding an adequate neutral port, their ultimate destination became the British base of Scapa Flow. One important effect of this prolonged discussion was that the terms to Germany were not settled until Austria had capitulated – an effect which, as Lloyd George shrewdly foresaw, enabled the Allies to 'put stiffer terms to Germany' with less chance of refusal.

The Germans' acceptance of these severe terms was hastened less by the existing situation on the Western Front than by the collapse of the 'home front', coupled with exposure to a new thrust in rear through Austria. The Allied advance in the west was still continuing, in some parts seeming to gather pace in the last days, but the main German forces had escaped from the perilous salient, and their complete destruction of roads and railways made it impossible for supplies to keep pace with the advancing troops. A pause must come while these communications were being repaired, and thus the Germans would have breathing space to rally their resistance. The advance reached the line Pont à Mousson–Sedan–Mézières–Mons–Ghent by November 11th – the line of the opening battles in 1914 – but strategically it had come to a standstill.

It is true that, to meet this situation, Foch had concentrated a large Franco-American force to strike below Metz directly east into Lorraine. As the general Allied advance had almost absorbed the enemy's reserves, this stroke, if driven in deeply and rapidly, promised the chance of turning the whole of this new line of defence along the Meuse to Antwerp and might even upset his orderly retreat to the Rhine. But

31 ☐   Vimy ●   6 A
BR. 1st. ARMY 62 ☐
●   Douai
56 ☐   17 A
R. Scarpe
Arras ● ☐ Gd   R. Sensée
15 ☐
3 ☐
34 ☐   Cambrai ◇
59 ☐   6 ☐ 51 ☐   2 A
Vaulx Vraucourt   17 ☐   Le Câteau ●
25 ☐   69 ☐
Bapaume ●   ☐ 19   47 ☐
BR. 3rd. ARMY 2 ☐   9 ☐
21 ☐
☐ 41   Epehy ● 16 ☐
Albert ●   ☐ 39   6 ☐
R. Ancre   Ronssoy ●
1 CAV   24 ☐
Amiens ●   R. Somme   61 ☐   18 A
R. Somme   St.
R. Somme   Quentin
● Villers-Bretonneux   30 ☐
R. Luce   ☐ 3 CAV.   36 ☐
58 ☐   14 ☐
BR. 5 th. ARMY   18 ☐
● Moreuil   Ham ●   Essigny ●
Jussy ● CROZAT CANAL
R. Avre   ● Roye   20 ☐   58 ☐
2 CAV   La Fère ●
Cantigny ●   ● Montdidier
Chauny ●   7 A
Noyon ●   Barisis ●
R. Oise   FR. 6 th. ARMY

GERMAN
OFFENSIVE
March, 1918

━━━━	Original Line on 21st. March
━ ━ ━	Line on evening 21st. March
••••••	Line on evening 23 rd. March
━·━·━	Line on evening 25 th. March
▰▰▰▰	Line on evening 5 th. April

Divisions —
☐ British   ▰ German

0   5   10   15
Miles

it is unlikely that this Lorraine thrust, prepared for November 14th, would have solved the hitherto insoluble problem of maintaining the initial momentum of advance after an initial breakthrough. Foch did not think so. For when asked how long it would take to drive the Germans back across the Rhine if they refused the armistice terms, he replied – 'Maybe three, maybe four or five months. Who knows?' And his post-war comment on this Lorraine offensive was – 'Its importance has always been exaggerated. It is regarded as the irresistible blow that was to fell and administer the knock out to the Boche. That's nonsense. The Lorraine offensive was *not* in itself any more important than the attack then being prepared in Belgium, on the Lys.'

More truly significant was the decision on November 4th, after Austria's surrender, to prepare a concentric advance on Munich by three Allied armies, which would be assembled on the Austro-German frontier within five weeks. In addition Trenchard's Independent Air Force was about to bomb Berlin on a scale hitherto unattempted in air warfare. And the number of American troops in Europe had now risen to 2,085,000, and the number of divisions to forty-two, of which thirty-two were ready for battle. The internal situation and the obvious external developments which could be calculated were the factors which produced Germany's decision to capitulate – not any single and hypothetical blow on the strongest part of her front. With revolution at home, the gathering menace on their southern frontier and the continued strain on their western, the German delegates had no option but to accept the drastic terms of the armistice, which was signed in Foch's railway carriage in the Forest of Compiègne at 5 AM on November 11th. And at 11 o'clock that morning the World War came to an end.

CHAPTER EIGHT

SCENE 1

The First Breakthrough

At 4.30 AM, on March 21st, 1918, the sudden crash of some 4,000 German guns heralded the breaking of a storm which, in grandeur of scale, of awe, and of destruction, surpassed any other in the World War. By nightfall a German flood had inundated forty miles of the British front; a week later it had reached a depth of nearly forty miles, and was almost lapping the outskirts of Amiens; and in the ensuing weeks the Allied cause itself was almost submerged.

These weeks rank with those of the Marne in 1914 as the two gravest military crises of the World War. In them Germany came desperately near to regaining that lost chance, and best chance, of victory, which she had forfeited in early September, 1914. And to the people of Britain at least the risk seemed even worse, because more fully realized and because their stake was greater.

No episode of the war is so studded with question marks as that on which the curtain rose, March 21st, 1918. Why, when the Allies had been attacking with superior force for two years, were they suddenly fighting 'with their backs to the wall'? Why, after the public had been assured that inter-Allied cooperation was assured and a generalissimo unnecessary, was one urgently demanded and appointed? Why, when the Allies had made so little visible impression on the German front in two years of constant offensive, were the Germans able to tear a huge hole in the Allied front within a few days? Why, as this breach so far exceeded in size the dream-aims of its Allied forerunners, did it fail to obtain any decisive results? In seeking the answers to these several 'whys' lies the main interest of March 21st for history.

The primary cause of the sudden British change from the offensive to the defensive lay in the fact that the German fighting strength on the Western Front was increased by 30 per cent between November, 1917, and March 21st, 1918, while the British strength fell by 25 per cent, compared with the previous summer. The bulk of these fresh German troops were transferred from the Russian front, where Ludendorff, as a preliminary to his great bid for victory in the west, had wrung a definite peace from the Bolshevik Government, and also from Rumania. But if these facts explain the change, the causes of its abruptness and extent lie beneath the surface. Chief among them was that the British Command had dissipated its credit, both in balance of man power and with the Government. This doubly unfortunate result was due to the strategy which can be summarized adequately in a single word, manifold in its ill-omened significance – 'Passchendaele'.

Conscious of his responsibility to the nation, and personally distrustful of Haig's judgement, Mr Lloyd George placed a firm check on the flow of reinforcements to France lest they should be poured down another offensive drainpipe. Friction between the two was almost inevitable, because of their extreme contrast of temperament and training. The one a volatile Welshman, and the other a stubborn and taciturn Scot. The one with a magnetic power of drawing even the unwilling to him; the other with an impregnable capacity for holding even the most willing at a distance. The one infinitely adaptable, the other inflexibly consistent, and persistent. In the one, speech and thought so closely coincided that they became fused, while with the other the opening of the mouth automatically cut out the action of the brain. Anecdotes of Haig's inarticulateness, to the point of unintelligibility, are many. One of the best is of the occasion when, presenting the prizes to an Aldershot cross-country team, all that he could get out was – 'I congratulate you on your running. You have run well. I hope you will run as well in the presence of the enemy.'

Again, Lloyd George was as receptive to ideas as he was critical of the pretensions of hierarchical wisdom, and he constantly sought to gather a variety and diversity of opinions as a broad basis for judgement. Haig, as his own admiring biographer, General Charteris, confesses, 'had not a critical mind', and neither knowledge of, nor interest in, affairs outside his own military work. And he took over the command 'genuinely convinced that the position to which he had now been called was one which he, and he alone in the British Army, could fill'. When to his rigidly disciplined outlook was added this feeling of divine right, it raised an almost impassable barrier of character between him and the Prime Minister. Neither made much effort to surmount it, and growing distrust on both sides – a distrust of Haig's military and Lloyd George's personal methods – steadily heightened it.

Throughout the months following Passchendaele and preceding the

German offensive, Lloyd George was assiduously seeking to create a power above Haig, as dismissal would have raised a political storm. His solution was the Supreme War Council in control of a general inter-Allied reserve. But the scheme was thwarted by Haig's action. For, having no belief in the method of battle control by committee, he shattered it by his refusal to contribute his small quota of nine divisions. Whatever the just strength of his objection to the method on principle, his action is not easy either to understand or to justify. For, convinced as he was that the German attack was coming on his front, and conscious of his shortage of reserves, it seems curious that he should not risk a contribution of nine divisions in order to draw from a pool of thirty. He chose, instead, to rely on an arrangement with Pétain for mutual support, whereby in case of need he might be reinforced by six to eight French divisions. This was far less than Haig could hope for from the general reserve, if formed. Moreover, Haig's distrust of French fulfilment of such promises had for years been so marked, his tongue so caustic about them, that it is astonishing that he should have pinned his faith to a small and purely French promise when he could have had a much larger promise from a board on which there was a British representative.

This excessive trust on the part of the British Command, like the Government's withholding of reinforcements, may well have been due to an apparently well-grounded belief in the power of their defence to stop a German attack. Why should the Germans succeed where the British had so often failed? The only close approach to a breakthrough by the British had been at Cambrai, with the tanks – and Haig knew the it was almost impossible for the Germans to have built tanks in quantity.

But in his defensive calculations, as in his offensive actions throughout the past two years, he seems to have underrated the infinite value of surprise, which for 3,000 years of recorded warfare has proved the master key to victory. The real significance of the Cambrai attack on November 20th previous had been that it had revived the use of such a key, forging it from an amalgam of armour and the caterpillar track. Unhappily, the effect of this tank key was largely lost because when inserted in the lock Haig had not the power to turn it fully, through exhausting his strength in the Passchendaele mud.

In the counter-attack of November 30th the Germans had used a key similar in principle if different in design – a short sharp bombardment with gas and smoke shell, followed up by an inrush of infantry, specially trained in the new infiltration tactics. It would seem that by the following March the British had not sufficiently taken this lesson to heart. For, though the Fifth Army's subsequent excuses of weak numbers and a long line had some justification, Gough had expressed confidence beforehand in his power to resist the onslaught.

But when Gough's original front was forced, an inadequate preparation and coordination of the measures to block the enemy's path farther back was revealed. He had failed to arrange for the blowing up of certain causeways and General Headquarters had not given him a definite order. Worse still was the confusion caused by the fact that in the case of the more important railway bridges, this duty was entrusted to the French railway authorities instead of the Fifth Army, and in this way the vital railway bridge at Péronne was allowed to fall undestroyed into German hands.

A similar haziness appeared in the GHQ instructions for the conduct of the defensive battle, for in one place Gough was told 'we should make our preparations to fight east of the Somme', and in another 'it may well be desirable to fall back to the rearward defences of Péronne and the Somme'. To reconcile these alternatives was not easy. It would have been simpler to have forestalled the Germans' attack by a withdrawal similar to their own in 1917, accepting the necessary sacrifice of ground: although political considerations and military sentiments tended to hinder such a course. Adaptation of plan to circumstance may be necessary, and often more advantageous, but it is the hardest test of generalship, and thus demands the clearest thought among those who attempt it. The fog of war is bad enough without being thickened by obscure phrasing: battles may be lost by lack of lucidity as well as by lack of tenacity. The effect of these instructions to the Fifth Army was that labour had to be divided between the alternative defence lines, without time for the satisfactory organization of either. Moreover, a withdrawal to the line of the Somme while the battle was actually in progress demanded a high capacity for rearguard action, and for this the officers and men of the Fifth Army as a whole were neither prepared nor practised. To quote from among many witnesses – Colonel Rowland Feilding has recorded: 'A retreat was the one possibility that had never occurred to us, and, unfortunately, it involves a kind of manoeuvring in which we are unversed, in spite of all our experience.' There is indirect proof of this statement in the fact that no less than 500 guns were abandoned to the enemy in the first two days.

The chance of avoiding a retreat was diminished, as its execution was endangered, because of the scarcity of reserves behind Gough's front and of the way that General Headquarters refused his request to move these nearer the front before the battle. And when it opened he was told that he would have to wait for one extra division until the first four available had been sent to the Third Army. These facts give point to his remark – 'It is impossible for me to say that GHQ showed a full understanding of the circumstances and progress of the battle.' And a chance of improving it was lost because – 'During the whole eight days' battle, the only member of GHQ who came to see and hear things for himself was Haig. He came and saw me once – on Saturday, 23rd. We did not go at all into details of the situation, nor of the action of the Third Army.'

On the eve of the German onslaught, only three out of the eighteen British divisions in reserve were disposed behind the Fifth Army front. Six were behind the Third Army, and the rest were still farther north, where no attack came or was by then expected. Haig's justification for keeping his reserves in the north until he was absolutely certain of the German aim lay in the narrowness of the space that there intervened between the front and the Channel ports. But it is not a complete explanation of his attitude. That was influenced to some extent by his prolonged doubt of the German intentions: at a conference of his army commanders on February 16th he expressed the view that the main blow, if the Germans attacked early, would probably be made against the French. 'Indications from the British front are that no attack in strength in Flanders is possible at the moment, and that there are at present no signs of any big offensive being imminent on the rest of the British front.' A small attack on the First Army front near Lens was a 'possibility'. GHQ was certainly slow to react to the warnings furnished by air reports and by the Fifth Army. At a further conference on March 2nd the likelihood of early attack was recognized but with no greater object than that of 'cutting off the Cambrai salient and drawing in our reserves'. And even on March 8th it was stated that there were no indications of an enemy attack south of St Quentin.

Haig's sense of the key importance of the Arras bastion was justified by the event. But, in keeping the bulk of his reserves in the north, he risked the security of the already thin Fifth Army in order to have ample insurance against a less probable risk to the Channel ports. One reason was that he felt he could better afford to yield ground in front of Amiens than elsewhere. Another was a confidence, which the event unhappily refuted, that the German advance would not go far enough to become a menace to the general situation. Calculated risks are inherent in generalship; the questions that linger in the mind are whether Haig's miscalculation was avoidable and whether he did all that was possible to cover the risks that his dispositions involved. It is at least clear that he preferred to risk his junction with the French rather than his hold on the Channel ports; and that his dispositions eased the task of the enemy more than they could have expected.

If this was good luck for the Germans, their thorough and skilful preparations for the initial assault had earned them success – although here again fortune favoured them.

For the effect of the gas-gained surprise was immensely increased by nature, which in the early hours of March 21st provided a thick mist that cloaked the infiltrating assailants as much as it masked the defending machine guns. Without this aid it is questionable how far the German tactical surprise would have succeeded, and in this lay the essential inferiority of the German means of surprise, compared with that at Cambrai, and later, on August 8th, 1918, which was achieved by armoured machines.

These not only formed the main material from which the key was manufactured but provided the power to press it home and turn it. In contrast, Ludendorff had to depend on unarmoured infantry to exploit the opening created by the brief but intense bombardment with gas shell. For he had failed to grasp the significance of the tank and neglected to develop it in time; only in August, 1918, when it was used to strike him a mortal blow did he put it in the 'urgent' class of war material.

But the German plan was distinguished by a research for tactical surprise more thorough and far-reaching than in any of the earlier operations of the war. The Germans significantly record that 'Haig's dispatches dealing with the attacks of 1917 were found most valuable, because they showed how not to do it'. To Ludendorff's credit he realized that the obvious is an obstacle that superior weight cannot compensate, and, once created, can rarely overcome. And he sought to effect and develop surprise by a compound of many deceptive elements. It is to his credit also that, unlike Falkenhayn, who merely wanted officer clerks, he surrounded himself with able assistants. Captain Geyer compiled the new training handbooks, while Colonel Bruchmüller had emerged from retirement to become the famous artillery 'battle-piece' producer. With a prophetic play upon his name he was known as 'Durchbruchmüller' – Breakthrough Müller. Under his superintendence the masses of artillery were brought up close to the front line in concealment, and opened fire without previous 'registration' through the method he had introduced. The infantry were trained in new infiltrating tactics, of which the guiding idea was that the leading troops should probe and penetrate the weak points of the defence while the reserves were directed to back up success, not to redeem failure. Special reconnaissance parties were assigned simply for the task of sending back early news of progress. The ordinary lines of attacking infantry were preceded by a dispersed chain of 'storm' groups, with automatic rifles, machine guns and light mortars. These groups were to push straight through wherever they could find an opening and leave the defenders' 'strong points' to be dealt with by the succeeding lines. The fastest, not the slowest, must set the pace, and no effort was made to keep a uniform alignment. Further 'the inclination of leaders to assemble their troops and get them in hand after a certain objective has been reached must be suppressed'. 'If the troops know the instructions of the commanders they can go on of themselves.' The assaulting divisions were brought up overnight, those of the second line to a position only about a mile behind the first, and the third only ten miles back. All reserves started moving forward at zero, so as to be at hand when wanted. And when a second-line division was so used it came under the control, not of a higher commander sitting in rear, but of the first-line division commander, who had his finger on the pulse of the battle.

On November 11th at Mons – prophetic date and place – the German 'leaders' had met in conclave to decide on the date and place of the forthcoming offensive. Naturally, according to German custom, the issue was thrashed out, not between the nominal commanders, but between their chiefs of staff – Ludendorff, Kuhl (Crown Prince Rupprecht's), Schulenberg (German Crown Prince's), together with Ludendorff's own strategical adviser, Major Wetzell. Kuhl and Schulenberg each wanted the attack to be made on the front of their own army groups – Kuhl indicating Flanders and Schulenberg the Verdun sector. Wetzell was inclined to support Schulenberg, arguing that an attack on the flanks of Verdun, a salient, would forestall any future Franco-American offensive at that delicate point, and, after defeating the French, the whole German strength could be turned against the British. Ludendorff, however, rejected this scheme on the score that the ground was unfavourable, that a breakthrough at Verdun would lead nowhere decisive, and that the French army had recuperated too well after nearly a year's undisturbed convalescence. He laid down as a first principle that 'the British must be defeated', and thought that the drain of Passchendaele would make them an easy prey. But he disagreed with Kuhl's proposal to strike, between Ypres and Lens, towards Hazebrouck as it would meet the main mass of the British, and this low ground would be long in drying. He favoured instead an attack around

St Quentin, although Wetzell contended that it would be slowed down in crossing the old devastated area on the Somme, and was within easy reach of French reinforcements. A final decision was put off and Rupprecht noted in his diary 'Ludendorff underestimates the toughness of the British'.

In December, Wetzell tried to reconcile, and sagely combine, the two projects, by dividing the offensive into two acts – first, a wide-front attack on both sides of St Quentin, and, second, a fortnight later, a breakthrough in Flanders towards Hazebrouck. The first act was only to be carried far enough to draw the British reserves southward. Wetzell summed up:

> We shall not, in my opinion, succeed in obtaining our object by *one* great attack at *one* place, however carefully it is prepared ... we can only shatter their front by a clever combination of successive, definitely related, mutually reacting attacks on different parts of the front, finally in the direction of Hazebrouck.

It was to be left to Foch to adopt his method without acknowledgement. For, after further conferences, Ludendorff decided on January 27th in favour of the St Quentin attack (known by the code name 'Michael') and against the Hazebrouck attack 'St George' which was only kept in mind and not in immediate readiness.

A further complication arose. The front from the Belgian coast to St Quentin was under Rupprecht, and for political as well as personal reasons it was considered necessary to give the German Crown Prince a chance of redeeming the credit he had lost in the struggle at Verdun in 1916. Hence he was given a share in the offensive by employing the Eighteenth Army (Hutier), which belonged to his army group, on the southern flank of the main offensive. It is a moot question whether he could not have helped better, if less gloriously, by using it for a diversion at Verdun, in order to draw the French reserves away from, instead of towards, the intended breach in the British front.

In a broad sense, Ludendorff's chosen sector, which extended from Arras to La Fère, fulfilled his new principle of taking the line of least resistance, for it was the weakest in defences, defenders, and reserves. Moreover, it was close to the joint between the French and British armies, and so lent itself to a separation. But although it was true, as a generalization, that this sector was comparatively weak, the classification was loose and inaccurate. The northerly third of it was strong and strongly held, by Byng's Third Army, with fourteen divisions (six in reserve), while the bulk of the British reserves were on this flank, which also could and did receive support more quickly from the other British armies which lay to the north. The remaining two-thirds of the sector upon which the German blow fell was held by Gough's Fifth Army. The central part facing Marwitz's army was held by seven divisions (two in reserve). The southern part facing Hutier's army was also held by seven divisions (one in reserve).

But Ludendorff gave Below's army near Arras nineteen divisions for the initial attack, by its left wing only, on a nine and a half miles' frontage. South of it came Marwitz's army. As the British salient towards Cambrai was not to be attacked directly, but pinched out, this four-mile stretch was adequately occupied by two German divisions, and Marwitz had eighteen divisions for his nine-and-a-half-mile attack frontage. On the extreme south, either side of St Quentin, came Hutier's army. Ludendorff gave it only twenty-four divisions to attack on a twenty-mile frontage. Hence we see that it had only half the proportionate strength of the other armies. Despite his principle, he was distributing his strength according to the enemy's strength and not concentrating against the weakest resistance. The direction given in his orders emphasized this still more. The main effort was to be exerted north of the Somme for, after breaking through, Below and Marwitz were to wheel north-west, rolling up the British front, while the river and Hutier formed a screen to cover their flank. Hutier's army was merely an offensive flank guard. This plan was to be radically changed in execution, and to have the appearance of following the line of least resistance, because Ludendorff gained rapid success where he desired it little and failed to gain success where he wanted it most.

What of the British meantime? As the result of a war game played at Versailles Sir Henry Wilson had forecasted that the enemy attack would come on the Cambrai–Lens sector, but that the Germans would wait to deliver it until about July 1st, when their training and accumulation of forces would be complete. Wilson was somewhat outside the mark in place and still more out in time. Haig's intelligence was more accurate, although it did not foresee the full southward extension of the attack. As the time drew near signs multiplied sufficiently to enable Haig to calculate the date. On March 18th German prisoners captured near St Quentin gave the date as the 21st, and on the evening of the 20th Maxse's XVIII Corps was able through raiding to establish the certainty of the morrow's attack.

Thus it is true to say that no strategic surprise was obtained. Nor was it even obtainable under the conditions of 1918 in France. But with the opposing armies spread out in contact along the far-flung line of entrenchments, a quick breakthrough followed by a rapid exploitation along the line of least resistance might promise such a decisive upset as normally is only attainable by choosing the line of least expectation. The hurricane bombardment opened at 4.30 AM on the 21st, concentrating for two hours on the British artillery and then, reinforced by mortars, turning on the trenches. Almost all telephone cables were severed and wireless sets destroyed, while the fog made visual signalling impossible. Thus the troops were made dumb and the commanders blind. At 9.40 AM, or in some parts earlier, the German infantry advanced under cover of a creeping barrage, supplemented by low-flying aircraft.

The British outpost zone was overrun almost everywhere by midday, but this was inevitable and had been foreseen. But the northern attack met such stubborn resistance against the right of Byng's army that it had not seriously penetrated the main battle zone even by the night of the 22nd, and, despite putting in successive reinforcements, the capture of Vaulx-Vraucourt was then the high-water mark of its progress. On most parts of Gough's army front the battle-zone resistance was just as firm, but the flood found a way through on the 21st near La Fère, on the extreme right, at Essigny and at Ronssoy. The resistance of the 21st Division at Epéhy for a time checked this last breach from spreading northward, but it began to crumble so deeply that the neighbouring sectors were affected. Southward, again near St Quentin, the line sagged still more deeply, and on the night of the 22nd Gough was driven to order a general retirement to the line of the Somme. He was hurried into this precipitate decision by a mistaken report that the enemy was already across the Crozat Canal at Jussy and so behind his right flank. Early next morning the Péronne bridgehead was abandoned. Several of Gough's subordinate commanders were even more vague or misled as to the situation, control lapsed, and gaps occurred. The worst was at the joint between Byng's and Gough's armies and this the Germans speedily accentuated. And a new danger arose farther south at the joint between the British and French.

But Ludendorff, continuing to ignore his new principle, was only intent to nourish the attack near Arras, where progress was disappointing. Meantime Hutier, once across the Crozat Canal, was pressing swiftly forward, almost without check save from his own limited role. On the 23rd Ludendorff again emphasizes in his orders that Below's is the principal effort, reinforces it by three divisions, and indicates that the Sixth and Fourth Armies, still more to the north, will chime in to help it. Two days later, when the check to Below has become still clearer, Ludendorff arranges that Below's hitherto passive right wing shall strike direct at Arras on the 28th, in order to overcome this strong place which is hampering and enfilading Below's attacking left wing. And on the 29th the Sixth Army, reinforced by six or seven divisions, is to extend the attack northwards between Arras and Lens – with Boulogne as its goal! Meanwhile Hutier is actually told not to pass the line Noyon–Roye for the time being.

On the 26th Ludendorff begins to doubt Below's chances and to turn his eyes south. But, instead of throwing his weight thither, he merely makes it a second principal effort. And, even so, it is to be towards Amiens by Marwitz's army, while Hutier is told not to cross the Avre without fresh orders. This means that the army which has all the difficult ground of the old 1916 Somme battlefields to cross is pushed on while the army that has a smoother path is held back. The apparent explanation, and the extraordinary flux of Ludendorff's thought, is revealed in a later sentence of the order which shows that he is contemplating a vast fanlike movement in which three armies are to wheel south towards Paris while Below and his neighbours wheel north to crush the British against the sea coast. The grandiose conception was far beyond Ludendorff's resources in reserves. It would seem that for the moment he was intoxicated with success, and, like Moltke in August, 1914, was counting his chickens before they were hatched. Another parallel with 1914 was that the army commanders' reports of progress outstripped their actual stages of advance. Even they, however, were less futuristic than the Kaiser who, according to Rupprecht, 'announced a complete victory' on March 21st.

On the 27th Hutier reached Montdidier, a penetration of nearly forty miles, but next day Ludendorff had a cold douche of reality when Below's Arras attack with nine divisions collapsed under a storm of fire from the expectant defence. No mist came to the aid of the attackers.

Ludendorff then put a belated stop to Below's vain efforts, and countermanded the Sixth Army's attack intended for the morrow. Amiens was made the main objective, and Marwitz was given all the reserves at hand – nine divisions. But Hutier had to pause for two days until four fresh divisions reached him. By this time the surge towards Amiens was almost stagnant, its impetus having slackened far less because of the resistance than because of the exhaustion of the troops and the difficulties of supply. Roads were blocked, transport scuppered, and reserves harassed by the British air attacks, which here played a vital part. When the attack was renewed on March 30th it had little force and made little progress in face of a resistance that had been afforded time to harden, helped by the cement of French reserves which were now being poured into the sagging wall. That day was the first on which their artillery, arriving later than the infantry, had come into action in force. Even so, there was a moment of crisis when the Germans captured the Moreuil Wood ridge, which was not only at the joint between the French and British but commanded the crossings of the Avre and Luce where they joined. And these covered the main Amiens–Paris railway. But the menace was warded off by a swift counterstroke of the Canadian Cavalry Brigade, made on the initiative of and led by General Seely, ex-War Minister turned Murat. The ridge was regained, and although lost again next day, by other troops, the coup seems to have extinguished the now flickering flame of German energy. Nearly a week passed before, on April 4th, a further German effort was made by fifteen divisions, of which only four were fresh. Meeting a reinforced defence, this had still less success.

Seeing that his new effort was too late, Ludendorff then suspended the attack towards Amiens. At no time had he thrown his weight along the line of fracture between the British and French armies. Yet on March 24th Pétain had intimated to Haig that if the Germans' progress continued along this line he would have to draw back the French reserves south-westwards to cover Paris. How little more German pressure would have been needed to turn the crack into a yawning chasm! The knowledge is one more testimony to the historical truth that a joint is the most sensitive and profitable point of attack.

The supreme features of this great offensive are, first, the immensity of its outward results compared with those of any previous offensive in the west; second, its ineffectiveness to attain decisive results. For the first it would be both unjust and untrue to blame the British troops. They achieved miracles of heroic endurance, and the prolonged resistance in most of the battle zone is the proof. The main cause of the subsequently rapid flow-back lay in the frequent breakdown of control and communication. During three years of trench warfare an elaborate and complex system, largely dependent on the telephone, had been built up, and when the static suddenly became fluid the British paid the inevitable penalty of violating that fundamental axiom of war – elasticity.

On the German side, Arras was the actual rock on which their plan broke. It is probable that military conservatism cost them dear. For Bruchmüller has revealed that while Hutier's army carried out his surprise bombardment designs, Below's in the north clung to their old-fashioned methods, refusing to dispense with preliminary ranging. Once again, and near the Somme again, Below's conventional military mind had proved the best asset to the British army.

But a more fundamental cause of the German failure was Ludendorff's own limitations. He had sufficient receptiveness to see a new truth but not sufficient elasticity or conviction to carry it out fully in practice. The principle of following the line of least resistance was too novel for one who from his youth had been saturated in the Clausewitzian doctrine of striking at the enemy's main force. 'The British must be defeated' was his catchword, his vision was bloodshot, and he could not realize that in strategy the longest way round is often the shortest way there – that a direct approach to the object exhausts the attacker and hardens the resistance by compression, whereas an indirect approach loosens the defender's hold by upsetting his balance.

In the actual execution of the offensive by the German troops there is another cause of failure that has been commonly overlooked and yet is of great significance. It is the physical effect on ill-nourished troops of breaking into an area full of well-filled supply depots, and the psychological effect of discovering that the enemy is so much better fed and equipped than themselves – that they have been nourished only with lies, about the result of the U-boat campaign and the enemy's economic condition. This dual effect is to be traced in many sources of evidence. One of the most illuminating and trustworthy is the war diary of the German poet and novelist, Rudolf Binding.

On March 27th he records:

Now we are already in the English back areas ... a land flowing with milk and honey. Marvellous people these, who will only equip themselves with the very best that the earth produces. Our men are hardly to be distinguished from English soldiers. Everyone wears at least a leather jerkin, a waterproof ... English boots or some other beautiful thing. The horses are feeding on masses of oats and gorgeous food-cake ... and there is no doubt the army is looting with some zest.

On the next day follows a highly significant entry:

Today the advance of our infantry suddenly stopped near Albert. Nobody could understand why. Our armies had reported no enemy between Albert and Amiens ... Our way seemed entirely clear. I jumped into a car with orders to find out what was causing the stoppage in front. Our division was right in front of the advance and could not possibly be tired out. It was quite fresh ...

As soon as I got near the town I began to see curious sights. Strange figures, which looked very little like soldiers, and certainly showed no sign of advancing, were making their way back out of the town. There were men driving cows ... others who carried a hen under one arm and a box of notepaper under the other. Men carrying a bottle of wine under their arm and another one open in their hand ... Men staggering. Men who could hardly walk. When I got into the town the streets were running with wine ...

I drove back to Divisional Headquarters with a fearful impression of the situation. The advance was held up, and there was no means of setting it going again for hours.

It proved hopeless, and the officers were powerless, to collect the troops that day, while the sequel he records was that 'the troops which moved out of Albert next day cheered with wine and in victorious spirits were mown down straight away on the railway embankment by a few English machine guns'.

But the intoxication due to loot was even greater and more general than that due to wine, and the fundamental cause of both was 'the general sense of years of privation'. A staff officer even stops a car, when on an urgent mission, to pick up an English waterproof from the ditch. And in this intoxication the Germans not only lose their chance of reaching Amiens, but ruin sources of supply invaluable to the maintenance of their own advance – wrecking waterworks for the sake of the brass taps. The cause of this senseless craving is revealed in their impression that 'the English made everything either out of rubber or brass, because these were the two materials which we had not seen for the longest time'. 'The madness, stupidity and indiscipline of the German troops is shown in other things as well. Any useless toy or trifle they seize and load onto their packs, anything useful which they cannot carry away they destroy.'

Once this plunder was exhausted the reaction was all the greater and the contrast of their own paucity with the enemy's plenty the more depressing. As hopes of military success fade, and with them the hope of again nourishing their stomachs, and souls, on the enemy's supplies, a moral rot sets in rapidly.

Anyone with personal experience of war knows how the thought of food and of civilized comfort fills the soldier's horizon. How far was the German army's sudden moral decline from July onward, when the last attack proved abortive, due not only to increasing hunger but to the eye-opening conviction of the enemy's greater material power of endurance?

Propaganda and censorship could hide the difference so long as the front was an inviolable wall of partition. But when the Germans broke through the British lines and into the back areas the truth was revealed to the German troops. Is the historical verdict, penetrating beneath the surface of military statistics and acreage to the psychological foundation, then to be that the British disaster of March, 1918, was a stroke of fortune for those who suffered it? If so, it seems a pity that the solution was not tried earlier. Instead of conducting unwilling 'frocks' round the front, the British Command might have arranged visits for Germans to its back areas – that 'land flowing with milk and honey'. Or at least it might have designedly released a proportion of its prisoners after they had been suitably entertained! Such a strategy would certainly have supplied the imagination which many found so lacking in the military leadership.

CHAPTER EIGHT

SCENE 2

The Breakthrough in Flanders

On April 9th, 1918, the first anniversary of the abortive British attempt to break through the deadlocked trench front in Artois, the Germans made a more successful attempt – in the reverse direction. This was the second move in Ludendorff's gigantic offensive campaign which had begun on March 21st. Springing from around Neuve Chapelle, where, three years before, the first British attempt to break the deadlock had penetrated half a mile deep in all, a narrow German jet of attack swept away the opposing Portuguese and before noon on the 9th had penetrated to a depth of over three miles. To the north, but happily not to the south, the flanks of the breach crumbled, and with fresh jets playing upon the British front more sectors gave way.

By the next day twenty-four miles of frontage had been engulfed and, on the 12th, Sir Douglas Haig issued his historic order of the day: 'There is no other course open to us but to fight it out. Every position must be held to the last man ... With our backs to the wall and believing in the justice of our cause, each one of us must fight on to the end.' To the British public, and even perhaps to the British forces, this message came like a thunderclap, awakening them to the graveness of the danger and seeming almost to convey a warning that hope had gone and only honour remained – to go down fighting with their faces to the foe.

Yet at that moment, and still more during the following days, it is probable that the least sanguine and most depressed man was not in the British ranks, but behind the advancing enemy – Ludendorff himself. On March 21st and the next days Ludendorff had seen his carefully contrived strategical plan – for his great bid for victory – going astray. The rapidity with which progress was made where he did not want it, and its slowness where he did want it, had driven him unwillingly to press on towards Amiens across the desert of the old Somme battle-

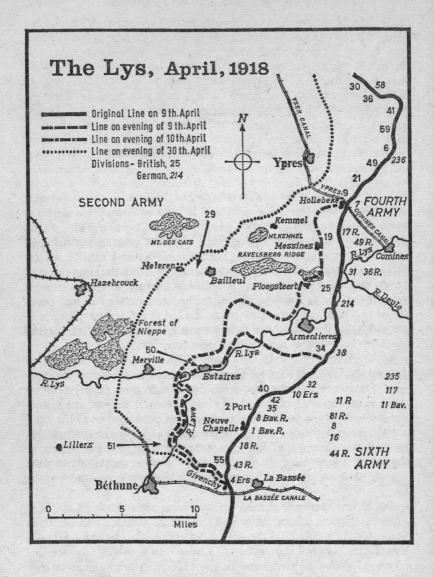

The Lys, April, 1918

————————	Original Line on 9th. April
————————	Line on evening of 9th. April
————————	Line on evening of 10th. April
••••••••••••	Line on evening of 30th. April

Divisions – British, 25
German, 214

N

SECOND ARMY

Ypres

YSER CANAL

30 58
36
41
59
6
49 236
21
YPRES-9
Hollebeke 7 FOURTH ARMY
17 R. COMINES CANAL
29 Kemmel
MT. KEMMEL 19 49 R.
Messines R. Lys
RAVELSBERG RIDGE 31 36 R. Comines
Meteren Bailleul Ploegsteert 25 R. Deule
MT. DES CATS 214

Hazebrouck Forest of Nieppe Armentieres 34 38
50 Merville R. Lys 235
R. Lys Estaires 40 32 117
2 Port. 42 10 Ers 11 R 11 Bav.
35
Neuve Chapelle 8 Bav. R. 81 R.
R. Lawe 1 Bav. R. 8
Lillers 51 18 R. 16
55 43 R. 44 R. SIXTH ARMY
Béthune Givenchy 4 Ers La Bassée
LA BASSÉE CANALE

0   5   10
Miles

fields, instead of wheeling northwards from the Somme. With the re-pulse of his delayed assault on the Arras bastion on March 28th he had been forced to relinquish definitely his plan of rolling up the flank of the British armies and penning them back against the coast, isolated from their Allies.

But his thrust towards Amiens failed, however narrowly, to reach its destination – through its belatedness and difficulties of supply. In desperation, rather than in reflection, Ludendorff clutched at Wet-zell's rejected scheme, and decided to launch the 'St George' attack against the Ypres–Lens sector. But he had pressed 'Michael' too long and too far. Not only was he short of reserves, but he had to accumulate fresh supplies and ammunition, and switch his heavy artillery north-wards. Conferences on April 1st and 2nd showed that the offensive could not be ready until the 9th; and, instead of thirty-five additional divisions, only eleven could be sent in time. With a sense of ironic humour the attack was rechristened 'Georgette'. Ludendorff was in luck at the start, but it was an elusive and delusive form of luck. The luck was that his opening blow fell on the front of the 2nd Portuguese Divi-sion, which was just about to be relieved by two British divisions, and had in the meanwhile been stretched to hold the whole corps sector.

The less agreeable aspect – for Ludendorff – of this piece of luck was somewhat unkindly epitomized in the comment that the Portuguese ruined Ludendorff and saved their Allies by running away. For although the extension and development of this attack was 'according to plan', Ludendorff never seems to have been wholehearted in pursuing it. From the point of view of his strategy, and its interests, he either pressed the attack too hard or did not press enough.

The clearest evidence of this irresolution – and depression – is to be found in the captured archives of the Fourth German Army, which attacked in this sector. And their evidence is a better guide than any carefully prepared post-war apologia. They have the further advantage that they fell into enemy hands before any judicious adulterations could be made in the interests of high commanders' reputations. These Ger-man records show the General Staff officers, Lossberg for the Fourth Army, Kuhl for the Army Group, and Ludendorff at the Supreme Command, settling all affairs without even the pretence of consulting their respective superiors, Sixt von Arnim, Rupprecht and Hindenburg. They also show Ludendorff doling out divisions with a parsimonious hand, usually too late and inadequate in number for real success; so apprehensive that his new bulge would become another sack that at the moment of supreme opportunity he stops the German advance for fear of a counter-attack.

But all this was hidden from the British commanders and men. They only knew the enemy's blows, not his doubts and disquietude. And if he felt himself in a sack, they felt themselves in a mincing machine – with an unpleasant likelihood of their minced remains being ejected into the sea. That is the sort of wall that an army does not relish having at its back. Whereas on the Somme there had at least been ample room to withdraw, in the north the British troops, bases, and communications were all crowded into and passed through a narrow 'throat' of land sensitive to the least pressure and all too easy to strangle. Apart from the coast railway, the only lateral line of communication ran through St Pol–Lillers–Hazebrouck, barely fifteen miles behind the front trenches. Thus it was that a ten-mile German penetration, reached on April 12th and, happily, never deepened appreciably, was as menacing, if not more so, than forty miles had been on the Somme.

The strain was all the more severe because it fell on troops already strained. Besides the Portuguese, all except one – the 55th – of the six British divisions between the La Bassée and the Ypres–Comines Canals were battle-worn, having come to this front on relief from the battle in the south. Strained, they were also stretched. The drain on Haig's reserves and the greater importance of the vital bastion of high ground, Arras Givenchy, had caused a distribution of strength by which this handful of divisions had to hold a front of twenty-four miles. Worst of all, the greatest stretching of all fell on those who could least bear it. The Portuguese Corps had been holding a six-mile front, on both sides of Neuve Chapelle. It had been in the line for a long time, and increasing cases of insubordination had been a warning of declining morale. General Horne, the First Army commander, reshuffling his dispositions, withdrew the 1st Portuguese Division from the line on April 5th. The 2nd also was to be relieved by British divisions on the night of April 9th, but meanwhile it was given the whole corps sector to hold, although one brigade of the 1st Portuguese was left in reserve near Lestrem, five miles behind the line. The 51st Division had been on the scene for several days and might have been used; indeed, its commander had proposed that he should take over the second line, a strongly concreted position easy to hold. But his request had not been granted. Yet Horne had been warned by his 'Q' staff that the convergence of German railways made the Lys sector the most probable point of attack; indeed, the only point where an attack could be mounted. They had, further, sought permission to prepare special supply dumps fifteen miles in rear to meet the danger of a breakthrough here, but had been rebuffed. Happily, they began preparations – without his knowledge. And the existence of these dumps helped to ease the emergency that followed.

If the state of the local preparations was Horne's responsibility, it is right to point out that he saw eye to eye with Haig in failing to read the writing on the wall-map. Rarely, if ever was this so clear: or surprise less warranted by the signs. For the Germans sacrificed concealment to speed in developing their new offensive. From March 31st onwards the British aircraft reported a general northward movement of the German reserves and artillery, by road and rail. On April 1st, as the Official Air History has revealed, one observer alone in a couple of hours 'counted fifty-five trains on the move along the lines feeding the La Bassée–Armentières front ... The air reports of the next few days, supplemented by air photographs, made it clear that the German concentration was of the most formidable kind'. The reason that GHQ failed to profit by the warning lay in its belief that the enemy would adhere to his original plan, and that the next step in furtherance of his Somme offensive would be a renewal of his attempt to break down the Arras bastion. It would seem that Haig credited Ludendorff with a persistency similar to his own at Passchendaele. Convinced that Ludendorff's correct course was to gain the key position of the Vimy ridge, even though it was the strongest part of his own front, Haig held fast to the idea that Ludendorff, despite his hard lesson on March 28th, was bound to try again.

As late as April 7th, in an appreciation of the situation, GHQ pinned its expectations to 'a converging attack on the Vimy ridge'. Yet, to quote the Air History again: 'There was nothing in the air reports and air photographs up to the 9th of April to support the view, held by General Headquarters, that a converging attack on the Vimy ridge was likely. On the contrary the air information showed that the German troops opposite Arras were being drawn upon to supply reinforcements for the north and should have left little doubt that the immediate enemy concentration was northwards from the La Bassée Canal.'

The air information has also a bearing on Horne's delayed action over the relief of the Portuguese. 'That the relief might come too late was indicated from the air. Throughout the morning of the 7th air observers reported the main roads immediately opposite the Portuguese to be full of moving transport, and ground observers told of men carrying ammunition into the German support lines. The impression conveyed by the combined air and ground reports was that the tactical concentration was nearing completion.' It did not, however, impress the men at the top – or they were slow in reaction.

For at 4.5 AM on the 9th an intense bombardment was opened on the eleven-mile front between the La Bassée Canal and Armentières; the flanks of this sector were deluged with mustard gas – an indication that they were to be paralysed but not immediately attacked. At 7.30 AM, after a slackening in the fire, small groups of German infantry began to move forward, and about 8.45 AM, after the bombardment had swelled again for an hour, the assault was launched by a mass of nine divisions of the German Sixth Army – against three. Once more, as on March 21st, nature afforded it a cloak in the form of a thick mist. At the southern extremity the 55th (a Lancashire Territorial division) held on to Givenchy firmly, opposing so unshakable a resistance as not only to break the attack, but to dissuade the German command from subsequent attempts to extend it southwards.

But in the centre the Germans swiftly overran the Portuguese positions. The Portuguese were temporarily holding a front more than double that of the 55th on their flank; although their strength per yard was not much less, comparison of quality made such a distribution risky – and the risk had matured. But the sturdy resistance of King Edward's Horse and the 11th Cyclist Battalion checked the German onrush, and helped, with that of the reserve brigade of the 55th Division, to prevent the Germans crumbling away the southern flank. This resistance, indeed, tended to shepherd the German advance into the north-westerly direction, which it took more and more.

But on the northern flank of the breakthrough, the 40th Division, its own flank laid bare, was partly overwhelmed by the combined pressure. The 51st and 50th Divisions, coming up to dam the breach, were delayed on roads encumbered with Portuguese and shattered vehicles, and, caught by the tide of battle before they reached their positions, could not prevent the Germans, now reinforced by seven divisions, attaining, and even crossing the line of the Lys and Lawe rivers. But next day their resistance so far stemmed the German tide that little more ground was lost except on the north of the original bulge.

That morning, however, the German attack had been extended northwards to the Ypres–Comines Canal, against the southern sector of the British Second Army (Plumer). It was akin to a left-fist followed by a right-fist punch, although this new punch was much lighter – by only four divisions of the German Fourth Army. This lightness was counterbalanced by the enforced diversion of part of the three British defending divisions to the breach made the previous day. The Germans broke through, and between the punches Armentières itself was pinched out, the 34th Division barely escaping from the bag. That night the breach was thirty miles in width, and by the 12th its depth was doubled.

This was the crisis. Less than five miles separated the Germans from Hazebrouck junction. On the 13th British and Australian reserves began to arrive from the south, and the German pressure to show signs of slackening – one self-confessed reason being their 'difficulties of supply under the increasing attacks from the air'. The approach to Hazebrouck, barred just in time by the 4th Guards Brigade, was now finally bolted by the 1st Australian Division, and the remaining German pressure was exerted almost entirely on the northern half of the breach.

Plumer now took over charge of all except the southern fringe of the battle area and, to shorten his line as well as to forestall a fresh extension of the German attack, he began an unhurried withdrawal from the Ypres salient to a line just in front of the immortal town. This was a wise and clear-sighted move, even though it abandoned the few square miles of mud which had been purchased at so terrible a price the previous autumn.

Although the enemy gained Bailleul and the Ravelsberg ridge on the 15th, he was then stopped at Meteren and in front of Kemmel Hill, and by the 18th the storm subsided. Meantime storms of another type had been raging behind the front. Foch's appointment as generalissimo did not seem to Haig to have brought him the prompt support he had expected. Ever since the 10th, and, indeed, before, he had been pressing Foch for French aid and active share in the battle. On the 14th an acrimonious conference took place at Abbeville, and next day Haig made the stricture 'that the arrangements made by the generalissimo were insufficient to meet the military situation'.

Foch, on the other hand, was, perhaps to the point of hazard, intent on husbanding his reserves for an offensive. In his opinion, on April 14th, 'la bataille du nord est finie' – where to many observers it looked rather as if the British Army was 'finie'. As usual he illustrated his opinion by a parable – of the rings made by dropping a stone into water, the successive rings growing less marked until the water became still. To hard-pressed Allies these parables were apt to be irritating. But his prediction proved right, even though, as at Ypres in 1914 and 1915, the British troops suffered a terrible strain in proving him right.

Contrary to what has been alleged, five French divisions arrived behind the British front as early as the 14th. But their intended counter-attacks, as at Ypres in 1915, did not at first materialize. Let it be said, however, in justice and as a matter of tactical interest, that British counter-attacks throughout this battle achieved consistently little gain, at heavy loss. On the 18th a French division took over Kemmel Hill, and next day the remainder entered the line. On the 25th the Germans resumed their offensive, but only on a limited front. The famous Kemmel Hill was captured from the French, and the British to the north were also forced back. For a few hours a last opportunity was vouchsafed to the Germans, but through Ludendorff's intervention they refrained from exploiting it. After a final, costly and more abortive assault on the 29th, the German offensive was abandoned.

As General Edmonds, the official historian, has penetratingly remarked, 'It is easy to see why Ludendorff collapsed after the 8th of August, 1918 - on the 29th of April he was already well on the way to despair.'

CHAPTER EIGHT

SCENE 3

The Breakthrough to the Marne

Four battle-worn British divisions were 'resting' in a quiet sector north of the Aisne, between Reims and Soissons, far detached from the rest of the army. They had been sent to the French front, after strenuous exertions in the battles of the Lys, in return for French reinforcements which had gone north to aid the British in the later stages of that 'backs to the wall' struggle. On the tranquil Aisne they could recuperate while still serving a useful purpose as guardians of the trench line.

It was too quiet to be true. But the uneasiness of the local British commanders – shared by certain of their French neighbours – was lightly discounted by their French superiors. On May 25th they received from French headquarters the message that 'in our opinion there are no indications that the enemy has made preparations which would enable him to attack tomorrow'. Next morning the French captured two prisoners who told of the impending attack, but the higher command had no plan to meet it, and, even so, did not warn the troops until late in the day. Too late!

For at 1 AM on May 27th, 1918, a terrific storm of fire burst on the Franco-British front between Reims and north of Soissons, along the famous Chemin-des-Dames; at 4.30 AM an overwhelming torrent of Germans swept over the front trenches; by midday it was pouring over the many unblown bridges of the Aisne, and by May 30th it had reached the Marne – site and symbol of the great ebb of 1914. After nearly four years a menace deemed for ever past had returned to a point that endowed it with demoralizing symbolism.

Happily, it proved to be 'thus far and no farther'. Like the two great preceding offensives of March 21st and April 9th, that of May 27th achieved astonishing captures of ground and prisoners, but it brought the Germans little nearer to their strategical object. And, even more than its predecessors, its very success paved the way for their downfall.

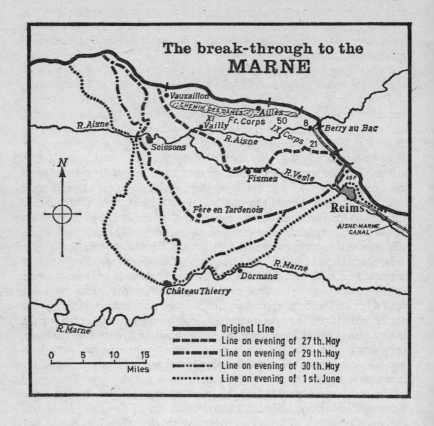

The break-through to the
MARNE

Vauxaillon
CHEMIN DES DAMES — Ailles
XI — Fr. Corps — 50 — 8
Vailly — IX Corps — 21 — Berry au Bac
R. Aisne
R. Aisne
Soissons
R. Vesle
Fismes — 45 F
Fère en Tardenois — Reims
AISNE-MARNE CANAL
R. Marne
Dormans
Château Thierry
R. Marne

N

	Original Line
	Line on evening of 27th. May
	Line on evening of 29th. May
	Line on evening of 30th. May
	Line on evening of 1st. June

0   5   10   15
Miles

To the reasons for this we shall come. But why, a month after the last onslaught, in the north, had come to an end; why, when there had been this long interval for preparation and for examination of the situation by a new unified command, should a surprise greater than any before have been possible? This is perhaps the most interesting historical question of the battle.

It has long been known, of course, that the French higher command, the one directly concerned with the safety of the Aisne sector, did not believe in the likelihood of an attack. Nor did the British higher command, which, however, was concerned with the front in the north, and expected a further onslaught there. If not justified by the event, the British had some cause for expecting it, as German disclosures have since attested.

But the Intelligence Service of another of the Allies, better placed to take a wide survey, did give the warning – only to be disregarded until too late. On May 13th, a fortnight after the fighting in Flanders had died away, the British Intelligence came to the conclusion that 'an attack on a broad front between Arras and Albert is intended'. Next day this was discussed at a conference of the Intelligence section of the American Expeditionary Force, and the head of the Battle-Order section, Major S. T. Hubbard, gave a contrary opinion, holding that the next attack would be against the Chemin-des-Dames sector, between May 25th and 30th. Among the reasons given were that, as surprise was the keynote of the German method, this sector was one of the few where it was now possible; that it was all the more likely to be chosen because regarded by the Allies as secure and as a resting ground for tired divisions; that its feasible frontage corresponded well with the limited German resources available at the moment, and that this hypothesis was confirmed by the ascertained location of the German troops, particularly of certain picked divisions.

The warning in detail was conveyed to the French General Headquarters, but fell on deaf ears. Why should credence be given to an opinion coming from such an amateur army, not yet tested in battle, over the verdict of war-tried and highly developed intelligence services? The warning was reiterated, however, and Colonel de Cointet, Chief of the French Intelligence, was won over to its acceptance. But now, as at Verdun two years before, the Operations branch opposed until too late the view of its own Intelligence. This time, however, it was less blameworthy, for it was tugged the other way by the comforting assurances of General Duchêne, commander of the Sixth French Army, in charge of the Chemin-des-Dames sector.

This General, indeed, bears a still heavier responsibility, for he insisted on the adoption of the long-exploded and wasteful system of massing the infantry of the defence in the forward positions. Besides giving the enemy guns a crowded and helpless target, this method ensured that once the German guns had made a bloated meal of this luckless cannon-fodder, the German infantry would find practically no local reserves to oppose their progress through the rear zones. In similar manner all the headquarters, communication centres, ammunition depots, and railheads were pushed close up, ready to be dislocated promptly by the enemy bombardment.

Pétain's instructions for a deep and elastic system of defence had evidently made no impression on General Duchêne, so that it was still less a matter for wonder that the protests of junior British commanders met with a rebuff - and the conclusive '*J'ai dit.*' It was unfortunate also, if perhaps less avoidable, that when the four British divisions forming the IX Corps (Hamilton-Gordon) arrived from the north at the end of April, their depleted ranks filled up with raw drafts from home, they were hurried straight into the line, as the best place to complete their training.

The central backbone of the Aisne defences was formed by the historic Chemin-des-Dames ridge north of the river. The eastern half of this 'hog's back' was to be held by the British, with the 50th Division (H. C. Jackson) on the left, next the 8th Division (Heneker), and beyond the end of the ridge, in the low ground from Berry-au-Bac along the Aisne and Marne canal, the 21st Division (D. G. M. Campbell), joining up with the French troops covering Reims. The infantry of the 25th Division (Bainbridge) was in reserve.

Altogether the French Sixth Army front was held by three French and three British divisions, with four and one respectively in reserve. Against these tired or raw troops, in the main attack from Berry-au-Bac westwards, fifteen German divisions, all but one brought up fresh, were to fall upon five, with two more for the subsidiary attack between Berry-au-Bac and Reims, while seven German divisions lay close up in support.

Even so, the Germans' superiority of numbers was not so pronounced as in the March and April offensives, whereas both the rapidity and the extent of their progress were greater. Once again the tactical surprise of the assault was aided by a thick ground mist, which wrapped the Germans' initial advance in a cloak of invisibility. But they had a series of extraordinarily difficult obstacles to cross - first, the Ailette stream in no-man's-land itself. The conclusion is, therefore, that the advantage was due in part to the strategic surprise – the greater unexpectedness of the time and place – and in part to the folly of exposing the defenders so completely to the demoralizing and paralysing effect of the German bombardment – by 3,719 guns on a front of thirty-eight miles. This last, indeed, was a form of surprise, for the object of all surprise is the dislocation of the enemy's morale and mind, and the effect is the same whether the enemy be caught napping by deception or allows himself to be trapped with his eyes open. Further, the German's success on May 27th, 1918, deserves study and comparison with their other offensives, whose success was almost in mathematical ratio to their degree of surprise. This final year, indeed, read in the light of previous years, affords fresh proof that surprise – or, more scientifically, the dislocation of the enemy's mental balance – is essential to true success in every operation of war. A lesson oft repeated, oft ignored. At the bar of history any commander who risks the lives of his men without seeking this preliminary guarantee is condemned.

Let us pass to the events of May 27th. For three and a half hours the unfortunate troops had to endure a bombardment unparalleled, according to the verdict of the more experienced sufferers, in its intensity. And the ordeal of those hours of helpless endurance, amid the ever-swelling litter of shattered dead and untended wounded, was made more trying by crouching, semi-suffocated in gas masks. Then the grey waves advanced – a relief, if only of action, at last. Three-quarters of an hour later they had reached the crest of the ridge in the centre, near Ailles. This uncovered the flank of the left British division, the 50th, forcing its survivors to fall back down the other slope. Next to it the 8th Division was being forced to give way, although two of its brigades held stubbornly for a time on the north bank of the Aisne.

Here the 2nd Devons earned imperishable glory and a citation in the French Orders of the Day – by sacrificing themselves almost to a man in a stand which gained breathing space for fresh resistance to take form in rear. On the British right, the attack on the 21st Division developed later; this division was awkwardly placed with the swampy Aisne and Marne canal running through the centre of its battle zone, but most of it was successfully extricated and withdrawn west of the canal. By midday the situation was that the Germans had reached and crossed at most points the Aisne from Berry-au-Bac to Vailly – helped by the fact that General Duchêne had been belated in giving the order to blow up the bridges. Hitherto the German progress had been evenly distributed, but in the afternoon a heavy sagging occurred in the centre, at the junction of the French and British wings, and the Germans pushed through as far as Fismes on the Vesle - twelve miles penetration in a single day. This central collapse was natural, both because it is an habitual tendency, and because the heaviest weight - more than four to one - of the assault had fallen on the two French divisions in the centre and the left of the 50th Division adjoining them.

This sagging, together with the renewed German pressure, compelled a drawing back of the flanks. On the east, or British flank, this operation was distinguished by a remarkable manoeuvre of the 21st Division, which wheeled back during the night through hilly wooded country, while pivotting on and keeping touch with the Algerian division, which formed the right of the army.

After forcing the passage of the Vesle and capturing the heights south of it, the Germans paused until fresh reinforcements reached them from Ludendorff. But on the 29th they made a vast bound, reaching Fère-en-Tardenois in the centre and capturing Soissons on the west, both important nodal points, which yielded them quantities of material. The German troops had even outstripped in their swift onrush the objectives assigned to them, and had done this despite the counterattacks which Pétain was now shrewdly directing against their sensitive right flank. On the 30th the German flood swept on to the Marne, fifteen miles beyond the Vesle. But it was now flowing in a narrowing central channel; and this day little ground was yielded by the Allied right flank, where the four British divisions - the 8th and 50th now merely remnants - had been reinforced by the 19th (Jeffreys), as well as by French divisions. Next day what remained of the original four was relieved by the French, who now took over command from the IX Corps, although fractions of them still remained in the fighting line for another three weeks as part of the 19th Division.

But from May 31st onwards the Germans, checked on the side of Reims and in front by the Marne, turned their efforts to a westward expansion of the great bulge - down the corridor between the Ourcq and the Marne towards Paris. Hitherto the French reserves had been thrown into the battle as they arrived, in an attempt to stem the flood, which usually resulted in their being caught up and carried back by it. On June 1st, however, Pétain issued orders for the further reserves coming up to form, instead, a ring in rear, digging themselves in and thus having ready before the German flood reached them a vast semicircular dam which would stop and confine its now slackening flow. When it beat against this in the first days of June its momentum was too diminished to make much impression, whereas the appearance and fierce counterattack of the 2nd American Division at the vital joint of

Château-Thierry was not only a material cement, but an inestimable moral tonic to their weary Allies.

Yet it would seem that the most valuable allies of all were the cellars of Champagne, reinforced by the vast stacks of supplies that the French abandoned to their destitute pursuers. At Soissons the desire for such loot brought the forfeit of opportunity. At Fismes there were 'drunken soldiers lying all over the road'. At Jonchery 'battalions stopped in the face of the slightest opposition and it was difficult to get them together again. Progress was very slow although there was no actual fighting. At the villages lamentable disorders took place. The officers could no longer keep control . . . a sorry picture of much drunkenness'.

In their victorious onrush, the Germans had taken some 65,000 prisoners, but whereas this human loss was soon to be more than made up by American reinforcements, strategically the Germans' success had merely placed themselves in a huge sack which was to prove their undoing less than two months later. As in each of the two previous offensives, the tactical success of the Germans on May 27th proved a strategical reverse, because the extent to which they surprised their enemy surprised, and so upset the balance of, their own command.

For, as the disclosures of General von Kuhl have revealed, the offensive of May 27th was intended merely as a diversion, to attract the Allied reserves thither preparatory to a final and decisive blow at the British front covering Hazebrouck. But its astonishing opening success tempted the German command to carry it too far and too long, the attraction of success attracting thither their own reserves as well as the enemy's. Nevertheless, we may justly speculate as to what might have resulted if the attack had begun on April 17th, as ordered, instead of being delayed until May 27th, before the preparations were complete. The Germans would have worn out fewer of their reserves in ineffectual prolongations of the Somme and Lys offensives, while the Allies would have still been waiting for the stiffening, moral and physical, of America's man power. Time and surprise are the two supreme factors in war. The Germans lost the first and forfeited the second by allowing their own surprise to surprise themselves.

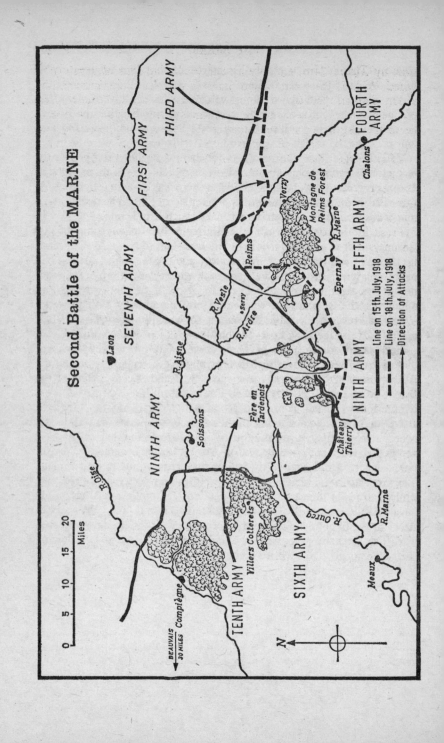

Second Battle of the MARNE

CHAPTER EIGHT

SCENE 4

The Second Battle of the Marne, July, 1918

How apt, if how strange, the historical coincidence by which, as the Marne had been the first high-water mark and witnessed the first ebb of the tide of invasion in 1914, so four years later it was destined to be the final high-water mark from which the decisive ebb began. For on July 15th, 1918, the shell-churned wastes around Reims were the scene of the last German offensive on the Western Front. The tide of German success was definitely stemmed and three days later the ebb began under pressure of the great Allied counterstroke.

But although the first day marked the last German bid for victory, the actual attack was by no means the Germans' supreme effort, nor had it the decisive aims popularly ascribed to it at the time. For Ludendorff still adhered to his guiding idea that the British, severely shaken in the great battles of March and April, should be the target for his decisive blow and that their front in Flanders should be the stage on which he would produce this final drama of victory.

Thus, as has already been told, the spectacular May 27th attack when the Germans, pouring over the Chemin-des-Dames, across the Aisne and to the Marne, seemed to menace Paris itself, was conceived merely as a diversion to draw the Allied reserves away from Flanders. And its rapid success, surprising Ludendorff as much as his attack surprised Foch, dug a pitfall for the Germans by luring their own reserves thither to exploit and retain this apparent windfall.

So also with the June 9th attack, less bountiful in its fruits, that had been launched near Compiègne to break down the buttress of Allied territory that lay between the huge salients created by the German 'pushes' of March and May. When, instead, this German attack was broken off by Ludendorff, with little gained but his own reserves still further drained, he considered 'the enemy in Flanders still so strong that the German army could not attack there yet'. So he planned a further diversion – to be made by forty-nine divisions attacking on either side of Reims. Another reason for this choice was that the German forces in the Marne salient depended on a single railway, the Laon–Soissons line, which was dangerously exposed both to air and artillery attack. The Chief of the Field Railway insisted that Reims must be captured in order to improve the communications. Otherwise the salient would become untenable – the Germans must get on or get out. Ludendorff chose to attack rather than to withdraw.

The plan was finally settled at a conference on June 18th. The principal blow was to be delivered by the First (Mudra) and Third (Einem) Armies, driving towards Châlons, while the Seventh Army (Boehm) sought to cross the Marne near Dormans and to converge with the main advance in the direction of Epernay.

Outwardly, Boehm's army seemed to have the most difficult problem to solve, having to cross a river eighty yards wide in face of the enemy. The designers relied for success on 'the unexampled boldness of the plan', aided by the methods of concealment which had triumphed on May 27th.

But the sands of time were slipping out for the Germans, and American reinforcements, like the sands of the shore in potential number, were slipping into the Allied line of battle, there to become a cement for this grievously strained rampart. Appreciating this, Ludendorff intended his Flanders attack, once more towards the nodal point of Hazebrouck, to follow on the 20th day, only five days after the Reims diversion. On July 16th actually, as soon as the Reims attack was under way, artillery and aircraft were sent off by train to the Flanders front, and Ludendorff himself moved to Tournai to supervise the staging and production of his decisive drama.

But the curtain was never to rise upon it. The Reims diversion had not even the brilliant opening success of its predecessors, and on July 18th the Allied counterstroke so jeopardized the Germans' situation that Ludendorff felt compelled to postpone, if not yet to abandon, the fulfilment of his dream. The reason why the German offensive 'fell flat' on July 15th was that east of Reims it was played to an empty 'first night' house. One of the great stories of the war which everybody knows is that of the 'elastic defence', in face of which the German onslaught lost its momentum, before it reached the real position of the French resistance. Statesmen and generals have vied with each other in acclaiming the brilliance of 'Gouraud's manoeuvre'. Alas! the story must be consigned to its place with many others in the museum of war legends.

The manoeuvre was entirely due to Pétain, that cool, unemotional company director of modern war, and shrewd economist of human lives, who, called to be Commander-in-Chief after the Nivelle fiasco of 1917, had systematically worked to rebuild the French Army and to restore the stability of its man power and morale that had been so undermined by the extravagant offensive policy of Joffre and Nivelle from 1914 to 1917.

Not content merely to reorganize, Pétain had set himself to insure against a recurrence of the trouble by tactics that should be both an economy of force and of the nervous force of the combatant. To this end, one method was an elastic defence in depth, allowing the initial shock and impetus of the enemy's attack to be absorbed by a thinly held forward position, and then to await him on a strong position in rear, when the enemy's troops would be beyond the range of the bulk of their supporting artillery.

This method Pétain had sought to apply against the German attack of June 9th, but, although partially successful, its full effect was lost through the reluctance of the local commanders, still clinging to their old offensive dogmas, to reconcile themselves to a voluntary yielding up of a few square miles of worthless ground. And before July 15th, when the coming German attack was definitely expected, a week's argument was required before Pétain could persuade the lion-hearted Gouraud, who commanded the French Fourth Army east of Reims, to adopt this elastic manoeuvre.

But even when we have ascribed it to the right source, the accumulation of historical error is not fully corrected. For the method was not the revolutionary innovation that it has been termed. The Germans, in fact, had used it on September 25th, 1915 – nearly three years before – to discomfit the great French autumn offensive in Champagne. And the underlying idea can be traced back 2,000 years – to Cannae, where Hannibal applied it against the Romans in a distinctly more subtle and decisive way.

But it sufficed, even in the mild way of 1918, to thwart the German attack east of Reims, where its effort was immeasurably strengthened by the German failure to achieve a surprise such as had marked their earlier offensives of 1918. Full warning of the coming blow was obtained by the French; the statements of prisoners taken from July 5th onwards being confirmed by air photographs of camouflaged ammunition dumps. And an evening raid on July 14th brought in a prisoner from whom, by withholding his gas mask, the French discovered the exact hour of the bombardment (1.10 AM). The French guns accordingly opened fire ten minutes earlier, and thus before the German infantry advanced from their trenches they had been trapped and riven by the French artillery counter-preparation. They withered away before the machine guns of the French outpost line, and the shrunken remnants that passed beyond failed to make even a crack in the main position.

But the dramatic nature of this repulse east of Reims has obscured the fact that it was not the whole battle. West of Reims the front had only been stabilized for a month since the last German thrust, and the newly improvised position was a handicap to the execution of the elastic method by commanders who were slow to grasp it. They chose to hold the forward position on the river line strongly, and their troops paid the penalty when the enemy's sudden deluge of gas shells caught them unawares. The Germans, in contrast, proved the value of taking the most obviously difficult, and hence most unlikely, course. Their infantry were ferried over the river under cover of darkness and a smoke screen, and then pushed forward to the attack, while a number of bridges were swiftly built under fire – an astonishing feat.

Thus here the German attack deepened the corner of the great bulge made in May, and not only pushed across the Marne but behind Reims, so that it threatened to undercut this pivot of the Allied resistance. If the threat had an important influence on the French plan for the counterstroke, its physical progress was stopped on July 16th. The German attack, unaided by pressure elsewhere, had degenerated into local actions, disconnected and therefore useless, while the French artillery and aircraft, by bombarding the Marne crossings, made it difficult for the Germans to obtain supplies. Next day a queer hush of expectation spread over the far-flung battlefield. The stage was set for the great 'revanche'.

In an event so significant for the history of the world, the main historical interest is to determine its causes. The chief among them is to be found not by any analysis of military art, but by a process far more true to the character of the World War – that of drawing up a balance sheet of the previous six months' transactions. When Ludendorff opened his campaign he had a credit balance of 207 divisions, 82 in reserve. Now he had only 66 'fit' divisions in reserve, most of them really so 'watered down' that they could hardly be counted as sound assets.

If these operations had made serious inroads into the Franco-British balance of man power, the Allies had at least averted liquidation, and now, in July, ample and increasing American drafts were being paid into their account. Like a promissory note, this American aid was of incalculable value in restoring their credit – their morale and confidence – even before it made good their material losses. Pétain, the military economist, had appreciated this primary factor long before, when he had said – 'If we can hold on until the end of June our situation will be excellent. In July we can resume the offensive; after that victory will be ours.'

If this simple calculation of time and numbers has the effect of attenuating the popular image of an inspired 'Foch counterstroke', wresting victory from the jaws of defeat, it is regrettable, but it is reality. Unfortunately, even what remains suffers in examination and, in the outcome, a further reduction. War is a masculine activity, and so it is perhaps natural that the feminine maxim, *'il faut souffrir pour être belle'*, should be inverted. For in military history it is both easy and pleasant for all concerned to make an image of beauty, whereas it is not only hard for the seeker to reach the truth but the subject usually suffers in consequence.

The riddle of July 18th, 1918, might aptly be put in terms of the old conundrum – 'When is a counterstroke not a counterstroke?' Foch's mystical faith in the almighty power of the offensive 'will to conquer' had long since been shown at the Marne in 1914 – where day after day he had ordered attacks, apparently oblivious of the reality that his exhausted troops could do and did nothing more than cling precariously to their ground.

Then at Ypres the same year he had spurred on Sir John French to order ambitious attacks, while actually the British troops were barely resisting superior numbers. On these occasions the result justified the spirit, if not the letter, of his instructions. But when the German gas attack made a hole in the Allied line at Ypres in April 1915, Foch's refrain of *'attaquez'*, and his unredeemed promises of a French attack, caused Sir John French to waver almost nightly from the resolve to withdraw and straighten out the line, as Smith-Dorrien, to his cost, urged from the outset. Thus, when this common-sense course was ultimately followed, the British had merely lost not only Smith-Dorrien's services but many lives to no purpose.

When Foch was rehabilitated in 1917 this 'offensive' instinct still dominated him, and when the crisis of March, 1918, called him to the Supreme Command he had hardly set about his unenviable task of restoring the battered front of the Allies before he was dreaming of fresh offensives. Even before the new collapse of the Aisne front in May he had issued *directives* to Haig and Pétain for attacks to free the lateral railway near Amiens and Hazebrouck.

If this project showed his practical belief in his theory of freedom of action, it is also evidence that he had no idea of luring the Germans into vast salients which he could cut off in flank – which was the conception subsequently extolled by popular propagandists. Similarly, the truth of the great counterstroke of July 18th is that it was not conceived, by Foch at least, as a counterstroke at all. But the refrain '*attaquez*' was chanted so continually that sooner or later it was bound to coincide with a 'psychological moment' – as on July 18th.

In the meantime Ludendorff's keenness in pursuing a similar policy, and the wariness of Pétain and Haig helped to prevent the Allied forces becoming seriously involved in a premature offensive before the balance of numbers changed. In contrast, it was the oft-derided economist, Pétain, the 'cautious', who had conceived the plan of the defensive-offensive battle as it was actually waged – first a parry to the enemy's thrust and then a riposte when he was off his balance. On June 4th he had asked Foch to assemble two groups of reserves at Beauvais and Epernay respectively with a view to a counterstroke against the flank of any fresh German advance. The first group, under Mangin, had been used to break the German attack of June 9th, and was then switched a little farther east to a position on the west flank of the German salient between Soissons and Reims which bulged towards the Marne.

Foch, however, planned to use it for the strictly offensive purpose of a push against the rail centre of Soissons. While this was being prepared, the Intelligence Service made it clear that the Germans were about to launch a fresh attack near Reims. Foch thereupon determined to anticipate it, not retort to it, by launching his offensive on July 12th. Pétain, however, had the contrary idea of first stopping and then smiting the enemy when the latter had entangled himself. And, perchance curiously, the French troops were not ready on July 12th, so that the battle was fought rather according to Pétain's than to Foch's conception. But not altogether. For Pétain's plan had comprised three phases – first, to hold up the German attack; second, to launch counterstrokes against the flanks of the fresh pockets it was likely to make on either side of Reims; third, and only third, when the German reserves had been fully drawn towards those pockets, to unleash Mangin's army in a big counter-offensive eastward along the baseline of the main bulge – the enemy's rear – and so close the neck of the vast sack in which the German forces south of the Aisne would be enclosed.

Events and Foch combined to modify this conception. As already narrated the German attack west of Reims had made an unpleasantly deep pocket, penetrating well over the Marne and threatening to take in rear the natural buttress formed by the Montagne de Reims. To avert the danger Pétain was driven to use most of the reserves he had intended for the second phase of the counterstroke; and to replace them he decided to draw from Mangin's army, and to postpone the latter's counter-offensive – already ordered by Foch for July 18th.

When Foch – full of eagerness and with his spirit still more fortified, if that was possible, by Haig's promise to send British reserves – heard of Pétain's action he promptly countermanded it. Hence on July 18th the French left wing* was launched to its counter-offensive while the defensive battle was still in progress in the centre and on the right wing. This meant that the second phase of Pétain's plan had to be dropped out, and instead of the right wing attracting the Germans' reserves in order to enable the left wing to fall on their naked back, the left wing's offensive eased the pressure on the right wing.

To compensate as far as possible the initial passivity of the right wing,† the British reserves (51st and 62nd Divisions) which were sent thither, were used to relieve the defending troops 'on the move', passing direct to an attack. In the centre,‡ American reserves were similarly used, and thus a general pressure began along the whole face of the great salient.

But this convergent pressure did not begin until July 20th, and by that time the opening surprise – due to the sudden release of a mass of tanks – was over and the left wing had lost its impetus. After advancing

* The spearhead of this consisted of Mangin's Tenth Army, which had ten divisions in the first line (including the American 1st and 2nd Divisions), six divisions and Robillot's Cavalry Corps in the second line, and the British 15th and 34th Divisions in reserve. At 4.35 AM on the dark and foggy morning of the 18th Mangin struck, using his massed tanks on the Cambrai method without any artillery preparation. The left of Degoutte's Sixth Army, on Mangin's inner flank, chimed in one and a half hours later, after a preliminary bombardment. Degoutte's subsidiary role was marked by the fact that he had only seven divisions (among them the American 4th and 26th) in the first line and one in the second; he was later reinforced by the American 42nd, 32nd and 28th divisions, which bore the main burden in the final stage of the advance to the Vesle. Five German divisions faced Mangin and six faced Degoutte; with six and two respectively in reserve. But all were weak and more than half had been reported as of little or no value.

† Berthelot's Fifth Army, comprising nine divisions. It was opposed by eleven German divisions, with one in reserve.

‡ De Mitry's Ninth Army, comprising six divisions (including the 3rd American), with the 28th American and a French one in reserve. It was opposed by six weak German divisions, with three in reserve.

about four miles on the 18th, and a little farther on the 19th, Mangin's army was brought to a standstill on the Soissons flank – near the jugular vein of the salient. Thus the Germans, fighting hard for breathing space, gained the time they required to draw the bulk of their forces out of the sack, even though they left 25,000 prisoners and much material behind. And once they were safely back on a straight and much-shortened line along the Vesle, Ludendorff felt able, on August 2nd, to order preparations to be resumed for fresh attacks in Flanders and east of Montdidier.

Six days later his offensive dreams were finally dissipated; but it is historically important to realize that it was not the second Battle of the Marne, 'Foch's great counterstroke', which dissipated them. This July 18th counterstroke, conceived as such by Pétain and amended by Foch, was by no means decisive in its results. It may be that Foch's impetuosity robbed him of such results; that Pétain's oft-criticized caution would have been more fruitful and collected a larger 'bag'.

Nevertheless, if the battle had no clearly decisive effect, the first taste of victory after such deep and bitter draughts of defeat was an incalculable moral stimulant to the Allies, and perchance its depressing effect on the German morale was more insidiously damaging than was at first visible. So that Foch, who was ever concerned only with moral factors, which cannot be mathematically calculated, may well have been content. He had gained the initiative, and he kept it – that was enough, results mattered little. For his strategy was simple, not the complex masterpiece of art which legend has ascribed to him. It was best expressed in his own vivid illustration – 'War is like this. Here is an inclined plane. An attack is like the ball rolling down it. It goes on gaining momentum and getting faster and faster on condition that you do not stop it. If you check it artificially you lose your momentum and have to begin all over again.'

CHAPTER EIGHT

SCENE 5

The 'Black Day' of the German Army – August 8th

August 8th, 1918, is a date which grows ever larger on the horizon of the historian. So far as any one event of the campaign in the west can be regarded as decisive, it is the great surprise east of Amiens that occurred on this day. And that decisiveness is above all a proof that the moral element dominates warfare.

For although August 8th was 'a famous victory', the most brilliant ever gained by British arms in the World War, and, better still, the most economical, neither its tactical nor its visible strategic results were sufficient to explain its moral effect. Its 16,000 prisoners on the first day, and 21,000 all told, were a handsome prize compared with that of any previous British offensive, but a trifle in proportion to the vast forces then deployed on the Western Front, and in relation to such triumphs of the past as Worcester, Blenheim, Rossbach, Austerlitz, or Sedan. Its initial penetration of six to eight miles, and ultimate twelve miles, were, again, excellent by 1915–17 standards, but in March the Germans had penetrated thirty-eight miles in the reverse direction without achieving any decisive result. Studied on the map, the advance of August 8th–21st merely flattened out the nose and indented one cheek of the shallow German salient Arras–Montdidier–Noyon. It was far from reaching any vital link of the enemy's communications, or even cutting off the troops in that salient.

Yet it unhinged the mind and morale of the German Supreme Command. It led the Kaiser to say – 'I see that we must strike a balance. We are at the end of our resources. The war must be ended.' It made Ludendorff take a similarly despondent view – 'The war would have to be ended.'

In comparing the impression made upon him by the dramatic counterstroke of July 18th on the Marne and that of August 8th, there

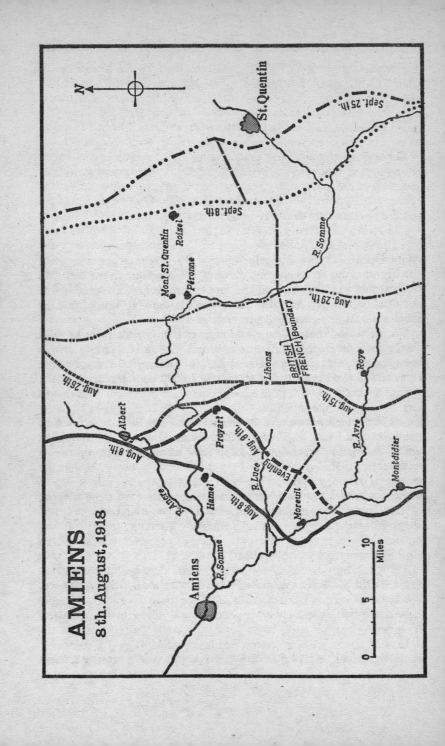

AMIENS
8th. August, 1918

is a remarkable contrast. And in this contrast lies the answer as to which was the more decisive of the two. For after July 18th he had by no means lost hope. He seems to have treated this reverse as hardly more than an unfortunate incident, and as late as August 2nd was ordering preparations for four fresh attacks, including his cherished Flanders blow, if on a reduced scale in comparison with his original intention.

But after August 8th these dreams vanish. There is an abandonment of any idea of returning to the offensive, and, more significant still, no adoption of an alternative strategy. Mere passive resistance to the enemy's kicks cannot be called a strategical plan. Only when it was too late did he formulate the design of a purposeful evacuation of France as a preliminary to a fresh campaign beyond the frontier. By then, however, the moral collapse of the German Command had spread to the German people.

After the war Ludendorff delivered his considered opinion that 'August 8th was the black day of the German Army in the history of the war'. The adjective 'black' is peculiarly apt, for when faintness follows a sudden shock the blackening of the vista is the symptom which precedes the loss of consciousness and the consequent paralysis of the faculties. Thus the primary interest in the story of August 8th is to trace how this shock came about. On July 12th Foch, irrepressibly eager to begin his cherished but oft-postponed idea of returning to the offensive, proposed to Haig that –

> The first offensive to be launched on the British front should be one starting from the front Festubert–Rebecq, with a view to freeing the Bruay mines and forbidding the communication centre of Estaires . . .

Five days later Haig replied that he saw 'no advantage in an advance over the flat and marshy region between Rebecq and Festubert', and suggested, instead, that —

> The operation, in my opinion, which is of the highest importance and which I proposed to you, as before, should be executed as soon as possible, is to push forward the Allied front to the east and south-east of Amiens so as to free that town and the railway. The best way to carry out this object is to make a combined Franco-British operation, the French attacking south of Moreuil and the British north of the Luce.
>
> To realize this project I am preparing plans secretly for an

offensive north of the Luce, direction east ... In liaison with this project the French forces should, in my opinion, carry out an operation between Moreuil and Montdidier ...

This letter, from the archives, sheds light on several momentous points of post-war controversy. First, as to the origin of the offensive, it shows not only that it was purely of British conception, but also that it was a 'limited' conception – a narrower-fronted 'shove' to secure for Amiens and the railway a rather wider margin of safety. The question is often mooted whether the idea sprang from the Commander-in-Chief, Haig, or from the Fourth Army commander, Rawlinson. Here the words 'as before' suggest that Haig had priority, for it was the brilliant little surprise operation at Hamel on July 4th and its revelation of the decline of German morale which inspired Rawlinson with the idea of a wider offensive.

However, there is little in the question of priority, for the defensive advantage of freeing Amiens was obvious. Indeed, the fact that Rawlinson's inspiration should not have come until after Hamel suggests his deeper appreciation of the moral element. The exploitation of an enemy's moral disintegration is fundamentally an offensive purpose.

Second, as to the plan of the offensive, the letter seems to contradict the claim, made in *Sir Douglas Haig's Command* and elsewhere, that the British were forced by Foch, against their will, to let the French share in the operation – thereby increasing what Clausewitz termed the inevitable 'friction' of war. Rawlinson certainly, and rightly, argued against it as inimical to the surprise he sought.

But the letter shows that it was Haig's proposal. It is true that he proposed leaving a gap a few miles between the French and British attacks. But both were purely frontal and strategically shoulder to shoulder. A richer offensive prospect was perhaps offered by a convergent attack on the two flanks of the salient, north of Albert and well south of Montdidier respectively. But, for the former, a trench-filled belt of the old Somme battlefields was a difficulty, and subsequent events do not support the view that another army would have brought off such a surprise as the Fourth did south of the Somme.

The enlargement of the original project was due to Foch, who, on August 5th, directed that if the initial attack was successful, it was to be continued by pushing south-east towards Ham. If the attacks against the southern flank of the salient which Humbert's and Mangin's armies began on August 10th and 17th respectively could have coincided with that of the British, greater material profits might have been yielded. As it was, the close cooperation of Debeney's army immediately adjoining the British did little to compensate its inevitable hindrance to the plan of surprise. For, lacking tanks, it could not dispense with a preliminary bombardment, and this could not begin, without forfeiting the general surprise, until the British advance started.

Greater material profits, however, could hardly have increased the moral effect of August 8th on the German Command. And this effect came from the shock of perhaps the most complete surprise of the war. How it was achieved is an object lesson for future soldiers, for, like all the masterpieces of moral dislocation in military history, it was a subtle compound of many deceptive factors. Too often surprise is treated as an incidental, to be gained by a simple choice of date or place.

Its foundation was the sudden loosing of a swarm of tanks – 456 in all – in place of any preliminary artillery bombardment.* This method, inaugurated at Cambrai the previous November, had been repeated by the French on July 18th. Before Amiens it was enhanced by manifold devices. Secrecy was sought by holding the preliminary conferences always at different places, by concealing reconnaissances, and by informing the executants at the latest moment compatible with readiness – divisional commanders did not know that an attack was intended until July 31st, and the fighting troops not until thirty-six hours before the start. Even the War Cabinet in London was kept in the dark, and in that august assembly the Australian Prime Minister, Mr Hughes, was in course of a vehement demand that the Australians should be taken out of the line, when a telegram brought the undreamt of news that the Australians were far on the other side of the line. On that same morning also, a general from the neighbouring army made a casual call at Rawlinson's headquarters on his way home for leave, and incidentally inquired why there was such a heavy sound of gunfire from the front.

Deception was sought by making all movements at night – with aeroplanes patrolling the area to check any exposure; by continuing work on the British rear defences until the last evening, by regulating the times and rates of fire of the artillery so that as more and more guns were slipped into concealed positions they registered without any apparent increase in the normal daily quantity of fire. By such means the strength

* In his analytical study of the war, General von Kuhl, the directing brain of the opposing Army Group, attributes the overwhelming effect of the attack to the fact that the British had 'learnt' how to achieve surprise; he adds that in this surprise 'the most important and decisive factor was the tanks'. This statement has the significance that belongs to a verdict in cool reflection, ten years after the event.

of the Fourth Army was roughly doubled – six fresh divisions, two cavalry divisions, nine tank battalions, and another 1,000 guns being concentrated in the area unsuspected by the enemy between August 1st and 8th. This involved the use of 290 special trains (sixty for ammunition and the rest for troops) – and only two lines of railway were available.

Thus by zero hour (4.20 AM) on August 8th, the Fourth Army strength had been raised to thirteen divisions, three cavalry divisions, seventeen air squadrons, ten heavy and two whippet tank battalions (totalling 360 heavy and 96 whippet tanks), and over 2,000 guns and howitzers, including 672 'heavies'. Two-thirds of the heavy artillery was allotted for counter-battery work, and effectively paralysed the hostile artillery.

Distraction also is an essential component of surprise, and in this case it centred round the introduction of the Canadians. Regarding them as storm troops, the enemy tended to greet their appearance as an omen of a coming attack. At the moment the Canadian Corps was near Arras and an aptly chosen fraction of it – two battalions, two casualty clearing stations, and its wireless section – was dispatched northwards to Kemmel in Flanders. There, also, other 'suggestions' of attack were conveyed by erecting extra aerodromes and cavalry wireless. Meanwhile the bulk of the Canadian Corps was filtered down to the Somme, where various ingenious rumours were circulated among the British troops to account for its appearance.

The Fourth Army dispositions were that the main punch was to be delivered south of the Somme, by the Canadian Corps (Currie) on the right and the Australian Corps (Monash) on the left, next the river whilst the III Corps (R. H. K. Butler) advanced north of the river to safeguard the flank of the main punch. But the Canadians did not move into the front line until a few hours before the assault, and meantime the Australians extended their front as far south as the Amiens–Roye road, relieving the French, and thereby lulling the Germans into a false sense of security. For what enemy would expect attack from a force which was spreading itself out defensively?

The whole front of attack was about fourteen miles long, and on the German side was held by six skeleton divisions (averaging barely 3,000 effectives apiece) of General von der Marwitz's Second Army. Their weakness of numbers was accentuated by weakness of defences, and in their rough forward line there were none of the usual deep dug-outs to safeguard morale until the hour of trial.

Five days before the attack an enemy raid captured an Australian post, and three days later a local attack fractured the III Corps front and took 200 prisoners. But such information as the enemy gained only deluded him further. Moreover, the German aircraft were so incessantly harried by the British that for several weeks they could not reconnoitre behind the British front. The only suspicious sign was a certain amount of noise at night. On several occasions the German troops reported that they heard the movement of tanks, but 'the army staff ridiculed the constantly recurring nervousness of the trench troops about tanks'. Actually, there were no tanks near the scene on the dates they were thus reported, and these cries of 'Wolf, Wolf,' hardened the German higher command in its attitude of disbelief and 'indifference'.

Thus when, an hour before sunrise on August 8th, the British tanks swept forward, with the barrage and infantry advance simultaneous, the blow had the maximum shock of surprise. Shrouded by a thick ground mist, it fell on an enemy who had done nothing to strengthen his position by entrenchments, and the Canadians and Australians – matchless attacking troops – surged irresistibly over the enemy's forward divisions. Only north of the Somme, where tanks were few, was there a partial check. To accelerate the momentum all reserves were set in motion at zero hour – copying the Germans' example of March 21st. Soon, too, armoured cars were racing down the roads, to spread confusion behind the German front, even shooting up an army corps staff at breakfast in Proyart.

The day's final objective (six to eight miles distant) was gained over most of the front except the extreme right and left. But the next day saw slight progress and rather spasmodic pressure, and thereafter the attack flickered out as rapidly as it had blazed up. Why this strange contrast? Why was not so complete a breakthrough completed by a dramatic finale? Partly, it would seem, because the advance had now reached the edge of the old Somme battlefields of 1916, a tangled waste of rusty wire and derelict trenches which was a brake on movement, reinforcement, and supply. It is well to remember that the problem of maintaining continuity of advance was never solved in the World War. Again, the original front of attack had not been wide, and it is significant that almost all successful advances in the World War seem to have been governed by a law of ratio, the depth of the penetration being roughly half of the frontage of attack.

Another reason was, as at Cambrai, the lack of reserves. The introduction of the local reserves of the Fourth Army was well timed but, when its thirteen divisions had been engaged, all that were available were three divisions assembled by Haig in the area. Moreover, the Germans, in contrast, succeeded in reinforcing their original six divisions with eighteen reserve divisions by August 11th – ten more than had been estimated.

A fourth cause of the stoppage was inherent in the form of the attack. For being strictly frontal the more it pushed back the enemy the more it consolidated their resistance. This is always the defect of a frontal attack unless an organized force can be rushed through and placed on the enemy's rear. The cavalry as usual were allotted the role of exploitation. This time they rendered serviceable help in gaining and holding certain localities until the infantry came up, but such help was but a slender thing compared with the true role of cavalry in past history. Greater results might have been attained if the ninety-six whippet tanks, instead of being tied to the cavalry, had been used independently to pass through the gap and make a concentrated thrust south-eastwards against the rear of the German army facing the French – as was suggested by the Tank Corps.

But from the broad strategic point of view there was, or was evolved, this time a method behind the lack of reserves. On August 10th Haig had visited this front and studied the situation at close quarters. In consequence, when Foch urged a continuance of the Fourth Army's frontal pressure, Haig demurred to it as a vain waste of life. In a letter of August 14th he told Foch that he had stopped the further attack prepared for next day, and that he was preparing an attack by the Third Army north of Albert.

Foch objected to the delay involved by this alternative step, but at a conference at Sarcus next day Haig stubbornly held to and gained his point. As a result the Third Army struck on August 21st, the First Army farther north on the 28th, while the Fourth Army seized the opportunity of this distraction of the enemy to resume their advance, the Australians gaining Mont St Quentin and Péronne on the 31st, and thereby turning the barrier of the upper Somme. These operations marked the new strategy of successive attacks at different but closely related points, each attack broken off and succeeded by a fresh as soon as its initial impetus was spent.

It would be unjust, as many British writers have done, to claim that Haig initiated this strategy. For it is to be clearly traced in the successive attacks already begun by the French to the south – Debeney's left wing on the 8th, his right on the 9th, Humbert's army on the 10th, and Mangin's on the 21st. But Haig appears to have appreciated first its potentialities for economy of force. While Foch was filled with the idea of maintaining the pressure, Haig was seized with the idea of pressure at the most economical expenditure of life. The Fourth Army's bag of 21,000 prisoners from August 8th–12th had cost only 20,000 casualties.

To the success of this strategy the surprise of August 8th and its effect on the German Command had contributed greatly. Their instinctive response to the shock was to hurry to the spot all possible reinforcements, and thereby they drained their reserve funds to bankruptcy point. The reserve divisions of the army group of Prince Rupprecht, which held the front from the sea to the Somme district, fell from thirty-six to nine by August 16th. Rupprecht's own resolution had done much to bring the British advance to a halt by preventing the local army commanders from carrying out their first panic decision to fall back behind the upper Somme. But this very resolution, perhaps, cost the Germans more in the end.

Thus, in sum, the decisiveness of August 8th came from its dislocation of thought or will, or both, throughout the whole hierarchy of the German Command. The history of 1914–18 repeated the experience of all history that, except against an exhausted or already demoralized foe, decisive success in war is only possible through surprise. And that surprise must be a compound of many subtle ingredients.

CHAPTER EIGHT

SCENE 6

Megiddo – The Annihilation of the Turkish Armies

On September 19th, 1918, began an operation which was both one of the most quickly decisive campaigns and the most completely decisive battles in all history. Within a few days the Turkish armies in Palestine had practically ceased to exist. Whether it should be regarded primarily as a campaign or as a battle completed by a pursuit is a moot question. For it opened with the forces in contact and hence would seem to fall into the category of a battle; but it was achieved mainly by strategic means, with fighting playing a minor part. This fact has tended to its disparagement in the sight of those who are obsessed with the Clausewitzian dogma that blood is the price of victory – and hold, as a corollary, that no victory is worthy of recognition which is not sanctified by a lavish oblation of blood. But Caesar's triumph at Ilerda, Scipio's near Utica, Cromwell's at Preston, and Moltke's, though opportunist rather than sought for, at Sedan, each had the same 'pale pink' complexion. In each, strategy was so effective that fighting was but incidental. Yet no one can deny their decisiveness both as victories and on the course of history. A more serious 'depreciation' of this final campaign-battle in Palestine lies in the fact that Allenby had a superiority of over two to one in numbers, and more in terms of weapon-values.* In addition the morale of the Turks had so declined that it is often argued that Allenby had merely to stretch out his hand for the Turkish army, like an overripe plum, to fall into it. There is force in these contentions; but most of the 'crowning mercies' of modern history, from Worcester to Sedan, have seen almost as great a disparity of

* Allenby's fighting strength was 12,000 sabres, 57,000 rifles and 540 guns. He estimated the Turkish strength at 3,000 sabres, 32,000 rifles and 402 guns. This figure is about double Liman von Sanders' estimate, which, however, seems to be a broad calculation, excluding machine-gun personnel.

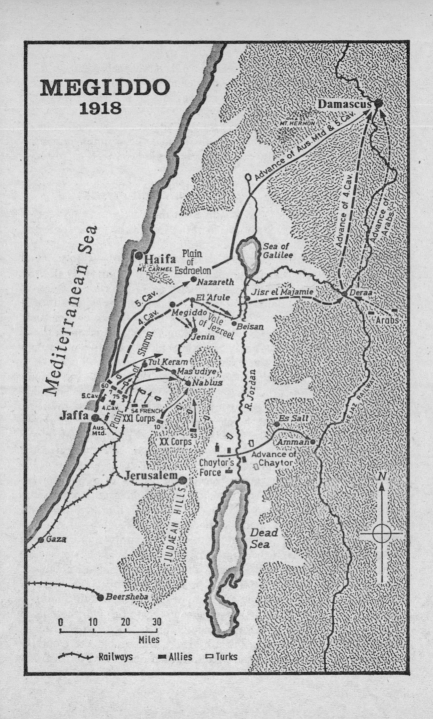

MEGIDDO
1918

Damascus

MT. HERMON

Advance of Aus. Mtd & 5 Cav.

Advance of 4. Cav.

Advance of Arabs

Sea of Galilee

Haifa
Plain of Esdraelon
MT. CARMEL

Nazareth

Jisr el Majamie

Deraa

5. Cav.

El 'Afule

Arabs

4. Cav.

Megiddo
Vale of Jezreel

Beisan

Mediterranean Sea

Jenin

Tul Keram

Mas'udiye

Nablus

R. Jordan

60

5.Cav.
7 5 3

Es Salt

Jaffa
Aus. Mtd.

4.Cav.

54 FRENCH

XXI Corps

10

53

XX Corps

Amman

Chaytor's Force

Advance of Chaytor

N

Jerusalem

Gaza

JUDAEAN HILLS

Dead Sea

HEJAZ RAILWAY

0   10   20   30
Miles

Beersheba

Railways   ▬ Allies   ▭ Turks

strength and morale between victors and vanquished. And in 1918 Allenby had to outwit such able commanders as Liman von Sanders and Mustapha Kemal, not such men as those who thrust their heads into the sack at Sedan.

When full deduction is made for the advantageous conditions of September, 1918, the conclusion remains that the triumph immortalized by the already immortal name of Megiddo is one of history's masterpieces by reason of the breadth of vision and treatment. If the subject was not a difficult one, the picture is almost unique as a perfect conception perfectly executed.

The question is often asked, – whose was the conception? Was it that of the titular commander? Or, did it spring from some gifted subordinate? When the victories of Hindenburg on the Russian front are discussed, even the man in the street speaks of Ludendorff's strategy – and the student of war goes still deeper, or lower, and muses on the unassessable influence of Hoffmann's military genius. But with Megiddo it is possible to dispel doubt, through the unanimous evidence of those most intimately concerned. The broad conception sprang entire from Allenby's mind, whatever the credit due to his assistants for working out its executive details. 'Grew', indeed, would be a better word than 'sprang', for the original conception was of more modest dimensions – to break through the Turkish front near the coast and, wheeling inwards, turn the flank of their forces in the Judaean Hills. But, returning one day from a ride during which he had been studying the problem, Allenby suddenly unfolded the plan as it was executed, in all its almost breath-taking scope. It abundantly fulfilled Napoleon's maxim that 'the whole secret of the art of war lies in making oneself master of the communications'. If Allenby had a superiority of strength he was going to use it to make himself master not of one, but of every one, of the Turkish communications. And the success of his attempt to do so owed much to the complementary fact that he had taken thorough measures to be master of his own communications

The three so-called Turkish 'armies', each hardly more than the strength of a division, drew nourishment through a single stem – the Hejaz railway running south from Damascus. At Deraa a branch ran out westwards; crossing the Jordan at Jisr el Mejamie, just north of Beisan, it forked at El Afule in the Plain of Esdraelon, one line going to the sea at Haifa and the other turning south again through the hills of Samaria to Messudieh Junction. This line fed the Seventh (Mustapha Kemal) and Eighth (Jevad) Turkish armies which held the front between the river Jordan and the Mediterranean Sea. The Fourth Army

(Jemal) east of the Jordan was fed by the main Hejaz railway.

Now, to cut an army's lines of communication is to dislocate its physical organization. To close its lines of retreat is to dislocate its morale. And to destroy its lines of 'inter-communication' – by which orders and reports pass – is to dislocate it mentally, by breaking the essential connexion between the brain and the body of an army. Allenby planned to achieve not a single but the triple dislocation, and the third element was not the least important to the success of his plan.

The convergence of both roads and railways made Deraa, El Afule, and, to a less extent, Beisan the vital points in the Turks' rear. To get a grip on El Afule and Beisan would sever the communications of the Seventh and Eighth Armies and also close their lines of retreat, except for the extremely difficult outlet to the desolate region across the Jordan eastwards. To get a grip on Deraa would sever the communications of all three armies and the best line of retreat of the Fourth. But it was considerably farther from the British front.

El Afule and Beisan, however, lay within a sixty-mile radius, and hence were within the range of a strategic cavalry 'bound', provided that these vital points could be reached without interruption or delay. The problem was, first, to find a line of approach unobstructed by nature, and, second, to ensure that the enemy could not block it by force. How was it solved? The flat coastal Plain of Sharon afforded a corridor to the Plain of Esdraelon and Vale of Jezreel, in which El Afule and Beisan respectively lay. This corridor was interrupted by only a single door, so far back that it was not guarded by the Turks, formed by the narrow mountain belt which separates the coastal Plain of Sharon from the inland Plain of Esdraelon. But the entrance to the corridor was firmly bolted and barred by the trenches of the Turkish front. Allenby planned to use his infantry to force this locked gate and swing it back, as on a hinge, north-eastwards, so leaving a clear path for his cavalry. But having passed through the front gate they would still have to get through the back door. This the Turks could easily close if they had time and warning. Speed on the part of the cavalry was essential. But not sufficient. The attention and reserves of the Turks must be distracted. Even so, there was still a risk. War experience had shown how easily cavalry could be stopped, and a handful of men and machine guns would suffice to block the two passes through the intermediate mountain belt. To avert this risk the Turkish Command must be made deaf and dumb as well as blind. In this complete paralysis of the Turkish Higher Command lies the main significance and the historical value of the victory of Megiddo.

Let us watch how it was achieved. For it, Allenby had two comparatively novel tools – aircraft and Arabs. Feisal's Arabs, under the
guiding brain of Colonel Lawrence, had long been harassing, im-
mobilizing and demoralizing the Turks along the main Hejaz railway.
Now they were to contribute more directly to the final stroke by the
British forces. On September 16th and 17th, emerging like phantoms
from the desert, they blew up the railway north, south, and west of
Deraa. This had the physical effect of shutting off the flow of Turkish
supplies temporarily – and 'temporarily' was all that mattered here. It
had the mental effect of persuading the Turkish Command to send part
of its scanty reserves towards Deraa.

The Air Force contribution was in two parts. First, by a sustained
campaign it drove the enemy's machines out of the air. This campaign
was carried so far that ultimately the fighters 'sat' above the Turkish
aerodrome at Jenin to prevent their machines even taking off. Thus
it closed the enemy's air eye during the period of preparation.
Secondly, when the moment came for the execution of Allenby's plan,
the Air Force made the enemy's command deaf and dumb – by
decisively bombing their main telegraph and telephone exchange at El
Afule, a stroke in which Ross-Smith, who later made history by his
flight to Australia, helped England to make history. In addition, the
enemy's two army headquarters at Nablus and Tul Keram were
bombed, and at the second, the more vital, the wires were so effectively
destroyed that it was cut off throughout the day both from Nazareth
and from its divisions in the coastal sector. Another and earlier form of
air activity was, if less military, perhaps of even wider strategic effect.
This was the dropping not of bombs but of an equal weight of illustrated pamphlets showing the physical comforts which the Turkish
soldier enjoyed as a prisoner of war. Its appeal to half-starved and
ragged men was none the less for being imponderable.

While the Arabs and the Air Force were perhaps the two most vital
factors in 'unhinging' the enemy preparatory to the actual push, the
plan had also the wide and purposeful variety of ruses which marks the
masterpieces of military history. By these Allenby sought to divert the
enemy's attention away from the coast to the Jordan flank. In this aim
he was helped by the very failure of two attempted advances east of the
Jordan, towards Amman and Es Salt, during the spring. Then,
throughout the summer he kept a cavalry force, periodically relieved, in
the stifling heat of the Jordan Valley to hold the enemy's attention.
When the cavalry were ultimately moved surreptitiously across to the
other flank, their camps were not only left standing but new ones added,

while 15,000 dummy horses of canvas filled the vacated horse-lines. Mule-drawn sleighs created dust clouds; battalions marched by day towards the valley – and returned by night in lorries to repeat this march of a stage army; a hotel was taken over in Jerusalem and elaborately prepared for the mythical reception of General Head-quarters; new bridging and wireless activity fostered the illusion; Lawrence sent agents to bargain for vast quantities of forage in the Amman district.

And all the time more and more troops were filtering down by night marches to the other flank near the sea, there to be concealed in orange groves or in camps already standing. By these means Allenby increased his two-to-one superiority, on the front as a whole, to a five-to-one superiority on the vital sector – unsuspected by the enemy. For some time Liman von Sanders had certainly anticipated a big attack, and indeed, had thought of frustrating it by a voluntary retirement to a rear line near the Sea of Galilee. 'I gave up the idea, because we would have had to relinquish the Hejaz railway ... and because we no longer could have stopped the progress of the Arab insurrection in rear of our army. On account of the limited marching capacity of the Turkish soldiers and of the very low mobility of all draft animals, I considered that the holding of our positions to the last gave us more favourable prospects than a long retirement with Turkish troops of impaired morale.'

Although he feared an attack near the coast, he feared still more the effect of one east of the Jordan, and even at the last hour the warning of the first given by an Indian deserter on September 17th was offset by the more positive news of the Arab attacks on the vital railway at Deraa. Deceived by his own preconceived idea, Liman von Sanders was, indeed, too ready to believe that this deserter was a tool of the British Intelligence, and his story a blind to cover Allenby's real purpose. Further, Liman von Sanders rejected the plea of Refet Bey, command-ing the coastal sector, who wished to withdraw his troops a mile so that the British bombardment might waste itself on empty trenches. For-bidding Refet to withdraw an inch, he ensured that he should go back 100 miles, to Tyre, leaving his army behind – dead or prisoners.

On the night of September 18th began what was both the last move of the 'distracting' preparation and the first move of the real action. The 53rd Division, which formed Allenby's extreme right, made a spring forward in the hills on the edge of the Jordan Valley. Thereby they would be a step on their way towards closing the only way of retreat – across the Jordan eastwards – left open to the Turks when the main move had fulfilled its encircling purpose.

Far away to the west by the sea all was quiet. But at 4.30 AM 385 guns opened fire on the selected frontage. For a quarter of an hour, only, they maintained an intense bombardment, and then the infantry advanced, under cover of a rapid lifting barrage. They swept, almost unchecked, over the stupefied defenders and broke through the two trench systems, shallow and slightly wired – by Western Front standards. Then they wheeled inland, like a huge door swinging on its hinges. On this door, a French contingent and the 54th Division formed the hinged end; then, with a five-mile interval, the 3rd Indian, 75th and 7th Indian Divisions, formed the middle panel; and the 60th Division, by the sea, the outside panel. The latter reached Tul Keram by nightfall. But what survived of the Turkish Eighth Army had long before been pouring back through the defile to Messudieh in a confused crowd of troops and transport. And upon this hapless mob the British aircraft had swept down with bombs and bullets.

Meantime, through the opened door had ridden the three cavalry divisions of the Desert Mounted Corps (Chauvel). By evening they had reached the Carmel Range, the 'intermediate door', sending detachments with their armoured cars to secure the two passes. By morning they were across. One brigade descended on Nazareth where the enemy's General Headquarters lay, ignorant of the events of the past twenty-four hours because cut off from all communication with its fighting body. Liman von Sanders, however, escaped through a failure to block the northern exit of the town, and after a vigorous street fight the cavalry were forced to retire.

The real strategic key, however, was now not at Nazareth but at El Afule and Beisan. These were reached at 8 AM and 4.30 PM respectively – to Beisan the 4th Cavalry Division had covered seventy miles in thirty-four hours. Passing through the Carmel Range in its wake, the Australian Mounted Division turned south to Jenin to place a closer barrier across the Turks' line of retreat. The enemy's only remaining bolt-hole was east over the Jordan – which flows swiftly, with few fords, through a deep and winding trough, 1,300 feet below sea level at the Dead Sea end. He might have reached this but for the Air Force, as the infantry advance was making slow progress through the hills in face of the stubborn Turkish rearguards. Early in the morning of September 21st, the British aircraft spotted a large column – practically all that survived of the two Turkish armies – winding down the steep gorge from Nablus to the Jordan. Four hours' continuous bombing and machine-gunning reduced this procession to stagnation, an inanimate chaos of guns and transport. Those who survived were merely scattered fugitives. From this moment may be timed the extinction of the Seventh and Eighth Turkish Armies. What followed was but a rounding up of 'cattle' by the cavalry.

Only the Fourth Army, east of the Jordan, remained. This, delaying too long, did not begin to retire until September 22nd. A broken railway and the Arabs lay across its line of retreat to Damascus. And four days later the 4th Cavalry Division moved east from Beisan to intercept it, while the other two converged directly on Damascus, its goal. Escape was impossible, but its fate was different from that of the other armies, a rapid attrition under constant pinpricks rather than a neat dispatch. In this pursuit the Desert Mounted Corps cooperated with, and for the first time met, their real desert allies, hitherto an invisible and intangible factor. Their presence, and identity, was disclosed when a messenger reported – 'There's an Arab on the top of the hill over there in a Rolls-Royce; talks English perfectly and in the hell of a rage!' For no pursuit could be fast enough to satisfy Lawrence's ardent spirit as he urged his Arabs on towards the city of desire. To a British cavalry officer with an apt gift of phrase their march looked 'like some strange oriental version of an old-time Epsom road on Derby Day', but they outpaced the 4th Cavalry Division.

The fragments of the Turkish Fourth Army were finally headed off and captured near Damascus, which was occupied on October 1st. On the previous day the garrison had been intercepted by the Australian Mounted Division as it was trying to escape through the Barada gorge (the Biblical 'Abana'). Sweeping the head of the fugitive stream with machine guns from the overhanging cliffs the Australian Light Horse rolled it back to Damascus, there to swell the 'bag' of prisoners to 20,000.

The next move was a fitting conclusion to this chapter of history. The 5th Cavalry Division was dispatched to advance on Aleppo, 200 miles distant, in conjunction with an Arab force. Its armoured cars led the way and dispersed such slight opposition as was met, reaching the outskirts of Aleppo on October 23rd. Two days later the leading cavalry brigade came up. A combined attack was arranged for next morning, but during the night the Arabs slipped into and captured the town on their own. The British force, too weak to press the retreat of the garrison, was awaiting reinforcements from Damascus when the capitulation of Turkey on October 31st wrote 'finis' to the campaign. During a brief span of thirty-eight days the British had advanced 350 miles and captured 75,000 prisoners – at a cost of less than 5,000 casualties.

In a war singularly barren of surprise and mobility, those keynotes of the art of war, their value had been signally vindicated at the last, and in one theatre at least. Surprise and mobility had virtually won the victory without a battle. And it is worth noting that the Turks were still capable of holding up the infantry attack until the 'strategic barrage' across their rear became known and produced its inevitable, and invariable, moral effect.

Because a preliminary condition of trench warfare existed the infantry and heavy artillery were necessary to break the lock. But, once the normal conditions of warfare were thus restored, the victory was achieved by the mobile elements – cavalry, aircraft, armoured cars and Arabs – which formed but a fraction of Allenby's total force. And it was achieved, not by physical force, but by the demoralizing application of mobility. A new light on Napoleon's dictum that the moral is to the physical as three to one.

CHAPTER EIGHT

SCENE 7

The Battle of a Dream – St Mihiel

For four years a wedge sixteen miles deep lay embedded in the flank of the main French armies. It was the most marked, and most 'ugly', feature of the whole irregular front between the Swiss border and the Belgian coast. Along this long irregular line of trenches salients were numerous, and of all sizes, but none was so acute as that which came down from the heights of the Woevre to the Meuse at St Mihiel – and even protruded beyond the river. All that time it galled France bodily and mentally, for although it was not in itself a convenient springboard for a fresh German offensive it might easily become a menace if a new wedge were driven in on the other side of Verdun; worse still, it crippled the prospects of any French offensive into Lorraine. For such an offensive, whether launched from the Verdun or from the Nancy sector, would not only suffer the menace of St Mihiel in its rear but would be difficult to nourish – because the St Mihiel salient interrupted the railways from Paris to Nancy and from Verdun to Nancy. This handicap was all too clearly manifest in 1916, when the army defending Verdun fought half choked and always in danger of being suddenly strangled.

For two more trying years the defenders of Verdun had to bear the semi-suffocation of their windpipe. And then, at the end of the first hour of September 12th, 1918, 3,000 guns pealed a message of deliverance. Four hours later, deafened yet exhilarated by the thunder of their guns, the infantry of the First American Army advanced from their own trenches across the pulverized earth that had held the enemy trenches. Twenty-four hours later the two sharp points of the American forceps, cutting into each side, met midway, and the ugly fang was removed.

America's First Army had fought its first battle and won its first victory, as an army. The achievement was not merely a good augury

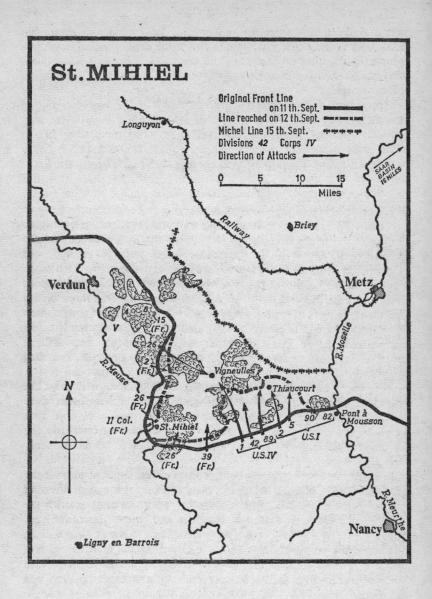

St.MIHIEL

Original Front Line
on 11th. Sept. ▬▬▬
Line reached on 12th.Sept. ▬ ▬ ▬ ▬
Michel Line 15 th. Sept. ◦◦◦ ◦◦◦ ◦◦◦ ◦◦◦
Divisions *42* Corps *IV*
Direction of Attacks ———→

0   5   10   15
                    Miles

SAAR
BASIN
16 MILES

Longuyon

Railway

Briey

Verdun

Metz

A B
15
(Fr.)

26

2
(Fr.)

R. Meuse

26
(Fr.)

Vigneulles

Thiaucourt

R. Moselle

II Col.
(Fr.)

St. Mihiel

N

26
(Fr.)

39
(Fr.)

1 42 89 2
U.S. IV

5

90 82

Pont à
Mousson

U.S. I

R. Meurthe

Nancy

Ligny en Barrois

but a vindication – especially of Pershing. And it was an invaluable tonic both to the army which fought and to the nation behind it, while a proportionate disillusionment to the Germans, who had questioned, even more strongly than her Allies, America's power to produce an effective army.

Apparently, the extraction of the St Mihiel fang was also one of the most perfectly complete pieces of strategic dentistry in the war. Actually, the operation was less satisfactory, and roots were left to cause trouble later. In part, the incompleteness was due to the faulty action of the forceps; in part to the dentist; but still more to the long-concealed fact that the dentist's arm was jogged. Yet there is still a question – whether the operation could have been more effective even if the dentist had not suffered interference.

To answer it, we must examine the cause and course of the operation. It was the fulfilment of a dream and a scheme which almost coincided with the entry of the United States into the war. Indeed, Pershing and his staff had come to Europe in June, 1917, with their eyes fixed on St Mihiel and their minds on Metz, behind it. The British, they knew, were committed to operations in Flanders and northern France, an area which, despite its drawbacks – mud especially – was nearest to their home base and gave them the shortest lines of communication with the Channel ports. The offensive operations of the French had all been carried out in the sector north of Paris and it was natural that they should concentrate to cover their capital.

The choice of the easterly sector facing and flanking Metz was the natural one for the Americans, because it clashed least with their Allies' lines of supply and was easiest of access from their own base ports in the Bay of Biscay. Moreover, this sector was obviously the Germans' most sensitive point, because a thrust there needed to penetrate only a short distance before it would imperil the stability of the whole German position in France – which formed a vast salient jutting southwards between Verdun and Ypres. For to sever the eastern end of the great lateral railway Metz–Maubeuge would at least restrict the free movement of reserves and supplies, and, more significant still, would 'turn' the flank of all the successive lines to which the German armies could withdraw short of their own frontier. Further, such a thrust promised the vital economic result of releasing the Briey iron region and threatening the Saar basin – upon which the Germans largely depended for their munitions. To pinch off the St Mihiel salient was not only a necessary preliminary to a secure offensive, but was a local operation well suited to the first test of a new force.

But the American Expeditionary Force was more intent to conserve its strength until maturity than had been the British. A year passed before it was ready, and before that the Germans had intervened elsewhere to compel a further postponement. Not until August, 1918, when the German tide had begun to ebb, was Pershing able to collect his scattered divisions – which had just helped in stemming it – and to form them into the first all-American army. And even so it had to depend on the French for most of its artillery and on the French and British for part of its aircraft.

On July 24th the commanders of the Allied armies met at Bombon to discuss their future action. The outcome was very modest. Foch did not choose to look far ahead and merely called for a series of local attacks to free his lateral railways. The first was delivered on August 8th in front of Amiens, and its dramatic evidence of the moral rot that had set in among the German troops changed the whole picture. On August 11th the newly formed staff of the First American Army moved to the St Mihiel area, and there developed their plan to a far more ambitious one than had been suggested at Bombon – from that of freeing the French lateral railways to that of threatening the German. Not merely to pinch off the salient but to break through its baseline, where ran the 'Michel' line as an inner barrier against any sudden rupture of the front. The plan framed by General Hugh Drum, the Chief of Staff, visualized the use of fifteen American divisions – each more than twice the strength of a French or British division – and four French divisions. Pershing approved the plan on August 15th and Foch two days later. Indeed, Foch added to it not only six more French divisions, but an extension of the frontage and the direction 'to strike the heaviest blow possible and secure the maximum results'.

But on August 30th Foch came to the American Headquarters at Ligny-en-Barrois with a radically different plan. The change was due to Haig's intervention. August 8th and its sequel had given him a clear perception of the German decline and, disregarding the cautious counsels of his government, he was now willing to test his judgement and risk his reputation by assaulting the ill-famed Hindenburg Line – the strongest defences on the whole German front. But he was anxious to reduce the risk of failure and increase the profit of success, and therefore urged Foch to change the main American attack from a divergent to a convergent direction. It would thus, he calculated, have a quicker and stronger reaction upon the German armies facing him, and by loosening their grip would ease his task – as he would similarly ease the Americans'.

Foch lent his ear the more readily to Haig's argument because his own horizon had enlarged. He now felt that the war might be finished in 1918, instead of 1919. And his enthusiastic assurance led him to transform his new method of alternating attacks at different points into a simultaneous general offensive – '*Tout le monde à la bataille.*' By it he seems to have hoped not merely to stretch and crack the German resistance, but even to cut off and surround the German armies between his converging pincers – British on one side and American on the other. Pétain, when consulted, was quite agreeable to the change of plan, which promised to draw the German reserves to either flank and leave the French a clearer path in the centre.

Thus when Foch came to Ligny-en-Barrois he proposed that the St Mihiel plan should be modified to a mere excision of the salient. This operation was to be a preliminary, and safeguard, to the rear of the American main attack – now to be launched north-west towards Mézières instead of north-east towards Metz. Foch further proposed that, while Pershing's army operated on the easier ground west of the Argonne, a Franco-American army under a French commander should attack the more difficult sector between the Argonne Forest and the Meuse. He also proposed to send General Degoutte to hold Pershing's hand and guide his tactical decisions.

The change of plan came as a shock to Pershing, and the other proposals as an affront. The interview was lively and the atmosphere grew heated. Foch hinted that he would appeal to President Wilson – and the threat had as little effect on Pershing as when previously used. Foch implied that Pershing was trying to shirk his share of the battle, and Pershing retorted that he was fully ready to fight 'as an American army'. Foch ironically suggested that even for St Mihiel Pershing could not raise an all-American army, but had to depend on his allies for guns, tanks and aircraft. Pershing retaliated with the reminder that by Allied request the Americans had shipped only infantry and machine guns during the spring crisis.

Foch wisely dropped the argument and left Pershing to 'chew the cud'. Next day Pershing, after reflection, wrote to Foch. He recognized the potential value of the convergent attack, but dwelt upon the difficulties of American participation. 'Since our arrival in France our plans ... have been based on the organization of the American army on the front St Mihiel–Belfort. All our depots, hospitals, training areas and other installations are located with reference to this front and a change of plans cannot be easily made.' Then he dealt with Foch's second proposal, contending that 'it is far more appropriate at the present moment for the Allies temporarily to furnish the American army with the services and auxiliaries it needs than for the Allies to expect further delay in the formation of the American army'.

Pershing did not attempt to hide his dislike of limiting the St Mihiel attack, and suggested that instead of switching at once to the Meuse–Argonne he should exploit the St Mihiel attack to the full and later, if necessary, mount a fresh attack 'either in the region of Belfort or Lunéville'. Not yet vouchsafed an intuition of victory that autumn, he suggested that these attacks would fit in with the ultimate American aim of taking charge 'during January and February' of 'the sector from St Mihiel to Switzerland'. 'However,' he said, 'it is your province to decide as to the strategy of operations, and I abide by your decision.'

On one question he was unshakable. 'I can no longer agree to any plan which involves the dispersion of our units.' 'Briefly, our officers and soldiers alike are, after one experience, no longer willing to be incorporated in other armies ... The danger of destroying by such dispersion the fine morale of the American soldiers is too great.' 'If you decide to utilize the American forces in attacking in the direction of Mézières I accept that decision, even though it complicates my supply system and the care of my sick and wounded, but I do insist that this American Army be employed as a whole.'

The result of this letter was a conference between Foch, Pétain and Pershing on September 2nd, whereat Pershing gave up his own plan for a share in Foch's and Foch conceded Pershing's claim to American unity. The concession was wrung from him by his own realization that without the Americans his right pincer would have a weak and worn point. And as Pershing preferred to attack east of Argonne, where supply would be easier although the ground was more difficult, he obtained his preference.

The one outstanding question was that of St Mihiel. Foch wanted the general offensive to open by September 20th at the latest, and suggested that the St Mihiel attack should be abandoned. Pershing and his staff decided that they must first cut off the St Mihiel wedge to safeguard the rear of their Meuse–Argonne attack. Again, their claim was conceded. But it meant that they would not switch divisions from one battle to the other in time, and that a number of raw divisions had to be used for the Meuse–Argonne attack. In addition, the St Mihiel attack was two days, and the Meuse–Argonne six days, behind timetable.

Each attack interfered with the other. And the consequences were compound, not simple. The first effect was upon the American dispositions. Instead of fifteen double-sized American divisions, which were available, only seven were used in the attack. Although this was a more than ample provision for the task, ensuring a numerical superiority of about eight to one over the Germans, the actual distribution was curious. For while six divisions (including two of Regulars) formed the right pincer, only one National Guard division formed the left. What had happened was that instead of reshuffling the entire dispositions the left pincer had been severely fined down, and the objectives rigorously limited. Foch, indeed, suggested that the left-wing attack should be abandoned.

The plan in detail was that Liggett's I Corps, on the extreme right nearest the hinge, and Dickman's IV Corps should attack the eastern face of the salient at 5 AM. Liggett would demonstrate with the 82nd Division against the hinge, while on its left his 90th, 5th, and 2nd Divisions thrust towards the baseline of the salient. Attacking next to them on the left were Dickman's 89th, 42nd and 1st Divisions. At 8 AM the 26th Division of Cameron's IV Corps would thrust into the western face of the salient, aiming to join hands with the 1st Division. Meantime the French would exert a gentle pressure on the nose of the salient to keep the defenders busy until their retreat was cut off.

But the Germans had for weeks been meditating and preparing to forestall the attack by a retreat. And when the Americans advanced to the assault on September 12th, the Germans had actually begun this withdrawal during the night. This fact has led to a satirical description of St Mihiel as 'the sector where the Americans relieved the Germans'. If there is some truth in the description, it is not the whole truth. Unlike the bigger strategic retreat to the Hindenburg Line in 1917, this withdrawal worked out to the disadvantage of those who planned it. Although the German command were as well aware of the impending blow as most of the population of France, and were not deceived by feints elsewhere, they hesitated too long over their decision and made their preparations too leisurely. Thus they were caught at a moment when part of their artillery had been withdrawn, and although a large part of the American bombardment – from 2,971 guns, mostly French – was wasted on empty trenches, the longer-range fire trapped some of the retiring Germans on the roads. Moreover, the comparative shortness of the bombardment, due largely to Liggett's insistence on the need for surprise, prevented the Germans gaining a comfortable start in their withdrawal. And the swift onrush of the American 2nd and 42nd Divisions, especially, upset their methodical arrangements.

But Pershing's plan was also too inelastic. Before midday Liggett's divisions had reached their final objectives and, soon after, their second day's objectives on the high ground north of Thaiucourt! The rapidity of their advance was accelerated by Liggett's instructions that units should press on as long as possible, without checking to keep alignment with their neighbours. Dazed and unsupported by their own artillery the Germans made practically no resistance. But Pershing felt himself tied by Foch's instructions and refused Liggett's plea for a further bound – which might have ruptured the Michel line. Dickman's and Cameron's converging corps reached their day's objectives with almost equal ease. But there, tied too closely to Pershing's apron strings, they came to a halt and awaited further orders.

Too late, Pershing tried to exploit his opportunity. If the German roads out of the salient were jammed, so also were his own roads into it. His orders for Dickman and Cameron to resume their advance did not reach the troops until after dark. And thus all but some four thousand of the forty or fifty thousand Germans in the bag slipped out before the neck was drawn tight by the junction of the two American corps at Vigneulles next morning. Nevertheless, Liggett had taken over 5,000 prisoners, and the other two corps, together with the French, had taken as many in their original advance. The total came to 15,000, and, more remarkable, 443 guns, for a cost of less than 8,000 casualties. If the result did not entirely satisfy the Americans, they could console themselves with the thought that this first attempt was no different from the past offensives of their Allies in failing to reap the harvest of an initial success.

During the 13th and 14th, Dickman and Cameron wheeled up, with the French 2nd Colonial Corps between, into alignment with Liggett facing the Michel line. Then, and there, the battle was broken off. The only serious fighting had been borne by Liggett's corps, which had met with counter-attacks owing to the menacing direction of its advance – the enemy was willing to evacuate the salient, but had no intention of allowing his baseline to be crossed.

What might have happened if Pershing had not been prevented from trying his original plan? There is no doubt that the Germans were immensely relieved that Pershing did not follow up his success; or that in their view a further advance in this direction would have been a greater menace than the Mézières direction of the Argonne offensive. Pershing's own view was emphatic – 'Without doubt, an immediate continuation of the advance would have carried us well beyond the Hindenburg line [the Michel line was an extension of the main Hindenburg line] and possibly into Metz.' Dickman was still more pungent – 'The failure to push north from St Mihiel with our overwhelming superiority in numbers will always be regarded by me as a strategical blunder for which Marshal Foch and his staff are responsible. It is a glaring example of the fallacy of the policy of limited objectives...'

On the other hand, Liggett, who proved himself perhaps the soundest reasoner and strongest realist in the American Army, has declared – 'The possibility of taking Metz and the rest of it, had the battle been fought on the original plan, existed, in my opinion, only on the supposition that our army was a well-oiled, fully coordinated machine – which it was not as yet.' He has also pointed out that although the attack between the Meuse and Argonne came as a greater surprise to the Germans they were able to throw in reserves so rapidly as to block the original breach by the third day. And even if the Michel line had been broken an advance from St Mihiel would then have met a fresh obstacle, especially on its right, in the defences of Metz. Significant also is the matured verdict of General von Gallwitz, the opposing German Army Group commander – 'An overrunning of the Michel position I consider out of the question. In order to capture this position a further ... operation on a very large scale would have been required.' It is well to remember that for decisive results Pershing would at least have had to reach the Longuyon–Thionville stretch of the lateral railway, a further twenty miles beyond the Michel line, and to have gone far enough beyond it to interrupt the line running back from Longuyon through Luxembourg. It would have demanded a penetration deeper and quicker than any yet achieved by the Allies on the Western Front. With an untried army this was surely a remote hope.

Yet there is one factor of which criticism has taken no account; a factor which endowed Pershing's original plan with a peculiar advantage. Almost every attempted breakthrough in the war had been based on the idea of a single penetration. Among the few exceptions had been the simultaneous Artois and Champagne attacks on September 25th, 1915. But although in form a dual penetration, the effect was that of two single ones, for they were too far apart to cause any prompt sagging and collapse of the sector between. The convergent Argonne and Cambrai thrusts of Foch's new plan had also the same appearance of duality but an even wider interval between them.

Now duality is the very essence of war, although curiously overlooked. Everyone recognizes the advantage which even a light-weight boxer has in using two fists against a one-armed opponent. So in war the power to use two fists is an inestimable asset. To feint with one fist and strike with the other yields an advantage, but a still greater advantage lies in being able to interchange them – to convert the feint into the real blow if the opponent uncovers himself. Nor should duality be limited to the force. Duality of objective, of which Sherman was the supreme exponent, enables the attacker to get his opponent on the horns of a dilemma, and, by mystifying him, to obtain the chance of surprising him, so that if the opponent concentrates in defence of one objective the attacker can seize the other. Only by this elasticity of aim can we truly attune ourselves to the uncertainty of war.

Returning from the general to the particular, we can recognize that the St Mihiel salient offered the chance of attempting the yet untried method of dual penetration under almost ideal conditions. If two powerful attacks had broken through the flanks of the salient – and better still, beyond them to right and left – the defenders in the centre would have dissolved into chaos – and been securely 'caged'. Through this collapsed centre a fresh force might then have driven, with a clear path between the two protecting wings. What we know of the incompleteness of the baseline defences and the time taken before they were completely garrisoned suggests that, on September 12th and 13th at least, they could have been ruptured on a wide front. On a smaller scale, the actual attack fulfilled this process as far as it went, but the wings were then held back and there was no fresh force to pass through the centre.

But it is still a question how far the Americans could have advanced beyond the breach. And here the main factor would not have been defences or defenders, but supplies. The road blocks and transport difficulties actually experienced in the limited advance do not encourage an optimistic answer. It is more likely that the eventual result would have justified Liggett's opinion – and Napoleon's axiom; 'With a new army it is possible to carry a formidable position, but not to carry out a plan or design.' And the last weeks of the war were to show that even experienced armies could not solve the problem of maintaining supplies during a sustained advance, even though almost unopposed. For bulk cancels out experience.

CHAPTER EIGHT

SCENE 8

The Battle of a Nightmare –
The Meuse-Argonne

Although a far greater battle in scale the Meuse-Argonne is less significant, except to the combatants, than St Mihiel. Strategically and historically it may even be viewed as an appendix to the unfinished and
partly unwritten story of St Mihiel.

In the first place, the ultimate aim was more idealistic than realistic.
It was based on the idea that the Ardennes formed an impenetrable
back wall to the great German salient in France, and that if the Allies
could reach and close the exits east and west they would cut off the
German armies in the salient. But the impossibility of the Ardennes
had been much exaggerated, especially in Haig's reports. Actually, the
Ardennes were traversed by numerous roads and several railways, so
that though the severance of the routes east and west might complicate
the German withdrawal this would be imperilled only if the objective
was attained very rapidly. As always in war, everything turned on the
time factor.

To reach the lateral railway from the Meuse-Argonne sector the
Americans would have to advance thirty miles. And to be effective they
would have to advance more rapidly than from the St Mihiel sector,
because their thrust would be aimed close to the main German armies
instead of, like the projected St Mihiel thrust, close to the German
frontier. The attempt, and hope, was fundamentally unreal. To cross
these thirty miles of difficult country, they would first have to break
through the German front and then, some eight miles behind it, would
meet the untouched defences of the Kriemhilde section of the Hindenburg Line. Pershing might have confidence in the capacity of his untried army, but his faith, like that of the French in 1914 and 1915, was
to founder on the rock of machine guns. Pétain, if he underestimated
the effect of other factors, was closer to reality when he predicted that
the Americans might cover a third of the distance before the winter.

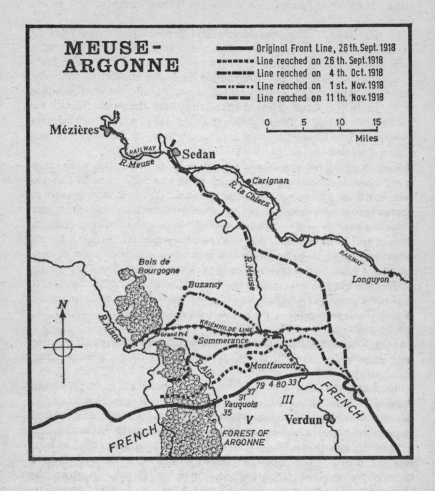

MEUSE-ARGONNE

Original Front Line, 26 th. Sept. 1918
Line reached on 26 th. Sept. 1918
Line reached on 4 th. Oct. 1918
Line reached on 1 st. Nov. 1918
Line reached on 11 th. Nov. 1918

0   5   10   15
Miles

Mézières

RAILWAY
R. Meuse
Sedan

Carignan
R. la Chiers

Bois de
Bourgogne

Buzancy

R. Meuse

RAILWAY
Longuyon

N

R. Aisne

KRIEMHILDE LINE
Grand Pré
Sommerance

R. Aire

Montfaucon

FRENCH

79 4 80 33
37
Vauquois 91
35

III

V   Verdun

77 28

I

FRENCH

FOREST OF
ARGONNE

That roughly was as far as their original attack reached, and there they stuck, until other factors, unforeseen by Pétain, intervened to relieve them.

In the second place, the Meuse-Argonne attack did not fulfil its immediate aim, the Haig-inspired aim for which Pershing had sacrificed his own plan. For the left-wing attack broke through the Cambrai–St Quentin section of the Hindenburg Line, the strongest artificially, before the Meuse-Argonne attack had drawn off any German divisions from the British front. Thus the result justified Haig's confidence but not his precaution, proving that his troops could break through without indirect help to ease their path. The strength of the defences was nullified by the weakening morale of the defenders.

The irony of the result was increased by the fact that while fifty-seven German divisions faced the left-wing attack by forty British and two American divisions, only twenty German divisions were present to oppose the right-wing attack by thirteen American and thirty-one French divisions – the equivalent of at least sixty ordinary-strength divisions. The difference of result may be explained, in part, by the differing degree of experience, and in part by the difference of conditions. The left-wing attack opened with the British close on the edge of the Hindenburg Line, while on the right wing the Americans had to conquer a deep series of defences before they could assault their section of the Hindenburg Line. And before they reached it their attack had lost its momentum.

Thereafter although stubborn American assaults at heavy cost caused the Germans to draw off, on balance, a further sixteen divisions from the French front, the strategic effect was small. For with shrewd strategic sense the French in the centre appreciated that decisive results depended on the rapid penetration and closing of the pincers, and so did not unduly hasten the retreat of the Germans facing them. In their skilful advance they usually kept a step in rear of their Allies on either flank, moving forward by successive bounds when the enemy had been shouldered back. For the first two years they had borne the main burden of the fighting. If their commanders had been slow to learn how to economize life, they, and still more their men, had learnt it now. Perhaps a shade too well. But it is not for those who were fresh in the evening of the war to complain of excess of caution in those who had suffered the full heat of the day, since dawn.

On the other hand, criticism of the disappointingly early check of the Meuse-Argonne attack has been too apt to overlook the handicap of excessive freshness. The trouble was not merely that the troops were fresh – perhaps it was mostly that the arrangements were fresh. The Americans had scarcely a week of real preparation – an astonishing contrast with the months which preceded the French and British offensives of 1915, 1916, and even 1917. Even though the German fighting power and morale were now in decline, such haste would have put an almost superhuman strain on any troops. Yet it was demanded of new troops with a new organization. Popular opinion might complain of the frequency with which the machine jammed; the miracle is that it did not collapse and, instead, was rapidly repaired to move forward anew.

It is equally creditable to the higher command that the opening attack achieved so high a degree of surprise. This preparatory success owed much to the ingenuity of the Intelligence section in creating the most artistic mirage of an offensive farther east, near the Vosges.

Thus when the real offensive was launched, the twenty-mile front of attack was held by only five German divisions, all emaciated, and all but one composed of low-grade troops. Against them were thrown nine American divisions, with three more in close reserve – a superiority in fighting strength of about eight to one. There were three more divisions in army reserve. But, owing to the difficulty of withdrawing and switching troops from St Mihiel, only one Regular division could be used at the outset, and only three had previous battle experience.

The attack was preceded by a three hours' intense bombardment from 2,700 guns and accompanied by 189 small tanks. It is significant to note that the proportion of tanks was much lower than in the Allied offensives of July 15th and August 8th. It is also noteworthy, in view of Pershing's pre-St Mihiel hint to Foch, that all the artillery was French-made, and half of it manned by the French, as also were forty-seven of the tanks.

Pershing's plan was far-reaching. It certainly cannot be criticized as circumscribed or shortsighted, for the attacking troops were expected to reach and break through the Kriemhilde line on the first day, an advance of over eight miles, and were to exploit the success during the night so that the second morning would find them in open country and almost halfway to Sedan and the lateral railway. Unfortunately, Pershing's orders were by no means clearly worded.

Foch in a personal note had intimated that the American Army must not let itself be tied by the pace of its neighbour, Gouraud's French Fourth Army, and added – 'There is no question of fixing ... fronts not to be passed without a new order – such a restrictive indication tending to prevent exploitation of opportunities ...'

Unfortunately, Pershing's orders to his corps had this very tendency, however far-reaching his aim. Bullard's III Corps on the right and Liggett's I Corps on the left, were to drive in wedges on either flank of the commanding height of Montfaucon, thus helping Cameron's V Corps in the centre, which was to sweep over Montfaucon and on to the Kriemhilde line 'without waiting for advance of the III and I Corps'. This provision was wise, but less happily their advance was to be 'based upon the V Corps'. Here lay the germ of paralysis.

For when the assault was launched, at 5.30 AM on September 26th, the V Corps, which had its flanks protected, made far less progress than its neighbours – although its left division, the 91st, was a happy exception. On the right of the V Corps the 4th (Regular) Division of Bullard's corps penetrated deeply past the flank of Montfaucon, while the 80th and 33rd near the Meuse made good progress. On the left wing of the army, which had the most difficult task and ground, Liggett's orders paved the way for a good start. Thus the 35th Division neatly circumvented the formidable obstacle of Vauquois by an encircling advance, and then, with the 28th Division on their left, drove a wedge nearly four miles deep up the Aire Valley just east of the Argonne Forest. Through the forest itself moved the 77th Division, which had the difficult task of linking up with the French on the west side.

Then, however, Pershing's orders for a halt, on reaching the corps' objective, were construed as putting a brake on the advance, and it was difficult to get up momentum again after the six hours' delay. A method that was sound in siege warfare was, as Liggett's insight told him, a mistake when faced with a weak and temporarily demoralized enemy. The Americans had, as yet, neither the training nor organization for methodical siege warfare, and the best chance of decisive success lay in swamping the defence by a human torrent in the first flush of surprise before the enemy could bring up reinforcements. With the brake put on prematurely, the advance thereafter slowed down and became spasmodic along the whole front. Guns could not get forward to support the infantry, control lapsed, and supplies frequently failed, through inexperience accentuating the natural difficulties of the ground.

All these factors helped the success of the Germans' own tactics in drawing the sting from the attack. For the Germans had repeated the method of elastic defence – with the real resistance some miles in rear. The unexpectant Americans ran into this cunningly woven belt of fire when their initial spurt was exhausted and their formation disordered. Although Montfaucon was taken – by the 79th Division – on the second day, the V Corps only came up level with the two flank corps, and they had made little further progress that day. The great offensive had practically shot its bolt and, in the days that followed, the arrival of fresh German divisions enabled the enemy to counter-attack and force back the disjointed attackers in places. A renewed general attack on October 4th made little progress, except on the left, and revealed once more the folly of trying to overthrow machine guns by sheer weight of human bodies without adequate fire support or surprise. But the value of training was also shown by the regular 1st Division in Liggett's corps which drove in a deep if narrow wedge on the east bank of the Aire. This enabled Liggett, on October 7th, to try a manoeuvre both original and daring; bringing the 82nd Division up in the wake of the 1st, he swung it against the enemy's flank west of the Aire and then northward. If the execution fell below the conception – only a tithe of the division came into action – so that the chance of cutting off the enemy troops in the Argonne was lost, the threat at least persuaded the enemy to retire from the forest while there was time, and by October 10th the American line had passed and was clear of this hampering obstacle.

Meantime, the all too obvious failure to fulfil the original plan had provoked widespread reactions behind the front. Clemenceau visited Foch and bitterly remarked – 'Those Americans will lose us our chance of a big victory before winter. They are all tangled up with themselves. You have tried to make Pershing see. Now let's put it up to President Wilson.' The complaint was rather unfair in view of the fact that the advance of Gouraud's army was well behind that of the American, if by design. But Foch was more generous – or more fully aware of the firmness of Pershing's position – and replied – 'The Americans have got to learn some time. They are learning now, rapidly.' Pétain, indeed, had made the strategically sound suggestion of giving charge of the Argonne Forest sector to a separate army, half French and half American, under General Hirschauer – but Pershing had seen in it only a fresh political manoeuvre, and had rejected it firmly.

Pershing, however, overhauled his own army – and its commanders. The inactive forces east of the Meuse were formed into the Second American Army, to be commanded by Bullard, while Liggett was given charge of the First and of the Meuse-Argonne attack. Pershing himself retained the superior direction of both and left Hugh Drum to continue as Chief of Staff to Liggett. Dickman succeeded Liggett in the I Corps, and Hines succeeded Bullard, while Cameron was replaced by Summerall. Other commanders of all grades fell beneath Pershing's sickle almost as fast as their men beneath the scythe of the German machine guns.

But for a time these changes made little impression on the Germans. The next general attack on October 14th achieved little at large cost – both of men's lives and generals' reputations – and with its failure even the higher command realized that the offensive had reached stalemate. An attempt to press on, with exhausted troops and disordered communications, could exercise no pressure adequate to be any appreciably greater relief to the other Allied armies. Moreover, the British left wing of the Allied offensive, in which the 27th and 30th American Divisions shared, had already broken through the last defences of the Hindenburg Line and by October 5th had emerged into open country, with only natural obstacles, mileage and a devastated area to hinder its advance.

Liggett, who now took charge, was wise to realize that in the circumstances it was far better to rest and reorganize his forces, for a sure bound as soon as possible, than to sacrifice lives in attempting the impossible. While utilizing the breathing space not only to replenish his ranks and supplies but to improve his communications and overhaul his organization, he carried out local operations to obtain a good jumping-off line for the fresh bound. Further, he recast not only the tactics but the plan. Pershing had proposed that the American left should strike first, followed in turn by the remaining corps to the right. This meant battering first at the naturally strong and heavily wooded Bois de Bourgogne area due north of the Argonne, where also the enemy were in strongest force. Liggett preferred to drive a broad wedge in the centre and so outflank the Bois de Bourgogne, threatening its encirclement in conjunction with the advance of the French Fourth Army to the west.

It was well conceived, for when Liggett unleashed his forces on November 1st, this area was the only one which showed resisting power, and by next day the enemy rearguards there had disappeared and were falling back as fast as on the rest of the American front. If the Germans were offering little resistance, the very rapidity of the pursuit – out-stripping the French on the flank – imposed almost as great a strain, and it was a tribute to the overhaul that the First Army machine functioned much more smoothly than in the earlier phase. And this despite the execution of a most difficult manoeuvre by which the whole army wheeled progressively to the right during the course of the pursuit, ready for an attack north-eastwards – against the strong position between the Meuse and Chiers rivers to which the enemy had retired. This wheel was a preliminary to an advance towards Metz, but the

Armistice now rang down the curtain.

Strategically this move was more important, because the Germans here were more sensitive, than the now incidental arrival of the left wing on the Carignan–Sedan section of the lateral railway. This railway had been brought under artillery fire as early as November 3rd, and had been reached by the infantry four days later, but the Germans had already slipped out of the bag. Indeed, the advance to this point, although an exhilarating finish, was chiefly significant in showing the 'liberties' that could be and were taken at the finish. With a somewhat brusque disregard of French feelings Pershing issued a message that he wished the American Army to have 'the honour of entering Sedan' – although it was now in the French sector of advance. Pershing added the encouragement or incitement – 'Boundaries will not be considered as binding.' The message was passed to the corps without being shown to Liggett, and as a result the 42nd Division on the left of the army raced for Sedan. But the vague wording produced a still more un-military – indeed, a burlesque– result. For the 1st Division – Pershing's favourite – from the centre corps had also started to race thither by night, crossing the divisions of the I Corps and throwing them into confusion as it impetuously swept through them. It capped the farce by taking prisoner the commander of the 42nd Division. Liggett, however, intervened with prompt action and vigorous language – to restrain both divisions and allow the French the courtesy of entering Sedan, thus to wipe out the bitter memory of 1870.

The historian who scans the whole horizon of the war must recognize that this last offensive, beginning on November 1st, had only a supplementary influence, for Ludendorff had fallen from power – his plea for a renewed stand on the German frontier rejected – and the enemy were already suing for peace before Liggett struck. Nevertheless it was well that the Armistice had tarried long enough to allow the offensive of November 1st to take place. For it provided a counterpoise to the bitter memories of the first phase – more truly, the first battle – of the Meuse-Argonne, and a proof that when purged and refined by experience the American army could produce leadership and staff work worthy of the gallant sacrifice of the fighting troops – the American nation in arms.

Epilogue

Every anniversary of the Armistice kindles emotions and memories such as no other day in the year has at present the power to do. For those who shared in the experiences of those four and a quarter years of struggle the commemoration does not stale with repetition. But the mood in which it is commemorated has undergone subtle changes. On the original Armistice itself the dominant note was a sigh of relief, of infinite volume, most restrained among those who had the most direct cause for relief, most exuberant, perhaps, among those who least appreciated the relief.

The earlier anniversaries were dominated by two opposite emotions. On the one hand grief, a keener sense, now that the storm had passed, of the vacant places in our midst. On the other hand, triumph, flamboyant only in rare cases, but nevertheless a heightened sense of victory, that the enemy had been laid low. That mood again has passed.

Armistice Day has become a commemoration instead of a celebration. The passage of time has refined and blended the earlier emotions, so that, without losing sense of the personal loss and quiet thankfulness that as a people we proved our continued power to meet a crisis graver than any in past annals, we are today conscious, above all, of the general effects on the world and on civilization. In this mood of reflection we are more ready to recognize both the achievements and the point of view of our late enemies, and perhaps all the more because we realize that both the causes and the course of war are determined by the folly and the frailty rather than by the deliberate evil of human nature.

The war has become history, and can be viewed in the perspective of history. For good it has deepened our sense of fellowship and community of interest, whether inside the nation or between nations. But, for good or bad, it has shattered our faith in idols, our hero-worshipping belief that great men are different clay from common men. Leaders are still necessary, perhaps more necessary, but our awakened realization of their common humanity is a safeguard against either expecting from them or trusting in them too much. It has been for the benefit both of history and of future generations that the past decade has seen such a flood of evidence and revelations, of documents and memoirs. That most of the actors are still alive provides an invaluable check in sifting the evidence, while the historians themselves have been so immersed in the atmosphere of war that they have a certain immunity from the abstract theorizing which an historian in his cloistered study fifty years later so easily contracts. We know nearly all that is to be known. The one drawback is that the flood has been so huge that only the student has been able to cope with its investigation.

What caused that astonishingly sudden collapse and surrender of Germany which, as by a miracle, so it seemed, lifted the nightmare load of war from Europe? To arrive at a satisfactory answer it is not sufficient to analyse the hectic weeks of negotiation and military success which preceded November 11th. Even in the military sphere we need to go back to August 8th, the day which filled the German command with the conviction of defeat, and to July 18th, which witnessed the visible turning of the tide. And if we go back thither we must go back further, to March 21st, for the decline of Germany's military power is not explicable without reference to the consummation of that military effort, and consumption of her military resources, in the great series of offensives which opened in the spring of 1918.

We ought, however, to go back further still. Indeed, if the historian of the future has to select one day as decisive for the outcome of the World War he will probably choose August 2nd, 1914 – before the war, for England, had yet begun – when Mr Winston Churchill, at 1.25 AM, sent the order to mobilize the British Navy. That Navy was to win no Trafalgar, but it was to do more than any other factor towards winning the war for the Allies. For the Navy was the instrument of the blockade, and as the fog of war disperses in the clearer light of these postwar years that blockade is seen to assume larger and larger proportions, to be more and more clearly the decisive agency in the struggle. Like those 'jackets' which used to be applied in American jails to refractory prisoners, as it was progressively tightened so did it first cramp the prisoner's movements and then stifle his breathing, while the tighter it became and the longer it continued the less became the prisoner's power of resistance and the more demoralizing the sense of constriction.

Helplessness induces hopelessness, and history attests that loss of hope and not loss of lives is what decides the issue of war. No historian would underrate the direct effect of the semi-starvation of the German people in causing the final collapse of the 'home front'. But leaving aside the question of how far the revolution caused the military defeat, instead of vice versa, the intangible all-pervading factor of the blockade intrudes into every consideration of the military situation.

This, during the last year of the war, is studded with 'ifs'. If Germany, instead of throwing all her military resources into a series of tremendous offensives in 1918, had stayed on the defensive in the west, while consolidating her gains in the east, could she have averted defeat? Militarily there seems little doubt that she could. In the light of the experience of 1915, when the Allies had 145 divisions in the west to Germany's 100, and when the German trench systems were a frail and shallow bulwark compared with those of 1918, it is difficult to see that the Allies could have breached it, even if they had waited until the inflowing tide of American man power had restored to them the relative numerical superiority that they had enjoyed in 1915.

And if so, in face of the accumulating cost of vain assaults, would they not eventually have inclined towards a compromise peace? A peace, peradventure, which, in return for the relinquishment of Belgium and Northern France, might have conceded to Germany part or the whole of her gains in the east. Yet as we ask the question, and militarily find an optimistic answer difficult, the factor of the command of the sea comes to mind. For it was the stranglehold of the British Navy which, in default of a serious peace move, constrained Germany to carry out that *felo de se* offensive of 1918. She was dogged by the spectre of slow enfeeblement ending in eventual collapse.

Perhaps if she had adopted such a war policy of defence in the west, offence in the east, after the Marne in 1914, or even, after 1915, continued the policy which she had that year temporarily adopted, her prospects might have been brighter and her story different; for, on the one hand, she could have consummated unquestionably the dream of 'Mittel-Europa', and on the other, the blockade was still a loose grip, and could hardly have been drawn effectively tight so long as the United States remained outside the conflict. But in 1918 the best chance had passed.

Another big 'if', often mooted, is the question whether even in the autumn of 1918 Germany could have avoided capitulation. Would the fighting front have collapsed if the war had gone on after November 11th? Was capitulation inevitable, or could the German armies have made good their retreat and stood firm on their own frontiers? German opinion largely says 'yes' to the latter question, and blames the surrender on the 'home front'. Many open-minded and diligent students of the war among the Allies are inclined to agree that it was possible from a military point of view. But again the naval aspect intervenes. Even if the German armies, and the German people, roused to a supreme effort in visible defence of their own soil, had managed to hold the Allies at bay, the end could only have been postponed. The most that history is likely to concede is that they might have held on long enough, tightening their belts, for the Allies, already weary, to sicken of the effort, and thus concede more favourable terms than those of Versailles.

Having disposed of the 'ifs', having emphasized the fundamental cause of the Armistice – Britain's sea power, her historic weapon, the deadliest weapon which any nation has wielded throughout history – let us turn to examine the immediate causes of the Armistice. How did victory come? Here military action bulks large. Other factors contributed, apart from the naval. If we do not accept entirely, we should not discount unduly the unwilling tribute paid by the Germans to the effectiveness of Allied, and especially of British, propaganda. In the later stages of the war it was skilfully directed and intensively developed.

If now, when passions are stilled, the memory of some of the 'facts' that were exploited is disturbing to our sense of fair play and lies uneasily on the stomach, we realize equally that such forms of propaganda neither stimulated our own people nor discouraged the enemy. It was the kernel of essential truth upon the bigger issues which was digested by the German people and, by leading them to question both the honesty of their leadership and the hope of success, weakened the will to continued sacrifice.

Nevertheless, though we should recognize the value of the more discriminating propaganda, its effect was rather in supplementing and completing the military successes than in paving the way for them, as German spokesmen have often contended. There is significant evidence on this point to be found in the memoirs of Prince Max of Baden, a man whose high-minded patriotism and sincerity command the respect of both friend and foe, and whose book is one of the most valuable of the war memoirs yet published. Unintentionally, and unconsciously, he shows in casual passages, easily missed, that when German arms were temporarily in the ascendant moderation was forgotten in exultation, even among the more sober.

In March, 1918, he quotes even a pacifist as exuberantly crying – 'Never worry! ... What an experience! ... World dominion.' And another representative of moderate opinion 'let the cat out of the bag' in saying meditatively – 'It would seem that we needn't say no to Briey and Longwy' – revealing that intoxication of spirit which, more fundamentally than any ill intention, was responsible for Germany's war guilt.

In face of such widespread intoxication, propaganda could only be secondary to military action. Thus we are left with the sure conclusion that the success of the Allied armies was chief among the immediate causes of Germany's capitulation on November 11th.

That conclusion does not necessarily, or even naturally, imply that at the moment of the Armistice the German armies were on the brink of collapse. Nor that the Armistice was a mistaken concession – as some among the Allies, usually those whose fighting was done with their tongue, were so loud in proclaiming at the time.

Rather does the record of the last 'hundred days', when thoroughly sifted, confirm the immemorial lesson of history – that the true aim in war is the mind of the enemy command and Government, not the bodies of their troops, that the balance between victory and defeat turns on mental impressions and only indirectly on physical blows. That in war, as Napoleon said and Foch endorsed, 'it is the man, not men, who counts'.

The reiteration of this great truth is to be found in the war's last phase. Great as was the stimulus and visible success of the tide-turning battle on the Marne in July, Ludendorff was still planning and preparing fresh offensives thereafter. If he was chagrined, he does not appear to have been so disillusioned as he had been after his own outwardly successful attack on the Lys in April.

But the Fourth Army surprise attack before Amiens on August 8th was a dislocating moral blow. Prince Max put August 8th in its true light psychologically, when he defined it as 'the turning point'. Even so, to develop the conviction of failure into the conviction of hopelessness required to compel surrender, something more was needed. It came not from the Western Front, but from a despised 'side-show' – Salonika, long condemned by Allied military opinion and scornfully ridiculed by the Germans as their 'largest internment camp'. With Bulgaria's collapse the back gate to Austria, as well as to Turkey, and through Austria to Germany, lay ajar.

The immediate issue of the war was decided on September 29th, decided in the mind of the German Command. Ludendorff and his associates had then 'cracked', and the sound went echoing backwards until it had resounded throughout the whole of Germany. Nothing could catch it or stop it. The Command might recover its nerve, the actual military position might improve, but the moral impression, as ever in war, was decisive.

Yet, let us once again emphasize that the fundamental causes of the decision are more various than the acts which immediately produced it.

The truth is that no one cause was, or could be, decisive. The Western Front, the Balkan front, the tank, the blockade and propaganda have all been claimed as the cause of victory. All claims are justified, none is wholly right, although the blockade ranks first and began first. In this warfare between nations victory was a cumulative effect, to which all weapons – military, economic, and psychological – contributed. Victory came, and could only come through the utilization and combination of all the resources existing in a modern nation, and the dividend of success depended on the way in which these manifold activities were coordinated.

It is even more futile to ask which country won the war. France did not win the war, but unless she had held the fort while the forces of Britain were preparing and those of America still a dream the release of civilization from this nightmare of militarism would have been impossible. Britain did not win the war, but without her command of the sea, her financial support, and her army, to take over the main burden of the struggle from 1916 onwards, defeat would have been inevitable. The United States did not win the war, but without their economic aid to ease the strain, without the arrival of their troops to turn the numerical balance, and, above all, without the moral tonic which their coming gave, victory would have been impossible. And let us not forget how many times Russia had sacrificed herself to save her allies; preparing the way for their ultimate victory as surely as for her own downfall. Finally, whatever be the verdict of history on her policy, unstinted tribute is due to the incomparable endurance and skill with which Germany more than held her own for four years against superior numbers – an epic of military and human achievement.

Bibliography

The appended list is, of course, far from a complete list of the books which have been read or consulted during the fifteen years since the war. Its purpose is to indicate those of main historical significance. It comprises those sources from which facts or quotations have been drawn for use herein, or which have directly helped in forming one's picture of the war. During these years one has also been privileged to see a number of documents, British and foreign, which have not yet been published or utilized, and to gather the personal evidence of those who participated in critical actions and in the taking of important decisions. Such sources, where they have contributed to the narrative, are referred to as either 'Unpublished Documents' or 'Personal Evidence'. Although it is not yet possible to give a fuller identification, all such sources have been recorded and privately catalogued for the eventual use of historical students.

In concluding this preface to the Bibliography I take the opportunity to acknowledge the great debt which all serious students of the war owe to the *Army Quarterly*, and especially its 'Notes on Foreign War Books'. This feature during the past ten years has been invaluable as a signpost and searchlight amid the vast and confusing mass of material that has been published. No periodical, military or historical, in any country has kept or marked so clear a track for students of the war.

Books published since 1930 are listed separately on pages 485–90, save in the case of a few continuing volumes of books published earlier.

CHAPTER I

ORIGINS

J. W. Headlam-Morley, *The Outbreak of War. Foreign Office Documents* (1926)

G. P. Gooch and H. Temperley, *British Documents on the Origins of the War*, vols i-v (1927)

Haldane (Viscount), *Before the War* (1920)

Grey of Fallodon (Viscount), *Twenty-Five Years, 1892–1916* (1925)

G. Buchanan, *My Mission to Russia* (1923)

H. Wickham Steed, *Through Thirty Years, 1892–1922* (1924)

R. W. Seton-Watson, *Sarajevo* (1926)

G. P. Gooch, *Recent Revelations of European Diplomacy* (1927)

H. W. Wilson, *The War Guilt* (1928)

B. Hendrick, *The Life and Letters of W. H. Page* (1922–5)

P. Renouvin, *Les Origines Immédiates de la Guerre* (1925)

R. Poincaré, *Au Service de la France*, vols i-iv (1926–7)

M. Paléologue, *An Ambassador's Memoirs* (Eng trans 1923–5)

German Foreign Office, *Die Grosse Politik der Europäischen Kabinette, 1871–1914* (1926) (Eng selection and trans in 4 vols *German Diplomatic Documents, 1871–1914*, 1928–)

K. Kautsky, M. Montgelas and W. Schücking, *Die Deutschen Dokumente zum Kriegsausbruch* (1919) (Eng trans 1924)

A. von Tirpitz, *Memoirs* (Eng trans 1919)

The Kaiser's Letters to the Tsar (Eng trans 1920)

M. Montgelas, *The Case for the Central Powers* (Eng trans 1925)

K. Lichnowsky, *My Mission to London, 1912–1914* (1918)

Generaloberst Helmuth von Moltke. Erinnerungen–Briefe–Dokumente 1877–1916 (1923)

W. von Schoen, *The Memoirs of an Ambassador* (Eng trans 1922)

Diplomatische Aktenstücke zur Vorgeschichte des Krieges, 1914 (1919) (Eng trans *Austrian Red Book*, 1920)

Conrad von Hötzendorf, *Aus meiner Dienstzeit*, vols i-iv (1922–5)

Czernin, *In the World War* (Eng trans 1920)

How the War began in 1914, being the diary of the Russian Foreign Office ... July, 1914 ... published by the Russian Soviet Government (Eng trans 1925)

S. Sazonov, *Fateful Years, 1909–1916* (Eng trans 1927)

Un Livre Noir, diplomatie d'avant guerre d'après les documents des archives russes (1922–3)

CHAPTERS II–VII

GENERAL

W. S. Churchill, *The World Crisis*, 4 vols (1923–7)

John Buchan, *A History of the Great War*, 4 vols (1921)

Oxford and Asquith (Earl of), *Memories and Reflections* (1928)

G. Arthur, *Life of Lord Kitchener*, vol iii (1920)

Esher (Viscount), *The Tragedy of Lord Kitchener* (1921)

C. à C. Repington, *The First World War, 1914–1918*, 2 vols (1920)

W. R. Robertson, *From Private to Field Marshal* (1921)
    Soldiers and Statesmen, 1914–1918 (1926)

Beaverbrook (Lord), *Politicians and the War, 1914–1916* (1928)

N. Macready, *Annals of an Active Life* (1926)

C. E. Callwell, *Experiences of a Dug-Out, 1914–1918* (1921)

C. P. Lucas, *The Empire at War*, 3 vols [covers war effort of Dominions and Colonies]

Royal Engineers' Institute, *The Work of the R.E. in the European War, 1914–1919*, 9 vols (1921–7)

War Office, *Statistics of the Military Effort of the British Empire, 1914–1920* (1922)

R. van Overstraeten, *Des Principes de la Guerre*, vol ii [vol ii covers World War]

C. Seymour, *The Intimate Papers of Colonel House*, 4 vols (1926–8)

J. W. Gerard, *My Four Years in Germany* (1927) [USA ambassador]

E. Ludendorff, *Urkunden der Obersten Heeresleitung, 1916–1918* (1920)

Kuhl, *Der Deutsche Generalstab in Vorbereitung und Durchführung des Weltkrieges* (1920) [French condensed trans my Douchy, *Le Grand État-Major Allemand avant et pendant la Guerre Mondiale*]

M. Erzberger, *Erlebnisse im Weltkrieg* (1921) [French trans *Souvenirs de guerre*]

J. V. Bredt, *Die Belgische Neutralität und der Schlieffensche Feldzugsplan* (1929) [excellent summary in *Army Quarterly*, July 1929]

E. von Falkenhayn, *General Headquarters, 1914–1916 and its Critical Decisions* (Eng trans 1919)

Stürgkh (Graf), *Im deutschen Grossen Hauptquartier* (1921) [intimate impressions and pen-portraits by the Austrian military representative]

Zwehl, *Erich von Falkenhayn* (1925) [contains extracts from diary]

Groener, *Das Testament des Grafen Schlieffen* (1927)

H. von Hentig, *Psychologische Strategie des Grossen Krieges* (1927) [criticism, usually acute, of the German war policy and strategy]

L. Gehre, *Die deutsche Kraftverteilung während des Weltkrieges* (1928) [gives location of all German divisions on 15th and last day of every month]

Bauer, *Der Grosse Krieg in Feld und Heimat* (1922) [intimate revelations of the German Supreme Command during the war]

M. Schwarte, *Der Grosse Krieg, 1914–1918*, 11 vols (1921–)

Buat, *L'Armée Allemande pendant la Guerre de 1914–1918* (1920)

WESTERN FRONT

J. E. Edmonds, *Military Operations, France and Belgium*, vols i–v (1922–32) [*British Official History*, vol i–ii, 1914; iii–iv, 1915; v, 1916]

The Despatches of Lord French, 1914–1915 (1917)

French (Viscount), *1914* (1919) [a record of his command, distinguished by inaccuracy]

J. H. Boraston (Ed.), *Sir D. Haig's Despatches, 1915–1919* (1919)

G. A. B. Dewar and J. H. Boraston, *Sir Douglas Haig's Command, 1915–1918* (1922)

H. L. Smith-Dorrien, *Memories of Forty-Eight Years' Service* (1925) [covers, if with extreme reserve, his service as corps and army commander in the first phase]

C. E. Callwell, *Field-Marshal Sir Henry Wilson*, 2 vols (1927) [extracts from an amazingly unreserved diary, 1914–19]

F. Maurice, *The Life of General Lord Rawlinson of Trent* (1928) [covers the whole war]

J. Charteris, *Field-Marshal Earl Haig* (1929)

Huguet, *Britain and the War* (Eng trans 1928) [impressions of French representative at British GHQ, 1914–15]

C. E. W. Bean, *The Australian Imperial Force in France, 1916* (1929) [Australian Official History]

J. Monash, *The Australian Victories in France in 1918* (1920)

A. W. Currie, *Canadian Corps Operations during 1918* (1920)

A. A. Montgomery, *The Story of the Fourth Army* (1920) [for last half of 1918 campaign]

A. de Schrÿver, *La Bataille de Liége* (1922) [by the Chief of Staff of the fortress]

Deguise, *La Defense de la Position Fortifiée d'Anvers en 1914* (1921) [by the Belgian commander]

E. Menzel, *La Vérité sur l'Évacuation d'Anvers en 1914* (1925)

C. Merzbach, *La Vérité sur la Défense de Namur en 1914* (1927)

Duvivier and Herbiet, *Du rôle de l'Armée de Champagne et des Forteresses Belges en 1914* (1929) [effect in detaining German forces]

Les Armées Françaises dans la Grande Guerre, Tome I, vol ii (covers operations up to eve of the Marne, 1914); Tome VII, vol i (covers period June 18th–September 25th, 1928) [French Official History]

B. E. Palat, *La Grande Guerre sur le Front Occidental*, 14 vols (1921–30)

P. Renouvin, *Les Formes du Gouvernement de Guerre* (1929) [relations between Government and commanders in France]

R. Poincaré, *Au service de la France*, vol v, *L'Invasion, 1914* (1929)

Lanrezac, *Le Plan de Campagne Français et le Premier Mois de Guerre* (1920)

V. Margueritte, *Au bord du Gouffre* (1920) [French plan for 1914]

F. Engerand, *La Bataille de la Frontière (août, 1914) Briey* (1920) [French plan for 1914]

Percin, *1914 Les Erreurs du Haut Commandement* (1922) [French plan for 1914]

Tanant, *La Troisième Armée dans la Bataille. Souvenirs d'un Chef d'État-Major* (1928) [special light on the opening battles of 1914]

Toussan, *Historique des Corps de Cavalerie commandé par le Général Conneau du 14 août 1914 au 2 mars 1917* (1924)

E. Valarché, *La Bataille de Guise* (1928)

A. Grouard, *La Conduite de la Guerre jusqu' à la Bataille de la Marne* (1922) [an acute criticism by a famous military critic who gave the French General Staff an unheeded warning of the German plan]

Camon, *L'Effondrement du Plan Allemand en Septembre 1914* (1925)

Mermeix, *Joffre–1er Crise du Commandement*
   Le Commandement Unique

Rousset, *La Bataille de l'Aisne* [Nivelle offensive, 1917]

P. Painlevé, *Comment j'ai nommé Foch et Pétain* (1924)

Laure, *Au 3ième Bureau du troisième G.O.C. 1917–1919* (1922)

L. Madelin, *La Bataille de France* [1918 campaign]

470 BIBLIOGRAPHY

Koeltz, *L'Offensive Allemande de 1918* (1928)
Jean de Pierrefeu, *G.Q.G. Secteur I*, 2 vols (1921)
  Plutarque a Menti (1923)
N. Domège, *En Marge de Plutarque*
Mordacq, *Le Commandement Unique. Comment il fut réalisé*
  La Vérité sur l'Armistice (1929)
Reichsarchiv, *Der Weltkrieg 1914–1918*, vols i, iii, v, vi (1924–29)
  [German Official History, covers 1914]; vii and viii [cover 1915]
Reichsarchiv, *Antwerpen, 1914* (1921) [German Official Monograph on
  siege]
Reichsarchiv, *Ypres, 1914* [German Official Monograph, Eng trans
  1919]
Crown Prince Rupprecht of Bavaria, *Mein Kriegstagebuch*, 3 vols
  (1928)
Krafft von Delmensingen, *Die Führung des Kronprinzen Rupprecht
  von Bayern auf dem linken deutschen Heeresflügel bis zur Schlacht
  in Lothringen im August, 1914* (1925) [light on opening battles in
  Lorraine]
Die Schlacht in Lothringen, (1929) [Bavarian Official History]
German Ex-Crown Prince, *Meine Erinnerungen aus Deutschlands Hel-
  denkampf* (1923)
*Generaloberst Helmuth von Moltke. Erinnerungen – Briefe – Doku-
  mente 1877–1916* (1923)
W. Foerster, *Graf Schlieffen und der Weltkrieg* (1920)
Kluck, *The March on Paris, 1914* (Eng trans 1920)
Army Quarterly, October, 1921, *General Ludendorff on the German
  Plan of Campaign, August, 1914* [extract from letter]
The Memoirs of Prince Max of Baden (Eng trans 1928) [especially for
  light on last phase of war]
Final Report of Gen. J. J. Pershing (1919)
First Army Report (printed 1923)
Shipley Thomas, *History of the American Expeditionary Force* (1920)
R. L. Bullard, *Personalities and Reminiscences of the War* (1925)
J. G. Harbord, *Leaves from a War Diary* (1926)
J. W. Thomason, *Fix Bayonets* (1927)
J. T. Dickman, *The Great Crusade* (1927)
Hunter Liggett, *Commanding an American Army* (1925)
  A.E.F. (1928)
T. M. Johnson, *Without Censor* (1928)
T. C. Lonergan, *It might have been lost* (1929) [extracts from British

Official documents dealing with Pershing's struggle to preserve the national unity of the AEF]

RUSSIAN FRONT
(See also Chapter III, Scene 2)

Reichsarchiv, *Der Weltkrieg, 1914–1918*, vol ii (1924); vol v (1929) [German Official History, covers 1914]

E. Ludendorff, *My War Memories* (Eng trans 1920)

P. von Hindenburg, *Out of my life* (Eng trans 1920)

A. von Cramon, *Quatre Ans au G.Q.G. Austro-Hongrois* (French trans. 1922)

M. Hoffmann, *The War of Lost Opportunities* (Eng trans 1924)
War Diaries and other Papers (Eng trans 1929)

Russian Historical Commission, *La Grande Guerre. Relation de l'État-Major Russe* (French trans 1927)

Conrad von Hötzendorf, *Aus meiner Dienstzeit*, vols iv–v (1925–6) [covers 1914 campaign]

François, *Gorlice, 1915* (1922) [the 1915 breakthrough]

A. Arz, *Zur Geschichte des Grossen Krieges, 1914–1918* [memoirs of Conrad's successor]

J. E. Edmonds in *Army Quarterly*, July, 1921, *The Austrian Plan of Campaign, 1914, and its development*

K. F. Novak, *Der Weg zur Katastrophe* (1920) (French trans) [Conrad's evidence]

Buat, *Hindenburg et Ludendorff Stratèges* (1923)

Camon, *Ludendorff sur le Front Russe 1914–1915* (1926)

Y. Danilov, *La Russie dans la Guerre Mondiale, 1914–1917* (French trans 1927)

Sukhomlinov, *Erinnerungen* (1924)

B. Gourko, *Russia in 1914–1917* (Eng trans 1918)

A. Knox, *With the Russian Army, 1914–1917* (1921)
Hindenburg's Second Offensive in Poland (in *Army Quarterly*, July, 1921) [Lodz]

C. E. Callwell, *Experiences of a Dug-Out, 1914–1918* (1921)

C. Maynard, *The Murmansk Venture* (1928)

ITALIAN FRONT

L. Cadorna, *La Guerra alla fronte Italiana* (1921)

Capello, *Note di Guerra* (1920–21)

Vigano, *La Nostra Guerra* (1921)

A. Tosti, *La Guerra Italo–Austriaca, 1915–1918* (1925)

Kuntz, *La Psychologie du G.Q.G. Italien sous le Général Cadorna* (1923)

A. Krauss, *Die Ursachen unserer Niederlage* (1921)

A. Arz, *Zur Geschichte des Grossen Krieges, 1914–1918* (1924) [covers 1917 and 1918]

A. von Cramon, *Quatre Ans au G.Q.G. Austro–Hongrois* (French trans 1922) [the chief German representative]

Kerchnawe, *Der Zusammenbruch der Oester–Ungar: Wehrmacht im Herbst* (1921) [Austrian documents]

J. F. Gathorne-Hardy in *Army Quarterly*, October, 1921, *A Summary of the Campaign in Italy and an Account of the Battle of Vittorio Veneto* [by the British Chief of Staff]

R. H. Beadon in *Army Quarterly*, Jan, 1925, *An Operation of War,* [British move to Italy after Caporetto]

BALKAN FRONT

Wolfgang Foerster, *Graf Schlieffen und der Weltkrieg*, Part III (1921)

O. Landfried, *Der Endkampf in Macedonien, 1918* (1925)

Nedeff, *Les Opérations en Macédoine. L'Épopée de Doiran, 1915–1918* (1927)

Feyler, *La Campagne de Macédoine*, vol i, 1915–16; vol ii, 1917–18 [from Serbian and Greek sources]

Jouinot-Gambetta, *Uskub ou du Rôle de la Cavalerie d'Afrique dans la Victoire* (1920) [final breakthrough]

Robert David, *Le Drame Ignoré de l'Armée d'Orient* (1928) [especially political side]

Les Armées Françaises dans la Grande Guerre, Tome VIII, vol i (1928)

Œhmichen, *Essai sur la Doctrine de Guerre des Coalitions. La Direction de la Guerre* (Nov, 1914–Mars, 1917) (1927) [Joffre's influence on Salonika campaign]

Sarrail, *Mon Commandement en Orient, 1916–1918* (1920)

L. Villari, *The Macedonian Campaign* (1922)

THE DARDANELLES
(See Chapter V, Scenes 1 and 2)

PALESTINE
(Including Egypt and Arabia)

G. MacMunn and C. Falls, *Military Operations Egypt and Palestine* (1928) [British Official History]

C. E. W. Bean, *Official History of Australia in the War*, vol i.

H. S. Gullet, *Official History of Australia in the War*, vol vii (1923)

A. P. Wavell, *The Palestine Campaigns* (1928)

R. M. P. Preston, *The Desert Mounted Corps* (1921)

T. E. Lawrence, *Revolt in the Desert*

T. E. Lawrence in *Army Quarterly*, October, 1920, *The Evolution of a Revolt*

W. T. Massey, *The Desert Campaigns* (1918)

M. Bowman-Manifold, *An Outline of the Egyptian and Palestine Campaigns* (1922)

G. E. Badcock, *History of the Transport Services of the E.E.F.*

Army, Navy and Air Force Gazette, 18th June, 1927

Reichsarchiv, *Yilderim* (1925)

Kress von Kressenstein, *Zwischen Kaukasus und Sinai* (1922) [covers the period 1915–17]

Liman von Sanders, *Five Years in Turkey* (Eng trans 1928) [covers 1918]

Rafael de Nogales, *Vier Jahren unter dem Halbmond* (1926)

MESOPOTAMIAN FRONT

F. J. Moberley, *The Mesopotomia Campaign, 1914–1918*, vols i–iv (1923–7) [British Official History]

Report of the Commission on Mesopotamia (1917)

C. V. F. Townshend, *My Campaign in Mesopotamia* (1920)

Erroll Sherson, *Townshend of Chitral and Kut* (1928)

Keisling, *Mit Feldmarshall von der Goltz Pascha in Mesopotamien und Persien* (1922)

Rafael de Nogales, *Vier Jahre unter dem Halbmond* (1926)

Schraudenbach, *Muharebe* (1926)

Gleich, *Vom Balkan nach Bagdad* (1922) [light on siege of Kut]

R. H. Dewing, *Army Quarterly*, January, April, July, 1927, *Some Aspects of Maude's Campaign in Mesopotamia*
Edmund Candler, *The Long Road to Baghdad*
L. C. Dunsterville, *The Adventures of Dunsterforce* (1921)
W. Marshall, *Memories of Four Fronts* (1929)
C. E. Callwell, *Life of Sir Stanley Maude* (1920)

NAVAL

J. S. Corbett, *History of the Great War (Naval Operations)* vols i–iii (1920–21)
H. Newbolt, *History of the Great War (Naval Operations)* vol iv (1928)
C. E. Fayle, *Seaborne Trade*, 3 vols (1920–)
A. Laurens, *Précis d'Histoire de la Guerre Navale* (1929)
W. S. Churchill, *The World Crisis*, 4 vols (1923–7)
Jellicoe (Viscount), *The Grand Fleet, 1914–1916* (1919)
J. E. T. Harper, *The Truth about Jutland* (1927)
G. Campbell, *My Mystery Ships* (1928)
W. S. Sims, *The Victory at Sea* (1920)
R. Scheer, *Germany's High Seas Fleet in the World War* (Eng trans 1920)
G. von Hase, *Kiel and Jutland* (Eng trans 1926)

AIR

W. A. Raleigh, *The War in the Air*, vol i (1922) (Official History)
H. A. Jones, *The War in the Air*, vol ii (1928); vol vii (1930) (Official History)
C. F. Snowden-Gamble, *The Story of a North Sea Air Station* (1928)
A. Rawlinson, *The Defence of London* (1923)
E. B. Ashmore, *Air Defence* (1929)
E. A. Lehmann, *The Zeppelins* (Eng trans 1928)
H. Ritter, *Der Luftkrieg* (1926)
Keller, *Die Heutige Wehrlosigkeit Deutschlands im Lichte seiner Verteidigung gegen Fliegerangriffe im Kriege, 1914–1918* (1926) [German Air Defence Organization]

PRESS AND PROPAGANDA

E. T. Cook, *The Press in War-Time* (1920)

C. Stuart, *Secrets of Crewe House* (1920)

N. Lytton, *The Press and the General Staff* (1921)

C. E. Callwell, *Experiences of a Dug-Out, 1914–1918* (1921)

H. D. Lasswell, *Propaganda Technique in the World War* (1926)

ECONOMIC AND HOME FRONT

M. Consett, *The Triumph of Unarmed Forces, 1914–1918* (1921)

R. H. Gretton, *A Modern History of the English People, 1910–22* (1929)

A. Hallays, *L'Opinion Allemande pendant la Guerre, 1914–1918* (1923)

CHAPTER IV

SCENE 1. THE MARNE

J. E. Edmonds, *Military Operations. France and Belgium*, vol i (British Official History)

Reichsarchiv, *Der Weltkrieg, 1914–1918*, vols iii and iv (1926) (German Official History)

Kluck, *The March on Paris, 1914* (Eng trans 1920)

J. E. Edmonds in *Army Quarterly*, January, 1921, *The Scapegoat of the Battle of the Marne*

Militär-Wochenblatt, 18th September, 1920 [court of inquiry on Col Hentsch's rôle]

M. von Poseck, *Die deutsche Kavallerie in Belgien und Frankreich, 1914* (1922)

Baumgarten-Crusius, *Marneschlacht, 1914* (1919)

Deutsche Heerführung im Marnefeldzug, 1914 (1921) [fuller extracts from Col Hentsch's report]

Bülow, *Mein Bericht zur Marneschlacht* (1920) (French trans)

Zwehl, *Maubeuge-Aisne-Verdun* (1921)

Helfferich, *Weltkrieg*, vol ii

Tappen, *Bis zur Marneschlacht*

François, *Marneschlacht und Tannenberg* (1920)

Foerster, *Graf Schlieffen und der Weltkrieg*, Part I (1920)

Kuhl, *Der Marnefeldzug, 1914* (1920) (French trans)

Crown Prince Rupprecht of Bavaria, *Mein Kriegstagebuch* (1928)

German Ex-Crown Prince, *Der Marnefeldzug, 1914* (1927)

Hausen, *Souvenirs de la Campagne de la Marne en 1914* (French trans 1922) [Saxon Third Army commander]

Reichsarchiv, *Das Marnedrama, 1914* (1928–9) [German Official Monographs, in five parts. Extensive summary in *Army Quarterly*, July, 1928, January, April, October, 1929, January, 1930]

Müller-Loebnitz, *Die Sendung des Oberstleutnants Hentsch* (1922) [official account of Hentsch's mission]

Generaloberst von Moltke, Erinnerungen–Briefe–Dokumente, 1877–1916 (1923)

Palat, *La Victoire de la Marne* (1921)

Dubail, *Journal du Campagne*, vol i, 1ere Armée

J. Charbonneau, *La Bataille des Frontières et la Bataille de la Marne vues par un Chef de Section* (1929)

Mémoires du Maréchal Galliéni Défense de Paris (25 août–sept 11 1914) (1926)

Clergerie and Delahaye d'Anglemont, *Le Rôle du Gouvernement Militaire de Paris de 1 au 12 septembre, 1914* (1920)

Marius—Ary le Blond, *Galliéni Parle* (1920)

Les Armées Françaises dans la Grande Guerre, Tome I, vol ii (1927) (French Official History)

Toussan, *Historique des corps de cavallerie commandés par le Général Conneau du 14 août au 2 mars, 1917* (1924)

J. de Pierrefeu, *Plutarque a menti* (1922)

Hirschauer and Klein, *Paris en État de Défense, 1914* (1928)

H. Carré, *La Véritable Histoire des Taxis de la Marne* (1921)

Boëlle, *Le 4e corps d'Armée sur l'Ourcq* (1925) [light on Maunoury's part]

Dubois, *Deux ans de Commandement sur le Front de France, 1914–1916* (1920) [light on Foch's part]

Bujac, *Le Général Eydoux et le XI Corps d'Armée* (1925) [light on Foch's part]

de Castelli, *Le VIIIe Corps en Lorraine août–octobre, 1914* (1926) [light on French right wing and on loss of St Mihiel]

Army Quarterly, October, 1922, *Another Legend of the Marne, 1914*

Private Evidence

CHAPTER IV

SCENE 2. TANNENBERG

Reichsarchiv, *Tannenberg* (1927) [German Official Monograph]
E. Ludendorff, *My War Memories* (Eng trans 1920)
P. von Hindenburg, *Out of my Life* (Eng trans 1920)
Army Quarterly, October, 1921, *An Echo of Tannenberg*
H. von François, *Marneschlacht und Tannenberg* (1920)
  Tannenberg (1926)
Y. Danilov, *La Russie dans la Guerre Mondiale* (French trans 1927)
M. Hoffmann, *The War of Lost Opportunities* (Eng trans 1924)
  Tannenberg wie es wirklich war (1927)
  War Diaries and other Papers (Eng trans 1929)
E. Ironside, *Tannenberg* (1925)
Russian Historical Commission, *La Grande Guerre. Relation de l'État-Major Russe* (French trans 1927)
Noskov, *Militär Wochenblatt* 1st August, 1926 [a Russian view]
A. Smirnoff in *Army Quarterly*, April, 1926, *A New Light upon the Invasion of East Prussia by the Russians in August, 1914*

CHAPTER V

SCENES 1 and 2. THE DARDANELLES

C. F. Aspinall-Oglander, *Military Operations, Gallipoli*, vol i (1929) (British Official History)
The Final Report of the Dardanelles Commission (1919)
Ian Hamilton, *A Gallipoli Diary*, 2 vols (1920)
C. E. Callwell, *Experiences of a Dug-Out, 1914–1918* (1921)
J. Masefield, *Gallipoli* (1923)
Wester Wemyss (Lord), *The Navy in the Dardanelles Campaign* (1924)
E. Ashmead-Bartlett, *The Uncensored Dardanelles* (1927)
W. Marshall, *Memories of Four Fronts* (1929)
Compton Mackenzie, *Gallipoli Memories* (1929)
Liman von Sanders, *Five Years in Turkey* (Eng trans 1928)
H. Kannengiesser, *The Campaign in Gallipoli* (Eng trans 1928)
Reichsarchiv, *Dardanellen, 1915* (1927)

Turkish Official History, *Campagne des Dardanelles* (1924) [extensive summary in *Army Quarterly*, January and April, 1926]

Army Quarterly, October, 1929, *The First Turkish Reinforcements at Suvla, August 7th–9th, 1915* [from Turkish sources]

The Times, February 14th, 1925, *The Suvla Bay Failure. New Evidence*

S. Sazonov, *Fateful Years, 1909–1916* (Eng trans 1927) [shows Russian attitude]

Les Armées Françaises dans la Grande Guerre, Tome VIII, vol i (1928) (French Official History)

Private Evidence

CHAPTER V

SCENE 3. THE GAS CLOUD AT YPRES

J. E. Edmonds, *Military Operations. France and Belgium, 1915*, vol iii

Les Armées Françaises dans la Grande Guerre, Tome III (1927)

Huguet, *Britain and the War*

C. E. Callwell, *Field-Marshal Sir Henry Wilson*, vol i

Volonté (Paris) April 25th, 1929, [account of Gen Ferry's warning]

Hanslian and Bergendorff, *Der Chemische Krieg*, (1925)

Falkenhayn, *General Headquarters, etc*

Unpublished Documents

Private Evidence

CHAPTER V

SCENE 4. LOOS

J. E. Edmonds, *Military Operations. France and Belgium, 1915*, vol iv

Les Armées Françaises dans la Grande Guerre, Tome III (1927)

Army Quarterly, July, 1924, *The Fight for Hill 70* [from German sources]

Crown Prince Rupprecht of Bavaria, *Mein Kriegstagebuch* (1928)

Palat, Vol ix. *Les Offensives de 1915*

Huguet, *Britain and the War*

Oxford and Asquith, *Memories and Reflections*

Maurice, *The Life of General Lord Rawlinson of Trent*

J. Charteris, *Field-Marshal Earl Haig*

Private Evidence

CHAPTER VI

SCENE 1. VERDUN

Reichsarchiv, *Die Tragödie von Verdun, 1916* (1926–9) (German Official)

Wolfgang Foerster, *Graf Schlieffen und der Weltkrieg*, Part III (1921)

German Ex-Crown Prince, *Memoirs*

Crown Prince Rupprecht, *Mein Kriegstagebuch*

Zwehl, *Maubeuge-Aisne-Verdun*

Ludwig Gehre, *Die deutsche Kraftverteilung während des Weltkrieges* (1928)

de Thomasson, *Les Préliminaires de Verdun, août, 1915–février 1916* (1921) [contains numerous documents]

Pétain, *La Bataille de Verdun* (1929)

J. Poirier, *La Bataille de Verdun* (1922)

A. Grasset, *Verdun, le Premier Choc à la 72e Division* (1926)

B. E. Palat, *La Ruée sur Verdun* (1925)

CHAPTER VI

SCENE 2. BRUSILOV OFFENSIVE

For sources see RUSSIAN FRONT

CHAPTER VI. SCENE 3. THE SOMME

C. E. W. Bean, *The Australian Imperial Force in France, 1916* (1929) [Australian Official History]

J. Charteris, *Life of Field-Marshal Earl Haig*

Maurice, *Life of Lord Rawlinson of Trent*

Dewar and Boraston, *Sir Douglas Haig's Command*

J. F. C. Fuller, *Tanks in the Great War*

Army Quarterly, January and July, 1924, *The German Defence during the Battle of the Somme* (July 1st)

Army Quarterly, January, 1925, *Mametz Wood and Contalmaison 9th–10th July, 1916*

Army Quarterly, October, 1925, *Delville Wood, 14th–19th July, 1916*

Army Quarterly, October, 1926, *The German Defence of Bernafoy and Trônes, 2nd–14th of July, 1916*

Palat, *Bataille de la Somme*

Schwarte, *Der Grosse Krieg*, vol ii

Reichsarchiv, *Somme-Nord 1 Theil* [July 13th]
  Somme-Nord 2 Theil [July 14th–31st]

Rupprecht, *Mein Kriegstagebuch*

Constantin Hierl, *Der Weltkrieg in Umrissen* (1927) [German methods of defence]

Unpublished Documents

Private Evidence

CHAPTER VI

SCENE 4. THE GROWING PAINS OF THE TANK

C. and A. Williams-Ellis, *The Tank Corps* (1919)

A. Stern, *Tanks, 1914–1918. The Log Book of a Pioneer* (1919)

J. F. C. Fuller, *Tanks in the Great War* (1920)

D. G. Browne, *The Tank in Action* (1920)

E. D. Swinton, *Tanks* [Encyclopaedia Britannica, 1922]

W. S. Churchill, *The World Crisis*

Evidence given before the Royal Commission on Awards to Inventors

Evidence given in the case of Bentley v The Crown, 1925

Unpublished Documents

Private Evidence

CHAPTER VI

SCENE 5. RUMANIA SWALLOWED

For sources see RUSSIAN FRONT, also

E. von Falkenhayn, *Der Feldzug der 9 Armée gegen die Rumanen und Russen, 1916–1917*, 2 vols (1921)

M. Sturdza, *Avec l'Armée Roumaine, 1916–1918*

CHAPTER VI

SCENE 6. THE CAPTURE OF BAGHDAD

For sources see MESOPOTAMIAN FRONT

CHAPTER VI

SCENE 7. JUTLAND

The Admiralty, *Official Documents and Despatches, Battle of Jutland* (1920)

J. S. Corbett, *History of the Great War (Naval Operations)* (1921)

Jellicoe (Viscount), *The Grand Fleet, 1914–1916* (1919)

C. Bellairs, *The Battle of Jutland* (1920)

R. Bacon, *The Jutland Scandal* (1925)

H. W. Wilson, *Battleships in Action* (1926)

J. E. T. Harper, *The Truth about Jutland* (1927)

W. S. Churchill, *The World Crisis, 1916–1918*, Part I (1927)

R. Bacon, *Mr Churchill and Jutland* (1927) [in *The World Crisis: A Criticism*]

H. S. Altham, *Jutland* [Encyclopaedia Britannica]

R. Scheer, *Germany's High Seas Fleet in the World War* (Eng trans 1920)

G. von Hase, *Kiel and Jutland* (Eng trans 1926)

CHAPTER VII

SCENES 1–4. ARRAS, MESSINES, PASSCHENDAELE, CAMBRAI

B. E. Palat, *La Grande Guerre sur le Front Occidental*, vol xii (1927)

Rousset, *La Bataille de l'Aisne*

R. Normand, *Déstructions et Dévastations au Course des Guerres* (1929)

W. S. Churchill, *The World Crisis*

Dewar and Boraston, *Sir Douglas Haig's Command*

J. F. C. Fuller, *Tanks in the Great War* (1920)

Reichsarchiv, *Flanders, 1917* (1919)

E. Ludendorff, *My War Memories*
Rupprecht, *Mein Kriegstagebuch*
C. E. Callwell, *Field-Marshal Sir Henry Wilson*
F. Maurice, *The Life of General Lord Rawlinson of Trent*
Laure, *Au 3ième Bureau du troisième G.Q.G.*
Mermeix, *Nivelle et Painlevé–2e Crise du Commandement*
P. Painlevé, *Comment j'ai nommé Foch et Pétain* (1924)
Unpublished Documents
Private Evidence

CHAPTER VII

SCENE 5. CAPORETTO

For sources see ITALIAN FRONT

Also Private Evidence

CHAPTER VII

SCENE 1. THE FIRST BREAKTHROUGH

E. Ludendorff, *My War Memories*
Rupprecht, *Mein Kriegstagebuch*
Wolfgang Foerster, *Graf Schlieffen und der Weltkrieg*, Part III
Albrecht Philip, *Ursachen des deutschen militärischen Zusammenbruch, 1918* (1925) [summary of Parliamentary inquiry]
Kuhl, *Entstehung, Durchführung und Zusammenbruch der Offensive von 1918* (1928)
Schwertfeger, *Die politischen und militärischen Verantwortlichkeiten im Verlaufe der Offensive von 1918* (1928)
Bruchmüller, *Die deutsche Artillerie in den Durchbruchschlachten des Weltkrieges* (1921)
Joachim, *Die Vorbereitung des deutschen Heeres für die Grosse Schlacht in Frankreich im Frühjahr 1918* (1927)
Fehr, *Die Märzoffensive 1918 an der Westfront* (1921) [reveals Wetzell's influence on Ludendorff's strategy]
Kuhl, *Der deutsche Generalstab*
German Ex-Crown Prince, *Memoirs*

M. Erzberger, *Erlebnisse im Weltkrieg*

E. Gugelmeier, *Das Schwarze Jahr* (1917) [food conditions]

Rudolf Binding, *A Fatalist at War* (Eng trans 1928)

Laure, *Au 3ième Bureau du troisième G.Q.G.*

Koeltz, *La Bataille de France, 21 mars–5 avril, 1918*
    L'Offensive Allemande de 1918

L. Madelin, *La Bataille de France*

Dewar and Boraston, *Sir Douglas Haig's Command*

C. E. Callwell, *Field Marshal Sir Henry Wilson*, vol ii

F. Maurice, *The Life of General Lord Rawlinson of Trent*

C. Falls, in *Nineteenth Century*, Oct–Nov 1921

C. à C. Repington, *The First World War, 1914–1918*, vol ii

J. Charteris, *Field Marshal Earl Haig*

Seymour, *The Intimate Papers of Colonel House*, vol. iii

Unpublished Documents

Private Evidence

CHAPTER VIII

SCENE 2. THE BREAKTHROUGH IN FLANDERS

Additional:

*La Bataille des Flandres d'après le journal de marche et les archives de
la IVe Armée Allemande (9–30 avril, 1918)* (1925) [French trans
of captured documents]

Unpublished Documents

CHAPTER VIII

SCENE 3. THE BREAKTHROUGH TO THE MARNE

Additional:

Unpublished Documents

Personal Evidence

CHAPTER VIII

SCENE 4. THE SECOND BATTLE OF THE MARNE

Additional:
Les Armées Françaises dans la Grande Guerre, Tome VII, vol i
  (French Official History)
Zwehl, *Die Schlachten im Sommer, 1918* (1922)
Private Evidence

CHAPTER VIII

SCENE 5. AUGUST 8th

Additional:
A. A. Montgomery, *The Story of the Fourth Army*
J. Monash, *The Australian Victories in 1918*
M. Daille, *La Bataille de Montdidier* (1922) [French share]
C. Falls in *Army Quarterly*, July, 1928, *An Aspect of the Battle of
  Amiens, 1918* [French cooperation]
Unpublished Documents
Personal Evidence

CHAPTER VIII

SCENES 7–8. ST MIHIEL AND MEUSE-ARGONNE

Final Report of Gen. John J. Pershing
First Army Report
Frederick Palmer, *Our Greatest Battle* (1919)
R. L. Bullard, *Personalities and Reminiscences of the War*
Hunter Liggett, *Commanding an American Army*
  A.E.F.
T. M. Johnson, *Without Censor*
J. G. Harbord, *Leaves from a War Diary*
J. T. Dickman, *The Great Crusade*
Wellmann, *Das I. Reserve-Korps in der letzten Schlacht* (1925)
Passaga, *Le Calvaire de Verdun* (1928)
Personal Evidence

ADDITIONAL. 1930–34

ORIGINS

Bülow (Prince von) *Memoirs* (Eng trans 1931)
Österreich-Ungarns Aussenpolitik von der Bosnischen Krise 1908 bis zum Kriegsausbruch 1914, 8 vols [Austro-Hungarian diplomatic papers]
Beyens, *Deux Années à Berlin, 1912–1914* (1932)

GENERAL

The War Memoirs of David Lloyd George, vols. i and ii (1933); iii and iv (1934)
C. Addison, *Four and a Half Years* (1934)
F. J. Moberly, *History of the Great War (Military Operations) Togoland and the Cameroons 1914–1916* (1931)
M. Paléologue, *Une Prélude à l'Invasion de las Belgique* (1933)
A. Neimann, *Kaiser und Heer* (1930) [an apologia which throws light on the Kaiser's influence on pre-war plans and war-time operations]
Schäfer, *Generalstab und Admiralstab* (1931)
Kuhl, *Der Weltkrieg, 1914–1918, dem deutschen Volk dargestellt* (1929). [précis in *Army Quarterly*, April 1930]
J. J. Pershing, *My Experiences in the World War* (1931)
Peyton C. March, *The Nation at War* (1932)
L. S. Viereck, *The Strangest Friendship in History–Woodrow Wilson and Colonel House* (1932)
C. Seymour, *American Diplomacy during the World War* (1934) [a most able and important summary of old and new evidence]

WESTERN FRONT

The Memoirs of Marshal Foch (Eng trans 1931)
Liddell Hart, *Foch–The Man of Orleans* (1931)
The Memoirs of Marshal Joffre (Eng trans 1932)
E. L. Spears, *Liaison, 1914* (1930)

J. Charteris, *At G.H.Q.* (1931)

C. B. Baker-Carr, *From Chauffeur to Brigadier* (1930)

Hubert Gough, *The Fifth Army* (1931)

C. E. W. Bean, *The Australian Imperial Force in France, vol. IV, 1917* (1933)

J. Fabry, *Joffre et son Destin* (1932)

G. Galliéni and P. B. Gheusi, *Les Carnets de Galliéni* (1932)

Les Armées Françaises dans la Grand Guerre. Tome II [covers the first phase of the deadlock, Nov 1914–May 1915, and reveals the fiasco of Joffre's attempt to stage a great offensive in Dec 1914]
   Tome IV, vol i [covers Feb–May 1916]

Mordacq, *Pouvait-on signer l'Armistice à Berlin* (1930) *Le Ministère Clemenceau. Journal d'un témoin* (1932)

General XXX, *La Crise du commandement unique. Le conflit Clemenceau, Foch, Haig, Pétain* (1931)

R. Poincaré, *Au service de la France*, vols vi, vii [1915]; and viii [1916] 1930–32)

Herbillon, *Du général en chef au gouvernement. Souvenirs d'une officier de liaison* (1930)

E. Mayer, *Nos Chefs de 1914*

F. Gazin, *La Cavalerie Française dans la Guerre Mondiale, 1914–1918* (1930)

Castelli, *Cinq Journées au 8e Corps* (1931) [deals with five critical episodes in 1914 when part of the French First Army]

Lucas, *Le 10e Corps à la Bataille de Charleroi* (1931)

J. Delmas, *Mes hommes au feu* (1931) [illuminating sidelights on the blundering French advance into Lorraine]
   L'Infanterie de la Victoire, 1918 (1932)

M. Caracciolo, *Le truppe Italiene in Francia*

P. Azan, *Les Belges sur l'Yser* (1930) [sheds some interesting light on Joffre's efforts to persuade King Albert to quit the coast for an inland advance in Oct 1914]

Galet, *Albert, King of the Belgians, in the Great War* (Eng trans 1931) [most important evidence on 1914]

Historical Section, Belgian General Staff, *La Défense de la Position Fortifiée de Namur en août, 1914* (1931)

A. Cerf, *La Guerre aux frontières du Jura* [some light on the possibilities of a German move through Switzerland]

Der Waffenstillstand, 1918–1919 (1931) [German Armistice documents, in 3 vols]

W. Foerster, *Aus der Gedankenwerkstatt des Deutschen Generalstabes*

(1931) [a comparative study of the influence of Schlieffen and Moltke]

Poseck, *The German Cavalry in Belgium and France, 1914* [Eng trans in US]

RUSSIAN FRONT

Army Quarterly, April and July 1931, *The Lemberg Campaign*

W. S. Churchill, *The World Crisis. The Eastern Front* (1931)

A. A. Brusilov, *A Soldier's Notebook, 1914–1918* (1931)

Danilov, *Grossfürst Nikolai Nikolajewitsch, Sein Leben und Wirken* (1931)

L. Trotsky, *The History of the Russian Revolution. Vol I* (Eng trans 1932)

Reicharsarchiv, *Gorlice* (1930) [German Official Monograph]

Österreich-Ungarns letzter Krieg, 1914–18 [Austrian Official History, vol i (1930) covers 1914; vol ii (1932) and vol iii (1933) cover 1915]

ITALIAN FRONT

L'Esercito Italiano nella Grande Guerra (1927) [Italian Official History, Vol i, preliminary. Vol ii, 1915]

L. Villari, *The War on the Italian Front* (1931)

BALKAN FRONT

C. Falls, *Military Operations; Macedonia. Vol I* (1933) [British Official History]

Cordonnier, *Ai-je trahi Sarrail?* (1932)

Pétin, *Le Drame Roumain, 1916–1918* (1933)

Österreich-Ungarns letzter Krieg, 1914–1918 [Austrian Official History, vol i (1929–30) Parts I and V]

PALESTINE

Liddell Hart, *'T. E. Lawrence'–In Arabia and After* (1934)

E. Brémond, *Le Hedjaz dans la Guerre Mondiale* (1932)

A. H. Burne, in *The Fighting Forces*, April 1932–Feb 1933, *Notes on the Palestine Campaign*

NAVAL

H. Newbolt, *History of the Great War (Naval Operations)*, vol. v (1931) [the Submarine Campaign and its frustration]

L. Guichard, *The Naval Blockade, 1914–1918* (Eng trans 1930)

A. Laurens, *Le Commandement Naval en Mediterranée pendant la Guerre de 1914–1918* (1933)

AIR

J. Poirier, *Les bombardements de Paris, 1914–1918* (1930)

C. F. Snowden Gamble, *The Air Weapon* (1931)

P. R. C. Groves, *Behind the Smoke Screen* (1-34) [important revelations on the misuse of air power in the war]

ECONOMIC AND HOME FRONT

W. Beveridge, *Food Control in War Time* (1928)

Landwehr, *Hunger die Erschöpfungsjahre der Mittelmächte, 1917–1918* (1931) [details of the famine-stricken state of Austria-Hungary]

Kohn and Mayendorff, *The Cost of the War to Russia* (1933)

THE MARNE

Liddell Hart, *Foch–The Man of Orleans* (1931)
   The British Way in Warfare (Chapter iii) (1932).

G. Lestien, *L'Action du Général Foch à la Bataille de la Marne* (1930)

Muller, *Joffre et la Marne* (1931) [important evidence from Joffre's aide-de-camp which goes far to confirm, by admission, previously disputed claims as to Galliéni's influence]

E. Valarché, *Le Combat du Petit Morin ... au 10e Corps d'Armée*

Koeltz, *L'armée von Kluck à la Bataille de la Marne* (1932)

A. H. Burne, in *The Cavalry Journal*, 1934, *The German Cavalry on the Marne* [an able analysis of the German evidence, bringing out the opportunities missed by the Allies]

TANNENBERG

W. Elze, Tannenberg [prints many documents, drawn from the German archives, which are not given in the official history]

THE DARDANELLES

C. F. Aspinall-Oglander, *Military Operations, Gallipoli, Vol II* (1932) [Official History]

THE GAS CLOUD AT YPRES

Les Armées Françaises dans la Grande Guerre. Tome II [this is worth comparative study, as an example of how official historians may falsify history on patriotic grounds]
Mordacq, *Le Drame de l'Yser. Surprise des gaz, Avril, 1915* (1933) [honest unofficial history by the commander of a brigade on the spot]

VERDUN

R. Poincaré, *Au service de la France, Vol VIII. Verdun 1916* (1932)
Paquet, *Verdun, Janvier-Février 1916. Le rôle de la Photographie et de l'Observation terrestre* (1930)
J. Rouquerol, *La Drame de Douaumont, 21 février–24 octobre, 1916*
H. Wendt, *Verdun, 1916* (1932) [reconciles the French and German accounts]

THE SOMME

J. E. Edmonds, *Military Operations. France and Belgium, 1916* (1932) [covers the launching of the Somme offensive]
Army Quarterly, July 1933, *The Somme: 15th of September, 1916*
January 1934, *The Capture of Thiepval, 20th of September, 1916*

THE GROWING PAINS OF THE TANK

E. D. Swinton, *Eyewitness* (1932)
R. Mortier, *Les Chars d'assaut. Comment ils furent realisés.* [sheds light on some French experiments in 1915 towards an armoured trench-crossing vehicle]

ARRAS, MESSINES, PASSCHENDAELE, CAMBRAI

C. E. W. Bean, *The Australian Imperial Force in France, Vol IV, 1917*
    (1933)
J. Charteris, *At G.H.Q.* (1931)
Hubert Gough, *The Fifth Army* (1931)
Army Quarterly, July 1930, *Cambrai: The Action of the German 107th
    Division*
Reichsarchiv (Official Monographs), *Die Tankschlacht bei Cambrai,
    1917* (1929)
    Die Osterschlacht bei Arras, 1917 (1930)

THE FIRST BREAKTHROUGH

Liddell Hart, *Foch – The Man of Orleans* (1931)
Hubert Gough, *The Fifth Army* (1931)
H. Rowan-Robinson, *Belated Comments on a Great Event* (1932)
Thierry d'Argenlieu, *La Bataille de l'Avre* [covers the operations of
    Debeney's army, which came up to the aid of the British]

THE BREAKTHROUGH TO THE MARNE

Reichsarchiv, *Deutsche Siege, 1918*
    *Das Verdringen der 7 Armee über Ailette, Aisne, Vesle und Ourcq
    bis zur Marne: 27 Mai bis 13 Juni* [German Official Monograph]
    Wachsende Schwierigkeiten, 1918 [covers the ineffectual attacks
    early in June between the Marne and Somme salients]

THE SECOND BATTLE OF THE MARNE

Reichsarchiv, *Der letzte deutsche Angriff. Reims 1918*
    Schicksalswende. Von der Marne dis zur Vesle, 1918 [German official
    monographs]

AUGUST 8th

Grasset, *Montdidier, le 8 août 1918 à la 42e Division* (1931)
Reichsarchiv, *Die Katastrophe des 8 August, 1918* (1932) [German
    Official Monograph]

Index

Index

GENERAL

Agadir, 15

Ahrenthal, Count, 13

Air operations, 76, 83, 85, 105, 110, 114, 163-4, 180, 312, 351, 355 ff, 375, 382, 388, 393, 394, 403, 418, 427; in Palestine, 436

Aisne (1914), 59-62, 94-5, 118, (1915), 134; French offensive, 1917, 321; German offensive, 1918, 371, 407 ff

Albania, 15

Albert, King, 61, 62, 119, 121, 130

Alderson, General, (Ypres II), 185

Alexander III, Emperor, 4

Alexeiev, General, 150, 228, 229

Allenby, General Sir E., (1914), 119, 123, 127; Somme, 233; (Arras), 301, 316 ff; (Palestine), 306-7, 378,432 ff

Amery, L. S., 35

Amiens, 60, 118, 369, 373, 427-8

Antwerp, 52, 55, 59, 61, 62, 80

Anzacs, the, (Gallipoli), 138, 173; (Messines), 248, 325; (Passchendaele), 333; (Palestine), 438

Aosta, Duke of, capture of Gorizia, 210

Aqaba, 212

Arabs, 211, 212, 307, 436, 439

Arish, El, 212

Armistice, discussion of terms, 379 ff

Army, Austro-Hungarian, 30, 107; British, 32-6, 45, 64, 65, 131, 143, 296-7, 364; French, 31, 248, 302, 329; German, 28-31, 49, 56, 125, 139, 395-6; Russian, 31-2, 139-40

Arras front, 62, 145, 206, 233, offensive, 301, 314-21; influence in 1918, 368, 369, 388, 392, 394, 395, 403

Artois, attacks in, 134, 149

Asiago region, 206

Aspinall-Oglander, General, 163

Asquith, H. H., forms Coalition Government, 155; resigns, 296

Aston, Brig-General, to Ostend, 80-1

Aubers ridge, battle of, 145, 181

Auffenberg, General, 112-16

Australian Army Corps, (Somme), 248; (Amiens), 428

Austria, and Three Emperors' Alliance, 2; annexes Bosnia and Herzegovina, 13; threatens Serbia, 1913, 15; declares war on Serbia, 1914, 21; mobilizes, 23; invaded by Italy, 150-1; project for combined attack on, 297; collapse of, 378-9

Baden-Powell, General, 35

Baghdad railway, 133

Baghdad, capture of, 211, 269-73

Bainbridge, General, 410

Balfourier, General, 186

Balkans, troubles of 1908, 13; war of 1912, 15-6; projects in 1915, 136-7. *See* names of countries

Barès, Colonel, on air strategy, 359

Barisis, 364

Basra, capture of, 154

Bauer, Major, 89

Bazentin-le-Grand Wood, 247

Bazentin-le-Petit Wood, 246

Beatty, Admiral, 73, (Jutland), 213, 279 ff

Beaumont Hamel, 242, 252

Beersheba, seized, 307

Belfort, 41, 205

Index

FACTORS

the Secret

the Secret

BEVERLY LEWIS

BETHANY HOUSE PUBLISHERS

Minneapolis, Minnesota

Published by Bethany House Publishers
11400 Hampshire Avenue South
Bloomington, Minnesota 55438

Bethany House Publishers is a division of
Baker Publishing Group, Grand Rapids, Michigan.

Printed in the United States of America

Library of Congress Cataloging-in-Publication Data

Lewis, Beverly.
    The secret / Beverly Lewis.
       p.   cm. — (Seasons of grace ; 1)
     ISBN 978-0-7642-0680-1 (alk. paper) — ISBN 978-0-7642-0571-2 (pbk.) — ISBN 978-0-7642-0681-8 (large-print pbk.)
    1. Amish—Fiction. I. Title.

    PS3562.E9383S43   2009
    813'.54—dc22

                                       2008051051

For
Judith Lovold,
devoted reader and friend.

By Beverly Lewis

THE HERITAGE OF LANCASTER COUNTY
The Shunning • *The Confession* • *The Reckoning*

....

ABRAM'S DAUGHTERS
The Covenant • *The Betrayal* • *The Sacrifice*
The Prodigal • *The Revelation*

....

ANNIE'S PEOPLE
The Preacher's Daughter • *The Englisher* • *The Brethren*

....

THE COURTSHIP OF NELLIE FISHER
The Parting • *The Forbidden* • *The Longing*

....

SEASONS OF GRACE
The Secret

....

The Postcard • *The Crossroad*

....

The Redemption of Sarah Cain
October Song • *Sanctuary** • *The Sunroom*

....

The Beverly Lewis Amish Heritage Cookbook

www.beverlylewis.com

*with David Lewis

BEVERLY LEWIS, born in the heart of Pennsylvania Dutch country, is *The New York Times* bestselling author of more than eighty books. Her stories have been published in nine languages worldwide. A keen interest in her mother's Plain heritage has inspired Beverly to write many Amish-related novels, beginning with *The Shunning*, which has sold more than one million copies. *The Brethren* was honored with a 2007 Christy Award.

Beverly lives with her husband, David, in Colorado.

Prologue

SPRING

Honestly, I thought the worst was past.

A full month has come and gone since the day of that chilly barn raising southeast of Strasburg. Mamma and I had traveled all that way, taking a hamper of food to help feed the men building the new barn. The plea to lend a hand had traveled along the Amish grapevine, which some said spread word faster than radio news.

There we were, sitting at the table with the other womenfolk, when Mamma let out a little gasp, jumped up, and rushed over to greet a woman I'd never seen in my life.

Then if she and that stranger didn't go off walking together for the longest time, just up and left without a word to me or anyone.

From then on my mother seemed preoccupied . . . even *ferhoodled*. Most worrisome of all, she began rising and wandering

outside in the middle of the night. Sometimes I would see her cutting through the cornfield, always going in the same direction until she disappeared from view. She leaned forward as if shouldering the weight of the world.

Here lately, though—in the past few days—she had begun to settle down some, cooking and cleaning and doing a bit of needlework. I'd even noticed her wearing an occasional smile, a sweet softness in her face once again.

But lo and behold, last night, when talk of my twenty-first birthday came up, silent tears streamed down her ivory face while she rinsed and stacked the dishes. My heart sank like a stone. "Mamma . . . what is it?"

She merely shrugged and I kept drying, squelching the flood of questions throbbing in my head.

Then today, while carrying a thermos of cold lemonade out to the sheep barn, I saw my older brother, Adam, over in the birthing stall with *Dat*. I heard Adam say in a low and serious voice, "Something's botherin' *Mamm*, ain't so?" My soon-to-be-wed brother must've assumed he was on equal footing, or about to be, to dare utter such a question to our father. Either that or he felt it safe to stick his neck out and speak man-to-man out there, surrounded by the musky, earthy smells, with only the sheep as witness.

I held my breath and kept myself hidden from view. A man of few words, Dat gave no immediate reply. I waited, hoping he might offer a reason for Mamma's behavior. Surely it was something connected to the stranger at the March barn raising. For as long as I remember, Mamma has always been somewhat moody, but I was just certain something had gone off-kilter that day. She kept to herself more and more—even staying away

twice from Sunday Preaching. *Jah*, there was much for me to ponder about my mother. And ponder I did.

Now, as I waited stubbornly for my father to acknowledge Adam's question, the only sound I heard was the laboring cry of the miserable ewe, her bleats signaling a difficult delivery. I swallowed my disappointment. But I shouldn't have been surprised that Dat made no response whatsoever. This was his way when cornered. Dat's way in general, especially with women.

I continued to stand motionless there in the stuffy sheep barn, observing my father's serious face, his down-turned mouth. Adam, blond and lean, knelt in the deep straw as he waited to assist the struggling ewe deliver the next wee lamb—a twin to the first one already wobbling onto its feet within moments of birth. Tenderness for my blue-eyed brother tugged at my heart. In no time, we'd be saying our good-byes, once Adam tied the knot with Henry Stahl's sister, nineteen-year-old Priscilla. I'd happened upon them the other evening while walking to visit my good friend Becky Riehl. Of course, I'm not supposed to know they are engaged till they are "published" in the fall, several Sundays before the wedding. Frankly I cringed when I saw Priscilla riding with Adam, and I wondered how my sensible brother had fallen for the biggest *Schnuffelbox* in all of Lancaster County. Everyone knew what a busybody she was.

Now I backed away from the barn door, still gripping the thermos. Perturbed by Dat's steadfast silence, I fled the sheep barn for the house.

Adam's obvious apprehension—and his unanswered question—plagued me long into the night as I pitched back and forth in bed, my cotton gown all bunched up in knots. In vain, I tried to fall asleep, wanting to be wide awake for work tomorrow.

After all, it would be a shame if I didn't preserve my reputation as an industrious part-time employee at Eli's Natural Foods. I might be especially glad for this job if I ended up a *Maidel*.

Being single was a concern for any young Amishwoman. But I supposed it wasn't the worst thing not to have a husband, even though I'd cared for Henry quite a while already. Sometimes it was just hard to tell if the feelings were mutual, perhaps because he was reticent by nature. In spite of that, he was a kind and faithful companion, and mighty *gut* at playing volleyball, too. If nothing more, I knew I could count on quiet Henry to be a devoted friend. He was as dependable as the daybreak.

Too restless to sleep, I rose and walked the length of the hallway. The dim glow from the full moon cast an eerie light at the end of the house, down where the dormers jutted out at the east end. From the window, I stared at the deserted yard below, looking for any sign of Mamma. But the road and yard were empty.

Downstairs the day clock began to chime, as if on cue. Mamma had stilled the pendulum, stopping the clock on the hour she learned her beloved sister Naomi had passed away, leaving it unwound for months. Now the brassy sound traveled up the steep staircase to my ears—twelve lingering chimes. Something about the marking of hours in the deep of night disturbed me.

I paced the hall, scooting past the narrow stairs leading to the third story, where Adam and Joe slept in two small rooms. Safely out of earshot of Mamma's mysterious comings and goings.

Was Dat such a sound sleeper that he didn't hear Mamma's footsteps?

What would cause her to be so restless? I'd asked myself a dozen times. Yet, as much as I longed to be privy to my mother's secrets, something told me I might come to wish I never knew.

The holiest of all holidays are those
Kept by ourselves in silence and apart;
The secret anniversaries of the heart.

—Henry Wadsworth Longfellow

chapter
....
one

April in Bird-in-Hand was heralded by brilliant sunrises and brisk, tingling evenings. Every thicket was alive with new greenery, and streams ran swift and clear.

Known for its fertile soil, the idyllic town nestled between the city of Lancaster on the west and the village of Intercourse to the east. In spite of the encroachment of town homes and newly developed subdivisions on nearly all sides, the fertile farmland remained as appealing to outsiders as it did to Judah Byler and his farming neighbors.

Judah's big white clapboard house was newer than most of the farmhouses in the area. Its double chimney and sweeping gables lent an air of style to the otherwise ordinary siding and black-shuttered windows. He'd drawn up the plans twenty-some years before, situating the house on a piece of property divided from a vast parcel of pastureland owned by his father. Judah took great care to locate an ideal sloping spot on which to pour the foundation, since the house would be situated on a floodplain. Together he and his *Daed* planted a windbreak of trees and erected several martin birdhouses in the yard. His

married brothers, father, and uncles had all pitched in and built the large ten-bedroom house. A house that, if cut in two, was identical on both sides.

Just after breaking ground, Judah took as his bride Lettie Esh, the prettiest girl in the church district. They'd lived with relatives for the first few months of their marriage, receiving numerous wedding gifts as they visited, until the house was completed.

Eyeing the place now, Judah was pleased the exterior paint was still good from three summers ago. He could put all of his energies into lambing this spring. It was still coat weather, and he breathed in the peppery scent of black earth this morning as he went to check on his new lambs again. He had risen numerous times in the night to make sure the ewes were nursing their babies. A newborn lamb was encouraged to nurse at will, at least as frequently as six to eight times in a twenty-four hour period.

Two plump robins strutted on the sidewalk, but Judah paid them little mind as he walked to the sheep barn, groggily recalling the day he'd carried Lettie's things up the stairs to the second floor. To the room that was to become their own. *As husband and wife*, he thought wryly.

Momentarily he considered Lettie's current dejected state, wondering if he shouldn't stay put today. But on second thought, he could not endure more questions from Adam or furtive glances from Grace. His eldest daughter had slipped into the barn last night and tried to hide in the shadows, as if wanting to inquire about Lettie, too. *Grace is as perceptive as her big brother is bold.*

At twenty-two Adam was the oldest of their four, and then

Grace, followed by nineteen-year-old Amanda—their Mandy—and fifteen-year-old Joseph, whom they called Joe. All of them still at home and mighty Plain clear down to their toes. Adam had joined church two years ago and Grace last September, along with Mandy, who'd always wanted to be baptized with her only sister. He was thankful indeed for his God-fearing offspring, having been privy to some of the fiery trials other parents suffered.

Is Lettie still grieving Naomi? Her sister had died in her sleep several years earlier, within days of Gracie's birthday, as he recalled. A heart attack, he'd heard it was. Poor Lettie had worn black for a full year to show her respect, twice as long as the expected time. There had been other signs, too, that she was locked up in sorrow for longer than most siblings might mourn. Lettie couldn't bring herself to speak of Naomi, which worried her parents, Jakob and Adah, who lived across the wide middle hall on their own side of Judah's house.

Presently Judah looked in on the ewe and her twin lambs, certain that Adam and Joe, with a little help from their grandfather Jakob, could tend to the newly birthed lambs, at least for today. When he was finished checking, he hurried back to the house. He'd seen Lettie stirring up eggs and milk for scrambling as he'd rushed past her to the side door. Disheveled and still in her bathrobe, her fair hair quickly pulled into a loose bun at the nape of her neck, she'd said nary a word.

Returning now, he made his way to the sink to wash up for the meal. Drying his hands, he moseyed over to the table, avoiding Lettie's solemn gaze as she set the table for his solitary early morning breakfast.

"S'pose we ought to have us a talk." Her big blue eyes nearly stared a hole in him.

"Well, I'll be leavin' soon for the animal auction up yonder," he replied.

She grimaced and placed two cups and saucers on the table before preparing to pour the coffee. "It shouldn't take much of your time."

His stomach tensed up and he motioned for her to sit. They bowed their heads for the silent prayer of blessing, which concluded when he uttered a quick amen. Judah reached for the eggs and generously salted them, then spread Lettie's raspberry jam on two pieces of toast. Out of the corner of his eye, he noticed his wife's occasional glance. She was scarcely eating.

When Lettie didn't say what was on her mind, he mentioned wanting to buy another mare for road driving. "I'll know for certain when I see what's up for auction this morning. We'll need another horse with Adam most likely marryin' come fall."

"Can't we rely on his horse later on?" she asked, her voice a thin, sad thread.

"A young man needs his own mare."

"Well, driving horses ain't on my mind today." She sighed loudly. "Judah . . . I need to tell you something."

He braced himself. "What is it?"

A long pause ensued as she attempted to gather herself. He wondered what had caused his wife to go from periodic moodiness to whatever this was. "You ain't sick, are ya, Lettie?"

"*Ach* no."

"*Des gut.*" Yet the tension hung in the air, nearly visible. Neither food nor drink eased the lingering silence.

"I truly do not know how . . . or where . . . to begin." She

did not raise her eyes to meet his as she drank her coffee, not until Judah was done eating and wiping his face on his sleeve. She glanced out the window, eyes glistening. "It's awful hard, really. . . ."

He folded his hands near his plate, waiting. Would she finally tell him what was bothering her—let down this everlasting barrier?

She opened her mouth to speak, lips parted as she turned to look at him. Then slowly she shook her head. "Perhaps it's better this way."

Better what way? Though she'd never before seemed as upset as she had these last few weeks, he'd tried before to pull answers from her but he scarcely ever knew what to say. Truth be known, he'd given up attempting conversation over the years—least where anything sticky was concerned. Nor did he have hope that things would change.

"Ach, you've got yourself a full day," she said again.

He leaned over the table, baffled by her deep sadness. "Keep yourself busy, won't ya?"

She looked his way and nodded. "Jah, we've both got our work. . . ."

He reached for his coffee, taking a slow swallow, and Lettie moved the sugar bowl closer to him. Suddenly, her cool hand was covering his, her eyes pleading. He tensed and withdrew his hand.

"Are you displeased, Judah?"

He saw the deep lines in her sallow face. "Displeased?"

"With *me*." She leaned her head into her hands.

He reached for the sugar bowl, at a loss for words. Then

she was on her feet and clearing the table, her face grim as she reached for his dirty plate.

Judah pushed back his chair. "Well, I s'pose I should be goin'." He made his way to the side door, still alert to her presence.

Taking the few steps gingerly, he was conscious of a painful gnawing in his stomach as he headed down the lane past the martin birdhouses. It was then that he realized he hadn't said good-bye.

With a small pang of regret, he was tempted to turn back . . . to say something to smooth things over, if that was even possible.

What good would it do? He stopped for a moment, then resumed his pace.

——— ··· ———

Grace Byler slipped into her cozy gray slippers and put on her white cotton bathrobe. Having awakened before the alarm, she lit the gas lantern on her dresser and set about redding up the room. She made her bed, then plumped her pale green and white crocheted pillows on the settee in the corner, where she liked to sit and read a psalm or two before dressing. Her favorite way to start the day.

She counted two clean dresses and matching aprons left for the weekend, each garment on its hanger on the wooden pegs along one wall. Going to sit on the settee, she reached for the Good Book.

When she finished reading, she dressed, weaving the straight pins sideways on the front of her loose-fitting bodice, hungry for a good breakfast. Last evening's supper seemed far too long ago

as she brushed her blond hair away from her face and wound its thickness into the customary bun. She set her *Kapp* on her head, letting its ties dangle free.

That done, she glanced in the dresser mirror and straightened her brown cape dress. Soon it would be time to sew up some new dresses. She yawned as she moved to the window and peered out at the rising sun. Her father stood at the end of the driveway, waving down a van. *Must be he's traveling farther than usual today.* Typically their family preferred to use the horse and carriage for transportation—the team—although Dat frequently used an English driver for longer distances.

Stepping away from the window, Grace was curious to know where he was headed so early, but her father rarely shared his comings and goings. She paused to smooth the lightweight bed quilt, made from an antique pattern they'd copied from Dat's mother. Grace recalled the fun she'd had piecing it together several years ago with Mamma, Mandy, and *Mammi* Adah.

Sweet memories.

On her way to the door, she eyed the braided rug between her bed and the dresser and decided it needed a good beating. She'd do that after breakfast, before Mamma and she took the horse and buggy into town to her job at Eli's. Mamma planned to stop at the general store.

Downstairs, she found her mother frying up eggs and sausage. "Mornin', Mamma," she said, surprised at her mother's already soiled black apron and unkempt hair. Stray strands of blond-gray hair were wispy at her neck, nothing like the neat bun Grace was used to seeing. "How'd ya sleep?" she asked.

"All right, I guess. You?"

"I've had better nights."

"Oh?" Mamma kept her eyes low, but she couldn't disguise their puffy redness.

Grace drew in a breath. Something was terribly wrong.

"You work so hard over at Eli's," her mother said. "You really need your rest, Gracie."

"We *all* do," she whispered. Then, going to the utensil drawer, she said, "I'll be home later than usual today, but I'll get a ride. You won't have to bother pickin' me up."

" 'Tis never a bother." Mamma adjusted the flame under a pot of stew for the noon meal. Quickly, she returned to kneading a mass of bread dough, her lips drawn in a taut line.

Oh, but Grace wanted to throw her arms around Mamma and tell her that everyone knew she was troubled, no matter how much she pretended otherwise. "I saw Dat out early, waitin' for a driver," she said, making small talk.

"Jah, and he was mighty hungry at breakfast." Mamma raised the lid on the pot filled with stew meat and vegetables, and a gust of steam rose out of the top.

"Dat sure enjoys your cooking." Grace was thankful for the gas that powered the range and oven, and the refrigerator and water heater, as well. The bishop had declared it acceptable to sell the old cookstove and icebox before she was born. That must have been a wonderful-good day for Mamma, who enjoyed working in the kitchen, whipping up one delicious meal after another. All the womenfolk had benefited in scores of ways.

She assumed someone had coaxed Dat to replace their kitchen appliances back then. Most likely her maternal grandmother, Mammi Adah, had stepped in to plead Mamma's case.

To this day an unspoken tension over such things continued between her standoffish father and outspoken grandmother.

Grace placed the knives, forks, and spoons around the table, glancing at her tired mother, still so pretty nearly everyone looked at her twice upon first meeting her. The milky blue of Mamma's eyes was remarkable, and sometimes Grace wondered if her mother knew just how striking she really was.

When Grace had poured the juice and milk, she called up the stairs to Mandy, their only sleepyhead. "Hurry, sister . . . breakfast is nearly ready."

At this hour Adam and Joe were out watering the sheep and looking after the newborn lambs, with more wee lambs on the way. Any minute, though, they would be in, hungry as ever, unless they'd eaten earlier with Dat.

"Your sister's ev'ry bit a slowpoke, just as she was as a schoolgirl," Mamma said while pouring coffee. "She's goin' to need more prodding, I daresay."

Grace wiped the counter and agreed. "Mandy's a good help, though, once the sleep's washed out of her eyes."

"Well, she's not near the worker you are."

Grace's breath caught in her throat. She stepped closer. "Ach, Mamma," she said, embarrassed.

Her mother offered a hint of her old warm smile and a good-natured wink. She carried her coffee cup over and sat at her regular spot next to the head of the table. "Best be callin' your brothers."

Heartened by the shift in Mamma's mood, Grace obliged and made her way out to the wide hallway, where pairs of shoes were neatly lined up on low wooden shelves. *More of Mammi Adah's doing.*

Along one wall of the entryway, Dat had positioned pegs for work coats, as well as sweaters, an equal distance apart. The sight of Dat's empty coat peg sobered her, and she wished she might brush away the heaviness she sensed in Mamma. If only Grace could manage the way her father somehow did, letting her mother's sadness slide off him. *Letting everything slide off, really.*

chapter
two

Out of sheer habit, Judah hailed the driver when the van was still a good ways down the road. Martin Puckett often came to pick him up, so there was sure to be a comfortable familiarity during the drive to Brownstown today.

Bending down, Judah picked up a pebble and turned it over in his hand, remembering last night. He hadn't known how to tell his firstborn that he had no answers. *This is just how things are. . . .*

He'd done what he did best, sinking within himself, where his son's thorny question vanished away. Where he daydreamed about raising sheep and providing a peaceful place for his family to live and enjoy the good fellowship of the People. Of growing old someday with grandchildren and greats, too, on his knee, all of them resembling beautiful Lettie.

My wife. Things would straighten out as a matter of course. In time, Lettie would return to some semblance of normalcy, just as she eventually had after the death of her sister Naomi. Naomi had never shared Lettie's tendency to moodiness, always behaving like a typical wife. He hoped young Grace, who was the

picture of health—both physically and emotionally—favored her aunt in that respect. *Especially if she's headed for marriage.*

The van slowed to a stop. Judah opened the front door and greeted the driver, "*Wie geht's!*"

Martin comically replied with a rather garbled line of Pennsylvania Dutch mixed with English—something about feeling as good as he ought to but not as good as he wished.

Judah reached for the seat belt and managed to offer a cheerful hello over his shoulder to the two middle-aged Amishwomen behind him.

Martin glanced his way. "Pretty soon, I'll have to start hiring *you* to take me on errands," he said, a grin on his ruddy cheeks. "Gas prices and all."

"So I hear." Judah liked Martin's frank way of speaking his mind, his spontaneous sense of humor, too. Martin's jovial nature was one reason Judah contacted the sixty-three-year-old first for transportation, before other drivers on his list. Anymore, the highways were unsafe for horses and carriages with so many impatient motorists rushing along the roads.

Martin shook his head. "Talk has it we'll be paying four dollars a gallon or more by summer."

"Guess you'll have to raise your fee per mile then, too." Judah hoped not. The price of feed and seed and just about everything else made for plenty of worrisome talk at suppertime.

"We'll just have to see." Martin glanced at his rearview mirror. "Where you heading to, ladies?" He tilted his head slightly.

"You can drop us off at market," one of them said.

"Well, I've never *dropped* anyone anywhere," Martin joked.

"Oh, for pity's sake!" the other woman said, laughing.

Judah joined in the frivolity. It felt surprisingly good to laugh again, especially with Martin. An imposing man in girth and stature, Martin had an enormous personality to match, and he had a handshake suggestive of a bear's paw. Talkative, too, he was a teller of often inspiring tales, and one of only a few English folk Judah enjoyed communicating with.

Looking out the window, Judah trained his sights on the splendor of the season on Beechdale Road. He noticed white rose arbors boasting their first coat of paint, accenting soon-to-be colorful flower beds along front and back porches and near small springhouses.

How Lettie loves her roses, he thought suddenly, wondering if their beauty might put a smile on her pretty face once again.

The way he was feeling, he didn't much care what Lettie did with her roses come June. They were her business, after all. But lest Judah allow his aggravation to make a nesting place in his soul, he pushed aside the leftover frustration. He'd had plenty of practice doing so over the past few weeks—no, nearly all their married life. What was another day?

He returned his attention to the road. Presently he would simply appreciate the speed with which he could get to his destination this morning, just as he enjoyed riding by car up to visit his older brother Potato John, near Akron. At less busy times of year, he also made trips south to Bart to see dozens of his father's Stoltzfus cousins. A quick and effortless way to escape concerns about Lettie.

Judah mustn't be gone too long today, however, with lambing well under way, though he was glad for a good excuse to clear his head for a few hours. He was headed to a private animal

auction, hoping to purchase another driving horse. The sale would be held in the barn of a Mennonite farmer in Browns-town who'd advertised in *Die Botschaft*, the weekly newspaper for the Plain community. Judah had attended the Mud Sales in Gordonville in mid-March—the fire department–sponsored horse auction—looking for just the right driving horse. He'd come up empty-handed. He knew what he wanted but wouldn't pay top dollar, not with feed prices going through the roof.

Hopefully I'll see something today. With marriage around the corner, it wouldn't be many more months before son Adam would need spirited Sassy, his sorrel, as well as another horse for himself. And their favorite driving horse, Willow—a gentle and big-eyed chestnut mare who was practically a family pet—was getting on in years and soon wouldn't be able to pull her weight around the farm. Or on the road. Judah had often observed Grace in the horse stable, grooming her, feeding her a carrot or apple, and talking up a storm.

Too bad she has to converse with a horse, he thought, wondering if Lettie might ever feel the need to resort to the same.

———···———

Gripping the banister, Adah moved slowly up the back stairs to Jakob. She'd cooked a hot breakfast—poached eggs and sausage patties, toast and apple butter—and it was all laid out, waiting for her husband to take his place at the head of the table. He was slower than usual this morning and, since Jakob's hearing had dimmed, she decided to go and find him.

The creaking staircase reminded her of the peculiar talking she had heard in the wee hours. Startled awake, she'd heard someone downstairs on their side of the house . . . jumbled-up

words mixed with weeping. She'd sat up in bed, straining to hear. Was it Lettie?

Curious, she'd crept down these steps, their squeaks more pronounced in the dead of night. She had stood in her large kitchen amidst strands of moonbeams, looking past the new-fangled stove she'd talked Judah into installing, identical to the one in Lettie's own kitchen. Standing before the front room window, her daughter had been hunched over as if she might be ill. A black silhouette against the white radiance of the night.

Not wanting to make her presence known, Adah had stayed put, not moving and scarcely breathing. A test of her will-power—her muscles, too. She did not want to risk the stairs creaking again. So Lettie was up and restless. Didn't all women-folk have the sniffles about something at least once during the month?

Surely that's all it was.

"All I hope it is. . . ."

Making her way into their bedroom, she tapped Jakob lightly on the knee as he read from his old, tattered German Bible. "Breakfast is on the table," she said.

He looked up, a twinkle in his eye. "Don't have to ask a hungry man twice." He heaved himself out of his chair and followed her to the stairs.

When they were seated and the silent blessing had been offered, she looked out the window and noticed Adam and Joe—the tall and the short of it—moseying toward the house. No doubt they had been bottle-feeding some of the weaker lambs, those rejected by the ewes. Since Judah had left the house so early, the care of the most recent newborns had fallen to the boys—at least for now.

"Our grandsons are plenty capable of lookin' after things." Jakob grinned at her. He'd caught her gawking and probably looking a bit worried, too. "Word has it Judah's Adam is soon goin' to have himself a farm of his own to look after."

"Oh?" This was news. "But the Stahls don't have land to spare, do they?"

Jakob shook his head, smacking his lips. "I didn't say they did."

So was Priscilla's father handing over the big farm to his son-in-law-to-be? If so, did Lettie have any inkling of this?

Lettie and Susannah Stahl had been friends since childhood, but Adah hadn't heard Lettie mention her much in recent years. Not since Naomi's sudden passing, when Lettie had become hopelessly withdrawn, despite Adah's efforts to get her out to quilting and canning bees.

"The way I heard it, the Stahl farm's bein' divided up again," Jakob explained, shaking pepper on his eggs. "Won't be much of it left if they keep on, but nobody asked me."

"Well, a Mennonite farmer down the way is sellin' off a small section of his land, Marian Riehl says. Four acres or so."

"A small plot like that makes no sense." Jakob shook his head.

"You'd think they'd want to pass it along to family . . . like you say Rudy Stahl's doin' with our Adam and his bride-to-be."

"Well, *that's* a good thirty acres, though. More than enough for a nice truck farm."

"A wonderful-*gut* wedding gift, I'll say."

Jakob chuckled. "Whoever thought a fella could keep his

30

weddin' plans a secret till the time of bein' published never had womenfolk lookin' over his shoulder, ain't?"

They laughed until Jakob had to pull a blue kerchief out of his pocket to wipe his blue-gray eyes.

"I'm guessin' Judah has to know somethin'," Adah said.

"If *we* know, then how on earth wouldn't he and Lettie know, or at least suspect it?"

"Seems to me Lettie has more on her mind than a weddin' dowry." Adah rose to get more sausage, still warming on the skillet. Jakob liked his meat plenty hot.

"You must've heard her last night, too." Jakob had never been one to beat around the bush, one of the reasons she'd liked him from the very start of their courtship, fifty-some years ago.

Adah stroked the top of his callused hand. "It's just not like her . . . not anymore, at least."

Jakob's eyes searched hers. *"Puh!* She's a woman, ain't she?"

"Oh, go on with ya, Jakob Esh!" She tugged at his cuff.

"Sure hope it ain't something cropping up 'tween her and Judah."

Adah's shoulders tensed. "Well, but . . . who's to say?"

"Ain't our business." He paused. "And it never was."

She nodded slowly. "The past is over and done with, thank the dear Lord."

At a loss for how to comfort her daughter, Adah decided to bake a loaf of fresh bread, then take it over to Lettie. *Poor thing.* A nice warm slice of buttered toast with some brown sugar and cinnamon would surely cheer her up right quick.

———— ··· ————

While she was still carrying breakfast dishes to the sink, Grace heard the side door open. Turning, she saw Becky Riehl standing there, a big smile on her rosy face, her dark hair pulled tight at the middle part. "Ach, hullo. So good to see ya!"

Becky glanced about the room, a joyful light evident in her soft brown eyes. "Are we alone?" she whispered.

Laughing, Grace said, "Sure looks like it." She put down the pile of dishes and went to her friend.

"You'll never believe this, Gracie."

"Jah?"

Becky looked about the room, as if confirming they were indeed by themselves. Then she said, "Yonnie Bontrager asked me to go walkin' with him after the next Singing!"

Grace wasn't at all surprised. "That's just wonderful-*gut*, Becky."

"Do you really think so?" Becky blew out a breath. "Do ya think I should go along? I mean . . . that makes me, what . . . the eighth girl he's asked?"

Grace suppressed a laugh. According to Yonnie's sister Mary Liz, her brother had made some sort of list of eligible girls from their church district, hoping to get acquainted with each one before deciding whom to seriously court.

"I think you should accept," Grace said.

"Honestly?"

Becky's dark eyes widened as Grace revealed what she'd heard from Mary Liz. "He made a *list*?" she exclaimed. "That's lots different than the way we do things here, jah? Do you suppose he got that idea from where he grew up in Indiana?"

Grace shrugged. "He'll likely run out of girls to choose

from," she said. "The longer he takes to decide, ya know, the more girls'll get snatched up by other fellas."

Becky paused, her eyes wistful. "Mighty puzzling, 'tis. If he wasn't so interesting, I might just decline."

Grace remembered Yonnie's appeal all too well.

"So, I guess I'm one of the last ones on that list of his," Becky said, shaking her head. "What do you think the chances are . . . ?"

It was clear to Grace that no matter her hesitance, Becky was indeed smitten. She smiled at her dearest friend. "You have every bit as good a chance of stealin' his heart as the next girl, Becky."

"Well, I don't know . . ."

Grace reached for her hand. "I'm tellin' ya, you *do*." She motioned for her to sit on the wooden bench. "Have a cinnamon bun with me," she coaxed. Secretly, she was surprised it had taken this long for Yonnie to work through his supposed list. As for herself, she was in love with Henry Stahl, who stuck closely to their courting rituals. Her Henry had a good head on his shoulders, and he was hardworking, too.

Just like Dat!

chapter
three

Judah was mighty glad the auction's makeshift registration window had opened early. He'd waited only a short time for his ID number, enjoying a cup of coffee and briefly chewing the fat with several Amish farmers. He'd even become acquainted with one intriguing *Englischer* from out of state—a friendly man in his early fifties or so who was sniffing out the area for a gentleman's farm to purchase. He'd given Judah his business card, but it was only printed with the man's name, *Roan Nelson*, and his email address. The man had immediately apologized, pointing out Judah was most likely not in a position to contact him that way. "Not without a computer," Roan had quipped.

Laughter followed, and for a time Judah and Roan strolled the grounds together, talking about the morning's offerings. Judah had been glad to oblige when Roan had asked more than a handful of questions about what qualities to look for in a good horse.

Presently Judah found himself shoulder to shoulder in the buzzing crowd, vying for the fine mare on the auction block. He caught the auctioneer's eye and then twitched his eyebrow—his

preferred way to bid. The mare, a young black Morgan named Maddie, had already stepped out nicely to demonstrate her road trot. This was one slick auctioneer, and Judah had to stay alert. Tough when his mind kept wandering.

Judah arched his eyebrow to the auctioneer, raising the bid. . . .

This morning's exchange with Lettie plagued him. He'd witnessed her occasional moodiness from early on in their marriage, although she'd done her best to conceal it. But in the past weeks her gloom had been more pronounced, and he had no idea what to do to make things better. He'd never had a good understanding of womenfolk.

The auctioneer looked to him for a third bid, and he nodded his head. He was staying in and soon would be the happy owner of this horse if the farmer over yonder bowed out. Even if the other bidder kept going, Judah was willing to go a bit higher. It wasn't that he was suddenly willing to pay a pretty penny for a horse, but he knew the value of a good mare.

His thoughts returned to Lettie. There had been times in the past when he'd wondered if her thinking was askew. After Naomi had died so unexpectedly, she'd gone to Ike, Naomi's husband, asking to go through her sister's personal effects. For a reason unknown to Judah, or even to Ike, Lettie had been particularly interested in some poetry books. She'd said merely that she wanted to have them, and she'd brought a collection of them home, placing them in the bedroom bookcase Judah had built as her engagement present. He knew the books were there, but he'd never looked at them. Never cared to. She was, after all, entitled to a measure of privacy.

Eventually, though, as time had passed, Lettie became less

sorrowful, apparently accepting her sister's untimely death. And once again, all seemed to be well.

But then came this year's blustery month of March, with its early spring barn raising down south. He had been too tied up to attend as he worked through his detailed records on his flock and plans for the year's breeding pairs—instructing Adam about the paper work involved. But looking back, he never should have allowed Lettie to go, because his wife had not returned the same woman.

He raised his eyebrow at the auctioneer yet again. Then came a pause as the auctioneer looked about the crowd, waiting for one more bid.

At last the wood gavel pounded. "Sold! To number eighty-three!"

Rejoicing with a nod of his head, Judah made his way to the cashier's table to pay for and claim his new horse. He spotted Roan Nelson on the fringe of the crowd. When he saw him, the man waved and called, "Did you get your horse?"

Judah nodded, surprised the Englischer thought enough to ask.

"Congratulations!"

"*Denki*," he called over his shoulder. While making his payment, he recalled hearing that a small parcel of land was up for sale—by word of mouth only—a mere two miles from his own farm. "Say, Roan," he said, turning, "if memory serves me, there's a piece of land available over on Gibbons Road, not far from the one-room Amish schoolhouse. A small swath is all, but it might serve your purpose."

Roan's eyes lit up. "Wonderful . . . thanks for the tip!"

Judah gave him directions and said if he ended up with it,

they'd almost be neighbors. "There's no house on that property, though," he added.

"Oh, that can come later." Roan was making note of the directions on a square-shaped gadget that looked like a small calculator with letters. "This sounds great. . . . I'll follow up today."

Mighty friendly for a city slicker, Judah thought, tipping his hat.

———— ··· ————

"It's s'posed to be nice all week." Grace smiled at her mother, who sat beside her on the right side of their family carriage, holding the reins. They'd chosen their gentle trotter, Willow, for the trip, and Grace was delighted to slip her some sugar cubes right after hitching up the buggy.

"Well, lookee there!" Mamma pointed to the purple ground cover near the neighbor's mailbox as they rode. "In full bloom already."

"Reminds me of my English lavender," Grace said.

"You and your herb garden." Mamma laughed softly, glancing her way. "You remember where your fascination with herbal remedies came from, don't ya?"

She'd heard it many times before, but she listened attentively now, because it had been a good while since her mother had been this talkative.

"Mammi Adah was the one who first taught you 'bout growin' herbs. I think you were around nine."

Grace cherished the memory. "I remember sitting beside Mammi out on the front porch swing on that hot and muggy summer day. Then, when it was close to sunset, we walked

hand in hand around her herb garden, and she named off each plant . . . and described the medicinal properties, too."

"That's right," said Mamma, a faraway look in her eyes. "And you were just ten when the two of you concocted a special tea for sore throats. Do you recall?"

"Jah, had some chamomile in it." Grace smiled to herself, tempted to lean closer to Mamma.

Maple Avenue was coming into view, and soon they made the turn east toward the store. "Denki for droppin' me off." Grace jumped down from the carriage, her apron floating up slightly.

"When did ya say you'll be home?"

"In time for a late supper." Grace held on to the buggy door, searching her mother's face.

"All right, then. I'll keep it hot for ya."

Reluctant as she was to end this pleasant interlude with Mamma, Grace turned toward the store. She wanted to be on time and preferred to be a few minutes early.

She looked back and noticed Mamma still sitting in the enclosed buggy, unmoving, like she was daydreaming. When at last Willow pulled forward and the black spokes on the buggy wheels turned, Mamma straightened to sit taller in her seat, her Kapp strings floating in the breeze.

Why's she sometimes so dear and other times so distant? Grace shook her head. If there was a way to make things better, she would certainly try.

— ··· —

As he was headed back toward Bird-in-Hand, Martin Puck- ett received a call on his cell phone. An Amish family of six

needed a ride down to Paradise. More than anything, Martin enjoyed driving Amish children, with their happy chatter in Pennsylvania Dutch. The things they said often brought a smile to his face.

"Okay. Off to meet the Zook family in front of the general store," he muttered to himself, thankful his Plain customers were becoming dependent on his transportation service. *Like a taxicab without the meter*, he thought, remembering what Judah Byler and he had discussed earlier that morning. The way the economy was heading had become the hot topic of conversation in households around the country, and his home was no exception. These days his wife was limiting her driving to only twice a week. Surprising, because she had been known to gallivant some with their married daughters—frequenting Root's Country Market and traveling nearly every Tuesday morning to Central Market at Lancaster's Penn Square. Before the gas crunch, they'd made a habit of driving up to the Green Dragon for Amish baked goods or homemade candies on Fridays.

Turning into the parking area in front of the general store, Martin spotted a vacant spot and pulled in. Next to him, a solemn-faced middle-aged Amishwoman stepped down from her buggy and went to tie the horse to the hitching post. She looked familiar, but not wanting to stare, he looked the other way as he turned off the ignition.

Martin leaned back on the headrest, twiddling his thumbs. Semiretirement was working out well, despite its coming on his doctor's orders. *"If you want to die of a heart attack, keep doing what you're doing."* His wife, Janet, was all for his switching gears from his former hectic job as an electrician to providing wheels for the "People," as some referred to Amish and "team

Mennonites." Both Plain groups set themselves apart from the modern world. Who else could pull off living and dressing like it was the 1800s while surrounded by all the modern trappings of the twenty-first century?

All of a sudden another Amishwoman came rushing out of the store, waving her hand in greeting to the woman tying up her horse. "Lettie . . . ach, is that you? It's been ever such a long time since you've come to quilting bees and whatnot all." The woman sounded as though she was a close friend or relative.

Lettie? Of course—he recognized her now. He'd driven Lettie Byler and her pretty blond daughters—Gracie, they called the older, and young Mandy—at least a dozen times in the past year. On occasion, Martin had even taken the whole family to see relatives southeast of Strasburg, near Bart.

While the two women visited on the porch of the store, he realized it had been weeks since he'd received a request for transportation from Lettie Byler and her girls.

But he *had* seen Lettie heading somewhere on foot. He'd observed her twice recently as she walked south on Church Road, past his own house. He would never have been up at that hour had he not suffered from insomnia and been doing a bit of walking himself—the full length of the first floor—waiting for his sleeping pill to take effect.

Watching her now, as Lettie stood silently listening to the other woman, her face impassive, he couldn't help but notice how ashen she was. Her vacant stare reminded him of his own sister's; she had seemingly walked in a daze for a year before a doctor prescribed depression medication.

Just then, the Zook family emerged from the store. Sadie Zook herded her brood toward his van, carrying a large sack.

"Hello there!" he greeted her and opened the passenger door for them, waiting as they climbed in. "Going to Paradise today?"

"No, no . . . I've changed my mind." Sadie fanned herself with a handkerchief after she got settled into the second seat with her youngest two, the sack of purchases on her lap. "Ain't much use runnin' ourselves ragged. We're all but tuckered out."

"*Un hungerich,*" the smallest boy declared, rubbing his stomach.

"Then to home it is. We'll have us a nice hot meal," said Sadie. Glancing up, she gasped when Lettie Byler hurried back to her carriage and climbed in. And she was openly staring at the sad-eyed woman as Martin pulled the door closed for her.

Martin was taken aback—even embarrassed—by Sadie Zook's gawking as he went around and got in behind the wheel. In his rearview mirror, he could see her craning her neck, eyes positively fixed on Lettie as he backed up and turned around to merge into traffic.

Has she also seen Lettie Byler out alone at night, walking? he wondered.

chapter
four

Heather Nelson sat on the lone chair across from the oncologist's desk. The room was spinning and she focused on her every breath. How many times had she walked into this doctor's office in the last six weeks? She'd come secretly, so as not to alarm her father, not wanting to burden him with this impossible situation.

Dr. O'Connor was talking again, but she had difficulty following him, especially after hearing the initial comment. "I'm sorry to tell you this. . . ."

Other worrisome phrases intermixed with his medical jargon: "lymph nodes . . . stage IIIA . . . radiation . . ."

Her lab results had come back startlingly bleak—a diagnosis precipitated by a physical after she'd discovered a couple of painless nodules in her right armpit.

Completely stunned now, she uncrossed her legs and leaned forward. She looked the doctor in the eye as he ceased his discourse. "This may sound presumptuous, but how can you be so sure, Dr. O'Connor? You say the areas of swelling in the lymph

node regions have spread, but I have no symptoms." She made herself slow down. "I mean, I feel perfectly fine."

Am I making any sense?

Dr. O'Connor wore an annoyed look, as if he'd heard this rebuttal before and did not appreciate being questioned. But didn't he understand she'd just had the living daylights knocked out of her?

He folded his well-manicured hands and leaned forward at his desk, more solemn than before. "There are four levels of this disease. And with each of the first three stages, many patients have few, if any, symptoms." He shook his head gravely. "After all the tests, Heather, I'm afraid the reports are quite conclusive."

You're afraid?

He continued on—something about a "nodular sclerosis variant in the late stage." He sounded too clinical . . . detached.

He must tell hundreds of patients similar news.

She wanted additional information, the kind that wasn't so quantifiable . . . and cold. Perhaps if she focused on the medical jargon—assuming she could—it would help her to make some sense of it. What exactly *had* the PET scan detected? Was it enough to know the medical imaging had shown increased glycolytic activity. . . and blood tests had found elevated levels of eosinophils?

She wanted to see these reports for herself, even though her brain was currently in freeze-up mode. *Was this how Mom felt?*

"Would you mind . . . starting over?" She blinked back tears.

The doctor nodded, offering a considerate smile. "I'll go over the initial biopsy results again and then the PET scan." He

turned a light on behind him and dimmed the canned lighting overhead.

She stood up to watch the screen, listening as her plans for a career, her perfect wedding, her future with the only guy she'd *really* loved—all of it—slipped away.

How can this be happening?

She was too young and too healthy—only twenty-four. The staggering news seemed far too pessimistic. Heather had always lived life with a cheerful outlook, even in spite of her darling mother's passing. She had been perpetually upbeat most of her life, even without the benefit of a serious date for high school prom or college sorority events. While she had a few casual friendships with a handful of girls, truly connecting with anyone, especially with guys, had always been difficult . . . if not impossible. But all that had changed when Devon Powers stared her down during an English Lit class in her final semester of undergraduate work. She'd promptly decided he was her one and only heart mate. Never before had she so thoroughly latched on to another human being, aside from her mother.

She had struggled through a challenging double major—sociology and English—at the College of William and Mary, near historic Williamsburg. The school was also her parents' alma mater, where they'd met their junior year and fallen in love, and within easy driving distance of Heather's childhood home. But she had spread her wings and lived in the dorm her freshman year, moving to a sorority house for the next three. Not so fond of hanging out with elitist roommates, she'd longed for her own place. Mom had always said Heather was happiest with her own company.

As eager as she was to make her way in the world following

her four-year degree, after a year's break Heather had opted to continue on, content to remain enmeshed in the academic mind-set as she worked toward a master's degree in American studies. She'd managed to work part-time all the while, editing Web content for a large telecom firm, not willing to mooch off her too-generous father, who'd received a significant sum from Mom's life insurance policy.

She jerked to attention. Was this a cruel twist of fate? *First Mom, now me?*

My poor dad, she thought as Dr. O'Connor droned on. Inhaling slowly, she folded her hands, as if clasping them together might help her through this painful maze. She paid close attention now: He was saying that medical imaging did not lie, walking her through even the smallest details as though trying to convince her things were as serious as he'd first said.

This doctor could definitely use some work on his bedside manner. *The grim reaper . . .*

In the midst of her fog, a tiny thought burst through: Maybe he was wrong. Shouldn't she get a second opinion? Or even a third? After all, she couldn't let this news destroy her dreams.

Dr. O'Connor had definitely made a mistake. But it wouldn't make sense to argue with him. He was obviously convinced of the diagnosis.

When the lights came up again, she could see the concern on his face. "I wish I had better news, Heather," he said, his mouth a tight line.

How old was this guy? Not much older than she was.

"But . . . I've got big plans." A surge of adrenaline made

her feel lippy. She was going to marry her fiancé one year from next month. "This isn't going to happen, okay?"

The doctor nodded as genuine relief spread across his face. "I wholeheartedly agree. You're a fighter, Heather. And this disease is highly curable." Pausing to shuffle through some papers on his desk, he quickly turned to his laptop. "I'll see about an opening for your first round of treatment."

Treatment? The word stopped her heart. She was well acquainted with the word and what it entailed—a combination of chemo and radiation. Her mom had endured the effects nobly, and according to her doctors it had extended her life a few months. But from what Heather had witnessed, the results had been dubious at best as her mother's quality of life dropped drastically. "Uh, no . . . I'm not interested in nuking my insides."

His look of astonishment was off-putting. "Well, let's talk about survival rates—"

"My mother was promised four more years."

"Your mother's cancer was quite different from yours. And she was twice your age." He drew a long breath, holding her gaze. "Why don't we set a time to discuss this further . . . perhaps after you've slept on it?"

I'm supposed to sleep?

"I don't think you understand, Doctor. I watched my mom die. I'm not sure what killed her, the cancer or the treatments."

He flinched at her comment. "Heather, I urge you to take some time to think about this. Without treatment the disease *will* progress . . . and you'll become very sick. Eventually it will take your life." He paused, his eyes small slits. "Of course, if

you're worried about fertility, most centers offer some preservation procedures."

She reached for her purse and slung it over her shoulder. As she got up, the floor seemed to slip from beneath her, and she leaned down to grip the chair to steady herself.

"Are you all right?"

"I'm fine." She forced a smile.

Perfectly fine.

"You're strong, Heather . . . and in otherwise good health," the doctor emphasized. "Every patient responds differently—there's no guarantee you would react to radiation the way your mother did."

There's no guarantee I'll be cured, either.

"Thanks anyway." *I'd rather not die before I'm dead.*

She didn't bother to pull the door shut behind her. Let him get up from beside his high and mighty desk and close it himself.

What must it be like playing God? The thought lingered as she hurried past the receptionist's desk where she'd made her co-pay.

They should be paying me! Glancing up at the clock, Heather was suddenly unable to suppress the lump in her throat. Overwhelmed, she pushed open the door, helpless to stop the tears spilling down her cheeks.

——— ··· ———

"Why, sure, we stock a large variety of herbs to help with digestion," Grace told her customer. She led the woman to the tonics and tea section of the store. "Here's what we have." She

reached for a popular herbal combination. "This one has a nice blend of herbs . . . it's helped lots of folk."

"Is this something you drink?" The woman turned the package over in her hands.

"Oh jah, and real tasty, too, I'm told. You can mix it with any kind of juice."

The dark-eyed woman took a moment to read the ingredients and compare the first suggestion to several other options, including bitter orange tea leaves. "Have you ever tried this?" she asked. Then, sputtering, she retracted her question. "Oh, well, I doubt *you* have stomach upsets."

Grace hardly knew what to say. There had been several times recently when she'd experienced queasiness, but it had nothing to do with indigestion. "You might want to just try one of these and see how it works for you."

The woman's face creased with uncertainty. "It's hard to decide."

"You're welcome to try one, and if it doesn't help, bring it back," Grace offered.

"Fair enough." The woman followed her to the cash register.

"Remember, if you have any questions at all, just ask. If I can answer them, I will. And if not, I'll find out the answer for you." Grace made change and counted it into the woman's hand. "Now that you know where we are, you'll have to come again."

The woman smiled. "You're very kind." She looked at Grace, her gaze drifting up to the head covering of white netting she wore from morning to night. "I've often wondered what it would be like to live as you do," she whispered.

Grace laughed softly. "Well, we're not as strange as you may think."

"But you don't drive cars or have electricity, do you?"

"Neither one, no."

"No phones or radios, either?" Looking chagrined, the woman said, "I don't mean to pry. Your ways *are* fascinating, though. You see"—and here she stepped closer—"I've always felt drawn to a simple life."

Grace rarely encountered this sort of open admiration among the English customers here or while tending the roadside vegetable stand in front of her family's house. Most Englischers were proud of their complicated lives with televisions, computers, cars, electricity, and whatnot. Uncertain how to reply, she only nodded in agreement.

"Oh goodness, I hope I didn't offend you, miss. I would just love to know more about Amish folk."

Grace thought of suggesting a book, but she certainly wasn't ready to offer the woman a tour of her father's house. "We live as our Anabaptist ancestors did." She suddenly remembered the cell phone one of her aunts was permitted to use for her quilting shop over in Honey Brook. "With some slight modifications."

"Oh really? Like what?"

The woman's fascination struck Grace as comical. She wondered, for a fleeting moment, if this customer with all her questions was somehow related to nosy Priscilla Stahl. "There are plenty of differences 'tween churches amongst the People. What's allowed from district to district is entirely up to the voting membership."

"Members are permitted to give their input?"

"Jah, we vote twice a year on our *Ordnung*."

The woman's bewilderment registered in her big brown eyes.

"The church ordinance," Grace added. "Our rules."

Another clerk came over to ask Grace something, and she was secretly relieved. "You'll have to excuse me." She smiled and scurried off to the other side of the store.

Such a curious soul!

She'd heard plenty of stories about pushy Englischers. But this woman had been the first Grace had ever met who'd seemed genuinely interested in their way of life. Of course, that didn't mean she was ready to join their ranks. All it took to discourage some outsiders was the thought of rising at four o'clock to milk a herd of dairy cows . . . *before* a hearty breakfast. That and having to learn the language of their forefathers, Pennsylvania Dutch.

Grace located the item the other clerk had wanted and wondered what might have prompted the customer's preference for all things simple. She recalled something Mammi Adah often said with a knowing smile on her wrinkled face: *"When you get what you want . . . do you want what you get?"* Grace assumed it was merely human to crave a different situation in life and not something unique to fancy folk.

— ... —

Adah stood out in the middle hallway and knocked and yoo-hooed to Lettie, the newly baked bread warm in her hand. She'd tried to make a point of respecting Judah and Lettie's privacy but knew she hadn't always succeeded since she and Jakob had moved into their side of the roomy house.

Lettie called back for her to let herself in. "You can just come over without askin', Mamm, you know that." Lettie had her hands in a wash pail and was down on the floor on all fours, looking up at her.

"I baked you some bread." Adah placed it on the table and sat down with a grunt as she observed Lettie wash the floor by hand. "Your Mandy ought to be helpin' with that."

Lettie kept on, her head down. "Sometimes doin' the work yourself is better."

"Does help occupy one's mind."

Lettie nodded slowly. "At times, jah . . ."

Not knowing how to broach the subject that nagged at her, Adah rose and walked to the side door, opened it, and looked out. She'd never been one to get anywhere with *this* daughter by making small talk. No, she had always had to take matters into her own hands . . . her own way. "Did I hear ya wanderin' the house and talkin' to yourself in the wee hours?" she asked, eyes still fixed on the pastureland to the south.

"Why do you ask?"

"Well, your father and I were talkin' and—"

"You know there's nothin' to gain from that."

Adah turned to see Lettie sitting upright in the middle of the floor, her bare feet peeking out from beneath the green choring dress spread out all around her. "I meant no harm, Lettie."

"Then say nothin' further." Lettie wiped her forehead with the back of her hand. "I have enough to think about just now."

She means without me poking my nose in. "All right, then." Adah glanced at the loaf she'd placed on the table. "I just

thought you might like some fresh bread this morning. Would you want me to slice a piece for ya?"

Lettie shook her head. "Denki, but I'll take a break when I'm *gut* and ready."

Adah forced a smile and said she had work to do, then left for her own kitchen. No matter her hopes, the tension between Lettie and herself had never lifted despite the passing of years. She could only wonder when, or if, her daughter might open up to her ever again.

chapter
five

Today the doctor informed me I'm dying. Someday, he's going to feel foolish for having ruined my day.

Heather stopped typing in her laptop journal, resting her fingers on the keyboard as she stared at the screen. She sat high on a barstool at the kitchen counter, one of several favorite spots in the house she'd shared with her parents for so many years. Pulling up her file of personal photos, she smiled as she stared at the most recent pictures of her and Devon, taken at Busch Gardens. *Before* climbing aboard the Loch Ness Monster, the most intense ride ever. She studied herself carefully. She looked exactly the same then as now, the picture of perfect health. Her shoulder-length brown hair with golden highlights gleamed in the sunlight, and her blue eyes sparkled with anticipation. Sure, she was tall and slender, but that was nothing new for her.

"See?" she said to a pair of matching black Persians. "I'm absolutely fine."

The cats had been a gift from her parents to each other on their twenty-fifth wedding anniversary. The big silver year was

celebrated by most couples with a trip to Hawaii or Cancun . . .
or silver jewelry and other finery.

But in spite of their practical approach to marriage, her
parents had always been anything but typical. For their special
anniversary they'd dipped into their savings and bought the
purebred kittens.

As cat lovers, they had already owned three beautiful cats
since saying "I do." Tiger's and Sasha's lives had been shortlived . . . but the sweetest cat of all, Kiki, had surprised even the
vet by living seventeen years before succumbing to old age. Mom
had been too heartbroken to replace Kiki right away, so they'd
waited a couple years to purchase the black feline siblings.

Heather nuzzled her face into Moe's gleaming fur. He always
seemed to know her mood and liked to meow-talk when alone
with her. She sighed and turned to scowl at the computer screen.
"Starting over." She selected what she'd just typed, then pressed
Delete. "Hypothetically speaking, if I *were* as sick as the doc
seems to think I am, what would I do?" She floated the question to the air.

Meow . . . mew.

She reached for Moe and held him close. "You silly cat."

What would Mom advise?

She recalled her mother's calm, sensible response to her
own diagnosis. While she had gone the route of modern medicine, in the end she'd wished there had been time to pursue an
alternative treatment method. *But Mom didn't have the luxury of
time. And she had numerous symptoms,* Heather thought, wanting
to quell the memories.

Still holding Moe, she got online and found a bunch of
emails from friends. The only one she really cared about was

from her fiancé, who was still frustrated about having been sent to Iraq. Looking on the bright side of things, though, today Devon had some good news. His tour of duty would be completed by Thanksgiving!

She hadn't forgotten the night six months ago when he'd made the upsetting announcement about his deployment. Back in his college days, he had thought it a good idea to join the National Guard and had assumed he'd only be gone on some weekends. But when his unit was called up and he was shipped off to Iraq via Texas, she'd inwardly recoiled, not wanting him to know how frightened she was.

Now she kissed Moe's furry head and decided not to tell Devon about her recent trips to the doctor. In fact, the more she considered it, the less she wanted to tell anyone. *Especially not Dad.*

He was still struggling over his grief—her depressing news would surely send him spiraling back down into a black tunnel of despair. She must spare her father that if possible.

Getting up, she went to pour some apple juice from the fridge and noticed a picture of the three of them, a magnet framing her parents and herself on the occasion of her college graduation. The grand brick buildings of William and Mary created an idyllic collegiate backdrop. The second-oldest school in the nation, it counted Thomas Jefferson among its distinguished graduates.

She flashed through her memories of her first year. She'd been so wet behind the ears and unsure of herself, looking back made her cringe at times.

"You never know what you'll accomplish if you don't take the first step." That was her dad's mantra, and a good one to live by,

too. Heather had succeeded as she lived out her academic dream at the challenging college. How she'd loved the feel of the old campus and the engaging professors—so much so she sometimes fantasized about becoming a perpetual student, maybe working toward her doctorate.

But then her mother had gotten sick . . . really sick. Heather had deferred her admission to the master's program and managed to get out of her apartment lease and move home, driving to and from work near Williamsburg. Based on the oncologist's prognosis, she'd had high hopes for her mother's recovery. All three of them had.

Even now, reflecting on the past, a plan began to churn in her head. The idea was quite appealing, actually. Why couldn't she simply drop out of her world for a while? With Devon serving overseas, who else would really notice?

Well, there was Dad, of course. He might notice if she disappeared, even though he was always preoccupied with work now that Mom was no longer around. He and Heather rarely bumped into each other at the house, which was just the way she liked it.

Frankly, her biggest obstacle to running away from it all was the timing. She was so close to the end of her final semester— just another week away. It would be smart to finish her work first, to keep her credits.

I'm fine, she reminded herself. *They just got my lab results mixed up.*

Second-guessing was her forte. What if someone else had gotten *her* report by mistake? She'd read about the frequency of misdiagnoses enough to know she wasn't borrowing trouble, yet . . .

Me and my overactive imagination. Most likely, they'd only misinterpreted her lab results . . . the other tests, too.

But what if they hadn't?

I have plenty of time to sort this out, she decided. Besides, from what she'd observed with Mom, if dying prematurely was absolutely in the cards, you couldn't argue with fate anyway. When your number was up, it was up.

Setting Moe down, she closed her laptop and headed outside to the two-tiered deck. She moved down the stairs to the large water feature her mom and their landscape architect had decided on before Mom died. The cascading mini falls reminded Heather of their many visits to Pennsylvania Amish country, where they had loved walking the back roads, stopping in at roadside stands, and enjoying the sound of gurgling creeks. *"Cricks,"* one Amish girl had called them, and Mom had looked at Heather with a twinkle in her eye, a smile on her pretty face. The three of them had frequently vacationed there, soaking up the tranquillity offered by rolling, picturesque farmland stretching in all directions.

I need something like that again.

Sipping her juice, Heather strolled through the grass, past the patio gardens and around to the front of the grand old colonial where she'd grown up.

"I miss you, Mom," she whispered.

She walked around to the opposite side of the house, taking her time as she pushed dry leaves out of the empty birdbath, wishing she could talk to her mom about Dr. O'Connor's diagnosis. The last thing she wanted was to be unreasonable. Maybe there was something else she could do . . . perhaps she could look into some naturopathic treatment alternatives

in Pennsylvania. There was a woman specialist somewhere in Lancaster whom Mom had wanted to see—Dr. Marshall, she recalled. According to the information Mom had jotted down and stuck on the fridge, her expertise was in stress relief, sleep disorders, cancer, headaches, and emotional well-being. Heather thought the list was still around.

Her mind was in a whirl as she slipped back into the house. Inside, she wandered down the hall to Dad's den. Somewhere in a drawer, waiting to be inserted into a photo album sleeve, there was a handful of brochures she and Mom had picked up and collected the last time they'd done something impulsive. They had planned the last-minute trip together, anxious to get away from the anxiety-ridden worlds of school and job and housework. Maxed out on stress, both of them had craved a serene spot that summer.

It would be like old times, visiting there. Heather recalled that her mom hadn't had a clue about her cancer then, though she'd been experiencing some weight loss and a puzzling lack of appetite. Her mom had been focused on nothing more serious than her obsession with heirloom quilts. While she'd never sewed herself, she loved seeing the quilts up close, even talking with expert quilters. On the final day of their trip, her mother had taken the plunge, purchasing the handmade Amish quilt that now adorned the guest bed downstairs.

"Think. Where *are* those brochures?" she muttered, aware of Moe's padding close behind her. Of the cat duo, Moe was more eager for company, following her from room to room as if he were her assigned shadow. "My constant companion, huh, Moe?"

She pulled out the top drawer of Dad's custom maple

built-ins. Beneath a road atlas, she found the pamphlets wrapped with a rubber band. "Jackpot!"

Heather curled up in her dad's recliner next to the bay window. Moe waited until she was settled, then jumped into her lap. "Well, aren't *you* needy," she joked. She flipped through flyers touting the Amish Farm and House on Route 30, J & B Quilts & Crafts, a strolling tour of Strasburg's historic district, and Wheatland, the historic mansion residence of President James Buchanan. She studied the words *Mennonite Information Center—welcome, let us help you feel at home*—and was captivated by the large barn and silo on the front of the brochure.

A page fell out onto her lap. It listed tourist homes in Lancaster County. She slid her finger down the list of people offering lodging in private family homes: Benners, Groffs, Rohrers, Wengers . . . Many families offered places to stay, some suggesting a "hands-on farming experience."

She sighed. "How cool is this? I might actually get to stay with an Amish family. That's something we never got to do. What do you think, Moe?"

The cat meowed twice loudly, and Heather gave him a pat. "Hey, now . . . I wish I could take you and Igor along, but I don't think any of these places accept cats." *Besides, there are probably zillions of Amish barn cats running around.*

The tilt of Moe's head seemed to indicate his displeasure. He was never too keen on sharing her with his brother, let alone anyone else.

Sighing, she decided to leave her father a note about her plan to take a break before working in earnest on her thesis . . . something vague like that. No need to concern him. And any-

way, he'd understand; lately he'd talked of getting away for a while himself.

"Terrific." She looked down the long list of accommodations, wondering how many phone numbers she'd have to try—didn't these people have Web sites or email?—before she landed a place to call home. *A place to defy gravity.*

Moe leaped off her lap, a black streak across the floor, and dashed into the hallway and out of sight. Headed for what, she had no idea. Maybe to find Igor, who was undoubtedly asleep on Dad's bed down the hall. Cats were weird like that, but these two were definitely family to her and Dad.

The elegant photo on Dad's desk caught her eye, and she leaned down to gaze at it. *Christmas past.* She'd had no problem returning to live at home, putting off her master's studies. Someone needed to be with Mom those final months and then keep Dad from becoming a total recluse during the first shock wave of grief. The emotional anesthesia they'd initially felt wore off quickly, following the funeral.

Then, a year or so ago, she'd moved into the spacious loft over the garage that connected to the rest of the house. The living arrangement allowed her to come and go as she pleased, which suited her need for seclusion.

I'm like Dad. We need our space. Lately, though, her father had begun to rally some, but just about the time you thought you were home free, waves of grief had an uncanny way of creeping up, building until they overtook like a tsunami. She'd discovered over the long months that one never fully recovered from losing a parent. And although Dad rarely talked about Mom's passing, she assumed it was even worse to lose a spouse.

Turning her attention again to the many addresses, she

enjoyed the quirky names of the towns—Ronks, Gap, Strasburg, Kinzers. Each had its own wonderful personality.

"Which one . . . and which host family?" Heather tried to imagine what it would be like to live with strangers, even for a few months.

What about Amish farmers? Maybe she'd help with the chores and get a reduction in boarding costs. She laughed at the image of herself perched on a stool beside a cow, bucket in hand. *Yeah, that'll be the day.*

She stared at the brochure, tracing the words with her finger.

Mom would never let me get away with this.

Her dad might not, either. But then, he wouldn't know. . . .

Her breath caught in her throat. It was one thing to talk bravely to herself or to a cat. But what if the diagnosis was correct? What if she *was* dying?

With just the end of this semester left to complete her M.A. course work, Heather decided to forge ahead and finish up. Nothing must keep her from that. Sick or not, she'd worked too hard to quit now. Meanwhile, she would take her exams next week, then go north to Lancaster County for some rest and relaxation before fall. If she felt up to it, she could work on her thesis there.

The list of names and addresses blurred suddenly. She'd held her emotions in check for this long since this morning's appointment. Wasn't she entitled to a good cry?

The tears fell fast, dripping onto the page . . . landing on the names Andy and Marian Riehl, who lived in a town called Bird-in-Hand. When at last Heather pulled herself together enough to call the number, a woman politely answered what

she later referred to as their "barn phone." And Marian's warm assurance that they had a place for her seemed like a sign.

——— ··· ———

Judah hired a Mennonite farmer to haul the new mare back to the house later that day, then bummed a ride with another English fellow heading his way.

During the drive, they traded stories of past auctions and talked some of a man near Gordonville who was doing a brisk business selling solar panels to Plain folk. "I've heard more and more these days that people see solar as an alternative to gas-powered generators," the Englischer said.

Judah nodded thoughtfully; he knew of the man, as well, and imagined the panels were fodder for discussion among the brethren of Bird-in-Hand.

They passed a sign advertising a new residential development, and the Englischer asked how Judah felt about the encroaching neighborhoods around his farmland.

"Well, none of us likes it," Judah said. "And we're losin' too many of our young folk to upstate New York and other areas round the country—Kentucky, Indiana, Virginia, and even farther south. Not sure where it'll end, all this movin' out to buy more land."

"Will the Amish end up being squeezed out of Lancaster County?"

"I'd hate to see it. But the reality is the outlet malls and the nursing homes are takin' over." He'd been hearing it for years already. If anything, more developers were building town houses and such than ever before.

The driver had a big talk going, but Judah preferred to mull

over the failed breakfast conversation with Lettie. "*S'pose we ought to have us a talk,*" she'd said. Despite his wife's behavior over the past month, he now realized there had been something different about her manner today, something more defined in her attempt to share whatever she'd had on her mind.

Yet he'd pulled his hand away when she'd clasped it, seemingly eager at last to open up. *Why now?* he wondered. He recalled finding her shivering downstairs in the front room on the hand-me-down sofa, all bundled up in quilts from her wedding hope chest. Other times, he'd seen her out walking through the cornfield, awake all hours. What was behind her apparent struggle?

He was pulled out of his musing when his driver asked, "Did you happen to notice that guy all dressed up in a sports coat and tie, walking around at the auction?"

"Jah—got his card right here. Name's Roan Nelson."

"That's right," the driver told him. "Evidently he's looking to buy a small hobby farm somewhere in the area."

Judah nodded. "That he is."

"He must not have heard of the land shortage here . . . that even some Amish farmers are going door-to-door asking if land might soon be available."

"Some folks inquire if the owner has passed away," Judah said.

The driver glanced at him. "That happened to my uncle and aunt. A young Amish farmer came knocking, said he'd heard the husband of the house was awful sick."

Judah shook his head but didn't mention the available plot, lest the Englischer have designs on it. For some reason, he didn't want Roan Nelson to miss out. "The man's a bit overzealous,

I daresay. Now, if he wanted to buy a bed-and-breakfast or a house without acreage, there are plenty of those for sale."

"A glut, I'd say."

They discussed the housing situation and how terrible it was for people to have the bottom fall out of what had previously been a thriving market. " 'Specially painful if you were hopin' to turn a profit right quick," Judah said.

"You can say that again. People used to be able to buy a house and flip it nearly right away."

They drove silently for a time, and then the driver spoke up again. "I don't know about you, but this Nelson fellow strikes me as odd."

"How so?" Judah looked at him.

"I just don't see how he's goin' to find what he's looking for round here. The way things are goin', it'll take a miracle."

Judah knew without a doubt the driver was quite right. Then, thinking once more of his wife, he wondered if it might not take another such miracle for Lettie to truly love him again.

chapter
six

Thursday morning, Martin pulled into the Bylers' driveway and parked, waiting for Grace. She'd called last evening to say almost apologetically that she wanted to go to Belmont Fabrics in Paradise to purchase dress material—and would it be all right if he picked up her friend Becky, too? She, like her mother, always planned multiple stops to accomplish more errands in a given day.

He found it curious how the Amishwomen expressed themselves and wondered if this tendency to overclarify was their way at home, as well.

"Good morning," he greeted Grace as she met him on the right side of the van.

"Hullo." She touched the top of her white head covering lightly as she got inside. He waited for her to put down her purse and get settled in the seat. "You won't forget to pick up Becky, will ya?" she asked, turning to smile at him.

"That's our next stop," he said and pulled the door shut.

On the short drive to the Riehls' dairy farm, he noticed Grace was jotting down a list of sorts on a piece of paper. He

wondered if it might be a shopping list—he'd known Amish women to go to that large fabric store and fill up the entire back of a van with dress material. Since there were only two of them shopping, he supposed that might not be the case today.

When he pulled into the Riehls' lane, he spotted Becky waiting near the sidewalk behind the house. She was wearing a blue dress and apron identical to Grace's. He wondered if they'd planned to match.

"Ach, looks like Becky needs plenty of sewing notions and whatnot," Grace said, probably because of the large, homemade bag flung over her friend's shoulder. "That or her Mamma does, maybe." She let out a little laugh. "Guess we'll be havin' us a big sewing frolic pretty soon."

"Before canning season?" He glanced back at Grace, who nodded before he got out to help open the heavy door.

Once Becky was buckled in, the girls spoke in whispers, mostly in their first language. Becky brought up a relative newcomer from Indiana, and a Yonnie Bontrager's name was soon accompanied by titters and soft laughter.

But the most remarkable comment of the trip was overhearing that this Yonnie was supposedly so smart he could "do crossword puzzles in his head." According to Becky, the young man had no need to ever fill in the blanks. The girl seemed quite taken with his intelligence and playful personality.

Martin smiled and glanced in the rearview mirror as the doting friends talked, their heads occasionally touching as they went from the topic of Yonnie to Grace's upcoming birthday next week.

Oh, to be young again, he thought with a quiet chuckle.

— ⋯ —

On the day before her birthday, Grace hurried downstairs to help with breakfast and found Mamma cooking up some potatoes in a large kettle. A heaping bowl of potato salad was a birthday tradition. No doubt her mother was off-kilter, perhaps thinking the birthday supper was this evening instead of tomorrow.

"Makin' boiled potatoes for the noon meal, perhaps?" she asked, cracking eggs into a bowl to make scrambled eggs.

Her mother looked momentarily confused. Then she let out a disgusted laugh. "Well, puh! I must've jumped ahead a whole day."

Grace frowned. It wasn't like Mamma to be so forgetful.

Shrugging, her mother continued. "Ach, my mind's on other things." For a quick moment, she looked at Grace—really stared—like there was something burning within her, something she needed to say. But when had Mamma taken anyone into her confidence? Other than Aunt Naomi, that is. Word was that her aunt had sat and listened to Mamma pour out her heart weeks before Aunt Naomi had died. Becky's mother, Marian, had bumped into them sitting in front of the springhouse, both Mamma and Aunt Naomi in tears and holding hands.

Grace felt terribly hesitant to pry but felt she had to make an attempt. Gently, she asked, "Mamma, would you mind terribly if I asked . . ."

Mamma shook her head, eyes misty. "What?"

Breathing in her courage, Grace looked up for a moment, staring at the day clock high on the shelf. "I hear ya walking round sometimes in the hallway," she said softly. "And down the stairs, too . . . late at night."

Her mother sighed audibly. "Now, Grace, is this anything to talk with your mother 'bout, really?"

"No, Mamma." It tore at her heart, knowing her parents must be at odds. Why else would Mamma be so out of sorts? And Dat wasn't one to say anything. Why, he hadn't budged an inch to answer Adam's inquiry out in the barn last week, either, and she doubted he'd said a word on that since.

Mamma glanced at the window, as if concerned someone might interrupt them. "After your birthday, we'll talk, all right?" She paused, making a slight movement toward Grace, like she might embrace her. Then she stepped away. "Isn't that soon enough?"

Grace nodded, more hopeful. "All right, then." She turned her attention to the meal planned for tomorrow. If the gathering turned out to be anything like last year's, it would resemble a party. Becky Riehl had given two quilted potholders for Grace's hope chest, and their English neighbors to the west of them had come to surprise her—childhood playmates Jessica and Brittany Spangler. The girls had brought yellow roses from a nearby florist and put them in a pretty blue vase. "*Cut flowers, indeed!*" Mamma had said, startling Grace. Her mother preferred to leave flowers in the ground, where the Lord intended them, but there was no sense in hurting their neighbors' feelings over that. To help smooth things over, Grace had thanked the girls repeatedly, admiring the pretty blooms and wondering what had come over Mamma to say such a thing.

With Mamma so distressed, who knows what tomorrow might bring? Grace thought now as she turned on the gas and found the frying pan for the scrambled eggs. Then, pouring the egg and milk mixture into the pan, she hurried to set the table.

—— ··· ——

Adah placed a full glass of water on the small table next to Jakob's chair, smiling at him even though he did not look up from reading the Good Book. She reached for her tatting, glad to rest here in their cozy front room after supper. The days were lengthening quickly now, and in two months they'd enjoy the longest day of the year. But late June was not the only thing she looked forward to in this fine season of newness. Tomorrow was Gracie's birthday.

She raised herself up a bit to glance out the window, noting Lettie out on the porch. *Des gut . . .*

"Gracie's friend Becky was over this afternoon, askin' for her," she said softly, eyes still on the window.

"What'd she want?" Jakob seemed preoccupied with his reading.

"They had themselves a phone call from a young woman in Virginia, Becky said. Lo and behold if she ain't comin' clear up here to stay for the whole summer."

"That's what happens when ya open up your house to strangers," said Jakob, looking up at her briefly before returning to the Bible.

"It does seem as if they have folk in all the time . . . some from even farther away." The Riehls had started doing this sort of thing a few years ago to bring in extra income. " 'Specially during the summer months, they're perty much full."

"But someone's staying all summer long?"

"That's what I heard," said Adah.

"When's this here woman s'posed to arrive?"

"Sometime next week." Adah picked up her tatting hook,

intent on finishing the pink edging on the pretty hankie for Grace. "The young woman's named for a flower, Becky said."

"Iris, maybe?" Jakob tilted his head down and looked at her over the top of his bifocals. "Black-eyed Susan?"

"Oh, for goodness' sake, Jakob . . . it's Heather." She couldn't help but laugh and wondered when he'd be saying she ought to hush now so he could read to her, like he always did in the evening.

"That *is* a nice name." He had his finger in his German Bible now and was eyeing her but good. "Ready to listen awhile, love?"

How well she knew him. Smiling, she nodded as he opened to the page he'd marked with his finger and began to read. Adah continued tatting as fast as she could, enjoying the sound of Jakob's dear voice and the way he shaped the words of the Lord.

——— ... ———

Grace eagerly turned in her time card and headed for the door to meet fellow Eli's employee Ruthie Weaver, a sweet Mennonite newlywed who'd offered to give her a ride home. She was conscious of the warm evening sun on her back as she hurried toward the waiting car.

Ruthie sat there behind the wheel, her window all the way down. "It was the nicest day so far this spring," she said, smiling. "And to think we spent it mostly indoors."

Grace could hear the redwing blackbirds congregating near the mill creek across the way. The air was so fresh, if not fragrant, and it held the promise of summer.

Ruthie offered Grace some raw nuts from a small plastic

container as she got in the front seat. "If you prefer salty snacks, you might not care much for these." Ruthie shifted the car into gear and pulled out of the parking lot.

"They're fine with or without salt. Denki." Grace took three. "My mother, though, loves her salt."

"Oh goodness, and so does my husband." Ruthie giggled, her face aglow. "He's downright dangerous with a salt shaker."

"I wonder if he craves iodine." Grace had read this sometimes explained people's hankering for salt.

"Wouldn't be surprised." Ruthie turned on the car radio and a clear soprano voice came through the speakers. "Oh, I've heard this woman before . . . wish I knew her name. Some folk say she has a special anointing."

Grace listened intently, soaking in the soul-stirring melody and the meaningful lyrics. "I see what you mean. 'Tis wonderful-*gut*."

Settling back, she enjoyed the lush landscape as they traveled past newly plowed fields and the wide millstream. Willow trees gracefully hovered near its banks, and cows dotted the pastureland in all directions. Such a short ride home by car, but she was glad not to have to walk today. Though she wouldn't dare complain, her feet hurt.

"You worked extra late, didn't you?" Ruthie said, reaching for more nuts.

"So I can take off a little early tomorrow . . . my birthday."

"Well . . . happy almost birthday!" Ruthie smiled. "And let me guess . . ."

Laughing, Grace waved her hand. "No, I didn't tell ya for any special attention."

Ruthie looked her way again. "Well, I'd say you're not a day over nineteen . . . if I was to try and guess."

"That's close enough."

"So, will there be a family get-together?"

"Just a few of us for supper, is all." Mamma most likely had invited Becky again, as well as the Spangler sisters from up the road. *Will Jessica and Brittany bring a plant this year?*

"Hope you have a real nice time."

Grace was relieved to see the house coming into view. Birthday or not, she was rather uncomfortable talking about herself.

"Here we are. Need a ride tomorrow?"

"Only if you'll let me help with gas." She pulled out several bills from her wallet.

"Thanks, but really, you're right on my way home, Grace."

"Won't ya please let me this time?"

"Put your money away." Ruthie pushed her long auburn hair back over her shoulder. "See you bright and early."

Grace opened the door, thanked her again, and said, "So long, then."

As she turned, she saw her mother standing on the front porch, near the mailbox mounted to the railing. Grace hoped for a smile or a wave, but Mamma appeared to be immobile, like she was glued to the porch.

"Hullo, Mamma!"

Slowly her mother turned. "Gracie? Aren't you home awful late?"

"I worked overtime to make up for tomorrow . . . remem-

ber?" She headed up the steps to the porch and opened the front door. "Come . . . let's go inside."

"No . . . no, you go on ahead."

Grace closed the door and touched her arm. "You all right?"

"I'll just sit here awhile." She smiled weakly and went to sit on the old wooden porch swing. Grace saw her chin quiver. "There are leftovers. . . ."

Grace went to sit beside her. "What's wrong?"

Mamma placed the mail in her lap and shook her head. "There's nothin' you can do. Nothin' at all."

"Well, no—not if you won't talk to me." She felt the sting of guilt for having spoken so bluntly. She'd never done so before to anyone, let alone to a parent.

"Go now and warm up your supper."

"But, Mamma . . ."

"I'm fine." Her mother added, "I just need some time alone."

Torn between obedience and concern, Grace rose and turned to look down at Mamma, sitting there so pitifully on the swing, completely still. She recalled how they'd swung there together, back and forth, free from all cares, so many summers ago, when Grace was little. Mamma looked as forlorn now as the day her sister had died.

Grace hadn't realized it, but she was holding her breath. Her mother seemed to look right past her, alert to something far beyond the porch. Grace felt compelled to turn and look, as well, but she saw only the first iris spears in the side garden near the springhouse and, farther away, Dat's flock of sheep. The new lambs followed the ewes ever so close.

Turning back to her mother, she noticed tears spilling down her face. "Aw, Mamma, won't ya say what's makin' you cry so?"

For a second, her mouth opened slightly, and Grace thought her mother might respond. But all she said was "You go on ahead now, Gracie."

"All right, then. I'll leave ya be." Despairing, she opened the screen door and slipped inside.

chapter

seven

Lettie watched her daughter go, her heart breaking. She pressed her bare feet against the wooden slats of the porch, painted white every year by dear Mandy, who had plenty to do since Grace had begun working at Eli's. The swing squeaked its familiar sound, bringing a sense of solitude to her mind, pushing her thoughts back to happier days.

We were happy . . . weren't we?

She'd sat on this swing—in this very spot—to rock tiny Gracie when she was brand-new. Oh, that first summer following her birth was a jumble of smiles and tears . . . and precious moments holding her daughter near, letting tiny Grace nurse at will. So happy she was to have another cuddly babe in arms. Adam, already a towheaded toddler of eighteen months, often crawled up and planted himself next to them, his sweaty little head against her arm, his skin nearly sticking to it at times, so close he was. The three of them swinging on the porch, waiting for a breeze.

Sometimes the neighbors would come bearing sweet, ripe watermelon. Thoughtful Marian Riehl had heard that Lettie

was suffering from the baby blues, no doubt. Marian and her husband, Andy, would cut generous slices of the cold fruit and perch themselves on the porch steps or the railing and eat clear down to the rind. Sometimes Judah and Andy would joke to see who could spit the seeds the farthest.

She smiled, remembering the fun they'd shared together, surrounded by laughter and stories. Marian's little Becky hadn't even been born then.

Becky, she thought now. *Not Rebekah, as anyone would have supposed.* Marian had come calling to ask her opinion on the name when the wee babe was just three days old. It seemed Marian and her husband were at odds on a name, and Marian wanted Lettie's say-so, too, which at the time had seemed down-right comical to her. Less comical, though, was Andy Riehl, who all too often looked for opportunities to dig in his heels, much to Marian's dismay. Lettie found little to like about the man. *Theirs is a thorny marriage*, she thought.

Shrugging the memory aside, she heard Grace's voice, mingled with those of her parents. And with a push of her big toe against the porch, she made the swing move faster and wished the crickets were out in full force this evening. Their refrain was sure to drown out any inside talk among Mamm, Dat, and Grace. Soon, very soon, the insects' chorus would return . . . come summer.

Lettie breathed in the cool evening air. How she needed solitude, craving it even more with Grace's coming milestone birthday.

Where have all the years flown?

Oh, but she knew. They'd vanished into the seasons, year after year . . . going the way of all good and lovely things.

Like love . . .

She could not even remember the last time she and Judah had given affection—not even a peck on the cheek. It wasn't that they'd meant to come to this place in their marriage; she guessed they'd simply fallen out of each other's hearts.

She covered her face with her hands, knowing what would happen if she was bold enough—and insensitive, too—if she were to reveal her heart to Grace. But no, her daughter couldn't begin to understand. And Judah? Doubtless her husband would simply view her revelation as yet another reason to retreat deeper into his own skin.

Judah's own world . . .

So, even though she'd given it great consideration since the barn raising last month, there was no question in her mind that she would be on precarious footing with everyone if her well-guarded secret was unveiled.

No, she must not take a risk like that.

Her husband, Jakob, wasn't but ten minutes into the reading when there stood Gracie in the doorway to the hall, coming slowly toward them.

"Just a minute, Jakob." Adah leaned forward in her chair, slipping her tatting behind her. "Gracie? You hungry, dear?"

"Mamma says there are leftovers. . . ."

Pity's sakes, the girl looked like she might cry.

"Aw, why don't you just have some of ours?" Adah reached for the nearby pillow and stuffed it behind her to better conceal the birthday hankie. She rose and motioned for Grace to follow her to the kitchen. "Your *Dawdi* was just reading Scripture, but

maybe he'll come join us, so you can hear, too." She said this louder than usual, hoping Jakob might take the hint.

When he did, Grace brightened and pulled out a chair. She sat down and leaned into her hands as Jakob came along and placed his big leather Bible on the table. "Haven't seen much of yous lately," Grace said, looking up at him.

"You're such a busy girl . . . all that workin' over at Eli's." Jakob sat down, giving her a sidewise smile. "What'd you bring me this time?"

"Oh, go on with ya," Adah said. "She doesn't have to bring free samples every day."

Grace was now smiling to beat the band, which pleased Adah. "I doubt you'd have wanted what they were samplin' today, Dawdi."

He looked at her, mischievous as all get out. "I guess I'll bite. . . . What was it?"

"Spicy beef jerky, the hottest you've ever tasted."

Jakob's head pushed back with laughter. "Well, you just never know till ya try something, ain't?"

Grace shook her head. "I spared you, Dawdi. I can guarantee you'd be havin' yourself a terrible sour stomach 'bout now."

"Then I guess I oughta be thankin' you, jah?" He reached for Grace's hand and squeezed it quickly, then let go, still beaming.

Adah reheated the tuna macaroni casserole and warmed up the remaining buttered peas in a smaller saucepan. From where she stood at the gas range, she could no longer see Lettie outside on the swing, but she would have heard her if she'd already come inside.

Stirring the macaroni, Adah wondered what it would take

to get things back on an even keel. Looking fondly at her granddaughter and husband sitting so comfortably, surrounded by the golden circle of light from the gas lamp overhead, she felt a little lump rise in her throat. Jakob's hair was peppered with gray, and these days he had to stand gingerly for a few seconds before proceeding to walk, his legs a bit wobbly after getting out of his chair. And their dear Grace, so full of youthful energy, surely ought to be getting married before too long.

She'll follow in her brother's footsteps, no doubt.

This minute, the warmth of family spread its wings over her . . . over the three of them. And Adah did not want a single thing to spoil its sweetness.

"You're comin' for supper tomorrow, *jah?*" asked Grace, breaking the stillness.

"Couldn't keep me away," Jakob said, looking at Adah.

"I'll bake your favorite dessert, Gracie," said Adah. "Carrot cake with butter frosting."

"Mamma doesn't like to make much to-do 'bout birthdays, ya know," Grace said unexpectedly.

"Well, if you could mark the day however you'd choose, what would ya do?" asked Adah.

Grace stared down at the table. "Well, let's see. You'd all sing the birthday song, for sure." She raised her head slowly. "I do like hearin' Mamma's perty voice rise up above all the others. Oh, ever so much."

That joyful side of Lettie's rarely seen anymore, thought Adah.

"And, without thinkin' too hard, I'd prob'ly like to spend a good part of the day with Becky." Grace squinted her eyes, as if expecting a retort. "And with Adam."

"In other words, with your closest friends," Adah said.

"Jah." Grace smiled warmly at them both. "But don't misunderstand, I'd take yous along, too, if I could."

"Take us where?" Jakob leaned forward again.

"To the ocean. Someday I want to see it for myself . . . not just in books." Grace glanced toward the window. "There must be something mighty special 'bout the roar of it, ya know?"

"And the extent of it," Adah added.

"To think you can see nearly forever . . . well, out to the edge of the world, so to speak." Grace was lost in a daydream, something Adah had never noticed before. *Thank goodness she's not the dreamer her mother always was!*

Jakob waved his hand. "Well, maybe that driver could take you to see that there horizon line you're talking 'bout. What's his name?"

"Martin Puckett?" said Grace. "A right cheerful fella, I'll say."

"Jah, that's who. Maybe Martin'll drive you, Becky, and Adam out to the ocean one of these days."

That brought the biggest smile to Grace's face, but it didn't last long, because just then Adah heard the front screen door smack shut. Grace's face paled, and her gaze found Adah's and held it awkwardly for a long time.

chapter
eight

Grace's birthday began like any other day except for one thing: She was awakened by Mandy, who slipped into the room and planted a kiss on her cheek. "Happy day . . . happy year, sister!" Mandy announced, all smiles.

Squinting up at her, Grace stretched and yawned. "Ach, you're up even before me."

Mandy sat on the edge of the bed, her long, reddish-blond hair flowing over her round shoulders, clear to her chubby waist. "I wanted to be the first to wish you a happy birthday, Gracie." She tried to suppress a yawn but did not succeed. Laughing softly, she said, "We have something special planned."

"Honestly?"

Mandy bobbed her head up and down, eyes shining. Then, pretending to seal her lips, she whispered, "That's all I'll say."

Grace loved her playful sister, who always seemed to have something interesting or mysterious up her sleeve. "Well, the day will go by quickly, I'm sure." She sat up and looked at the wind-up alarm clock on the small table next to her bed. "I best be getting ready for work."

Mandy stood up, still clad in her long white cotton night-gown. "And must you work tomorrow, too?"

"*Nee*—no, not that I know of."

"Well, *gut*, then . . . we'll have us some sister time, jah?" Mandy's sleepy eyes sparkled.

"What were ya thinkin'?"

Mandy walked to the doorway and turned, her face beaming. "How 'bout if we take Willow out to the meadow and ride her bareback? That'd be such fun!"

Their horses were meant for pulling carriages and market wagons, not riding, as Mandy well knew. Some bishops were rather opposed to the latter. "What would Dat say to that?" asked Grace.

Mandy wore a mischievous grin. "Well . . . if you must know, I already said something to Mamma."

"Jah? And?"

"She doesn't think it's anything to worry 'bout, as long as we aren't out on the road . . . ya know, showin' off."

"All right, then . . . if Mamma says not to flaunt, we won't."

Mandy fluttered her fingers in a little wave and left the room.

Grace jumped out of bed and closed the door. She picked up her brush and began counting the strokes as she brushed her hair. *What will come of this day?*

She knew one thing: She didn't feel a speck older than yesterday, even though the calendar said otherwise. She pulled on her robe and raised the green shade all the way, then sat near the window to read from the Psalms. When she was finished, she prayed a blessing on the day and for all those she might

encounter, gathered up her clean clothes, and headed downstairs for a warm bath before the rest of the family awakened. Her father had spent a lot of time and money putting two modern bathrooms in the house. One on their side and one over where Dawdi and Mammi lived. She sometimes wished for a wash-room upstairs, as well . . . just down the hall a few steps from Mandy's and her bedrooms. But Dat had said they must make do with what they had. As it was, Mammi Adah was mighty happy about having a fancy indoor bathroom. She enjoyed the convenience of a nice big tub and modern facilities, especially during winter months.

Grace reached for the shampoo and lathered up, taking special care with her hair, eager for it to be shiny and clean.

What will Henry do for my birthday?

She hurried along, stopping herself each time she felt the urge to hum, holding back. Truth was, she wondered if Henry's shyness, even awkwardness, might hinder him from wanting to celebrate.

Today she wished to get a head start on breakfast, even though Mamma might surely have something planned already. Still, Grace wanted to get the day off on the right foot to make certain things were just as they should be.

Several other years, on landmark birthdays such as six-teen—the start of courting age—her mother had surprised them with homemade waffles and specialty soufflés or, Grace's very favorite, cinnamon rolls and a spritz of chocolate syrup in her coffee.

Such happy memories of gathering round the table for a delicious birthday breakfast. She allowed herself to hum. *A few more minutes won't hurt,* she decided.

She thought again of Henry, who was the most handsome of all the fellows she'd known. So much so, she sometimes pinched herself. *Why did he pick me?*

She had been told by several young men that she was pretty. *"Mighty pleasing, in fact,"* Yonnie had once said right to her face during one of the three short evenings he had gone walking with Grace last year, before Henry had asked her out riding. Such compliments were foreign to the Plain way . . . leaving room for vanity to grow.

She had to smile as she recalled Yonnie's peculiar ways. Even then, he'd never bothered to take a horse or courting buggy to Singings or other youth gatherings; they'd walked everywhere. Never had she gotten more exercise in her life. Grace had sometimes thought that if the Lancaster bishops ever got wind of it, they might want to encourage this rather irregular way of courting—perhaps it might keep young folk more attentive to the youth in their own church district.

Plenty of stories floated around about young men who were sweet on several girls, so she supposed Yonnie wasn't unusual in taking his time to choose. And from what Mammi Adah had once hinted about Mamma's own courting days, Grace wondered if Yonnie and her own mother had something in common.

Dear Mamma . . .

Grace stepped out of the tub and dressed, then wrapped her hair in a towel. She opened the door, nearly bumping into Adam, who stood right outside. "Ach, you scared me . . . for goodness' sake!"

He grinned, his sleepy eyes meeting hers.

"Time to rise and shine." She moved away.

"I've risen . . . just not shinin' yet. 'Twas a rough night in the sheep barn." He wandered in and shut the door, and she heard the water running for his shave. Then, nearly as quickly, the door opened and he poked his head out. "Someone's a year older, and it sure ain't me!" With a sleepy-sounding chuckle, he again closed the door.

Grace felt warmed by her brother's humor as she rushed through the kitchen and sitting room toward the center hallway, making her way to the stairs. She flew to her room, needing to towel dry her hair before winding it into a bun. Letting it down long past her waist, she was glad it wasn't as thick and hard to untangle as Becky's or even Mandy's, who had the prettiest color she'd ever seen—like sun-kissed strawberries and harvested wheat all mixed together. Her sister certainly stood out in a crowd. Years ago, when Mandy was only fourteen, Mamma had complained about the number of times Mandy had sneaked away to Singings, hoping to pass herself off as older. *"All in harmless jest,"* Mandy had assured them when she'd been caught. Still, both Mamma and Dat had given her a good talking-to.

Even though Mandy presently had several nice fellows interested in her, Grace wasn't entirely sure whether her sister cared for any of them, or vice versa. She only knew what she'd observed at Singings, where the boys sought Mandy out. Her sister's popularity was no secret, but despite her cheerful birthday greeting, Mandy's pensive brown eyes revealed an uneasiness. One Grace had observed often lately.

She dealt with an uneasiness of her own. Life just felt so unpredictable. *Between Dat and Mamma, especially.* As much as she wished they'd be more content with each other, she'd seen

similar signs of aloofness in Becky's parents. She'd begun to worry that many married couples were equally distant.

I'd like something far better . . . if I ever marry.

When she heard Mamma cooking downstairs, Grace hurried back down, aware of the tantalizing smell of chocolate as she came to the landing. *Can it be?* She went through the sitting room, to the kitchen.

Seeing her, Mamma quickly attempted to hide the package of unsweetened chocolate.

"*Gut* mornin'," said Grace, trying not to smile too big.

"You weren't s'posed to sneak up on me," Mamma said, a sparkle in her eye. Gone was the sadness of the days before.

"I sure like your chocolate waffles."

Mamma gave a nod, her eyes still on Grace. "I made some peach delight for you to take with you to work, for your lunch today."

Grace was relieved that her mother was sounding—and acting—more like her old self.

"That'll be ever so tasty. Denki, Mamma."

So, Mandy was right—surprises a-plenty!

———··· ———

It was midmorning when Grace glanced up from the cans she was shelving and spied the top of a man's head. Rising to her tiptoes, she was startled to see Henry Stahl entering the store, his light brown hair combed ever so neatly.

She looked down at her hands and wondered what to do with the tins of tea. And why on earth was she shaking so?

Quickly placing the cans on the shelf out of order to be free of them, she moved down to the end of the aisle, near a

display of the *B* family of vitamins. Her heart sped up as she watched him move through the store.

Of all things, he's come to see me here!

"Oh, Grace . . . there you are." He glanced about, his eyes darting nervously. Standing there, she couldn't help wondering why he'd worn his for-good black trousers and vest for this unexpected visit. All that was missing from his regular Sunday Preaching attire was his thin black bow tie.

"What a nice surprise," she said softly.

He inhaled and straightened to his full height, squaring his shoulders—a tall man at six feet two. "I'm here to say happy birthday." He leaned closer and, lowering his voice, said, "Somethin's waiting for you . . . in the buggy." He moved his head slightly toward the door. "All right?"

Oh, this was beyond her expectations!

She glanced toward the counter and saw the manager give her a quick nod. "If it's just for a minute."

Henry's grin made her blush even more.

Outside, he led her around to the other side of the buggy, where they could escape the prying eyes of the other clerks. She was mighty sure if she glanced at the store window, Ruthie and the others would be watching. "I've got a present for ya." He raised the lap blanket and there, beneath it, was an unwrapped box with the words *chime clock* printed on it.

"Goodness, Henry!" She couldn't believe her eyes. A young man didn't give his girl a gift like this unless he was on the verge of proposing marriage.

Grace's heart flew into her throat, and for a moment she had trouble gathering her thoughts.

"I'd be happy to open it for you." He reached for the box,

turning it around to show her the picture of a beautiful golden clock with moving chimes encased in glass.

"No . . . let's keep it all wrapped up and safe." She shook her head as she looked at the picture of the lovely clock and then up at him. "It's ever so perty. I can't begin to say—"

He reached for her hand, the first time ever. Oh goodness, the feel of his warm, callused fingers made her smile right back at him.

She was suddenly too aware of the daylight. Had they ever been so close on their nighttime rides? She was quite sure they hadn't. But she liked the way their fingers entwined and being able to look into his gentle brown eyes. Well, up . . . up into them, as he was at least a half foot taller.

"Denki . . . I really like the clock, Henry," she said, still feeling awkward about anyone's witnessing their affection.

His eyes lingered on her. "You have a place for it?"

She paused, wondering what would be most appropriate to say. "Well, more than likely, it'll go in my room."

Till later . . .

He fell silent, looking down at her, more serious again.

"I'll hope to see it, then . . . one day." His face lit up.

She thrilled to his words. So he *was* going to shine his flashlight on her window and come calling. If he did, they would not remain alone in her room for more than a few minutes, as Mamma had always urged her and Mandy to entertain serious beaus in the kitchen, near the heat of the corner stove. Other families allowed courting couples to spend hours talking in the girl's room. Yet even as some church districts encouraged such activity, others frowned on it. Such distinctions in the Ordnung from church to church could be ever so confusing. Grace was

glad she'd grown up in this particular district, where caution in courting was urged and where folk spoke openly about the Lord, even offering prayers aloud at times.

She suspected she knew the reason why there was an emphasis on pure motives and holy living in their house church, which met every other Sunday. But she wouldn't give those rumors about other youth another thought. Not on this, her special day.

"Henry . . . I'm more than pleased. Truly, I am." She scarcely knew what to say to open his heart wider, if that was even possible.

He nodded and smiled warmly.

Glancing toward the store, she explained that her clock was ticking. Then she suppressed a laugh—that had not come out at all the way she'd meant it! "Ach, I hope you understand what I'm tryin' to say."

Again, he nodded. His eyes were merry, but he said nothing. Oh, how she would love to hear him laugh heartily.

Awkwardly, Henry climbed into his black open buggy and picked up the reins. "Have a nice day, Grace."

She blushed as she waved good-bye and returned to the store. The other girls attempted to keep from grinning but failed miserably. Ruthie was the worst of them, too cheerful and trying hard to bite back a smile. Surely every one of them knew that it was her soon-to-be-intended—her handsome Henry—who'd just visited.

chapter
nine

Grace counted the hours till she could head home, still delighted by Henry's visit and his generous gift. She couldn't possibly know when he might drop the chime clock off at the house. Since he wasn't one to make a spectacle, she doubted it would be in the daylight.

To contain her excitement, she kept busy with her store inventory list, documenting each item among all the varieties of food supplements and arranging them in alphabetical order. She smiled when she came to zinc, an essential mineral for building a strong immune system. It also helped reduce acne, according to Ruthie, who'd struggled with pimples—*"too much chocolate,"* she'd admitted, though after taking zinc for three months, her complexion now looked as clear as Grace's.

Mamma often said, "You are what you eat." Grace considered the kinds of fried foods and soda pop the Spangler girls preferred, yet *they* had perfect complexions. Did that alone refute Mamma's words?

Grace was not overly strict about her diet, as some were who now advocated eating only vegetables, grains, and legumes.

"*Rabbit chow*," Adam had jokingly said when she told him about some of the health fads making the rounds.

Thinking of vegetables, Grace missed helping with the gardens as much as she always had. The smell of freshly plowed soil was invigorating . . . that and deciding where to plant the various vegetables. She loved spending early morning hours weeding and harvesting a good variety of produce to eat, sell, and put up for the winter. Since starting to work at Eli's, she'd largely had to assign the weeding and tending of her herb garden to Mandy, though sometimes Becky came over to help on Grace's days off.

All the hot, humid hours of hoeing and watering rows of lettuce, snap beans, radishes, tomatoes, and squash were also times of laughter. But Mamma wasn't usually the one smiling— not lately. Oh, Grace could see that she attempted to enjoy herself and enter into the fun, but when all was said and done, Mamma seemed to hold back.

Presently, Grace moved on to the next shelf and began to alphabetize the many kinds of herbs, beginning with alfalfa, aloe, angelica, and anise. She refused to think about dismaying things, especially on such a fine day. Fretting over bygones had never proven to be helpful. Besides, Mammi Adah said dwelling on the past could become obsessive, even destructive.

Today, however, Grace had awakened to birdsong and brilliant blue skies—such a bright way to begin the day. The birds had come right up to the feeders she and Mandy had placed in strategic spots around the back and side yards. Avid bird watchers, the whole family enjoyed the robins, finches, blue jays, and chickadees that found sanctuary close to their house, though it was Mamma who loved observing them most of all, especially

from the back stoop. Her favorite was the gray-brown mourning dove, which produced multiple offspring each season. Mamma had taught her children to listen for the fluttering whistle its wings made when taking flight. *"But only the male makes the mournful-sounding call,"* her mother had said.

Recently there had been a good amount of rain, and robins could be seen searching for worms, making their songs even more plentiful. Or so Grace liked to think. Considering how the rain had greened the grazing land for Dat's sheep, she was doubly thankful for the ample moisture.

Grace had never questioned why her father was one of only a handful of Amish in the area who wasn't a dairy farmer. An exceptionally private man, her father's dawn-to-dusk approach to raising sheep earned him admiration from other farmers. Grace liked to observe his interaction with other men, because she gleaned more insight into her own father's thoughts than when he engaged in most family conversations. His tongue just seemed to loosen up as Grace listened in sheer amazement.

Now she'd come to the G herbs, including ginseng—one of Mammi Adah's favorites. She continued lining up the bottles in perfect order, hoping all would go well this evening. Secretly she once more pondered Henry's visit. *Of all things, coming here!*

———   ···   ———

When it was time to leave for home, Grace spotted her younger brother, Joe, waiting in Dat's buggy in the parking lot. Joe waved to her, a piece of straw dangling from his mouth as he sat on the right side of the family carriage. He often came to pick her up, relishing the freedom of driving, as if impatient for his own courting buggy once he turned sixteen next year.

The afternoon had been rather mild, with only the slightest hint of a breeze. She glimpsed through the stately trees a buildup of dark clouds in the west. Tossing her purse on the seat, she hopped into the carriage and noticed her favorite horse hitched to it. "Nice ya brought Willow," she said, smiling.

"Well, it was either her or Sassy, 'cause Dat's gone to the blacksmith with the new mare. And Adam put his foot down on usin' *his* horse."

"Why's that?"

"Said he needed to run a last-minute errand." Joe put on a straight face and looked back at the road.

"Wouldn't have anythin' to do with tonight, would it?"

Joe didn't flinch. "Why, what's goin' on?"

"Oh, you . . . don't ya know?"

Still keeping his face forward, he said, "You speaketh in riddles, Gracie."

Stifling a laugh, she turned to look at the landscape. She was ever so sure Joe and Mandy and Adam, too, were all in cahoots.

A sudden rumble of thunder caught her attention, and she leaned forward to survey the ominous sky. "Looks like a storm's comin'."

"A nice soaker would be right *gut*, 'specially since we just planted corn." Joe craned his neck to survey the wall of clouds.

Hope the rain's gone before supper. Grace envisioned the extra people who would gather at the table tonight. She looked forward to seeing Becky and the Spangler sisters again.

Joe clucked his tongue. "Seems Willow's out of sorts today."

"Just today?" She grimaced. "She's always slow, ain't so?"

"Well, she's got ev'ry right to be, old as she is."

She smiled and watched Willow's head rise and fall with each trot, her long, thick mane waving in the breeze. "She's been the best driving horse ever." Grace remembered Dat first bringing her home with an enormous smile on his ruddy face. They were having a picnic on Ascension Day, and here came Dat leading the beautiful young mare, showing her off. *"Lookee at what I've got,"* he'd said. *"This one's as gentle as they come."* Within days, the chestnut-colored horse had endeared herself to the entire family.

"Why'd you name her Willow back when?" Joe tossed the piece of straw onto the road.

"Because she was always graceful, whether she was trotting or eating feed. Like willow branches movin' in the wind."

He pulled on the reins to make the sharp right onto Church Road. "Jah, I guess I can see that."

"Willow just seemed like the perfect name—"

"For a perfect horse," Joe finished. They laughed at each other because this happened among the four siblings too often to ignore. They were all so closely linked as sisters and brothers and friends.

She'd often wondered about Becky's relationship with her brothers and sisters. Did most Plain families have such a close bond?

When Joe guided the horse and buggy into the driveway, everything looked to be ready for company. The lawn had been carefully mowed and manicured, and the pasture fence freshly painted white, thanks to Mandy and Joe.

Out front, Mamma glanced up from the porch, waving at

them. Seeing everything looking so spiffy—and Mamma waiting for them—was heartening to Grace.

"Mamma waits for the mail nearly ev'ry day," Joe said softly
as they headed up toward the horse stable.

"How do you know?"

"Well, I ain't blind, am I?" He leaped out of the buggy
and began unhitching Willow. Working around the horse, Joe
said with a grunt, just like Dat might have, "Happy birthday,
by the way."

Grace laughed out loud. What an unpredictable brother!

Lettie eyed the front porch swing, wishing she had time
to sit awhile. *Before the house is all filled up.* Sighing, she moved
toward the swing, thinking if she could just rest a bit, she might
feel better. *I'm so weary.*

More than anything, she wanted to reread the latest letter
from her Indiana cousin Hallie Troyer, who had scarcely a care
in the world. Or so it seemed from her frequent correspondence.
Lettie stared at the return address: *Nappanee, Indiana.*

She was thankful Adam had run to pick up a birthday card
for all of them to pass around and sign. She'd also asked him
to purchase some nice writing paper and two pretty pens for
Grace's gift.

Dear girl.

There was some indication from across the wide hall that
Mamm had made a small present for the birthday girl. *Why must
my mother spoil her so?* Lettie wondered, thinking Grace was much
too old to be given many gifts. But old-school though Mamm was
bred to be, she was also one to push the line, inching toward it
until it almost felt sometimes like they behaved like fancy folk.

"I mustn't let her get the upper hand ever again," Lettie muttered, pushing Cousin Hallie's letter deep into her pocket. She wished she might simply sit and write Hallie another note right back. But first things first.

She rose. Joe had arrived with Grace from work, and they were probably wondering why the table wasn't even set. No doubt, Grace was already tinkering around in the kitchen herself, if she wasn't upstairs brushing her hair and pinning it up fresh. It wasn't that Grace was known for vanity or putting on airs—far from it. She was one of the sweetest girls around, living up to the promise of her name early on.

Looking longingly at the porch swing again, Lettie knew she must make a quick phone call. Did she have time to hurry up the road to the community phone shanty? Hopefully the gloomy skies would hold off their rain for a few minutes yet.

Ach, I should've called sooner, she thought, knowing full well why she'd put it off this long.

She breathed a prayer for strength . . . both for the birthday feast and for whatever lay ahead.

For all of us.

chapter
··
ten

Judah removed his straw hat in the hallway and plopped it down on his own wooden peg—one he'd used for twenty-some years. He smelled the pot roast cooking and a thought crossed his mind: How had Lettie ever managed before the bishop gave the nod for them to get a gas range and oven? It was hard to remember the days before that time, although he was mighty sure his wife remembered quite well. Adam, too, since he'd had the daily chore of hauling in the wood for the cookstove.

He walked around to the kitchen, glad to see Mandy helping. *Where's Lettie?* he wondered, not bothering to ask Mandy or Adam, who just that minute had come indoors. Adam's unruly bangs were all combed down for a change. Seeing the washroom door standing open, Judah made his way inside and closed the door.

Removing his glasses, he filled the sink with warm water, grateful for the hot water directly from the spigot. Long gone the days of carrying water from the springhouse and waiting around for his parents to heat it up for baths and whatnot.

He splashed water on his face and lathered up with the

homemade soap Lettie purchased from Preacher Josiah Smucker's wife, Sally. The industrious woman had herself a small shop right in their house, out near the utility room. Being that she was married to one of the brethren, she'd gotten permission from the bishop himself to run the business. The man of God understood their plight.

The plight of many Amish . . . With farming land dwindling and being divided up among marrying-age sons, no wonder folk kept moving out of Lancaster County to other counties and states—some even out of the country to Canada. A good many, in fact, over the years.

He suspected several families in the church of scouting out places like Kentucky and Virginia to obtain farmland, places where Amish had already established small communities. Some had talked privately about starting a new church district down as far south as Georgia, and not only in Macon County. These days, it seemed there were Amish and Beachy Amish branching out nearly everywhere.

But for Judah's needs, Lancaster County was just fine. Really there was nowhere he'd rather be. Besides, with word from old Rudy Stahl that Adam was going to be given a good portion of Rudy's land, Judah had only to be concerned with young Joe's future land options.

Won't be long and I'll be turning my pockets inside out for yet another courting-age son, he mused. Truly he didn't mind seeing his offspring grow up and look ahead to starting their own families. And, just maybe, once he and Lettie had themselves an empty nest, they'd somehow manage to get things back on an even keel.

He dried his face and put his glasses back on, glancing in

the square mirror above the sink. "Goodness, but you're gettin' old," he muttered.

"Someone talkin' in there?" Adam called through the door.

"Can't a man have some peace?"

Adam chuckled. "Take your time, Dat. I just wondered . . . when's supper?"

Judah checked his watch. "Should be now." He opened the door. "Better ask your Mamma, though."

Adam shook his head. "Joe said he saw her out front on the porch a little bit ago, but she's not there now."

It wasn't like Lettie to invite guests and then dillydally about getting the table set and all done up. "Could be she's helpin' bring Dawdi Jacob over for supper," he suggested as they stepped into the kitchen.

Adam nodded thoughtfully, then showed him a birthday card. "Want to sign this now, before Gracie sees it?" Glancing over his shoulder, Adam indicated he should hurry.

Judah noticed the pen stuck atop Adam's ear and reached for it. *Happy birthday, Grace, from Dat,* he signed simply.

Adam retrieved the card and pen when Judah was done. He dashed out of the kitchen, leaving Judah there with Mandy, who was bustling about, checking on the roast and baked potatoes, carrots, and onions. Such tantalizing aromas—but where *was* Lettie?

Going to the side door, he looked out and saw, in the near distance, the English neighbor girls walking this way, each carrying a present, an umbrella at the ready. Becky Riehl was coming up the driveway, too. Had Lettie invited others besides these three?

He turned away from the door, wishing his wife were there to greet the young women. Feeling awkward, he was glad to see Adam returning and Jakob hobbling over from the other side of the house, through the sitting room. "Hullo there, Daed," he greeted him.

Adah and Lettie were right behind them, as was Joe, who sniffed the air, clearly ready to dig in to the delectable meal. "Looks like nearly all of us are here," Adam said, trying unsuccessfully to slip Grace's birthday card under her plate before she noticed. Mandy's eyes were wide with disapproval, but Grace flashed him a smile.

"Oh look! There's Becky . . . and the Spangler girls, too!" Grace rushed to the door and ran down the steps to greet them.

Judah looked at Lettie, who caught his eye and gave him a small smile, as if to say, *It's our daughter's birthday . . . let's be merry.*

He returned the smile, aware of a curious new light in her eyes.

Soon their guests were welcomed by Lettie herself, who stepped into her comfortable role as hostess. She and Mandy carried the food to the table in Grace's honor. They'd changed the normal seating arrangement considerably for the evening, putting Becky on one side of Grace, and Brittany Spangler—the darker haired of the two sisters—on the other side. Lettie, as always, sat to Judah's right.

"Time for the blessing." He bowed his head and remained so for longer than usual, adding a special silent prayer for good health for Grace—and for a hard-working husband for her

someday, too. Then he made a little cough and raised his head as he always did to signal the end of the prayer.

Lettie reached immediately for the large platter and sliced an ample portion of roast for him first. Then she asked Grace to hold her plate and served another smaller portion to her. The two English girls glanced at each other, and Becky engaged them in casual conversation as Lettie saw to everyone's plate, making sure each one had plenty.

Seeing her so caught up in her hostess role, Judah couldn't help wondering how long it might be before she grew weary of wandering about at night. How long before Lettie behaved like a good wife?

He picked up his fork and cut the roast with it, so tender it was. Focusing now on the delicious meal at hand, he dismissed his scattered thoughts, falling into the pleasure of this fine feast.

The talk around the table quickly caught Grace's attention. Becky hadn't waited long to begin describing several new quilts she'd put in the frame with her mother. Neither of them cared much for finishing off quilts, sometimes letting several sit around before finally stopping everything to sew the binding at last—"all at once, to get it over with."

"Oh goodness, I don't mind doin' bindings," Mandy spoke up.

"Well, piece work's more fun," Grace said, glad for Becky's presence.

"Hard work, though," Becky replied. "But I like choosin' the colors."

"Me too." Mandy leaned over the table. It was obvious from

her attempts to be part of the conversation that she wished she'd been seated closer to them.

After a short lull, Jessica Spangler announced her plans to marry her college sweetheart during Christmas break. "A festive time for a wedding, don't you think?" At that, all the women at the table, including Mamma and Mandy, nodded in agreement. Adam, Joe, and Dat continued eating as if merely onlookers, present only in body.

Then Mammi Adah surprised Grace by talking of Grace's childhood and "her many firsts," as her grandmother liked to refer to her little-girl antics. Grace cringed a bit, hoping Mammi would not take this too far. "The first time Gracie ever went off to school, her Mamma and I stood like two protective doe on the porch, creepin' down the steps, then eventually out to the lane . . . watching our Gracie walk up the road with her big brother. She looked awful tiny to be a first grader."

"Too tiny, really," Mamma added.

"Kids *all* look that small when they first start out," Joe piped up.

"Did ya take a lunch bucket to school?" asked Becky, her brown eyes curious.

Brittany laughed. "Sure she did—Grace used my old one that whole year." She covered her mouth, trying to subdue her giggle. "Remember it, Grace?"

"How can I forget?"

"It was one of those funky California Raisins lunch boxes, and Grace couldn't part with it when she came to play at our house." Brittany leaned forward next to her sister, who was also nodding. "So I let her keep it."

Jessica continued. "It pictured a raisin singing into a

microphone, and three girl raisins singing backup. It was too cute."

Half the table was snickering, and Grace couldn't help laughing herself. When she looked toward the hushed end of the table, she noticed a small smile on Mamma's face, but there was no hint of the same on Dat's. His attention appeared set on the spread of food before him—all that mattered.

As for Grace, she had two birthday wishes: She wished that the evening might last long past the supper hour. And she wished that Mamma might remain as happy as she seemingly was this very moment.

——— ··· ———

The sky hung low in the trees bordering the side yard and the pastureland where Judah's sheep grazed all day. Now that the rain had passed, a dark blue band lined the horizon to the east.

Lettie forced her gaze away from the window as she helped Mandy clear the table. Grace's friends had left for home, and Lettie wanted to give her birthday girl some time to do as she pleased.

Mamm and Dat had surprised Lettie by staying around longer than usual following such a big gathering. Lettie felt both appreciative and perturbed. Glad, because her mother had an uncanny way of drawing any attention away from Lettie, and fairly annoyed because more than a full hour ago she'd hoped to write another letter.

She assumed Grace's supper had been everything her daughter had hoped for. Grace had been so cordial, accepting the tatted hankie from her grandmother with a pleasing smile, and

later, offering plenty of *oohs* and *ahs* when the Spangler sisters each presented a gift—a floral-covered book of blank pages and a long, thin case of colored pencils. The latter was something Lettie could not imagine Grace using, or even wanting.

Becky had held to tradition, giving Grace a simple homemade card, just as Judah and the boys and Mandy had—except their card had been store-bought. Regrettably Lettie had failed to sign it, thanks to her ill-timed phone call. She hoped Grace hadn't noticed . . . but then, Grace noticed nearly everything. That was precisely why Lettie felt so anxious now as she inspected the kitchen and went to the next room to pull out a writing tablet, one of three she stored in the corner hutch drawer. She'd always kept stationery there, as well as a few nicer pens.

The pretty yellow lined paper would help to keep her hand straight. Truth be told, she had much to make up for with dear Grace. *With all of them, really.*

Grace and Mandy were curled up on the floor in the front room, playing checkers. Judah and the boys had naturally been in a big hurry to return to the barn, what with more lambs on the way. It was something of a rarity to have the kitchen table all to herself.

Sighing, Lettie thought again of Cousin Hallie and the appealing way she described her loving marriage in her weekly letters. Was it truly possible for anyone to be so happy?

— ⋯ —

Heather carried her laptop out to the deck and settled into her mother's comfy chaise. She yearned to be close to nature, already anticipating the upcoming Pennsylvania trip. Opening her laptop, she began to write.

Seven days have passed since my diagnosis, and I still feel perfectly fine. The whites of my eyes haven't turned yellow, no fever yet, and I have zero pain.
Hard to believe I'm supposed to be dying.
Well, we're ALL dying, aren't we, from the second we're born. But only some of us get to actually live a full life. . . .

She glanced up and watched a bird in flight, its wings seemingly so fragile. Yet the delicate creature managed to fly using the wind current and its own strength.

"Flying strong . . . just like me," she whispered, although that wasn't even remotely true.

Her stuporlike cloud of denial had finally lifted that morning, and Heather wanted to know what she was up against. If she procrastinated on getting her treatment started, what symptoms had the doctor warned might develop?

She typed in the address for WebMD, a credible online resource, and soon discovered her symptoms might someday include weight loss—up to ten percent of her total body weight—heavy night sweats, fevers with no apparent cause, itching, and a cough or breathlessness.

She was confused because she had none of these symptoms, even though the oncologist had told her she was in stage IIIA. That meant the disease had spread to three lymph regions in her body, though the nodes remained small and painless.

One thing led to another, and soon Heather was reading Web pages for holistic alternative treatment centers around the country, and even one in Salzburg, Austria. Wow, there was one situated on a private island in the Caribbean, too. *Who wouldn't feel better just being there?* She spent the next hour online, viewing sites for fasting weekends, day spas, Candida cleanses,

and alternative treatments ranging from detoxes to therapeutic massages and thermal water cures.

Quite the gamut, she thought, baffled. One YouTube clip actually featured a man vowing his water diet would cure anyone of anything.

Heather shook her head, sighing. Some of this was almost laughable. But people did impulsive things when their life was in jeopardy. How was it possible to sift the scams from what was legitimate, especially when so many of these places were charging an arm and a leg? *They're certainly not covered by insurance.*

She closed the laptop and stared at the sky. Despite her initial denial, she was ready now to make some choices based on her diagnosis. Closing her eyes, she reveled in the springtime sounds and smells. Didn't she owe it to herself and to her family to give natural methods a try, at least for the summer?

Yes, she definitely wanted to experiment with a natural approach before getting a second opinion from a medical doctor later. The Lancaster naturopath came to mind once again, and she decided to call Dr. Marshall's office for an appointment.

She might've helped Mom, if it hadn't been too late. . . .

——— ··· ———

While Grace waited for Mandy to determine the next move of her king on the checkerboard, she admired again the cute card from Becky. A hummingbird fed from a single pink flower, a vibrant sea of flower cups opening to the sun in the background. A legend she'd heard as a girl said that a hummingbird's flight was unfettered by space and time . . . and carried all one's hopes for lasting affection, greatest joy, and merriment. Grace

paused to consider it, looking fondly at the expertly rendered likeness.

Becky's a wonder. . . .

It was evident how many hours her friend had put into the picture. Grace almost felt guilty for having received the many multicolored pencils in the fancy case from Jessica. Surely they were something Becky might better enjoy.

"Your move." Mandy looked up, eyes mischievous.

Grace laughed. "Nice try. I see you're goin' to double jump me!"

"If you're not careful."

She smiled at her sister, then made her move.

"You're partial to board games, ain't?"

"Any time you want to play, I'm willing." Grace also enjoyed cross-stitching and tatting, just as Mammi Adah did. And, on occasion, she liked to spin wool on an old treadle wheel Brittany and her mom had purchased at a flea market—a most unique hobby.

"Are we still taking Willow for a ride tomorrow?" Mandy asked.

"Fine with me." She waited for her sister to move her checker.

Mandy folded her arms, grinning because she'd made the perfect setup to block Grace. "There . . . how'd ya like that?"

Not ready to be outwitted, Grace leaned closer to the board, studying her options. "Do you think our grandparents had a *gut* time tonight?" she asked.

"Jah, why?"

Grace shrugged, reaching across the board to move her king backward. Truth was, she worried all the foolish bantering

at the table had not been overlooked by either her parents or her grandparents. But each year they put up with it, and rather graciously at that. Next year, though, things would be different with Jessica Spangler married and living elsewhere. And who could know about Becky? Mandy, too, for that matter.

Grace did not include herself in the group of potential brides, although she wondered if she would still be residing in her father's house on her twenty-second birthday. Would Henry decide to make her his wife at last?

Mrs. Grace Stahl . . . She considered Henry's family name. There were plenty of Stahls locally, but they weren't Amish, except for Henry's extended family. His grandfather had settled in Bird-in-Hand from south of Somerset County, where Stahl was a common Amish name. Sighing while Mandy decided where to move her only king, Grace was drawn to the card Adam had slipped under her plate before supper. A placid ocean scene with a lone seabird walking the shoreline. He knew well her desire to see the ocean for herself one day. She hadn't paid close attention to the inside of the card, at least not until now. Adam's note made her smile: *If you keep having birthdays, you'll soon catch up to me. Your older brother, Adam.*

Joe had made a squiggly, smiling figure beside his name, and Mandy had signed, *With love to my best sister, Mandy.*

"How silly," she said, showing Mandy what she'd written. "I'm your only sister, in case you forgot."

Mandy pulled a face, which made Grace laugh even more. Then, looking for her grandparents' names, she was delighted to see Mammi Adah's shaky hand. *Yet the Lord will command his loving-kindness in the day time, and in the night his song shall be with me, and my prayer unto the God of my life.*

"My favorite verse . . . she remembered," Grace said, showing Mandy. "Psalm 42:8."

"Mammi Adah always writes Scripture in her cards," Mandy said, all smiles. "What did Mamma write?"

Grace searched the card, blinking . . . looking. "Well, that's odd."

Mandy reached for it. "Let me see."

"She must've forgotten," Grace said, befuddled.

Mammi Adah had once told her, during last September's walnut-picking time—their hands stained brown from the nuts—that it wasn't what you intended to do in life that mattered, but what you actually did. "I'm sure Mamma meant to sign it," she said.

"Ain't *gut* enough." Mandy got up, waving the card.

"What're you doin'?"

Mandy marched straight to the kitchen. "Mamma?"

"Ach no . . ." Grace's voice faded to a whisper, her heart sinking. Mamma had seemed so content earlier. She hadn't wanted anything to ruin this day.

chapter
eleven

Grace had just curled up on her little love seat to write in the pages of her new blank book when her mother knocked on the slightly open door.

"Come in, Mamma."

Her mother wore a tentative expression as she lingered in the doorway. Then she slowly moved toward the dresser, where the birthday cards were lined up, returning the card given to Grace by her family.

That done, she made her way to the bed and sat down gingerly, drawing in a long breath. "I'd planned to sign your card before supper," Mamma said softly, a little hitch in her voice. "Truly, I did."

Grace suddenly felt sorry for her. "You had a lot on your mind."

"Well, seems the time got away from me." Her mother looked as embarrassed now as Grace had been earlier at the thought of Mandy's bringing the card to Mamma's attention.

"The supper was wonderful-*gut*," Grace said, changing the subject. "Denki, Mamma."

"You certainly seemed to enjoy yourself."

Grace smiled. "Mammi Adah told some stories on me, jah?"

"We all have stories. . . ." Mamma paused and a frown crossed her brow. "Gracie, there's something I've been wanting to ask you."

Grace caught her breath. Never had Mamma looked so serious. Was she about to reveal her heart at last?

Mamma straightened and folded her hands. "I don't mean to seem nosy, dear. But I've guessed that Henry Stahl might be courtin' you."

Grace didn't feel comfortable letting on that the hunch was correct, but she was curious as to what her mother might say.

"Now, I know he's a nice boy . . . his parents are hardworkin' and God-fearin' and all, but—"

"But what, Mamma?"

Her mother looked down at her hands for a moment. "It's just that . . . well, have you thought what it might be like, marryin' someone so reserved?" Mamma brushed her hand against her face, her expression sad. "I've noticed he's awfully quiet—even awkward—around everyone. Is he that way with you, Grace?"

"Ach, Mamma . . ."

Her mother's tone was almost apologetic as she continued. "I know it's awfully bold of me. Mind you, I don't mean to criticize Henry in any way. I'm just lookin' out for you . . . making sure you're thinking things through, is all."

She should've been glad for this mother-daughter talk, but Grace was more bemused than happy—there seemed to be much

more on Mamma's mind than Henry. Her blue eyes were too solemn.

"A reserved man can be hard to live with," Mamma said softly. "A woman might never know where she stands."

Grace sighed sadly, reading between the lines. She had worried that Mamma's melancholy—and her nighttime wanderings—had something to do with Dat and the state of their marriage.

" 'Tween you and me, Mamma, I care for Henry," she whispered. The past eight months together had been pleasant and a longer time than most couples spent courting.

Mamma blinked her eyes, then rose. "Just please think 'bout it, won't ya?" With that she kissed Grace's forehead and patted her face. "Sleep well, dear one."

Her mother left the room, and Grace heard the familiar footsteps in the hall. Out of curiosity, she got up to look at the now-signed card standing next to Becky's hummingbird on the dresser. Opening it, she was surprised to see what Mamma had written: *You came into my life just in time, Grace. I will always love you. Your mother.*

Tears sprang to her eyes. "Oh, Mamma . . ." Struggling not to weep, she placed the card in the center of the birthday wishes.

I will always love you, too.

Slowly, she began to remove her hairpins, one at a time. When she'd finished, she shook out her long tresses, the length falling around her like a thick shelter. Reaching for her brush, she began to count the strokes. Soon she would dress for bed, but tonight she wanted to burn the lamp oil a bit longer.

It's my birthday, after all.

She paused her brushing and glanced out into the hall, noting her parents' door was closed.

How long before Mamma goes walking tonight?

Grace resumed brushing her hair until her scalp tingled. Then she settled back down on the settee to write, still pondering the surprising things Mamma had said.

——— ··· ———

Judah sat in his chair near the bedroom window in his pajamas, the old German *Biewel* open on his lap. He looked out at the moonlit sky and heard Lettie open, then close the door behind her.

Without acknowledging her, he turned back to the Good Book. Quietly, she moved to sit across from him. "Judah . . . I don't want to interrupt your reading, but . . ."

He raised his head to see the dark circles beneath her tearful eyes, her face so drawn. Another moment passed as Lettie appeared to gather herself.

Judah felt the old, familiar tension in his gut. How long had their conversations been something akin to the birthing of a stillborn lamb? Without thinking, he said, "Whatever's wrong . . . well, it's awful hard on the children, Lettie."

She frowned, her hands folded on her lap. "What is?"

"The past month."

She seemed to bristle. "Well, I've tried to explain, Judah. Truly, I have."

"You've tried, *jah*. Perhaps you might try talkin' to someone besides me."

Instantly, he regretted his words. He didn't wish to speak harshly—her pained expression bored a hole into his soul. She

withered before him, and he felt guilty again. Guilty for every conversation that had gone miserably awry. And yet, hadn't he waited in vain for her to speak her mind, only for her to shrink back time and again? He'd learned as a young husband that his bride harbored something deep within, something she could not seem to share.

Now, quietly, he waited again, searching for the right words to make things easier for her. But the moment was tense, even draining. He leaned forward. "What is it, Lettie? What's botherin' you?"

She fixed her eyes on him, her words coming with slow deliberation. "I want you to hear this from me, Judah. . . ." She paused again, and Judah felt the blood drain from his face. After weeks of wandering the night, was she finally about to say what troubled her?

Suddenly, a series of loud thuds came from downstairs. He jerked his head toward the door.

"Judah . . ." Lettie whispered, her pretty eyes brimming with tears.

Adam's voice rang out. "Dat, *kumm schnell*—come quick!"

Judah turned back to his wife. "Ach, the ewes!"

"Dat! You awake?" Adam's voice was closer now, his footsteps in the hall.

"Let Adam manage for a few minutes," she pleaded. "Won't ya hear me out, Judah?"

He stood up, pulled away by his own insensible need to go. "I should see about this."

"Please?" Her voice was a mere whisper.

Swiftly, he pulled on his work trousers over his pajamas. "I'll be right back," he said, dashing out the door.

Downstairs, he cringed at his cowardly reaction but hardened his resolve, hurrying outside. Whatever was on Lettie's mind could wait till morning.

Tomorrow, he promised himself. *We'll get to it then.*

Lettie closed her eyes as she lay in bed. She should have gone out to help her husband. More times than she could count, she'd assisted with pregnant ewes struggling in their labor. But now she felt depleted of energy, too exhausted to walk across the room, let alone to the barn.

"It's awful hard on the children," Judah had said, referring to these recent weeks.

"Ach, such trouble in my spirit," she whispered.

The memory of Judah's fiery eyes remained before her, yet her own emotions were torn between what she recalled of their former love and the present reality. Oh, she knew he'd cared for her early on. But now?

Still fully dressed, Lettie lay there, waiting for her husband's return.

———···———

Along about ten o'clock, when she'd filled several pages of her new journal, Grace was startled by a bright light climbing slowly up the windowpane, then swimming crazily across it. As the light moved in a circular motion, she realized what this might be. Going to the window, she raised it high enough to poke out her head.

She looked down and saw Henry standing far below, shining the light on his face.

"I've brought the clock," he whispered, cupping a hand

around his mouth. Then, catching himself, he added, "Hullo again, Grace."

"Henry?" She hardly knew what else to say. He was standing clear down there, directly below her window. Chime clock aside, that could only mean one thing.

Glory be! Is this the night?

"Is now all right . . . I mean, for a visit?"

Goodness, he could scarcely get the words out. Was he that nervous?

"I'll meet you at the side door," she said, then slowly closed the window.

Heart in her throat, Grace wound her hair back up into the best bun she could manage quickly, her hands trembling. Her mind raced as she twisted the sides of her hair and pinned it quickly, then secured her reverent white Kapp. As excited as she was for this moment, she worried Henry had arrived too early, before everyone was sound asleep—especially Mamma.

She looked closely at her room, glad she had not put on nightclothes or rumpled her bed just yet. Oh, to think Henry had come calling here!

Scarcely able to believe it, she took the stairs quietly, then once she was down, she flew through the sitting room and into the kitchen.

She opened the side door and stood waiting as he carried the chime clock up the steps. "Please, come inside," she said, unsure of herself.

"I best be takin' the clock out of the box first," he said, and she wondered if he was concerned about the chimes making a ruckus. As was the age-old custom, they mustn't draw any

attention to themselves whatsoever—all of it an overture to the most wonderful-good part of all.

Soon . . . very soon!

— ··· —

Heather finished studying for tomorrow's exam and decided to incorporate some additional ideas into her master's thesis, titled *Patriarchy in the Writings of Colonial Williamsburg.* Her fingers tapped out her thoughts, racing over the keyboard as she added a few more pages. Soon she would have to begin the dreaded chore of double-checking the latest footnotes.

Stretching, she looked at the digital clock on the microwave. *Dad should be home by now.* She hadn't expected him to call; he rarely did. She assumed he'd picked up dinner or ordered take-out for the office. *"Eat on the run or go hungry,"* he'd once said in reference to his demanding schedule.

She thumbed through two research books—one focusing on the patriarchal ideal and reality, and the other on the function of the colonial family making sure she'd accurately documented everything. A desire for top marks had always been her priority, and that had not changed, even with Dr. O'Connor's words still ricocheting in her head. *Even now,* she thought, shrugging away the dreadful diagnosis. *I've no time for doom and gloom.*

For the time being she was determined to cap off her last semester by acing her exams. After that she would head to Amish country for a great escape, leaving next Tuesday—in six days. She hoped to further her work on her thesis and oral presentation at the Riehls' quiet tourist home.

When she'd tweaked the first twenty pages for the ump-teenth time, Heather was satisfied . . . for now. Tomorrow she

would print out what she had and work off the hard copy, obsessing as always. After all, anything written late at night often looked entirely too disappointing in the daylight.

She was tempted to call it a night and head off to bed, but something urged her to check her email . . . see if Devon had written. She still was not totally clear about what the time difference was between Virginia and Iraq. She was sure he was in Baghdad, but his company was constantly moving, and for security reasons he wasn't allowed to disclose his location.

Her heart slammed hard when she saw who'd written: Devon's battle buddy, he'd called him. *If anything happens to me, you'll hear from Don Hirsch first,* he'd written soon after deployment. The words had sounded so ominous.

And now here was Don's email address showing up like a bomb in her in-box. She could hardly breathe as she read. *Hey, Heather, don't freak. . . . Devon's sick, but he's gonna be okay.*

She squinted back tears to read more. *There's a weird virus floating around,* Don explained.

"Aw, poor guy . . ." she groaned.

They'll keep an eye on him at the military hospital for a few days, so he won't be online for a while. He says not to worry and sends his love "to his sweet babe"—and I quote.

"Um, how do I not worry?" she sputtered, and Moe meowed loudly. She leaned down to pick up her favorite cat. "Devon's real sick," she whispered. "Can he get well fast without us, huh?"

Moe began to purr, rolling over on his back as he lay on her lap. She rubbed his tummy, thinking all the while about her fiancé's being so ill he had to go to a hospital. *Where?* She felt

helpless not knowing . . . not being able to visualize any of it. She really wanted to hop on a plane and fly over there.

Shoot, he'd signed up for guard duty and gotten *this?* It still baffled her why he'd signed up at all.

Hey, Don, she began to type, expressing her gratitude for his email, jarring as it had been to receive it. *Tell Devon I love him, and I'm really sorry he's sick. Please keep the updates coming. Thanks!*

She stopped typing, frustrated with the immense distance between them. *My incredible guy . . . so ill!*

She wished she could do this entire year over, starting from the day Devon had held her in his arms at the airport. She'd gotten a gate pass so she could go with him through security to his departing gate. In the end, it might have been easier if they'd said their *good-byes* and *I love yous* a dozen times in the terminal. But no, she'd had to see him off completely.

"I really despise this war," Heather muttered, hitting Send. She shut down the laptop and shuffled off to her room. *I'll be lucky to get any sleep tonight.*

——— ··· ———

Henry carried the clock up the stairs without the chimes ringing even once. Grace shyly led the way to her room, leaving the door slightly open as Mamma would expect.

Whispering now, she moved the birthday cards off the dresser. "For the time being, it can go here."

Henry placed the small, gleaming clock in the center, in front of the mirror on her long doily runner. He seemed stiff, standing there in the middle of her room.

She felt just as ill at ease—so much so that she nearly forgot

what to do next. Thankfully, Henry motioned toward the hope chest at the foot of her bed. "Oh . . . jah," she said, still concerned their talking might disturb the family. "Would you like to see what I've made?"

He moved to the padded settee and silently sat down.

"I embroidered these pillow slips," she began, wondering if he expected her to describe each item. She'd never done this before. Of course, neither had he, and she smiled at the lovely thought.

Next came the woolen shawl she'd made several years ago, when she'd first learned to spin wool with Jessica. And the woolen lap afghan for chilly days.

Henry regarded each item with seeming interest, and Grace hurried along, showing him the four winter-weight quilts she and Mamma had made, and another one made by Mammi Adah. There were quilted potholders and placemats, too, and dozens of linens—many of which were treasured family heirlooms—towels, bed coverlets, and even a cradle quilt done in lovely pastels. She told him about her sewing equipment and cooking utensils, all packed away in boxes in the attic for now.

When she'd displayed everything, she carefully returned the items to the chest and closed the lid. She sat there, heart pounding as Henry gave a slow smile and held out his hand. She rose and went to his side.

"Sit here . . . with me." He released her hand. "Denki for showin' me all your nice things."

She nodded, still feeling awkward and shy. "Happy to."

He faced her, his dark eyes serious. "You must know I'm quite fond of you, Grace."

She looked into his face, smiling . . . soaking up his attention. "I love you, too," she said in a whisper.

" 'Tis mighty *gut*, then." He lifted her hand to his lips and held it there, eyes fixed on her. Then he kissed her hand. "Will you agree to be my bride?"

My bride . . .

She could hardly keep from bursting out in laughter . . . no, in tears. This was the most wonderful moment ever. "I'd be honored to marry you, Henry. Jah!"

Still clasping her hand, he nodded his pleasure, and she cherished the feel of her small hand in his big, work-roughened one. "We'll tie the knot sometime this fall."

She gave him her sweetest smile. "All right."

His eyes searched hers and his head tilted sideways for a moment, as if he might say more. But when his gaze became uncomfortable, she looked down, not sure what to say next. She didn't want to rush him out in an unfeeling sort of way, yet their time here together should come to an end.

"God be with ya, Henry," she said kindly, hoping he'd take the hint.

He did. He rose and walked to the door, turning briefly to look once again at the chime clock. "Looks right nice there," he said.

She agreed and followed him downstairs, both of them tiptoeing as they went.

When they were outdoors, she saw that he had not parked his buggy in the lane. "It was awful nice seein' you twice in one day," she ventured, hoping it didn't sound forward.

He leaned down and kissed her cheek. "Good night, Grace."

"G'night." She broke into a smile as the feel of his kiss lingered on her face. Waving now, she watched him hurry away, out to the road.

Good-bye, my love . . .

Reluctantly she turned and walked toward the dark house.

chapter
twelve

Grace dropped off to sleep after lying awake for a short time, reliving the last hours of this wonderful-good day. Later, she dreamed of walking with Henry along a path strewn with bright yellow rose petals. She could not, however, hear what he was saying no matter how she strained to listen.

Eventually the dream floated away to nothingness and she slept more soundly. But in her haze, she sensed someone kissing her cheek.

It was still dark out when she awakened. She had not heard her mother's footsteps in the night, and Grace marveled at how soundly she must have slept.

Turning over, she looked at her dresser and saw what appeared to be an unopened envelope propped up against her dresser mirror, to the left of the chime clock. She leaned up, rubbing her eyes. The house was still quiet; it was too early to get up.

Lying back down, she glimpsed the small alarm clock on the bedside table and saw that it was only ten minutes before five. She looked again at her dresser, wondering where the

envelope had come from—had someone placed it there while she slept?

Her curiosity got the best of her, and she went to look. She carried the letter to the window and opened the shade slightly, letting in the waning moonlight. The words *To Grace* were written in her mother's handwriting on the envelope.

Quickly, she tore it open.

My dear Grace,

You looked ever so happy tonight on your birthday. I know you enjoyed the supper and your time with our family and the neighbor friends.

I promised to tell you what is bothering me, but now, frankly, I can't find the words in me. I've seen the concern on your face since we helped at the big barn raising last month—heard your gentle prodding, too. Your caring heart is such a dear part of who you are.

It's very late, and all of you are sleeping as I write. I trust you will share my thoughts here with your brothers and Mandy, as well as with your father. I know if I'd told all of you my plans in person, I would not have had the courage to leave.

"What on earth?" Grace whispered, her breath coming in short, panicked bursts as she read on.

I fear that what I'm writing makes little sense and will change your birthday joy to sadness. For that, I'm very sorry, Grace.

You see, there's another whole side to this, and such pain comes with all of it. But I cannot spell it out just now. In time, you will understand, I promise. Perhaps all of you will. Even so, my leaving will bring shame to my family . . . and sorrow, too.

I hope you will not despise this hard thing I must do. My heart is ever so tender, if not breaking. Yet go I must. I love you.

Always,
Mamma

"She's leaving?" Clutching the letter, Grace fled the room, peering first through her parents' open door. Dat lay crosswise on the bed, sound asleep. Rushing downstairs, she looked everywhere for her mother, including the cold cellar in the basement, then clear out to the barn, near Willow's stall.

Not finding Mamma, she went all the way around the house to the front porch, still pondering the strange letter . . . ever so mysterious. She turned and looked toward the field, where Mamma often walked. How many times had she seen her out there, wrapped in moonbeams, her arms tight around her middle, as if she were holding herself together?

Breathlessly, Grace returned to her room, where Henry had proposed just hours before. *Does Dat know any of this?* Looking at the letter again, she read it more slowly and began crying.

Baffled and confused, she rose once more and headed for the hallway. This time she stopped to look in on Mandy, her arm flung over her head, sound asleep.

Poor sister, what will she think?

And what about Dat? Apparently Mamma had written a letter only to *her* . . . but why?

Walking to the dormer windows, she peered out and, to her fright, saw what she hadn't seen before—a faraway dark figure walking briskly from the house, heading west toward Route 340. *Can it be?* She leaned forward, squinting to see.

Grace darted back to her room and tossed the letter onto the bedside table, atop the envelope. She yanked her bathrobe off the wooden peg and put it on, not bothering to tie the belt. Then, rushing outside, she dashed past the well-groomed lawns and the pasture fence near the road.

Grace stumbled and caught herself, running as she tied a knot in her robe. She was gaining some ground, getting closer, desperately hoping that the distant black silhouette was *not* her mother. That this whole thing was some horrid mistake. Surely her mother wouldn't just up and leave while everyone was sleeping. Would she?

Through a blur of tears, she saw a car heading this way, then slowing and coming to a stop.

There's another whole side to this, Mamma had written. Grace couldn't imagine what that meant, or even what it *could* mean.

The moon moved out from behind a cloud, making it easier to see more clearly now. The figure was definitely a woman. Suddenly it was unmistakable: Mamma was practically running toward the car, her head covered by a heavy black outer bonnet, something bulky at her side.

The car door opened. Grace sucked in her breath and nearly choked when she realized what was in her mother's hand. Their old brown suitcase!

"Mamma!" she called, gasping for breath. "Come back! Please, come back!"

Slipping inside the car, her mother did not stop or even turn to look back. *Can't she hear me?*

The door slammed shut, its echo reaching Grace with a final thud. *No, this can't be!* Stunned, she slowed to a walk, holding her sides and breathing fast . . . then she stopped completely, unable to go on.

I hope you will not despise this hard thing I must do, Mamma had written.

"No, Mamma . . ." wept Grace as the vehicle sped away. "Why must you go?"

Judah awakened with a jolt. He thought he'd heard someone rushing about. Alarmed, he pulled himself out of bed to flounder down the hall to look in on the children.

Strange, he thought, *I still think of them that way. Especially the girls.*

He peered through the open door at Amanda, who was softly snoring in her sleep, recalling that it was Lettie who'd always done this sort of checking. He would sometimes awaken as she returned to bed.

Before she started wandering all hours, he thought, still feeling guilty for his own cowardice last night. He headed slowly up the narrow staircase that led to the boys' rooms on the third floor. All was well.

Back on the second floor, he noticed Grace's door ajar, and when he looked in, he saw that her bedclothes were thrown back. "Odd," he said, but on second thought he wondered if she'd gone out to meet her beau.

He was about to head to the main floor and have a look outside when he noticed a letter lying close to the edge of Grace's bedside table, as if flung there. Not given to reading other people's mail, he hesitated. Then, thinking that it was out in the open, he looked at it more closely and immediately recognized Lettie's handwriting. He shrank back then, thinking of just leaving it there . . . letting it be.

But something stirred within and he reached for it. He carried the letter back to his room, scanning the first line as he went.

Then, with a great sigh, Judah closed the door and sat down to read what appeared to be Lettie's farewell to them all.

Grace trudged along the road, her mind in a dither. She was scarcely able to see the road through her tears as she made her way home. And she found herself wrapping her arms around her stomach, just as she'd seen Mamma do.

In the midst of her grief, her favorite psalm came to mind— the one Mammi Adah had scrawled on Grace's birthday card. *In the night his song shall be with me. . . .* The words went round and round in her head as she plodded toward the house.

What will Dat say? she thought, at a loss for how to tell him.

None of the family would believe it. Even Mammi Adah would look at her askance if Grace was brave enough to reveal what she'd just witnessed.

Had Mamma been rehearsing her quick escape those other nights? Had she been getting up the courage to walk away . . . escape from her family, maybe?

Escape? It was downright strange to be thinking of such a word. "Escape from what?" she said into the chilly air.

Plain wives and mothers simply did not leave their families. Even when there was trouble in marriages, divorce was unheard of among the People. Only on rare occasions were there even whispered comments about legal separations. No, married folk somehow made do, or they found a way in spite of their difficulties.

Surely Mamma has only gone to visit someone. Surely . . .

But the words of her mother's own heartbreaking letter belied Grace's hopes, and she trembled.

—— ··· ——

Martin Puckett had been somewhat surprised by Lettie Byler's call early yesterday evening. She'd sounded distraught as she asked him to pick her up at an appointed spot and time.

"Just before 5:00 AM tomorrow . . ."

He'd had a hard time convincing his wife that it wasn't out of the ordinary to leave the house when it was still dark to pick up an Amishwoman. "She needs to catch a train," he'd explained.

So here he was, behind the wheel of his car, with Lettie sitting in the front seat, a position she'd never occupied while traveling with either Judah or the rest of her family. She'd hopped right in, as if eager to get to her destination.

He could hear her muttering in *Deitsch* as he drove toward Lancaster, something about being worried she was doing the right thing by Judah. "I tried to tell him," she said in her first language. The children, too, were apparently heavy on her mind.

"Are you all right, Lettie?" He glanced at her.

She waved her hand. "Ach, don't mind me."

He'd never thought twice about driving the Amish, least of all at an hour when it would seem dangerous to travel with horse and buggy. "You'll be mighty early to the train station," he mentioned.

"I don't yet have a reservation."

He hoped she would be okay traveling alone, as bleak as her face looked. But it was not his place to pry. *Unless she is in danger . . .*

When he arrived at the Amtrak station in Lancaster, he stopped in front and got out to retrieve her suitcase. She stood at the door, waiting. "I'd like you to keep mum 'bout this, if you don't mind," she said.

He'd never heard her, or any Amishwoman, speak so point-edly to a man. Nor speak with such determination.

"You mean Judah doesn't know about your trip?" he asked, suddenly more concerned.

She hung her head. "I best not say."

"Lettie," he pressed her, "does *anyone* know of your travel plans?"

Her desperate look when he set the suitcase down told him all he needed to know. "Have you thought this through?"

"Ain't anyone else's business. Please keep this mum."

At a complete loss as to what should be done, Martin stepped back. "Now, you know I can't do that," he told her. "In fact, I have a mind to take you right back and—"

"No . . . please." She shook her head. "Someone's meeting me . . . where I'm goin'. Not to worry."

Relatives? he wondered. But it wasn't his place to ask.

"As I said, please keep this hush-hush, Martin."

"Well, your husband is a friend of mine. If he asks me whether I drove you here, I won't lie."

Worry swept her face and she held out his pay for the trip in rolled-up bills. He stepped forward to take it, then withdrew quickly. "Have a safe trip . . . wherever you're going."

"Ever so kind of you."

He offered to carry her suitcase inside, but Lettie declined. "No need, but thank you." Then she said a quick good-bye.

Her dejected tone made him shudder as she clutched her suitcase and resolutely walked into the station.

chapter
....
thirteen

As panicked as she was at the sight of her mother's leaving, Grace was also terribly upset at not finding Mamma's letter in her room when she returned. Mentally retracing her steps, she remembered staring out the hallway window, seeing her mother's dark silhouette. . . . Then hadn't she tossed it into her bedroom?

But rechecking her room—and the hallway—the letter was nowhere in sight.

She made her way downstairs and looked in the front sitting room, searching even on the china hutch, where Mamma displayed her prettiest teacups and saucers and plates. Breathlessly she hurried into the kitchen to look on the table and counter—every imaginable spot she might have inadvertently left it during her rush out the door.

Could it have been taken? But who would do that?

And anyway, everyone was sleeping.

She crawled into bed, still wearing her robe, shaking with a bad case of nerves. She'd witnessed her mother leaving, carrying

a suitcase . . . getting into a car even as Grace pleaded for her to stay. Was it possible to ever wipe away that image?

Doubting she would fall back to sleep, she prayed. Only the dear Lord knew what she should tell Mandy and the boys at the breakfast table, when they discovered Mamma gone. And Dat? What could she possibly say to him?

She rolled over and covered her head with the quilt. *What would cause Mamma to do such a thing?* It was incomprehensible, and now she couldn't even reread the letter . . . unless it had fallen under the bed.

Tossing off the covers, she got out of bed and peered beneath. Not finding the letter there, either, she opened the narrow drawer on the small round table next to her bed, her heart racing. She slipped her hand inside but found nothing.

Reaching under the bedside table, she discovered only a coating of dust—she must remember to push the dry mop under there later. Weeping silently, Grace returned to bed and curled up in a tight ball as she recalled the dear way Mamma had signed off: *My heart is ever so tender, if not breaking. . . . I love you.*

Oh, Mamma, she cried silently, *but it's my heart that is breaking now.*

Judah's hand trembled as he held the letter. He hadn't been able to put it down.

"Lettie," he whispered, head throbbing. "Why?"

He stared at the bare wooden pegs on their bedroom wall where her dresses and black aprons had been and remembered their awkward discussion last night. Something compelled him

to open her dresser drawers, though he felt oddly intrusive about that. Each one was empty.

Earlier, he'd searched the house and outdoor perimeter for her, shining his lantern over the pastureland, spreading its light over the area. He'd walked the road, too, heading north, thinking surely she would not go on foot out toward the highway. Route 340 was much too dangerous.

He'd wanted urgently to call out her name, but that was impractical. Besides, he didn't want to raise the neighbors. They'd all know soon enough, come daylight.

Bad news travels faster than good.

For now, though, his knowledge of her intentions belonged to him alone. Or to him and Grace, if she'd even read her mother's letter yet. Most likely she had been out with her beau. If so, Grace knew nothing of Lettie's leaving . . . or the letter.

Assuming he was correct in his thinking, the best thing to do was to keep the letter hidden for now. That way Grace would be spared having to read it, although Lettie's words to her daughter were as tender as any he'd heard uttered from her lips.

"She's miffed at me," he said. Maybe she'd simply gone walking in the wee hours and would return when she was ready to forgive him. Certainly, he had offended her.

After daylight, he thought, *I'll go and find her . . . bring her home.* In his bewilderment, he read the letter again, searching for a clue—anything at all.

But as he reread the puzzling words, it seemed even Lettie was unsure about her destination. Her desperate plea last night rang in his ears. *"Won't ya hear me out, Judah?"*

No, this letter was no mere attempt to get his attention.

Martin Puckett hadn't driven but two miles when he noticed something Lettie Byler had dropped on the floor. At the nearest stop sign, he leaned down to get it and saw several phone numbers—all outside the 717 area code. Just what part of the country they were from he did not know. But they were undoubtedly important to Lettie, so he turned around and headed back to the Lancaster train station.

Under different circumstances, he would have enjoyed seeing the historic station again. Now, still pensive about Lettie's troubling request, he almost timidly entered the nearly palatial-looking terminal. The place seemed to be in the process of restoration. He recalled having read something about the restoration online, as well as in the *Lancaster New Era*.

The ceiling soared to a glass-paned insert high overhead, and the words *To Trains* were engraved on the wall over a portico. Even at this hour, the waiting area was scattered with would-be travelers, and he spotted Lettie over in the far corner, sitting alone on a tall-backed wooden bench. She was crocheting a scarf. He considered her forlorn state momentarily, noticing the streaks of gray in her blond hair for the first time. Then, pulling the piece of paper from his pocket, he slowly approached her. "Excuse me, Lettie." He reached down to give her the paper.

She started, obviously surprised to see him.

"I found this in my car. Is it yours?"

A light came into her sad eyes. "Ach, I would be a cooked goose without it." She smiled broadly. "Ever so *gut* of you to bring it."

Still anxious about her safety, he felt compelled to sit with her. "I thought it might come in handy," he said.

She nodded, obviously pleased. "Oh my, you have no idea. . . ."

"Well, I'm glad it's helpful." She hadn't invited him to sit, but there he was all the same. "Lettie . . . I . . ." He paused, cautious as to what he should say. "I'm concerned for you."

She looked down at her hands, the crochet hook poised to make the next loop. "You mustn't be. Really."

He noticed her sack lunch and the book she'd brought. "I don't wish to meddle." He assumed Judah and Lettie Byler were as amicable at home as they appeared to be in public. Yet if so, why was she here in secret?

She smiled weakly, then began crocheting again. Instinctively, he sensed their conversation was over.

Not thinking, he touched her arm. "If you ever need help— from either my wife or me—please don't think twice about calling."

Slowly, as if painfully, she nodded, lifting her eyes to his. He saw tears wetting her cheeks and took his handkerchief from his pocket and handed it to her. "You're very kind," she said, accepting it and dabbing at her face. "Very kind."

"I mean it . . . no matter where you're going," he emphasized. Then, when she'd returned his handkerchief, he remained there awhile, temporarily unable to say yet another good-bye.

At last he rose and walked across the marble floor. It was then he recognized Sadie Zook's cousin among those waiting for trains. Pete Bernhardt traveled weekly to the Big Apple on business and was sitting across the way, his briefcase propped near his feet.

Because he'd known Pete for many years, Martin was about to head over and say hello, but Pete glanced up furtively and quickly looked away. Confused by that, Martin hesitated. *Why so distant?*

Then it struck him—had Pete witnessed his exchange with Lettie Byler?

Offering a wave, Martin felt quite embarrassed by what Pete might presume to have seen. He made his way out the door and down to the parking lot, mortified for having taken even the most benign liberty with Judah's attractive wife—sitting beside her, offering his handkerchief.

Martin opened his car door and got in. Janet would be up making breakfast before she put the finishing touches on their packing. They were eager to get an early start to their own out-of-town trip today. He needed to do his part in fueling up and having the car washed, the reason he'd chosen to drive the car instead of his usual van.

As he turned the key in the ignition, he found himself breathing a prayer for Lettie, a vulnerable Amishwoman traveling quite alone.

chapter
fourteen

Grace awakened with a jolt, having fallen back to sleep. Still wearing her robe beneath the covers, she was vaguely aware of the sound of steady rain on the roof. She stretched but instead of relief came a profound feeling of melancholy and fatigue. Bits and pieces of the predawn hours slowly emerged in her memory. *Finding a letter from Mamma . . . racing down the road . . . watching helplessly as Mamma stepped into a strange car.*

Grace sat up in bed, her heart pounding. Had she simply dreamed this nightmare?

Moments passed as she attempted to sort through the panic. But no, it was true. She hadn't imagined it at all.

Grace peered with one eye at her exquisite chime clock. Seven o'clock. *Ach, I overslept.*

Leaping out of bed, she nearly tripped on her robe and could not find her slippers. *I'm misplacing too many things.* She thought again of Mamma's letter as she moved to the window and looked out on a dim and foggy morning. It was impossible to see even to the edge of the yard, let alone out to the road. She

pressed her fingers against the pane, feeling the chill through it and remembering Henry's visit.

How overjoyed she had been. Now she felt so grief stricken in comparison as the recent events of her life mingled—Henry's proposal and her mother's departure—like the intricate weaving of a variegated rag rug.

Grace felt terribly out of sorts. Something had gone completely off beam for Mamma to pack a suitcase and leave.

After forcing herself to go through the motions of getting dressed, she hurried downstairs to start breakfast, late as it was, and realized Mandy was still asleep. A glance around the corner into the front hall revealed her father's and brothers' work boots were missing. The men had already gone to look after the baby lambs. New ones were arriving every few days now, just as Dat had planned it. The round-the-clock checking on the expectant ewes kept him and the boys up off and on during the night.

Didn't they wonder about breakfast—why Mamma wasn't up and cooking? She found it curious no one had even called to awaken her for the task. What did they make of Mamma's absence? Did they assume she, too, had overslept?

Hearing sounds coming from the kitchen on the other side of the house, she guessed Mammi Adah was making eggs for Dawdi Jakob. The air caught in her throat as she thought how saddened they also would be by Mamma's disappearance.

Once it's known.

Turning on the faucet, Grace filled the kettle, thinking that on such a dismal and rainy day the men would want coffee. The mid-spring day more resembled autumn in temperature and dampness.

Glad that Mandy had gathered the eggs yesterday, she brought out the bowl filled with fresh ones and set it down on the counter. She turned on a burner and set the frying pan on the stove, plopping a chunk of butter in the center. Dat's stomach would be growling and so would Adam's and Joe's. They liked scrambled eggs made with bits of bacon and cheese, but today she wouldn't take the time for any of that. *Fried eggs are quicker.*

Still in disbelief, Grace gritted her teeth and wished she might know what to say when they came in. Suddenly she realized she'd stepped immediately into Mamma's role without even considering it.

She set the flame to a gentle heat, then cracked the eggs against the edge of the pan before dropping them in. Placing a lid on top, she turned to stare out the window. Still not hearing Mandy, she walked to the bottom of the stairs. "Daylight's a-wastin'!" she called, waiting to hear the thud of her sister's feet on the floor before she resumed cooking.

In a few minutes, Mandy came dragging down, barefoot and in her bathrobe. "Why'd ya let me sleep in?" she asked, sounding nearly accusing.

"I overslept, too."

Mandy slumped onto the bench next to the table, leaning her head into her hand. "I'm so tired . . . can't seem to wake up."

"Jah, the weather's downright gloomy."

Mandy looked out the window. "It's really makin' down."

"Well, we need rain." Bracing herself for the question that was sure to come, Grace faced the stove, putting salt and pepper on the yolks, which were now nearly done. Dat liked his slightly runny, but everyone else wanted their yolks firm.

"Would you mind toasting some bread right quick?" she asked Mandy. "Wash your hands first, though."

"Ach, you sound like Mamma." Mandy sauntered to the sink and turned on the water. "Why're you cookin' breakfast anyway?"

"Why not?"

Just then, Adam and Joe came in through the side door, even though Dat always urged them to use the front door that led to the hallway, with its specified places for work boots and outerwear.

"Is Dat with you?" Grace asked, glancing toward the door.

"He took off with Sassy and the buggy earlier . . . didn't say where he was headed," Adam said, referring to his own driving horse.

"He was in a big hurry. Must be an important errand," Joe said as he clumped over to the sink, where Mandy was standing, drying her hands.

"So early?" Mandy said. "What's open this time of day?"

Grace cut in, "Better take off your boots. Leave 'em outside."

"They'll get rained on," Joe said, removing his and leaving them on the oval rug near the door. He looked up at the three of them . . . minus their mother. "Where's Mamma?"

Grace glanced at Adam, who seemed oblivious. "Well, she's not here," she said, heart sinking.

She's left us. . . .

"So *you're* makin' breakfast?" Joe said. "It better be *gut*."

She took the spatula and lifted the eggs out of the pan and set them on plates. "How many eggs can ya eat?" she asked Adam, then Joe.

They each claimed their usual three, along with two pieces of the buttered toast that Mandy provided.

"Maybe Dat went to fetch Mamma," said Mandy out of the blue as they all sat down.

Grace was caught by surprise. What did her sister mean?

"She's not in the barn," said Adam. "Has *anyone* seen her?"

"Not this mornin'," Mandy said.

"Could be Dat's taken her to visit one of her sisters," Joe suggested.

Grace squeezed her hands tightly beneath the table and looked to Adam for the table blessing, since he was the oldest male present. She bowed her head when he did, praying the silent rote prayer she'd learned as a child.

"Why would ya say that . . . what you said before?" Joe asked Mandy when they started eating. "That Dat went to fetch Mamma?"

"Because," Mandy replied. "Don't ya know she goes out walkin' at—"

"Mandy, you'd best be eatin'," Grace interrupted.

Her sister frowned, clearly resenting Grace's rebuke. "We *all* best dig in now," Grace suggested, feeling sick to her stomach.

——— ... ———

Judah was on his third pass down the road and garnering stares from the neighbors. He'd even ventured as far east as Monterey Road, near Eli's Natural Foods store and back, keeping his eye out for any sign of Lettie. He'd driven past several of her cousins' houses, as well as all of her siblings', not stopping to inquire after her . . . not wanting to worry anyone needlessly.

But he assumed if Lettie had gone merely to visit, someone would've come out to hail him.

Feeling mighty weak now, he knew he ought to head home. Yet he was hardly ready to face questions from Adam or the others, and surely there would be some.

Waving at the neighbor up the way, Judah tipped his hat when he was greeted with *"Guder Mariye"* and a big wave.

If Lettie's gone, my children won't be the only ones asking questions.

"And I have nothin' to appease their curiosity." He clucked his tongue to spur Sassy onward, observing his fine sheep grazing in the distance.

He waved to the next neighbor, Marian Riehl, who was out on her porch, beating rag rugs. He'd heard from someone, he didn't recall who, that the Riehls were getting a long-term paying guest. This struck him as both curious and practical. Andy and Marian were hard-pressed to make ends meet, as many were. Plain folk were thinking twice these days about having gas-run appliances—some wished they could return to wood-fed stoves.

He wondered how his mother-in-law must be feeling *now* about her doggedness in wanting more modern kitchen appliances.

Shaking his head, he also considered what Adah Esh would think if she'd received the kind of letter Lettie had written to Grace. Perhaps Lettie *had* shared her plan with someone besides Grace.

If Naomi were still alive, she would undoubtedly know.

As Judah surveyed the rain-drenched landscape, he could see patches on the ground where samara had fallen last year

and were already beginning to take root. He was anxious for the sunny days of May, another week away.

Lettie will miss watching her beloved mourning doves if she stays away too long. He recalled her fascination last spring as she'd observed the males accompanying their mates to possible nesting sites, the male birds gathering twigs and other material for the female that built the nest. Lettie had stood and watched at the kitchen window for nearly half an hour just after dawn one day. Judah had offered to make a ground feeding tray for them, since they weren't hoppers like some birds, and Lettie had been so pleased, giving him a rare smile.

Will she miss the late-blooming honey locust? he wondered. *Surely she'll return for harvesting elderberries and peaches. Surely . . .*

He rubbed his neck and shoulders—the pain at the nape of his neck had become a searing ache. No more putting off the dreaded breakfast scene. It was past time to head home. By all indications, his wife had flown the coop. For how long, Judah did not know.

— ··· —

Dat took his time unhitching Sassy from the family buggy, then headed toward the house, cutting across the drive and through the side yard. Grace noticed he'd worn his winter hat instead of the straw one and was all dressed in black. *Like for Preaching service,* she thought, stepping away from the window, her heart pounding.

He looked ashen as he came into the kitchen. Grace had cleaned off the table and washed the dishes, not knowing when he might return. With Mandy upstairs making her bed and straightening her room and the boys back in the barn monitoring

the new lambs, the house was uncomfortably quiet. She felt ever so strange, knowing all she did about Mamma . . . wondering what her father knew, if anything.

She moved silently to the cupboard and again took out the frying pan, ready to make breakfast for Dat if he wanted it. Mandy would be down soon enough, she was sure, which would help things along, as well. Unless Mandy once more brought up Mamma's absence.

Dat had broken his own rule about not using the side door. He'd come in stocking footed, having removed his work boots and left them outside since the rain had stopped. "Am I too late for some eggs and toast?" he asked, his face angst ridden.

"Not at all." She turned and set the gas flame where she liked it. She longed to fill up the dreadful void, the aching emptiness between them, but she knew better than to ask where Mamma was. That would be deceitful. Yet, because he didn't utter a word about her taking over the cooking duties, she guessed he knew something. Perhaps they'd had words in the night?

Dat went into the washroom and decisively closed the door. She heard the click of the lock, as well, which was not at all like him. He—all of them—simply shut the door. The whole family respected a closed door, no matter the room. "*A closed door is closed for a reason*," Mamma had often said when they were little.

By the time Dat appeared again and took his place at the head of the table, Mandy reappeared in the doorway of the kitchen, wearing a scowl. "Did ya find her?" She planted herself next to their father.

"Your Mamma, you mean?" Dat eyed them both.

Grace carried the food over, the eggs cooked to Dat's liking,

and put the plate in front of him. She waited, wondering what more he might request. And if he might say where he'd gone.

"She's nowhere to be found." Mandy leaned forward, her elbows on the table, hands supporting her chin. "Where on earth could she be?"

"I don't know," Dat muttered.

"She's not usually gone first thing in the morning," Mandy declared, turning to look at Grace.

Dat bowed his head for the blessing, squeezing his eyes tightly shut. When he'd said amen and picked up his fork, he whispered, " 'Tis a mystery."

"Well, where do ya *think* she is?" Mandy folded her hands on the table.

Grace gently touched her shoulder. "Let Dat eat in peace."

Mandy frowned at her, getting up. "Sorry," she muttered and left by way of the side door.

Dat continued eating, his eyes fixed on his plate while Grace went to scrub out the frying pan for the second time. In spite of her father's blank expression, she sensed he knew something.

She turned, her hands still in the sudsy water. "Mamma wrote me a letter 'bout her leaving." Pausing, she quickly dried her hands and crossed the room to him. "She must've left it on my dresser in the wee hours."

A flicker of surprise crossed Dat's face, and then he nodded. "I saw it."

"You read it, then?"

"Jah."

He must've taken it.

Grace sensed how awkward he surely felt. "Well, I never

would've known how to share it with you, Dat, anyway. None of it made sense."

His eyes were sad, and she lowered herself to sit on the wooden bench to the left of her father, in Adam's spot. "I went lookin' for her right away, all through the house."

"So did I," he said.

"And then I saw her running up the road. A car stopped to pick her up. I could hardly believe my eyes."

At that, he frowned and ran his hand over his untrimmed beard. He sighed ever so deeply.

"Where do ya think she went, Dat?"

He sat motionless. "Haven't the slightest notion."

She heard him breathing, yet he said no more. So many questions ran through her mind, but he was clearly in no shape to tend to them just now. Surely he had dozens of his own.

Getting up, she returned to the sink.

"*A reserved man can be hard to live with. . . . A woman might never know where she stands,*" Mamma had said. At the time, Grace had hoped her mother was referring only to Henry.

chapter
fifteen

When Adah wandered across the downstairs hall and into the kitchen through Lettie's sitting room, she was surprised to see Grace wiping off the counters. "A bit late to be cleanin' up after breakfast, jah?" she teased.

Grace nodded and kept cleaning.

"Is your Mamma around?" Adah asked, then noticed her granddaughter's peaked face. "Ach, girl . . . are you feelin' all right?"

"Just a little tired, I guess."

"Well, if you see her, tell her I'd like some help with a quilt top I've been puttin' off."

"Mamma's not here." Grace's lower lip trembled. "She's gone."

"Gone where?"

Grace stopped scrubbing and folded her dishrag. "Wish I knew."

Has Lettie taken one of her long walks? Adah wondered. "Come, sit . . . let's talk." She gestured to Grace.

They moved into the cozy sitting room. Grace sat on one of

153

the hard cane chairs, while Adah sank down into an upholstered one. The spacious square room was darker than the kitchen, which gave it a feeling of confidentiality. "Why do you say your mother's left?"

Grace inhaled slowly. "I saw her go."

Adah had known Lettie to traipse around outside after Judah was sleeping. Why would Grace think this was different from other nights?

"You saw her . . . just like other times—is that what ya mean?"

"No, I don't think you understand, Mammi. I saw her get into a car."

"Maybe you were dreamin', dear," suggested Adah.

"Honestly, I might've thought that, too . . . 'cept Mamma left me a good-bye note."

A note?

"Ach, we'd best slow down." Adah fanned herself with the white hankie she'd pulled from beneath her sleeve. "You have something from your Mamma in writing?"

Grace nodded, explaining also that she'd seen her mother running away from the house, carrying a large suitcase. "She went down toward Route 340."

This made not a whit of sense. *Lettie left?*

"I wish I'd imagined it," Grace said softly, her eyes moist.

"Has your father gone looking for her?"

"Jah. Adam and Joe said he left early this morning, even before takin' his turn with the newborn lambs. He didn't find her, though."

Adah had a dark, sinking feeling and leaned her head back against the wing of the chair for a moment.

"You all right?" Grace came to kneel beside her.

"The room's turnin' awful fast."

"You take it easy," Grace said. "I'll get some water."

Adah took several slow, deep breaths. "If I can just sit here quietlike . . ."

She fanned herself, trying to remain calm. Truth be told, Lettie's disappearance was the last thing she'd expected from this daughter.

The very last thing.

Grace hurried to get a glass from the cupboard, letting the water run. *I could get cooler water from the springhouse,* she thought. But no, her grandmother shouldn't be left alone. Not as dizzy as she was.

The pain and fright of early this morning came rushing back. Tears sprang to her eyes, and she leaned her head against the cupboard. She struggled to control her emotions, wanting to be strong for her grandmother, who was clearly as distraught as Grace herself.

Not willing to be gone for long, she wiped her eyes and dabbed at her wet cheeks with her apron hem. Taking a long breath, she carried the glass of water back to the sitting room.

Adah was relieved when Grace returned. Merely seeing her granddaughter again helped Adah regain her own composure, and she accepted the water. "Denki, Gracie."

"You feelin' a little better now, Mammi?" Grace asked once Adah had taken a few sips.

Adah finished a long drink, then said, "You're not to worry,

dear." She leaned forward to look in the direction of the kitchen but saw no one. "Where's your father now?"

"Must be out with Adam in the barn," Grace said softly, appearing very much as though she was trying not to cry again.

Adah reached out her hand. "Everything's going to be just fine, ya hear?" Grace came over and took her hand, regarding her with those tender eyes. Adah recalled having to help Lettie through the dreadful loss of Naomi. How difficult that had been to bear! "We'll be all right," she said again, assuring herself as much as her granddaughter.

Grace's lips parted, but she looked away, falling silent.

"What is it, dear?"

Shrugging, Grace hesitated at first. Then she knelt beside Adah's chair, her hands on the upholstered arm. "I wanted to share somethin' wonderful-*gut* with Mamma. Something important." Tears welled up in her eyes. "And now I can't."

"Aw, honey-girl." She was fairly certain Grace's news involved a serious beau, but she wouldn't think of assuming Lettie's rightful place as confidante. "Your Mamma will be delighted 'bout your news when she returns. Whatever 'tis."

Shaking her head, Grace wiped away her tears. "I don't want to foster unkind feelings toward her, Mammi. Never . . ."

"Of course not." The sound of the day clock in the kitchen, its pendulum ticking, was unmistakable in the quiet. Adah's heart was ever so heavy for Grace . . . and for her daughter, too. "I'm sure she'll return right quick."

After a time, with Grace's help, Adah got up from her chair. She made her way to Lettie's gas stove and set the teakettle on the burner. "Would ya like some tea?"

"No." Grace said she had work to catch up on. "If you'd like, I'll help finish your quilt top later, though."

Adah nodded. "That'd be mighty nice."

"All right, then." Grace headed for the arched doorway and out into the hallway.

Adah heard the front door open and close. *Poor, dear thing.*

Pushing her hankie back up her sleeve, she was nervous about Lettie's rash decision. More than anything, she hoped Lettie hadn't gotten a bee in her bonnet and let her curiosity overtake her. She'd been known to be an impulsive sort. But now Lettie was older . . . and a good deal wiser.

———— ··· ————

Moving through the morning like a swimmer in a pond, tangled up in willow roots, Grace longed to be free of the mental weights—the wearisome questions. All of them devoid of answers. She could not voice her concerns further to Dat or to Mammi Adah. She worked quickly, yet carefully, on the quilt with Mammi, glad her grandmother was also silent. Deep in thought, no doubt, as they sat together in the cozy third-floor sewing room on Mammi's side of the house.

Later, when it came time to put food on the table at noon, Grace carried the baked chicken and rice casserole from the counter. She placed it near Dat's spot, the way Mamma always served the hot dish.

After the blessing, Mandy spoke up about Mamma again. "It's not like her to disappear in the daylight, too," she said once they'd helped themselves to the large casserole.

"Sure ain't." Adam looked up, then back down at his plate.

Dat said nothing, his eyes vacant as he occupied himself with buttering his bread and salting his green beans.

It wasn't until close to dessert that Adam asked, "Haven't we all known Mamma wasn't herself lately?"

Joe and Mandy nodded. "Jah, like she's not feelin' so well," Joe suggested.

Adam turned toward Dat. "Could she be visitin' one of her sisters . . . for a bit of rest?"

Dat nodded slowly. "Might be."

"Did she say anything to you, Dat?" asked Mandy, her fork clinking on the plate as she set it down. "She would, wouldn't she? I mean, if she was goin' to go off visiting somewhere?"

"You'd think so." Joe glanced at Mandy while Adam's face grew more flushed by the second.

"None of us knows where Mamma is . . . or when she'll return," Grace intervened, studying first Adam and then Dat. She felt she must interject lest the talk get out of hand. No need to jump to conclusions.

"What should we tell our neighbors . . . our friends?" asked Mandy, her face knit into a tight frown. "With Preachin' being held here, everyone will know come Sunday . . . unless Mamma returns before then."

"I doubt she'll be back anytime soon," Dat surprised them by saying.

Grace gripped her fork. She'd assumed as much from the size of the suitcase Mamma had hauled up the road.

Dat continued. "Your mother wrote a note . . . to Grace."

Startled at having this dumped in her lap, Grace stiffened.

Mandy shook her head, as if uncomprehending. "Well, what did it say?"

Quickly, Grace replied, "Mamma didn't reveal where she was going or why . . . something 'bout not having the courage to leave if she talked with Dat . . . or us."

Grace saw her father's pained grimace.

Adam leaped up from his spot on the wooden bench, glaring at Dat. "Mamma didn't tell *you?*" He wore a fierce frown. "Why not?"

Their father shook his head.

"Was it 'cause she didn't think you'd listen?" Adam was red in the face now, his right foot planted on the bench as he bent forward.

Grace cringed, her feet curling tightly beneath the table.

"What'll we do without her?" Mandy sniffled.

"Oh, for pity's sake, Mandy," Adam said, raising his voice. "Ain't like you need takin' care of . . . or do ya?" He ran his hand through his thick shock of blond hair. "You're grown now. We all are."

Grace saw her opportunity. "Adam's right." She directed her comment to her sister. "Besides, this isn't the time to worry 'bout ourselves, jah?"

Dat set down his knife and fork and folded his hands as he would if he were ready for the final prayer. Yet they hadn't finished the main meal, let alone dessert. Leaning back in his chair, he slowly spoke in a low, measured tone, ignoring Adam's accusations. "Above all, we must pray for your mother's safety. That is what the Lord requires of us."

Mandy's face clearly registered her pain.

Dissatisfied with Dat's lack of response to Adam, Grace felt

only frustration with her father's suggestion that they commit Mamma into Providential care. She wanted to know when their mother was coming home, for goodness' sake!

When they were washing dishes—Mandy was drying and chattering anxiously about where Mamma might be—Grace merely listened to her sister, lost in thought. Had her father no opinion about what had transpired to make Mamma leave?

Throughout the meal, Grace had noticed how he'd often stopped to swallow before speaking. That and the unmistakable misery in his eyes combined to encourage Grace somewhat. In a peculiar sort of way, Dat's struggle gave her heart. *He's missing Mamma, just like the rest of us.*

She lifted the last plate out of the hot, soapy water and began scrubbing the large pots and pans, glad this chore was nearly done.

The minute the last pan was dried, Mandy flew out the door, not staying to help sweep the floor or gather up the trash. Secretly, though, Grace was pleased to be alone.

She went to get all the throw rugs on the first floor and lugged them out front, draping them over the porch railing. When they were lined up, she beat them with the broom. With each blow, she contemplated Henry's marriage proposal, his reticent manner even at this most joyful moment.

"*I'm fond of you,*" he'd told her.

Oh, how happy she'd been last night. Any thought of being passed over as a bride had vanished with his visit. And then, within hours, so much had changed. Now she pondered whether it wasn't best to talk to Henry about postponing the wedding, at least till Mamma could be present. Yet the wedding season was

some months away. Surely her mother would come to her senses before then. Grace could only hope for that, but the contents of the letter—and Dat's bleak outlook—made her wonder.

As for Adam, she was sure he hadn't meant to lose his temper at the table. *So unlike him.* The whole family was on edge, and no wonder.

Yearning for peace, she remembered Becky's hummingbird birthday card, drawn with such care. She dried her hands and ran upstairs to look at it once again.

Unfettered by the earth and its woes, hummingbirds fly free.

Upstairs, she was surprised to see Mamma's letter lying on her dresser. She sat down with it, anxious to read her mother's words yet again, searching each one for an answer.

—— ··· ——

The rhythmic sway of the train lulled Lettie into a more restful state than she'd experienced since first boarding. Closing her eyes, she attempted to block out the memory of Grace's cries on the road. *"Mamma, please . . . don't leave!"*

She shuddered. She'd refused her dear girl, of all horrid things. Grace would surely question everything Lettie had written in the hasty letter, based on her apparent rejection. And how unthinking she had been, failing to write in Grace's birthday card till Mandy had come waving it at her, all upset. To think she'd chosen to run off to the phone shanty to call for a driver instead of staying put at home, where she could have signed it.

What's come over me?

She dared to think of her husband; she hadn't even taken time to write a good-bye note to him. She'd simply run out of

time . . . and felt helpless to put her thoughts into words. Well, on paper anyway.

She pressed her book—a collection of favorite poems—close to her heart. She'd been ever so nervous about not having made a reservation ahead of time for the 1:52 PM departure for Pittsburg. How could she, without causing more of a ruckus than she already had? And dear Grace had seen her go—unthinkable!

I never wanted that.

Suddenly she felt lightheaded—she'd allowed herself only a few hours of sleep, then sat in the train station for hours, eating her sack lunch there, too, and reading from the poetry book. More than six hours of waiting in all—simply because she could never have slipped away with a suitcase in broad daylight.

Even now, rest was elusive. Weary from planning this day, Lettie offered a prayer for strength. *Help me, Lord, to do this difficult thing.*

She had a long trip ahead. Sighing, she opened the book to its flyleaf and read the inscription written so very long ago. *On your sixteenth birthday.*

She pressed her lips firmly together to keep them from trembling. To keep the tears in check.

Gently she placed her hand on the precious words: *To my dearest Lettie . . . with all my love, Samuel.*

chapter
sixteen

Heather detested the evening rush hour, but she made good use of her time while sitting in bumper-to-bumper traffic, typing out a text message and sending it to Devon's email address. He'd get it later, once he was released from the hospital.

Not hearing anything more from his buddy Don was both nerve-racking and reassuring. Heather hoped her fiancé would defy the viral infection and soon return to health once again.

As terrific as I feel . . . She was still baffled by her energy level and good appetite. Mom had always said you were healthy if you were hungry.

The traffic inched forward and she flicked on the radio to drown out her worry for Devon . . . and her own insidious apprehension.

She'd hung around longer than she'd planned after her exam and now it was close to five-thirty. No wonder she was parked here on I-64. She'd run into several classmates and had mentioned her plans to go north next week, instead of sticking around for the summer to finish her thesis, like most students in her program. Despite their pleas—"*Aw, stay with us . . . we'll*

do the beach and boardwalk scene"—she dug in her heels, not wavering.

She didn't have the heart to dampen their enthusiasm by dumping the terminally ill news on them. Who would believe it anyway? Heather was having a hard time buying the doctor's diagnosis herself.

When she finally arrived home, tired of fighting traffic, she called for her dad, on the off chance he'd come home early. She wandered through the house, looking for signs of life. But his bed was still unmade and the same socks were strewn on the floor near his bureau. "Weird," she said, going into the master bathroom and finding his shaving kit missing. *Must be on a business trip and forgot to tell me.*

If true, she was disturbed at the thought. Her father came and went quite a lot, but since she'd moved back home, he'd never before neglected to tell her about an overnight trip. After Mom had passed away, he'd poured himself into his work more than ever, keeping constantly preoccupied—his way of dealing with grief. Most of the time, the approach seemed to work for him.

Going into the den now, she noticed his executive-style desk looked the same as it had the other day, when she'd come searching for the Lancaster County brochures and stopped to admire her mother's picture.

She felt uneasy not knowing her dad's whereabouts and then realized she'd intended to do the same thing, taking off for Pennsylvania without letting him know.

At least I planned to leave a note!

"Am I that disconnected from my own dad?" she whispered.

Moe and Igor came padding into the room, both meowing.

She reached down and picked Moe up, holding him in front of her face and looking into his copper-colored eyes. "Have you seen Dad lately?"

Moe stared back.

"Okay . . . don't tell me." She laughed softly, yet inwardly, she sensed something amiss. But she had little time to finish studying for her last exam tomorrow, although she felt confident she was ready.

If Dad didn't show up in the next couple of days, she would call him, find out where he was holed up. Or send a text message, even though he disliked the whole idea of "reverting" to what he said was an archaic shorthand—*"too slow,"* he often joked with her, insisting she stick with a phone call. *"So nineties,"* she'd reply. At this, he'd roll his eyes and she'd pretend to be appalled until he let loose his infectious laughter.

Slipping into her dad's desk chair, Heather leaned back as she swiveled around in a full circle. She touched his lamp and the light came on—simple . . . easy—just the way he liked things. Mom's death had been much too complicated. It had really messed up everything about their lives.

But the final trip she and Mom had taken to Lancaster County had been effortless. Things had fallen into place so quickly, Mom had even remarked about it—how often did anyone acquire such perfect accommodations at the last minute? The day before they'd headed out by car, Mom had urged her to take along a nice dress and heels.

"We're going dancing?" Heather had joked, knowing better.

"We're going to celebrate us, and that's all I'll say." Her mother had been comically mysterious. Heather had played along, enjoying the fun.

Moe jumped up into her lap, interrupting her reminiscing. "Hey, you!" She stroked his neck and he stretched forward, leaning hard against her fingers. "I'll miss you . . . and Igor. You'll be good for the cat-sitter, right?"

Not responding with his usual meowsy reply, he snuggled close as she hugged him. She was glad she'd already made the call to the Lancaster naturopath. Getting in for an appointment would take nearly a full month, but she'd asked to be put on a waiting list. You never knew when someone might cancel.

———···———

After evening prayers, Grace caught Adam's sleeve before he headed to the stairs. "Let's go walkin' sometime tomorrow," she said.

"I'll have to see." He gave her a thoughtful smile. "You goin' to be all right?" he whispered.

She shrugged. "Honestly, I think someone should go and look for Mamma."

His eyes searched hers. "Remember what Dat said, though?"

"Jah." While she would indeed pray for Mamma's safety, she could hardly stand the thought of doing nothing else.

"Can we talk 'bout it tomorrow?" he asked.

"Sure . . . whenever you're free." She watched him hurry up the stairs, feeling renewed sadness at the thought of losing him to marriage. Not as depressing as losing Mamma's presence from home but a great loss all the same.

Yet tomorrow was a new day, as Mamma often said in an attempt to soften the blow of things gone awry.

Grace saw that Dat had gone outside instead of retiring for

the night like the rest of the family. She could only imagine the pain of rejection *he* must be feeling.

After today, everyone will know Mamma's gone.

In time, no doubt, the bishop would come to speak privately with Dat. Deacon Amos, too—all the ministerial brethren would converge here, as was their way.

Missing Mamma, she went to her parents' bedroom yet again and slid open the drawer where her mother's hankies were kept. The slight scent of her sachets wafted upward. She'd looked for Mamma's things earlier today, but just now she wanted to breathe in the faint scent left over from the plump pillows of potpourri her mother was so fond of. All of them gone, just like Mamma's personal items.

Turning to look around the room, Grace cried for the loneliness her mother must have experienced. What was in Mamma's mind and heart that made her believe she had to go away? The question plagued her as she turned toward the bookcase—Mamma's pride and joy, she'd always said of it—handmade by Dat not long after they'd become betrothed.

Bending down, she noticed a space where several books had stood. Mamma had often talked of her beloved poetry, though not recently. Grace could see that a few, perhaps two or three volumes, were missing.

She must've taken them along. Why? Were they more precious than her own children?

Grace dried her eyes and left for her room.

——— ··· ———

Unable to sleep, Adah sat up in bed, careful not to disturb Jakob. Dear man, he had not felt well all day. Truth be told,

neither had she. The whole house seemed to resound with Lettie's absence.

She couldn't help but wonder where her willful daughter was sleeping this night. Any number of places, she assumed. Lettie had as many Plain relatives as the rest of them. Enough to form an entire church district if all of the aunts, uncles, and first cousins were to assemble in one place. And dozens of second cousins were scattered out all over the country—some in Holmes and Wayne counties in Ohio, and a good many in Indiana, too. She wished she'd kept in touch with some of her own first cousins who might have a clue as to Lettie's whereabouts—*if* Lettie had indeed gone to visit one of them. Adah was not at all eager to get the rumor mill churning. But heavens, would it be stirred up, beginning tomorrow, when Lettie's sisters Mary Beth and Lavina arrived to help wash down walls and whatnot to get Judah's side of the house ready for worship this coming Sunday.

Didn't Lettie consider this? Adah knew she mustn't permit herself to fall into the snare of aggravation, which led too quickly to anger. *Let not the sun go down upon your wrath,* from Ephesians, was one of the first verses her own mother, Esther Mae, had taught her so many years ago.

Adah refused to let her daughter's foolishness dictate her emotions, no matter that she wished to goodness she hadn't been so awful harsh with Lettie down through the years. Or so insistent, back when.

——— ··· ———

Nighttime had always been the pits during her mom's excruciating disease, especially the final weeks. Even now, as Heather

brushed her teeth and prepared for bed, she had difficulty dismissing the memories of her own insomnia during that wretched time. Alarmed by her mom's steady decline, there were nights when Heather had wandered into the family room, only to find Mom reclining on the sectional, her legs stretched the full length of it, her head propped up. Always, she wore her pale pink fleece robe, even though the temperature in the house felt comfortable to everyone else. But Mom's circulation was poor, and she was continually chilly, particularly at night.

One evening, Heather had tucked her feet under her and sat up late, keeping her mother company long into the dark hours, trying not to think about the inevitable. In spite of her attempts to divert her mom's thoughts, somehow they managed to revisit the diagnosis—the ugly way it had slashed into their lives. *"My good life,"* Mom said, not in defiance but doing her best to embrace the reality of her cancer.

Heather had wanted to carry some of the suffering, thinking that if her mother's debilitating pain was so intense that it could seep over into her daughter's emotions, Heather just might be able to impart something positive in return. So she'd offered her optimism. They were like vessels spilling over onto each other—one draining herself of suffering, one filling the other's heart with hope. And so they'd passed those final fragile months.

Heather had memorized the words her mother had written in a "just because" card some weeks before her passing: *I've always felt so well loved by you, Heather. What a beautiful mother-daughter bond we've had. In so many ways, you've taught me how to love more fully . . . as a parent and as a friend. With love, Mom.*

Presently Heather pulled up the blanket, encouraging both

Moe and Igor to hop onto it. She smiled at them as their glowing eyes stared her down. "You guys are the best little pals ever," she said, turning out the light.

Tomorrow she hoped to hear again from Devon's buddy Don, anxious for an update. *Surely if he was worse, I would have heard.*

When she dreamed, both Devon and her mom were talking together, and she woke with a start, afraid the dream had some predictive meaning.

No . . . She groaned and reached to move Moe closer, until once again she fell asleep.

— ··· —

Lettie felt the sway of the train, the near-mesmerizing rhythm of the *clackety-clack* of wheels on the rails. She'd endured the stares of Englischers and the strong smell of cigarette smoke in Pittsburg upon disembarking. Thankfully, she had little trouble locating her second train. The connection in Pittsburg had been more nerve-racking than her boarding in Lancaster—so many more passengers. She'd found herself breathing a prayer when her fear began to rise, and somehow, she'd kept her wits.

Settling deeper into her coach seat, she exhaled, glad for the empty spot beside her on the train to Alliance, Ohio. Her head bobbed repeatedly until she eventually yielded to the sandpaper feel beneath her eyelids and fell asleep at last.

While she slept, she dreamed happily of bygone days—of gripping the softball bat in her youthful hands . . . swinging it hard and hearing the *crack* as the ball connected with the wood. That ball had sailed high over the girls' outhouse, sending the

boys jumping the fence. They were late for the clanging bell at the end of recess.

In her dream, she was a tomboy once again, just as she'd been right into her early teens. But that had changed after Samuel Graber's twinkling hazel eyes met hers during eighth grade, before graduation their final year at the Amish schoolhouse. Oh, how her heart had ached with longing when he looked her way and smiled across the one-room school. Samuel . . . her first true love.

When Lettie awakened, the train was pulling into the Alliance station, and she realized yet again just what she'd done to get this far. Looking at her watch, she saw that it was 1:30 AM. Most likely Judah would be up, spending time in the barn with his newborn lambs, a chore he hadn't asked her to share of late. She'd had her own responsibilities indoors.

Responsibilities I've left behind . . .

Her guilty conscience gnawed at her as she reached for her book and woolen shawl, gathering up the things she'd brought on board. All too soon, a time of reckoning would come.

chapter

seventeen

"Mamma *won't be back anytime soon*," Dat kept saying in the dream. Over and over the phrase was repeated till Grace awakened with a start. It was well after midnight, and she rose and reached for her robe at the foot of her bed.

Creeping down the steps and into the kitchen, she noticed the door was ajar, and peering out, she saw that the barn door was open, as well. Still feeling drowsy, she decided to take a look. In the past, they'd had lambs stolen—not by anyone among the People, she was sure, but newborn lambs had gone missing all the same.

Moving slowly across the backyard, she took in the night sky. Was Mamma looking at the moon and the sweep of stars tonight, too? Somewhere . . . wherever she'd run off to?

More than likely at this hour, her mother was fast asleep, and Grace wished she, too, might fall into a peaceful slumber. But a bitter root had taken hold in her, planted when Mamma did not turn to acknowledge her out on the road. She knew enough not to nurture it, to allow the memory to entangle her

heart. Even so, the knowing and the doing were two different things.

Surprised to hear her father's voice, tentative and low, coming from the barn, she went in search of him and caught her breath when she spotted his dim silhouette, there in the faint light of the moon. He stood near Willow, his hand stroking her long neck. "Things are in a terrible mess, old girl," he confessed. " 'Tis my fault . . . and there's no goin' back."

Grace had never known her father to express himself so openly to anyone. Yet there he was near beautiful Willow, pouring out his regret.

She stepped back against the gate. Would there be no end to her family's pain?

——— ··· ———

Hours later, Grace awakened in her bed, still mulling over what she'd witnessed in the barn. She wished the dawn away as she lay stretching in her bed—she possessed little courage for what was sure to be a difficult day ahead, what with two of Mamma's older sisters coming. Lavina and younger sister Mary Beth were expected to arrive after breakfast. They would surely wonder why everyone in the house looked to be in mourning. She was fearful, too, of their reaction—what would they think? Would Mamma be harshly judged?

In her mistiness, Grace dozed off again. When the alarm awakened her, she sat up and reached for the Good Book, turning to the Psalms. Mamma had always loved reading them. *"Scripture set to poetry,"* she liked to say.

Grace finished and marked her place, pondering her upcoming talk with Adam. She wondered what he would advise

about her engagement to Henry during such a time as this. Of course, by tomorrow the grapevine might already be rippling with the news of Mamma . . . so it wouldn't surprise her if it was Henry who decided to postpone their wedding, or even cut off their engagement. She truly hoped he would see fit to stand by her for as long as it took.

She leaned up on her elbows and peered into the dresser mirror. With Mamma gone, it somehow seemed all right to sit and stare at herself. So much had altered so quickly. She thought again of Dat speaking to Willow, of all peculiar things.

When Willow dies, many secrets will go with her, she thought as she got out of bed to brush her hair. She moved to the window, brush in hand, and raised up the blind. Looking out, she remembered the thrill of seeing Henry's light swirling on the windowpane just the night before last. Setting her brush on the windowsill, she leaned down and opened the window, then knelt there. Deeply, she breathed in the clean morning air. The faint scent of fresh beeswax wafted downwind from their beekeeping neighbors across the road.

She stayed on her knees till they ached. What had kept Mamma from saying she was leaving that night, here in the room where Grace had been so eager to listen? Instead, Mamma had written a puzzling letter . . . one that revealed so little.

She picked up her brush and finished counting the strokes, watching for a glimpse of a hummingbird just outside the window.

— ··· —

Judah moved slowly among his grazing sheep and the older lambs. Voices came from the road, and he looked to see two

of Lettie's sisters—Mary Beth and Lavina—coming this way from the Riehls' place. He surmised their driver had dropped them off after picking up Andy, who'd planned to visit an ailing brother at Lancaster General Hospital.

Hearing the women's animated chatter, Judah was certain they knew nothing of Lettie's sudden and mysterious departure. He could only imagine how quickly their lightheartedness might turn to shock, and he wished he might soften the wallop they were soon to receive. It made not a lick of sense, Lettie's going away. Especially not with all the new lambs coming on.

Lettie's sisters continued their prattle as they made the turn toward the driveway. They waved to Adam and Joe, hauling feed, and his sons waved back, glancing at each other as if concerned for what their mother's sisters were about to discover.

Watching the women make their way toward the house, Judah pushed his hands into his pockets. Steeling his resolve, he hurried across the pasture to the side yard.

From the kitchen window, Grace saw her aunts headed toward the door. She had been watching for them and was surprised to see Dat running across the walk, calling to her aunts. She heard him ask if he might speak with them "before you's head inside."

She was tempted to stay right there, but she went upstairs to overhear her father's explanation through the open hallway window.

Dat's tone was ever so solemn as he relayed the news, sparing them all but the most pertinent details. "I'm sorry to have to be the one to tell ya," he said finally.

"Well, what the world's wrong with Lettie?" *Aendi* Lavina whimpered softly.

"Is she just wore out, maybe?" asked Mary Beth.

"You'll go and find her, won't ya, Judah?" Lavina asked, sounding all out of sorts.

Grace had wondered that, too, and waited for Dat to continue, but it was Mary Beth who spoke next. "Our Lettie's just upset, ain't so? What else could it be?"

"Hard to know," Dat replied, ending the conversation with an awkward thanks for their help today. He turned and headed for the barn, leaving Mamma's sisters to stand on the stoop, blowing their noses and drying their eyes.

They were whispering to each other now. "You don't think Lettie's first beau has surfaced, do ya?" Lavina said—at least that's what Grace thought she heard.

What a wretched thing to say! She refused to think less than respectfully of Mamma. Surely no one threatened her devotion to Dat!

When she heard the kitchen door open, Grace hurried downstairs to meet them, plastering on a smile.

Aunt Mary Beth had on her rattiest old brown dress and apron, but her hair looked nice and clean, pulled back in the usual tight hair bun, her Kapp strings tied loosely in back. Aunt Lavina's dark brown hair was already coming free of its bun, stray strands falling on the sides as though she'd been in a hurry to put it up. She wore a maroon dress and faded black apron, her smile too broad for the news she'd just received.

"Denki for comin' to help redd up," Grace said, suddenly conscious of the lump that threatened her voice.

"Oh, we're mighty glad to . . . 'specially now." Mary Beth's eyes locked with Grace's. "Let's get started upstairs."

Grace nodded. "Mammi Adah will be over in short order; she'll lend a hand. So will Mandy."

"Jah, *gut* . . . the more, the merrier," said Lavina. She caught herself and said, "Ach, sorry."

Struggling to remain composed, Grace called for Mandy, who promptly came over from the other side of the house. "Time to fill the buckets with lots of warm, soapy water. We've got plenty of scrubbin' to do," she said as the aunts hugged and kissed Mandy more fondly than Grace had ever remembered.

Mandy's chin quivered when Mary Beth put her arm around her. "Now, honey-girl, you just remember how much your mamma loves you. Always has."

"And always will," added Lavina.

Mandy nodded tearfully. But her eyes asked the question they all were thinking: *Then why would she leave?*

Lavina took some old rags out of the cupboard. "We've got work to do."

Grace reached a hand to Mandy. "Mamma always said to work hard when things are troubling, ain't so?"

Mandy nodded and followed dutifully, dabbing at her nose with a hankie. And at that moment, Grace felt as if she'd wholly taken over her mother's place, uncomfortable though it was.

——— ... ———

Around ten-thirty, Grace and the other women stopped washing and sweeping and began cooking the noon meal. Earlier, Grace had laid out three pounds of lean ground beef to thaw—meat they'd purchased from the Stoltzfus cousins. She

planned to make porcupine meatballs using Mamma's pressure cooker. Mandy set to peeling potatoes, and Mary Beth and Lavina brought up canned vegetables—asparagus, corn, and beets—from the cold cellar.

Gut, thought Grace, wanting to provide a delicious dinner for her father and brothers. "Be sure and invite Dawdi and Mammi over to eat with us, too," Grace told Mandy. She'd kept a watchful eye on her sister all morning.

It helps to have Mamma's sisters here, she thought.

"We'll have us a feast," Mandy said, offering a brief smile at Grace, who began to shape the meatballs.

A dinner without our mother . . .

She wondered if Mamma was safe and sound. Everything felt so strange and out of whack without her. Grace supposed they'd feel this way for as long as Mamma was gone from them, however long that might be.

chapter
eighteen

Every decorative plate and each of Mamma's teacups and saucers had been washed and dried and put back in their exact locations on the sideboard and china hutch. The furniture was polished to a sheen, and overall the house was spotless . . . gleaming from the rafters down to the smallest corner. Their abode was well prepared to become the temporary house of worship on Sunday. Now all Grace needed were cold cuts and freshly baked bread to serve two hundred souls—that and the benches and the old hymnals the bench wagon would bring tomorrow evening.

Grace had been particularly grateful for the extra cleaning help earlier, and although presently it was a bit chilly outdoors, she pulled on a sweater and went to sit on the front porch swing. There, sitting where Mamma had sat three evenings ago, she waited for Adam to finish up his after-supper chores.

She could easily have gone to see Becky, but she wanted to talk with her brother first. Mandy was much too upset to attempt any sort of meaningful communication, on the verge of tears much of the time. Grace had offered understanding

to her sensitive sister—all of them had. It was hard to see Mandy cry.

All day Lavina and Mary Beth had carried their dread and disbelief in their eyes, the color nearly all washed out. Yet they'd worked as hard as they had every other time before Preaching service here. By now they would have surely whispered their worries to their husbands at home and possibly their older children, who, in turn, would tell others. Soon, all of Bird-in-Hand would hear of Lettie Byler's departure. And there was very little, if anything, Grace could do about it.

"Hullo there, sis."

She jumped, startled out of her reverie, and turned to see Adam draping his long arms over the porch railing.

"Ach, you must be ready, then?" She felt relieved to see him, knowing she could fully share her heart.

He nodded. "We'd better get goin' before I'm too tired to put one foot in front of the other. These nights of lambin' are catching up with me."

She rose and hurried down the porch steps to the lawn. "Where should we walk?"

He paused to deliberate, then suggested, "Let's take Sassy instead and go for a root beer."

"Sure, I'll forfeit the walk—for soda pop!"

Sassy was already hitched to the enclosed family buggy. Grace was glad Adam had thought to take that instead of his open courting buggy. She felt self-conscious just thinking about being seen out riding when the Amish grapevine might already be whispering about Mamma.

"So your hard work's finished, ain't?" he asked, referring to the thorough housecleaning.

"Sure feels *gut*, I'll say."

"And dinner was mighty tasty at noon, too." He let the reins lie loose on his knees. "You're nearly as *gut* a cook as—"

"Adam, don't say that," she broke in.

He frowned, shaking his head. "Honestly, I almost forgot Mamma was gone."

Naturally he would say that. He and Dat and Joe worked long hours outdoors this time of year, so Mamma's not being around wouldn't affect them as much as it did her and Mandy.

And Mammi Adah.

"Any idea where she might be?" Adam turned toward her, his straw hat tipped back.

"No." Grace shook her head. "This sort of thing doesn't happen amongst the People."

"And a mighty *gut* thing, too."

She wasn't about to divulge what Aunt Lavina had said to her sister. No point in that. Besides, it couldn't possibly be true—Mamma interested in an old beau?

"Dat's more than ferhoodled." Adam removed his hat and set it on his leg. "I've never seen him so confused." He explained that he'd had to rewrite some of the feeding charts today, erasing many of Dat's entries. "Ain't at all himself."

"I can't imagine what he's feelin'."

Adam shook his head. "Me neither."

The horse pulled the buggy into the drive-through at the fast food place, where they stopped and placed their order for a single root beer. "You want one straw?" Adam asked.

"I'd like my own, please," she said, smiling. Her brother must've momentarily thought they were going to share, like

he probably did with Priscilla. Like Grace did sometimes with Henry. "You're as ferhoodled as Dat."

He laughed, a light glinting in his blue eyes. "Fact is, we're all a mess, jah?"

She couldn't agree more.

When he handed her the frosty root beer, she took a long, slow drink. As they headed back, she soon began to shiver from the cold beverage. "I do hope *you'll* be happy when you're married, Adam," she said softly.

Happier than Mamma . . .

"And you, too." He smiled. "I'd best be fessin' up, Grace."

"Oh?"

"Well, your Henry told me he was comin' to visit the other night. He swore me to secrecy a few days before."

She listened, not sure what to say. Was Henry's and her courtship becoming common knowledge?

"So did he ask you?"

She nodded. "Jah, he did."

Adam stared at her. "And . . . ?"

She laughed at his eagerness. "I accepted, but now . . . with Mamma gone away and all, I wonder if we shouldn't hold off for a while."

"Aw, don't be takin' back your word, Gracie. What sort of girl does that?"

Sighing, she realized he hadn't understood. "I didn't say I was breakin' it off with him. Just that things are up in the air now."

"Jah, but do you think Mamma will be gone that long?"

"From what little he's said, Dat seems to think so."

Adam grimaced. "Still, I think you'll be all right with Henry," he said, his tone confident. "Let Dat and Mamma's problems stay put with them. You . . . me, we have our whole lives ahead of us, Gracie. And just think—our children will be closer than your average cousins. I mean, with you marrying Priscilla's brother and all. It'll be fun raisin' them together. Nearly like siblings, don't ya think?"

For once, he hadn't heard her heart. She wasn't talking about breaking her engagement, rather simply waiting till she was sure Mamma'd be there for the wedding. All Adam seemed to care about was their marrying siblings—and this fall, too—so that Adam's children with Priscilla would be close cousins to Henry's and her own.

Grace sighed inwardly. *I should've kept my thoughts to myself.*

——— ··· ———

Distracted during evening prayers later, Grace pondered her conversation with Adam. Because of his failure to understand her, she thought it best not to tell of her new idea brewing. Her mind was already in a whirl, flying back to the day of the barn raising—the day that had brought on so many changes.

Dat seemed lost in a haze, too busy with daily chores to actively search for their mother. Worse, he seemed resigned to her absence, hoping for the best but braced for the worst.

Hoping was far better, and in addition to her rote prayer, Grace whispered, *Please help us know what to do, Lord. Amen.*

Her idea came back to her: What if she could actually find Mamma—talk to her and convince her to return home?

At first the notion had struck her as silly. Other than horse

and buggy—or calling for a hired driver—she had no access to transportation. Her ongoing domestic responsibilities, indoors and out, presented another problem—it wouldn't be fair to leave when Dat was so shorthanded with the lambing.

Even so, Grace felt she ought to do something, small though it might be.

With how close Mamma and Aunt Naomi always were, I wonder if Uncle Ike knows anything. Or maybe I should start by finding out who Mamma went walking with that day of the barn raising.

Despite her sadness, Grace found a sense of anticipation, even hope in this. The woe-is-me pit of misery Mandy and Dat had fallen into was not for her. She would rise to the occasion and find their mother, bringing her home where she belonged. Thinking back to Aunt Lavina's comment, Grace decided to talk first with Mammi Adah. She had a feeling her grandmother knew more than she was saying.

Possibly a lot more.

—— ··· ——

Saturday morning Grace and Mandy, along with Mammi Adah, baked oodles of loaves of bread for the common meal tomorrow, to be served following Preaching. All the while, Grace did her best to be attentive to Mandy. Before she left, Mamma had suggested that Mandy would need extra prodding, but Grace couldn't see doing that now. Grace fully understood her sister's sorrow but didn't dare let their loss freeze up her own ability to think and feel. Especially not with so much to be done before the Lord's Day. They were also hosting the bi-monthly Singing tomorrow evening, which meant Dat and her brothers would sweep out the whole second level of the barn this afternoon.

Along with putting in her hours at Eli's store, Grace would now have to juggle doing all that Mamma had done, too. Monday's day of washing and ironing would be followed by Tuesday's mending and darning of socks, as well as finishing up any stray ironing. Dat and her brothers would need socks without holes in them for the upcoming sheepshearing day next week. The sheep's heavy coats required cutting before the summer, when they would shed much of the valuable wool. The sheep would also have their hooves clipped at the time of that all-day affair.

As for herself, the early morning hours next Wednesday would be spent weeding the family and charity vegetable gardens, as well as the long rows of berry bushes all along the rock wall out back. Thursday was the only weekday Grace might squeeze in time to go down to Bart, assuming her talk with Mammi didn't turn up enough to go on. She shuddered at the thought of asking questions about her mother, yet she would not shirk from it.

Has the grapevine found its way that far south?

Prior to making that trip, though, she first wanted to visit Uncle Ike Peachey. After all, Mamma had gone through all of Naomi's books and personal things, carrying home several poetry books, some of which were now missing. Grace had read from some of them, but she couldn't see why they were so highly cherished by her mother.

Do they have something to do with a first beau? She hated to even think the thought.

Perhaps now, since four years had passed since Aunt Naomi's death, her husband might be willing to give Grace something more to go on.

She sighed. Truly the biggest hurdle in all this was her daily chores. Next Friday she and Mandy would clean this big old house once again, and Saturday was another baking day. And next Sunday, although not a Preaching day, was a time set aside to rest, read, write letters, and go visiting relatives and friends— the latter something they usually did as a family.

Presently, Grace turned her attention to starting the noon meal while the many loaves of bread cooled. Mandy would have to wash and dry dishes on her own, since Grace was scheduled to work at Eli's this afternoon. How strange it would be to venture away from the house alone for the first time since rushing up the road after Mamma.

She glanced at Mandy, glad her sister would be sheltered here at home from the endless stream of questions. *For the time being.*

chapter
nineteen

The parking area at Eli's was filled with cars and Amish carriages alike. Suddenly wary, Grace smoothed her skirt and sat for a few seconds after they arrived, not budging.

Adam glanced at her kindly. "No matter what, Gracie, don't let the rumors sting you." He leaned forward, one hand holding both the driving lines connected to Sassy. "Mamma has a mind of her own—and what she's done, well, it's not what we'd do . . . not Dat, either." He looked away, glancing across the road to the east, then back. "So don't let the gossip hurt you is all I'm sayin'." He smiled, which gave her courage.

In the store, she signed in and set to work right away, holding her breath when Nancy and Sylvia Fisher—two Amish girls from her church district—looked her way. She responded in kind when Ruthie Weaver waved and smiled across the store at her.

Remember what Adam said, she reminded herself. His words had the power to both sting and cheer her. He hadn't bothered to listen to her heart yesterday when they'd talked, but she

wouldn't hold that against him, and she certainly didn't want to borrow trouble. They had more than enough of that already.

———···———

Grace was thankful Ruthie did not show her face that afternoon in the small room set aside for coffee breaks. She pressed the button on the water cooler, waiting while the paper cup filled. She then moved to the doorway to look out at the expanse of the store while she drank her water, its coldness seeping down inside her. She slipped away from the room while the other breaking employees talked a blue streak.

Strolling the back aisle of the store, she looked over the selection of herbs she'd recently inventoried. She knew which ones were reported to elevate the mood and was picking up a bottle of valerian root and a box of passion flower herb, thinking of her despairing sister, when Nancy Fisher slowly approached her.

Ach no . . . Grace groaned inwardly.

———···———

Adah turned her teacup around slowly, disturbed by the bewildering news Marian Riehl had shared. "It's beyond me, what you're sayin'," she told her neighbor.

"Jah, 'tis hard to believe." Marian stirred more sugar into her tea. "I'd like to think there's no truth in it, but . . ."

"Martin Puckett, you say?" Adah frowned, stunned. "Seems like an honorable man . . . and a driver lots of folk hire."

"We've called him, too."

Adah stared at her. "You say he took Lettie to the train station in the wee hours?"

"That's what I heard."

"And he sat right with her, waiting for her train for how long?"

"Hours, was what was said. And the man's been gone ever since, too."

Adah shook her head. "Puh! Doesn't sound right to me."

The sun broke through the clouds and shone through the kitchen window, glinting off the edge of the gas range. Marian turned and looked outside, so dramatic was the change in the room's light. "But Lettie *was* known to—"

"No, now, you listen here," Adah said. "Lettie's married to Judah and has been for a good, long time. *Married*, I say."

"Then why on earth would she leave him?" Marian's words hung in the air.

Why, indeed? Adah pursed her lips.

Their time of tea and cookies was cut short when Jakob wandered in, looking bright-eyed from his afternoon nap. Adah was so relieved she let out an immense sigh, which Marian must have noticed, because she quickly pushed back her chair and excused herself for home.

——— ··· ———

"Frankly, I hate to even whisper what I heard," Nancy Fisher was saying.

"Well then, you best not," Grace replied, the bottle of valerian root still gripped in her hand.

Nancy's round face drooped, her frown creasing her brow. "All I'm askin' is, can any of this be true?" She continued recounting the rumors.

Martin Puckett held my mother's hand at the train station?

"Oh, this is ever so awkward," Nancy said.

Grace could hold back her frustration no longer. "Awkward for you, Nancy? I have no idea where you heard any of this nonsense, but if I were you, I'd be careful 'bout repeating things that are false."

"Well, is your mamma at home or not?" Nancy paused. "Priscilla Stahl says she's left. And Martin Puckett's nowhere to be found!"

Adam's fiancée's talking like that about her future mother-in-law?

Without a further word, Grace headed for the front door. She needed some air, lest she become as dizzy as Mammi Adah had been earlier this week. The last thing she wanted was to be carried back to the coffee break room and stretched out on the small sofa, being fussed over.

—— ··· ——

"What on earth?" Jakob asked Adah while she carried the teacups and saucers to the sink. "Marian looked mighty befuddled."

"Well, I guess some folk have little to do but flap their tongues." She would not repeat what Marian had said she'd heard from Sadie Zook, whose Englischer cousin, Pete Bernhardt, had supposedly witnessed the distasteful scene.

Why was Lettie at the train station? Where'd she go, for pity's sake?

"Ain't becoming of Marian a'tall," he said, indicating he'd overheard at least part of their neighbor's accusation.

Adah nodded. The gossip their neighbor had relayed was downright malicious. The way Adah saw it, it was wise of her

to come over and get things straight from the horse's mouth, so such talk could be brought to a standstill. Except that Jakob had interrupted them before she'd had a chance to set Marian straight.

Lettie is quite respectable, she thought defiantly. *At least now she is!*

Even these many years past, Adah remembered all too clearly how Lettie's behavior as a youth had felt like a smack in the face—*her* face. How many times had she caught her daughter in the haymow with that one fellow? Sure, they'd merely sat out there talking and reading poetry to each other, of all strange things. But they couldn't seem to stay apart for more than a day or so, and he'd be right back with his books. Word had it Samuel Graber was already on his way out of the church even then. He'd ended up renouncing Amish ways soon after, when his family had pulled up roots and left for another state. Even so, while they were courting, Lettie had never smiled so much in her life.

Oh, but Adah was delighted when the whole lot of them moved away. The thought of Lettie's first beau made her blood pressure rise. Adah was better off not contemplating the no-good boy. She reached for the dish towel, the cloth loose in her hand as she stared out the window to the west, spotting Judah out there carrying one of his baby lambs. A right good man, tending his sheep with such care. She'd never regretted Lettie's marrying him. Jakob, too, had observed all those years ago how conscientious and steady Judah Byler was. *Still is.* The fact that he said very little didn't bother them much—not compared to Samuel, who was yakking nearly all the time.

Thinking again of the outlandish rumors, Adah felt disgusted

at the grapevine's speed and influence. *I'll march right over to Marian's tomorrow, after Preaching,* she decided. Someone had to put out the brush fire before it got to the ministers' ears.

But as she washed her delicate teacup, Adah couldn't help worrying that Lettie's reckless youth had caught up with her at last.

———···———

The pretty boardinghouse was set back from the road in a small hollow. Lettie made herself read in her comfortable room, looking up to take in the view of towering maple trees that grew in a haphazard zigzag behind the three-story house. The sky was the color of the sea.

She set the book aside and went to sit at the small writing desk and picked up the pen, feeling its smoothness between her fingers. With everything in her, she wished she could simply call Judah and let him know she was all right.

Still weary from her travels, Lettie was glad she wasn't in the habit of making such journeys. What a long trip she'd taken, arriving in the middle of the night in Alliance, Ohio. And she'd sat and waited a good while for the driver the innkeepers had arranged at her request. It was another nearly hour-long car ride before she'd observed yesterday morning's sunrise in the picturesque town of Kidron, where she had made a reservation at this charming inn.

She tore out a single page from her writing tablet and pressed her pen to the page. *My dear family,* she wrote.

Would they believe she truly thought of them as dear and always had? It pained her to consider what they must be feeling and thinking now. They all would know of her

disappearance, even her parents. She especially hated what it might do to them, frail as her father was. Even Mamm wasn't so strong now.

And Judah?

A large fist seemed to grip her heart. She could not write what she ought, no more than she had been able to say it to his face. Oh, she'd tried, but she hadn't the grit . . . nor, in the end, had he. Had it been better to spare him?

To think they'd bickered the night before her leaving. And what would it possibly accomplish now for Judah to read her explanation on a page? Wasn't the damage done?

She hadn't been able to open her heart to him, because any sharing felt like tossing words at a windmill. And, early on, given her despair over losing Samuel, she'd felt it best for Judah to be kept in the dark about her deep love for her first beau . . . and his for her. But being so detached from her own husband over the years had caused permanent harm to their marriage.

She crumpled up the stationery. This was not at all the right way to do things. She must simply wait and tell Judah to his face.

When I can help him fully understand, I will.

——— ... ———

Needing something to quench his thirst, Judah walked toward the house early Saturday evening. He was halfway across the backyard when he saw the bench wagon coming. Deacon Amos rode high at the reins but did not remove his hat, nor did he wave, as was his usual way. Today his face was austere as he climbed down and tied up his horse.

Judah reached back and massaged his neck, the burning pain growing more intense each hour. Seeing Amos's grandsons jump down and start the process of unloading the benches, he pushed down his hat and strode forward.

The deacon's bringing the bench wagon was no doubt intentional. *We'll have us a very different Lord's Day*, Judah thought, picking up one end of a long bench, which would also serve tomorrow as a tabletop. Adah, Grace, and Mandy had the food all lined up, Grace had told him, thanks to some help from Marian Riehl. He'd seen their kindly neighbor arrive earlier to visit with Adah and Jakob. *Could be she's gotten word about Lettie.*

Just now the air was stiff with undeclared inquiry. He was relieved when Adam and Joe came running out of the barn and pitched in to help. Soon, Grace and Mandy stepped outside, as well, wiping their hands on their aprons, having just finished up in the kitchen.

No one had yet spoken to him directly about the calamity that had befallen his household, but he sensed it coming now as Deacon Amos caught his eye, a severe frown on his sunburned face.

"After a bit, it'd be best if we moseyed out behind the barn," Amos said in a low voice.

He nodded. His wife had brought disgrace to the Byler name, and he'd have no choice but to own up to his own grim part in the quarrel. Surely that's all her departure was— Lettie's response to their unfinished argument. So many years of unspoken tension. She had done strange things before— hiding letters that came for her alone, for one.

She had behaved curiously about attending the barn

raising, too, he recalled. Someone—he didn't know who—had put a bug in her ear about taking food down there. That much he knew. When she'd first talked about wanting to go, she hadn't included Grace in the plans. It had been Judah who had insisted if she was going that far, she ought not be alone with Martin Puckett. It just didn't look right. Not that he didn't trust Lettie—of course he did. It was the appearance of evil that weighed on him . . . so he'd sent Grace out the door with her.

Now, though, it was clear Lettie shouldn't have gone at all. She'd returned moody and agitated, unable to lie still for a moment's rest. Unable, it seemed, to even remain at home. *Where she belongs.*

He set down his end of the heavy bench in the front room and followed meekly as Amos made his way out the door and down the front porch steps. Amos walked briskly around the side yard, then waited for him to catch up as they neared the barn.

"Do you know where Lettie is?" Amos had never been one to hem or haw. His eyes held Judah's, unrelenting.

"No."

"She's run off, then?"

"Might be."

"And you have no idea where to?"

Judah shook his head.

"All right, then . . . I must bring up the rumors that're flyin'."

Puzzled, he braced himself.

"One of the local drivers, Martin Puckett, was last seen in

Lancaster with your missus in the early mornin' hours this past Thursday. He also seems to have disappeared."

This was the first Judah had heard such a thing.

"Why do ya think Martin would accompany your wife somewhere, Judah?" Amos's slightly sunken gray eyes looked increasingly weary as he spoke, as if he hadn't slept much.

Truth was, Martin was one of the men Lettie felt most comfortable with driving her—Judah felt the same way. In his opinion, Martin was a fine man. And his Lettie had never given him any reason to doubt her fidelity.

"You'd have to ask Martin 'bout this," Judah replied.

Amos glared. "You ain't much help."

"Well, I know nothing 'bout it."

"Surely you realize that Lettie's rebellion is an outward show of disobedience to you, her husband, as well as to her parents, who raised her to be a God-fearing woman. We'll investigate this further." Amos turned away.

Judah matched the deacon's pace. He noticed Andy Riehl's horses out grazing, several of them standing head to tail.

"The ministerial brethren will be lookin' to me for a report of our discussion," Amos added.

"Do as you must," Judah said, uncertain why Amos seemed bent on trying to put the fear of God in him.

"Preacher Smucker will seek you out tomorrow, followin' the common meal."

Nodding, Judah said that was just fine. In all truth, he'd much prefer talking things over with Josiah, the younger of their two preachers, if he was to own up to his fault in the matter. No sense putting off that confession. Some ministers in other districts could be downright domineering, even

specifying how often the marital bed was to be used for the purpose of procreation—but neither of their preachers was that outspoken. Still, Judah knew he had some personal fessing up to do.

chapter

twenty

Grace stood beside her grandparents' front room window, watching two squirrels give chase. They pattered across the front walk, up the steps, and over to the porch swing. Anymore, each time she looked at the swing, she thought of Mamma.

"What's on your mind?" her grandmother asked from her chair behind Grace.

Turning, she went to sit next to Mammi Adah, watching the tatting hook fairly fly across the border of a pretty yellow hankie. Her own birthday handkerchief had not been used at all since the wonderful supper Mamma had cooked. Grace had nearly forgotten about it and her other gifts. Nearly everything had stopped when her mother had gone away.

"I heard some awful things today," Grace whispered.

A softness came over her grandmother's wrinkled face. "I think I might've heard some of that, too."

"Well, it ain't true . . . is it? Mamma'd never do such a thing." Something powerful rose up in Grace. "I'm goin' to go and talk to Dat's cousins, the Stoltzfuses, down south."

"Ach, why?"

"Because surely one of them knows who all was there for the March barn raising."

Mammi's face fell.

"There was a woman I'd never seen before."

"Why, sure . . . a *gut* many folk, I 'spect." Mammi's voice sounded strained.

"Jah, but this woman seemed to know Mamma. She went off walkin' with her."

Mammi's tatting hook hung loose in her hand as she took that in for a moment. Then she asked, "Do ya recall what she looked like?"

"Not sure I can describe her, really. Her Kapp was altogether different from any around here, so I figured she was from elsewhere, but I don't know for sure." She sighed. "Frankly, I don't know at all."

"And that's why you want to see your father's cousins?"

Grace wondered why Mammi Adah was so full of questions. "Ach, you should've seen Mamma jump up during the noon meal to go to her."

"So ya think there might be a connection 'tween that day—and the strange woman—and your mother's leaving?"

"Sure seems like it." She hadn't meant to sound wavering, but she hadn't expected her grandmother to take such a disbelieving tone.

"Oh, Grace, I hate to dampen your spirits, but I just don't see how that can be."

"Well, I want to find Mamma."

"Why, of course you do . . . we *all* do."

Her grandmother's petite features and light hair made her look nearly angelic. Or at least like some of the delicate pictures

of angels Grace had seen in one of the poetry books Mamma had brought home from Aunt Naomi's bookshelf. One of the missing books, in fact.

Grace scratched her head through her Kapp. "You must not think it's a *gut* idea, then?"

"I'm saying we ought to leave your Mamma be" came the surprising response.

"Maybe she just needs rest, jah?" Grace suggested. After all, Mammi Adah should know Mamma best . . . aside from Dat.

"Well, she doesn't need you or anyone beggin' her to come home, I daresay."

Grace was astonished. "So ya think she'll return on her own?"

"Perhaps . . . when she's ready."

Fear pricked her chest, making it suddenly tight . . . so tight Grace thought she might not be able to draw her next breath. *What exactly does Mammi Adah know?*

Once Grace left, Adah went straight to the kitchen. She stood at the sink and ran cold water over her wrists, hoping to slow her pulse. Why should Grace, or anyone, go looking for Lettie? Wasn't there too much to be done here? And wouldn't Grace risk losing her job at Eli's?

The coolness soothed her as she leaned against the sink, staring out at the two-story barn beyond the yard. Ever so slowly, she began to feel calmer. No, all the work here was not the biggest argument against Grace's searching for Lettie. Not at all.

She wiped her hands on a small towel, then patted her face, as well. Calling for Jakob, she made her way upstairs to find

her husband reading the Sugarcreek-based paper, *The Budget.* "We might have us a problem," she said, recounting Grace's earlier announcement.

"Well, she's Lettie's daughter, so there's no stoppin' her." Jakob looked up with worried eyes.

She sat in the chair next to him, wishing Lettie had just stayed put. This was more than a mere complication. "We need to discourage Grace somehow."

"Jah." He closed the paper and folded it in half. "No tellin' what poor Gracie might discover out there."

She gasped. "So you must think Lettie's gone back to Ohio?"

"We live life as though it matters, jah?" he said mildly. "And since we believe it does matter . . . then in Lettie's mind *all* of it must count for something."

She understood perfectly. And it was precisely what she feared . . . that Lettie was suddenly determined to undo her past. "Do ya think she's goin' to make things right, once and for all?"

"What other explanation is there?" he asked, his chest rising and falling rapidly.

She hadn't known until now how much she looked to Jakob for his opinion. How much she depended on his levelheaded point of view . . . his cautious yet deliberate manner. If only she'd paid more attention to his advice on handling Lettie's teenage whims.

Given the chance, Adah realized she'd go back and do everything differently. Just as she feared Lettie had now decided to do.

Lord, help her!

— ⋯ —

Grace headed outside to see how many more dozens of hymnals were yet to be unloaded. Deep in thought, she inadvertently brushed against Mandy, not seeing her.

"Ach, Gracie?"

She turned.

"You ain't ignorin' me, are ya?" Mandy's face scrunched up.

"Sorry, sister." She touched Mandy's arm. "You all right?"

"Truthfully, I've never . . ."

"Aw, Mandy." She led her around to the front porch. "Let's sit awhile."

Mandy chose Mamma's spot on the porch swing, and Grace sat across from her in the wicker chair, Mammi Adah's favorite. "Now, tell me, what's a-matter?"

"What *isn't*?" Mandy muttered, not looking at her. "Things are even worse than I feared. It's all over the place that Mamma has run off with another man."

Grace folded her arms tightly. "You can't believe everything you hear," she said. "We have to cling to what we know, Mandy. Remember that."

"But nearly everyone's sayin' it."

"Well, *we* aren't. . . . We know it has to be a lie."

"Then where is she?"

"Time will tell that." Grace shifted her position, not wanting to reveal her desire to find Mamma and bring her home. "Meanwhile, we've a lot to do round here. Adam and Joe could use some help deworming the sheep next week, for one."

"I hate helpin' with that." Mandy got up and sat on the railing. "And the sheep hate it, too."

Grace subdued a smile. She had seen Dat and Adam—Joe, too—firmly holding the sheep as they fought having the syringe stuck in their mouths. The sheep bore no love for shearing, either. Some of them nearly fainted during the process, and Dat kept water in a bucket close by to revive them if they did.

Always before, Mamma had assisted with the lambing. Every year, as far back as she could remember, Mamma had taken her turn at night, checking to make sure the wee ones were nursing frequently. Despite some rough patches, she and Dat had always made an attempt to demonstrate their silent unity in that and other things—at least up until last month.

It seemed her sister needed continual reminders that life must move ahead with or without Mamma, for as long as that might be.

"There's lots more work . . . with Mamma absent," Mandy said glumly.

"Well, and we all have to pull our share," Grace replied.

"Sure doesn't seem fair, does it?"

"Sometimes life just isn't."

"You'd think Mamma would send word. Tell us she's all right." Mandy's voice was muffled.

"We'll just keep praying for her safety. Something's troubling her, that's certain."

The floodgates opened, and Mandy bowed low into her hands, sobbing like her heart had broken into more pieces than could ever be mended.

Grace rushed to her side and rubbed her back like Mamma would have. And Mandy reached for Grace's hand and held on for dear life.

— ··· —

When Becky came over to lend a hand with the setup for Preaching, Grace suddenly felt tense, worried she'd come to discuss Mamma's absence. But her friend surprised her by simply carrying in hymnals from the bench wagon. She also brought word that her mother was getting some additional help with baking pies for the common meal tomorrow.

"This'll be *gut*," she told Becky as they placed the hymnals on the end of the wooden benches, along the center aisle.

"Well, we want to help." Becky's eyes were moist. "Trust me, we do."

Grace gave her friend a quick hug and whispered, "Denki . . . ever so much."

——— ··· ———

"Pocketful of Sunshine" began playing on her iPhone, and Heather reached to see who'd sent her an email. "Don!" she shouted.

Unsure what to think, she opened the update from halfway around the world. It looked from Don's email like Devon was back on his feet and should be returning to the base soon. *I'm sure he'll be in touch*, he concluded.

"And Dad thinks this is all so primitive," she scoffed, wondering again where her father was.

Her thumbs flew over the surface of the digital keypad as she typed back a swift response. *Thanks. Great to hear it!*

The phone beeped and it was her dad. "Where've you been?" she answered.

He was laughing . . . really laughing, like she hadn't heard for a while. "You'll never believe this," he said.

"Um . . . what?"

"I just bought some land in the middle of Amish country. How weird is that?"

She nearly shrieked. "You what?!"

"You heard me." He was still laughing, and it made her smile.

"Well, where?" There were numerous Plain communities around the country.

"Just north of Bird-in-Hand. You must see it sometime," he said. "I'm in Lancaster County now—remember all the summers here?"

"Hey, cool, Dad." This was just too coincidental. She couldn't believe it. "So you bought land for what?"

"I don't know—I'll have a hobby farm or plant vegetables."

"Dad . . ."

"I'm serious."

"So, you're moving there?"

"First I have to put a house on it." He mentioned using some of the proceeds from Mom's life insurance policy. "Of course, I could sign the land over to you, Heather . . . for your wedding dowry." He chuckled into the phone. "Like the Amish."

She laughed at the thought. *Dad and his crazy ideas . . .*

"I'll be home in a few days."

And I'll be leaving. . . .

She was still surprised he was calling from Pennsylvania. "Uh, Dad?" Should she tell him she was heading there, too?

"Look, honey, I've got to run. We'll talk again soon."

"Okay. See ya." She found this all so amazing. *Wow, to think we're on the same wavelength for the first time. How weird is this?*

Wondering if Don was still at his computer, she sent him another message: *So terrific hearing from you! You guys be safe.*

Hoping for more, she carried her phone around for the rest of the evening. But she heard nothing further as she added another few pages to her thesis.

— ··· —

Judah spent a good part of Saturday night looking in on his lambs. He'd given Adam and Joe the night off—they needed to catch up on sleep. And it wasn't fair to ask Grace and Mandy to help outside, since they'd done so much to get the house and barn ready for tomorrow's Preaching.

It was his responsibility to make sure this brand-new set of twins survived and were not rejected by their mother— although he was seeing signs of that already. At least one of the newborns might have to be adopted by another ewe, which meant even more hands-on work. He was willing and able to do it, but the prospect of the continuing lack of sleep was daunting right now.

Recalling Lettie's restlessness, he wondered if her exhaustion had been part of the reason for her depression. Judah let out his air in one long breath. It was impossible to know what had been on her mind. He rubbed his sore neck, thinking back to the evening before his wife had left.

"I want you to hear this from me," she'd said, eyes intent on him.

Hear what? That she loved someone else?

Impossible, he thought. A desperate lump of regret churned in his gut, devouring him.

"Was it 'cause she didn't think you'd listen?" Adam had boldly asked at the table, in the hearing of his brother and sisters.

And none of them, not even Grace or Mandy, had defended their father.

What if he *had* stayed to hear her out? Would Lettie still be here? He shook his head. *I can't change the past.* The thought gave him no consolation, and he was consumed with worry for his troubled wife, out there alone somewhere in the modern and wicked world.

He hoped, if nothing else, she was getting some rest at last. Sleep, and the Lord's watch care, might just work wonders.

Long after the newborn lambs had finished nursing, Judah remained there in the hay, soon limp with sleep.

——— ··· ———

Andy Riehl's rooster crowed and awakened Judah with a start. It was the Lord's Day, and he rose, shaking the straw off, aware again of the shooting pain in his upper back and neck. But he couldn't let it slow him down; he must begin a flurry of chores, just as on a weekday.

He made haste to the house and got Adam and Joe up and going. He didn't need to prompt Grace, who would be rising soon to start breakfast, rousing Mandy once the meal was underway. His younger daughter wasn't much for rising early. He remembered once smiling with Lettie about that.

He wondered if his wife was up and dressing for Preaching, wherever she was staying. He opened the pasture gate and let the sheep out to graze, watching the mighty frisky baby lambs bob after their mothers. The smallest ones worried him most. Keeping them alive was sometimes a chore and a half.

Adam and Joe came downstairs quickly, no dillydallying. The Lord had given him some mighty fine sons and daughters.

A good thing, too, because there was much work to be done. He expected a good forty or so lambs this spring, assuming they all survived.

He glanced at Adam and Joe as they headed to the sheep barn. They'd need to freshen the straw for the new mothers-to-be. He hoped none of the ewes would go into labor today, with church being held here.

There was the not-so-small matter of Preacher Josiah Smucker, too. Anticipating the coming confrontation drained him, and he hoped whatever Josiah had to say wouldn't take up too much time. Truth was, Judah had neither knowledge nor time to spare. He thought of calling Martin Puckett tomorrow to see if he'd drive him over to the blacksmith shop first thing—although word had it Martin had disappeared the same day Lettie had. All that hearsay seemed out-and-out strange. Martin and Lettie?

He would not allow the ridiculous murmurings to cloud his judgment. Lettie—and Martin, too—were surely innocent of any wrongdoing. Might be a good thing to let the unsuspecting fellow know what was being said about him.

Reaching for his hayfork, Judah shook his head. *Des hot ken Verschtand!*—*This is absurd!* He wondered if Lettie had any idea what a hornet's nest her departure had stirred.

chapter
twenty-one

Sometimes innocent things done in a spirit of kindness—even out of intended care—came back to bite you. Martin pondered this on the drive to the church where he and Janet had attended all their married life. He'd gone to this church even longer, having joined at seventeen. *Nearly an eon ago.*

Keeping his hands at ten and two o'clock on the steering wheel, he wondered if something was up with his Amish regulars. Despite his having been out of town for several days, he had returned to find not a single message requesting transportation from any of the Bird-in-Hand folk. Even those who called from farther to the west—Intercourse—and to the north, from Stumptown, had not contacted him since last Thursday.

He thought again of Lettie Byler . . . and of Pete Bernhardt's standoffishness at Penn Station. Had Pete anything to do with the major drop-off in business? Martin certainly hoped not.

Pulling into the church parking lot, he spotted Victor Murray, one of their longtime ushers, and waved. He got out and hurried around to open Janet's car door.

If Martin didn't hear something soon from either Andy Riehl or Judah Byler himself, he'd have to wander over there and make small talk. The silence was not only disconcerting but utterly deafening.

———···———

Judah hung back a ways from the house, fanning himself with his straw hat. From the backyard, he observed Adam and Joe, along with their boy cousins, greeting the People as they pulled into the driveway in their buggies. Adam had designated certain lads to help unhitch horses and lead them to the barn for water.

Judah was mighty pleased at the efficient assembly line before him, considering what his sons were going through. Folk looked right through to your heart at a time like this, and Judah himself was ready to have the day over and done with. He reached back to rub his neck; the pain was nearly unbearable now.

Here came Josiah, waving him down. "Mind if we have a word, Judah?" The preacher had caught him off guard in the yard where the menfolk lined up to file into the house for the Lord's Day gathering.

"Jah, fine." He followed the younger man out to the barn. It was important to demonstrate a willing spirit, even though he was already becoming weary of the questions. No matter how many were asked, none could bring Lettie back.

They walked to the sheep side of the barn and Preacher Josiah asked to see the newest set of twin lambs. A Scripture verse came to mind, one Judah had read so many times he'd committed it to memory without even trying. *They that wait*

upon the Lord shall renew their strength . . . they shall run, and not be weary.

Judah felt tense as the preacher made small talk about the weather for longer than necessary. Unlike the deacon, Josiah had never been one to leap into a particular topic but rather preferred to wander around to it. So, biding his time, Judah remained patient as they walked toward the pasture.

Judah noticed the last few horses were being unhitched, back in the driveway. Most of the membership had arrived, and he wondered if the preacher might be setting him up as an example. *Hard to imagine that of Preacher Josiah, though.*

He kept up with the preacher's long stride, and finally Josiah got to the point. "Your wife's been absent from Preaching off and on since March," he began.

"Jah, twice."

"For health reasons, would ya say?"

The hair on Judah's arms prickled. "She never said."

The morning sun cast a wan light over the grazing sheep. Kindly, the minister placed a hand on Judah's shoulder. "I take it Lettie didn't say she was leavin'?"

Judah shook his head.

Preacher Smucker looked down at his feet, shifted them, and removed his straw hat. "Well, I don't mean to put you on the spot. You've heard the rumors 'bout Lettie and another man." His voice was quiet. "Would you know of any reason for your wife to go away?"

Judah resisted the question. Up until now, he'd refused to consider the possibility. But what if the rumors were true?

He recalled how affectionate he had been with Lettie early

on in their marriage, like any young couple. Those days of passion had produced four healthy children.

He glanced toward the house, bustling with activity as the crowd swelled. Drawing a long breath, he removed his hat, holding it in front of him. "I've been remiss as to my wife," he confessed. "Not as attentive as I should be . . . confidentially speaking."

A slow frown gathered on Preacher's brow. "Husbands are not to deprive their wives, and vice versa—except, as the Scripture says, to 'give yourselves to fasting and prayer.' "

Judah bristled. In his defense, he might have mentioned that raising sheep took every ounce of his energy—had for years. He was no longer a young buck. Sure, he could offer any number of legitimate excuses, but none would hold up in Josiah's eyes.

Nor the Lord's.

"I can assure you, Lettie's not the sort to stray" was all he could manage to say.

"I see." The preacher straightened. "If what you say is true, then surely she'll return. And we'll discuss this further at that time, if need be."

Josiah extended his hand and Judah shook it.

Preacher raised his hat to his head and set it down on his thinning hair. "I won't be speakin' with the brethren on this," he said, his gaze fixed on Judah.

Judah's throat felt as dry as dust, his mouth too parched to speak. He nodded his appreciation, then watched the kindly minister hurry back toward the house.

Running his fingers over the edge of his hat, he felt the

relief of having come clean, his transgression laid bare before the man of God.

Judah put on his hat and headed to the barn to check on his expectant ewes once more before the start of Preaching.

Grace saw her father walking back from the barn, his shoulders visibly slumped. She'd noticed Preacher Smucker strolling with him earlier, though the man had returned to the other ministerial brethren some minutes ago, ready to get church underway.

He's heard about Mamma. She swallowed hard. *Has everyone?*

She saw Henry arriving with his family, and when he looked her way, he smiled faintly and gave a quick, discreet nod of the head. There was no way to tell from his cautious gestures if he was upset at the news swirling about Mamma's disappearance, since Henry had always been prudent in his greeting at Preaching services. Even at Singings, he was subdued.

Will he want to marry into the Byler family now?

It would certainly make an upstanding young man think twice, she guessed. She had better dismiss the niggling thought, or her ability to pay close attention today would be out the window.

Glancing over her shoulder, Grace saw Henry line up to enter, his face hidden from view.

———— ··· ————

Heather spent Sunday morning sleeping in, vaguely aware of her dad's arrival sometime after midnight. The garage door's

rumble had awakened her momentarily, but she'd fallen back into slumber.

She dreamed of a long weekend with her mother in Amish country, and in the dream Mom, completely well again, was pointing out some beautiful blossoming pink and yellow plants. There was the sound of water trickling, lending a peace to their surroundings. All was well . . . Heather and her mother were relaxed and happy, together once again.

When she awakened, Heather wondered if the dream was confirmation she was doing the right thing by returning to Pennsylvania to get well.

Later, at breakfast, which was late enough to be brunch, she sat with her dad, watching him eat his usual sugar-laden cereal, with a small dish of applesauce—cinnamon sprinkled on top. "The works," he said, wearing navy sweats, his dark hair rumpled. He took a sip of his coffee and set it down next to his OJ. "Feels great to be home."

"I was beginning to think you'd gone on a never-ending trip." She leaned forward, blowing on her coffee. "Sounds like you succumbed to an impulse purchase."

His sleepy eyes shone as he described the parcel of land, which the former owners had reluctantly carved from their larger acreage. "They were in need of emergency cash, and they sold as little as they could—only four acres. I guess back there, that's really too small for a farmer to do much with."

"So what are *you* going to do with it?" She ran her fingers through her hair, still damp from her shower. "Are you serious about a hobby farm?"

He smiled, radiating confidence. "I'm leaning more toward

growing potatoes. You might be surprised at how much fun it could be. I think you'd like it, too."

"I have a phobia about dirt under my fingernails and multi-legged creatures that fly, don't forget."

"Well, *I'm* ready for the next chapter in my life. I've had it with the corporate fast track, for one, and besides . . ." Here, he paused for so long she wondered if he'd forgotten what was on his mind. "Your mother was crazy about that area. She told me countless times she wanted to retire there someday."

She agreed. "Obsessed with the place, yeah . . ."

"I'll start building a house in a while." His face was alight with the possibility. "Will you help come up with a plan for a small, old-style farmhouse? The kind of house unique to the back roads?" He paused, a faraway look in his eyes. "Doesn't make sense to build something contemporary in Amish country, does it?"

"Sure, I'll help you design it." Heather got up for more coffee. If she stayed sitting, she might easily cry. That would never do, not today. Nope, for the first time since Mom's passing, Dad's sights were set on the future, and no way would she interfere with that.

———— ... ————

Grace appreciated all the help from the womenfolk during and after the common meal. Marian Riehl, along with Aunts Lavina and Mary Beth, acted as self-appointed shadows.

Opening the side door to the kitchen, Grace propped it wide with the doorstop. Several blossoming lilac bushes she

and Mamma had planted years before gave the air a delightful sweetness.

She glanced down at the springhouse and saw Yonnie Bontrager talking with Becky. It was a little odd to see them together in such seclusion, but who could resist Yonnie's contagious laughter and merry spirit?

Looking away to give them privacy, she noticed Henry out near the woodshed with several other young fellows. And surely plenty of gossip was spreading now that everyone had seen for themselves that Mamma was nowhere around.

There was much left to do to clean up after the big meal, what with a record attendance this Lord's Day. Uncanny, really. The sadness—even disbelief—of nearly every woman present had been overwhelmingly apparent.

Returning to the kitchen to help wipe down the tabletops, each comprised of several benches, Grace was relieved to see Mammi Adah talking with Deacon Amos's mother. She and Dawdi Jakob both seemed quieter than usual, sitting at the table with the eldest of the group, finishing up their slices of snitz. Becky, her mother, and many of their extended family had baked many pies for the occasion, and Grace went over to offer her thanks.

One of the kindest neighbors ever.

She finished drying off the tables, except where the older folk still lingered, and was just returning to the sink when Becky came up behind her, face beaming.

Becky tugged on her sleeve gently. "Come! I must talk to ya." Her friend led her outside and down the driveway a bit, past the front porch and the mailbox. Grace would check it again tomorrow for word from Mamma.

"Ach, can ya keep a secret?" Becky's big eyes twinkled her joy.

"Well, don't you look awful pleased this Lord's Day," Grace said.

Becky gripped her hand, pulling her closer. "Yonnie's close to decidin' who he'll court."

"He told you this outright?" Grace thought it presumptuous.

Becky laughed and shook her head. "That's just his way. Truth is, I have a feelin' I just might be one of the girls he's considerin'. Oh, Gracie—can it be?"

"Well, you know what I think already."

"But not what *Yonnie* thinks."

Grace laughed. "I say you'll be surprised when he makes his choice. You wait and see if I'm not right."

"You're a peach." Becky kissed her cheek. Then quickly her expression changed to concern. "Ach, I shouldn't be goin' on so . . . not with you—"

"Now, don't even mention it. I'm awful happy for ya, honest."

"You goin' to be all right?" Becky asked, her eyes solemn.

"Why, sure." Grace remembered something. "Becky, can you come up to my room real quick?" They hurried back to the house and up the stairs to Grace's room. She showed her the case of colored pencils. "Remember these?"

"Jah. And goodness, they're just beautiful. . . ." Becky lifted out the pale blue pencil and held it in her hand.

"I want you to have them."

"Oh, Gracie—are ya sure? They were *your* birthday gift, after all."

Nodding, Grace gave her the case. "Make more pictures of hummingbirds, if you want to. I'd love that."

Becky smiled, eyes blinking. "I can hardly believe this. Denki!" She gave Grace a quick hug.

"Might be best not to tell the Spangler girls, ya know."

"I'll keep mum, not to worry." Becky eyed her. "You *sure* you'll be all right?"

"I live each day as it comes." Grace wanted to be strong. "But it's just like you to be so caring."

An hour later, after Becky had run off to find her family and head home, Grace realized she'd forgotten to tell her friend her own good news.

She smiled at Yonnie's unique—even peculiar—approach to finding a life mate. Curious as it seemed to some, there was something to be said for taking one's time in the matter. *For sure and for certain, he'll make Becky mighty happy.*

———···———

Heather leaned close to the laptop screen, trying to make sense of what she was reading. She gathered her hair in a high ponytail and sighed. "So Devon *wasn't* really sick."

She should've suspected something like this. Deep in her psyche, hadn't she feared this very thing? She read the email again, shaking her head repeatedly.

How could I have been such an idiot?

Reliving even their slightest disagreements now, she could not come up with a single issue that would have pointed to this. Why had she been so naïve, trusting him with her feelings? How could she have so completely missed who Devon Powers was?

Obviously, he wasn't the man of her dreams after all. In the blink of an eye, he'd found someone new—*someone from my unit. We didn't plan this—it just happened. It's unbelievable how much we have in common,* he wrote.

"Yeah, I'll bet!" She wanted to throw something. "So now I'm chopped sushi?"

She wanted to leap through the computer screen. "This is what I get for being loyal?"

I really hate to hit you with this, but face it, Heather . . . I'm halfway around the world, and we haven't seen each other in months. It's not like your life will change. He signed off with nothing more than his name.

She closed her laptop. "You can have your soldier girl," she whispered.

She'd heard enough sob stories from her sorority sisters to know this was how things went for some people—a never-ending rotation of new relationships and breakups. For some, it was actually the thrill of starting up a relationship that did it for them.

But *she'd* wanted a long and committed love. None of the casual boy-meets-girl stuff of the campus scene.

And here I thought I'd found it. . . .

She clicked on her phone, needing a tune. The louder and more teeth rattling the better—anything to get through the first night. She marched through the house, a fitting angry-girls-who-hate-guys band cranked up.

She forced a laugh. Devon was a total jerk.

"I messed up," she whispered through tears, realizing there wasn't a single shoulder to cry on. No one she felt like telling. Devon had been her best friend, her first and only true

boyfriend. That kind of relationship was hard to come by, at least for her.

It was definitely time to get away.

Great timing, Devon, Heather thought angrily. *If only you knew* . . .

chapter

twenty-two

Despite her heart-to-heart talk with Adam over root beer, Grace could not shake off her inner concerns about a fall wedding. Watching her father slowly unravel over Mamma's absence fed her worries. Was it just the timing of her engagement to Henry, or was it the idea of marriage itself that made her shiver?

She pondered this all through the fast songs at Singing as she sat among the girls on one side of the long stretch of tables. Nearly as many fellows mirrored them on the opposite side.

Henry sat directly across from her, as if sending an uncharacteristically bold signal to the other fellows that he'd made his choice. Interestingly, Adam never once sat near Priscilla at Singings . . . and wasn't tonight, either. Rather, her brother had planted himself across from Mandy and was making faces at her, no doubt trying to cheer her up.

Maybe that's *why.*

Priscilla Stahl was seated farther down, surrounded by her close-in-age sisters and girl cousins. Becky Riehl sat next to Grace, leaning near every so often, as if to show her care. Grace treasured Becky's devoted presence.

Yonnie Bontrager kept to himself at the far right end of the boys' side of the table, sporting a broad smile at no one in particular. She hoped Becky wouldn't be hurt by this young man and his unusual ways.

She glanced at her friend, not surprised at all that Yonnie, or any boy, would like her. Becky was, after all, a spontaneous and fun-loving young woman.

Turning, she saw Henry staring at her. She felt surprised by his noticeable attention and quickly looked away.

What must be going through his mind?

While her courting-age grandchildren sang in unison with the other youth in the old bank barn, Adah sat on the front porch with Jakob and Judah, enjoying the voices drifting their way. Adah recalled having gone down to talk straight to Marian Riehl this afternoon, once the house cleared out from Preaching. She'd felt the need to speak her mind about Lettie to her neighbor, dear as any friend she'd ever had. Not surprisingly, Marian had looked askance, but not for long. And Adah had made her attempt to put a stop to the senseless rumor.

At least that one, she thought now.

Jakob's head bobbed to the melody, and his upper torso swayed now and then as he obviously enjoyed the sound of music coming from the upper level of the barn built into the side of a hill.

"Sounds right *gut*," Jakob commented, looking at Judah, who nodded.

"First time we've had us a Singing in a while," Adah mentioned, hoping to get her son-in-law talking.

"Do ya think young Joe's out there, too, even though he

ain't courting age just yet?" Jakob ran his long fingers through
his graying hair.

Adah waited to see if Judah might bite. "Wouldn't be surprised if Joe's hidin' away somewheres, observing high in the
haymow." She paused—goodness' sakes, Judah was quieter than
usual. *To be expected, I guess.* "Joe idolizes Adam, ya know."

Jakob nodded several times, as though deep in thought.
"Both fine boys, I'll say."

Sighing, Adah felt the familiar frustration of trying to carry
on a conversation with Judah—one reason for Lettie's own
frequent irritation. "Grace has a mind to go lookin' for Lettie,"
she said. "What do you think of that, Judah?"

He planted his elbows on his knees and bowed his head.
"All this talk about Lettie has me ill," he said. "That's what I
think."

She folded her arms, peering over her glasses at him.

And there you have it.

Truth was, all their finagling to get Lettie and Judah together—
mostly Jakob's doing—had returned to haunt them.

Judah excused himself and headed into the house, going
directly to the hallway stairs. Adam would see to extinguishing
all the lanterns and latching the barn door once Singing ended.
Judah feebly made his way to his bedroom, still exhausted from
the previous night.

The day had been a long one—too long. The endless stares,
the worried looks on the faces of so many womenfolk.

Out of the blue, he remembered an especially carefree
moment when his wife's eyes had lit up with delight as they rode
home from visiting one Sunday afternoon not long ago. Lettie

had spotted their Englischer neighbors, the Spanglers, outdoors with two of their toddler-age nephews, all of them laughing and playing fetch with their golden Labrador retriever.

Are her eyes filled with sadness or joy right now? he wondered.

He recalled the lovely way Lettie's unpinned hair fell around her shoulders in blond waves after being done up all day in the unyielding bun. He'd never felt the need to say much with his wife. Her presence in the house was nearly enough to bring him contentment. *Not so for her, it seems. . . .*

He looked out the window, still able to make out the tall, pointed shadows of the windbreak of trees. Shaking his head, he found it annoying how Lettie's mother had pried shamelessly on the porch tonight, trying every which way to snoop enough to get him talking. He hadn't refused out of stubbornness, though it may have seemed that way. Honestly, he had felt he might keel over from the aching in his head and neck. It had been weeks since he'd slept through a single night. The way he saw it, rest was a gift from God's own hand, just as the Psalms stated: *He giveth his beloved sleep.*

Quickly closing the door, Judah went to the dresser and pulled out his pajamas. Once changed, he drew back the covers and slipped in. He stared at Lettie's pillow, then reached for it to clench it to his chest, the sound of youthful singing still wending its way from the barn to his open window.

— ⋯ —

After Singing, Grace accepted Henry's invitation to go riding in his fine black buggy. The old stone wall and the fields across the road were still visible in the fading light. As the crescent

moon rose on the thin horizon line to the far east, its light cast an eerie stream across the now-silvery fields.

She got into the open carriage and sat to his left. She'd worn her best maroon dress, nearly violet in color, with Mammi Adah's birthday hankie tucked into the pocket. So far the night was only slightly chilly, but she'd brought along her woolen shawl, just in case.

Henry's flashlight lay on the seat between them, the very light that had brought their relationship to this point. How swiftly she'd forgotten the excitement of seeing him standing outside last Wednesday night.

Four long days ago!

Henry reached for her hand as soon as they were on their way. Since they rarely made more than a little small talk, enjoying the quiet of each other's company instead, this night was much the same as all the others.

The moon had moved above the row of pin oaks on the east side of the road, near where the Amish schoolhouse sat silhouetted on Gibbons Road.

Out of the blue, Henry steered the horse onto the shoulder of the road and parked in front of the schoolyard where they'd both attended all eight grades. Was he feeling sentimental, even romantic? She found it hard to believe this of Henry. Maybe he *did* have an impractical side.

He helped her down, and they walked toward the little one-room school together, side by side. All around the perimeter, they strolled in silence.

After a time, they made their way to the area where they'd played baseball as children, though, not being much of a

tomboy, Grace had preferred to jump rope or, when she was younger, play with her faceless cloth doll.

When it seemed as if Henry had in mind only to walk in a pleasant setting, she could hold back no longer. "You must've heard 'bout my mother," she ventured to say.

"I did."

"Then you understand why things are so *verkehrt* these days. For me . . . for my family?"

He barely nodded.

"It's downright upsetting." She sighed, frustrated. "Everything's all jumbled up."

He looked at her. "But life keeps on going, jah?"

She shivered. Was that all he could say?

"You're shearin' sheep, birthing lambs, ain't?" he said unexpectedly.

"Keepin' mighty busy, jah."

They walked over near the swings. "No word from her?" he asked.

"Not yet, but I'm sure we'll hear soon." She moved to sit on one of the swings, and Henry did the same. "I don't know how you feel 'bout this," she said, "but I wonder if we shouldn't postpone things. For now."

"Why?"

"Till all this is past," she explained.

"Ain't necessary, is it?" Henry's quick reply surprised her. "Surely your mother will return in time for the wedding. November is seven months away yet."

So he doesn't think ill of me. . . . The thought brought her a measure of reassurance as she pulled her shawl around her,

then clutched the chains of the swing. "All right, then, we'll leave things be."

He paused, turning in the swing next to her, his expression hard to make out in the dimness. "Remember, you're not like your mother, Grace."

She let out a little gasp, not knowing what to think. If he'd meant to compliment her, he was certainly going about it all wrong.

Perhaps sensing something was amiss, Henry quickly rose and went to her, reaching for her hand to help her from the swing. "We should head home," he said. And that was that.

———— ··· ————

Grace noticed a light still burning in her grandparents' front room after Henry dropped her off. She longed to visit with Mammi Adah, wanted to curl up in her loving arms and be rocked to sleep like a young child.

But she was a grown woman, and she must weather this storm. Even so, she might glean some wisdom—perhaps even some comfort—from Mammi Adah tonight.

If she's the one up.

Surely her always-sympathetic grandmother would understand her unease over what to do about her engagement. Grace had welcomed Dawdi and Mammi's presence since they'd moved into her father's three-story farmhouse several years ago. And even though Mamma and Mammi Adah were apparently on edge much of the time, Grace's seventy-year-old grandmother was ever ready to help. Mostly, though, she stayed busy taking care of Dawdi Jakob, who'd slowed down considerably in recent years. Rarely did they share meals with the rest of the family,

other than birthdays and holidays, and the arrangement seemed to suit Dat and Mamma just fine.

Grace moved silently through the lawn and up the few steps to Dawdi's back door, letting herself in. She saw that while a gas lamp remained lit, no one was nearby in either the kitchen or the wide front room, where Dawdi and Mammi liked to sit and talk and read after supper.

She noticed her grandfather's big German Biewel on the sofa, as well as Mammi Adah's tatting hook and a handkerchief in the process of being finished. Calling softly, she assumed Mammi had failed to outen the light, and she was moving to do so when a letter sticking out of the Bible caught her eye. She glanced at it and saw it was addressed to Mrs. Adah Esh and Miss Lettie Esh, at a street somewhere in Kidron, Ohio.

Opening the Bible, she peered more closely at the envelope, recognizing now that it was a steadier version of her grandfather's writing. The return address was her grandparents' former home on Weavertown Road, where they'd resided prior to moving here.

Curious, she tried to see the postmark but could not make it out. Hearing someone on the steps, she quickly pushed the letter back inside the Bible and closed it, then hurried out to the hall.

"Well, Grace . . . it's you. I thought I heard someone." Mammi Adah looked tired, her hair flowing like silk all around her, clear to her knees. "You're gettin' in a bit early from a date, jah?" Mammi glanced at her.

Grace nodded. "I ought to just head off to bed."

"But you're here now. . . ." Mammi said. "Care to sit awhile?"

"Well, it *is* late . . . 'specially for you."

Mammi shook her head, eyes softening. "Never too late for my Gracie."

She could not resist, so she sat in Dawdi's upholstered chair while Mammi got settled on the small sofa, next to the Bible with its odd letter. She glanced at the Good Book, wishing she could get up the nerve to ask Mammi Adah about the letter inside. The strange Ohio address had filled her with questions, yet the peculiar way Mammi had acted about Grace's idea to search for her mother made her hesitant to ask. Besides, she had a more pressing matter on her mind tonight.

"Have you ever done something you wished you hadn't?" Grace asked.

Her grandmother's smile faded and she picked up her tatting. "I daresay we all do such things—ofttimes when we're young—and even after we're all grown up, too."

"Things that might hurt another, even though we don't mean to?"

Mammi nodded. "Why do you ask?"

Grace truly wanted to preserve something of Henry's and her privacy, but she also was anxious for Mammi Adah's advice. "Can you keep a secret?"

Mammi nodded. "You have my word, dear."

"Well, even though my beau doesn't agree, I wonder if we're doin' the right thing by goin' ahead with our wedding this fall."

Mammi smiled. "So this must be the news you wanted to share with your Mamma."

"Jah, 'cept now . . . well, bein' engaged doesn't feel quite right . . . with Mamma gone."

"I see why you might feel thataway."

After a moment, Grace said quietly, "I'm not all that sure 'bout things in general, truth be told."

"About marriage?"

Nodding, Grace recalled how she'd felt when Henry had offered his hand tonight, when she was sitting on the swing in their old school yard. There were times when she believed she had done the right thing by saying yes to his proposal. But lately so many doubts had begun to surface—beginning the night of Mamma's talk with her about Henry's reserved nature.

The night of my birthday . . . before Henry came to propose.

"Well, I'll be the first to say 'tis a challenge," Mammi said. "There's nothin' easy 'bout puttin' two people under one roof as husband and wife, tryin' to make heads 'n' tails out of living together and raising a family."

Grace considered the blunt words and wondered about her grandparents' courtship. "Dawdi must've loved *you* an awful lot."

"Why, sure. But love's altogether different when you first meet and court and all. It changes and deepens into something that can withstand the storms, ya know—something worth fighting for as you grow older." She paused to look up from her tatting. "Or it doesn't grow at all."

She understands, for sure and for certain.

Mammi continued. "Course, some folk might begin to appreciate each other again, but it takes time." She kept tatting, more slowly now. "But some marriages are merely tolerated," Mammi Adah ended in a whisper.

Grace stared at the afghan lying on the ottoman, the one Mammi had made specifically to keep Dawdi's unsteady legs

warm. "Did you know for sure . . . I mean, when Dawdi asked you to marry him, did you know . . . ?"

"That he was the right one?"

"Jah." Grace blinked away her tears.

"Honestly, Jakob couldn't keep his eyes off me—wanted to come and tell me things first before anyone else. And we always enjoyed each other's company. There were lots of strong signs such as that."

"Tell me things first . . ."

Henry was not the first person Grace longed to share with, she suddenly realized. In fact, she scarcely ever thought to confide in him. And since he rarely spoke his mind to her, evidently she was not his first choice, either.

Like Mamma and Dat, she thought sadly.

Grace ran her fingers over the hem of her apron, deep in thought. "I'm glad you left your gas lamp on, Mammi."

"Well, bless your heart . . . so am I." With that, her grandmother rose, smiling. "I'll leave ya be for now."

"See you in the mornin'." Grace remained seated.

"Jah . . . and sleep well, dear."

If I can. She glanced at the Bible, still curious about what lay tucked between its pages.

chapter
twenty-three

On washday morning, Grace took time to shake each wet garment carefully before pressing the shoulder seam or waistline to the clothesline. She secured each item with wooden clothespins, using only two of the several lines today. Mamma's clothes were distinctly missing.

When she'd finished, Grace hurried down the road to the shanty phone and dialed the number she'd memorized. Martin Puckett answered on the second ring.

"Hullo. It's Grace Byler."

"Why, yes." He sounded exceptionally pleased. "How can I help you?"

"I need a ride to Orchard Road."

"What time would you like to be picked up and where?"

"Out at the end of the driveway is just fine," she told him. "And as soon as possible."

"Is twenty minutes from now soon enough?"

"That'll be *gut*. Denki."

"All right, I'll be there."

She said good-bye and hung up, hoping she wouldn't soon

become the topic of a new wave of gossip by being seen alone with her mother's early morning driver.

Frowning at her own cynicism, she scurried back to the house to give Mandy instructions for dinner at noon, in case Grace wasn't able to return in time. But when she arrived, Mandy was nowhere to be found. She wrote her a note instead, then dashed out to the barn, where it turned out Mandy was helping with a difficult delivery—triplet lambs.

Reassured that all was in order, Grace stepped inside to the main hall to get her shawl and once again left the house. Walking along the roadside, she discovered she'd picked up her mother's wrap by mistake, but she kept going, not wanting to keep Martin Puckett waiting. "If only wearing it could help me understand what Mamma's been thinkin'," she whispered.

She dug into her shoulder purse, glad she'd remembered to bring the payment for the driver. It wasn't a long ride over to Uncle Ike's place, and he would probably be surprised to see her. She could only hope she'd find him home, so as not to waste her hard-earned money. It wasn't like her to make a trip with a single stop.

When she spied Martin's van, she felt sure this had not been the vehicle she'd seen when Mamma left. If he had indeed driven her mother, why had he chosen to take a car?

"Good morning." She waited for him to slide open the passenger door.

"Such a nice day." He stepped aside as she got in.

She nodded, wanting so badly to ask if he'd taken Mamma to the train station, as the rumors had it. But she spared him the embarrassment of facing up to the gossip. No matter the

usual poison of the grapevine, it was beyond her how all this had gotten started.

"Where would you like to go today?" asked Martin. She gave him the address. "Ah, to your mother's kin." He nodded. "I recall the place."

"If you can return for me, I'd be grateful," she added quickly. "I'll be there only about an hour or so."

He glanced in the rearview mirror, his eyes kind. "Very well."

She tried to ignore her unasked question by taking in the sights of fertile fields and babbling creeks as she rode. Spotting a robin landing on a neighbor's birdbath and shaking its wings, she thought again of Mamma.

They rode for a ways without more conversation, until Grace could hold it in no longer. She simply had to know. "Ach, Martin, I hate bringin' this up, but there's word you drove my mother to the train station last Thursday," she said. "Do you happen to know where she might've been headed so early in the mornin'?"

Their eyes met in the rearview mirror again. "Your mother was quite upset." He looked back at the road. "I tried to talk her into staying, but she was insistent about going. I've no idea where she was headed."

He turned slightly to look over his shoulder, as if uncomfortable about divulging more. "She asked me not to say anything." He paused. "So then, she hasn't returned?"

"Not yet . . . and none of us have heard from her, either." Grace sighed, feeling too tenderhearted to mention the rumors flying about Martin and Mamma. *No need*, she thought. It was quite clear from what he'd said that Martin hadn't gone

anywhere with her mother, though Grace didn't understand why she'd wanted him to conceal her trip.

"I hope she's all right." His voice was thick with concern. "Frankly, I worried about her traveling alone like that."

"Well, I pray the Lord's watchin' over her." Looking out her window again, she tried to appreciate all the beauty around her—the morning skies were clear, promising sunshine. Yet the world seemed cold and bleak.

Thinking now of Uncle Ike, she hoped that he might know something to lead her to Mamma. "I mean to find my mother and bring her home," she stated suddenly.

Martin's head bobbed. "For your sake and your family's, I hope you will."

Ike Peachy's farmhouse was coming into view, and even before Martin got out of the van, he promised to return as she'd requested. Grace waited for him to come around and push open the heavy door before she stepped out. "Denki, ever so much," she said.

Ain't a speck wrong with Martin Puckett, she decided.

Martin backed up and turned around before pulling onto the road, relieved that Grace Byler had been so sympathetic toward him. Lettie's disappearance had evidently caused her daughter great confusion and grief—her bloodshot eyes gave that away. He wished he might somehow alleviate the family's pain.

I should've tried harder to keep Lettie from going. . . .

He drove to Ronks, south of Route 340, to pick up several Amish ladies who wanted to go to Belmont Fabrics in Paradise. Grace's request for him to come back for her in an hour or so

made for perfect timing. He was definitely using plenty of gas by juggling customers, but he was glad to be busy today after a weekend without any calls—at least none that had reached his voice mail. And since Grace had phoned him and spoken directly about last Thursday, Martin began to feel less concerned that the weekend's quiet had anything to do with Lettie Byler.

———···———

Judah could bear it no longer. Dejected, he left the birthing stall. He pushed open the barn door and walked across the yard, toward the road. He and Adam had done everything in their power to save the third lamb. *Triplets . . . ach, think of it.* But the more he pondered whatever had gone wrong, the more miserable he felt.

Not caring where he walked, he muttered to himself, "If Lettie had been here, things might've turned out better." From the early days of their marriage, she'd always been so gentle and caring with the ewes. She'd spent hours with him in the barn, or checked on the newborns herself to spell him.

What happened in March that changed her so much? He shook his head, not wanting to entertain irritating thoughts about his wife, the beautiful bride of his youth. Lettie had not always been a worry to him. No, there had been many pleasant days.

How long had she been gone? Seemed awful long already. He felt as helpless now as he had watching the smallest lamb struggle for air, the will to live so strong in the poor, tiny thing.

"Mornin', Judah!"

He looked up to see Andy Riehl and two of his older sons out planting corn. Judah waved and spotted Andy's nephews in the field to the east of their house, spreading manure. Looking

toward the Riehls' house, he realized he'd turned left on the road and come this way in the midst of his daze. Marian and Becky were hanging out the last few trousers on the clothesline.

Washday, he thought. *Where's Grace?*

The sun felt warm on his aching neck and shoulders as he walked past the Riehls'. If anything, the pain was increasing, rather than diminishing as he'd hoped. He ought to return to the barn and help Adam dispose of the dead lamb, yet he was not up to taking on that chore just now. His children needed at least one confident parent around these days. Perhaps he would return stronger for the walking.

Suddenly he understood something of Lettie's need to walk at night: It was so she could manage to keep her chin up all day long. *Helped her hide whatever was troubling her.*

He began to run, swinging his arms, work boots pounding against the road . . . his breath coming faster. All the way to Preacher Smucker's house he went—a good half mile or so. Buggies clattered up and down the road, some folk waving and calling to him, some rattling past.

Let them think what they will.

Judah wasn't sure if the moistness in his eyes was perspiration or tears, but he kept up his pace, unable to stop.

—— ··· ——

Grace could hear voices inside Uncle Ike's house, so she didn't bother to knock but rather made her way in through the summer porch, where she noticed thick cobwebs in one corner. *Aunt Naomi would never have allowed that.* She turned toward the kitchen, and there she found Uncle Ike having a breakfast

of fried scrapple, eggs, and toast. Two of Grace's elderly great-aunts sat at the table with him.

Lest she startle them, she coughed softly. All three turned to look her way. "Well, lookee there . . . it's Judah's Gracie." Ike half rose out of his chair, then just as quickly sat down. "Come . . . come and eat with us."

The older women smiled and nodded before returning their attention to breakfast. "What brings ya?" asked the older one, her fork midway between her plate and mouth.

"Just wanted to talk with Uncle Ike a bit." She sat where Aunt Naomi had always sat, the seat still vacant after her passing. "Would ya mind?" she asked.

"Not if you don't sit and stare at me all through my breakfast." His eyes twinkled mischievously, and he reached for his coffee. "What would ya like to eat?"

Since she'd already eaten, she wasn't much hungry. But she supposed if she was to get any information, she was going to have to politely settle in with a plate of food and visit first. *Unless* . . . "My driver's comin' back for me in an hour," Grace said, hoping that might hurry things along.

Ike glanced at the window. "Wasn't that Martin Puckett I saw bringin' you?"

She straightened. "Was indeed."

"Well, why would ya want to—"

"Ain't a thing wrong with Mamma callin' on Martin to take her to catch a train, is there?"

"Well, it was wrong of her to leave town, ain't so?" Ike said, wiping his plate clean with a crust of toast. He took a final swallow of his coffee and stiffly rose out of his chair, motioning Grace into the front room to sit down.

Grace quickly changed the subject. "I know you're busy, but I thought you might be able to fill in some pieces of a very big puzzle for me," she told him.

"Which puzzle's that?" Like so many farmers, his cheeks were ruddy from many years of working in the sun. His puffy lids nearly covered his eyes; his age showed since Naomi's death.

"Well, the puzzle of Mamma's earlier years." Grace explained that she felt sure her mother had cherished the poetry books Aunt Naomi had once kept. "Did Aunt Naomi ever tell you where the books came from?"

The whites of his eyes glistened suddenly. "I wish I could help ya, Grace, but I'm afraid I have nothing to tell. Naomi never did say why she had those books, and I never thought to ask." He paused, his eyes searching hers. "Do you really think some old poetry books are important?"

Grace hesitated to tell her uncle her suspicions, fearing it might open her mother up to further criticism. "I just can't see why Mamma would have bothered to bring them home if they didn't have some special meaning for her."

Uncle Ike sighed. "I'm sorry ya had to come over here for nothin'. S'pose you found it hard to get away with so much to keep you busy these days."

Grace gave a small nod, her thoughts still on Mamma as her uncle began to speak of spring planting and whatnot.

——— ··· ———

Set back from the road and nestled in its private grove, the boardinghouse looked surprisingly the same as it had years ago.

Even the paint on the outside was exactly the same color, Lettie recalled, although the front porch had been extended.

Nowadays a much younger couple, Carl and Tracie Gordon, ran the quaint inn. Lettie was thankful for that, as well as for having gotten an upstairs room, so she wouldn't have to hear latecomers tramping overhead.

Four days since the train left Lancaster, she thought, both dread and anticipation filling her. It had taken this long to discover Samuel's exact home address from a handful of leads, beginning with someone her cousin Hallie had recently mentioned in a letter. Aside from the innkeeper's phone number and the driver they'd recommended, the list of telephone numbers she'd brought along had proved little help. Although the innkeeper's wife had gently suggested that if Lettie had attempted to access a computer, she might have found Samuel's address more quickly.

In such a small town, she'd expected her search to be far easier. But Samuel hadn't belonged to an Amish group for years—not since his family had left Bird-in-Hand so long ago.

She was astonished at how many listings for Samuel Grabers there were in the area. By the time she'd worked her way down the directory, calling one number after another using the Gordons' telephone, she was discouraged.

To think I had such high hopes of walking right up to his door and ringing the bell!

But today she had a new lead and new hope that she might finally see her former beau, a recent widower after twenty years of marriage.

The bishop's long-ago words to her rang in her ears: *"Do*

you accept this man as your husband, and do you promise not to leave him until death separates you?"

Lettie pushed away the remembrance and straightened the bed. She was glad for a bright corner room. Not so different from the one she'd stayed in before in this historic inn. She and her mother had come at the recommendation of dear friends, Mamma had explained to her that bitter winter's day. And they'd stayed only a short time, if her memory served her now.

She looked about. The pale green-striped wallpaper was attractive, although some of it was peeling off near the wide doorframe. Surely she would have recognized the color if this were the same room.

She went to the door and glanced back at the small dresser, where she'd stowed away her personal things—plenty of space for the time being.

"What God hath joined together, let not man put asunder. . . ."

Sighing, Lettie sat next to the window, there in her private haven. She reached for her beloved poetry book and leisurely read the last few pages. Then, clutching the slip of paper, she stared longingly at the address. "My last hope."

chapter
twenty-four

Heather brushed away tears as she backed out of the curved driveway, casting a pensive look at her family's red-brick colonial house.

I'm doing this for you, too, Dad. She stared up at her window over the garage—that sweet and cozy spot she and her father had created just for her.

She'd hardly taken any time at all to pack, piling a bunch of clothes and personal stuff into the trunk of the car and the backseat before heading off in search of a stress-free summer. As she saw it, serenity was the first ingredient necessary to health. Lancaster County, the Garden Spot of the World, would perfectly fill the bill. For her, gardens equaled tranquillity . . . and tranquillity, wholeness. Not that she was going to start espousing that Mother Earth mumbo jumbo, but nature was natural, after all.

Glad for the GPS mapping system on her iPhone, she'd have no trouble navigating her way to Pennsylvania. The map routed her up to Interstate 95 through Baltimore and then she would take Interstate 83 into Pennsylvania.

Listening to one song after another, Heather already felt herself relaxing. She was eager to meet Marian Riehl, who had been so accommodating by phone, even to the point of suggesting Heather pay by the week. *"We'll give you a nice discount as a long-term guest . . . and remember, we don't charge on the Lord's Day."*

She'd never heard anyone refer to Sundays like that and found it charming, even intriguing.

——— ··· ———

Hours later, as she took the exit off of Highway 30 and turned onto 340, Heather wondered if her dad had spotted her note by now. Glancing at the digital clock, she realized he wouldn't have seen it propped up on his desk as of yet.

Four o'clock. He's still at work. . . .

He really didn't need to know the hard facts about her leaving, except that she was on a self-imposed getaway. She'd made it clear she would keep in touch and had decided at the last minute to take her phone along. She couldn't imagine living without Twitter or instant messaging or email.

She had been quick to delete a former draft of an email she'd written to Devon last week, telling him she would be tied up for a while—*going to hang out in an exotic community for the summer*. Now that he'd dropped his bombshell, her only love would never know of her plans—or of her disease.

Suddenly she noticed a real live horse pulling a quaint gray buggy in front of her car. She let out a gasp and remembered how remarkable this old-fashioned sight had been the very first time she'd visited here with her family, as a girl. Seeing the Amish

mode of transportation so very close brought it all back . . . the reason they'd kept returning here.

Gone now were Heather's health concerns . . . gone her perplexity over Devon's choosing someone else over her. At this moment she was zeroed in on the incredible sight before her eyes. She never got past the awe no matter how many times she'd come here. This was, after all, the twenty-first century, even though she felt like she'd fallen through a time warp somewhere between Virginia and here.

Heather stared at the red triangle on the back of the buggy and noticed the thin, wobbling carriage wheels on either side. *No chance of surviving against a speeding car.* Cringing, she crept along at less than ten miles per hour behind the boxlike carriage, traveling that way all the way to Bird-in-Hand. Nervous for the family inside, she could see several towheaded children peeking out from the back. She checked her rearview mirror, aware of the lineup of cars behind her.

They're content to go at a snail's pace, she thought.

The GPS indicated how many feet she had to travel before turning. She marveled at this cool technology while her car followed the horse and buggy. "Okay, now for the turnoff."

Almost there . . .

Once more a small face turned to look at her through the rear buggy opening. She got a glimpse of corn-silk hair and wide eyes, and a sudden knife of pain sliced at her heart. Dr. O'Connor had said she might never have a child of her own now.

A wall of fear rose up and towered over her. Had she done the right thing in refusing conventional medical treatment?

But no, she wanted to at least try to conquer the disease her way. She wouldn't second-guess her decision. She mustn't.

This trip was all about her . . . and about the path her mom wished she'd chosen. Heather could nearly pinpoint the moment when she'd turned so inward, or whatever it was referred to by more charitable people. After all, someone had to look out for her now. If Heather didn't, then who would?

Again she considered Devon's blunt email. If she didn't view prayer as an overall waste of time, she would send one up for his new girlfriend, asking God to protect her from Devon the Terrible, who broke female hearts at will.

It wasn't as if she didn't know firsthand about faith. Her greatest hope had been dashed when God ignored her pleas to spare Mom's life. He must've been too caught up in other more important things, too busy to heal Mom through the treatments the doctors had claimed were essential.

In the end, the treatments had been stronger than her mother. *Yeah, they worked all right. Like killing a fly on the wall with a shotgun.*

Making the turn north onto Beechdale Road, she felt conflicted. Sure, she had run away, but she hoped to recapture some semblance of peace here. She hoped, too, that the naturopath—Dr. Marshall—might be optimistic about her chances for recovery.

She spotted the old stone farmhouse, described to a tee by Marian. Vines clung to the exterior all across the expanse of the front porch, with its white railing. Heather noted several smaller houses adjoined the main one, something she'd seen before in this area. A long clothesline stretched across the side yard, much like her grandparents' place years ago.

A plump chicken crossed the driveway and two chubby

girls with pigtails wrapped around their heads went chasing after it.

This could be fun. She opened the car door and breathed in the fresh smells of the farm, replete with cow manure. And she laughed.

——— ... ———

Ever so glad for the referral for a driver, Lettie was headed to Fredericksburg, just south of Kidron, the location of the Gordons' inn. She was on her way at last.

She felt a pang of guilt for leaving Judah on such shaky ground.

Will he ever forgive me?

Recalling the strain between them, she regretted their final disappointing conversation. How much better would it have been if she'd simply kept quiet? Absolutely nothing had been accomplished this past month by her repeated attempts to talk to her husband.

And what of Grace and Mandy? She'd thought so many times of the cooking duties and other chores thrust suddenly upon her girls, and Grace having to squeeze in her hours at Eli's, too.

My family must think little of me now. . . .

——— ... ———

Willing herself to breathe more slowly, Lettie double-checked the numbers on the mailbox in front of the bungalow-style house—Samuel's house, supposedly. The front door stood open, the screen door dimming her view inside as she walked up the porch steps.

Two clay pots filled with red Dragon Wing Begonias bloomed profusely on either side of the doorway. *Samuel always loved bright colors*, she recalled, a wind chime dinging softly on its hook in the corner of the porch.

She straightened to her full height, inhaled deeply, and reached for the doorbell—then hesitated. She could not bear to hear a loud ring today. Gently she rapped instead on the unlatched screen door, which bounced a bit. She heard a woman's voice calling, "Just a minute . . . my hands are full."

Samuel's twin—Sarah? She couldn't be sure, and the woman was not visible.

Patiently waiting, Lettie wondered if the woman might've mistakenly gone around to the back door.

"Hello there," a blond English woman said as she rushed to the door. "Sorry to keep you . . . just here watering plants."

"Oh, not to worry." Lettie stepped back as the young woman opened the door. "Is this Samuel Graber's house?" Her voice was a mere breath.

The woman smiled. "He's out of town—left just yesterday. Helping redo a friend's roof."

Lettie nodded, disappointment washing through her. She'd come all this way. . . .

"Is there something I can do for you?"

"Do you happen to know when he'll return?"

"Sometime this weekend. Would you like to leave a message?"

"No . . . no," Lettie said, putting on a smile. "I'll return another time. Denki—er, thank you."

The day suddenly seemed very long. She trudged back down

the newly painted porch steps, wanting to glance back and take in the full effect of the pretty sitting area on Samuel's porch.

Will we sit together there when we talk . . . at long last?

Lettie had rehearsed such a private meeting dozens of times in her mind. But now she was forced to wait longer to tell him what she yearned to say—if she did not lose heart by then.

chapter
twenty-five

"Come in . . . come in. *Willkumm* to our home, Heather." The lady of the house, Marian Riehl, was well into middle age, Heather guessed, yet she insisted on carrying in two pieces of luggage at once. Heather protested repeatedly, but Marian appeared determined to roll out the carpet of hospitality.

Heather paused to take in the vast reach of sky and land— lush green fields and majestic silver silos marked the iconic landscape. The setting was something out of a movie—a windmill, woodshed, milk house, and even a hand pump to the well, not far from the back door. "Beyond amazing," she told Marian as she followed her into the house. If the place had been advertised online, she'd never have gotten a room—the Riehls would be booked up for years.

"Would ya care for some warm chocolate chip cookies and fresh lemonade?" Marian asked, showing Heather into the spacious kitchen.

"I really shouldn't, but . . . well, okay!" She laughed and accepted a glass of lemonade, as well as a cookie from the plate of homemade treats. The table, adorned with a red- and

white-checked oilcloth, stretched for yards in the center of the large room, and a gas lamp dangled over its middle.

"Just make yourself at home," Marian said. "For as long as you're here, our home is your home, too."

Heather realized again how completely removed from the real world she felt. Modern society as she'd known it had vanished, replaced by old-time surroundings and a pleasing level of hospitality. As many visits as she'd made to Lancaster County through the years, she had never actually stayed with an Amish family.

"Have you ever heard of a Dr. Marshall?" she asked as she appraised Marian's attire—her bare feet poked out from beneath the long green dress and full apron.

"We certainly have. Miss Marshall's treating our minister's wife." Marian's eyes brightened as she found a tablet and pencil in a drawer. She began to sketch a map without Heather's asking, finishing quickly. "You shouldn't have a speck of trouble findin' her office—smack-dab in downtown Lancaster."

Heather smiled her thanks, hoping she hadn't grinned too broadly. With Marian's quaint speech, twinkling blue eyes, and the rosiest cheeks on record, the woman was as delightful as a storybook character.

"I'll take you to your room," Marian said after greeting two other guests that came into the kitchen, her face alight. "If you're ready."

Heather followed, making note of the lack of wall pictures and not a single electric light fixture. A tall corner cupboard stood in a smaller room off the kitchen, and she wondered if this was the dining room, minus the table, or simply a place to display more teacups and saucers than she'd ever seen.

Decorative plates stood on edge on a wooden ledge that ran all across the wall.

Strange as it seemed, Heather already felt completely at home here, in this place she'd never before stepped foot in.

Maybe this wasn't such a crazy idea, after all!

——— ··· ———

Adah loved everything about the way sticky buns smelled— and oh, the texture, too. She removed a large baking pan from the gas-fired oven, smiling at the remarkable convenience of it all as the yeasty-sweet fragrance permeated the room. She had half a mind to call Jakob and give him a taste, but he'd already exceeded his daily sugar limit, what with his penchant for dunking a pastry into his coffee first thing of a morning.

But Marian Riehl . . . now *there* was a woman who could use a few extra pounds, wiry as she was. Besides, Adah was itching to get outdoors, such a pretty day it was. So once the buns had cooled slightly, she would go and surprise their neighbor, who was expecting their new guest sometime this afternoon.

Imagine always havin' strangers for company. . . .

Adah went to the front room window, which faced east, and looked down toward the Riehls' treed lane. Sure enough, a navy blue car was parked there.

Not wanting to admit that it was more out of curiosity than benevolence, Adah gathered up enough sticky buns to feed all of Marian's big family, as well as their several overnight patrons.

When she arrived at the Riehls' back door, she called to Marian, who came rushing to open it. "Hullo. Wie geht's, Adah . . . come in and sit awhile."

"How've you been?" She set the basket of warm breakfast rolls on the table.

"Just fine," Marian said, eyeing the delicious goodies and grinning. "You shouldn't have, ya know . . . but smells mighty *gut*."

Adah nodded and uncovered the basket, and Marian bent low to breathe in the delicious aroma. "You won't have to bake so much for tomorrow, jah?"

Marian replaced the basket lid. "Ach, I don't mind bakin'. But this here's ever so nice of you." She motioned for Adah to sit down. "I'll pour ya some tea, how 'bout?"

"Sounds fine."

"I'd like you to meet our newest guest. The one I mentioned last week . . . remember?"

Adah didn't admit to being eager to meet the young woman with the shiny blue car. She merely nodded.

"Well, round the time you and I are finished havin' our tea—you watch—she'll be back downstairs." Marian's eyes glinted with delight. "I can tell she likes it here already, and she's only just come."

"Why, sure she does. Just as all of your guests enjoy your warm hospitality." Smiling, Adah smoothed her dress, daintily crossing her bare feet beneath the table.

They talked all around Lettie—in circles, really—and Adah found it silly. Marian asked about Judah, Adam, Grace, and the rest . . . even Jakob, but never a peep about the *missing one*.

Adah was stirring sugar and several droplets of cream into her hot tea when in came the tallest young woman she'd ever seen. Why, the girl had to be nearly six feet in height, with

golden-brown hair and a smile that undoubtedly would stop a young man in his tracks.

Quickly Marian introduced her. "This is Heather Nelson, from Virginia."

"Very nice to meet you, Heather," said Adah, enjoying this.

"And, Heather, I'd like you to meet my longtime friend, who also happens to be my neighbor . . . Adah Esh." Marian motioned for Heather to join them. "Care for some tea?"

"Thanks." The young woman nodded and smiled. Adah and Marian were both wearing dark green cape dresses with an apron to match, and Heather appeared to be taking it all in. "Your kitchen smells fabulous," Heather said, sitting at the table.

"Guess we should offer Heather some of your delicious pastries," Marian said, opening the basket. "After all, they won't be this warm tomorrow . . . or near as fresh."

Heather laughed softly—like she was singing—before reaching in to pull out a great big bun, oozing sugar.

"Nobody can eat just one," Adah said right quick, glancing at Marian.

Heather bit into the bun and her eyes grew as wide as quarters. She nodded her head again and again, apparently unable to speak. When she was finally able, she said, "Wow. A person could get addicted to this rich stuff."

"Ain't that the truth," said Adah.

"None of us should eat so much fat . . . or sugar," Marian added.

"What we *should* do and what we do are often very different," Adah put in. Goodness, but she'd surprised herself by saying right out what was in the depths of her heart. *Oh,*

Lettie . . . She realized anew how empty Judah's big house must seem to him and the children.

How very empty. And for a moment, she felt nearly afraid.

Heather found herself completely taken in by the backwoodsy talk at Marian Riehl's table. She loved the comical topsy-turvy idioms of the Amish. Things like, "throw the horse over the stall some hay," or "those naughty boys oughta get more birchings—switchings!" and "outen the light." To think she was going to spend her summer in the middle of all this charm!

Although Marian was a real sweetie, Adah Esh's spunk and folksy wit appealed more to her. The way the older woman paused before speaking, her lips parted, seemingly thinking how best to express herself, caught her attention. She could just imagine Adah's thoughts swirling . . . and what striking gray eyes!

"Your last name's Nelson?" Adah asked her during a lull.

"That's right."

Marian raised her cup to her lips. "We don't hear that name much round here."

"You know, I heard a man named Nelson bought a small piece of land up a ways." Adah tilted her head. "Could it be someone you know?"

The grandmotherly woman put things together faster than an e-book could download. "Might be my dad."

The Amishwomen looked at each other.

"Unless there's other land for sale nearby."

Marian shook her head. "Land's at a premium anymore—

you just can't get your hands on it. I'd say your dad's mighty fortunate, if true."

"What's your father's name?" asked Adah.

"Roan Nelson," replied Heather. "He's talked of building an Amish-style farmhouse on the four acres."

"Oh?" Marian's eyes brightened. "Will the house have electric?"

Heather laughed. "I sure hope so!"

"Will you raise a few head of cattle or have a dairy cow or two, then, also?" Adah asked.

"Neither one, I'd guess."

This brought a trill of laughter, and Heather could see they were equally as interested in her as she was in them—if not more so.

— ··· —

Grace's younger brother, Joe, came in for a drink of water, and she leaned against the counter, listening to him talk about the Riehls' latest boarder. "Mammi Adah says she brought all kinds of stuff with her," Joe said, talking up a storm.

"What sorts of things?"

"Armloads of books, mainly, Mammi said." He scratched his head. "You must've heard 'bout this Virginia girl already, jah?"

"Mammi told me she was coming."

Joe gulped down a tall glass of water and went to the sink for more. "Mammi says she's come to stay put for a while. Has something called a thesis to write."

Grace hadn't heard this. "Must be highly schooled, then."

"It'll be interesting having another Englischer in the neighborhood, jah?"

Grace thought suddenly of Martin Puckett, certainly considered English, too. "Listen, Joe, I want you to help me stamp out the rumors 'bout Mamma and Martin Puckett. Okay?"

He nodded. "I was thinkin' the same thing at Preachin'. He's such a nice man . . . always so helpful to us."

"Gut, then. Tell everyone you know that Martin's at home and not off with Mamma. He never was, either." Just saying it made her feel queasy.

Joe frowned, rubbing his chin. "Well, that might quiet the tittle-tattle where Martin's concerned, but Mamma's still gone. That much ain't a rumor!"

"Gone, jah." *Though hopefully I can change that.*

chapter
twenty-six

The uncommon stillness awakened Heather the morning after her arrival. She lay in bed, pressing her fingers gently into her armpits to find the same tiny nodules—still no pain. She moved her hand along her rib cage, relieved there were no changes there, either. Her getting away might prove to be truly therapeutic. That, and being free from a deceitful toad of a fiancé!

She lay there relaxing, stretching, and pleasantly aware of the comfortable surroundings. She sighed, realizing she'd never again be held in Devon's strong arms.

Where did I go wrong with Devon?

But she couldn't let herself think of him anymore. He was out of her life through his own actions. Wasn't it better this way than finding out later, closer to the wedding . . . or worse yet, even after?

She rolled over, fighting back a jumble of emotions—anger and sadness and bewilderment—and reached for her phone.

Sitting up, she checked for any missed calls during the night, never having been one to sleep with her phone on—and without electricity here, she needed to conserve her battery. She was

glad to have brought along several replacement batteries for her laptop, but the phone had little power left, thanks to using the GPS so much yesterday. She'd have to go out and charge it up at a coffee shop somewhere, maybe look into getting a charger to use in her car, too.

When I'm back in real time, she thought ironically, surprised at her own reluctance to venture away from the Riehls' insulated setting.

At that moment, her dad's cell number showed up and she listened to her voice mail. *"Why such a cryptic note, Heather? Where'd you go? Please call."*

Hearing his voice made her unexpectedly homesick. He was all she had now. But if he was true to form, he had a zillion office projects to see to—he wouldn't have been home much even if she'd stayed. And who knows? If she kept feeling this great, she'd keep her word and help him come up with a plan for his new house. *Right down the road . . .*

Perhaps one of the Riehls might direct her to Dad's land. Or better yet, take her there in a buggy.

Heather switched off her phone to preserve the power. Who could go for long disconnected from cyberspace? Could she live without all the bells and whistles of her modern life for several months?

Getting out of bed, she staggered to the window and immersed herself in the refreshing view. Yet in some inexplicable way, the loveliness of the landscape heightened the lingering hurt she felt at receiving Devon's jolting email.

She turned away from the window and from the splendor of farmland, sky, and trees. Returning to bed, she fell back onto

the pillow. "I'm in the most peaceful place on the planet, and I really just need a shrink."

So is it God who lets this stuff happen? Losing Mom and then Devon? Not to mention some doctor says I'm going to die if I don't get treatment. Yet if I do get it, I could end up like Mom . . . sicker because of the things that are supposed to help me. And all this is okay with God?

Burying her face in the pillow, Heather managed to pull herself together. By the time she'd showered—in record time, since she had to share a bathroom with three other guests—she was pretty sure her eyes were no longer lobster red.

When she called her dad, she hoped her voice sounded less froggy, too. Her call went directly to his voice mail, so she left a quick message.

"Hey, Dad . . . I've escaped to another era." She laughed softly. "I needed a break after the last semester, like I said in my note. Maybe I can get out in a horse and buggy to search for the land you purchased. Well, my batteries are dying and electricity is forbidden here, so we'll have to catch up later. Bye!"

Downstairs, at breakfast, she was surprised at the spread of food—like the ultimate bed-and-breakfast experience, only better. A fluffy omelet with fresh steamed asparagus and topped with cream cheese, a platter heaped with sausages, three kinds of sweet breads, every imaginable jam and spread, and the same decadent sticky buns that Adah Esh had invited her to preview yesterday.

The other guests seemed equally astonished at the offerings as they talked and chewed and passed food. One guest—an attractive man in his thirties—singled her out with his gorgeous

hazel eyes, even winking at one point when he thanked her for passing the cream for his coffee.

Real men don't use cream!

She enjoyed observing Becky and her mom . . . and the lineup of Becky's six siblings. Who had *this* many children in a single lifetime? She remembered reading the average Amish family had eight children, with some having fifteen and more.

Becky Riehl was as delightful as her mother. After getting settled yesterday in her small, cozy room under the eaves—given the small amount of bureau space and zero closet space, that proved a challenge—Heather had accepted a buggy ride with Becky. They'd driven past the general store and the Bird-in-Hand farmers' market, as well as another place Becky thought might interest her, Eli's Natural Foods. *"You'll find plenty of health foods and supplements at Eli's,"* Becky had said with a Dutchy accent.

Now, taking her first bite of the delectable omelet, Heather was doubly glad her dad wanted to build a house nearby. Maybe Becky could teach her how to cook like this!

She cut into her sausage patty and thought how foolish she was to assume that Becky Riehl might view her as a good choice for a friend.

Not if she really knew me . . .

— ... —

Dat began shearing the sheep right after breakfast. Grace and Mandy rushed out to help once the dishes were cleaned, dried, and put away. Grace had gotten up early to weed and hoe the vegetable garden, knowing the rest of the day would be taken up with helping to trim the sheep's hooves—Mandy's

and Joe's and her chore today. Dat, Adam, and Uncle Ike were
the brawny ones who could steady the sheep for the yearly
shearing. It was important to shear in the springtime, once the
weather was warm enough for the animals to do without their
fleece, yet before the hot summer sun had a chance to burn the
sheep's skin.

"Ten minutes per sheep," Mandy told her. "That's what
Dat wants to try and get the time down to."

"Even so, it'll be a long day." Grace recalled how in previous years Mamma was always one of the first ones outdoors
on such a day, murmuring softly to the young ewes while she
worked.

"What do you think Mamma's doin' right now?" asked
Mandy, as if sensing Grace's thoughts.

Grace kept her eyes on the sheep's feet. "Depends on where
she is."

"Well, where do *you* think she went?"

"Far enough away to take a train," Grace answered.

That was all they said about it. Mandy worked her mouth,
as if trying not to cry. Dwelling on the negative aspects of
their lives was no help to either of them. And Grace needed
to work fast today so she had time tomorrow to go to the town
of Bart. Maybe there she would have more success than she'd
had with Uncle Ike, who had shed no light on the significance
of the poetry books or anything else related to Grace's search
for Mamma.

Surely it's worth a try. . . .

Grace was relieved to see her grandmother come outside to
stuff stray clumps of wool into bags. *Many hands make lighter*

work, Mamma had always said. And Mammi Adah—and for a very short time, Dawdi Jakob, as well—helped in this way while the assembly line of sheep, clippers, and shearers streamed along.

Around half past eleven, Aunt Lavina brought over two large pans of Busy Day casserole, with cubed ham and diced vegetables, topped with biscuit dough and grated cheese. The work came to a swift halt as all of them headed indoors to wash up. Grace and Mandy set the table right quick, then put out two kinds of dinner rolls, along with butter, strawberry jam, and apple butter. There was also a large crock of coleslaw and some chowchow, too—a fine feast of a meal, thanks to Mamma's days of canning last summer . . . and her sister's thoughtfulness in bringing the main dish.

Later, when the men had resumed the shearing, and Lavina, Mandy, and Grace were cleaning up in the quiet of the kitchen, their aunt asked about Mamma. "Have you heard anything?"

"Not yet, if you must know." Mandy had never been so pointed with their aunt, nor had she looked so pale.

"Oh, sister," said Grace, chagrined.

"*Es dutt mir leed*—I'm sorry." Mandy looked first at Aunt Lavina, then at Grace. She sighed. "Guess I'm feelin' under the weather."

"Of course you are, dear." Aunt Lavina reached for a tea towel and began to dry the plates. "I shouldn't have asked."

"No . . . no, it's only natural you'd wonder," said Grace, putting her hands back in the dishwater.

"She's *your* family, too," Mandy added.

"If . . . or *when* we hear something, I'll tell you right away."

Grace carefully placed each glass in the hot rinse water on the right side of the double sink.

Lavina's oval face broke into an encouraged smile. "I'll be holdin' my breath, then."

Nodding, Grace said she hoped they'd hear something soon. Anything to end the not knowing.

chapter
twenty-seven

Later that afternoon, Heather headed out to her car to explore the back roads. She glanced toward the little chicken house, her digital camera case slung over her shoulder. One of these days, she hoped to feed the hens with Becky.

The sights and smells of farm life captivated her as she looked toward the south, taking in the fields of newly planted corn. Birds twittered and called back and forth in the trees and beyond. This would be a great day to locate a coffee shop. After that, she wanted to drive the byways she and her parents had explored together in the past.

She was just getting into the car when Becky came running out, feet bare, skirts flying. "Wait . . . Heather!"

"Yes?"

"I . . . well, I just wondered if you'd like to go on another ride, maybe." Becky's eyes sparkled with excitement. "I'd be ever so happy to take ya."

Heather hadn't expected this; she could always drive to Lancaster later. "Sure. That'd be super."

"Come, I'll show you how to hitch the horse up to the buggy." Becky laughed. "If you want to watch, that is."

"I never pass up a guided tour." She closed the car door, not bothering to lock it. She'd heard Marian tell the flirtatious man at breakfast this morning that nobody locked anything here. "*Not even your house?*" one of the other two women guests had asked. Marian had seemed nearly offended at the question, which got the two women talking at once. The room had seemed as chaotic as a group of CNN pundits hashing out the current political landscape.

Didn't outsiders pose a single threat? The idea was nearly as startling as the earthy smell rising from the nearby manure pit. But even the strange smells added to her carefree feeling—she felt alive, in spite of everything that was so completely wrong with her life.

"Come, Heather!" Becky was calling for her.

"Jah, comin'," she whispered, smiling to herself.

——— ··· ———

Judah was happy to see his neighbor Andy Riehl walking across the pasture to help with the shearing. Having rushed back and forth between the newborn lambs, the pregnant ewes, and the shearing, he was nearly ready for another fine dinner—and a good long nap, too. Yet here it was only three o'clock, and three agitated ewes were complicating things by showing signs of early labor. They'd isolated themselves from the herd, refusing feed, Adam reported when checking on their latest arrivals.

A while later, when he and Andy were hand pumping well water for a drink, Andy himself brought up what had become the consensus among the community. Judah's ire rose quickly.

"Listen here, Andy: I don't want ya speakin' so about my wife and Martin. Both of them are good folk. You must continue to call Martin for transportation." He shook his head. "It just ain't right not to."

Andy removed his straw hat. "But—"

"No buts to it. I know my wife . . . and I know Martin. Just shut the People up 'bout this, ya hear?" Judah strode away, down toward the springhouse. "What's come over me?" he muttered.

He'd never spouted off to Andy like that . . . nor to anyone else.

Is this how I am without Lettie?

—— ... ——

Heather was surprised at how quickly Becky Riehl located Dad's plot of land.

She reined the horse over to the side of the road so Heather could get a better view. "I wonder where we'll build." Heather surveyed the sweep of grassy field.

"Well, I see several choices, really." Becky pointed out the various locations. "It would be nice, though, to have the house shifted off to one side of the property—maybe over there by the trees. A *gut* windbreak, I daresay. And if you do plant anything, you should rotate crops so as not to wear out the soil."

Heather laughed and explained that her dad would need plenty of advice about such things. "You know . . . my mom would have liked this idea of his."

"Your mother's not living?"

Heather shook her head.

"Ach, so sorry."

"I am, too." *Every single day* . . .

"Was it recent?" Becky's face was somber.

"Still feels like it." Heather nodded. "She passed away eighteen months ago."

Becky appeared to take that in. "Grief's harder for some than others," she said thoughtfully. Then she asked if Heather had seen enough of her father's new place. "If you like, we can circle around Bird-in-Hand."

"Sure, I'd like that. And if it wouldn't be too much trouble, I need to find a spot to recharge my phone." She smiled a little, saying this to a conventional Amish girl.

"I know just the place." Becky picked up the reins and urged the horse into a trot.

Looking over her shoulder at the piece of land, Heather could hardly believe Dad was embarking on this extraordinary adventure. She stared until her neck got a kink, then turned to face the road. "I feel like I've been missing out on something my whole life," she blurted, her emotions dictating her words. "Ever feel like that?"

Becky shrugged. "Around here, we just take things in stride." She glanced at Heather. "Maybe that's not what you meant."

"I'm the only child in my family. Maybe that's why."

A sympathetic look spread over Becky's face. "Aw . . . no wonder, then." She paused. "Maybe you know that Plain folk are surrounded by lots of siblings and family, grandparents included. And we look after each other."

Heather asked, "Is everything really family focused, then?"

"Pretty much." Becky smiled. "And I'd say we're more about the whole community, though families are mighty important. The ministerial brethren oversee each church district, and their

word comes down to the family through the heads of each household. It's the menfolk who rule . . . some more kindly than others."

So much for freethinking women. Heather could not believe how similar this system was to the one she was addressing in her master's thesis, on the patriarchy of colonial days. For a moment, she wished there was time to change the topic to the role of the Amish patriarch, since she was here, living the research.

"The oldest men in the church district have the biggest say—'the most clout,' Mamma likes to say, always with a twinkle in her eye." Becky covered her mouth, stifling her laugh. "But 'tis ever so true."

"What about women—do they have any choice on personal preferences?"

This brought more laughter from Becky. "Such as what?"

"You know, things like fabric colors for dresses or quilts, or who to name their babies after."

Becky's eyes lit up. "To tell you the truth, Mamma's well known round here as good at namin' babies." She explained how her mother had once given some suggestions to their neighbor when her first daughter was born—"my *gut* friend, who lives in the first house to the west of us. Her name's Grace. She was the first of many children Mamma helped to name."

Heather had no idea what Becky meant. "So . . . do the People have some sort of old-time naming ritual?"

"Well, let me tell ya . . . Mamma holds the baby up and turns around three times. Then she closes her eyes real tight, says the alphabet backward and—" Becky's face burst into a grin. "No, I'm just pullin' your leg, Heather. All she does is look at a new infant to see if a particular name fits. That's all."

"But who would let someone else name their baby?" Heather asked, hoping she wasn't corrupting Becky with her modern mind.

"Oh, no one. People do ask her for ideas, though. Lettie Byler would never have come up with Grace on her own. Ain't such a common name amongst us." Becky glanced at her. "Sorry . . . we joke a lot round here."

They continued to ride through the farmland, abounding with willow trees and laced with a wide, flowing creek. They saw dozens and dozens of grazing cows as, at Heather's insistence, they kept discussing community versus the individual. She wished she had her laptop along to take notes when Becky made an interesting comment: "God put in the heart of His creation—in all of us—the need to belong. Husbands to wives, families to one another, and all of us to our heavenly Father." Becky said this with such wide-eyed conviction, Heather scarcely knew what to think.

Soon, they arrived at a small house set near the road, with a sign out front: *Emma's Cupboard.* "My mother's cousin has electric here," Becky said. "Emma's Mennonite. She'll be happy to let you charge up your phone or whatnot all."

Heather was glad for this chance, but if asked she would have admitted to not missing her phone at all today. Quite satisfied with her decision to come to Amish country, she followed Becky into the adorable white clapboard shop with black shutters.

— ··· —

That evening Heather sat at the long kitchen table with Becky, who was drawing with colored pencils. Three hummingbirds in flight, each subsequently larger than the other.

Heather had decided to chronicle her trip longhand, with the plan to transcribe it to her journal file on her laptop later in her room. She continued writing about her day and the collision of emotions she'd experienced while sorting through her feelings about her illness and Devon in this almost magical setting.

It's the last day of April, and I've been in Lancaster County for only a little more than twenty-four hours. Mom loved coming here so much, yet I miss her less here than when I'm home.

Well, about my first day back in Plain country. I observed marked differences between Emma, a Mennonite shopkeeper who allowed me to recharge my phone, and Becky, with her Amish customs. Becky wouldn't think of owning or driving a car, or having anything run on electricity.

As much as I love my high-tech toys, there's an undeniable appeal to the simple life. That's saying a lot for moi!

I do think it's a good thing I was born modern, though. I couldn't tolerate living in this thoroughly male-dominated society, even with the trade-offs. Getting to run barefoot half the year sounds good to me!

Of course, I plan to indulge my modern side, too. The thirty-two shops at the Kitchen Kettle Village await. Looks like a hoppin' place!

I've already pinpointed three additional things I'd like to do—"must-sees," according to Marian and Becky. First are the back-roads tours offered by the Mennonite Information Center; the second, a visit to Central Market, on the square in downtown Lancaster. And finally, the Landis Valley Museum looks fascinating. Mom and Dad took me there when I was nine, I think. I loved it then, and I'm sure I'll enjoy it even more now. This is definitely what the doctor ordered. (Well, not exactly!)

Heather glanced across the table at Becky, who had almost completed her drawing. Maybe this trip wasn't what the

doctor had ordered, but for today, it was all the medicine she needed.

— ··· —

Judah stood at the footboard and stared at Lettie's side of the bed, his eyes lingering on her pillow. How long had it been since they'd held each other? Turning, he reached for the Good Book, bearing its weight to his chair near the bureau. He sat with a groan. Opening to the Proverbs, he read: *"A soft answer turneth away wrath: but grievous words stir up anger."*

The lantern on the dresser shone brightly, yet in it he saw his future, which looked downright lonely. If Lettie did not return, she would eventually be cut off by the church—no matter that she was already estranged from him.

No wonder . . . the peculiar way we started out, he recalled. At the first Jakob Esh had been something of a go-between for Lettie and himself. Not that Judah hadn't laid eyes on her years before and decided she was something to behold—a real catch and a natural with a baseball bat. He would have pursued her then, except she was only fourteen. Her pretty face—*ach, her eyes*—he'd carried the memory into his dreams. He'd set his sights on her as the girl he wanted to wed and settle down with to have a family. But being two years older, he'd waited for her, without making his intentions known.

My first mistake, he'd thought many times since.

Lettie, it turned out, had a mind of her own when it came to boys. Judah hadn't foreseen that Samuel Graber, with all his fancy leanings, would beat him to the punch.

Little good it did him in the end, he thought.

Sitting in the stillness of his room now, Judah knew it

wouldn't have mattered a whit back then had he realized how off-putting Lettie might become. He'd loved her in spite of her sullenness and determination to have her own way. Besides, now that they were married, what could he do about it? Under God, they were joined till death separated them.

He wiped his brow. It was one thing to speak downright pointedly to Andy Riehl, admonishing him not to put credence in gossip. It was quite another to chop off the grapevine at its root.

chapter
twenty-eight

Heather pulled on her jeans, peering down at the loose-fitting waistband. This pair had fit well the last time she'd worn them, so why were they getting baggy now, after all the rich Amish food she'd been eating since arriving two days ago? Saggy jeans annoyed her, and these certainly were getting there.

How had she managed to drop a few pounds—every girl's ambition—while pigging out on Marian's mouthwatering meals? Was this proof that a disease actually lurked within her body?

Once downstairs, she followed Becky out to the chicken house, where she watched her scatter chicken feed. Heather reached into her own bucket and mimicked Becky, enjoying the swarm of chickens near her feet, some flying with a great *swoosh* through the air. "Wow, are they starving or what?"

Becky laughed. "You'd think we never feed 'em." She explained that as a young girl she'd been afraid to carry them water or to throw feed from her apron. "The chickens would fly right at me," she said. "Nearly knocked me down."

These were definitely some ravenous critters. *Puck, puck,* they carried on, feisty in their frenzied pecking of feed.

"Come, let's water the horses next." Becky motioned to Heather and glanced at her tennies. "You might want to wear older shoes or my brother's boots, maybe?"

"Or run barefoot?" Heather couldn't help it; she giggled just like Becky. She tried to ignore the fears brought on by her weight loss—at least till her appointment with Dr. Marshall.

———···———

Thursday was typically market day, but Grace was scheduled to work at Eli's later this afternoon. Since she was needed at home to cook the noon meal, going straight to Bart after breakfast would work best.

On the way to the phone shanty, she was surprised to see Dat just hanging up the receiver. His hair was all clean and shiny, minus his straw hat. "You must be headin' somewhere, too," she said.

"Martin's comin' by in a few minutes," he replied.

"Oh, would ya mind if I share the ride?"

Dat shook his head. "Might as well kill two birds with one stone."

They turned back toward the house, walking along the left side of the road, as she'd always walked to school. Here lately, those days seemed like another lifetime ago.

Dat didn't mention where he was heading, so she decided not to mention her destination, either—not unless he asked outright. She wondered how he'd react if he knew. *Likely he won't say anything.*

Her father's lack of communication could be maddening at times—Mamma had all but admitted to feeling the same. Like any married couple, she and Dat had experienced disagreements. Why was it, once two people tied the knot, their troubles seemed to surface?

Grace had secretly read a love poem in one of Mamma's books. According to that, marital happiness was simply a matter of being willing to give yourself fully to your beloved. Had Mamma read it, too?

Something akin to dying to one's self, as the Lord commands?

She walked silently with Dat, pondering these things and wondering if she might ever feel so terribly frustrated with Henry . . . years from now.

Enough to leave him?

——— ··· ———

Once again, Grace was amazed by how talkative Dat could be as he hashed over the planting season and the weather with Martin Puckett while they rode. Was he bending over backward to indulge their driver because of the appalling rumors?

It surprised her, as well, to see what a short distance Dat was going today by van. Normally he'd hitch up the horse and buggy to go to the bank, his first destination. He mentioned to Martin he needed to withdraw some cash to pay his bill at the harness shop, which was his next stop.

Martin pulled over and parked.

"Won't be but a minute," Dat said.

Even though she was anxious to get to Bart, Grace didn't mind sitting and waiting for her father. His errands wouldn't

take long, and it would be no time before she and Martin were on their way south.

The banking line was longer than usual, and here Judah had been so sure he'd beat the morning crowd. He had filled out his withdrawal slip before ever leaving the house, and he noticed several other Plain folk ahead of him, mostly young mothers with children in tow.

Where are you today, Lettie? he wondered while watching two small girls play behind their mother's long skirt.

When he stepped up to the teller window, he handed the clerk his withdrawal slip with the requested amount and his account number, along with his pictureless ID—like a driver's license of sorts, without the photograph. The English locals had made this provision for the many Amish residents, and he was mighty grateful not to have to squabble over the church ordinance on yet another issue. Enough of that went on already.

"I'll need your code word, please, Mr. Byler," the clerk said, sliding a small blank piece of paper toward him.

Quickly he scribbled the name of Grace's beloved horse, *Willow,* and returned it to the clerk. She counted out the bills and handed him a receipt and a printout of the balance of his account.

Looking at it, he realized there had been a mistake. "Excuse me," he said. "The balance is too low." He leaned forward, not wanting to make a scene. "Much lower than I expected."

The clerk asked if he wanted to see a list of his recent account activity, to which he nodded. She ran it through the printer, and he glanced over his shoulder to see Martin's van in the parking lot. He almost wished he'd come by horse and buggy

instead, not wanting to keep Martin—and Grace—waiting. Of course, he couldn't have predicted the bank mix-up. The nagging pain in his neck worsened.

The clerk handed him the sheet and pointed to the transaction for Wednesday, April 23. Five thousand dollars had been withdrawn in the form of cash that day.

His breath caught in his throat, but he managed to thank the clerk and move away from the teller window.

Lettie?

Staring at the printout, he shuddered to think his wife had withdrawn money from their joint account without asking, or even mentioning it after the fact. Nearly the sum total of her earnings from last summer's market sales had vanished on the day of Grace's birthday.

So, Lettie must've planned her trip down to the penny, Judah thought. Truly, it appeared she was not coming home any time soon . . . if ever.

When Dat appeared at the bank entrance, looking ashen, Grace wondered if perhaps there had been a problem. But he quietly got in the front seat next to Martin without saying a peep about anything amiss.

Naturally, he wouldn't, she decided. Yet it seemed odd that he had ceased his previous chatter.

By the time they arrived at the harness shop, Grace wondered if her father might be feeling ill. As Martin turned into the parking area for the harness shop, Dat said, "Listen, Martin, I think I'll stay round here for a while."

"Fine by me," Martin replied.

"What do I owe ya for Gracie and me?"

Martin told him the amount, then added, "It'll be a while before I get back here to pick you up, if that suits you."

"Oh, I can easily hitchhike a buggy ride home." Dat glanced at Grace just then. "I'll see ya for dinner at noon, jah?"

That was all he said—no inquiry about where she might be going today. *Doesn't he care to know?*

She nodded and forced a smile. Mamma had always said Dat's appetite for food was one of his primary concerns. When he closed the door, she felt overwhelmed by sadness.

As they rode, Grace observed the familiar landmarks on South Ronks Road . . . then Fairview Road and eventually down to the main street in Strasburg. She looked longingly at the creamery on the northeast corner as they waited for the red light. Henry had taken her there late last summer, when they'd first started dating, coming all this way for ice cream on a Saturday night. He'd been so uncomfortable and shy, he'd said scarcely one word that evening, she recalled.

Sighing, she leaned her head against the window, not sure who baffled her more these days: her father or her fiancé.

——— ··· ———

Judah breathed in the rich, leathery scent of the harness shop. It was one of his favorite places for that reason alone. Intensely aware of his mounting neck pain, he wondered if he might be on the verge of a stroke. His great-aunt had suffered with such pain for months prior to the brainstem bleed that eventually took her life.

There were times when he could not make sense of what he truly felt about Lettie's departure. And now this—it was unthinkable for her to withdraw such a large sum without

discussing it. Was her need for money the reason she'd struggled so to tell him? And why hadn't she contacted him or anyone else since leaving? Her exasperating silence struck him as uncaring and downright cold.

He reached in his pocket to fish for an aspirin and found none. If the excruciating pain didn't subside soon, he'd have to see a doctor. *Prob'ly should've before now*, he thought, waiting his turn for the smithy, who was finishing shoeing a horse.

Hurry up and wait today . . .

Hazily, he heard his name spoken behind him.

"Judah Byler! I was hopin' to see you this week."

Turning, Judah saw a tall blond man in his early twenties. He'd slipped in the door unnoticed till now.

"Yonnie Bontrager." The young fellow offered an engaging smile and a solid handshake in return. "Will you spare me a minute, sir?" He explained that he'd planned to stop by the house. "But since you're here . . ."

Judah nodded, unsure what the boy could want.

"*Gut*, then." Yonnie's grin was infectious. "I'll wait out by my buggy."

When the smithy finished up with his other customer, he caught Judah's eye and hurried to the back room to get Judah's repaired harness. Soon he returned, hauling it out and laying it down on the long table. "You'll be glad to know the amount came to less than we'd agreed on. Don't hear that too often, *jah*?"

Judah nodded and pulled out his wallet. *Every little bit helps . . . 'specially now*, he thought. While tallying up the correct amount of cash, he recalled the bank clerk's hushed counting of these same bills. And his sinking feeling when he realized Lettie had taken so much for herself.

He slung the harness over his shoulder and headed outside. Yonnie stood near his horse and open carriage.

"Here, let me help." Yonnie took the harness and carried it to his own buggy, lugging it inside. "Looks like you could use a ride home." Going around to the driver's side, he hopped into the courting buggy. "That is, if you don't mind ridin' in my new wheels."

One ride's as good as another, Judah decided and got in.

Yonnie's eyes grew serious now as he reached for the reins. "If it's not too forward, I'd like to ask you something."

"Speak your mind," Judah said absently.

Yonnie pulled out onto the road, letting the horse trot a ways before speaking again. "Would it be too much to ask . . . well, to give your blessing for me to court your daughter Grace?"

Judah had never heard of such a request. Certainly, among some of the more conservative Mennonites—even the Brethren folk—the potential groom was expected to ask the girl's father for her hand in marriage but not prior to merely courting. "I believe Grace is spoken for," said Judah, looking at Yonnie.

"Puh! I'm too late, then?"

"You'd know better 'bout who's pairing up at Singings and whatnot."

Yonnie raised his eyebrows. "Glory be, if Grace's spoken for, she doesn't look too happy 'bout it."

Judah flinched. Grace *was* carrying the weight of the world on her shoulders, but not for the reason Yonnie now assumed. "Tell you what: I won't stand in your way if Grace wants ya. How's that?"

Yonnie patted his hat and gave a whoop. He clucked his tongue and the horse moved from a trot to a near gallop.

Now, here's a boy in love, thought Judah, thinking back to his own courting days.

There had been a mighty stir among the area youth when Samuel Graber started showing up at Singings before the appointed time. He was only fifteen, if that, when he first came and sat high on the bales of hay, just watching the youth sing. Nearly staring them down, some said. Gawking, said others.

Then, when some of the couples started pairing up, Samuel wandered around the barn, always with a book tucked under his arm and a pencil stuck atop his ear. Some of the girls thought he was getting ideas for poetry, but Judah didn't know what to make of that. Sometimes he struck up a conversation with a couple, or several girls, and other times he simply strolled along the perimeter of the social gathering. Then, after a time, he went and sat again, making drawings of faces and profiles in his notebook, or writing snippets of rhyme.

There was enough hearsay to know this Samuel was mighty strange. And Samuel seemed to know, somehow, that he wasn't truly accepted by the other youth, but that didn't seem to discourage him one iota. He continued to overstep his bounds by attending all the youth-related events.

Then, along about the time Lettie Esh started attending the get-togethers, Samuel suddenly quit coming. Later, word had it he was seeing Lettie on the sly at her house—according to two of her sisters, anyway. Samuel was known to go over there several times a week, which was considered giving a girl the rush—nobody did anything like that. Not that Judah had heard of, anyway. Still, none of that seemed to matter to Lettie, and the two of them were frequently seen after the common

meal on Sundays, their heads nearly touching as she sat behind the barn with him, watching him write in his so-called poetry book.

Meanwhile, Judah realized he'd dallied and hadn't acted quickly enough. More of an observer than a go-getter, he'd lost his chance with Lettie—and to Samuel, of all fellows. Samuel, who wasn't too keen on following the Lord in holy baptism, or taking the required instruction to join church. Some said he was working on getting Lettie to "see the light, too" and making other disturbing remarks against the church.

Judah figured if that was the kind of fellow he was, then Lettie must be on the fringes, too, or heading there. So Judah began seeing other girls, hoping to find a devout, hard-working wife from among the remaining group of eligible young women.

Months passed, and by the time he heard that Lettie Esh and her mother had gone to assist an ailing aunt out in Ohio for a time, Samuel Graber and his poetry books were long gone.

Meanwhile, Judah was dating a new girl, though not one nearly as pretty as Lettie. It was much later that Jakob Esh came knocking one morning, and they went talking, man to man. Although he'd thought at the time how unusual it was for a father to play such a role, Judah was still plenty interested in having a chance to court Lettie—willing and ready, in fact, having never forgotten her. And while he was nothing like Samuel, he hoped she might come to love him. Judah's talent was laboring with his hands and by the sweat of his brow—he had never read a poem to a girl or even to himself, let alone written one. At only eighteen, he worked the soil hard and tended to sheep.

Once he started seriously courting seventeen-year-old Lettie, he gave her the courtesy of not speaking about Samuel.

For her part, she, too, never uttered his name. At least, not intentionally.

There were times, though, when Lettie sometimes whispered Samuel's name while she lay sleeping. Judah had refused to let it bother him. He knew as well as the next fellow that plenty of young folk didn't end up hitched to the first girl or fellow they took a shine to.

Most important, Lettie had agreed to marry *him*. And nearly ten months later, she bore him a fine and healthy son. The Lord had been good, seeing fit to give them four wonderful children and twenty-three years of marriage.

Till now . . .

—— ··· ——

Grace was greeted warmly at the back door of the Stoltzfus home. Cousin Rose actually threw her arms around her. "Oh, it's so nice to see ya!"

"And you, too." She was glad when Rose suggested they go walking on the road, which was rather unlike their own busy street. The unpaved road more resembled a private lane, and Grace began to relax, the warmth of the sun on her face as Cousin Rose chattered away. Grace was surprised—and pleased—when she realized the grapevine had not wended its way this far concerning Mamma. It made things much easier all around.

At last Grace hesitantly asked Rose about Mamma's friend at the barn raising. "Do you remember the woman? She wasn't from around here, I don't think."

"Goodness, I believe I *do* know who you mean," said Rose. "That was Sarah Graber, visiting from Ohio, though I can't

be sure of the exact city. Might be in Wayne County." Rose fanned herself with a hankie. "She lives *somewhere* out there, anyway."

"Is she related to you . . . or to Mamma?"

"Not to me, no. She was in town to see her grand-niece's baby, is what I heard." A sudden frown appeared on Rose's plump face. "Ach . . . I 'spect you might not know who Sarah's twin is, then."

"No."

"Well, that would be your mother's first beau, Samuel Graber. He was already on his way out of the church right around the time he and your mother started courtin'." Rose paused and drew in a slow breath. "Seems from what was said back then, he had a real hankering for fancy, modern books—poetry and whatnot. Even wrote some himself. I believe I've got that right . . . so long ago now."

That explained the books Mamma had retrieved from Uncle Ike's; they must've come from Samuel. *But how odd that Mamma wanted to keep them.* Grace blinked her eyes, trying to absorb the news. "Why didn't they marry?"

"Well, like I said, Samuel wasn't much interested in joinin' church. And your mother surely was."

Mamma certainly had married someone devoted to God and the church. "She's been a stickler for goin' to Preaching all my life." *Just not so much recently,* thought Grace, not knowing what to make of all this. She'd never heard Mamma breathe a word about her first beau, yet she'd chosen to keep the poetry books . . . even taking some away with her. *Of all things!*

Rose asked in a roundabout way about Grace's relationship with her parents, and Grace saw through it. No doubt Rose

wondered why Grace had come all this way to ask something her own mother could have answered.

"Your Mamma was better off without Samuel, I'll say," Rose added. "Some called him a troublemaker."

Grace knew she ought to be heading home right quick. "Denki ever so much, Cousin Rose, but it's 'bout time for me to start back—I have dinner to make."

Now Rose was frowning to beat the band, staring over her glasses at her. "Is your mamma too sick to cook today? You can certainly stay and eat with us . . . that'd be just right fine."

She had slipped up but good. "Another time, maybe," Grace said quickly. "My driver will be returning soon. It's kind of you to visit with me. Thank you again ever so much."

"Anytime, Grace . . . just anytime at all." Rose took off her glasses and cleaned them with her hankie. "Tell your family hullo from all of us down here. We sure miss the Sunday visits."

Nodding, Grace told how busy they were now, what with lambing. She hoped Rose wouldn't ask specifically again about Mamma and open up that can of worms.

Very soon, Martin Puckett's van came inching along the narrow lane. *Just in time, too.*

——— ⋯ ———

All the way home, Grace could not begin to understand what her mother and the twin sister of Mamma's first beau could have had to talk about on their long walk. It seemed very awkward.

Has Mamma kept in touch with Sarah through the years? Could that be?

If so, she felt it was a prickly thing—nearly inappropriate.

She stared out at the sky, glad to be sitting behind Martin as he drove. That way he wouldn't feel at liberty to talk as they traveled, nor to make eye contact in his rearview mirror. There was so much to ponder now, her head all filled up with strange names and odd circumstances. Hearing about Samuel was jarring, especially since Joe said Mamma had been hovering near the mailbox all those days before she escaped.

Who was she expecting to hear from . . . and was it related to her leaving?

Aunt Lavina's vague comment about Mamma's first beau rang in Grace's memory. Oh, but she did not want Martin Puckett to glimpse her face now. She was afraid that the confusion all tangled up in her heart would surely be registered there.

chapter
twenty-nine

Martin's wife called him on his cell phone, asking if he would like to come home for lunch. "I've made a nice batch of chicken salad," she said, enticing him with one of his very favorites.

He agreed to head right there. And while doing so, he considered Judah Byler's upbeat attitude earlier today and, in contrast, his daughter Grace's sullenness. He couldn't get over why she'd wanted to travel so far for such a short visit, but that was neither here nor there. He was just pleased for the opportunity to be working again, because the calls from the Amish—especially those in Bird-in-Hand—were still far fewer than usual.

Janet had the round table in the dining cove set and ready when he arrived. He kissed her and went to wash his hands at the sink.

"Business picking up?" she asked.

"Only two passengers so far." He reached for the towel and dried his hands.

"Might be the last two," she said softly, "from what I heard at the spa." Janet had gone for a facial and overheard two women

talking about a silly rumor that had turned into a mountain of a story.

"Well, for goodness' sake!" His heart sank as he pulled out his chair and sat down.

"Seems more like the doings of small-town busybodies than a typical Amish community." Janet reached for her napkin and placed it on her lap.

"Plenty of gossip everywhere, I suppose."

Janet was staring at him now. "It's tantalizing to pass along something seen at a train station, I guess."

He squeezed his lips together. So she'd heard what *must* have originated with Pete Bernhardt that day. "Well, not *all* of it is fact."

She leaned over the table, reaching for his hand. "You didn't run off with an Amishwoman, did you?"

He laughed. "Not unless *you're* Amish."

She leaned back and sighed. "Considering we left for our long weekend that day, I'd already figured *that*."

"Evidently someone needs more than a little amusement." He shook his head. "At my expense."

"And Lettie Byler's. How must her husband feel?"

No way did Martin think Judah Byler believed any of those rumors. Not as friendly as he'd been on the way to the bank today.

"The whole thing will die down," Martin said. "Except for the fact that I did drive Lettie Byler to Lancaster, as you know." He explained that Lettie had left a slip of paper with several phone numbers on it, so he'd gone in to return it to her. He leaned over and kissed Janet's cheek. "You have nothing to worry about, love."

She smiled back. "What can we do to put a stop to all this?"

"Live our lives honestly, just as we do."

She reached for the salt and pepper. "Have you thought of addressing the rumors with her husband?"

He considered it, but Judah wasn't one to make a to-do over something. And Judah trusted Martin with Grace, so why not with Lettie? No, it seemed clear Judah Byler did not believe the rumors. *He's too sensible to believe hearsay.* "If he brings it up, I'll tell Judah my side of things. How's that?"

Janet didn't question his response, and they continued the lunch by talking about their married son's plans to visit next week. Later, Janet's face glowed as she shared a description of her hour-long facial. "I wouldn't mind going every few months," she added. "If it doesn't tax our budget."

Martin nodded, trying to think of ways to woo back his Amish customers. *Janet's spa habit will keep me working!*

———··· ———

Grace had left lean ground beef to thaw on the counter while she was in Bart. When she returned to the kitchen, she was happy to see Mandy already assembling the ingredients for the meatloaf. She stood in the doorway between their large sitting room and the kitchen, watching her sister stir together the eggs, oatmeal, mustard, onions, ketchup, and tomato juice to add to the meat, then prepare to shape the finished mixture into a mound.

"Ach, you're doin' such a nice job," she said, finally moving into the kitchen.

Mandy looked up, smiling. "You were planning on having meatloaf today, weren't you?"

"That'll be fine," Grace said, going to get some pinto beans out of the pantry. She enjoyed working side by side with her sister. Grace put the beans in a pot with some smoked meat, brown sugar, mustard, onions, catsup, vinegar, and other seasonings to make the baked bean side dish.

The way Mamma always makes them.

When she'd put the beans in the oven, she headed up the stairs to change into an older gray choring dress. She would simply change back into the better blue one as the time came closer to heading for work.

In her room she sat on the settee near the window and reread Mamma's letter. The thought nagged at her that she ought to share at least some of what Mamma had written with poor Mandy. Yet she feared doing so would stir up more sadness in her sister, just as it would in any of them.

"Did it in Dat?" she whispered, gazing out the window.

It was nearly impossible to understand how her father could talk so animatedly with Martin Puckett so soon after practically ignoring his own daughter on their walk back from the phone shanty. She would almost prefer him moping around the way Mandy did, carrying such pain in her eyes. Truth be told, that was the way she felt, too, though she kept her saddest emotions hidden for the sake of her family.

Returning the letter to its hiding place, she decided to seek wise counsel from her grandmother. Mammi Adah would know best.

And, too, Grace hadn't forgotten about the old letter stuck in Dawdi's Bible. Why on earth had Dawdi and Mammi saved it?

Back downstairs, Grace began to peel, then boil a heap of

potatoes for mashing. Next she finished making the brown gravy. Hurrying to the cold cellar below, she chose a canning jar of chowchow and one of red beets to round out their meal.

Close to noon, she noticed Dat and her brothers emerging from the barn. They stood outside talking—what about, she couldn't guess. "Remember to put on the bread and butter," she told Mandy, placing the hot dishes on the table.

"Dat likes his apple butter, ain't?" Mandy asked.

"He plain loves to eat." Grace returned to the sink area and gave her sister a sideways glance. "What would ya say 'bout takin' turns cooking?"

"Actually, today in the barn Dat suggested I help you more. Did you say somethin', maybe?"

Grace shook her head. "Nary a word." She was frankly surprised their father had noticed her plight.

"Well, I'm sure willing to pitch in more." Mandy began slicing a loaf of bread on the large cutting board. "Just wish there was more I could do to help Dat. 'Tween you and me, I think he's ever so miserable."

"No doubt."

Mandy continued. "I was really tuckered out myself for a few days there, Gracie. I felt I couldn't keep goin', sad as I was." Mandy stacked the slices of bread on a plate. "But you know what? I've decided not to be so glum anymore," she said. "I don't understand why Mamma left, and I don't like it one bit. But if she doesn't want us to know where she's gone—or why—then she must have a *gut* reason."

Grace looked at her sister. Hers was an interesting view. As for herself, she couldn't simply dismiss Mamma's strange

behavior—or the tragedy of her abandoning them. "It's hard to know what Mamma's thinkin'," she said.

"Jah, but if we ponder it too hard, it'll just drive us all mad, ain't?"

Grace had fought through anguished moments in the night when she thought she might awaken the house if she gave in to sobbing. "Think I'll go over to see if Dawdi and Mammi want to join us for dinner today," she said.

"Jah. They ought to join us every day," Mandy agreed. "Seems odd for them to live under the same roof but only eat with us once in a blue moon."

Mamma's doing, thought Grace, though to her sister she said, "That's a wonderful-*gut* idea, Mandy." With that she hurried through the sitting room and across the hallway to their grandparents' side.

During the tasty meatloaf dinner, Grace noticed Mandy seemed more like her old self. No doubt she had happily noticed all the lip-smacking at the table.

Later Grace helped Dawdi Jakob back across the house to his favorite chair in the sitting room. Once he was settled, Mammi motioned her into the kitchen so she could look at a new cookie recipe.

"I received it in a circle letter from one of my cousin's friends," Mammi Adah told her.

Grace looked at the recipe and smiled. "A healthy cookie?" She'd seen them at Eli's, all packaged up in cellophane near the cashier. She'd even tasted one.

Mammi Adah asked what she thought of substituting agave nectar for sugar, as called for in the cookie recipe. "You would

need less of it, for one thing . . . and for another, the texture would be more cake-like," Grace told her.

But as interesting as the recipe was, Grace was anxious to discuss other things. And the minute Mammi put the recipe on the kitchen counter, Grace said, "I've been holdin' on to Mamma's note to me, not sure what to do." She explained her uncertainty, how she feared it might especially affect sensitive Mandy. "Dat's read it, though."

Mammi frowned. "Does it explain why your father thinks Lettie's not comin' back?" Her voice was flat.

"Might be. But it's hard to say, really."

Mammi Adah's eyes were somber. "Would ya mind if I read it?"

"Well, only if it won't make you feel awful blue. I'd hate to—"

"No . . . don't think that." Mammi reached out a hand. "You're a gracious soul, dear."

She felt embarrassed but squeezed Mammi's hand. "There's something else on my mind, Mammi."

"Jah?"

Slowly, choosing her words carefully, she began to share what she'd learned from Dat's cousin Rose about Mamma and her long-ago beau. "Now that I know who Sarah Graber is, I'm still befuddled as to Mamma's excitement at seeing her down at the barn raising."

Her grandmother sighed softly, and pretty soon big tears slipped down her wrinkled cheeks.

Grace felt the tight, prickly feeling in her stomach again.

"So, dare I ask you . . . why would Mamma be so thrilled to see Samuel Graber's sister?"

Adah had to be careful what she revealed to Grace about her mother and Samuel. The last thing she wanted was to influence her granddaughter in any negative way. No, Grace mustn't think any less of her Mamma for her youthful interest in worldly young Samuel.

Grace's blue eyes were wide as she waited for an answer. She crossed her legs and leaned forward intently, a bare foot sticking out from beneath the hem of her choring dress.

"My dear girl, I have no idea why your mother was so happy to see Samuel's sister." Adah was conscious of the beating of her own heart.

"Ever so peculiar, ain't so?"

Adah straightened her apron and willed herself to remain calm. "I wish I could tell you that your mother fell first for a devout boy, heading toward church baptism. But, alas, Samuel would have taken her away from the church." She patted her face with her hankie. "It was providential that one of Dawdi Jakob's elderly relatives—your mother's great-aunt—needed some live-in care in Ohio. Your Mamma and I went there to assist her for a few months . . . till she died."

"But was it also to get my mother away from Samuel?"

"Well, by the time we returned home, Samuel and his family had surprisingly moved away. Your mother was heart-broken beyond belief, but your Dawdi and I were relieved." Adah brushed away her tears. "Not a soul approved of Samuel courtin' our Lettie, including Dawdi and me."

"So the People knew of their courtship, then? It wasn't a secret, like we keep it nowadays?"

"Oh, it was meant to be secret, all right, but the few who knew how much time Samuel was spending with your mother each week were concerned."

Grace looked surprised. "Who else knew?"

"The ministerial brethren had gotten word, for one."

"Did Dawdi Jakob tell them?"

Adah bowed her head. That had been her doing, as she recalled—such a painful position to be in. "I daresay we've talked enough 'bout the past, dear one."

Grace rose and walked the length of the kitchen with a determined look and glanced toward the sitting room.

Adah assumed she was looking to see if Jakob had nodded off to sleep in his chair. "Ach, Gracie, you mustn't let this trouble you so."

"I must confess somethin'," Grace said suddenly.

Adah jerked her head fully upright. "Oh?"

"I saw an envelope sticking out of Dawdi's Bible the night I came in to see you, all discouraged after a date. Remember?"

"Jah." Adah's heart was pounding faster now.

"I don't want to snoop, Mammi, so I'm askin' for permission to read the letter Dawdi Jakob sent to you and my mother in Kidron." Grace blinked her eyes too quickly. "All right?"

"Why, dear?"

Grace shrugged. "There must be a reason you or Dawdi saved it, jah?"

Adah sighed. "Best not, Gracie." She tried to keep her emotions steady, but Grace was pushing much too hard for her own good.

chapter
thirty

Judah awakened from a fitful sleep, glad his inner clock hadn't failed him. His turn to check on the lambs. *Can't afford to lose another one*, he thought, fumbling for his robe in the darkness.

He staggered down the stairs to the hallway and sat on the deacon's bench to pull on his work boots over bare feet. Although still in something of a stupor, he managed to get to the barn, where he made his way to the lambing pen. There he monitored the two-day-old twins, born Wednesday afternoon while he and Andy Riehl sheared the rest of the sheep. Thankfully, Adam and Joe had kept watch over the laboring ewe, and there had been no complications.

Unable now to repress his feelings of anxiety, Judah knelt in the hay. The pain in his neck had developed into a constant torment, a continual reminder of his loss. Blame saddled him down with a weight he felt powerless to escape.

What Judah wouldn't do for some rest . . . deep, restorative sleep to submerge the memories and ease the enduring pain.

Let us lay aside every weight, and the sin which doth so easily beset us . . .

He mustered up the energy to inspect the two remaining triplet lambs, as well—one of which needed frequent bottle-feeding. That done, he slid open the barn door, closed it again, and slogged back to the house. He kicked off his dirty boots, then gripping the banister, he pulled himself back up the stairs to his room.

Almost too tired to move, Judah fell into bed with his robe still tied at the waist. His feet hung off Lettie's side of the bed.

Dear wife of mine . . .

— ... —

The sun peeked over the distant green hills, and Heather was awake enough to turn on her phone to check her email. Several college acquaintances had sent updates in an attempt to get her to return for some summer fun.

Fleetingly, she wished she had a sister. It would be a relief to have someone to confide in, whether about Devon or about her diagnosis and the upcoming appointment with the naturopath. It wasn't that she questioned her decisions; she just felt so alone in the world.

When she heard a knock on her door, she set aside her phone. She really needed to work on her thesis today, once she got her inbox down to zero.

She opened the door and there stood Becky, dressed for the day in a dark green dress with an apron to match. "Would ya want to come help make chocolate waffles, Heather?" she asked, eyes shining.

Heather had indicated an interest yesterday, but this minute? She craved some time alone. She had enjoyed Becky's company, but as was her usual way with potential friendships, she felt herself backing away, even though her initial connection with Becky Riehl had been so strong.

"Heather?" Becky repeated.

"Maybe another time?"

Becky's smile faded.

Heather felt bad—she hadn't wanted to hurt the younger girl's feelings. "I just need to keep working, that's all." The explanation sounded lame even to her ears.

"I'll call ya when breakfast is ready, then."

"Thanks. I appreciate it." Heather closed the door.

She shook her head. *Why do I always do that?*

Heather crawled back onto the bed with what looked to be her best friend in the world right now—her phone.

———···———

Surprised to see Dat's door wide open, Grace looked in on her father, who was still sleeping. She'd come up to check on him after Adam and Joe asked why he hadn't gone directly to the barn after dawn, their usual habit.

She didn't have the heart to waken him as he slept crisscross on the bed. *Must have checked on the lambs earlier.* Thinking it best to leave him be, as weary as he'd been for the past week, she softly closed the door and tiptoed downstairs to put breakfast on the table.

Dawdi and Mammi came over without being asked today . . . quite cheerfully, too. Evidently they were all for Mandy's suggestion they take meals together as one big family.

"Dat's under the weather," Grace said as they sat. Then they bowed their heads, ready for Dawdi Jakob's blessing.

Grace placed her left hand on Mamma's vacant chair and asked the Lord to look after her while offering her own silent thanks. Dat had instructed them to remember Mamma and her safety in their prayers. She was tempted to pray for a safe and quick return, too.

After the blessing, Mammi Adah looked at Dat's empty chair before mentioning the coming no-Preaching Sunday. Dawdi Jakob also entered into the discussion. "Any suggestions who we should go visit?" he asked. "Has your Dat talked of anyone?"

Both Adam and Joe shook their heads.

"Well, we can't all fit in one carriage," Mammi said, "but Adam could take his courtin' buggy and put the girls in it."

"That'd be fun," Mandy piped up, her fork resting between her fingers.

"It's been the longest time since we've seen Dat's cousins in Bart," suggested Joe.

Grace sucked in a breath. "But . . . without Mamma?"

Adam locked his gaze on Grace's. "Jah . . . those cousins probably aren't the best choice this time."

"Might just get things stirred up worse than they are," Dawdi agreed, wiping crumbs from his gray beard.

"What about Dat's parents, then?" Joe asked. "We could go down near Ronks to see them . . . then come back and visit the Bontragers, maybe."

"Two families in one afternoon." Mandy smiled and looked back and forth between Grace and Joe.

Grace studied her younger brother. What was he up to? Was
he sweet on Yonnie's younger sister Mary Liz, just maybe?

Adam suggested they wait to see what Dat wanted to do.
"He's not sick, is he, Grace?" he asked, frowning.

"Considering everything, I'd say he's all tuckered out," she
replied.

At that, everyone nodded, seemingly in unison. Truth was,
and she could see it in their eyes, they were all worried Dat was
pining hard for Mamma.

———— ··· ————

Jessica and Brittany Spangler stopped by with three loaves
of banana nut bread midmorning. Such kind and caring neighbors, as always. "Thought you maybe could use an extra bit of
baking," Brittany said, looking much too serious.

Grace assumed they'd heard by now of Mamma's leaving.
How could they not? Even though nothing was said about it,
she'd have to be blind not to see the knowing glint in their
made-up eyes. "Come see us, Grace!" they urged before saying
good-bye.

So the news had traveled even farther than the People.
Surely the most remarkable tittle-tattle to hit the area in recent
years.

Grace ambled through the kitchen and across the hall, heading upstairs to Mammi Adah's sewing room. Earlier, Mammi
had asked Grace to help cut yard lengths of thread for quilting, and Grace had agreed. She greeted her grandmother and
settled in across the worktable from her, all the while knowing
it was time to come clean. "I hope you know I didn't just let

Mamma go that night," she finally said. "Not without calling to her. Well, pleading . . . truly."

"Of course you tried to stop her." Mammi sighed, her bosom rising slowly. "I'm sure you did, dear, just as I would've."

"There's something else," Grace said, nearly in a whisper.

Mammi looked up, scissors and thread in hand.

"I went looking for your letter in the night," Grace said, swallowing hard. "It was wrong of me. . . . I'm sorry."

Mammi's eyes grew wide.

"I can't stop thinking 'bout Mamma. If the letter Dawdi wrote to you and Mamma might help . . . well, why not let me read it?" Grace began to cry. "Oh, Mammi . . . I just thought, maybe . . . Ach, I'm ever so sorry."

"There, there, honey-girl." Mammi Adah reached across the table and touched her hand.

She wept softly, wishing she could get ahold of herself. After a time, when she'd wiped her eyes and blown her nose, Grace caught her breath. "Could the address on the envelope be the same as Mamma's present location?"

Mammi Adah nodded slowly. "I can't tell ya how many times I've wondered that myself since she left." She fidgeted.

"If so, Dat could just go and bring Mamma home."

"Well, if your mother's gone there, I can tell you she would not want any of us followin' her." Mammi's breathing was audible as she resumed her measuring and cutting. "It's best we leave things with the Lord."

Grace pondered this and stretched the measuring tape along the thread. She wasn't content to do as Mammi suggested. What if Dat did travel out to Ohio, only to be rebuffed as Grace had been the day Mamma left?

Suddenly, Dawdi Jakob called up the stairs, "Ach, the breth-ren have come to see Judah!" and Mammi excused herself right quick, looking quite distressed.

Grace's heart beat hard, yet she made herself stay sitting quietly in the tranquil room where her mother had sometimes come to work. Mammi's old treadle sewing machine stood silently in the corner like an old friend.

The psalm she'd read early this morning came to mind: *Trust in him at all times . . . pour out your heart before him.*

She bowed her head to pray.

Judah had awakened with a jolt, flabbergasted to find himself still in bed at this late hour. He'd quickly gone downstairs to shower and dress and was just coming out of the washroom when Adah motioned him to the back door. "The ministers are here to see you, Judah." She stepped aside and swiftly left the kitchen.

If it's not one thing . . .

He inhaled deeply, uncertain what was ahead. He went to the door and took the steps slowly, not trusting his legs. In spite of his unintentional long rest, they were as unreliable as rubber.

"Mornin', Judah," Preacher Smucker said, the first to greet him.

Judah gave a nod but made no effort to speak, preserving his energy for whatever was to be addressed. And surely there was trouble ahead, with all four ministers in his yard—the bishop, two preachers, and Deacon Amos.

The bishop took the lead. "We've come to offer our help," he said, glancing toward the barn. "If you want to try to locate your wife."

She doesn't want to be found, he thought bitterly.

Judah spied part of Joe's face peeking out from behind the barn door. He frowned at his son, who immediately disappeared inside.

"I have many new lambs. . . ." Surely the brethren realized that to go now would put his very livelihood at stake.

"Even so, perhaps you could be doing more to find her," Deacon Amos suggested.

The intimation seemed harsh to Judah's ears, and it was all he could do to stand upright.

"Preacher Smucker says you have no clear understanding as to where she's gone. Is that it?" The bishop looked at him, his brow pinched into a frown. The oldest man of the group, his beard was long and wispy and as white as washed wool.

Breaking into a cold sweat now, Judah mumbled that he knew nothing of Lettie's whereabouts or motives. And the deacon's remark caused him further embarrassment—was Amos questioning the quality of his marriage? Were all of them?

He'd kept secrets from them, from his family, too. Yet was it anyone's business that Lettie had taken money from their account? As far as he could tell from that, she had no intention of returning home, even if found.

"Judah?" The bishop was awaiting a response.

Judah opened his mouth, and the backyard whirled as if he alone were caught on a windmill.

He gasped and reached out a hand to Amos to steady himself. But he missed, and his legs were suddenly too weak to hold him. "Oh . . ." He stumbled backward and fell to the ground, the sky a spinning bluish gray. The sum total of four beards,

four faces, and four straw hats hovered over him, all part of the churning background.

"Judah, what's happening?" asked Preacher Josiah Smucker.

"Ain't rightly sure. . . ." He uttered words that made no sense, as though someone else were speaking for him.

Great drops fell from his eyes, down his face, and into the thickness of his beard. He crossed his arms over his chest while his sorrow and confusion poured forth.

"I cannot go on. . . ." His breath no longer supported his words. And he was sobbing.

"He needs rest" came the kindly voice of Preacher Josiah—Judah knew that much. But he did not comprehend much else as the men linked arms, raising him up to carry him into his house.

chapter
thirty-one

From the sewing room window, Grace could see her father encircled by the brethren, though it appeared that only the bishop and the deacon were doing the talking. Unexpectedly Dat teetered to the left, clutching for Amos before stumbling back and falling to the grass.

"Oh . . . Dat, no!" she cried, horrified.

Quickly, the ministerial brethren surrounded him. Then, with great care, they lifted him into their arms and collectively carried Dat toward the door.

Grace flew down the stairs, meeting them as they brought Dat, pale and trembling, into the front room. They laid him out on the only sofa in the room, his feet hanging off the end.

Preacher Josiah rushed off to alert their neighbor Mrs. Spangler, a registered nurse. After he'd gone, Deacon Amos suggested calling an ambulance, but the bishop said to wait for the nurse's opinion on that, not wanting to get more Englischers involved "unless necessary."

Grace knelt and touched her father's forehead. "I'm right

here, Dat," she whispered, leaning near to his face. "It's Grace . . .
I'm here with you."

When she realized she was alone with her father—no doubt
the others were waiting outdoors for Preacher Josiah to return
with Mrs. Spangler—Grace raised the hem of her apron and
gently dabbed his dear face, spotty with perspiration. Her poor,
grief-stricken father had silently borne his anguish, and now . . .
"Sleep," she said, caressing his cheek with the back of her hand.
"Just sleep."

His eyes fluttered but did not open. He raised one hand
momentarily, and she clasped it in both of her own. "Grace . . .
denki," he managed to say.

She covered her mouth with her hand, not wanting to cry
again. Broken in mind and spirit, Dat had asked them to pray
for Mamma's safety, and oh, she had. But now someone must
carry her father's great need to the Almighty.

*O Lord, look down on Dat here . . . and grant him health and
peace.*

Rising quietly to avoid distressing him further, she backed
out of the room and dashed off to find Adam and the others.

———— ... ————

For several hours, Dat slept under Grace's watchful eye.
Mrs. Spangler had taken his vitals and determined that he most
likely was suffering from sheer exhaustion and dire stress—the
latter she confided softly to Grace alone.

Mammi Adah assigned Mandy to help her prepare the
meals, for the time being. And Adam and Joe solicited help
with the lambing and the barn chores from the ministers and
other Amish neighbors.

Word of their father's collapse spread swiftly. To prevent unnecessary disturbances, Mandy posted signs on the main door and side kitchen door, alerting would-be visitors or well-wishers not to knock or raise their voices. And come they did, bearing hot casseroles, canned fruits, meats, and even monetary gifts. Preacher Smucker stopped by, as well, speaking quietly to Grace, expressing both his concern for her father and his hope that he might be able to speak with him again soon.

When Dat awakened for the first time, he asked to be helped upstairs to bed, and his sons supported him on either side. Grace held her breath the whole way, following close behind.

Ach, Mamma, if you only knew . . .

Adam helped him undress as Grace and Joe waited in the hallway, exchanging anxious glances. Then, when Adam emerged with concern etched on his face, Grace asked if he thought she should go inside.

"Just see what else he might need." Adam worked his jaw, fighting back tears.

She touched his arm and thanked him, even though it seemed odd for her to do so. After all, she was as apprehensive as he. Now, however, she was determined to oversee Dat's recovery, not allowing a single hitch in his getting the restful, healing sleep he required.

Pulling a chair next to his bed, she asked what he wanted to drink. "You'll need something sooner or later." He had not eaten since breakfast.

"Just water . . ." He struggled to keep his eyes open, then his hand went limp, and she realized he'd already given in to slumber once again.

Finding a quilted coverlet in Mamma's blanket chest, Grace

spread it gently over her father. She moved silently to the door and, with one more glance, slipped out of the room.

———···———

The late afternoon sun spread a golden light over Dat's grazing land, where a half dozen new lambs romped about, trailing their mothers. Needing some time outside, Grace watched the younger, more playful lambs bounding over the dark green meadow, soon to be teeming with a sea of golden dandelions.

To her, spring had always signaled the advent of new life. And it was nearly impossible to contemplate the rolling landscape before her without realizing anew how it altered so completely with the movement of the seasons.

Time and nature were tied together somehow. She'd once read about the change from winter to spring . . . that the shift had the power to jumble up people's emotions. She wondered if it affected the sheep Dat raised in the same way.

She was amused by the animals' hesitancy around strangers. They backed away quickly, only one of the older rams brave enough to inch forward at the sight of someone new.

Looking toward the road, she spotted a young woman—an Englischer—coming up from the Riehls' place. She was sniffling and wiping her eyes with her fingers. Grace wondered if this was the young woman staying at the Riehls' for the summer.

The woman began to run hard, like a runner in a race, and Grace could hear her sobs. She appeared to catch herself and slowed again to a walk, wrapping her arms around her middle. She reached up a hand to brush back more tears, her shoulders rising and falling.

Grace's heart went out to the jean-clad girl. And she wished she could help somehow.

——— ··· ———

Judah rolled over in the big bed to reach for Lettie's pillow, scarcely conscious of the hour before again falling quickly into the enticing comfort of sleep. He was only faintly mindful of Grace when she appeared now and then with cold water in a glass or to check his pulse. Did she think he'd expired?

It was the Lord's Day, the second morning following his collapse, and Judah crept his way downstairs to bathe and shave. But not to dress.

Grace was in the kitchen with Mandy and came out to assure him he need not check on the animals. "We've ample help." No mention was made of their visiting relatives or friends this particular Sunday, and he felt sorry for putting a damper on the family day.

He took the stairs carefully again, without help, pleased at this small feat. Strength was slow in coming, yet returning all the same. He savored the smallest progress as he sat in his chair near the window, sunshine pouring in.

He opened the Good Book and found his place. *I was dumb with silence, I held my peace, even from good; and my sorrow was stirred.* The relevance of what he read struck him, and Judah was moved to pray, grateful to God and his family for their tenderness toward him.

Grace brought his dinner up soon after and placed the tray by his side. He thought of telling her how much her care meant to him, but the words were lost somewhere inside him.

——— ... ———

Judah slept again, waking up just as night began to fall, surprised at the stillness in his usually bustling house. What had his children done to create such tranquillity?

For the first time since his collapse, he thought of Lettie's parents. Was Grace looking after them, too?

Getting up, he moved gingerly to the edge of his bed. He had a hankering to slip into his trousers, to know how good it might feel to be fully dressed again. "Tomorrow," he promised himself.

He rose to walk the length of the hallway and did not see a soul. Then footsteps broke the quiet.

"Oh, Dat, so good to see you up again and walkin'," Grace said as she came to check on him. A full smile lit her dear face.

"My legs are finally cooperating." He was surprised when she linked her arm through his and walked back with him. "Guess I just needed some rest."

"That and some tender loving care." She looked away, but he'd seen her tears. "You had us awful scared, Dat."

He sighed, winded, and sat down on his chair. "Shouldn't it be mornin' instead of dusk?" He stared out at the darkening sky and stretched his legs before him.

"Hungry?"

He nodded up at her as his daughter moved to the doorway. *Ach, she radiates goodness.* "You're a fine nurse, Gracie."

She smiled again; he had used Lettie's nickname for her, and she'd noticed. "Do you want pie or cookies and ice cream for dessert?"

"I'll eat whatever you bring." He turned back to the window. The birdbath Lettie had chosen for the side yard was nearly invisible in the graying twilight.

Leaning closer to the window, he saw his own reflection on the pane, faint yet recognizable. And he felt a sudden wave of relief come over him. He was going to be all right.

——— ··· ———

As she began to take down her hair, Lettie was struck by the thought that she simply could not wait any longer. She'd napped soundly that afternoon, falling into a sleep fraught with dreams. So many dreams of her family, especially her children. An urgency stirred within her as she'd awakened—she must get word to them that she was safe.

Quickly winding her hair back into a makeshift bun, she pinned it up and hurried downstairs to the common area, where a telephone was available for the guests. She'd brought along a card with prepaid minutes and had used it only once since leaving home.

Martin Puckett urged me to call for any reason, Lettie remembered, not wanting to contact Marian Riehl on her barn phone . . . afraid her neighbor friend might take the opportunity to scold her. She couldn't bear that now.

Going to the chair near the fireplace, she reached for the receiver.

Martin heard the phone ring and was glad Janet answered, leaving him to watch his news show. His feet propped up on the ottoman, he leaned back in his lounge chair and enjoyed a

bowl of popcorn Janet had made the old-fashioned way—in a pan, on the stove.

"Martin," she called, her voice strained. "It's Lettie Byler. Sounds like she's crying."

"Well, good night . . . What's this?" He reached for the portable phone on the lamp table. "Hello?"

"Ach, Martin, I hate to call you so late and all. I'm truly sorry."

"This is fine . . . just fine." He paused, not wanting to sound too relieved to hear from her. "Are you all right?"

"I . . . just . . ." She sniffled, then spoke again. "Would it be too much trouble to ask you to get a message to my family— 'specially to Judah?"

"No trouble, Lettie. What would you like me to say?"

Janet had come into the TV room and stood in the doorway, facing him with a quizzical expression.

"Could ya just tell him I'm safe?" Lettie asked.

"Anything else?" Martin asked. She sounded as tense now as she had at the train station, and he waited for more. Something solid to go on—where she was staying, perhaps . . . when she planned to return.

"Tell my husband I'll be in contact later."

He was baffled by her still-distant tone. "I'll deliver your message first thing tomorrow."

"Denki, Martin. Again, I hope I didn't disturb your evening."

"You take care now."

She said good-bye and hung up.

He switched off the phone. "She's all right."

"Sure didn't sound like it." Janet frowned. "Why would she call here?"

"Her family has no house phone, you must remember."

His wife nodded as if it hadn't occurred to her.

"When I took her to the train station, I suggested she call here if she needed help." He added, "It seemed like the right thing to do."

"Well, of course." Janet sat on the ottoman and touched his knee. "You're a good man, Martin."

He reached for the remote. "She must be visiting someone."

"She didn't say?"

"Well, when she left she had a list of phone numbers and said someone was meeting her." He was glad to see the assurance return to Janet's eyes. She'd had no reason to ever be uneasy.

Tomorrow he must deliver Lettie's message to Judah— and explain why she'd contacted him instead of any of her people.

———— ··· ————

Grace had seen Martin Puckett pull into the drive numer- ous times before, so she didn't think anything of it when he arrived after she'd finished hanging out the Monday washing. She assumed Adam needed transportation, because she had not phoned Martin, and Dat was in no shape to go anywhere.

Martin got out of the van and came around to the side door.

"Goodness, this is service," she said, welcoming him inside.

"I won't stay but a minute." He stepped into the kitchen but glanced back at the door. "I see your sign. Is someone ill?"

She explained that Dat had been sick but was improving. "He's still not takin' visitors, though . . . and he'll be sorry to miss you."

Martin's concerned look caused her to offer him a seat at the table and some cookies, which he declined. "I came to bring you news from your mother," he said, continuing on without waiting for a response. "She wants your father to know she's all right."

Grace tried but could not speak.

"Will you relay the message?" She nodded and he explained that he and his wife had received a call last night. "I don't know where she was calling from—the number was blocked."

Grace managed to thank him. "I'll tell Dat you dropped by."

Mamma says she's all right. But where?

Irritation grew within her—why hadn't her mother said where she was? Did she always have to be so mysterious?

Grace could think of only one way to quell her intense anger. Only one.

— ··· —

While her hearty vegetable soup simmered on low, Grace saw her chance to leave for a walk. The morning was warming up—already the fifth day of May. A light breeze swayed the tops of trees, and the windmills in the distance moved steadily. She was glad for the fresh air on her face after rushing around to get breakfast and then assisting Mammi Adah with some piecework for a quilt after cleaning her father's bedroom and doing laundry.

Dat had declared he was strong enough to wander out to the barn, with Adam and Joe keeping close watch. It did her

good to see the color returning to his cheeks. They'd all had a bad scare.

One Mamma might never know about, she thought, resentment rising.

The road was as empty now as at that dark hour when she'd run after Mamma . . . ignored, despite her pleas. Grace looked all around her, assuming she'd found the very spot.

Then, folding her hands, she bowed her head and voiced the prayer she'd contemplated since seeing Dat fall at the feet of the brethren, shattered by his own grief.

"I'm here, Lord, because I'm weary of my bitterness. And I want to ask forgiveness." She paused. "No, that ain't quite right. . . ."

She struggled against every bit of frustration pent up inside her. "I want to forgive my Mamma," she said, lifting her eyes. In her mind, she saw again her mother hustling away from her with the bulky suitcase, filled with nearly every bit of clothing she owned. "I'm askin' you to carry away my anger, Lord. And the resentment I feel every time I think of that awful moment."

She was weeping now, unable to stop. "I'm sorry for the ugly feelings I've kept inside me, nurturin' them." Stopping her prayer, she went to lean against the sheep fence. "Oh, Mamma, I don't understand why you had to go. But with God's help, I won't tend this bitter root in me any longer."

She wiped her wet face on the handkerchief she'd tucked into the sleeve of her dress and sighed as she glanced back at Dat's big house in the distance.

She was surprised, but she already felt ever so much lighter.

Forgiven.

She thought of the hummingbird drawing Becky had slipped beneath the side door yesterday. A thoughtful thing for her friend to do, knowing Grace was sitting nearly round the clock at Dat's bedside. Mandy had brought the drawing upstairs to her, not speaking, only pointing to Becky's lovely handiwork. Made just for her with those pretty birthday pencils Grace had given her friend.

No wonder Mamma loves hummingbirds. They're unfettered and free.

She thought again of her own struggles. Only through daily and deliberate forgiveness could she, too, find freedom. *Just as Mamma taught me . . .*

She turned toward home. As much as she understood about forgiveness, Grace knew it would take time for healing to come.

She was nearing the turnoff into the driveway when she noticed Henry and his sister Priscilla riding together in the market wagon. The minute Priscilla spotted her, she began waving excitedly. Grace waved back, pleased to see them.

Henry, however, sat as straight as a stick, both hands on the reins, offering merely a half smile as they approached.

She instantly felt glum. *Why can't he be more like his sister?* she wondered as they passed by. *Isn't he happy to see me?*

Mamma had once told her, "*Dat loves us, even though he doesn't say it.*"

"Like Henry?" Grace blurted aloud now, recalling the way he'd asked her to marry him, not saying he loved her even then.

In that painful moment, the disappointments of the past months caught up with her. Was this the reason she'd awakened the morning after Henry proposed with so little joy about their

coming union? Had she subconsciously known she was headed for a cheerless marriage . . . like Mamma's?

For sure and for certain, she'd made excuses for herself—for Henry, too, initially thinking her ho-hum feelings stemmed from her disillusionment over Mamma's leaving. But she knew there was far more to it. And seeing Henry just now and the way he'd looked right through her triggered an onslaught of suppressed feelings.

Somehow she'd managed to overlook his shy nature from the first date on, hoping that in time he might open his heart. Plenty of men were like that, including Dat. Yet the way she felt right now, it was hard to think of living out her years with a husband like her father. *Hard . . . if not impossible.*

Grace stubbed her toe as she turned into the driveway. In all truth, she found not a speck of pleasure in the thought of being engaged to Henry Stahl. If anything, she was panicked by it.

chapter
thirty-two

Washday in Ohio fell on the same day as back home, though here Lettie had no access to a wringer-washer or a clothesline. For that reason, she offered to pay Tracie Gordon for the use of the inn's automatic washer and dryer.

"I wouldn't think of charging you," the younger woman said. "You just help yourself whenever you're ready. There's an iron and ironing board in there, too, if you need them."

Lettie had assumed the facilities would be in use to wash the inn's soiled linens and towels. But later, while sorting her own clothes, she discovered from the housekeeper that she was the only weekday guest. The tidy little laundry room was all hers.

Once her washing was folded and pressed, she returned to her room and smoothed down her hair at the middle part. Then she bathed and chose a clean dress and matching apron.

She'd felt queasy all morning—a bad case of nerves. Samuel, being a recent widower, might be too grief stricken to welcome a visit from her. She had no way of knowing how things might turn out between them. They'd cared so deeply for each other. But that was long ago.

Lettie hoped her second car trip down to Fredericksburg would not be in vain. The drivers here were as expensive as in Lancaster County, but that wasn't the only reason she hoped she might find Samuel Graber at home this time.

Her heart felt like it might beat right out of her chest as she stood waiting beside the front room window for her ride. For weeks her emotions had been nearly raw, yet as she pondered what she was about to do, she felt more vulnerable than heartbroken. Tears slipped from her eyes, and the tree-lined street became a shimmering stream.

How will Samuel receive me?

——— ··· ———

The afternoon sun cast a gentle light over the narrow street as the driver parked two doors away and opposite from the house belonging to Samuel. Lettie spotted a man pulling weeds in the front yard, and her breath caught in her throat when she realized it was indeed Samuel.

Dressed like an Englischer, she thought, reminding herself to breathe.

His fancy attire wasn't the only thing that had changed since their courting days. His face was somewhat fuller, his light brown hair peppered with gray on the sides.

She paid the driver and stepped out of the van. Her pulse raced as she made her way up the street, feeling her weight on the sidewalk as she took each step approaching the front yard. Once again she admired the overall attractiveness of the place, and she prayed for courage.

I'm this far. . . .

Meanwhile, Samuel moved up to the front porch, unaware

of her as he pinched off dried blossoms from the begonias in matching pots. She stood quietly at the foot of the steps, suddenly too bashful to announce herself.

Ach, what have I done?

Just when she'd thought she might simply retreat, he turned and saw her there—an unexpected sight to be sure. She was, after all, wearing her Amish garb, her hair in the traditional bun.

"Hullo, Samuel," she said, offering a smile.

He squinted and straightened. Then, suddenly, his eyes grew wide and twinkled in recognition as a smile spread across his face. "Lettie? Is it you?"

She smiled back, nodding. "Jah, 'tis."

"Goodness, what a surprise!" His laughter rekindled so many fond memories. "Well, for Pete's sake!" He stood back and appraised her.

"Nice to see you again, Samuel." She felt slightly more confident now that he seemed so delighted.

He apologized for having forgotten his manners. "Please . . . won't you come inside?" He motioned toward the door, holding it for her.

"Denki." She let the word slip.

In the house, she inhaled slowly . . . deeply. *Here at last.*

"Make yourself at home," he said, a curious smile on his face.

She looked around, taking in the comfortable room. It had the look of a small library or perhaps a den, as she'd heard some fancy folk call such a room. Plenty large enough for two upholstered chairs—one a soft green, the other eggshell in color—with an oak lamp table between them. The chairs were situated facing

a small glassed-in fireplace, and books, dozens of them, lined the shelves, one side reaching to the ceiling.

Samuel waited till she was seated before he moved the decorative pillow from his chair and sat down, too, still simply beaming. "Goodness, how long has it been?" he asked, his eyes fixed on her. "Twenty-some years."

"At least." But she knew precisely. A girl never forgot her first love.

He leaned back. "What brings you to Ohio? Business or pleasure?"

My visit with you, she thought.

Her mind—no, her heart—was whirling. So much to say. "Well, I'm in the area for several reasons," she managed to respond, embarrassed at his keen attention.

"You've come alone?"

She nodded. "This trip, jah."

"You must still live in Bird-in-Hand, I assume?"

She said she did. "I married Judah Byler," she added quickly.

"Judah?" He glanced at the ceiling, as if trying to place him. "Why, sure . . . I remember now. He was kind of a reserved fellow, wasn't he?"

She nodded only slightly, wanting to change the subject . . . needing to. "I heard of your wife's passing from Sarah, when your sister was visiting in Bart some weeks back. I'm so sorry to hear it."

He thanked her, saying that Emmie's passing was something of a blessing, because she'd suffered for so long. Then he went on. "Well, I'll be . . . I had no idea Sarah was back there. When was this?"

"In March . . . she came to see a relative's new baby."

"Ah yes, our grand-niece." He scratched his head. "Guess I failed to even send them a card. Emmie handled that sort of thing, you know." He chuckled. "I've got so much to catch up on."

"Have you lived in Fredericksburg very long?" she ventured.

"Three years now," he said. "I'd always wanted to own a welding shop, and when this one came up for sale—less than four miles away—I snatched it right up." He rose suddenly, going to his books. "Here's another one of my dreams come true," he said, waving his hand at the shelves of books. "Would you care to see some of my favorites?"

"Poetry?"

"Is there anything else?" He laughed and the sound brought her joy. "Emmie used to say my poetry books were my Bible, but that was only a joke." Still, he was obviously attached to his fine collection of Browning, Frost, Dickinson, and several other poets she hadn't heard of.

He brought Alfred Lord Tennyson to her and ran his finger down the list of poems on the first page—"Audley Court," "The Beggar Maid," "The Blackbird," "The Charge of the Light Brigade." . . .

" 'A hundred summers! can it be?' " he quoted from "The Day-Dream."

Oh, she was sixteen again . . . shooing flies away from her face as she sat high in the haymow, listening intently to the rhythmic sway of his voice, the mesmerizing way he had with each stanza and measure of phrase. As if he were born to read poetry to her and to her alone.

"Emmie said I was a dichotomy—part grease monkey, part rhymester." He glanced toward the window, surely thinking of her just now. "Not sure where she ever heard that."

"Rhymester?" Lettie asked.

He nodded. "Guess it's strange, but I never wrote a poem for my late wife. Wasn't much good at it, I guess."

He was, after all, more an interpreter of poets, she remembered, though he'd tried his hand at rhymes.

"I once wrote a decent one, though," he said quietly. His gaze found her. "It was the day my father told us we were leaving Lancaster County."

She sighed, heavyhearted now at the prospect of hearing what she knew he was about to say.

"I wrote the poem for you, Lettie." He rubbed his hands back and forth on the arms of his chair. "I had no way of knowing how to get in touch," he said. "No one seemed to know where you'd gone, or why you'd left."

"I was out here, in Ohio . . . came with my mother to help my father's very ill aunt." She took a long breath. "But that wasn't the only reason we came, Samuel."

She'd imagined this very moment for more than a month— had even practiced her words. Somewhere in Samuel's dining room, a clock was ticking. And out on the pretty porch the wind chime tinkled, the sound ever so haunting as it drifted through the window screen.

Samuel's face was pensive now.

Ach, how I loved him.

Pursing her lips, she tumbled over the waterfall of the past. "The reason I'm here is to make a confession. One I should've made years ago."

Seeing his furrowed brow, she paused and felt the distance of their years apart.

"Lettie?" He leaned forward, his hands on his knees. "What is it?"

She swallowed hard, willing herself to find the courage. "Truth is, I never should've left you, Samuel. Not without tellin' you the truth."

His fingers fidgeted on the piping along the edge of the chair.

"Ach, but I was so deceitful. And I have paid dearly for it. And . . . I'm ever so sorry."

He frowned tenderly. "Whatever you have to say . . . please, feel free to say it, Lettie."

Samuel had always made it easy for her to speak her mind. Her heart. "I had a baby," she said softly. "*Ours.*"

He sat motionless, eyes wide. "We . . . have a child?"

She bowed her head, staring at her folded hands. "It was wrong of me not to tell you." She was afraid she might cry. "I was nearly five months along when Mamm and I went to Kidron to stay . . . where I gave birth."

"Oh, Lettie, I wish I'd known."

She shook her head, drawing a shallow breath. "It was never my idea to keep such a secret—or to give up the baby." She pulled a hankie from her sleeve. "Ach, this has weighed on me for so long."

His face was drawn, pale. "Who else knew?"

"Only my parents at first." She sighed heavily. "And of course my great-aunt. Then, much later, I confided in my clos- est sister, Naomi, but she passed away several years ago." She

told him how she'd stayed then at the same inn she'd chosen this visit, having the baby there.

"A boy or a girl?" he asked tentatively.

"Mamma hired an Amish midwife, and together they decided it was best, all round, that I wasn't told. I never even got to see or hold the baby," she said sadly. "Honestly, though, I had a strong feeling I'd birthed a son."

"This is all so shocking." Samuel's face was filled with angst. "You see, Emmie and I always wanted children. Very much so," he said quietly. "We yearned for our own, but Emmie wasn't well for much of our marriage. And now you say that I had a child all along." He pressed his fingers against his temples. "And I missed it all, all the growing-up years."

"I know, Samuel. I know. . . ."

She'd heard of Samuel and Emmie's childless marriage from Sarah, who'd revealed the sad news when they walked together at the barn raising. "This is one of the reasons why I came lookin' for you," she said. "My heart broke for you, Samuel, when Sarah said you'd lost your dear wife . . . and you'd never had children."

He glanced at the window, eyes blinking as he seemed to calculate the years. "Our child must be close to twenty-four by now."

Brushing away tears, she nodded. "Born April twenty-ninth that year."

Six days later than Grace's own birthday . . . and only two days from the anniversary of Naomi's passing. Tears slid down Lettie's cheeks.

His eyes probed hers. "Do you have any idea where he or she might be?"

She explained that she'd hoped to find the midwife while in Kidron, with no success. "I wanted to find our child first, before coming to see you.".

A way to attempt to bridge the chasm between them, she'd realized. Oh, but their unresolved parting had taken its dreadful toll on her. And after stumbling upon Samuel's sister, Lettie had purposed in her heart to find both Samuel and their child, to set things right. During the long nights of wandering, she'd prayed for both her child and for Samuel. Deep in thought, she'd wished for a way to find their child, but had no idea where to look. Aside from Kidron, Ohio.

"That was very thoughtful of you . . . and generous, too," he said.

"Well, I'm still searching for the midwife—anyone who might know something, but I'm discovering there are many hurdles." Lettie closed her eyes, reliving the questions that continually plagued her. *Does my child know how much he or she was loved? Is my son or daughter happy? Healthy?*

"I would have helped you raise the baby . . . would have married you." Samuel's voice was strained. "That was my intention, Lettie, you must know. But I was young and my father moved us away in a failed attempt to keep his wayward son in the church," he said. "Poor excuses, I know, but I was under my father's roof then."

She understood. "I, too, was under the control of my parents." A little sob escaped. "Ach, Samuel, believe me, I wanted to keep the baby, but my parents—*my mother*—forced me to give the child away."

He shook his head sadly.

"A private adoption was arranged by a local doctor after the midwife took the baby away . . . that day."

"I'm so very sorry," he said. "What you went through . . . alone."

"It was a closed adoption, too, which is why this has taken much longer than I first expected. I immediately began making contacts after seeing your sister Sarah." She paused. "I have no idea how long it'll take."

Samuel grew silent again, unquestionably lost in a blur of musings.

A lengthy silence prevailed; then he rose and went to stand near the bookshelves. "I took advantage of you, Lettie . . . when we were young. I apologize for that."

"We both knew better."

He walked to the window, his hands in his trouser pockets. "I'd like to help with your search," he said. "But I'm tied to my work here. Perhaps I can at least assist with your travel costs."

"Mighty kind of you, but that's not necessary, really." She thought of the money she'd withdrawn for the purpose of supporting her search. "Besides, my husband would not approve."

His eyebrows rose. "Judah didn't accompany you to Kidron, then?"

"It's lambing season." She gave her best excuse, not wanting to admit to having kept Judah in the dark about the trip. And the bigger secret—her child out of wedlock. "Well, I've taken up enough of your time." She rose and made her way to the door.

"Please, Lettie, let's stay in touch." He followed her outside to the porch. "How can I contact you?"

She mentioned the inn. "But I won't be there much longer. So it's best if I contact you, all right?"

He nodded and smiled sadly. "I appreciate your coming." He touched her elbow. "I'm sure you've considered this, but you have to realize there's always the possibility our child doesn't wish to be found."

"Such news could turn a person's life upside-down, for certain," she agreed. "Might find it horribly upsetting . . . even reject the notion."

"And . . . what if he or she doesn't know about being adopted? It's a terrible risk."

"Jah, 'tis." Overhead, the wind chime was surprisingly still. "And I can't be gone from my family indefinitely." She was needed at home, for gardening and canning . . . and for the fall wedding season.

For Adam's wedding. And for Judah.

Oh, how much she had to share with her husband. He wasn't the easiest to talk to, but he was a good man, and he'd weathered her ups and downs through the years. Judah had no knowledge whatsoever of the baby she'd conceived with Samuel—her cherished secret.

I owe Judah an apology, too. . . .

"Well, I really must be goin'." She moved toward the steps.

"I'll look forward to hearing from you," he said. "Be safe, Lettie."

She turned to wave. Then, seeing her driver parked across

the street, she hurried to the van, breathing more freely now. She'd accomplished what she'd come to do.

The first of many difficult steps.

———— ··· ————

That night Lettie dreamed of Judah and saw his dear face once again. He was carrying a wee lamb in his arms, giving it a baby bottle to spare the lamb's life.

Your father's such a gentle shepherd, Lettie had once said at the table in front of all of them, even though he was truly considered a sheep farmer. Adam had nodded, looking right quick at Grace.

When she awakened, she felt the familiar pangs of home-sickness. Yet her long journey had just begun. She would search for her firstborn child, the newborn taken from her much too quickly. Torn away from her . . . out of her life.

She wept for the infant she'd lost. Mamm had deprived her of laying eyes on that sweet bundle—*"the sinful result of forbid-den love,"* she'd said so many times Lettie believed she was, in fact, consigned to hell.

"I must forgive Mamm, too," she said, rising to meet the day. "And Daed."

There were times when she honestly wondered if her hus-band and children would even want her back . . . if they knew her secret. And if she didn't return soon, there'd be dire talk of the *Bann*, too. She could easily fall into despair thinking about all that her family must be struggling with now, in her absence. And not just the amount of work left over from her leaving. No, there must be a terrible sense of rejection and the

anguish of not knowing where she was or why she'd want to abandon them.

Yet, on the other hand, Lettie felt strangely relieved, as if a very heavy burden had been lifted from her. Not allowing herself to dwell on bleak thoughts, she opened the window and welcomed the warm May morning, a breeze catching the curtain, making it flutter.

I've come this far!

On a tree branch nearby, a jenny wren chirped happily. Then, moving away from the window, Lettie gathered up her clothes and began to pack to the cheerful song of the little bird. She was determined to locate the Amish midwife. Somehow, she would.

A favorite verse of Judah's came to mind—one from the prophet Isaiah, in the Old Testament. *And the Lord shall guide thee continually.*

Bowing her head, she asked God to do just that.

chapter
thirty-three

Grace could hear the muted sound of voices coming from the Singing as she slipped around the back of Deacon Amos's barn and leaned hard against a tree trunk facing the cornfield. The bark was still warm from the sun, fair as this Lord's Day had been. Yet the day had also been a difficult one.

Sighing, she gathered her wits. She'd exited the barn without Henry, who had been milling about with a group of singles—fellows who were not yet engaged or seriously courting anyone. Surprisingly, Yonnie Bontrager had been among them. *Surely he and Becky will pair up, like usual,* she thought, glad for this moment of respite behind the barn. There, where the ministerial brethren sometimes came and stood in a cluster, hashing out church issues and whatnot.

Pressing her hands against the tree's rough bark, she soaked up the quiet. It was impossible not to contemplate the thorny evening ahead of her—ahead of *them*. She'd glanced at Henry several times as they were singing with the rest of the group, pondering how best to do what she knew she must. She'd waited

too long already, and she wondered what he might think of her when all was said and done.

Henry has no passion for life, she thought. *Nor for me . . .*

She stared at the night sky, letting her gaze drift over the wide expanse of stars and the blackness beyond. With all of her heart, she'd wanted their relationship to be mutually affectionate. And she had waited for him to make the first move toward marriage, all those months after they'd become serious . . . yearning for his marriage proposal. To think all the while Mamma had been silently suffering her own relationship problems.

The stars seemed much farther away this night, and she found herself reaching up and pinching her fingers to frame an especially bright one. Some of them were six million light years away, she'd read in a school book. In that moment, surrounded by the majesty of God's creation, she felt ever so small.

Ach, my wants and wishes seem petty just now.

She willed herself to be content with her soon-to-be lot, since breaking up with Henry Stahl would mean certain Maidelhood.

"A reserved man can be hard to live with," Mamma had said. Remembering bolstered Grace's courage. Mamma would be in favor of her breakup with Henry.

Just then, she heard voices coming from the side of the barn. Right away she knew it was Adam and his fiancée, Priscilla. Grace leaned to peer around the tree and held her breath to listen.

"You *were* gawking at me," Priscilla spouted off. "And your face was none too approving."

"Aw, now, Prissy . . ."

The sound of sniffles traveled to Grace. "You must not

like the color of my dress," Priscilla continued. "Is that so, Adam?"

"Never said that."

She heard rustling now, like one of them was pacing in the tall grass a few yards from her hiding place.

They're arguing like this . . . over a dress? She wondered if Adam had endured other such sassy encounters.

Grace had recently seen her sister, Mandy, with a new beau, Becky Riehl's cousin. Mandy had seemed so comfortable, even joyful. In fact, this very night after the singing portion of the gathering was through, Grace had noticed several other blissfully happy couples . . . talking face to face, smiling and laughing.

Grace shook her head, annoyed at her brother for putting up with such an outspoken girl. Adam deserved better.

Then and there, the thought of so many lacking relationships weighed on her, and she hurried away from her spot to find Henry before she lost her nerve.

More than a half hour later, Grace was still waiting for Henry. He was certainly taking his time. Was he discussing fieldwork with the other fellows, perhaps? She'd considered simply leaving and walking home, but she made herself stay put right near the barn door.

Dozens of couples streamed out from the Singing as the night progressed. And such a lovely evening it was . . . still mild from the balmy day. Mandy and her beau strolled out through the open barn door, laughing and holding hands.

Waiting with as much patience as she could muster, Grace noticed Yonnie Bontrager walk through the door by himself. How peculiar it seemed, since she was accustomed to seeing

him with Becky. Glancing over her shoulder, she looked for her friend, having seen her earlier in the long line of girls. But Becky was nowhere around.

Unexpectedly, Yonnie turned and looked at Grace just then. A smile spread across his face, and his eyes caught hers if but for a moment. Then, still smiling, he gave a nod and turned to make his way toward the lane. *On foot, like always,* she thought, still surprised he was alone.

Quickly, Grace dismissed his gaze and too-broad smile, and she wandered toward Henry's open buggy, more than ready to have the evening behind her.

——— ··· ———

Heather clicked the safety latch on her mother's bracelet, then slid it up her arm. Eyes woozy from hours of thesis work, she went out the door, pleased at having written five new pages. A break was well deserved. She was beginning to feel confined and was curious about a funky little coffee shop she'd spotted the other day, so she decided to venture there. *Hopefully it's still open. . . .*

Her dad had left another voice mail, saying he wanted to see her. "To get your input on several ideas swimming in my head about that farmhouse we're going to build," he'd said, laughing. "I'm coming your way in a few weeks, once I wrap up this project. Okay with you?"

His coming might not be such a bad idea. That way she could ask him to bring some of her more casual dresses and skirts, since not a single pair of jeans fit right anymore. Of course, with summer coming, she could just invest in a few shorts and

tops at the outlet malls, which were as plentiful around here as eggs in the Riehls' hen house.

And, too, these past few days observing Andy and Marian Riehl interact with their large family made Heather wonder if maybe she shouldn't try to gently level with her dad—tell him the real reason why she'd run away.

——— ... ———

Grace drew in a small breath when at last she saw Henry coming out through the barn door, glancing from side to side. *Looking for me*, she thought, suddenly sad.

She would not enjoy another Singing for a long time, she was quite sure. Why would she care to attend the cheery gatherings when, in all truth, she would feel anything but cheerful?

"Henry?" she called softly from where she stood near his buggy. "I'm here."

To think she was about to inflict on him a pain similar to that Mamma had inflicted on Dat. Cringing, she knew it was not wise to ride with Henry tonight—even for one last time. No, she must speak to him now and let him go home alone.

"Henry . . . I'd like to talk to you," she said, her throat husky as she moved toward him.

He nodded and motioned for her to get into his open carriage.

"No, I mean here," she said, her body tense. "Do you mind?"

He shrugged.

"Can we walk that way . . . toward the cornfield?" she asked, feeling strangely forward as he fell into step with her. "Over yonder."

She wondered if he might ask what was on her mind, but as was typical, he left it to her to take the lead. Yet now instead of experiencing her former melancholy, she was nearly encompassed with anger.

"It's not right," she said suddenly.

He turned, studying her in the dim light of the quarter moon. "What ain't?"

She paused to consider her words. "Our engagement." She took a few more steps before she stopped and faced him. "Maybe we moved too quickly," she said more quietly.

"You're not makin' sense, Grace."

Unsure of herself now, she did not want to sound ungrateful . . . or even unkind. "I shouldn't have said yes to your proposal, Henry." She looked at the sky. "Ach, but this is ever so hard."

"Wait—you're sorry you said you'd marry me?" His voice was tinged with resentment.

She nodded slowly and looked beyond his shoulders.

His face fell, and she felt horrid. Henry was a good, dependable man. She hoped her rejection would not lead to bitterness. She knew too well how the emotion could fester and eventually overtake a person.

She recalled their first dates, the slow-paced buggy rides long into the night—how he was content to be silent for as long as an hour at a time. Once she'd turned to him and asked, *"What're you thinking 'bout?"* and he'd said simply, *"You, Grace."*

She'd thought it an endearing, even a tender thing to say. But his inability to express anything more made her certain, without a doubt, that Henry Stahl did not possess what she longed for in a husband.

"I honestly believe we made a mistake," she said. "And I'm so sorry to say it."

He didn't attempt to change her mind, nor did he offer a good-bye kiss on her cheek. He merely bowed his head for a moment, then took a slow, deep breath. "All right, then," he said, turning away. "If this is what you want." And without another word, he headed back, climbed into his buggy, and drove away. Grace followed with her eyes until the horse and carriage were two black silhouettes on the road.

"Good-bye, Henry," she whispered, half wishing he had put up a fight for her.

Walking home by the shimmer of moonlight on Deacon Amos's silo, Grace felt a strange kinship with the night's stillness. Contentment came so quickly it surprised her, reassuring her that she had done the right thing for both Henry and for herself.

chapter
thirty-four

The next morning, once the washing was hung out across the clotheslines, Grace asked her brother if he'd mind returning the gift Henry had given her. "Please, will ya, Adam?" she pleaded when immediate opposition registered on his face. "You don't have to say one word to Henry 'bout the clock—I'm not askin' for that."

While she had no regrets, she truly felt weary. The bold action would surely lock the door on any hope of future reconciliation.

Adam's face scrunched into a tight frown. "Ain't becoming of you, Gracie."

"Well, it's the hardest thing, I know that."

"So think about what you're doin', then."

She sighed. "I have, Adam. And . . . I expect Henry will be waitin' for the clock."

"Then you must've had words last night."

"Only mine."

Adam shook his head. "I hope you at least apologized. It wasn't fair to say yes if ya weren't certain."

351

"Jah, you're right. And I was as kind as anyone could be."

He grimaced. "Then so be it." Her brother followed her upstairs and took from her room the most beautiful chiming clock she'd ever seen, carrying it down to his open buggy. Lifting it high, he placed it gently inside, then looked back at her. "I can't change your mind?" he said. "No parting words to give Henry some hope, just maybe?"

"This ain't some snap decision, Adam," she said. "I've been a-ponderin' it for quite some time."

"Well, then, if you're mighty sure." He gave her a tender smile, pushed his straw hat forward slightly on his head, and made one leap up into the buggy.

Grateful for her brother's support, grudging as it was, she said, "Denki for makin' the delivery." She was relieved Adam did not despise either her or what she'd done.

"Consider it done." Adam waved, then picked up the reins and clucked his tongue. And old Willow, *bless her heart*, moved forward, pulling the carriage down the driveway to the road.

——— ⋯ ———

Heather politely refused Becky's invitation to run an errand midmorning, again using her thesis as an excuse to stay in her room. She glanced out the window, waiting until Becky had hitched up the horse and buggy and left before she ventured from the house to her car, hoping to slip away unnoticed.

She wanted to drive over to her father's land and poke around there. How glad she was that her dad was pulling out of his initial grief. Or so it seemed. A breeze shuffled the leaves in the nearby maples, and she noticed a fragrant aroma coming from Mill Creek, to the south. She'd walked along the wide

stream at dusk several times, musing on her decision to abandon her summer plans to escape her grim diagnosis.

Now, as she drove the short distance, she noticed a van parked in a narrow lane, an Amishwoman and her young children filing in while an older man in jeans and a striped shirt stood near. Was he the driver? She'd heard from Marian Riehl of Mennonites and others making a living driving the Amish. She found it fascinating that a people who were prohibited to own or drive cars were permitted to pay others to drive them places. Another riddle of this Plain culture.

When Dad's land came into view, she pulled onto the shoulder and parked. Getting out, she walked to the passenger side of the car, leaned against it, and stared in awe. This was the perfect place for her dad to recover from his great loss.

And mine. She realized how very lonely she had been since her mother's death. Yet she felt powerless to stop pushing would-be friends away—a lifelong pattern.

"At least I'll have an idyllic spot to return home to, when I want to visit Dad," she muttered, making her way across the fertile green field.

Imagine Dad growing potatoes . . . She walked the perimeter of the acreage, thinking again of her mother. Forever missing the only person she'd ever opened up to fully.

Enjoying the breeze on her face—the sky was such a profound blue—Heather realized her mother would be happy if she could see her now. "She'd be ecstatic that I've come here," she said aloud, thinking ahead to her appointment with the alternative doctor.

And, looking across the field to the farmhouses dotting the land, Heather felt as if they were all inviting her inside . . . as if

she were being made welcome in this rural, back-roads place. Here, where dairy cows roamed free from constraint, munching leisurely in deep pasture grass, and where field crickets sang a familiar refrain each evening. Once she'd nearly lost her breath to the beauty of the moment as she watched a giant red sun drop gradually over faraway hills.

A subtle yet potent anticipation stirred within. And for the first time since arriving here, she wondered if there was something to Becky's talk of Providence. Had she been led here by an unseen hand?

Heather smiled at the thought, surprised by a sense of hope for the future.

Whatever it may bring.

——— ··· ———

While refilling Jakob's coffee cup, Adah glanced out the kitchen window. After a full morning of doing laundry, Grace was presently down near the springhouse, weeding her herb garden. *Working her heart out.*

How she loved the little plot, and she could just imagine the lively flavors in their salads, come June.

It seemed like just yesterday when she'd helped young Grace make the first plantings of chives and thyme and other herbs. Lettie had been there, too, looking on and encouraging them in the process. Grace had marveled at their herb garden springing to life year after year, with many varieties reseeding themselves.

Presently, Grace stopped hoeing to look at the sky, and Adah realized anew the incredible strain on her granddaughter of late. All the energy it took to attempt to hold the family together—she was doing a fine job of it, too.

Grace wants to find her mother and bring her home. . . .

Adah had awakened with a bad dream in the night, wondering if it was an omen of sorts. She hadn't wanted to go into much detail with Jakob, but sitting here at the table now, she felt she should ask her husband if she was making a mistake by keeping the Ohio letter hidden.

—— ··· ——

Grace saw Mammi Adah coming out the door, waving to her. Briefly, she considered confiding in Mammi about Henry; then she thought better of it. If Mamma were here and knew of her decision, she would surely agree that letting Henry go was the right thing.

"You're out here early," her grandmother said, bringing her own hoe.

"Wanted to get a head start on the day."

"Ach, you sound like your mother—she says the same thing. . . . I mean—"

"It's all right. I understand what you meant." A knowing look passed between them, and Grace stood tall and stretched her back. "I spoke with Dat privately this morning, out in the barn. He's agreed, though reluctantly, that I can leave to look for Mamma once lambing's over—that is, if the market lambs are fast gainers."

"Well, someone ought to look for her, I s'pose." Mammi nodded slowly.

"Dat also says I mustn't go alone in my search, though."

"Sensible enough." Her grandmother leaned on her hoe, her expression thoughtful. "So . . . who do ya think might go with you?"

355

"I really haven't gotten that far yet," Grace admitted. "There's a little time to think on that, what with the lambs still comin'."

Mammi reached into the folds of her dress to remove a slip of paper. She held it out to Grace, her eyes bright with tears. "Sounds like you might be needing this."

Grace accepted the paper and opened it, startled to see the address for an inn in Kidron, Ohio. "Is this . . . ?"

"Jah . . . the address where your mother and I stayed in Ohio all those years ago. I talked to your Dawdi 'bout it, and he agreed you should have it." Mammi paused a moment, then added, "We both hope it leads you to her."

She was surprised by the sudden change in her Mammi's attitude. "So you don't mind anymore?"

Mammi gave her hand a quick squeeze, her eyes still brimming with tears. "If you're successful, perhaps your mother will be home in plenty of time for wedding season. Or sooner . . . hopefully." She stooped again to return to weeding around the chives.

Grace felt sure that was possible. How hard could it be to find someone in Ohio Amish country anyway?

—— ··· ——

Judah cradled his newest lamb as he squatted in the hay. He kept his distance from the ewe for a time as she rested from the birth. New life had been springing forth almost daily now, and he was mighty grateful for so many healthy lambs.

He'd gone for another walk earlier today—pushing away the underbrush with his arms to make his way through a less-traveled path in a wooded area near Mill Creek. This time, he

did not flail and lash out but rather offered a simple prayer that Lettie might know, somehow, that he loved her.

Stroking the lamb in his arms, he considered Grace's eagerness to begin her search. And he could kick himself for relenting. *Where will she look?* He had no idea himself. The rigid stipulations he'd put on the whole thing were his saving grace, because not a soul would be willing or able to leave family and farm chores behind to accompany Grace next month.

Yet what if she does find Lettie? The possibility nagged at him. Not that he didn't want his wife to return—with everything in him, he did. But he longed for Lettie to come home on her own, not due to pleading. Nor because of Grace's attempt. Judah wanted the bride of his youth to decide to come back because she loved them . . . loved *him.*

In his mind's eye he pictured Lettie walking up their driveway, the worn brown leather suitcase in hand. She might simply slip into the house unnoticed, before any of them began to stir, just as she had gone away in that dreadful darkness while they'd slumbered so soundly.

And wandering down to the kitchen, ready to greet a new day, Judah would see her there, back where she belonged, and the words locked away for much too long would tumble at last from his lips.

Epilogue

....

Tonight the rain was a mere drizzle as I went out front to sit on the porch swing. Soon, though, it started making down harder, splashing on the railing . . . and at times, onto me. Still, I stayed put in Mamma's spot, curling up there, pulling my bare feet beneath my long dress. Creating a shelter, of sorts. And, ach, how I needed it!

I couldn't help thinking of Becky's short visit here earlier today, when she shared how befuddled she was over their Virginia guest, Heather. The young woman has suddenly become distant and even looked to be crying one afternoon, according to Becky, who wonders if she is heartbroken or maybe ill. Now I knew that must have been the woman I saw crying and running down the road that day. Honestly, as Becky described the way she isolates herself most of the time, I couldn't help feeling sad for the girl called Heather.

But knowing Becky and her family, surely they'll draw her out in due time.

I told Becky about my own growing eagerness to go looking for Mamma. I asked her what *she'd* do, but it's awful hard

for a person to know something like that. Becky looked all thunderstruck and said, "Oh, Grace . . . your family needs you here now more than ever." Of course, it wouldn't do for both Mamma *and* me to be away—least not till after lambing season, like Dat suggested. I'm glad he's agreeable, but I heard all too clearly the hesitancy in his words. If only he hadn't made it near impossible for me. 'Twill be nothing short of a miracle to find someone to accompany me.

Yet find someone I must, for all our sakes—Dat's especially. Who would've thought Mamma's leaving would get the best of him, putting him flat on his back?

Something must've happened while he slept away the days. There are times now when he'll utter more than five words in a row, as if he regrets being so quiet with Mamma. And so it seems good can rise out of turmoil and disappointment. So many feelings we've all experienced since Mamma's leaving. All's forgiven on my part, but I know I'll be offering up a prayer for a forgiving heart yet again tomorrow . . . and the next day. I only hope Mamma doesn't turn silent on us again, after her one and only phone call.

Mammi Adah's reaction to the whole thing continues to bewilder me. For sure and for certain, I'm thankful to her for giving me the address of the Ohio inn. But why should I suspect Mamma might have gone there? And why doesn't Mammi Adah seem surprised by my mother's need for a secretive journey?

The way Mammi Adah stares at me sometimes—it's unnerving, to say the least. I can't help thinking she might know why my mother would wish so hard for something she didn't have here in Bird-in-Hand. What would compel a forty-year-old wife and mother to rush out into the world like that?

Mammi says it's human nature to wish for more than we have. The thought convicts me, if only briefly, when I think of Henry's and my brief betrothal . . . and my failure to go ahead with the wedding. Was I wrong to hope for something more? Truly I don't think so. These past few days since we've parted, my heart is at peace with what I did. If I am to live out my life as a Maidel, then so be it.

On the porch, the wind suddenly gusted, and the rain became a real downpour, forcing me inside, lest I "catch my death," as Mamma used to warn—back when things were a bit calmer under our roof. Yet even then, there was a charged atmosphere, a buildup to our present storm.

Retreating to my room, I wrapped up in a cozy afghan and enjoyed looking at Becky's recent drawing of three humming-birds. I traced the outline of the smallest one and imagined it coming to life, hovering near Mamma's feeders out back. I'd always wondered why I was so keen on these delicate birds, and now I thought I knew. It was much more than their freedom of flight; it was their persistent search for the sweetness that sustained them.

I found myself reciting a stanza from a poem Mamma had taught me from one of the McGuffey's Readers.

Quickly, I opened my dresser drawer and reached for the journal presented to me on my birthday. Filled with an unexpected sense of hope, I wrote the beautiful words from "April Day."

> The very earth, the steamy air,
> Is all with fragrance rife!
> And grace and beauty everywhere
> Are flushing into life.

I held my pen and again studied my friend's lovely drawing. Becky's ongoing friendship is ever so dear.

Eventually, I dressed for bed and then brushed my hair. Mandy called softly from across the hall, and I hurried to meet her—going and sitting on her bed for a while, before time to outen the lanterns. Together we joined our hearts in earnest prayer for our mother, just as we do each and every night, waiting not so patiently for her return.

Acknowledgments

Creating a new series is always a special beginning—the joy of the fresh slate of characters and their circumstances. *The Secret* is not based on any particular true story or life event shared by any of my Amish friends or Plain relatives. It is rather the collective story of countless women who have given up a child at birth to adoption, either willingly or otherwise. Lettie Byler's heartrending journey, and her daughter Grace's response to it, is particularly dear to my heart as an adoptive mother.

During the writing of this novel, numerous people offered their assistance and encouragement. Their input is so essential that they really deserve their own paragraph!

My ongoing thanks to my husband, Dave, who loves the brainstorming process as much as I do. And to our daughter Julie, who lives and breathes my first drafts and is, thankfully, not reticent to point out embarrassing mistakes!

I offer heartfelt appreciation to my outstanding editorial team and reviewers—David Horton, Rochelle Glöege, Julie Klassen, Ann Parrish, and Jolene Steffer.

Thanks also to my clever cousin Kendra Verhage, an artist

in her own right, for naming the Bylers' beloved mare, Willow, during Thanksgiving last year—so much fun! And to her sweet mother, my auntie Judy, who offered prayerful support during the final weeks of my writing deadline.

To my astute and ever helpful consultants in Lancaster County—both Plain and English—your prompt responses still astonish me and are a great blessing. Also, many thanks to Barbara Birch, proofreader extraordinaire. And to John Henderson, as well as the Mennonite Information Center and the Lancaster Historical Society.

To Carolene Robinson and Sandi Heisler, dear friends and medical consultants, your insight and knowledge are vital to this series. Thank you!

For the faithful prayers and quick feedback to title ideas, I send not-so-cyber hugs to Dave and Janet Buchwalter, Debra Larsen, Donna De For, Bob and Aleta Hirschberg, Iris Jones, Jeanne Pallos, Barbara and Lizzie, and to my own little grand-girls, who say the sweetest prayers. And, last, though he should be first, I give my love to my dear dad. Your prayers are precious!

All honor and praise to our heavenly Father, Creator and ultimate Mender of broken hearts, without whom no story would be possible.

Looking for More Good Books to Read?

You can find out what is new and exciting with
previews, descriptions, and reviews by signing up for
Bethany House newsletters at

www.bethanynewsletters.com

We will send you updates for as many authors or
categories as you desire so you get only the
information you really want.

Sign up today!

Martin Seymour-Smith
An Introduction to
Fifty European Novels £1.95

The novel first appeared in European literature following the
emergence of printing technology, with Rabelais and Cervantes
producing the first recognizable European novels. Martin Seymour-
Smith's Literature Guide traces the history of the *genre* from
those early landmarks to the established modern classics. Work by
Voltaire, Stendhal, Balzac, Dostoevsky, Kafka, Camus, Gunther
Grass and Solzhenitsyn is included along with many other of the
greatest European novels.

Michael Schmidt
An Introduction to Fifty British Poets
1300–1900 £1.95

Through the literary heritage of six centuries, the tradition of
English verse runs as a rich and fruitful seam. Each historical period
has produced its own great names of poetry and distinctive schools
of poetic thought. Michael Schmidt's Literature Guide examines
the life and work of fifty key poets, from the earliest poetry of Gower,
Langland and Chaucer through Donne and the Metaphysicals, the
eighteenth century and the Romantic movement, to the Victorian
heyday of Tennyson and Browning.

You can buy these and other Pan Books from booksellers and
newsagents ; or direct from the following address :
Pan Books, Sales Office, Cavaye Place, London SW10 9PG
Send purchase price plus 20p for the first book and 10p for
each additional book, to allow for postage and packing
Prices quoted are applicable in the UK

edited by Elaine Steinbeck and Robert Wallsten
Steinbeck: A Life in Letters £3.95

'The letters of John Steinbeck provide an insight into the mind
and life of a writer : the compulsion to write, perpetual planning of
new books, the build-up of work, the danger of the crack-up ...
The Nobel Prize was well awarded, for Steinbeck must be listed
among those writers who effectively convey their understanding of
life, and their emotional, exuberant delight in its complexities. He
had, in sixty years, left a lot of tracks : and we can retrace them through
the outspoken letters he wrote' YORKSHIRE POST

'His friend and his widow have raised a fitting memorial, carved from
his own words, to both his life and his art' OBSERVER

Francis Hitching
The World Atlas of Mysteries £4.50

From the origins of the universe and terrestrial life, through the unique
development of man, to the secrets of ancient civilizations and
bizarre phenomena in the sky and beyond — the enormous scope of
this encyclopedia, its exhaustive research and copious illustrations
(maps, photographs, diagrams) make it a unique and fascinating
book. Francis Hitching, author of *Earth Magic*, is one of the world's
authorities on the inexplicable and the unexplained.

'A book of absorbing interest to anyone who believes that there are
more things in heaven and earth than science will recognize'
DR KIT PEDLER (creator of DOOMWATCH), EVENING NEWS

Elspeth Huxley
Scott of the Antarctic £1.95

Through a close study of Scott's diaries and letters, those of his colleagues and reports of his expeditions, Elspeth Huxley has produced a splendid narrative that follows Scott's progress to his tragic end in the iceworld of Antarctica. A powerful portrait of the great doomed hero of polar endeavour.

'A story not only exciting but pathetic . . . direct and straightforward . . . totally absorbing' EVENING STANDARD

'By far the best account of Scott's life and death that has so far been written' SUNDAY TIMES

G. H. Jansen
Militant Islam £1.25

Militant Islam is a force shaping the world from North Africa to South East Asia. Beset by the sudden transformations brought about by 20th-century oil wealth, Islam has been under religious, political and cultural assault from the West since the Crusades.

G. H. Jansen's analysis examines the militancy of Islam since 1800, emphasizing its resurgence in the last decade. He contrasts the traditionalists such as Iran's Ayatollah Khomeini and Pakistan's General Zia with the reformers trying to adapt the faith to the modern world, and assesses Islam's future for the last quarter of our century.

Sir Basil Liddell Hart
History of the Second World War £2.50

'The greatest military thinker of this century' SOLDIER

'The most civilized and compassionate military historian' THE TIMES

Liddell Hart brought his brilliant and original mind to this magnificent narrative of the war, a task which occupied him for over twenty years. Trenchant, searching, thought-provoking, it is military history written with realism and learning and illuminated by flashes of insight.

'The book has the mark of the author's genius — a lucidity and insight such as no other military writer can match . . . it will long be read with profit and enjoyment by all interested in the military art' ARMY QUARTERLY

'Unlikely to be surpassed' SUNDAY TELEGRAPH

'On the level of operational military history the best book we are ever likely to see' SUNDAY TIMES

William L. Schirer
The Rise and Fall of the Third Reich £3.25

The world-famous history of Nazi Germany.

'A magnificent work . . . documented, reasoned, objective and never dull . . . the standard, indeed the classic, history of Nazism'
HUGH TREVOR-ROPER, SUNDAY TIMES

'I can think of no book I would rather put into the hands of anyone who wanted to find out what happened in Germany between 1930 and 1945' ALAN BULLOCK, GUARDIAN